STOMP ROCKETS, CATAPULTS, AND KALEIDOSCOPES

STOMP ROCKETS, CATAPULTS, AND KALEIDOSCOPES

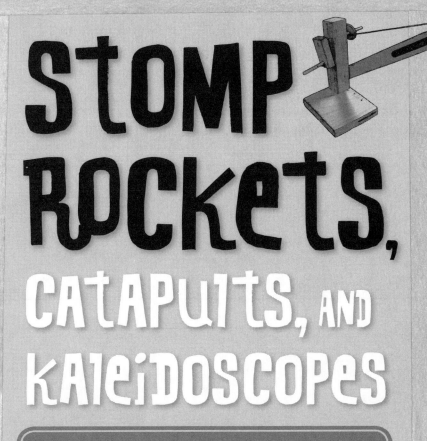

30+ Amazing Science Projects You Can Build for LESS THAN $1

Curt Gabrielson

CHICAGO
REVIEW
PRESS

Library of Congress Cataloging-in-Publication Data

Gabrielson, Curt.

 Stomp rockets, catapults, and kaleidoscopes : 30+ amazing science projects you can build for less than $1 / Curt Gabrielson. — 1st ed.

  p. cm.

 Includes index.

 ISBN 978-1-55652-737-1

 1. Science—Experiments—Juvenile literature. 2. Scientific recreations—Juvenile literature. I. Title.

Q164.G23 2008
507.8—dc22

2007037917

Cover and interior design: Monica Baziuk

© 2008 by the City of Watsonville
First edition
Published by Chicago Review Press, Incorporated
814 North Franklin Street
Chicago, Illinois 60610
ISBN 978-1-55652-737-1
Printed in the United States of America

5 4 3 2 1

To the kids of Watsonville, California.
Here's to many more years of great ideas
and science projects!

ACKNOWLEDGMENTS

I HAD THE PRIVILEGE of working with many fine people to make this book happen. Juan Jose Padilla and Lorena Onofre of our Students Teaching Project shot and posed for many of the photos. Gustavo Hernandez, my assistant extraordinaire, shot and posed for many photos, did a lot of editing, and kept hundreds of projects and parts organized in our cramped space. Araceli and Frankie Ortiz and Erick Torres also helped with some photos.

Paul Doherty of the Exploratorium Teacher Institute kindly proofed these activities for content, and Pat Murphy in Exploratorium Publications (and of the Brazen Hussies!) gave a lot of useful advice.

Much appreciation goes to my wise superiors in the City of Watsonville's Department of Public Works and Utilities—Tami Stolzenthaler, Nancy Lockwood, Bob Geyer, David Koch—and also to Carol Thomas and Al Smith, all of whom gave great support for this book. Thanks also to Watsonville city manager Carlos Palacios and the city council for all their support of the Watsonville Environmental Science Workshop past and future. Finally, thanks for the support and ideas from other community science workshop directors across the country.

Most of the ideas here originated or were significantly developed by students and staff at the Watsonville Environmental Science Workshop. Like folk tunes, science projects such as these are constantly being changed and improved upon as they pass from hand to hand, shop to shop. I've given credit within the chapter for ideas that I recall picking up from a distinct person or place, whether or not that was the true origin.

CONTENTS

⚲ Fluids and Aerodynamics

⚲ Biology

⚲ Chemistry

Appendixes

iNtRODUCtiON

ALL NATURAL THINGS—SOLAR SYSTEMS, volcanoes, glaciers, tornadoes, camels, live oak trees, sea turtles, algae, cardiovascular systems, silicon nuclei—just work, without any human effort. On the other hand, most of the gadgets that you use each day, both high and low tech, have been *made* to work by people. When you cry out "It doesn't work!" you should remember that *not* working is actually a gadget's default condition.

To make something work is exceptional—it takes know-how and ingenuity. Ten thousand years ago, every family knew more or less how to make everything work that was necessary for their existence: where to find the materials, how to put them together, how to use the finished product. People in many so-called backward places in the world can still do this today. But here in our "advanced" society, where we're up to our ears in technology? I challenge you to think of three things you depend on daily that you could create from scratch, even given all the materials set out in front of you. We are clearly losing our touch.

This book will show you how to build more than 30 amazing science toys. You will learn a lot as you build them, about science and about making things work. You can work with friends or alone. Adults are helpful to have around, but don't let them take over your project!

You can build these toys in any order, and don't feel like you have to follow these directions precisely. If you do, you'll end up with a fine working project, but if you can see a better way to do it, go for it. The toys here are all open-ended, so you can keep on going and make more amazing stuff. In fact, many of these projects were developed from kids' ideas. If you come up with a brilliant idea in the process of building these projects, send it to me. I probably won't make you rich and famous, but I'll pass your idea on to thousands of other kids, who will then have a chance to improve it even more.

The toys here will cost you about 75¢ each. If you can't squeeze that out of your parents, you need to work on your technique. Many of the materials you'll need you can get for free from a garbage can or recycling bin or find lying around the house. To get a few of the materials, you may have to go to a specialty shop or order them from a catalog or over the Internet. Some sources are listed at the end of Appendix A, "Bringing These Projects into the Classroom."

You'll need some basic tools to construct these toys. Definitely get your parents to help you gather these tools—don't just help yourself to your mom's tool cabinet. The most complex tool required in these projects is a hand drill. If you have a thick piece of wood or several pieces fastened together for a drill platform, the projects can be done on any table without damaging the surface. Several of the projects should be done outside, owing to noise or messiness. Here's a list of common tools you may need for these projects. Each project will have a list of any additional special tools you will need.

TOOLBOX

⚒ Knife	⚒ Hot glue gun (low-temperature
⚒ Side cutters	models work fine and are much safer)
⚒ Needle-nose pliers	⚒ Hot glue sticks (plenty!)
⚒ Scissors	⚒ Markers or paint
⚒ Ruler	⚒ Decorations of various kinds
⚒ File	⚒ Masking tape
⚒ Scraper	⚒ Black tape
⚒ Hacksaw	⚒ Duct tape
⚒ Wood saw	⚒ Hand drill with variable speed
⚒ Vise or C-clamp	⚒ At least these drill bits: $15/64$-inch,*
⚒ Flat-blade screwdriver	$19/64$-inch,* $1/2$-inch
⚒ Phillips screwdriver	⚒ A few nails to serve as tiny drill bits
⚒ Hammer	("nail bits")

* Dowels of $1/4$ inches and $5/16$ inches are used in many projects and often inserted into holes. If you make a hole $1/64$ of an inch smaller than the dowel, then hammer the dowel in, it will fit nice and tightly. This is also a good opportunity to practice your fractions: $1/4 - 1/64 = 15/64$ and $5/16 - 1/64 = 19/64$.

You'll also want a few boxes to store materials and tools in; then when you go to work on future projects, you'll have all sorts of supplies ready at hand. If possible, you'll want to set up all your stuff in a corner with a table or workbench where you don't have to clean it up each time you stop working. It's an adult secret I'll clue you in on right now: real scientists and engineers and artists hardly *ever* clean up—they just organize the mess in the direction of the next project. You can quote me on that.

Finally, remember, **SAFETY IS FIRST!** What kind of fun will you have if you rip a big gash in your finger or poke a hole in your eye? Always be careful, and never joke around when it comes to safety.

Building things is great fun. Making things work and fixing things are not only satisfying but also can save you money and teach you all kinds of stuff in interesting ways. You may not get much of a chance to do these sorts of things at school these days, but you shouldn't be waiting for school to teach you what you want to know anyway.

Happy building!!

A Note to Adults

The projects in this book do not include laboratory exercises, structured discovery lessons, or experiments in the formal sense of the word. Students learn from firsthand experience in the process of trying to build the projects and make them work. Each project demonstrates several science or math concepts that can be found in most curricula and lists of standards. Each project has been tested in between 10 and 30 classes over the course of four years. I can be confident when I say: the projects work.

You can have great times with your kid while building stuff. Here are some pointers to make the process work:

↗ **Don't take over your kid's project.** If you get so excited about it that you grab it from them to do the next step, you've overstepped

continued...

your mandate. There are safety issues to be sure, but don't let the off chance of a small cut or scrape stand in the way of your youngster's learning to use a new tool or build a great project.

🪓 **Don't demand perfection.** Even built crudely, most of these toys will work. Polish comes with practice. The kid's pride in completion is the priority.

🪓 **Let kids make mistakes.** Many times a mistake will teach more than will a first-time success.

🪓 **Know your role: you are the *assistant*.** If you want to build your own toys, wait until your kid goes to bed. I'm serious: if your kid sees your success to be better than his or her own, the child may be put off from trying another project. But if you can work together with your kid in a way that demonstrates you're helping without taking the lead, you'll have hours of fun together. I find a good technique is to be fiddling with something unrelated nearby. That way I can easily step in and out of the kids' work with advice and help, without having to twiddle my thumbs as they slowly learn how to do something I already know.

The toys here span the technical subjects: physics (including sound, light, mechanics, electricity, and magnetism), chemistry, geology, and biology. Usually several topics can be explored with a single project. The toys are ideal for sparking students' interest in a concept area, and can be used as stepping-stones toward more learning.

Happy assisting!

STOMP ROCKETS, CATAPULTS, AND KALEIDOSCOPES

hOliDAY light CiRCUit

A 9-volt battery will light these tiny bulbs, if you hook them up right.

PARTS	
2 film canisters or wood blocks	Weight (nut or bolt)
Baseboard	9-volt battery
½ paint paddle	Battery snap, or two small paper clips
Craft stick	File folders or stiff paper
3 8-inch wires, thin, with insulation	
1–3 holiday lights in a row, cut from a standard string of small holiday lights	

The Basic Concepts

Electricity has to have a complete path in order to travel from one side of a battery to the other. This path is called a circuit. A switch "breaks"—or opens—the circuit and stops the electricity flowing. A battery "pushes" the electricity around the circuit. When the chemical reaction within the battery runs out of chemicals, the battery is dead and can't push anymore.

Glue a film canister to the middle of one edge of the baseboard. Cut a paint paddle to be about 9 inches long. Glue a craft stick to one end of the paint paddle.

Glue the other end of the paint paddle to the edge of the baseboard and also to the film canister. Glue the other film canister on the opposite edge of the baseboard, as shown.

Strip the insulation off both ends of three 8-inch wires. Strip both ends of the holiday light wires.

Connect one 8-inch wire to each end of the holiday light wires. One of these wires will go directly to the battery, the other to the craft stick.

Drape a second 8-inch wire over the craft stick and wrap it around once. Tie the weight to this wire near the bottom. Wrap the third 8-inch wire around the paint paddle and make a loop that encompasses the hanging wire. This wire will go directly to the battery. These two wires need to be stripped about 5 inches from one end. When the hanging wire swings, it should contact the loop wire.

Put a battery in the film canister near the paint paddle. Use a 9-volt battery snap if you have one. If not, connect one paper clip to the loop wire and one to the wire coming from the lights. Connect the paper clips to the battery snaps, taking care not to let them touch each other. When you're finished, there should be a single series circuit: from one side of the battery, to the holiday lights, to the swinging wire, to the loop of wire, and back to the battery.

Draw a picture of a snowman (or whatever you'd like) on the file folder or thin cardboard and cut it out. Make a hole in the picture with a screwdriver for each light. Each hole must be big enough to hold the light firmly. Insert the lights, and glue them in place if they do not stay by themselves.

Glue the figure to the front film canister.

Add craft sticks for rigidity if it does not stand up on its own. Swing the weight back and forth. The lights will flash every time the dangling wire touches the loop completing the circuit.

More to Think About and Try

- ✦ What happens when one light goes out?
- ✦ If you put more lights in the circuit, would they be brighter or dimmer?
- ✦ How could you make it blink longer?
- ✦ How could you make it blink faster?

A Little Background

Wire is the conductor through which the electricity travels in this circuit. Air, on the other hand, is a pretty good insulator. So when the weight is swinging and the wire is not touching the loop, electricity does not travel through the circuit. This is known as an open circuit and is exactly the arrangement in a light switch when you shut off the light.

When the wire holding the weight touches the loop wire, the circuit is complete and electricity can travel through it. The lights glow. This is called a closed circuit.

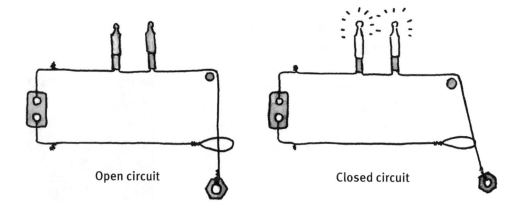

Open circuit   Closed circuit

If you happen to cross the two bare ends of the holiday light wires, the lights will go out but the battery will continue pushing electricity around a circuit. Since there are no lights and just wire in this new circuit, it is smaller, that is, shorter, than the one you had before you touched the wires. This situation is called a short circuit.

The lights that went out when you shorted them had some resistance, which limited the amount of electricity that could flow through them. When the circuit is shorted, this resistance is gone and much more electricity can travel around the circuit. In this project the worst that will happen with this type of short circuit is that the battery will get warm and go dead rapidly. However, if the battery was much bigger and could supply a lot of electricity, this would be a dangerous situation. The wires or other components of the circuit could become hot and perhaps explode. This is why homes have fuses or circuit breakers. Both of these instruments open a circuit that suddenly has too much electricity traveling through it, usually due to a short circuit.

Electric circuits come in two varieties: series and parallel. Try taking one lightbulb in a string of holiday lights out of its socket. The other bulbs should go out. Bulbs in a series circuit act this way. The electricity goes through each bulb, one by one; if you take one out, you have opened the circuit. Bulbs wired in series have to share the total voltage of the circuit. For this reason, you can use these lightbulbs with a 9-volt battery when they were designed to be used with a 120-volt wall outlet. You used only two or three, whereas in their original circuit, there were perhaps 50 bulbs sharing the 120 volts.

You can also wire holiday lights in parallel—try it! Set it up like the drawing on p. 5. Cut two lightbulbs out separately and strip the wires on

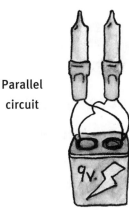

Series circuit

Parallel circuit

either side of them. Connect one wire from one bulb to one wire from the battery, and then connect the other wire from that bulb to the other battery wire. That bulb should light up. Then connect one wire from the other bulb to one of the connections you just made and the other to the other. Both lights should now glow.

Now try removing one bulb. The other should stay lit. This is because each bulb has its own path in a parallel circuit. Each type of circuit has its advantages. You may notice that the bulbs wired in parallel glow more brightly. This is because they each get the full voltage of the battery. On the other hand, they'll use more electricity and the battery will go dead sooner.

In a series circuit, if you have fewer lights, each will shine brighter. Each additional light adds more resistance, which results in less electricity flowing. To get them to blink faster, you'd need a shorter wire on the pendulum through the loop. A heavier weight would help them to continue blinking longer.

CRANE

Magnets are more useful if you can turn them off and on.

PARTS	
3-inch 1-by-2 wood	Baseboard
6-inch dowel (¼-inch diameter)	6-foot magnet wire (around #30)
Paint paddle	Bolt, screw, or nail (1 inch)
6-inch 2-by-2 wood	2 18-inch wires, thin, with insulation
2 nails, thin (1¼-inch)	Aluminum foil
#6 washer	C battery
String	Paper clips or small nails
Film canister with lid	
TOOLS	
Wire strippers	Sandpaper for stripping magnet wire

The Basic Concepts

Moving electricity creates a magnetic field. If you make electricity run around and around in a coil of wire, you can concentrate the magnetic field and create a strong electromagnet. An electromagnet is much like a permanent one but with an added benefit: you can also turn it off and on at will.

Build It!

Cut a 1-by-2 to be 3 inches long. With a $^{15}/_{64}$-inch bit, drill two holes at each end of it. Cut two pieces of ¼-inch dowel, about 4 inches and 2 inches. Hammer them in the two holes so that they stick out of opposite sides.

Drill a $^{15}/_{64}$-inch hole near one end of a paint paddle.

With a nail bit, drill a small hole near the other end of the paddle. Drill a $^{19}/_{64}$-inch hole near one end of a 6-inch 2-by-2.

Hammer a nail with a washer through the hole in the paint paddle into the 2-by-2 near the end without the hole. Don't hammer it in tightly— the paint paddle must be able to pivot around this nail easily.

Cut a piece of string a bit longer than the paint paddle.

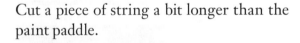

Tie the string to the hole on the free end of the paint paddle. Slide the long dowel through the hole in the 2-by-2. With the paint paddle at about 90 degrees to the 2-by-2, tie the free end of the string around the dowel. This should be on the same side of the 2-by-2 as the nail with washer.

Drill a ¹⁵⁄₆₄-inch hole in a film canister lid. Press it on the dowel so that the string is restricted to a small space between the lid and the 2-by-2.

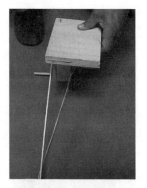

On the table or floor, start a nail into the baseboard near one corner. Turn your 2-by-2 upside down and finish pounding the nail through the baseboard into the end of the 2-by-2.

Turn it over and the mechanical part of your crane is finished.

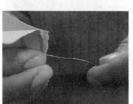

To build the electro-magnet, cut about 6 feet of magnet wire. Sand off about 1 inch of insulation (lacquer) at both ends.

Wind the magnet wire around the bolt, leaving both ends sticking out a bit. Twist them to prevent unwinding.

Strip both ends of both thin wires and con-nect them tightly to

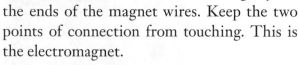

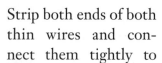

the ends of the magnet wires. Keep the two points of connection from touching. This is the electromagnet.

Dangle the electro-magnet from the tip of the paint paddle. Tape it on.

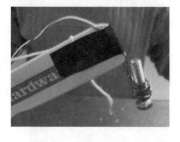

Run the wire down the paint paddle, then off to the side. Glue the film canister down to the base beside the 2-by-2. Fold some aluminum foil onto the end of one wire and stick it into the film canister. Put the battery in the film canister so that it rests on the wad of aluminum foil.

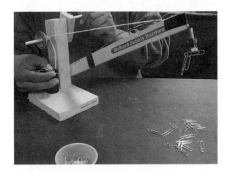

Place some paper clips or small nails on the table. Reel your crane down so that the electromagnet touches the pile of paper clips. To turn it on, connect the stripped end of the free wire to the top of the battery. When you see the paper clips sticking to the electromagnet, reel your crane up.

Pivot the 2-by-2 to swing the crane to the side. When the electromagnet is over the place you want to drop the paper clips, release the wire from the top of the battery and they should fall.

More to Think About and Try

- How is this project different from a real crane?
- How could you tell if a nail or bolt has become permanently magnetized?
- What do you think would happen if you hook up a car battery to the electromagnet you made?
- If you don't use wire with insulation, your electromagnet won't work. Why do you think that is?

A Little Background

Atoms of all elements have magnetic fields associated with them. These fields arise from quantum effects (having to do with electron orbits and spins—very difficult to explain) and are very small for most atoms. Iron atoms, and to a lesser degree cobalt and nickel atoms, have special structures that make a large magnetic field possible. These elements can become the permanent magnets you may find holding up a photo on a refrigerator door.

Electrons are subatomic particles that are less tightly bound to an individual atom than the more massive particles at the atom's center. Electrons may travel from one atom to another, and when they do, that movement is called an electric current. Every electric current creates a magnetic field. In this project you've made an electric current flow many times around a bolt. This "organizes" the magnetic field and results in two distinct poles at either end of the bolt. The bolt also increases the strength of the magnet; if you take it out, the electromagnet will be much weaker.

It is easy to increase the current to your crane, making the magnet stronger: just add more batteries. But if you hook your crane up to a car battery, which can provide enough current to turn an entire car engine, you'll rapidly have an extremely hot coil. The wire will likely melt down at its weakest point. (In addition, car batteries are dangerous. They are filled with acid strong enough to burn you and they sometimes produce hydrogen gas, which can make the battery explode and spray acid all over your face. If you want to increase the current, it is safer to use lantern batteries or line up several D cells than mess with a car battery.)

If your nail or bolt sticks to other iron objects after you switch off the electromagnet, you've transformed it into a permanent magnet. If you used wire with no insulation, when the electricity came to the coil, it would not need to go around and around along the wire. Instead, it could jump sideways from loop to loop until it came to the wire leading back to the battery. Electricity looks for the easiest path and will not go running around loops if there is a faster path—that is, a short circuit. Insulation keeps the current traveling down the wire so that it goes around the coil.

Electromagnets are generally used to move iron or steel objects. Some machines that sort recycled materials use magnets, and cranes such as this model use magnets to transport heavy iron or steel objects. But all materials are magnetic at a much lower level—that is, you can't often move them with magnets. The medical procedure known as magnetic resonance imaging (MRI) is performed by placing a person inside an enormous electromagnet, switching it on and off, and looking at the way the various atoms of the human body respond to the magnetic field.

eleCtRiC CAR

A small motor and a small battery will make a small car go fast.

PARTS	
2 craft sticks	2 wires, thin, with insulation
Drinking straw	Aluminum foil
3 film canister lids (or other circles for wheels)	AA battery
	2 paper clips (small)
Bamboo skewer	Wire and paper for flag
Hobby motor, 1.5–3 volts	
TOOLS	
Nail for making axle holes	Wire strippers

The Basic Concepts

The car in this project gets its energy from a battery. The motor will work only if it's connected in a complete circuit to the two sides of the battery. If you reverse the wires, the motor will go in the opposite direction.

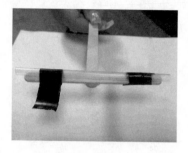

Hot glue the tip of one craft stick to the center of another craft stick in the form of a T. Cut a drinking straw a little bit longer than the craft stick; then tape the straw to the craft stick as shown. It is best to make the straw stick out over both ends so that the wheels will rub on the straw and not the craft stick.

Make a hole in the center of three film canister lids with a small nail. Slide a bamboo skewer inside the drinking straw. Then put one wheel onto each end of the skewer. Cut the excess length, including the dangerous point, off the bamboo skewer.

Hot glue the motor to the end of the craft stick so that the shaft is exactly 90 degrees to the stick.

Press the last wheel onto the motor's shaft. If necessary, add glue to the end of the shaft to secure the film canister lid. Be careful not to let the glue cause the shaft to stick to the motor housing.

Strip the insulation off both ends of two wires. Connect the wires to the motor and wrap the excess wire around the craft stick.

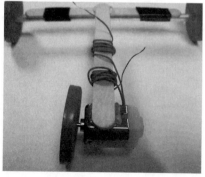

Cut two pieces of aluminum foil and fold them several times into long rectangular shapes. Tape the pieces of aluminum foil tightly to the battery, leaving a bit of foil sticking up on each side.

Hot glue the battery to the top of the craft stick. Connect paper clips to the ends of both of the wires.

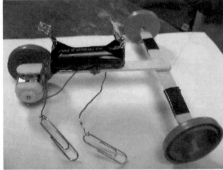

Connect the paper clips to the foil pieces sticking up off the battery. The car should go! Reverse the wires and watch what happens. If you want, make a flag from wire and paper and attach it to the back of the car as shown.

More to Think About and Try

- Where does the car get its energy?
- How can you make the car turn corners?
- How could you make the car go even faster?
- What can you do to make your car change directions?

A Little Background

Batteries store energy. There are two chemical reactions ready and waiting to happen in every battery. One of them creates excess electrons, and the other requires the addition of electrons. If you connect a battery's positive and negative terminals, the reactions begin happening and electrons go racing through the wire from the negative terminal to the positive one. This is electric current.

The wire you use to connect the terminals may get quite hot if you make a direct connection across your battery. The battery will also go dead quickly because all the chemicals are used up quickly in the reactions. To get some work out of the battery, you would need to send the current through something that will make use of the current, such as a motor.

Take apart a motor to see what is inside. You will find little coils of wire and little permanent magnets. When the motor has current running through it, those little coils turn into electromagnets. They then push and pull on the permanent magnets, making the motor turn. The electromagnets are turned off and on at just the right time by tiny brushes touching the shaft of the motor. When the electric current is going through the electromagnets in the opposite direction, they push and pull in the opposite direction and the motor turns in reverse.

By gluing either the front or back wheels at an angle, the car can be made to turn. If you had another motor to control the turn, you could make a remote-controlled car. If you want your motor to go faster, you could put on another battery, but that would also make it heavier. Heavier things generally have more friction, so it may not go faster after all.

electrostatics

**Build up a charge, and
you will feel the force!**

PARTS	
Rubbed Balloon	
Balloon	Pencil
Piece of wool	Aluminum can
Hair	Plastic bottle
Bits of paper	Kite string
Salt	½ CD case
Pepper	
Flying Hydra	
Plastic string (or a very thin plastic bag)	Balloon
Piece of wool	
Small Spark	
Aluminum pie plate	Balloon
Large plastic cup	
Tape Testers	
Two pieces of 5-inch frosted "invisible" tape	"Small Spark" cup-and-plate setup
	Balloon

The Basic Concepts

Electrostatic charge builds up when you rub two insulators together. Conductors carry electricity; insulators usually just hold it. But everything becomes a conductor if you "push" electricity through it hard enough.

A spark is electricity passing through the air, just like lightning.

Opposite electric charges attract, and likes repel, just as with magnetic poles. Charged objects also attract neutral ones. For each activity, you can decide whether it is an example of opposites attracting, likes repelling, or a charged object attracting a neutral object.

Build It!

Rubbed Balloon

Blow up a balloon and rub it with a piece of wool. See what items you can attract to the balloon: hair, bits of paper, salt, pepper, pencils, aluminum cans, plastic bottles, kite string, and so on.

Cover some of the items with half of a CD case and try to attract them to the balloon through the cover. Carefully watch their behavior as you hold the balloon close by.

Flying Hydra

Cut a piece of plastic packing string about 4 inches long. Unwrap it so that it is only one layer. If you can't find this sort of string, you can use a small piece of the thinnest plastic bag you can find. Hold one end down on the table and score the other end with scissors so that it turns ragged with tiny strings. This is the "hydra." Rub it with a piece of wool.

Rub the balloon again and throw the hydra into the air. Put the rubbed spot of the balloon directly under the hydra and it should push the hydra up. Move the balloon around to keep the hydra floating. This activity works well with two people—one rubbing the hydra and throwing it, one rubbing the balloon and floating the hydra.

Small Spark

Hot glue an aluminum pie plate to the top of a plastic cup. Place it away from other objects on the desk.

There are four steps to the process that can be repeated over and over. First, bring the balloon up close or even touching the pie plate. Then, touch the pie plate with a finger to get the first spark.

Remove the finger first, then the balloon. And finally, touch the pie plate again to get the second spark.

After that you can begin all over again. See how many times you can do it.

Tape Testers

Stick one 5-inch piece of "invisible" tape to the table so that it extends over the edge. Stick another directly on top of it, but leave the tail end separate. Mark a T for "top" on the top one.

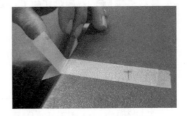

Lift the bottom piece off the desk, and hold one with each hand. Rip them apart rapidly. Bring them back close together and see if they attract each other. They should. They should also attract almost anything you bring

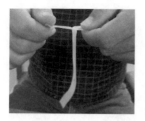 

close to them. Try it! These two tape pieces are oppositely charged and can be used to test any object for its electric charge.

Charge up the pie plate by getting the first spark from it. Bring the top tape close to it; it should probably attract. Bring the top tape close to the balloon in the place where you rubbed it; it should probably repel, and it should definitely have the opposite reaction it did with the pie plate. The bottom tape should have the opposite reaction to these two objects.

More to Think About and Try

- How could you get your balloon to make an even bigger shock?
- Can you get a shock through your clothes?
- Can you get a shock if you touch the pie plate with a paper clip or nail?
- Do the tape pieces that you pulled apart attract and repel the same from both sides?

A Little Background

Here are some observations that you should be able to confirm yourself:

- When you rub a balloon with wool, the balloon attracts and is attracted to many things, including the piece of wool you rubbed it with.
- If you also rub a bit of plastic string with wool, it will repel the balloon.

18

- If you bring the rubbed balloon close to the pie tin, insulated on a cup, you can get a small spark upon touching the pie tin.
- If you stick two pieces of tape together and then rip them apart, you can see that they'll attract and repel various things. Sometimes they'll both attract something, but you'll never find them both repelling the same thing.

These observations can provide proof of the theory of electrostatics.

This project is about the behavior of charged objects. "Charged" means they hold a net electric charge. Scientists often talk about making or *generating* static charge, but more accurately, they are *separating* the two types of charge. The two types are called positive and negative. Benjamin Franklin came up with these names, and it is good to remember that there is nothing particularly positive or negative about the kinds of charge—they are merely different and opposite. He could have called them black and white or hot and cold.

Before you rubbed the balloon and wool, they were neutral, meaning they contained an equal amount of positive and negative charges. But while you were rubbing, one of the materials pulled harder on the negatives and the other on the positives so that there was a movement of charges, resulting in a net difference in electric charge.

Then—and this is a key point—the charge that moved could not move back to where it came from. It stayed there as a "static" electric charge. That is why this type of electricity is called static electricity. When you touch a highly charged object, such as the pie plate, you can see a spark. This is what you may think of in relation to static electricity, but the spark means charge is actually flowing, as opposed to sitting in one place. Most of the charges in this activity couldn't move because you were using insulators and not conductors. In the pie plate activity, the pie plate is a conductor, and charge is free to move.

The charged balloon exerted force as follows:

- A pull on neutral objects (salt, string)
- A pull on objects charged the opposite way (wool, one of the tape pieces)
- A push on objects charged the same way (rubbed plastic string, the other tape piece)

This is the fundamental law of electric charges. You have heard some of it before: "Opposites attract; likes repel." You don't often hear that charged objects can also attract neutral objects, but this is equally true. The mechanism is called electrical induction.

The tape testers become charged when you rip them apart, one positive and one negative. They'll attract any object with the opposite charge *and* any neutral object. Thus, you can't tell much from attraction. But when you see one repelling another object, you will know it has the same charge as that object. The rubbed balloon usually has the same charge as the top piece of tape. The charged tape pieces generally attract and repel the same on both sides.

A built-up electric charge will always try to flow to the ground or to some large neutral object. You yourself are usually a large neutral object connected to ground (but not if you've been scooting your shoes around on carpet on a dry day or sliding down a plastic slide—then you're highly charged), and if you rub your balloon and then touch it all over with your hands, you can remove the charge.

Try to explain each of the observations you make in terms of the theory described above.

Thanks to Paul Doherty and others at the Exploratorium Teacher Institute for several of these electrostatics ideas.

MAGNETIC SPINNER

It looks like magic, but it's only magnets pushing and pulling on each other.

PARTS	
½ paint paddle	Drinking straw
Baseboard (at least 8 inches by 3 inches, ½-inch thick)	Ring magnet (¾-inch diameter, ³⁄₁₆-inch thick, ¼-inch hole in center)
2 block magnets (1 inch by ¾ inch, ³⁄₁₆-inch thick)	Film canister base (or lid with large divot)
	Color wheel
12-inch dowel (¼-inch diameter)	
TOOLS	
Pencil sharpener	

The Basic Concepts

Magnets can exert force on iron and other magnets without touching them. This is called a magnetic field.

Magnets have two sides called north and south. Like sides push on each other, opposite sides pull on each other, and both sides pull on iron.

When something is supported by magnetic repulsion, there is very little friction. This is the way magnetic levitation trains work.

Cut about 4 inches of a paint paddle. Hot glue the paint paddle to the short edge of the baseboard.

Cut two 1-inch pieces of a dowel. Hot glue these pieces, slightly off center, to the rectangular (block) magnets. *Important:* The magnets' faces (opposite the dowels) must push on each other. If they don't (if they attract), take off one dowel and put it on the other side of the magnet; then check it again.

Draw a straight line from the center of the paint paddle to the opposite end of the baseboard.

Put one of the magnets on this line, centered, and mark both sides of it. Glue the magnets down symmetrically as shown above right, each with one edge on the lines you just made. Again, be sure the faces repel each other—the project will not work if they are attracting.

Cut a dowel at least 1 inch longer than your baseboard. Sharpen it to a fine point. Cut 1 inch of a drinking straw. Insert the straw into the ring magnet; then insert the sharpened dowel. The straw should hold the magnet firmly on the dowel.

The magnet must slide up and down the dowel but only when you push on it. Put the sharp point of the dowel up against the paint paddle and begin experimenting with the stick to get it to float horizontally. To get the ring magnet in exactly the right spot on the dowel is quite a trick. The correct side of the magnet must be facing toward the paint paddle, and you can determine the correct side only by trying. If you try for a while and it's not working, remove the ring magnet, flip it around, thread it back on, and try again.

Once you have the dowel floating horizontally, mark the spot where the dowel point is touching the paint paddle.

Cut the bottom out of a film canister with a knife or scissors. You may use a film canister lid instead

if it has a significant divot or dent in the center. Hot glue the circle with the divot to the paint paddle in exactly the spot you marked. Set the dowel up again, now with the point in the divot. You may need to adjust the ring magnet again, since the width of the film canister plastic forces the dowel farther out.

Add a colored circle of paper on the end of the dowel to make the spinning more conspicuous. Alternating colors on this paper will mix when it is spun rapidly.

Once the dowel spins stably, stick a piece of tape on it near the magnets. This is to blow on, either directly or through a straw, to keep the dowel spinning.

More to Think About and Try

- ✦ How can you make the magnetic spinner float higher?
- ✦ What happens if you tip it up vertically?

➤ Why do you think we had to put a point on the tip of the dowel?

➤ Why does the spinner stop spinning eventually?

A Little Background

The shaft of the magnetic spinner is not really levitating: the sharpened point is touching the paint paddle and spinning with very little friction. But if one were to try to replace that point of contact with another magnet or array of magnets, it would be impossible to make it levitate. (Don't take my word for it—give it a try!) This is simply the way magnetic fields behave. It can be compared to trying to balance a basketball on a racket ball. In both cases stable equilibrium is not possible.

Magnetic levitation trains and other systems that float on magnetic fields need not have a point of contact, because the magnets they use are electromagnets controlled by computers that use rapid feedback circuits to maintain balance. You can balance a basketball on a racket ball if you are holding the racket ball and changing its position fast enough to stay under the basketball.

If a magnet had only one pole, it would be called a magnetic monopole and have very different properties. No one has ever discovered such a magnet, though, despite decades of searching. All known magnets, from atoms to stars, have a north pole and a south pole. The names "North" and "South" are arbitrary—the important thing to understand is that the two poles are fundamentally different. The only way to determine which pole you are dealing with is to expose it to a known pole of the same type and witness it repelling. If it attracts a known pole, you may have the opposite pole of a magnet or you may have a bit of iron. If you have two identical objects that attract each other from all sides (not repelling at all), it is impossible to know which one is the magnet without bringing in another magnet.

Stronger magnets will make the spinner float higher. If you tip it toward the vertical, it should work until it falls over. If you stick the shaft in a cup and put magnets all around the rim, it will work fine vertically.

The point on the tip of the stick minimizes friction as it spins. There is still some friction, though, which is why it always stops eventually.

Thanks to Tien Huynh-Dinh of the Exploratorium Teacher Institute for proving that even normal humans can make magnetic levitation devices.

SOLENOID AND SPEAKER

Electromagnetism works for us every day.

PARTS	
Solenoid	
6-foot magnet wire (#30 or a bit larger)	C or D battery
Drinking straw	Paper clips or small nails to pick up
Aluminum foil	Nail, large
Speaker	
40-foot magnet wire (#30 or a bit larger)	2 magnets (round works well)
3-inch PVC tube (½-inch diameter, to make wire coil)	Paint paddle
	2 paper fasteners (brads)
Paper cup with raised bottom	Rubber band (medium)
Mono plug	
TOOLS	
Sandpaper, small bits	Amplifier (optional)
Radio	

The Basic Concepts

A solenoid is an electromagnet with a hole in the center. When connected, it will suck iron objects into the hole.

Every common speaker has a coil and a magnet. The coil becomes an electromagnet when electricity passes through it. The two magnets then push and pull on each other to make a vibration, which is the sound you hear.

The cup in this speaker works like the diaphragm in a normal speaker: it takes a small vibration from the coil and magnet, and transfers it to the air so that a listener can hear it better.

Build It!

Solenoid

Cut at least 6 inches of magnet wire (the longer it is, the stronger the solenoid will be). Use sandpaper to strip the varnish insulation from both ends of the wire. Leaving a tail of about 4 inches, wrap the wire around the straw near the end.

Leave a 4-inch tail on the other end as well. Twist the two wire ends together so that the coil stays together.

Fold two pieces of aluminum foil around the two stripped ends so that the wire can make better contact with the battery—to be added next. Tape the shorter end tightly onto one end of the battery.

Tape the battery onto the straw just above the coil. The other end of the wire should just reach to the other end of the battery. This is the switch: when it touches the battery, the solenoid will be on.

Unbend one side of a paper clip and "feed" it into the end of the straw while pinching the aluminum foil to the battery. The paper clip should be sucked quickly into the straw and held even when you turn it upside down. The same should happen with a small nail. When you release the battery, the objects should drop out.

Wrap tape around a larger nail until it wedges snugly when inserted into the end of the straw. This is now an electromagnet. You can pick up paper clips, nails, or other small iron objects. When you disconnect the wire from the battery, they should drop off.

Speaker

Cut 40 feet of magnet wire and wind it around the PVC tube to form a tight coil. Leave at least 1 foot on each of the ends sticking out. Remove the wire from the tube and wrap the ends around the coil so that it holds its shape.

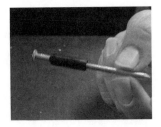

Hot glue the coil securely to the bottom of the paper cup. Sand the varnish insulation off the tips of both ends of the coil.

Take the plastic sheath off a mono plug. You can thread it on the wires to be screwed back on when the connection is made, or just discard it. Connect one end of the wire to each of the terminals of the plug. Note that each of the terminals is connected to one of the two segments of the plug, which are separated by a black band of insulation. The wires can't be touching each other where they have been stripped, nor can the terminals touch. Tape each one separately to avoid a short circuit.

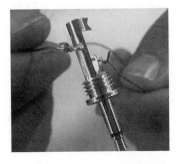

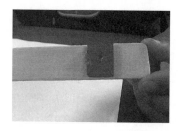

This is the coil and the diaphragm for your speaker. The next step will involve adding the magnet. Glue a magnet onto a paint paddle near the end but not flush. A magnet that fits inside the coil will work best, but any magnet will do.

Poke paper fasteners into either side of the cup near the bottom. Bend them over inside the cup. Stretch the rubber band over the base of the cup and loop one end of it around the heads of each fastener.

Lift the rubber band and slide the paint paddle with magnet under it. The rubber band should hold the magnet near to or touching the coil. Turn a radio up loud and plug the speaker in. You should be able to hear the radio if you put your ear close to the cup. If you make the coil and magnet fit together very well, you may be able to hear it across the room.

If you have a small amplifier, plug the speaker into its input jack. Now you have a microphone. Speak into the cup, and someone else will hear your voice coming from the amplifier.

More to Think About and Try

- ☙ Will the solenoid work if you "feed" a toothpick into it instead of a paper clip or nail?
- ☙ How could you make the speaker louder?
- ☙ What happens if the magnet is too far away from the coil of wire?
- ☙ How is your speaker different from a real one?

A Little Background

You can make a simpler electromagnet with just a nail or bolt wrapped with a bit of wire. The solenoid is more interesting because you can see that the magnetic field is strongest in the center of the coil. When you put a nail in the center, the iron atoms of that nail become magnetically aligned and the nail becomes a magnet. If you put in something that is not attracted to a magnet, like a toothpick, nothing will happen.

Trace the sound from an announcer's voice in the radio studio to the speaker you just made. The announcer's vocal chords vibrate when she pushes air past them. This vibration pushes on air, and sound waves are set up, moving out in all directions from her mouth and vocal chords. Some of these sound waves hit the microphone in front of her. The function of a microphone is to turn sound waves into electric impulses, called a signal. This signal then gets sent to the radio station's transmitter and antenna, where it is converted into radio waves. All the information from the original sound is contained in these radio waves, which get broadcast out in all directions.

If some of these radio waves make it to your radio before they lose their energy, your radio will receive them, convert that information back into an electric signal, amplify it, and send it to the speaker. The function of a speaker is exactly opposite that of a microphone: to turn electric impulses into sound waves. Speakers do this by means of two magnets pulling and pushing on each other. One is an electromagnet, whose strength and direction of magnetism depend on the electric signal that the radio is giving it. All the information from the original sound is contained in that signal, so the electromagnet pulls and pushes on the permanent magnet to create the same vibration that the microphone originally received.

Either the coil or the permanent magnet is connected to the diaphragm of the speaker. When the diaphragm starts vibrating, it pushes on the air and sends out a sound wave. If that sound wave makes it to your ear, you can hear what the announcer is saying.

Speakers can be made louder by amplifying the signal sent to them, by increasing the size of the coil or the permanent magnet, or by making them of higher quality, with less distance between the magnet and coil. The best speakers are still very similar to the one you made, but are constructed so that the coil and magnet are extremely close together. If they are too far apart, the magnetic field decreases in strength and they cannot push and pull as hard on each other. The shapes of the box and diaphragm also are crucial in determining the final sound of a speaker.

CHIRPING BIRD AND CUICA

A traditional toy from China and a musical instrument from Brazil will help to explain earthquakes.

PARTS	
Chirping Bird	
File folder or stiff paper	2 straight pins
Drinking straw	String
Bamboo skewer	12-inch dowel (¼-inch diameter)
Fender washer (into which the glue stick tightly fits)*	
Cuica	
Large nail to make hole	Water
Clear plastic cup	Paper towel
String	Pinch of sand (for demonstration of vibration)
Small nail or toothpick (to tie string onto)	
TOOLS	
Chirping Bird	
Stapler with staples	Hole punch
* It is also possible, though a bit trickier, to use a bottle cap, smashed and sanded, in place of the fender washer.	

The Basic Concepts

Sound is created when vibration occurs. In the chirping bird experiment, the pin does not slide smoothly on the fender washer—both rub together in a slip/stick motion. In the cuica, the paper moves on the string in the same way. This slip/stick motion is also what produces sound when a bow moves across a stringed instrument. And earthquakes occur when the Earth's tectonic plates, which have been sticking together and building up pressure, suddenly slip.

The volume of a given sound depends on various factors, including how large the object vibrating is and how it makes contact with the air around it.

Build It!

Chirping Bird

Cut a file folder in half. Fold one piece of the file folder in half. Follow the template on the next page to draw the head and wings of the bird, or draw a bird of your own design. Make sure the long side is on the folded edge. The head needs to be big enough for an eyehole. Cut out the shape through both sides of the folder, leaving the folded edge intact.

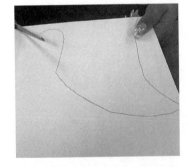

On the other half of the file folder, draw and cut the tail of the bird. Fold the ends back in opposite directions.

Head and wings template

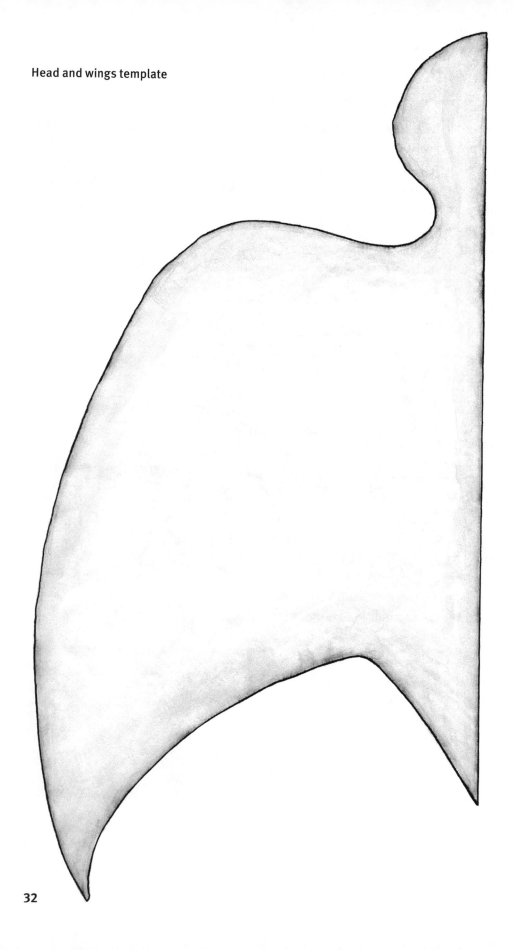

Tail template

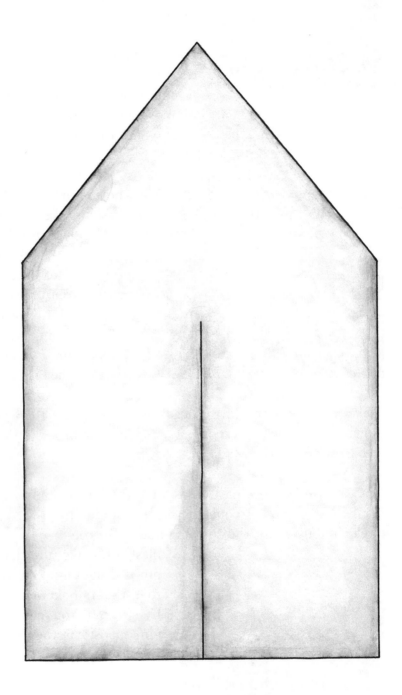

Cut the drinking straw so it is a little bit longer than the body of the bird. Insert the bamboo skewer through the straw. Put the straw in the middle of the bird.

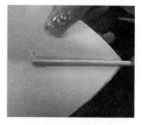

Fold the body around the straw and staple it several times so that it grips the straw tightly but does not stop the skewer from spinning. Hot glue the back end of the bamboo skewer in the center of the tail.

Cut a short piece of hot glue stick. Drill a hole in the piece of glue stick with a large nail. Insert the sharp end of the bamboo skewer into the piece of the hot glue stick. Then, push the piece of hot glue stick through the hole

of the #10 fender washer. Hot glue a straight pin onto the head of the bird so that it extends out in front of the head. The pin must touch the washer, or the bird will not work.

Make a hole on the bird's head with the hole punch. Cut 18 inches of string. Thread one end of the string through the hole and tie it securely.

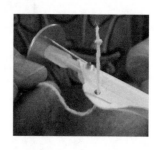

Cut at least 6 inches of a dowel. Tie the string firmly to the dowel. To operate the bird, spin it in circles and listen for the chirping noise. To trou-

bleshoot, make sure that the tip of the pin is dragging along the washer and that the tail-skewer-washer piece is free to spin. You may also add another pin, opposite to the first.

Cuica

Make a hole with a nail in the center of the base of a clear plastic cup. Cut a piece of string 2 to 3 feet long and pass it through the hole.

Tie the string to the nail on the inside of the cup. The nail will hold the string tightly inside the cup.

Wet a piece of paper towel. Holding the cup with one hand, gently squeeze the string with the wet paper towel and pull the towel down the string. It should make an interesting sound. Drop a pinch of sand into the cuica and watch it dance while you stroke the string.

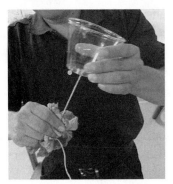

More to Think About and Try

- ➤ How does the bird make noise?
- ➤ How could you make the bird louder?
- ➤ What would happen if you made a very small tail?
- ➤ What do you think would happen if you made the cuica out of a big drum?

A Little Background

The chirping bird and cuica make sound in a very distinct way. The slip/stick motion of the pin tip scratching along the washer is very similar to that of the wet paper towel sliding on the cuica string, chalk screeching on a chalkboard, a violin bow on violin strings, and tectonic plates moving beside each other. There is a period of no motion as tension builds up, then a period of great motion as the two items move from a high-energy state to a low-energy state, then a return to no motion and the slow buildup of tension. With earthquakes, one cycle takes years, decades, or millennia. With a violin, the process happens many times per second.

In both the bird and cuica, the "sounding board" principle is important. On the cuica, try holding the string alone and pulling down on the wet paper. The sound is there, but it is much less intense. The cup helps to connect the vibration from the string to the air. It touches and pushes on more air than does the string alone, and it sends out sound waves with much more energy than just a vibrating string. This is one reason behind the big box of a guitar, and the reason real cuicas (very loud!) are as large as 5-gallon pails. A chirping bird made with a large body may be louder because the body of the bird is the sounding board for the tiny vibrating pin.

The bird may also be louder if it's made with two pins. If you make the tail very small, not much air pushes on it as it flies, so it may not have enough force to spin the washer around. A big tail comes in contact with more air and gives plenty of force to make the pin slide on the washer.

Thanks to an anonymous street vendor in Zhongguancun, China, for the fine Chirping Bird idea. Thanks to the Math and Science Across Culture focus group of teachers at the Exploratorium for the Cuica idea.

MUSiCA:

SAXOPhONe, hARMONiCA, gUiTAR, bUll ROAReR, ObOe, AND SUCkeR

There is more than one way to make music.

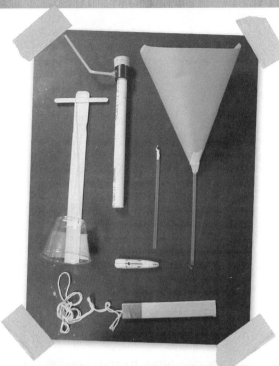

PARTS	
Saxophone	
10-inch PVC tube (½-inch diameter)	Rubber band
Film canister	Drinking straw
Latex glove	
Harmonica	
Clothespin	Rubber band (fat)
Guitar	
Paint paddle	Rubber band (skinny)
Clear plastic cup	Craft stick
Nail (to make hole and to hold rubber band inside cup)	
Bull Roarer	
Paint paddle	Strong string
Oboe	
Drinking straw	Colored paper

PARTS *Continued*	
Sucker	
Paper, any kind	Drinking straw
TOOLS	
Saxophone	
PVC cutter (or hacksaw)	Small drill bit (the same size as drinking straw)
13⁄16-inch paddle bit	

The Basic Concepts

Sound comes from vibrations. The vibrations push on air and make sound waves that travel through the air to your ear. The frequency of a sound vibration is called pitch. The pitch of an instrument is related to its size: large things generally have lower pitch, small things higher pitch. The amplitude of a sound vibration is called volume. The higher the amplitude of vibration, the louder it is.

Build It!

Saxophone

Cut around 10 inches of PVC tube (almost any length works). Make a hole on the side of the film canister. The size of the hole should be exactly the size of the straw.

Use the 13⁄16-inch paddle bit *without the drill* to make a hole in the bottom of the film canister. (Paddle bits can be dangerous when used in the hand drill.)

Cut a finger off a latex glove. Stretch the finger over the top of the film canister, but do not cover the side hole.

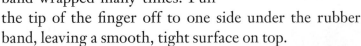

Secure the finger with a rubber band wrapped many times. Pull the tip of the finger off to one side under the rubber band, leaving a smooth, tight surface on top.

Insert the PVC tube into the ¹³⁄₁₆-inch hole until it contacts the stretched glove. Insert a drinking straw into the side hole. It should extend inside only a tiny bit—not tight against the PVC tube. Glue the straw in.

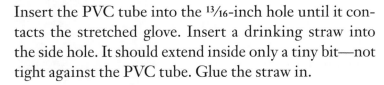

Drill holes in the PVC tube with a small bit. You can put nails into the drill platform to help hold the PVC tube and keep it from turning when drilling these holes. Be sure you can reach the holes with your fingers. Blow through the straw to make music.

Harmonica

Take apart the wooden clothespin. Wrap masking tape about six times around the ends of the two wood pieces. The tape must allow a small gap between the wood pieces when you sandwich them together. At one end, the tape should be at the tip of the wood piece. At the other end, there should be a bit of wood sticking out beyond the tape. Make both pieces this way.

Carefully stretch a rubber band around one wood piece. Then, put the other wood piece back-to-back with the first one, sandwiching one length of the rubber band between the wood pieces. Pinching them together, carefully twist the rubber band at one end and loop it back over both wood pieces.

There should be one layer of rubber band between the two clothespin pieces, one on one side and two on the other. Blow through the small hole in the center. To change the sound, pinch the tips that extend from the tape on one side.

Guitar

Hot glue and then tape a full-length paint paddle to the clear plastic cup.

Make a hole with a small nail in the middle of the cup. Poke a rubber band down through the hole.

Thread the nail through the loop in the rubber band inside the cup. Pull up on the rubber band to tighten the nail against the inside of the cup. Glue a craft stick crossways to the other end of the paint paddle. Stretch

the rubber band up and loop it around the craft stick. Wrap it several times around the craft stick to get the right tightness and tone.

Pluck the rubber band to play the guitar. Put the cup to your ear to hear it louder.

Bull Roarer

Cut a paint paddle in half. Glue and/or tape the two halves together. Drill a hole near one end of the paint paddle. Then, tie a string to the paddles. Make the knot very strong, and reinforce with tape if there is any doubt.

Tie a knot on the other end of the string in order to hold it securely. Find an open space and spin it hard. Listen to a roaring sound that starts and stops. Look at the angle of the string as the toy is roaring.

Oboe

Chew on the end of a straw gently to make it flat. Then cut small triangles from each edge near the end, making a sort of dull point. This is the "double reed" of the oboe.

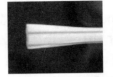 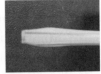

Stick this end in your mouth and blow. If there is no sound, chew it slightly in various directions until a sound comes out.

To make the sound louder, tape together a paper cone for the oboe.

Sucker

Cut a tiny rectangular piece of paper. Stick it on a small piece of tape (any kind). Tape it so that it sticks out over the end of a drinking straw.

Fold the paper out and then back over the opening. The paper flap should cover the opening if pushed toward it but then spring back a bit when released.

Suck on the straw from the other end and continue to adjust the paper flap until it vibrates and a sound occurs.

More to Think About and Try

- In each instrument, what is vibrating?
- How could you change each instrument's pitch?
- How could you make each instrument louder?
- What happens if you just stretch a rubber band across the paint paddle—without the cup—in the guitar project?

A Little Background

Musical instruments make sound in many different ways, but in each one something is vibrating. In the saxophone the piece of glove is going up and down—feel it with your finger as you blow. This simple instrument is called a saxophone because it sounds like one. In reality, a saxophone has a single reed vibrating against a mouthpiece, not a piece of latex vibrating against a tube.

The harmonica's rubber band stretched between the two halves of the clothespin also vibrates up and down—you can feel it with your tongue. The guitar also has rubber bands vibrating, which then make the cup vibrate. The bull roarer is spinning around, beating the air like a helicopter. In the oboe the sides of the straw vibrate against each other just like a real oboe or bassoon. It is called a double reed mouthpiece. The sucker makes all its noise from that tiny piece of paper banging again and again against the end of the straw.

The pitch of an instrument is its frequency, or how fast the vibration is going: faster is higher pitch, slower is lower. You can easily change the pitch of most of these instruments. You can stretch rubber bands or rubber gloves tighter to raise the pitch. On the saxophone you can also cover the holes in the tube. The air in the tube up to the first hole vibrates together with the glove, so the longer that this tube is, the more air that needs to vibrate and the longer it takes to vibrate back and forth. The bull roarer has a higher pitch if you swing it harder, because it is spinning faster. The oboe and sucker are harder to change. You can change the pitch by cutting the drinking straw or making tiny holes. Since the straw is full of air, different lengths of straw will give different pitches, just as in the saxophone.

To change the volume passing through the instrument is even easier: just do what you do more vigorously. If the amplitude of vibration goes up, the volume increases.

The cup on the guitar vibrates along with the stretched rubber bands. The cup can push more air than the rubber band does, so it sends out more sound waves into the air. The cup serves the same purpose as the box on a guitar. Without it, you'll have a pathetic little sound from your instrument.

Thanks to teachers and staff at the Exploratorium Teacher Institute for the oboe, sucker, harmonica, and saxophone ideas, and to Modesto Tamez for a killer performance on the harmonica.

XYlOPhONe AND MARiMbA

Both wood and metal make interesting sounds when they vibrate.

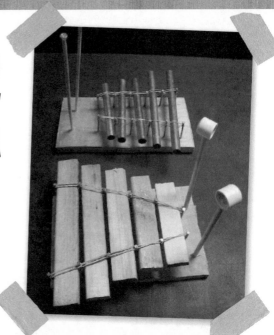

PARTS	
Xylophone or Marimba	
Baseboard (at least 12 inches by 6 inches and at least 5/8-inch thick)	Rubber bands (small)
	2 8-inch dowels (1/4-inch diameter)
12 nails (two-headed concrete form type works best)	Cardboard (for feet)
Xylophone	
40-inch steel conduit pipe	2 nuts (1/4 inch)
Marimba	
45-inch 1-by-2 wood	2 PVC pipe caps (1/2-inch diameter)
TOOLS	
Xylophone	
Pipe cutter	
Marimba	
File or sandpaper	

The Basic Concepts

Sound comes from vibrations. If you hear sound, something is vibrating. Sticks of wood and metal vibrate and make sound when you hit them. The frequency, or pitch, of this sound depends on the composition of the material and the length of it. The volume of the sound depends on the amplitude of vibration, which is determined in large part by how hard you hit the material.

Build It!

Xylophone

At one end of the baseboard, make a mark 1 inch in both directions from the two corners.

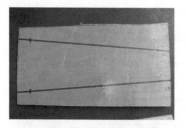

Lay the ruler so that it starts at one of these marks and angles down toward the center (but not quite at the center) of the other end. Draw a line along the ruler; then draw another one more or less symmetrical with the first, starting at the other mark.

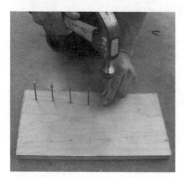

Using the original marks as zeros, mark every 1½ inches down each of the lines until you have six dots. (This is to create five spaces for five pipes. Of course, you can make more if you have the material.) Hammer a nail in at each of the marks.

String two sets of rubber bands along the nails between the two heads.

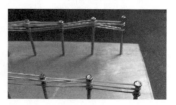

Mark and cut pipes (from the steel conduit) to the lengths you wish, but make them all different lengths. (Segments of 10, 9, 8, 7, and 6 inches work well.) A pipe cutter works by your tightening it snugly, turning it around the pipe two times, tightening it another one-quarter around, turning around the pipe two more times, and on and on until

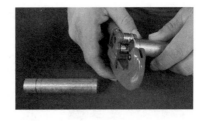

the circular blade has cut through the conduit. But be careful—if you tighten it too much, it is bad for the blade and impossible to turn the pipe.

Slide the pipes between the two sets of rubber bands.

Place the longer pipes on the end with the nails farther apart.

To make playing mallets, cut two dowels around 8 inches long. Slightly sharpen one end of each with a pencil sharpener or knife, then thread on a ¼-inch nut until it is tight.

Cut out and glue on small squares of cardboard for feet. These feet have two

functions — to avoid scratching the table with any nail tips that protrude through the

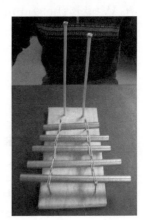

bottom of the baseboard and to prevent the baseboard from rattling on the table when it is played.

Drill two ¹⁹⁄₆₄-inch holes in one end of the baseboard to hold the playing mallets when not in use.

Marimba

The marimba uses a base with nails in the same manner as the xylophone. The marimba merely replaces the sections of conduit pipe with pieces of wood. The nails on the marimba base must be farther apart, at least

2 inches. The bottom row of rubber bands may be below the double heads of the nails. Cut the 1-by-2 pieces to length with a saw (segments of 11, 10, 9, 8, and 7 inches work well.), and then file or sand off the rough spots for a better look and a better sound.

To make marimba mallets, drill a $^{15}\!/_{64}$-inch hole in two PVC pipe caps. Then, hammer a ¼-inch dowel into each hole.

Use the rounded back of the pipe cap to hit the pieces of wood.

More to Think About and Try

- ✐ What happens if you hold a pipe or stick when you hit it?
- ✐ How can you make the sound last longer after you strike the pipe or stick?
- ✐ Why is the sound different when you hit the pipe or stick with the wooden side of the mallet?
- ✐ What happens if one of the pipes or sticks is pressed up against one of the nails?

A Little Background

When you hit something, it tends to start vibrating. Originally the object is deformed; then it springs back to its original position, goes a bit farther because of momentum, stops, starts back the way it came, and on and on. Some materials have little or no elasticity, or spring (water, clay, leather, loose fabric), so when you hit them, they do not vibrate. But most woods and metals do.

A stick of anything may vibrate in several different ways. In one of the primary vibrations, the ends go up and down as the center bulges up and down in the opposite direction. There is a point at about one-quarter of the length of the stick from each end that hardly moves at all as the ends and center vibrate up and down. This place is called a "node of motion," and this is where you want to hold the stick if you are looking to sustain its vibrations. The closer to a node you can support the stick, the longer it will vibrate. The V pattern of the nails on the board is an attempt to support the pipes and sticks more or less at that quarter-length point.

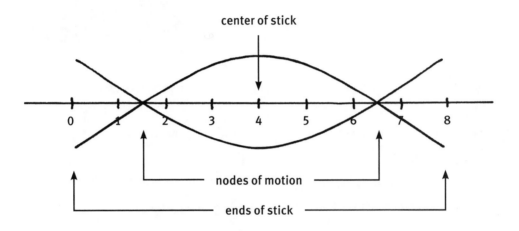

An exaggerated drawing of a vibrating stick in its two positions of "maximum deformation"—that is, the maximum that the stick is able to move when bent like this.

If you hold the pipe or stick anywhere else than at the quarter-length point, or if it is touching something else (such as a nail), the vibrations will be dampened (reduced). If you hold it with something elastic though, such as a rubber band, the stick will be free to vibrate. Thus, you don't need to find the precise node in this project because you are supporting the pipes and sticks with rubber bands.

The material used to hit these instruments also helps determine what kind of vibration will arise and what sound will come out. You can try hitting your xylophone or marimba with many different materials and thinking about why the sounds are different. Using harder objects to hit with will start vibrations faster; softer ones will start vibrations gradually.

KALEIDOSCOPE

If you give it the right mirrors, light will just keep bouncing.

PARTS

3 plastic mirrors (1 inch by 4 inch)	2 washers ($^5/_{16}$ inch)
2-inch 1-by-2 wood	5-inch clear, flexible tubing ($^5/_{16}$-inch inner diameter, $^1/_2$-inch outer diameter)
10-inch dowel ($^5/_{16}$-inch diameter, for glitter rod, spinner rod, and plugs in tubing)	
	Large cup to trace for circle
Binder clip (large)	White paper
Glitter	Pushpin
Food coloring (or liquid watercolor)	Clear marble

The Basic Concepts

Light reflects from almost everything. When the light that reflects off something enters your eye, you see that thing. Mirrors reflect differently from most things: they reflect at only one angle. Water and glass reflect, too, but not as well as a mirror. Light can reflect from mirrors many times, each time losing a bit of its intensity.

Build It!

Cut a small piece of duct tape and lay it sticky side up on the table. Put one mirror in the center of the duct tape.

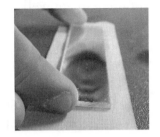 

Attach the other two mirrors to the tape on either side of the first mirror, but leave some space between them. Cut off any tape that sticks out around the edges.

Fold the mirrors into a triangle and tape them together, mirrored side in.

Cut about 2 inches of 1-by-2 wood. Glue it on one of the mirrors, close to the end.

Cut two pieces of a 5/16-inch dowel about 4 inches long. Glue one on between the mirrors and the wood piece so that it sticks out past the end of the mirrors.

Glue a binder clip onto the front of the piece of 1-by-2 wood. The opening of the binder clip should be exactly in the center of the opening of the kaleidoscope.

Put a 5/16-inch washer onto the second dowel about an inch from the end. Put hot glue on the short end and dip the dowel in some glitter.

Cut two pieces of a ⁵⁄₁₆-inch dowel about 1 inch long. Insert one of the dowels into one end of the tubing. Glue it well.

Put some glitter and a bit of food coloring inside the tube. Then fill the tube with water.

Put the other piece of dowel in the other end of the tube and seal it with hot glue. Try not to capture any air, but a small bubble inside is OK.

Draw a circle on a piece of paper and cut it out. Decorate it however you want.

Glue a washer to the center of the circle. Insert a pushpin in the center of the circle.

Push the pin into the end of the dowel sticking out beyond the mirrors. The decorated side should be toward the mirrors.

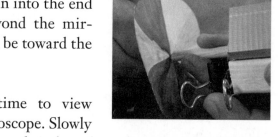

Now it's time to view your kaleidoscope. Slowly spin the colored circle and see the patterns by looking through the other end of the kaleidoscope.

Take the circle off and insert the dowel into the binder clip with the glittered end up. Spin it slowly as you view it. Then, take the dowel out and insert the glitter tube into the binder clip. Turn the kaleidoscope over and over and watch the glitter fall

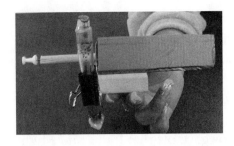

through the water past the opening in the mirrors.

Take the tube out and put a marble at the opening and view it, or instead of a marble, look at anything you want: your finger, your friend, a tree, and so on. The more light that gets into the kaleidoscope, the better it works; so look toward a window or go outside—***but don't look at the sun!***

More to Think About and Try

* When you put the marble in the end and look through the kaleidoscope, how many marbles can you see altogether?
* What do you think would happen if you put four mirrors together into a kaleidoscope?
* What do you think would happen if you used the kaleidoscope at night?
* What do you see if you don't put anything at the end of the kaleidoscope but instead rotate the whole thing as you look through it.

A Little Background

Some things give off light: the sun and stars, candles and other flames, lightbulbs, and glowing things. If something gives off its own light, you see it when some of its light enters your eye.

Most things do not give off their own light. You can see these things because they reflect light that is given off by other things. Most things reflect light in many directions. A whole crowd of people can see a rock star on stage because light given off by the spotlights is reflecting off the singer into each of their eyes.

Mirrors are different. They reflect light at only one angle. The angle of reflection happens to be the same as the angle of incidence, that is, the angle the light came in at.

When you look at a mirror, at any given spot on that mirror you'll see one thing. The light coming from that thing (either given off or reflected by it) hit the mirror, bounced off at the same angle as it hit, and then went into your eye.

If you have two or more mirrors, some light may hit one, reflect to the other, and continue to go back and forth. If that light then gets into your eye, you can see the object that reflected or gave off that light. Since light comes off things at all different angles, many different bits of light can take various paths back and forth between the mirrors and then get into your eye. This is how you can see multiple images of the same object.

Each time light reflects off a mirror, it loses a bit of intensity. That's why the images that result from fewer reflections tend to be brighter, while the images that result from many reflections tend to be dimmer. Thus the images seen near the center of the kaleidoscope tend to be crisp, and those seen farther out are not as clear.

How many images you can see depends on the angle between the mirrors, how many mirrors you have, where you put your eye, and where you put the object you are viewing. For each image that you see, you can try to work out which mirror or mirrors the light has bounced off.

thAUMAtRope

Your eye and brain are just slow enough to see several things at once.

PARTS
Paint paddle
Baseboard
2 craft sticks
Cardboard (thin)
White paper
Rubber bands (medium)
TOOLS
Stapler with staples

The Basic Concepts

Your eye has limits to how fast it can see two distinct pictures. When pictures are moving through the same area too fast, they get "mixed" in your eye. Movies and video screens use this concept. A movie is actually a lot of nonmoving images flashing quickly across the screen. Human eyes can't distinguish the individual images fast enough, so it looks like everything is moving smoothly.

Build It!

Cut a paint paddle in half. Hot glue each half to one end of the baseboard on the same side. Hot glue craft sticks in triangles for braces.

Cut a piece of cardboard that will fit between the two vertical paint paddle pieces. Cut white paper pieces of the same size and glue them to the cardboard on either side.

Slip a rubber band around the resulting sandwich. Move the rubber band exactly to the center and staple it in place. The staple may straddle the rubber band, or it may penetrate it, as shown here.

Draw one half of a picture (such as a face) on one side of cardboard. Flip the piece vertically and draw the other half of the picture (such as a head). Do this carefully, flipping it back and forth in the same way that it will flip on its stand, to be sure it will look right. Draw two halves of a picture that will roughly fit together well; it is hard to make a very precise fit.

Stretch the rubber band from one paint paddle to the other. Twist the two-sided picture over and check them both again. Both pictures should be right-side up as you look at them.

Wind the cardboard up and let it go. If the two halves don't fit together

well, you may have to make another try at the drawing. You can make several cardboard pieces with different pictures to use on your base.

More to Think About and Try

- ✗ What would happen if you had three or four sides to the thaumatrope?
- ✗ Do you think the thaumatrope would work better with a bright light or a dim light?
- ✗ How could you see the picture on the thaumatrope upside down?
- ✗ Why do you think we used small rubber bands on the thaumatrope?

A Little Background

Television programs and movies consist of images flashed on the screen 60 to 72 times per second. In the early days of movies, the images were flashed much less often, giving a flickering effect. ("Let's go see a flick!") The reason video images appear to move is that your eyes have a limit as to how fast they can resolve and distinguish flashing images. Flashing images in a film present motion in small increments. Your eye-brain system puts these images back together into realistic looking motion.

In the thaumatrope, you see the two images from opposite sides of the paper at the same time because the cardboard is rotating so fast. If you look at the back side, the images are upside down. If you put a large rubber band on, the cardboard rotates even faster. If it turns too fast, the drawings present themselves for too short a time and are less clear. If there were several sides instead of just two, you might be able to make a real movie, but there are several factors making this difficult. The images have to be exactly in the same spot when they come around, and there has to be a moment of relative darkness between the pictures or the eye-brain system will blur them. In the two-sided thaumatrope, this moment of darkness happens as the edge of the cardboard swings by.

bALANCiNg ACtS

Watch your center of mass, or you'll fall over.

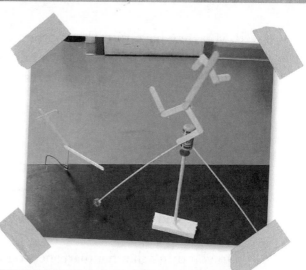

PARTS	
Dancer on a Table	
Craft sticks	Nut (⅜ inch or larger)
Baling wire	
Dancer on a Tack	
Small baseboard	Cork
8-inch dowel (¼-inch diameter)	2 bamboo skewers
Penny	2 nuts (⅜ inch or larger)
Craft sticks	Tack

The Basic Concepts

Everything has a point called its center of gravity, or center of mass. You can think of all the mass of the object concentrated there. An object standing on the ground will balance only if its center of mass is directly above a point that is within the boundaries of its support points. For example, if you lean too far forward, you'll fall over unless you move a foot or hand underneath you.

An object hanging will fall and/or rotate until its support point is directly above its center of mass. For example, if you hang from your hands you'll hang straight down, but if you raise your legs out in front of you, your torso will swing back a bit.

Build It!

Dancer on the Table

Construct a small figure, as shown, with craft sticks and hot glue.

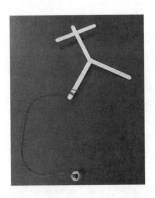 

Cut about 12 inches of baling wire. Wrap about 1 inch of the wire around the tip of one of the figure's legs. Then connect a nut or something heavy to the other end of the wire. Bend the wire in a curve such that the craft figure stands up by itself. It can stand on either leg if you bend the wire correctly.

Dancer on a Tack

First, drill a $^{15}/_{64}$-inch hole into the baseboard. Cut a piece of ¼-inch dowel about 8 inches long. Hammer it into the hole. If it is not tight, hot glue it.

Glue a penny flat on the tip of the dowel, with the Lincoln Memorial faceup.

Make a figure—any shape, but not too heavy—with craft sticks and hot glue. On the left is one example.

Use a nail as a drill bit and make two holes in opposite sides of a cork. The holes should be angled upward, so that when you insert the sharp ends of two bamboo skewers into the holes they angle upward, as shown.

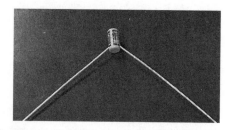

Glue nuts to the unsharpened ends of the bamboo skewers. Glue the cork to the lower most stick on your figure.

Glue a tack to the bottom of the cork so that the point is sticking out.

Balance the figure by the tip of the tack pin on the penny. Give it a spin. If it tips too much, glue more weight on the ends of the skewers.

More to Think About and Try

- If your Dancer on the Table doesn't balance right, what can you do to change it?
- If a larger kid and a smaller kid use a seesaw, who should sit closer to the center?
- Why is it harder to walk on high heels than on regular shoes?
- Why would you want to carry two buckets half full of water instead of one bucket full of water?

A Little Background

These projects are about optical illusions as well as center of mass. Since the nuts are small and the figures are large, it looks as if they should fall over. But the nuts are heavy for their size and the figures are light, so it makes sense that the heavy parts will swing to the bottom. If you made the figures from thick wood, they would probably fall over because they would be heavier than the nuts.

Your body has a center of mass, too. While standing, your feet always stay directly under your center of mass. If you try to stand on your hands, you may notice that your hands are not as big as your feet, and you will have to work harder to keep them under your center of mass. To walk in high heels can be hard because your points of support on the ground are so very small. It is easy for your center of gravity to move outside those points of support, at which time you'll stumble or fall. Similarly, if you want a table to be very stable, you'll put the legs far apart. Tall, slender tables with legs close together fall over easily.

If you try to hang from your hands, it will be easy. Gravity just pulls your center of mass directly under the pole you are hanging from. In physics this is called "stable equilibrium," and it occurs whenever you hang something. Think of the exact same system upside down—that is, standing on your hands on a bar. There will still be a point of equilibrium—when your mass is balanced above the point of support on the bar—but it will not be very stable because the bar is so narrow. Instead, you will tend to fall and swing around until you reach stable equilibrium again.

If your dancer on the table is not working, you can bend the wire and weight around so that the center of gravity is below the point of support. A seesaw works because it is balanced on the center pivot. If one kid is a lot heavier, it will not be balanced, so that kid will always be on the ground. But if she moves toward the center, there will be a point where she is balanced with the other kid around the central pivot. Carrying one full bucket of water requires leaning and bending so that you don't fall over. Two buckets of water, one hanging from each hand, are much easier to balance.

CATAPUlT

Learn physics from very old military science.

PARTS	
32-inch 1-by-2 wood (cut to 9-inch, 11-inch, and 12-inch sections)	3 nails, small
	Bottle cap, film canister, or any small cup (for the bean)
Screw (#8, 1½ inches long)	
2 nuts (#8)	2 rubber bands
2 fender washers (#8)	Cardboard
2 paint paddles	Beans
2 small binder clips	
TOOLS	
Tin snips for cutting cardboard	

The Basic Concepts

There are two important lengths on a lever: between the weight (bean) and the fulcrum (the point around which the lever turns), and between the fulcrum and the force (rubber band). If you change the two lengths, the catapult will shoot differently. There is some combination of these two lengths that will make the weight shoot the farthest.

Triangles are very important in construction. The triangular cardboard supports are crucial to the catapult's stability.

Build It!

Cut three pieces of 1-by-2: 12 inches, 11 inches, and 9 inches. Then, drill a ¹⁵⁄₆₄-inch hole near the top of the longest piece. Glue the 9-inch piece to the 12-inch one, face-to-face, with ends matching.

Glue the bottom of those two pieces to the middle of the 11-inch 1-by-2.

Insert the screw into the hole at the top of the longest piece. Put on one nut until tight. Put the fender washer outside the nut.

Glue two paint paddles together face-to-face. Clip one binder clip at one end and one at the middle of the paint paddles. Check to be sure the middle binder clip can slide from side to side.

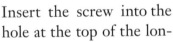

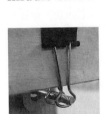 

Insert the two handles of the middle binder clip on the screw. Then put on a second washer and then a second nut, finger tight.

Hammer a small nail into the end of the 11-inch (base) 1-by-2 piece on the same end as the binder clip and at the end of the paint paddles.

On the opposite side of the paint paddles (where there is no clip), hot glue a bottle cap.

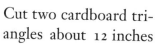

Tie two rubber bands together; then tie them to the handle of the binder clip at the end of the paint paddle.

Cut two cardboard triangles about 12 inches long and 5 inches high. Glue one triangle to each side of the wood base.

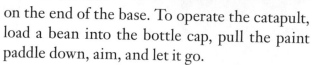

Tie the rubber band to the nail on the end of the base. To operate the catapult, load a bean into the bottle cap, pull the paint paddle down, aim, and let it go.

To improve your shot, slide the center binder clip to a new position and try it again.

More to Think About and Try

- What can you do to make the catapult shoot farther?
- Does it shoot farther with a longer arm on the rubber band side, or a shorter one?
- What is the function of the cardboard? What would happen if you didn't put it on?
- How could you make the catapult shoot straight up?

A Little Background

The catapult is a lever with an adjustable fulcrum. This makes the total length of the force arm and the effort arm a constant: when one gets bigger, the other gets smaller. Another lever is a seesaw. On a seesaw the fulcrum is fixed in the middle of the board, but you can effectively shorten one of the sides by having one person sit closer to the middle.

This is a good project to do a short experiment with. If you mark off the throwing arm every inch and then shoot three times with the fulcrum at each mark, you can average the results for each mark and can find out what the optimal place is for the fulcrum. You can then graph it to see it in a different way.

To make the catapult shoot farther, you can add more rubber bands, shoot a smaller weight, or try to optimize the ratio of lengths between the force and effort arms. The cardboard triangles keep the vertical pieces from bending over when you pull one way or another. To make the catapult shoot up, you just need to rotate the catapult so that the base is vertical.

DANGLING SPINNER

A fraction of a wave is a beautiful thing.

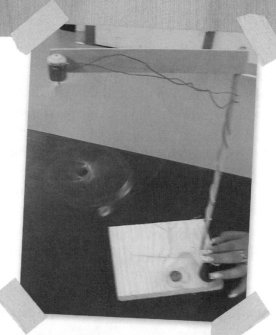

PARTS	
16-inch dowel (5⁄16-inch diameter)	2 2-foot wires, thin, with insulation
Baseboard	Film canister
Paint paddle	Aluminum foil
Hobby motor, 1.5–3 volts	C battery
Colored string and yarn of different thicknesses	7-inch resistance wire
	Paper clips
Craft sticks	
3 different washers (such as #10, ¼ inch, ⅜ inch)	
TOOLS	
Wire strippers	

The Basic Concepts

A wave on a string can be driven from one end. The motor provides the force and the battery provides the energy. When something is moving fast, your eyes can't follow it. It becomes a blur in the shape of its entire path.

By putting more resistance in the circuit with the motor, a motor will go slower.

Build It!

Cut the dowel to about 16 inches. Drill a $^{19}\!/_{64}$-inch hole in the baseboard. Hammer the dowel into the hole.

Cut the paint paddle at about 10 inches. Hot glue the paint paddle to the top of the dowel. Then hot glue the motor to the tip of the paint paddle.

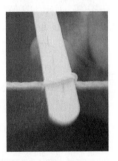

Tie a string firmly on one of the edges of a craft stick. Tie a washer on the other end of the string. (Start with one string on one end of the stick, for simplicity. You can add another to the other end later.)

Gently drill a hole in the center of the craft stick with a nail bit that is slightly smaller than motor shaft. Insert the shaft of the motor through the hole. If it doesn't hold, add glue to the tip of the motor shaft to hold it in place. You can glue the string onto the stick as shown, or you can use a paper clip to leave open the possibility of exchanging strings (see p. 66).

Strip both ends of the wires. Connect the wires to the terminals of the motor. Run the wires back down the paint paddle and then down the dowel.

Hot glue the film canister to the baseboard near the dowel. This is the battery holder. At the other end of one of the wires tightly fold a piece of aluminum foil. This makes for a better connection for the battery.

Insert the wire end with the aluminum foil in the film canister, all the way to the bottom. Put the battery inside so that it rests on the foil, making a solid connection.

Connect about 6 inches of resistance wire to the other free end of wire. To make the toy spin, press the resistance wire to the top of the battery. The resistance wire will control the speed of the motor depending on where you connect the battery to it. Take out the resistance wire and connect the battery directly to the other wire for maximum speed.

You can create several strings. Instead of gluing them to the craft stick, tie each string to a paper clip then clip it to the craft stick.

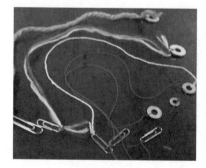

Try it with different sized washers and with no washer.

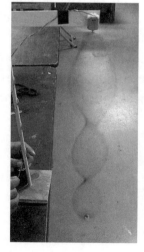

You can make many different shapes. Other variables you can adjust: speed, string size, washer size, position of paper clip on craft stick, and number of strings hanging.

More to Think About and Try

- Which parts of the string go inward, toward the center of the circle when the toy spins, and which move away from the centerline?
- What difference does the length make in how the strings spin?
- What do you think would happen if you put two batteries on the toy?
- What do you think would happen if you tipped the whole thing sideways?

A Little Background

Waves have points of maximum movement and nodes of minimal movement. There is a node at the top of this project where the string attaches to the craft stick on the motor shaft. At the bottom there may be a node if a washer is tied on, or a maximum if there is no washer and the tip of the string flies out to the side as it spins.

Waves produced by this project can be divided into two categories. Waves in multiples of ½ (½, 1, and ³⁄₂) can be produced with a washer tied on the bottom end (creating a node), and waves in odd multiples of ¼ (¼, ¾, and ⁵⁄₄) can be produced with no washer on the end (creating a maximum).

One full wave will include a node to a maximum to a node to another maximum and back to a node.

One maximum surrounded by two nodes make half a wave.

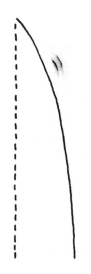

A node and a maximum alone make a quarter wave.

Try to make various combinations of these. Here is one and a quarter waves.

Heavier things, such as the washers, tend to stay in toward the center-line of a wave, while lighter things, such as the string, fly out away from the centerline. Different lengths of string give different wave patterns. I have seen students stand up on tables and use 6-foot-long strings to make astonishing kinetic art from their dangling spinners. More batteries give the motor more force to spin. If you can figure out some way of holding the bottom tip of the string but still allowing it to turn, you can tip the whole project on its side. Since both ends are restricted to be nodes in this arrangement, you'll be able to make waves only in multiples of ½.

The resistance wire is like the dimmer switch on a light. It can only resist (or restrict) the amount of electricity going to the motor, not increase it, so it can only make the motor slow down. The more resistance wire the electricity has to go through, the slower the motor goes.

MiNi-bOt

It bounces around a lot, but can you control it?

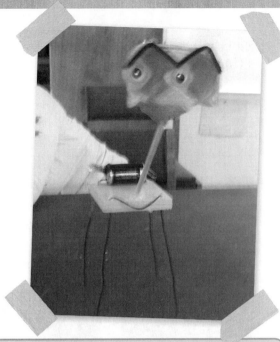

PARTS	
Baseboard (2 inches by 2 inches and thin)	C or AA battery
Baling wire	6-inch dowel (¼-inch diameter)
2 wires, thin, with insulation	Egg carton
Hobby motor, 1.5–3 volts	Pipe cleaners
2 paper clips	Yarn
Aluminum foil	Plastic eyes
TOOLS	
Wire strippers	

The Basic Concepts

The motor does not make contact with the ground, but it gives force to make the mini-bot move. The piece of glue stick on the motor shaft is not balanced, so when it spins, it sets up a vibration. And as Newton said, for every action there is an equal and opposite reaction. When the glue stick spins to one side, the mini-bot hops to the other side. When the glue stick swings down, the mini-bot hops up, and so on.

Build It!

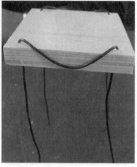

Drill four holes in the baseboard with a large nail bit, one in each corner. Cut a piece of baling wire, bend it, and force both ends through the holes. Make the wires stay on the board by bending or adding some hot glue.

Strip both ends of both insulated wires. Connect them to the

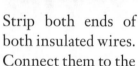

motor. Glue the motor onto the baseboard in any position you think will work.

Connect a paper clip to the free end of both wires. Fold two pieces of aluminum foil. Tape them tightly to the ends of the battery.

Glue the battery to the baseboard.

If you want a neck and head, cut a short piece of dowel. Drill a $^{15}/_{64}$-inch hole in the piece of wood at an angle and insert the dowel.

Build a head and face using an egg carton, pipe cleaners, yarn, and plastic eyes.

70

Cut a piece of hot glue stick. Drill a hole with a small nail bit in the side of the piece of glue stick, *off center*. Press it on the motor shaft.

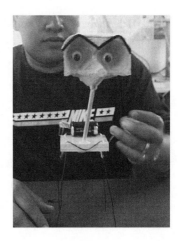

Connect the paper clips to the bits of aluminum foil and watch it hop. Try to figure out how to control its motion.

More to Think About and Try

- ☙ What happens if you attach the motor to the glue stick in exactly the center?
- ☙ What can you do to change the direction in which the mini-bot hops?
- ☙ What would happen if you put on a very large weight instead of the piece of glue?
- ☙ What would happen if you made only three legs?

A Little Background

You may never have seen anything powered in this manner, and the reason is clear: it is nearly impossible to control. Because the motor does not touch the ground or blow on air, the mini-bot is limited to hopping. The direction of each hop is determined by the swing of the piece of glue stick, the weight and balance of its body, the angle of each leg, and its friction with the ground.

If you put a hole right in the center of the glue stick and attach it to the motor shaft—you should try this—the glue stick will spin very smoothly but the mini-bot will not move. It is only when the glue stick is off center that the jumping occurs.

Think about when an adult swings a child around by the hands. The adult cannot be exactly vertical; he or she must lean back in opposition to the direction the child is swinging. On the mini-bot, the body and legs move in opposition to the glue stick.

If you switch the wires on the motor or the battery, the motor will turn in the opposite direction. This will have an impact on the direction the mini-bot hops, though it is not always predicable. The larger the weight spinning on the motor shaft, the harder the motor will have to work to spin it and so the slower it will spin. Different numbers of legs may make the mini-bot act differently, but mini-bots made with no legs—just a flat base—also work. If you make the legs using markers, your mini-bot will scribble you a picture on the table.

Thanks to the students and staff at the Mission Science Workshop in San Francisco for the original idea of locomotion by hop.

RUbbeR bAND RACeR

The answer to rising gas prices?

PARTS	
Cardboard (approximately 10 inches by 6 inches)	2 film canister lids (or plastic circles)
	Aluminum soda can
4 bamboo skewers	3 rubber bands (medium)
Drinking straw	

The Basic Concepts

If something that is not moving starts to move, energy is being used and a force exists in the direction of the motion. Energy can be stored by twisting a rubber band. This kind of energy is called "potential energy." When the car is all wound up, it has potential energy.

Energy that is moving is called "kinetic energy." When the car is moving, it has kinetic energy.

Cut a piece of cardboard such that its width is less than the length of the bamboo skewers. Slide two bamboo skewers into the corrugation holes of the cardboard.

Cut a drinking straw in half. Slide another bamboo skewer through both pieces of straw. Tape both straw pieces to the cardboard, as shown.

Punch or drill holes with nail bit in the center of the film canister lids. Put one on each end of the axle skewer. Glue them if they do not fit tightly, but glue only on the outside so that the glue does not get near the straw or cardboard.

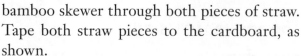

Get a soda can and make a hole with a Phillips screwdriver on top of the can across from the drinking hole. Then make two more holes on the bottom of the soda can.

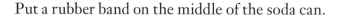

Put a rubber band on the middle of the soda can.

Get another rubber band and insert one end into the small hole in the top of the soda can. Fish the same end out of the larger hole with the remaining bamboo skewer.

Put one end of the rubber band through the other end. Loop this around one of the bamboo skewers sticking out the front of the cardboard.

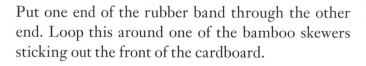

Do the same on the other side. Your racer should now look like this.

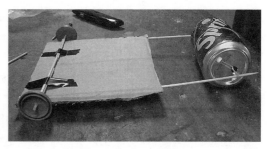

Twist the can many times to wind up the rubber bands then put it on the table and let it run. Turn the car over and see what happens.

More to Think About and Try

- ⚒ How could you make a rubber band–powered car go even farther?
- ⚒ Where does this car get its energy?
- ⚒ Where does a real car get its energy?
- ⚒ What is the purpose of the rubber band wrapped around the middle of the can?

A Little Background

Rubber (and synthetic rubber) is made from molecules that can stretch or deform a lot before they break apart. When they get deformed, such as when you stretch or twist a rubber band, molecular forces try to reshape them. In this way, you can store energy in rubber. Many materials have this property, but few can stretch as far as rubber without breaking.

In this project you can follow the energy step-by-step. For this project, start at the end and work backward. When the racer stops moving, it has lost all its energy. When it was still moving, it had energy of motion, called kinetic energy. Before it began moving it had no kinetic energy, but since the rubber bands were twisted tightly, they held potential energy. As you wound the rubber bands up, you and the racer had kinetic energy and steadily gave the rubber bands potential energy.

Before you picked up the racer, you had potential energy in your body. This energy was stored in your cells in the form of chemical bonds. This energy came from the food you ate. The food was from either plant or animal. If it was from an animal, it got its energy from a plant, just like you can. The plants in turn got their energy from the sun, through photosynthesis. From one point of view, then, this is a solar-powered car.

If you trace the energy in most things, you can trace it back to the sun. Real cars use gas, which came from plant matter tens of millions of years ago. Those plants also got their energy from the sun. The sun obtains its energy from nuclear reactions—the splitting and forming of the nuclei of dozens of atoms. These atoms in turn got their energy in the formation of the universe.

The rubber band wrapped around the center of the can increased the friction between the car and the ground. This is interesting because usually we try hard to reduce friction so as not to waste energy. But some friction is good. If a car's tires had no friction with the road, the car could not push off and begin to move. When it is time to stop, the car needs as much friction with the road as possible. On an ice-covered road it is impossible to get friction, so cars will continue moving until they hit something.

To make the racer go farther, wind the rubber bands more. If you make a very wide car, you can install longer rubber bands, which can store more energy. You can also install thicker rubber bands, but if the car has too much force, it will not have enough friction with the ground and it will just spin its wheels. You can solve that problem by increasing the weight of the car, which will increase the friction it has with the ground.

VOIADORES DE PAPANTIA

("biRDMeN OF PAPANTIA")

This ancient ritual is actually full of physics.

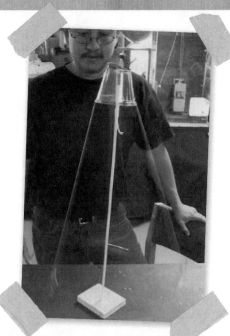

PARTS	
Baseboard	Bead
24-inch dowel (¼-inch diameter)	12-foot kite string
Toothpick	5 machine screws (¼-inch by 1¼-inches long)
1-by-2 scrap wood piece for drilling holes in cup	
	Pipe cleaners
Clear plastic cup (short works well)	

The Basic Concepts

By winding the four strings on the dowel, you raise the screws and give them energy. This energy is called "potential energy," or stored energy. The force of gravity pulls the screws down to the ground and makes them and the cup spin. When the screws are spinning and falling, they have energy of motion, or "kinetic energy." Even though gravity pulls only straight down, the toy spins because the strings put a force on the central stick at its edge. This gives a torque that pulls the cup around.

The Voladores de Papantla ("Bird Men of Papantla") is a ritual originating in pre-Columbian times. A small ethnic group called the Totonacas, who lived in the area of Veracruz, Mexico, performed this ritual for the sun god, asking for good harvest and fertility. The post for this experiment can be over 50 feet tall.

➔ *Voladores de Papantla at the Forum de Barcelona 2004, Marcelo Aurelio—Nocturama Fotoblog, www.arte-redes.com/nocturama*

Build It!

  Drill a ¹⁵⁄₆₄-inch hole in the middle of a baseboard, as straight vertically as possible. Hammer the 24-inch dowel into the hole. Tape a toothpick to the top of the dowel such that it sticks up an inch or so.

Clamp a scrap 1-by-2 to extend over the end of the worktable. Drill 4 holes symmetrically in the sides of the cup, near the rim. Make one hole, then the one opposite it; then split the difference on each side. Glue a bead inside the base of the cup in the center.

Cut four strings, each one a few inches longer than the dowel is tall. Make them all exactly the same length. Tape one end of each string to a machine screw. First tape it on so that a

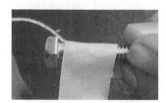  

tail extends over the head of the screw. Then double the tail back and tape over that tail. This will keep the string from sliding out from under the tape and will avoid tying any knots.

Insert the free end of each string through one of the holes in the side of the cup, from the outside in. Put the ends together and tie them in a simple knot.

Tape these four strings and the knot to the dowel up near the toothpick. The exact place is not important, as long as the screws can all reach the ground. Put the cup on the top of the dowel with the toothpick sticking into the bead. If one of the screws is a lot longer than the rest, pull its string from inside the cup and tape a bit of it to the dowel.

Attach pipe cleaners to the machine screws as shown to form four fliers. Use an additional machine screw and pipe cleaners to create a "flute-playing priest" atop the cup.

Wind up the fliers. Slowly turn the cup, and they will rise; however, the fliers tend to get tangled up using this method. A better way is to hold the cup steady and twist the dowel and base.

When the fliers are at the top, make sure the toothpick is still in the bead and release the cup.

More to Think About and Try

- ✦ What would happen if you had only three or two *voladores*?
- ✦ How could you make the *voladores* spin faster?
- ✦ What would happen if you had a smaller cup, or a larger central shaft?
- ✦ What would happen to the other *voladores* if one string broke halfway down?

A Little Background

This may look like a simple toy, but the physics is astonishingly complex. Consider that once you've added your energy and it is all wound up, the only force driving it is the Earth's gravity, which always pulls straight down. Most times gravity leads to a downward acceleration, but the motion of this device is both downward and rotational and at a nearly constant speed. Furthermore, the *voladores* (seen as screws) do not travel straight down as they spin but rather swing out to a certain angle with the central dowel.

You may conduct small experiments to see what difference various factors make. Some possibilities are to make the *voladores* heavier (tape two more screws onto each one), use a thicker central dowel or wrap the dowel with tape or paper to make it thicker, use a larger or smaller cup, tie more or fewer *voladores*, or make the pole longer. In each experiment you will need to do two trials with only one factor changed between them. For example, if you want to see the effect of the weight of the *voladores*, it is best to get two setups with the cups, central dowels, and strings exactly the same; then change just the weight. Once you have two devices with one different variable, let them go and time how long it takes for them to get down, as well as noting any other differences: the angle that the screws swing out to, how long it takes them to get up to speed, what happens when they are down, and so forth. If you have only one setup, you can watch it carefully in one trial, then change one variable, and then watch it carefully as you do it again.

Force that makes something turn is called "torque." The strings exert torque on the central stick in this project, but the stick is fastened down, so the cup ends up turning. The torque results from the strings pulling on the edge, or circumference, of the central stick. If they were fastened directly to the center of the stick, there would be no motion.

The angle that the *voladores* swing out to depends on the speed at which they turn, which depends on the torque of the strings, which depends on the weight of the *voladores*. The rotational speed also depends on the angular momentum, which is determined by the weight and the distance of the weight from the center. So the bigger the screws, the harder they pull; but the bigger the screws, the harder it is to spin them around. Our group found that the weight makes very little difference in how fast the *voladores* spin.

On the other hand, the size of both the central shaft and the cup makes a huge difference. If you make the shaft larger by wrapping it with tape or paper, or just by using a larger cylinder, such as a film canister, the torque alone increases and the *voladores* go spinning down much more rapidly. The same thing happens if you use a smaller cup.

You can wind the toy up halfway, cut one of the strings, and then continue to wind it to the top. When you let go, it works fine until halfway down, when the one *volador* goes flying to its demise. You can then see what happens to the others. They may still live!

Thanks to Gustavo Hernandez for conceiving and developing this project.

AiRPlANes

Amazing flights are possible with a simple folded paper.

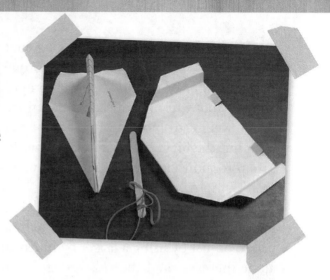

PARTS	
Airplane with Bottom Fold	
Paper	Paper clip
Glider with Flat Bottom	
Paper	Tack
Craft stick	Index cards
Launcher	
Rubber bands (medium)	Craft stick

The Basic Concepts

There are two main factors that will change the way the plane flies: the weight in the front, and the angle of the elevators. Elevators are the horizontal surfaces on the back of a plane that change its angle as it flies. That said, every surface is important; a good plane will be beautiful and perfectly symmetric.

You can have great fun and learn a lot with paper airplanes flown by hand. It is also nice to launch them with rubber bands. Nearly any paper plane can be altered to make it rubber band launched.

Build It!

Airplane with Bottom Fold

Fold the sheet in half the long way. Open it again. Fold the two top corners into the centerline. Then fold the top point over.

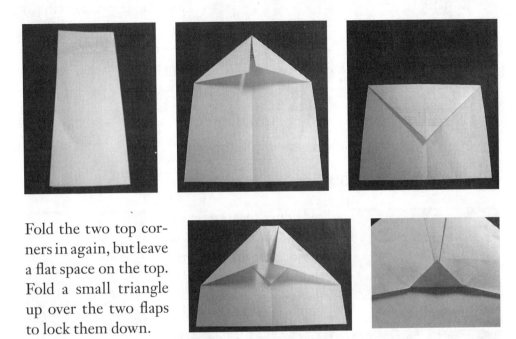

Fold the two top corners in again, but leave a flat space on the top. Fold a small triangle up over the two flaps to lock them down.

Fold along the centerline then fold the wings back down. The points at the back of the wings function as the elevators. If your plane goes up too fast, bend them down; if it goes down too fast, bend them up. Folding one up and one down will make the plane turn and possibly corkscrew.

If you want to prepare your plane for the launcher attachment (see p. 85), unfold the long end of the paper clip 90 degrees. Put the paper clip in the center slightly toward the front of the airplane. Poke the open end of the paper clip through the middle crease, so that it sticks out below the airplane.

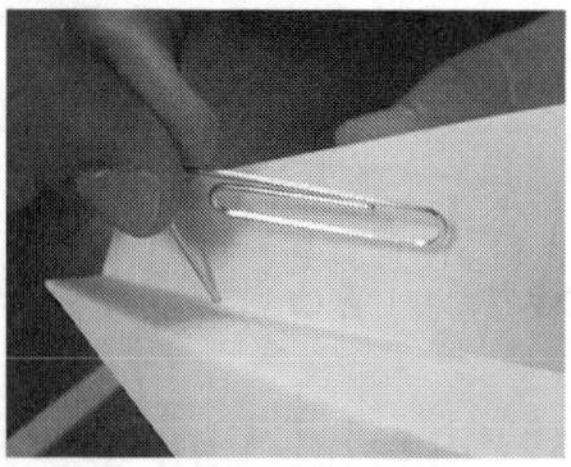

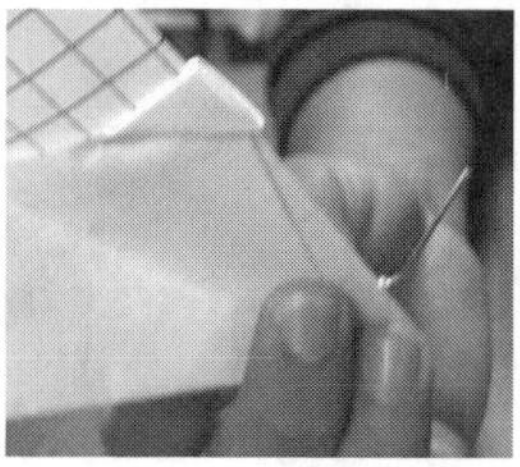

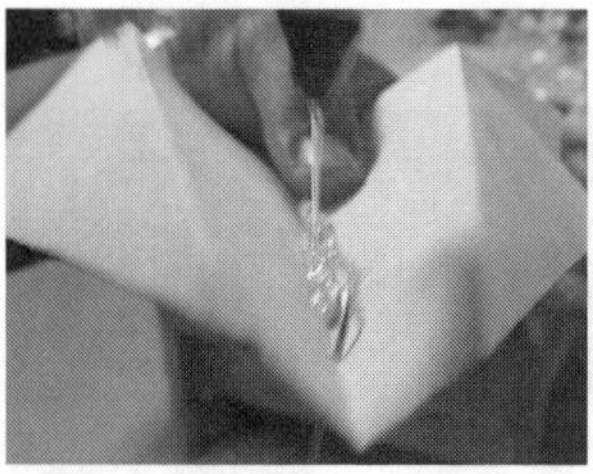

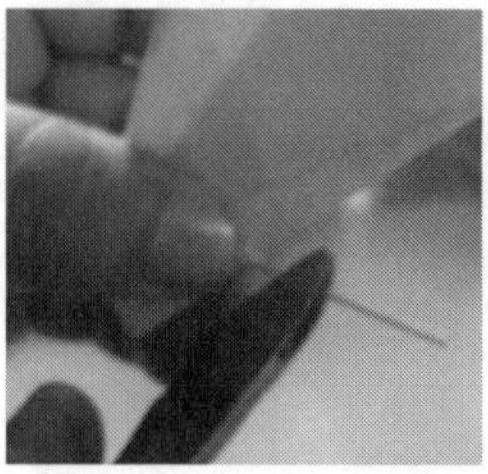

Hot glue the paper clip in place, closing the fold of the airplane. Cut most of the paper clip off, leaving enough to hook a rubber band.

Glider with Flat Bottom

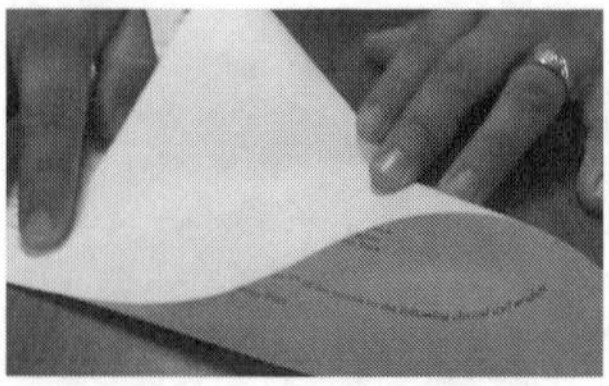

Fold one of the top corners to the opposite edge and unfold. Repeat with the other top corner, creating intersecting creases.

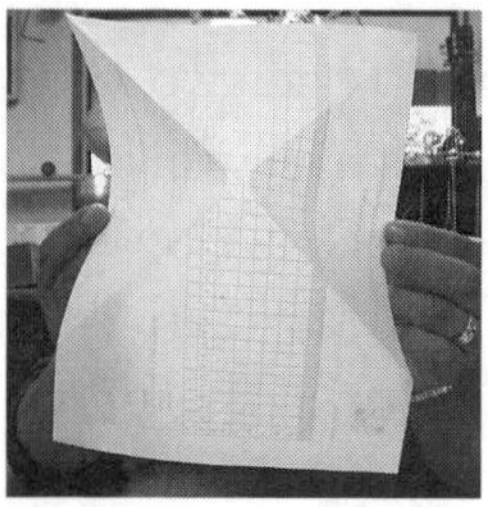

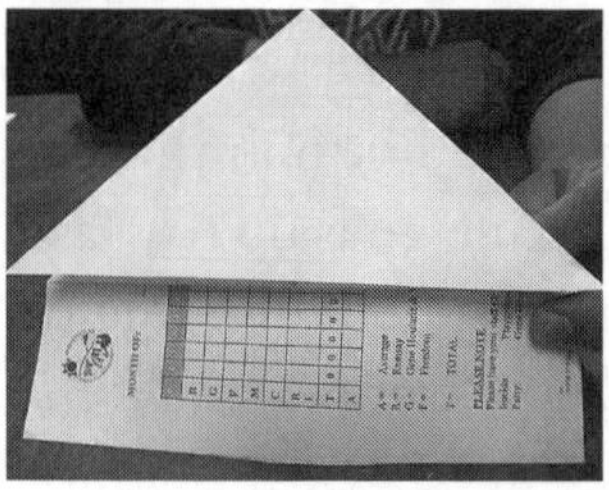

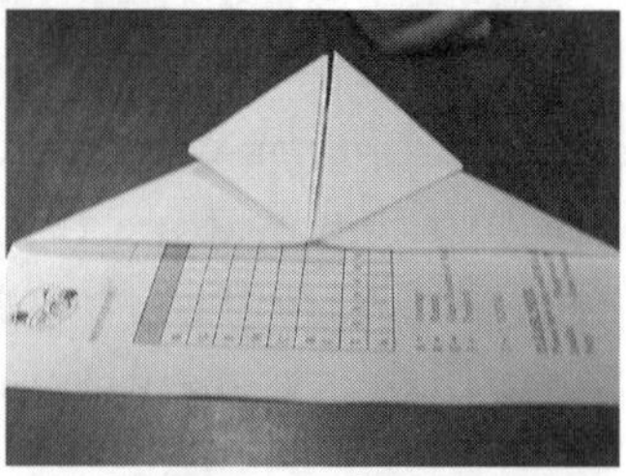

Fold the side creases in, making a pointy top. Fold the bottom tips back up to the top.

Fold the top point down and the two side points up so that they meet. Crease them well. Find the pockets in the top point and insert the two side points into these pockets.

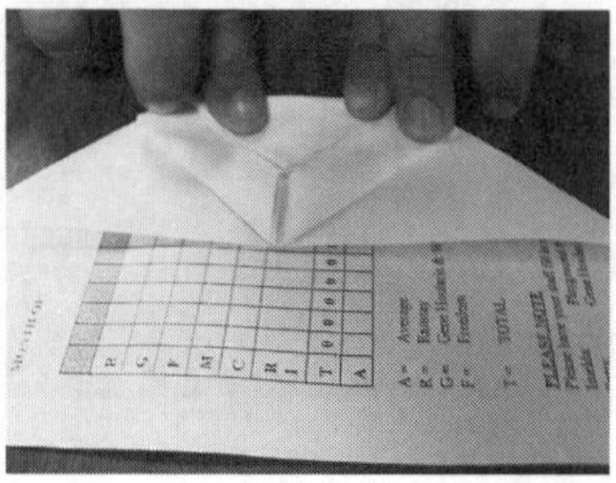

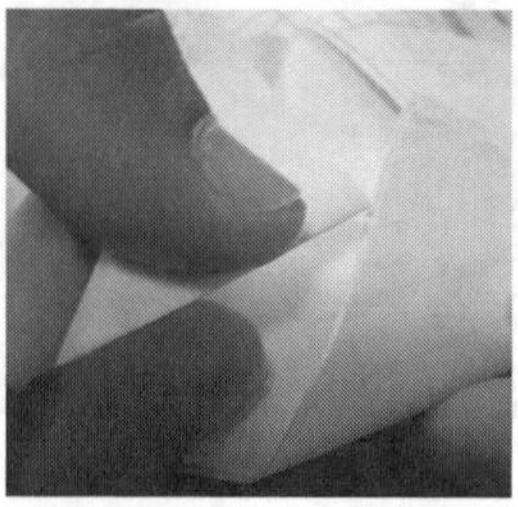

Flip over the airplane. Fold both side edges up a bit to make vertical stabilizers.

Make small cuts on the tail with scissors. Fold the small rectangular section up a bit. These are the elevators.

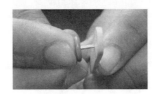

If you want to prepare your glider for the launcher attachment (see below), make a hole in the craft stick with a tack. Take the tack out, then glue it back in.

Put hot glue on top of the craft stick. Glue it to the bottom of the airplane, exactly in the middle, with the head sticking out just a bit.

Launcher

Connect the two rubber bands together, as shown. Then connect them to the craft stick.

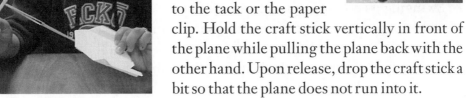

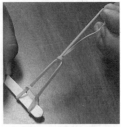

Hook the rubber bands to the tack or the paper clip. Hold the craft stick vertically in front of the plane while pulling the plane back with the other hand. Upon release, drop the craft stick a bit so that the plane does not run into it.

More to Think About and Try

❧ What do you think would happen if you made a plane out of aluminum foil?

❧ What do you think would happen if you put more rubber bands on the stick?

❧ How do you think these airplanes would work on the moon?

❧ Where does the energy come from to make these airplanes fly?

A Little Background

Aerodynamics and fluid mechanics can get very complicated, but it is quite simple to think about what makes these paper airplanes fly the way they do. When you toss a paper plane, you give it forward motion. Air is the fluid that the plane is flying through—the air will hit the surfaces of the plane just as water would. The angle of the surface will determine the force the air puts on the plane.

If the elevators are sticking up, the air will hit them and push the rear of the plane down. The nose of the plane will then stick up, sending the plane upward. If the elevators are sticking down, the opposite will happen.

A real airplane has at least three control surfaces, one for each of the dimensions in which it is free to travel. On the ground, we are used to traveling in two dimensions: forward/backward and right/left. Airplanes have an additional one: up/down. Whereas a car can turn only right or left, an airplane can turn on each of its three axes:

❧ Tilting its nose up or down is called "pitch" and is controlled by the elevators.

❧ Swinging its nose right or left is called "yaw" and is controlled by the rudder, which is part of the vertical surface on the tail of the plane.

❧ Tilting one wing up and the other down is called "roll" and is controlled by the ailerons, which are on the trailing edge of the two wing tips and which move in opposition to each other—when one goes up, the other goes down.

Some people call the elevators on these paper airplanes "elevons" because they can make the plane roll as well as pitch. An additional complexity is that airplanes actually use ailerons to make turns, "flying around the corner," so to speak. This is different from a boat, which uses the rudder to turn.

Many airplanes have a fourth control surface called the "flaps." Like ailerons, flaps are on the trailing edge of the wings, but normally close by the fuselage (or body) of the airplane. These go up and down together and are used to change the shape of the wing to enable more stable flight at low speeds, usually in preparation for landing.

The materials and construction of a plane are extremely important because the overall weight and the distribution of weight on an airplane will determine whether it will fly. It is possible to make a few airplanes from aluminum foil, especially gliders. If you put too many rubber bands on the stick, the plane will be torn apart as it launches. On the moon there is no air, so the planes would not fly at all but instead behave just as if you had thrown a rock. You provide the energy to make the planes fly, and you get your energy from food, which in turn gets its energy from the sun.

FlYiNG FiSh

If you want to go forward, throw something back.

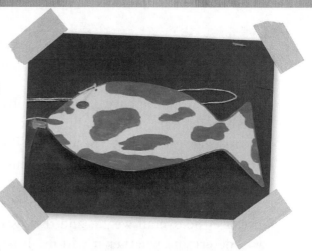

PARTS	
File folders or stiff paper	Paper clips
2-liter plastic bottle (for propeller)	Craft stick
Aluminum foil	String
AA battery	Ribbons
Hobby motor, 1.5–3 volts	Long ⁵⁄₁₆-inch dowels (for hanging the fish)
Wires, thin, with insulation	
TOOLS	
Hole punch	Wire strippers

The Basic Concepts

Propellers "throw" air (or any fluid) backward or forward. (Impellers, like in the Tornado project, throw fluid outward.) To make something move forward from rest requires a forward force. But a forward force always comes together with a backward force. This is Newton's third law: for every action there is an equal and opposite reaction.

The energy for making the fish fly comes from the battery. The force comes from the motor and propeller.

Draw a fish (or any other long, slender figure) on stiff paper. It should be around 6 to 8 inches long. Cut it out.

  Draw lines on a 2-liter bottle *along a slight incline.* This incline provides the twist for the propeller. Cut out a single segment.

Fold two pieces of aluminum foil and tape them tightly to the ends of the battery with black tape.

 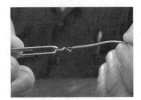 Strip both wires at both ends and attach them to the motor. Attach paper clips to the other ends of the wires.

Hot glue the motor to the end of a craft stick so that the shaft sticks off the end.

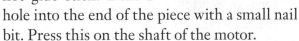

 Cut a ½-inch piece of hot glue stick. Drill a hole into the end of the piece with a small nail bit. Press this on the shaft of the motor.

Glue the propeller onto the bit of glue stick. Make sure it is exactly in the center, and don't let it get deformed by the hot glue. You may need to wait a few seconds for the glue to cool down a bit before pressing the propeller on.

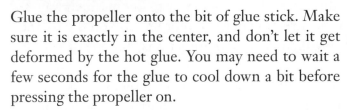

Glue the battery onto the craft stick; then glue the craft stick onto the fish, with the propeller at the nose.

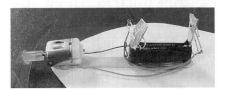

With a hole punch, punch a hole near the top of the fish so that the fish will hang level, that is, without pointing its head too far up or down. Tie a length of string through the hole.

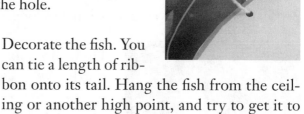

Decorate the fish. You can tie a length of ribbon onto its tail. Hang the fish from the ceiling or another high point, and try to get it to fly around. Launch it straight down the circular path it will follow.

Sometimes it is tricky to get the fish to fly. Here are some troubleshooting steps:

- When the propeller is spinning, it should be blowing air *back* across the fish. Check this by putting your hand by the fish to feel for the air.
- If you can't feel air blowing back, it may be blowing forward. Check this by putting your hand in front of the propeller. If you can feel the air blowing forward, change the wires on the battery to make the motor spin in the other direction.
- If the air does not seem to be blowing forward either, the propeller may not be bent correctly. Both sides should be twisted slightly, just like a real propeller or fan blades. Bend it more if it needs it.
- If it is blowing air backward, but not much, you can tighten your battery connections with tape and twist your wires a bit tighter. Be sure the battery is not dying.
- Once you can feel air blowing back over the fish, you need to launch the fish in the right direction. There is no way to know which way is right. It depends on the direction of the motor but also on the balance of the fish. A few fish will circle in both directions, but one direction is always faster.
- Try launching the fish at different angles and different speeds.
- One other variable to adjust is the length of the string. The fish and string will trace out a cone when flying. The angle that the fish hangs at depends on the size of this cone. Sometimes a different angle will make a fish fly better.

More to Think About and Try

- 🔧 What makes the fish fly through the air?
- 🔧 Can you make the fish go in both directions?
- 🔧 What would happen if you put another battery on the fish?
- 🔧 Why is it hard to make a real airplane with an electric motor?

A Little Background

Propellers and fans push air. They go around in circles, but they push air perpendicular to the plane of rotation. Most people are more familiar with fans than with airplane propellers, but they are essentially the same. Fan blades are at an angle such that each bit of air they encounter bounces off toward the front or back. If something perfectly flat, such as a craft stick, goes in circles, it does not push much air and thus would not make the fish move.

In this toy the propeller can push air forward away from the fish or back across the fish, depending on which way the motor is turning. Newton said that for every action there is an equal and opposite reaction. In this project, the action is the propeller pushing the air back across the fish; the reaction is the fish being pushed forward through the air.

Gyroscopic effects (strange forces on spinning objects) and center of mass also play into this project. It gets a bit complicated, but for most fish one direction of flight is much more stable than the other direction. The body of the fish is not symmetric; that is, the batteries and motor put nearly all the weight on one side. The orientation of the fish is diagonal as it traces out its circular flight path, and usually the fish is most stable if the battery side is down. But the rotation of the motor-propeller system makes gyroscopic forces that also affect which direction is more stable. This is an example of a complex combination of linear and rotational motion.

The battery provides the energy for this process. The motor takes the energy from the battery and gives force to the propeller. The propeller then gives force to the air (action), which also pushes back on the propeller (reaction) to make the fish move through the air. Thus, the air coming off the propeller pushes the fish forward, much the same way a rocket is pushed forward by the air it is expelling backward through the rocket nozzle.

An electric airplane needs a powerful battery, and that usually means a lot of weight. With cheap hobby motors and normal batteries, you'll never get enough force to make an airplane fly on its own. You can sometimes get a motor and a propeller to fly like a helicopter if you hook up a strong battery, hold the battery, and run thin wires to the motor. Recently some powerful batteries and high-torque motors have been developed that allow for electric remote-controlled airplanes.

heliCOPteRS

What happens when a helicopter's engine quits?

PARTS	
Indoor Helicopter	
File folder or stiff paper	Pennies
Craft stick	
Outdoor Helicopter	
¾-inch PVC tube (½-inch diameter)	2-liter plastic bottle (for wings)
8-inch dowel (¼-inch diameter)	
Outdoor Helicopter Launcher	
2 rubber bands (large)	Craft stick
TOOLS	
Outdoor Helicopter	
PVC cutter (or hacksaw)	
Large pliers (to hold PVC piece while drilling)	

The Basic Concepts

Air is real. You can't see it, but it moves things. The rubber band in this project gives the force that makes the helicopter go up. Gravity gives the force that makes it come back down. The air that it encounters makes it spin around and fall slower. If the blades are bent correctly, the air pushes them to make the helicopter go around.

Build It!

Indoor Helicopter

Cut a helicopter shape out of thick paper or file folder. The simplest shape can be a rectangle with a slit cut down the center. The blades are the pieces on each side of the slit. You can make the blades any size you like.

On the other end of the piece, fold the corners of the rectangle in toward the center. Then glue a craft stick on the center.

Glue one or two or more pennies to the other end of the craft stick.

Throw it up, and it should spin on the way down.

Outdoor Helicopter

Cut a piece of PVC, about ¾-inch long. With a sharp drill bit, drill a ¹⁵⁄₆₄-inch hole into the center of the PVC while holding it tightly with pliers. You can punch a shallow hole in the PVC with a nail to get the bit started.

Cut about 8 inches of a ¼-inch dowel. Hammer it into the hole in the PVC.

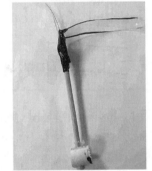

Put some hot glue around the dowel, especially inside the tube. This will keep the dowel from flying out when you launch the helicopter.

Draw slanted lines on a 2-liter bottle. Cut along the lines on the bottle until you have two strips. These will be the blades.

Put hot glue on the dowel. Allow the glue to cool for a few seconds so it does not melt the plastic. Then press the blades onto the glue so that they stick up, in the same direction as the dowel.

Tape around the blades to reinforce the glue. Fold the wings a bit toward the outside and make them symmetric.

Outdoor Helicopter Launcher

Tie two rubber bands together.

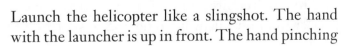

Tie the rubber bands to the tip of the craft stick. The launcher is finished.

Launch the helicopter like a slingshot. The hand with the launcher is up in front. The hand pinching the blades is down in back. The rubber band is looped around the end of the tube, pulled toward your body. To launch the helicopter, let go of the blades and move the launcher hand away slightly so that the helicopter does not hit it.

If the helicopter does not spin on its way back down, make sure the blades are symmetric, twisted slightly, and bent opposite each other.

More to Think About and Try

- What do you think would happen if you made the helicopter even heavier at the bottom?
- How could you make the helicopter go up farther?
- What are some differences between this helicopter and a real helicopter?
- What could you change to make the helicopter spin faster?

A Little Background

The helicopter's blades encounter air as it falls. The blades are at an angle, so that each little bit of air that hits them bounces off and pushes them to the side. If you have them bent correctly, each one will be pushed around in the same direction, causing the helicopter to spin. The air also pushes up the blades, causing the helicopter to fall more slowly.

Real helicopters do this in emergencies. If a helicopter's engine fails, the recovery procedure is to begin "autorotation." This simply means that instead of the engine turning the blades, the air flowing past the falling craft will turn the blades. In most cases, this provides enough upward force to slow the descent, allowing the pilot to find a suitable space below for an emergency landing.

This toy requires air to function. If you tried it on the moon, here is what would happen: It would rise to six times the height it rises to on

Earth, because the moon's gravity is six times less than the Earth's. Then it would fall back to the Earth without any spinning at all, because there is no air on the moon.

Let's follow the energy used in this project. You provide the original energy to stretch the rubber band. Your body got this energy by metabolizing the food you ate earlier. When the rubber band is stretched, it holds potential energy. When released, it gives this energy to the helicopter. The helicopter begins accelerating upward. As the helicopter leaves the rubber band, it is traveling as fast as it will go during its flight. The potential energy of the rubber band has been converted into kinetic energy.

The helicopter slows down as it continues upward because gravity is pulling steadily downward on it. It loses kinetic energy as it gains potential energy of height. At its highest point, it stops moving up and has lost all kinetic energy. It holds the maximum potential energy of height it will have. It then starts down.

If the blades spring out properly, they encounter air, which pushes them around. As the helicopter begins rotating, it gains rotational kinetic energy, which uses up some of the potential energy. Some of the helicopter's potential energy is also given to the air, heating it up a bit. Because of these losses, the speed (and kinetic energy) of the helicopter is a bit less on the way down than it was on the way up. Upon impact with the ground, all remaining energy is converted to heat. You won't feel this heat because there is not much energy involved.

hYDRAULiC bUtteRFly

A crude mechanical model of the graceful insect.

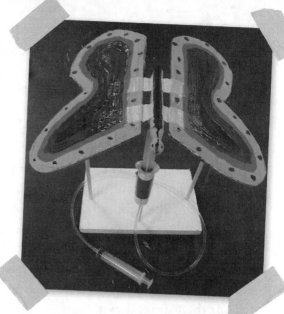

PARTS	
Baseboard	One-piece wooden clothespin
24-inch dowel (¼-inch diameter)	2 feet of clear, flexible tubing (⅛-inch diameter)
2 syringes	
Cardboard	2 craft sticks

The Basic Concepts

Air is compressible (squeezable.) When you squeeze it, it gets smaller. Water does not. Hydraulic systems are often used to give a strong force across a short distance. When driven by a hydraulic pump, the butterfly's body goes up and down as the wings go down and up.

Build It!

Drill three ¹⁵⁄₆₄-inch holes on the baseboard near the edges in a triangular pattern.

Cut the ¼-inch dowel in three pieces: two of them the same size

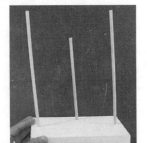

and the third at least an inch shorter than the other two. Hammer the dowels into the holes, with the short one in the middle.

Duct tape one syringe to the top of the middle dowel. Its handle should be about even with the tops of the other dowels.

Using the template on the next page or a design of your own, draw one butterfly wing on a piece of cardboard and cut it out. Trace this first wing to create a second, identical wing, and cut it out as well.

Put the wooden clothespin between the straight sides of the two wings. Tape them together as shown, leaving a space that allows the wings to flap up and down.

Cut 2 feet of ⅛-inch tubing and press it onto the tip of another syringe.

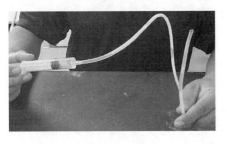

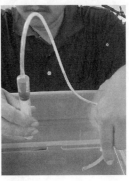

Over a basin, suck water into the syringe then invert it to expel the air. Do this a few times to get all the air out.

Wing template

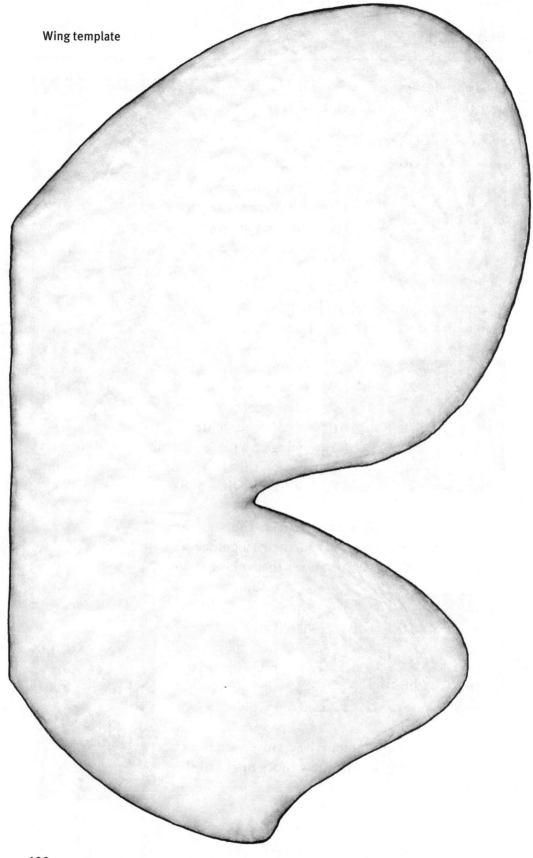

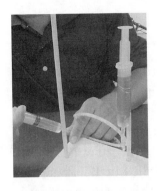

When there is no air in the syringe and tube, connect it to the syringe taped to the dowel. This syringe should be completely closed when you press on the tubing, to avoid air in the system. Compress the free syringe and be sure the piston of the stationary syringe moves up.

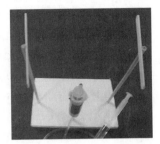

Glue craft sticks to the tops of the two side dowels. Hold them steady until the glue is dry.

Put hot glue on top of the stationary syringe and glue on the butterfly's body (the clothespin).

Decorate the butterfly.

Push the syringe up and down to make the butterfly's wings flap.

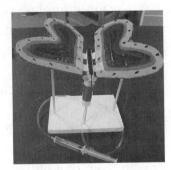

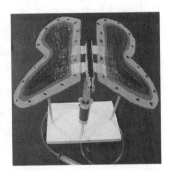

More to Think About and Try

- Why do you think oil is used instead of water in most hydraulic systems?
- What do you think would happen if the tube were very long, perhaps a half-mile long?
- Why do nurses tap on the tubes of syringes and IVs when they are getting ready to give you an injection or set up an IV?
- What happens if there is just air in the syringes?

A Little Background

A simple demonstration will help illuminate this project. Find two identical plastic bottles with lids. Fill one completely up with water—no air bubbles—and leave the other one empty. Tighten the lids and put one in each hand. Now squeeze as hard as you can on the bottles and notice the difference. The bottle full of water will hardly squeeze at all. What squeezing can be done is due to the deformation of the bottle. The other bottle will squeeze quite a bit. It is key to realize that this bottle is not actually empty; it is full of air. When you squeeze air, it gets smaller. When you squeeze water, nothing happens at all. If you were to put the bottle full of water into a giant smashing machine, the bottle would break long before the water would decrease its volume by even 0.01 percent.

This compressibility property reflects the different way molecules behave in liquids and gases. In a gas the molecules are flying freely, bouncing off walls and other molecules. Between these wild flying gas molecules is only space. If you find a way to press on them, such as squeezing them in a closed bottle, you can reduce the amount of space they have. Pneumatic systems (like the ones used in those loud power-wrenches at auto shops) use a gas (usually air) and exploit this cushiony property.

Liquids and solids, on the other hand, have closely packed molecules, bound together much more tightly than gas molecules are. If you push on them, very little happens. You can think about pushing down on a pile of blocks—it doesn't matter how hard you push, nothing much will happen. If you push hard enough on only one end of a pile of blocks, though, the pile will move, and whatever is in front of it will move, too.

In this project you push on one end of a system of liquid. The walls enclosing the liquid all feel the same pressure (force per unit area) as the pressure you give the piston in the syringe. The one "wall" that is free to move—the other piston—then gives way to push your butterfly up. When you decrease pressure by pulling on the piston, the same thing happens in reverse, with the atmosphere pushing the other piston (connected to the butterfly) down into the syringe again.

Hydraulic systems are good at giving a lot of force over a short distance. You find them on construction and manufacturing machines. It is harder to make hydraulic systems move over great distances. Hydraulic motors do exist, making rotating applications available.

Hydraulic systems use oil instead of water because oil doesn't cause metal to rust and because it automatically lubricates the system. If a hydraulic system is very long, many small losses in the tube (such as holes or elasticity) will add up to a greater loss of motion, but the pressure at the point of use will still equal, approximately, the pressure applied.

When getting the air out of your system, you use gravity and buoyancy. Air bubbles will rise to the top, and if they stick to the side, you have to tap them a bit to get them to rise. Nurses do the same before giving a shot or setting up an IV because they don't want air in your blood vessels. If you don't get all the air out of your butterfly syringe, or if you don't put any water in, you will have, instead, a pneumatic system: much less responsive, cushiony motion.

A butterfly's weight is distributed across its body and wings. As the wings move down, the body goes up a bit, and vice versa. The resulting motion is the crazy, fluttery path that a butterfly travels. This toy replicates that motion well.

Thanks to Manuel Hernandez and other staff of the Fresno Community Science Workshop for the remarkable idea of putting hydraulics on a butterfly.

STOMP ROCKETS

The foot goes down, and the rocket goes up.

PARTS	
Plastic bottle (2-liter size works well)	Paper (8½ by 11 or larger)
Bicycle inner tube (10 inch, more or less)	12-inch dowel (¼-inch diameter, for pushing through nose cone)
2-foot PVC tube (more or less), ½- or ¾-inch diameter	
	Yarn (for target)
File folders or stiff paper	
TOOLS	
PVC cutter (or hacksaw)	

The Basic Concepts

Air gets forced out of the bottle when you reduce the bottle's volume by smashing it. This escaping air pushes the rocket up. After the rocket leaves the tube, it doesn't get pushed anymore. The rocket is going as fast as it will go just as it comes off the tube. It will rise slower and slower until it stops going up altogether; then it will accelerate as it falls back toward the ground.

Force the mouth of a plastic bottle into a length of inner tube. Tape it tightly with duct tape.

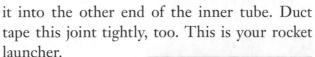

Cut a 2-foot piece of PVC and insert it into the other end of the inner tube. Duct tape this joint tightly, too. This is your rocket launcher.

Roll a piece of stiff paper around the PVC. Make it tight but not so tight that it cannot slide easily up and down the PVC. The paper shown here is being rolled lengthwise, but rolling the other direction to make a longer rocket also works. Add masking tape along the length of the tube to hold the paper closed.

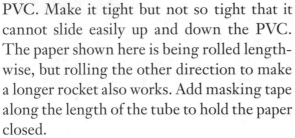

Using a sheet of stiff paper, make at least three fins and glue them on the lower end of the rocket.

Make a cone from a piece of stiff paper. Tape it tightly.

Insert it into the rocket and cut it off flush. Use the dowel to push the cone through the tube until it sticks out the opposite end.

Pull the cone out until it is just about to pop out of the tube. Position it correctly and hot glue it into position. There should be no holes for air to escape.

Take the rocket outside to launch. Slide the rocket onto the PVC.

Hold the PVC below the rocket and stomp on the bottle. Be careful not to shoot yourself in the face.

Two people can launch very well: one to stomp and one to aim. Lay yarn out in a circle, 5 or 10 feet in diameter, and try to hit this target with rockets from a distance.

More to Think About and Try

- Why do you think the rocket goes up when you stomp on the bottle?
- How does the speed of the rocket as it hits the ground at the end of its flight compare to its speed as it leaves the tube?
- Why might a big bottle work better than a small bottle?
- What do you think would happen if you made the tube a lot longer?

A Little Background

The force that pushes this rocket up comes from the air escaping from the bottle. When you stomp the bottle, its volume decreases. This increases the pressure of the air inside the bottle, and that air takes the only route of escape: out the neck and through the tube. Then it encounters the rocket. It has to push up on the rocket to get out of the launcher tube.

The rocket is pushed for the length of time it is on the PVC tube and then is blown for a few more inches after it comes off. After that there is no more push. In other words, it is less like a rocket and more like a bullet or a ball being thrown. Projectiles that don't have their own energy source accelerate only while they are in contact with their launcher. This is an example of Newton's second law: an object will accelerate according to how much force is put on it, and when the force is no longer there, it will no longer accelerate. The stomp rocket is going as fast as it ever will go just as it comes off the end of the tube. Real rockets will continue to accelerate as long as there is hot gas escaping from their rocket nozzles.

You can divide the motion of the rocket into vertical and horizontal elements. In physics these are called "vectors." If you think about only the vertical element—a flight straight up and straight down—it is easier to understand the motion. As soon as the rocket leaves the tube it has no more force pushing it up, but gravity is always pulling it down. The rocket begins to slow down and continues slowing until it stops at the top of its path. Then, it begins accelerating again toward the ground, this time powered entirely by gravity. If there were no air resistance on the rocket, the speed of the rocket when it hit the ground would be exactly what it was when it left the ground on its way up.

It is harder to consider the sideways vector alone because we have no experience living without gravity or air. If one were to launch this rocket in space, where there is no gravity or air, it would accelerate for the length of the PVC, attain its maximum speed, and then continue on with that speed until it hit something. This is an example of Newton's first law: objects in motion tend to stay in motion and objects at rest tend to stay at rest. Here on Earth, the air that the rocket encounters slows its sideways motion and it always returns to hit the ground and stop.

The result of these two different vectors of motion is a curved path called a "parabola." Everything thrown up from the Earth follows a parabola (if you ignore influence from the air). You can see it in ball games, fireworks blasts, and when you throw a rock.

A bigger bottle would have more air and thus should be able to give more force to the rocket. The longer the tube is, the more air is inside it, and the more air must be pushed. Air is springy (unlike water) and so is the bicycle inner tube, so the longer the tube is, the less directly the air will be pushing on the rocket. With a very long tube, there would be a delay between the stomp of the bottle and the launch of the rocket.

toilet

A fully flushing model of an important modern convenience.

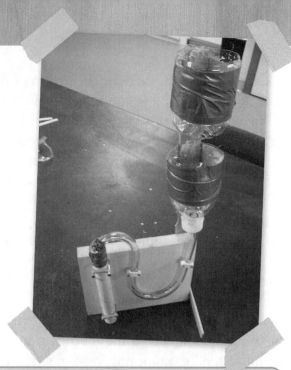

PARTS	
8-inch PVC tube, ½-inch diameter	2 paint paddles
Baseboard	3 two-nail cable clips
Nails (approximately 1¾ inch)	6-inch dowel (⁵⁄₁₆-inch diameter)
Rubber bands	Drinking cup
18-inch clear, flexible tubing (½-inch outer diameter, ⁵⁄₁₆-inch inner diameter)	Toilet-testing dye or food coloring (or liquid watercolor)
Single-size plastic drink bottle, with cap	

TOOLS	
Flapper valve (for demonstration)	PVC cutter (or hacksaw)
Bucket or basin (for testing)	

The Basic Concepts

Water "seeks its level." This means that if two places are connected and full of water, and are open to the atmosphere, the water level will be at the same level at both places.

A trap system is used to keep the air in the sewer from coming into your house, as well as to catch jewelry you accidentally drop in the sink (or toilet).

If your toilet's flapper valve is leaking, you will waste a lot of water and money each year. You can test this with the dye tablets.

Build It!

Cut a length of PVC tubing at least 8 inches long. Place the PVC on the baseboard near one edge and drive two nails into the baseboard, one on each side of the PVC, at both ends of the  baseboard. Hook rubber bands around the nail heads to hold the tubing in place but make it able to slide up and down.

 Cut at least 18 inches of flexible tubing. Cut a drink bottle exactly in half through the middle with a knife or pair of scissors. Then, drill a ¹⁹⁄₆₄-inch hole in the bottom of the bottle.

Drill a ½-inch hole in the bottle cap. Insert the flex-  ible tubing a little ways into the hole in the bottle cap. Hot glue around the flexible tubing inside and outside the cap. This joint needs to be watertight.

 Glue half a paint paddle perpendicular to the side of the baseboard, along the edge at the bottom, on the end *opposite* the PVC. This should make the toilet model stand up, with the PVC pipe vertical.

 Glue a paint paddle vertically to the baseboard, at the opposite end to the PVC, on the opposite *side* of the baseboard. It should be sticking up above the board and be strong enough to support the tank.

Glue the top half of the bottle onto the paint paddle, just above the baseboard, with the cap (and the inserted tubing) pointing down. This is the toilet's bowl. (When gluing anything to a plastic bottle, always put the glue on the other material first; then press the bottle onto the glue. This will avoid deforming the plastic with the heat of the glue.)

Glue the bottom half of the bottle to the top end of the paint paddle so that when the board is standing vertical, the water will drain from it into the bowl. This top half is the toilet's tank.

Hammer a cable clip around the flexible tubing to hold it in position.

Make an S with the tubing so that it ends up inserted into the top of the PVC pipe, facing down. You can use duct tape to secure the flexible tubing into the PVC pipe, but leave a hole so that air can get in. (This hole acts like the vents that go from the drainpipe of a house up through the roof.)

Attach the flexible tubing to the baseboard with cable clips. The cable clips should be horizontally arranged and not hammered in too tightly, so that the tubing is adjustable up and down through them.

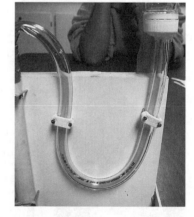

Cut at least 6 inches of a $5/16$-inch dowel. Insert it into the tank's hole (from above) as a plug. It should prevent the water from leaking out the hole in the bottom of the water tank. (This dowel acts like the flapper valve in a real toilet.)

Place the toilet on the edge of a table so that the PVC pipe sticks down, over the edge of the table. Fill the tank with water. Hold a drinking cup under the PVC pipe to catch the water; then pull out the dowel and the toilet should flush.

You can pour the water you collected in the cup back into the tank for another flush. (It takes a couple of flushes to get the air bubbles out of the system.)

To show how dye tablets work, arrange the dowel so that there is a small leak from the tank into the bowl, then put a dye tablet or food coloring into the tank. As it dissolves, the tank water will turn blue, and then the bowl water also will turn blue.

More to Think About and Try

- ➤ How could you make the water level in the toilet bowl stay higher?
- ➤ How could you make the water flush faster?
- ➤ What would make it clog up and not go down?
- ➤ How is a real toilet different from this one?

A Little Background

Every sink and toilet in your house has a trap—check for yourself. These S-shaped traps are useful if you drop jewelry down the drain, but the main purpose is to keep the sewer air from coming up into the house. If a big storm, tornado, or hurricane changes the pressure in a house enough, it can push the water out of these traps. The home's residents will know this has happened as the smell of the sewer fills the house.

The water level is the same on both sides of the trap. This is the physical property of water "seeking its level." It happens because gravity pulls the whole mass of water down to its lowest level.

Real toilets have automatic float and valve systems so that the tank is filled again with water after each flush. Toilets also have a somewhat complex device in the tank that fills the bowl to the highest possible level while it is refilling the tank. If you add more water to your toilet bowl you will notice that the level of water in the bowl never rises. This is because every time you add more in the bowl a bit more flows down into the sewer from the back.

So, if your flapper valve is leaking, water from the tank continually leaks into the bowl but the bowl's water level never increases. Thus you may never notice the leak. The float system will periodically spurt a bit more water into the tank, and you may hear this if you are observant. A sure way to test it is to put color dye into the tank (but don't flush!) and wait to see if it appears in the bowl. If it does, you need to replace your flapper valve.

The water level in the toilet bowl can be raised only by making the backside of the trap higher. In a porcelain toilet, this trap level is fixed, but in our model, you just need to raise the PVC to get more water to remain in the bowl after a flush. The size of the hole in a toilet bowl will limit the speed of the flush—if you put in too much water too fast, the bowl will just overflow. Any large object stuck in the hole will clog it up.

TORNADO

Better than a ship in a bottle!

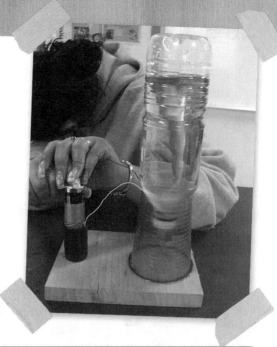

PARTS	
Bottle with lid (big is better)	Small pieces of Styrofoam packing
Hobby motor, 1.5–3 volts	Baseboard
2 wires, thin, with insulation	Aluminum foil
Large plastic cup	Film canister (no lid necessary)
Food coloring (or liquid watercolor)	2 C batteries
Glitter	Resistance wire
TOOLS	
Rasp or coarse sandpaper (to roughen up the cap)	Wire strippers

The Basic Concepts

Fluids—liquids or gases (vapors)—flow within the vessel that contains them. Tornados, hurricanes, and whirlpools all have the same sort of motion. In these natural cases the rotation is caused by pressure differences. In this project the rotation is caused by the bottle and the impeller. An impeller throws fluids outward. Propellers throw fluids forward or backward.

Build It!

Make a ¹⁹/₆₄-inch hole exactly in the middle of a bottle cap.

Scratch the top of the cap with a rasp so the glue will stick to it better. Then put glue around the hole and press the motor firmly into the hole. Add more glue around the joint between the cap and the motor so that it is very strong. It is important to get this right the first time, because it will not glue well after it gets wet. But be careful not to get any glue inside the cap, on the turning shaft.

Strip both ends of two wires. Connect them to the motor.

Cut at least 1 inch of a hot glue stick. Drill a hole in the end of it with a small nail bit. Cut a slit into the other tip of the glue stick.

Cut a tiny piece of plastic either from the base of your cup or from another bottle, and insert it into the slit. This is the impeller. Push the motor shaft into the hole at the other end of the glue stick.

Fill the bottle about three-quarters full with water. Add a bit of food coloring—too much and you can't see the tornado inside the bottle. A bit of glitter and tiny pieces of Styrofoam are interesting too.

Tightly screw on the cap (with motor attached).

Check out your cup and bottle sizes. Make sure the bottle will sit nicely, cap-and-motor-end down, on the cup, without the motor touching the baseboard. These photos show a small bottle and a large cup. We cut off the bottom of the cup and glued it to the baseboard upside down. For 2-liter-bottle tornados, often the mouth of the cup works to support the bottle, and the cup is glued to the baseboard right side up.

Put a piece of aluminum foil around one end of one wire. Jam the aluminum foil and wire into the bottom of the film canister and glue the film canister to the baseboard.

Tape two batteries together and slide one end of them inside the film canister.

Touch the other wire to the top of the batteries and the tornado should begin.

To change the speed of the tornado, connect a piece of resistance wire to the free insulated wire. For full speed, connect the free wire straight to the battery without using the resistance wire. To slow it down, touch the battery with the resistance wire, causing the electricity to pass through a bit of it. The more of the resistance wire the electricity needs to pass through, the slower the motor will go.

More to Think About and Try

- ❧ How could you make the tornado spin faster?
- ❧ What would happen if you fill the bottle with water so that there is no air in it?
- ❧ What would happen if you put the impeller and lid on a different sized bottle?
- ❧ Consider a tiny piece of glitter swirling in the tornado: what is its path through the bottle as the tornado spins?

A Little Background

A battery powers this tornado. The sun powers real tornados and all weather patterns. Radiation from the sun warms the Earth differently according to many factors, such as reflectivity of the surface and cloud cover. Hot areas and cold areas then lead to different air pressures. Wind is basically air moving from high to low pressure, and the greater the difference, the stronger the wind. Hurricanes and tornadoes are special situations where a local area of very low pressure (a large area for a hurricane and a small one for a tornado) becomes the center of strong rotating winds.

Why do the winds blow around in circles? Rotation is a common, stable situation in nature. For example, all known planets and their satellites are rotating. For another example, try to shake a bottle of water or soda from side to side, and then hold it still. Invariably, the liquid is rotating when you finish. In technical terms, the winds of hurricanes and tornados are merely conserving their momentum, as all things must.

Adding more batteries will make the motor spin faster; weaker batteries make it spin slower. Changing the size of the impeller is more complex. A very large impeller turns slowly because it has to push a lot of water, and the motor is not strong at slow speeds. A very small impeller turns fast but can push only a tiny bit of water, so it can't get the whole bottle of water moving fast. The optimal size is somewhere in between. The shape also is important. A boat's propeller is much smaller and shaped differently than an airplane's. The best size and shape depend on what kind of fluid is being pushed and at what speed the motor is most efficient.

Changing the wire connections on the battery will make the motor and tornado turn in the opposite direction. In this project, and in most human-made vortexes (whirlpools), your hemisphere is not important; the vortex turns in the direction that you drive it. But your hemisphere is important when considering hurricanes and all large pressure systems. Large low-pressure systems in the Northern Hemisphere turn counterclockwise because they occur on the surface of a spinning sphere—the Earth. The force that makes this happen is called the Coriolis force.

Tornadoes are much smaller and localized than hurricanes. Most often they are formed from the midst of a single thunderstorm and last only minutes. Most in the Northern Hemisphere rotate counterclockwise, but some have been seen to go the other way.

If you put some glitter or bits of paper in the bottle and follow them, you'll see that they are going around and around but also up and down; the up-and-down motion is also circular. They go down near the center of the bottle and back up near the outside. A larger bottle has a similar pattern, just bigger.

eye MODeI

Step inside your eye to see where the light goes.

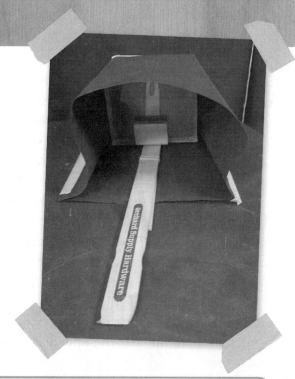

PARTS	
CD case (two transparent sides and black middle insert)	Sheet of black paper (9 inches by 12 inches)
Magnifying glass (small)	Sheet of black paper (12 inches by 18 inches)
2 wood blocks (or film canisters)	
2 paint paddles	Set of colored lights on sockets with power strip
Waxed paper	
Rubber band (small)	

The Basic Concepts

The front surface of the eye is called the cornea. It is hard, and it protects the inside of the eye. The inside back surface of the eye is called the retina. It is made up of nerves that receive the image made by the lens and send the information on to the brain. The eye changes focus to see things far and near. A real eye does this with muscles that change the shape of the lens.

Build It!

Separate the two sides of the CD case and remove the black insert. Use needle-nose pliers or scissors to break off the fringes and widen the hole in the black insert.

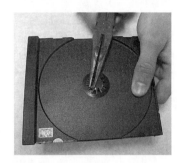

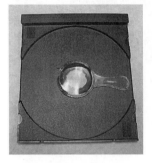

Hot glue the magnifying glass to the inside of the black insert.

Pop the black insert back into the transparent cover. This part of the project represents the cornea (clear case), iris (black insert), pupil (hole), and lens (magnifying glass).

Hot glue a wood block (or film canister) to the end of a paint paddle. Then hot glue the cornea/lens setup to the wood block, with the lens side toward the paint paddle.

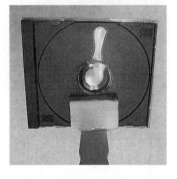

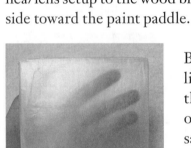

Break off the two little hinge tabs of the remaining side of the CD case. Cut a piece of waxed paper the same size as the case, and tape the waxed paper on it without making any creases or folds. This is the retina.

Hot glue another wood block (or film canister) to the end of another paint paddle. Then hot glue the retina setup to the wood block.

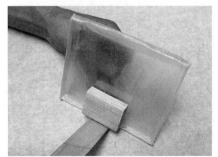

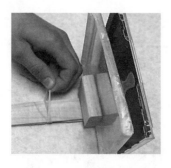

Put the paint paddle with the retina on top of the paint paddle with the cornea/lens. Secure the paddles together with a rubber band, loose enough that they can slide back and forth to vary the distance between the lens and retina.

Now you will enclose this setup with black paper. Begin by applying hot glue to the bottom of the cornea CD case. Then stick this in the center of one end of the small (9-by-12) black paper.

 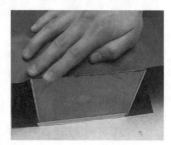

Apply glue to the top edge of the cornea CD case. Stick that to the center of one long edge of the large (12-by-18) black paper.

Wrap the top sheet of paper all the way around until it meets the paper at the bottom. Glue and/or tape all these edges to the case so that light cannot enter. The retina setup should be able to slide back and forth within the enclosure of the black paper.

Tape together the edges of the two black sheets of paper, all the way to the back. Point the model eye to a strong source of light, such as a lightbulb, a window, or a door. Grasp the bottom paint paddle (connected to the cornea/lens and the paper enclosure) with one hand and the top paint paddle (connected to the retina) with the other. Move the retina back and forth until the image is clear.

More to Think About and Try

- How are the models like your eye, and how are they different?
- Why do you need the black paper?
- What happens to the image on the waxed paper if you cover part of the hole letting the light through the lens?
- What if you remove the lens?

A Little Background

Humans gain most information through their eyes. Scientists try hard to understand the eye because sometimes it can trick the brain. This model works well to show the cornea (front half of the CD case), the iris (black plastic insert from CD case), pupil (hole in the black insert), lens (magnifying glass), and retina (other half of the CD case with the waxed paper). The black paper represents the globe of the eyeball but has another function as well.

It is always useful to consider the limitations of a model. In this model, focusing is achieved by moving the lens with respect to the waxed paper. In your eye the lens itself can change shape, thus changing its focal length. In your eye there are two types of transparent fluid: "aqueous humor," between the cornea and lens, and "vitreous humor," filling up the majority of the eye globe between the lens and the retina. There is no one standing behind your eye to report on the image that falls on the retina. The retina is composed of many tiny light-sensitive nerves (the highest concentration of nerves in the body), which are connected to the brain by way of the optic nerve.

If you can obtain a cow's or sheep's eye, you can dissect it to see all these parts. Cut a small hole in the side of the cow eyeball before you start and then shine a light in the pupil. You will be able to see the upside-down image of that light on the retina. Once you remove the lens from a cow's eye, you can use it to project an upside-down image on a piece of paper.

The function of the black paper in this model, and the purpose of the large black cloak used 100 years ago by photographers, is to block out other light in order to see the dim image on the screen (retina). Let's say you are viewing a sunlit stop sign with your eye model. The image you see is made up of light that came from the sun, bounced off the sign, and then entered the eye model through the hole (pupil) and lens. If sunlight were allowed to reach the retina directly, it would overwhelm the dim image of the stop sign.

If you cover part of the pupil, less light gets in, so the image is not as bright. At the same time, it may be clearer because a smaller part of the imperfect lens was traveled across.

The translucent waxed paper serves an important purpose: when an image falls on it, we can view it from either side. Old-time photographers used frosted glass for the same purpose. An image will form on anything placed at the proper distance behind the lens, but most things, such as a piece of white paper, would display the image to viewers only on the lens-side of the paper.

It is possible to build a model like this that would be large enough to seat several people within. The people then sit with their backs to the lens and view the image on a white screen. This is known as "camera obscura." You don't need a lens; you can make one in your own room if you can get it dark enough, and then leave a tiny hole in one window. You'll see the scene outside the window, projected on the opposite wall, only upside down. If you removed the lens from this model and reduced the size of the hole, it would still work, though the image would be much dimmer. This is known as the "pinhole phenomenon," and it is quite interesting in its own right.

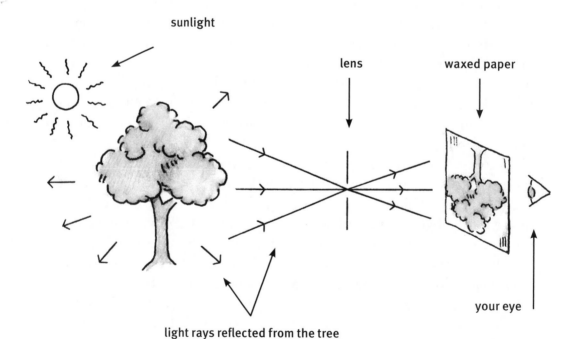

light rays reflected from the tree

Why are the images on the waxed paper upside down and reversed right to left? To understand, we must consider the path of the light from start to finish.

In the drawing on p. 122, the light from the sun hits the tree and is reflected in all directions. If you are viewing the tree with the eye model, a few rays of reflected light will pass into the model through the lens. Lenses bend light as it passes through them, so the light coming from the top of the tree is bent up a bit as it goes through the lens, but still ends up near the bottom of the waxed paper. The light coming from the bottom of the tree is bent down a bit as it goes through the lens, but still ends up near the top of the paper. Meanwhile, the light ray going exactly through the center of the lens does not bend at all and ends up in the center of the paper. The end result is an upside-down image. This happens both on the wax paper of this model and on the retina of your eye.

This same process would happen with just a pinhole and no lens. In that case, however, the light rays would not bend at all.

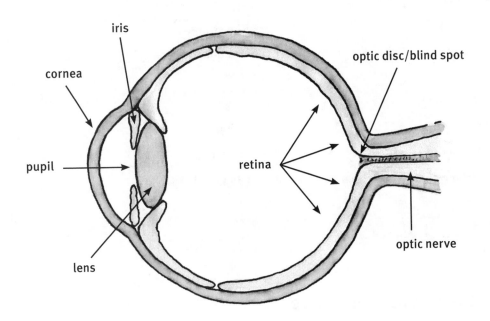

FiNGeRS OF the hAND

These fingers really work. Make four with a thumb and you have a model of a hand!

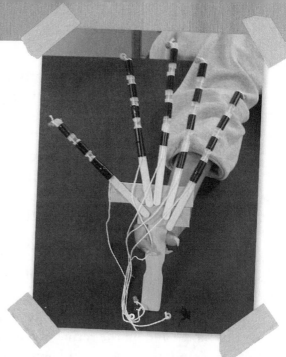

PARTS	
One Finger	
2 craft sticks	Kite string
2 drinking straws (fairly large in diameter)	Bamboo skewer
Bead	
The Whole Hand	
Paint paddle	10 beads
10 craft sticks	Kite string
10 drinking straws (fairly large in diameter)	Bamboo skewer

The Basic Concepts

Craft sticks represent the bones in this project; they give the hand its structure. The strings represent the hand's tendons; they connect the bones to the muscles. And pulling the strings represents the contraction of the muscles. There are actually few muscles in a hand—the muscles in the *arm* pull on the tendons that make a hand move.

Build It!

Note Before Building

You may be frustrated by not being able to finish an entire hand; this takes a long time. To get around this, the instructions below show you how to make a single finger. If you have the stamina, you can build five to complete an entire hand. A single finger is still very nice.

One Finger

Cut a craft stick into three roughly equal pieces. Then cut three lengths of a drinking straw, each slightly shorter than the three cut sticks.

  Use hot glue to affix a piece of drinking straw to a craft stick piece. Put the glue on the craft stick, *not* the drinking straw, or the straw may melt. Repeat this for the remaining two pieces.

 Glue all three stick segments onto one end of a full drinking straw, but leave a small space in between each segment so that bending is possible at each joint. The sticks will be sandwiched between the straws when you are finished.

Cut the other end of the full straw, leaving 3 inches to glue onto a full-length craft stick. Glue one more straw segment onto the top of the full-length craft stick in line with the other three segments, as shown.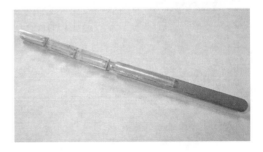

Tie a bead onto one end of 10-inch-long piece of string. Use a bamboo skewer to push the other end of the string through all four short straw segments.

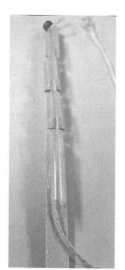

Tie another bead onto the other end of the string.

Wrap each segment with tape to reinforce the glue. Masking tape works, but black tape looks nicer. Alternatively, you can use only tape and no glue, to avoid burns, but it is harder to hold the small sections in the correct position as you tape them together. Pre-bend the finger at each joint. You have now completed one finger.

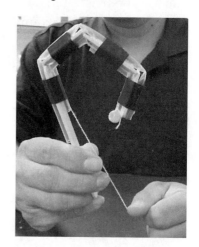

You should be able to hold the long stick and pull the string to make the finger bend.

The Whole Hand

Cut a paint paddle in half; then cut one half into two pieces, one about an inch shorter than the other. Glue the larger piece to the top of the full half of the paint paddle to form a T. Glue the smaller piece just underneath it.

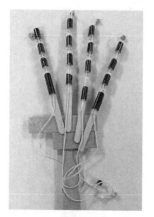

Build three more fingers and a thumb. The thumb has one less segment than the other fingers. Now glue the fingers to the paint paddle frame.

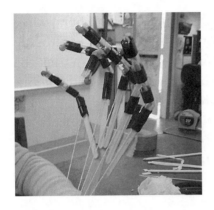

Glue on the thumb toward the side of the hand. Each finger should move when pulling on its string.

More to Think About and Try

- What are some differences between this hand and your hand?
- Human hands have two sets of tendons, one in front of the bones and one in back. What are the ones in back for?
- What happens if your tendons break?
- Ligaments hook bones to other bones. What are the ligaments in this project?

A Little Background

You move your body when your muscles pull on your bones. Ligaments attach bones to bones, and tendons attach bones to muscles. Most of the muscles that pull on each segment of your fingers are actually in your forearm. If you put your hand palm up on the table and move one finger at a time, you can see narrow lengths of muscles move in your forearm. Each of these muscles is connected to one bone in your hand through long tendons. The tendons move from the arm to the hand through the carpel tunnel.

In science, models help you understand the real thing. A model is similar to the real thing, but every model has its limitations. As you work with a model, you must always think about what is similar and what is different from the real thing.

There are several major differences between this model and a real hand. For each of your fingers on your hand, there are actually three muscles, one for each of the three bones. You usually use them all together, so like most people you are probably not able to move a single bone in, say, the tip of a finger. Also, when you stop bending a finger, it doesn't snap back the way a model finger does. You also have another set of muscles and tendons going down the back of each finger to re-extend it on demand.

If a tendon breaks, sometimes a doctor can repair it. Ligaments are much more difficult to heal. The ligaments in this model are the long straws connecting the bones in the back of the finger. Muscles, bones, tendons, and ligaments always work together, and if there is too much force put on the system, any of them may break.

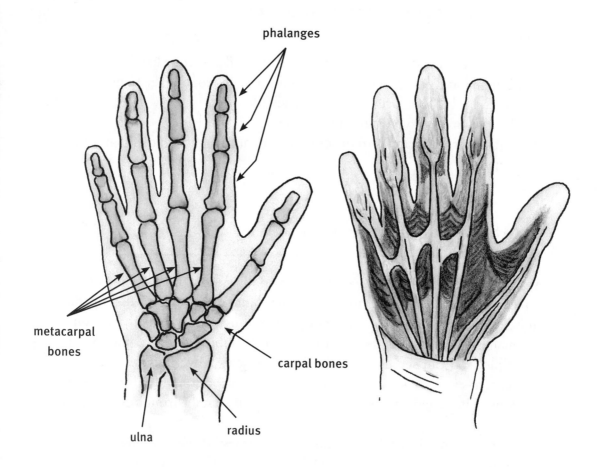

phalanges

metacarpal
bones

carpal bones

ulna

radius

hEARt PUMP

Your life depends on a reciprocating pump just like this.

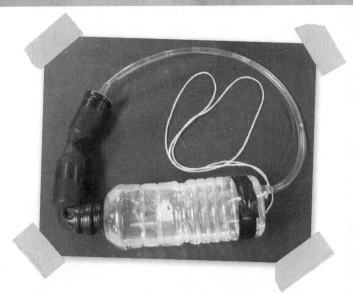

PARTS	
2 film canisters	1-inch flexible tube (³⁄₁₆-inch outer diameter, to fit snugly into long one)
Film canister lid	
Single-size plastic drink bottle (no lid necessary)	1-inch flexible tube into which the long one fits snugly (⁵⁄₁₆-inch inner diameter, ½-inch outer diameter)
7-inch bicycle inner tube (1¼-inch diameter works well; film canister must fit completely inside it)	
	String
	Red food coloring (or liquid watercolor)
2 pennies	
18-inch flexible tube (³⁄₁₆-inch inner diameter, ⁵⁄₁₆-inch outer diameter)	
TOOLS	
Sandpaper	

The Basic Concepts

The heart is a muscle that pumps blood through the body and back, then through the lungs and back. Pumps like the two in your heart have two one-way valves, so that the liquid can go in only one direction. The human heart has four chambers: two that work together to pump blood to the lungs and two that work together to pump blood to the rest of the body. Birds have only two chambers, like this model.

Build It!

Drill ¹⁹⁄₆₄-inch holes in the bases of two film canisters and one film canister lid. Check to be sure there are no burrs or rough edges around the holes inside of the film canisters. (The pennies must be able to lay flat across the holes.)

Drill another ¹⁹⁄₆₄-inch hole in the bottom of the bottle halfway between the center and the edge. Change to the ½-inch bit and enlarge the bottle's hole. (The bottle often rips if you drill directly with the ½-inch bit.)

Cut 7 inches of bicycle inner tube. Push one of the film canisters into the center of the inner tube.

Tape this film canister in tightly with black tape.

Pull the inner tube over the mouth and neck of the bottle as far as it will go. The film canister within the inner tube should be with its mouth up. Tape this joint tightly with black tape. The bottle and inner tube up to this first film canister represent the atrium. Blood gathers here as it arrives back at the heart.

Drop a penny into the film canister within the inner tube. This will be the first valve, between the atrium and ventricle.

Push the second film canister into the top of the inner tube, almost to the rim. Drop another penny into it. This will be the second valve, between the ventricle and the body. The short length of inner tube between the two film canisters represents the ventricle. This is the chamber that does most of the pumping.

Cap the film canister. Tape the inner tube tightly to this film canister and tape its lid on.

Prepare your flexible tubing. Cut 1-inch pieces from each of three sizes, then a 17-inch piece from the medium-diameter tubing. Sand the short pieces of large-diameter and medium-diameter tubing so that they are rough all

over. This will make the hot glue stick to them better. The tubing collectively represents all the vessels in the body.

Hot glue the short medium-diameter piece into the hole in the film canister lid. Insert the small-diameter piece into the short medium-diameter piece.

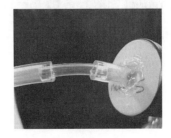

Stick the 17-inch piece over the small-diameter piece. When you take apart this joint later, the small-diameter piece should remain stuck in the piece glued to the film canister lid. This will be your squirter. (You could also drill a smaller hole into the film canister lid and insert the small-diameter piece directly. The way it is shown here requires only two drill bits.) Sand the bottle around the hole in the base, again to make the hot glue stick better.

Insert the large-diameter piece into this hole and hot glue it in. Do a good job on this joint because once the glue is wet, it will no longer stick. Examine it for tiny holes and add more glue until you are sure it won't leak. (If it does leak, the project still works—you will just get wet as it works.)

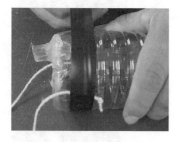

Cut about 24 inches of string and tie knots at both ends. Tape them so that the loop extends over the bottom of the bottle.

Put the loop over your neck to hold the pump when you're not using it. Fill the pump through the large tube in the base with water until it is almost completely full. You will need to hold the long tube up, or the water will leak out as you are filling it. This process is easiest done at a sink.

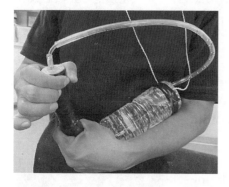

Cradle the bottle in one arm and grasp the inner film canister with that hand. Grasp the outer film canister with the other. Begin a systematic pumping action, first pulling the two film canisters apart, then pushing them firmly back together. The film canisters should be more or less vertical as you do this, to make the penny valves work properly. You should be able to see and feel the water being pumped around the tubing and into the base of the bottle again. This is the heart model working. Color the water red for an added effect.

To convert the heart pump into a squirt gun, remove the long tube from the smallest piece and fire away.

More to Think About and Try

- ✈ How could you make the pump stronger?
- ✈ Where would the lungs be in this system?
- ✈ When you push the two film canisters together and that part of the inner tube gets smashed smaller, what happens to the other part?
- ✈ What would happen if there was a hole in the thin tubing?

A Little Background

When talking about the function of the heart, it is important to consider the lungs at the same time. The importance of the heart and lungs can be seen from their position in the body. They are behind the rib cage and thus are protected more than any other organ aside from the brain. If you damage your heart or lungs, you'll die in minutes, whereas if you damage your other organs, you'll have more time on your side.

The function of the heart and lungs (along with the entire circulatory and respiratory systems) is to supply each cell in the body with oxygen and nutrients and also to remove waste materials and carbon dioxide. Both organs work involuntarily; that is, you don't have to think about them. You keep breathing and your heart keeps pumping even while you're sleeping. The heart is a muscle that is controlled by tiny electric signals.

It is always useful to think about where a scientific model is accurate and where it breaks down. In this heart pump model, the inner tube section between the two film canisters is like the ventricle. It does most of the pumping. The bottle and the other inner tube section are like the atrium; they receive the water when it comes back from the tube. You can watch this section of the inner tube get bigger and smaller in opposition to the one that you are pumping. The clear tube is like the blood vessels. As the blood flows away from the heart, it is in vessels called arteries, so the first part of the tube is like the arteries. Blood then flows into smaller and smaller vessels, which are called capillaries and which lead to every cell in the body. Finally, blood starts back to the heart in vessels called veins. So, the tube is like a vein as it flows back into the bottle. If there was a hole in the tubing, the water would be pumped out of the system. This is similar to when a person loses blood.

There are several things missing from the heart model. There is only one short blood vessel. Even a tiny animal's system of blood vessels is extraordinarily complex as it connects up with each cell in the body. Also, even in a bird's heart, which has only two chambers, there are two different routes for the blood: one through the lungs and one to the rest of the body. Our heart model doesn't represent lungs at all (though a lung model follows this project); there would need to be an entirely separate pump with valves and tubes running to the lungs.

The penny valves are very simple models of a real heart's valves. As the water comes into the first film canister, it blasts the penny out of the way. Then, as the ventricle chamber is compressed, the pressure rises and the water pushes that penny back down to cover the hole. But the penny in the other film canister is blasted up, allowing the water to go in only one direction. When the ventricle is expanded again, that penny is sucked back down to cover that hole while the penny in the first film canister is blasted up again allowing water to flow in. This is the way most reciprocating pumps work.

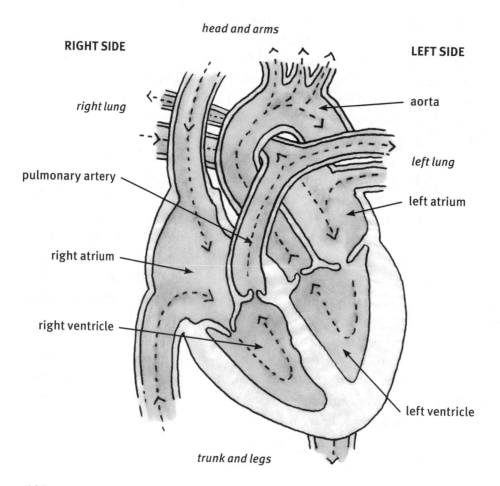

134

LUNG MODEL

Breathe deep as you inflate a balloon inside a bottle.

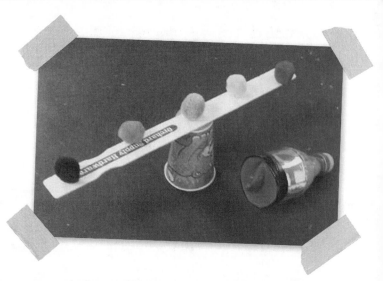

PARTS	
Single-size plastic drink bottle (no lid necessary; soda bottles are stronger and work better than water bottles)	Craft pom-poms
	Paint paddle
	Cup
2 balloons	

The Basic Concepts

Lungs are basically sacks full of many smaller sacks, all connected together like branches of a tree. Air passes through the mouth and into these sacks, and blood circulates in the walls. Carbon dioxide is transferred from the blood to the air, and oxygen is transferred from the air to the blood.

Lungs are not muscles. The diaphragm is the muscle that moves up and down and draws air into the lungs. In this project the balloon over the bottom half of the bottle is like the diaphragm.

Cut a plastic bottle in half. Cut the mouth and neck off a balloon; then stretch the remaining half over the bottom of the bottle. It helps to have someone hold the bottle while you do this. If you do it right, the bottle will not collapse on itself. This balloon represents the diaphragm.

Tape the balloon to the bottle.

Stuff another balloon in through the mouth of the bottle. Wrap the mouth of the balloon over the mouth of the bottle. This balloon represents a lung.

To make your model exhale, push the diaphragm up into the bottle. The lung balloon will shrink. To make it inhale, pull down on the diaphragm. The lung balloon will expand.

When you are done experimenting with your lung model, take out the lung balloon, and you will have an air gun. Set up a shooting range with a

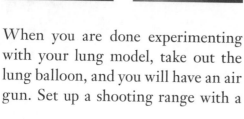

cup and paint paddle. Place small objects such as craft pom-poms on top and try to knock them off. Pull back on the diaphragm and let it go. The gun also works well for blowing out candles.

More to Think About and Try

- What happens to your diaphragm when you take a very deep breath?
- Why do you think the heart is made of muscle but the lung is not?
- Why can some people hold their breath longer than others?
- If you breathe into a bag without letting any air escape, after a minute or so you start feeling like you're not getting any air, even though you're breathing normally. What is going on?

A Little Background

To fully understand how your lungs work within your body, reread the previous project's background on the heart. Unlike your heart, your lungs are not muscles—they can't move by themselves. The diaphragm muscle makes them work. This muscle is a bit different from the heart in that you can consciously control your diaphragm for a few minutes, such as when you hold your breath or blow out a candle. But as soon as you forget about it, it goes back to working on its own.

The lung model in this project is very simple, and surprisingly accurate. The top balloon is like your lungs: it inflates when the bottom balloon, which is similar to the diaphragm, is lowered. The bottle itself is like the rib cage, protecting the lungs. It would be more accurate if there were two lungs instead of one, if there was a heart in there with the lungs, if there were blood vessels connected to the balloons, and if the balloons were actually composed of millions of tiny balloons.

Different people have different sized lungs, and different people use oxygen at different rates. Pearl divers can have lungs much larger than usual, the result of breathing very deep in order to raise their oxygen capacity and maximize their time under water. If you breathe into a bag, you will soon convert all the oxygen in that volume of air into water and carbon dioxide. You need oxygen to live, so your body will begin to give you signals that you need more.

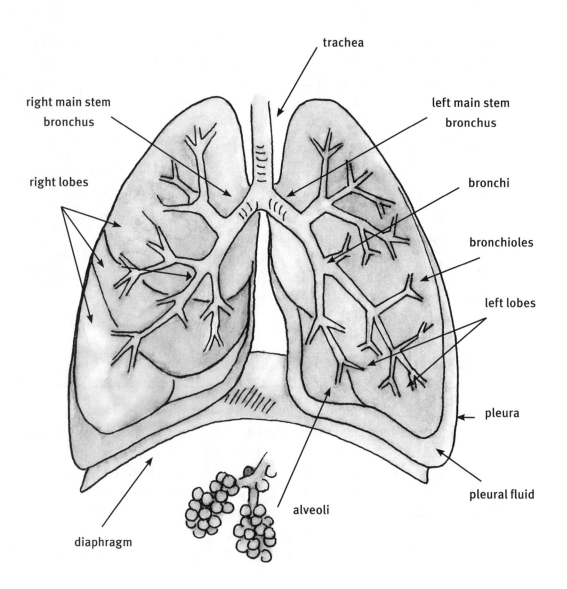

trachea

right main stem
bronchus

left main stem
bronchus

right lobes

bronchi

bronchioles

left lobes

pleura

pleural fluid

alveoli

diaphragm

CARTESIAN DiVERS

Density determines whether they float or sink.

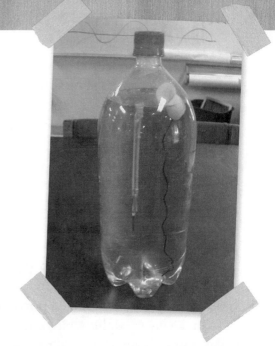

PARTS	
2 drinking straws (transparent or translucent)	2-liter bottle with lid
	Thin wire (for making hoop in bottle)
4 rubber bands (small)	Piece of Styrofoam packing material
6 paper clips (small)	
Large pitcher, bottle, or bucket with open top (for testing)	

The Basic Concepts

Things float when they are less dense than the fluid surrounding them. Things sink when they are denser than the fluid surrounding them. Knowing either the weight or size (volume) alone is not enough to determine whether something will sink or float. You have to know both, and that will tell you the density. (Something small may sink, but something big may float, whether it be liquid or solid.)

When you squeeze the bottle in this project, the air inside gets pressed into a smaller space. The space the water takes up doesn't change. Because of that, some water goes into the straw, making it heavier. Since the straw's size (volume) did not change, its density increased.

Build It!

Cut a 5- or 6-inch piece of drinking straw. Fold a little bit back from one end and wrap a rubber band very tightly around the doubled portion. To make it very tight, wrap only half

the rubber band, then fold the end of the straw again and wrap the rest of the rubber band so that the rubber band holds down two folds, as shown. Slide several paper clips inside the open end of straw. This is your first diver; make at least one more.

Test the divers in an open vessel. For a diver to work, it must have enough weight so that it just barely floats. When you tap it from above, it should sink and then rise again slowly. If it sinks and doesn't come back up, you have too many paper clips. Add or subtract paper clips until the divers work correctly.

When they work, drop the divers in a bottle almost full of water and cap it tightly. Squeeze the bottle, and the divers should sink. Release it, and they should rise. Look at the straw very carefully to see what is happening to make the diver sink and rise.

To make a game with the divers, add a wire hoop to the bottle. Wrap a length of wire around a Styrofoam packing peanut. At the other end make a loop that is just small enough to fit through the mouth of the bottle. The loop should 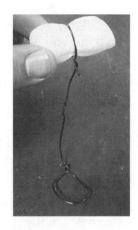 be perpendicular to the rest of the wire so that the divers can go down through it. The wire hoop assembly should be just shorter than the height of the water in the bottle. Drop it into the bottle.

When you squeeze the bottle, try to get the diver to pass through the loop on its way to the bottom.

More to Think About and Try

- What happens inside the straw diver when you squeeze the bottle?
- Why do you think the diver goes down?
- What would happen if you filled the diver bottle only half full?
- Could you make the straw diver go down even if the bottom of the straw were sealed off?

A Little Background

Throw a small grain of sand into the ocean, and it will sink. Throw an enormous tree in, and it will float. What matters is not the weight (or mass) or the size (or volume), but the amount of mass in a given volume. That is the definition of "density." It is easiest to think about if you hold one of these constant. For example, if you have two identical bottles, one full of sand and one full of air, their volumes are the same, but since the mass is different, the densities are different. A little piece of wood would have less mass than the same sized little piece of sand. It would take many cups of Styrofoam packing pieces to equal the weight of one cup of water because the water is denser.

Density is a property of all materials. You can compare the density of a solid and a fluid by checking to see if the solid floats. Floating is the opposite of sinking, and sinking is just gravity pulling something down. You could even say that we have all sunk to the bottom of the atmosphere. This is because we all have densities greater than the gas that makes up the atmosphere.

Think of all the things that you have seen float or sink. It is all due to different densities: Helium and hot air balloons are less dense than air, so they float. Bubbles are less dense than water, so they float. Boats are less dense than water, so they float unless they are filled with water, in which case they usually become denser than water and sink. Ice is less dense than water, so it floats. Sugar is denser than water, so it sinks until it dissolves, at which time it has made the water itself denser.

In this Cartesian divers toy, the straw floats when it is less dense than water and sinks when it is denser than water. Its density changes when you squeeze the bottle. Air is made of gasses, and gas molecules are farther apart than liquid molecules. If you press on them, they will get closer together. Liquid and solid molecules are close together already, and if you press on them, nothing much happens. You can feel this by squeezing on two identical bottles, one all full of air and the other completely full of water.

If you look very carefully at the bottom end of the straw when you squeeze the Cartesian diver bottle, you'll see water going up into it. If you look at the top of the water in the bottle, you may also notice it move up a bit in the neck when you squeeze. This is because all the air trapped in the bottle is compressed when you squeeze and the water is not. The water moves up to take the place of the air.

When water enters the straw, the straw's mass goes up while its volume stays the same, so its density goes up, too. When its density gets larger than that of water, it will sink. If the bottom of the straw were sealed off, it would still move down when you squeezed the bottle. The straw would be squashed a bit as you squeezed. Now the diver's mass would not change but its volume would decrease, making its density increase.

It is unclear how Cartesian divers got their name. The word "Cartesian" generally refers to something connected to the great scientist/philosopher/mathematician René Descartes (1596–1650), but in fact it was a student of another pioneering scientist, Galileo, who originally described this toy in 1648. See www.ed.uiuc.edu/courses/CI241-science-Sp95/resources/philoToy/philoToy.html for more information.

Oil ON WATER

Density works the same way with two liquids.

PARTS	
Single-size plastic drink bottle, with cap	3 film canisters
Water	Bamboo skewer
10 ounces oil, any transparent type	Plastic bag
Food coloring (or liquid watercolor)	Baseboard
TOOLS	
Funnel	Long stick or tweezers
Nail, large (to make hole for boat's mast)	Stapler with staples

The Basic Concepts

Like solids, liquids float and sink depending on their densities. The density of a material does not depend on how much of it is present, so a tiny drop of one liquid will act the same as a large quantity when added to another liquid.

In this project, the water is denser than the boat, which is denser than the oil.

Build It!

Pour water into a small plastic bottle until it is just under half full. Then add oil until it is almost full. Lastly, add several drops of food coloring and watch what happens.

Make a small boat to float inside the bottle. Cut the hull of the boat from a plastic film canister. The boat's hull must be small enough to fit through the mouth of the bottle. Place the hull on top of a film canister lid and punch a hole in the center with a nail.

Cut a small piece of bamboo skewer for the boat's mast. Carefully cut a small slit in one end of the bamboo piece.

Next, cut a piece of a plastic bag for a flag and insert it into the slit.

Insert the mast into the hole in the hull.

Put the boat into the bottle. If it doesn't sink to the water, fish it out with a long stick or tweezers and put a staple into it. Before capping the bottle tightly, fill it all the way to the top with either water or oil. It looks best without an air bubble.

To make a stand for your project, hot glue a film canister to a baseboard.

Then cut the bottom off another film canister, and cut it down one side. Glue it to the top of the other canister, so that it opens up to receive the bottle. Balance the bottle on the stand.

The boat should float in the center.

More to Think About and Try

* What would happen if you made a boat entirely out of wood and put it in the bottle of oil and water?
* What about a boat made of wire?
* If you put a drop of water in a bucket of oil, would it sink or stay on top?
* How about a drop of oil in a bucket of water?

A Little Background

Density is a property of all materials, whether they are solid, liquid, or gas. Two liquids or two gases together will find their places according to their density, just like a solid in a liquid. In this project, water sinks below the oil because it is denser. The food coloring is water-based, not oil-based, so it sinks through the oil without coloring it, yet mixes well when it hits the water.

The boat also sinks in the oil, but then floats on the water. If your mast is too large it may decrease the density of the boat so much that it floats on the top of the oil. Adding staples increases the density, because metal is denser than any of the other materials used.

If you made a boat from wood or Styrofoam, it would probably float above the oil as well. On the other hand, a boat made from wire would likely sink beneath the water. Try both and see!

Density is defined as the amount of mass in a given volume. This doesn't change if you cut something in half or otherwise reduce the *amount* of it. As you observed, a drop of water will move to the bottom of a pool of oil, just as a drop of oil will remain on top of a bucket of water.

gak and Oobleck

Renegade materials on the loose!

PARTS	
Gak	
Borax	About 2 ounces glue
Large plastic cup for Borax solution	Food coloring (or liquid watercolor)
Film canister, no lid	Paint paddle
Short clear plastic cup	Ziploc bag
Oobleck	
About 2 ounces cornstarch	Food coloring (or liquid watercolor)
Short clear plastic cup	

The Basic Concepts

Some things are not exactly a liquid and not exactly a solid. Both Gak and Oobleck act like solids if you move them fast, but act like liquids if you let them move slowly.

Gak is a polymer, meaning it has long molecules that can slide back and forth beside one another while still holding together. Oobleck is a mixture of a liquid and tiny particles of a solid. The solid particles in Oobleck are normally lubricated by the liquid and slide together smoothly, but when Oobleck is pressed, the solid particles rub against one another and move less fluidly.

Two substances may just blend together when they combine, forming a mixture, or a chemical reaction may take place between them, creating one or more new substances. The substances created in a chemical reaction may have very different properties than either of the original two substances.

Build It!

Gak

Put some borax in a large cup, about a half-inch in the bottom. Fill the cup up with water.

Stir with paint paddle to make a borax solution. The undissolved borax at the bottom is evidence that the liquid on top is a saturated solution. Once the liquid borax solution has been used up (in the steps below), add more water and stir again to get more solution.

Pour one film canister of glue into a short cup. Add a film canister of water to the glue.

Add a few drops of coloring. Mix these three ingredients together with a paint paddle.

Add a film canister of the borax solution. Stir it all together. The chemical reaction takes place in this step. Remove the Gak from the cup and play with it. It will get drier as you play.

When you are done playing, put it in a Ziploc bag. (Gak can be very messy on fabrics.) Write on the Ziploc bag how many cans of glue, water, and borax solution you put in. Then make another batch, but instead of using a 1 to 1 to 1 mixture, change one of the variables to see what happens, or change the order of adding the different ingredients.

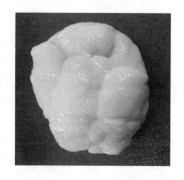

You can do many experiments with Gak to learn its strange properties. For example, put the Gak near the edge of a table and wait to see what happens.

Put the Gak inside different objects, such as a film canister. As you squish it in, listen to the interesting noises it makes. Or put the Gak on top of a cup and see what happens to it.

Stretch your Gak to see how far it goes; then measure it.

Oobleck

Put cornstarch in a short cup. Add a tiny bit of water and mix them together.

Add more water bit by bit until something interesting begins to happen.

Play with it: poke it, stir it, hit it, squeeze it, pick it up, pour it. You can also add food coloring.

More to Think About and Try

- ➤ What is the longest you can pull your Gak without breaking it?
- ➤ What happens if you just leave your Gak sitting on the edge of a table?
- ➤ What do you think would happen if you got your Gak warmer or froze it?
- ➤ How could you make your Oobleck harder?

A Little Background

Most people learn the three states of matter: solid, liquid, and gas. This is only a part of the picture. First of all, scientists believe most (over 90 percent) of the visible universe is made up of none of these but rather a fourth state called "plasma." Most of the visible mass of the universe is contained in stars. Stars are powered by nuclear reactions so hot that the basic structure of atoms changes. The result is a state of matter called plasma, which is very hot and has a different distribution of electric charge. This situation is created for some electronic devices (plasma balls, plasma screens) and occurs naturally here on Earth in the form of lightning and other spark discharges.

The substances in this activity straddle the line between solid and liquid. Gak does so because of its long polymer molecules sliding past one another like wet noodles. Oobleck has this property because the shape of the cornstarch particles allows water between them. The water can act as a lubricant and aid the particles in slipping beside one another. When you push hard and fast, however, the particles themselves touch and don't slip nearly as easily. A similar situation can exist in wet sand. You may have noticed the water being pressed out of wet sand if you have ever walked on a shore. Wet sand has properties very different from dry sand.

Oobleck is just a mixture. If you let the water evaporate, you have the original cornstarch again. If you let your ball of Gak dry out, you have dry Gak—nothing at all like the glue or borax you put in. Chemicals in the glue and borax reacted to give a fundamentally different substance. If you make some Gak without color and then add the food coloring, the ball of Gak will not take in the color. The reaction has already happened, and the new substance does not absorb the watery food coloring.

Gak made with more water tends to be gooier, and with less water tends to be harder. Making Gak with no water aside from that in the glue and borax solution can give you a tight substance that bounces like a rubber ball. But leave that ball on the table for a few hours and it "spills" like milk; it behaves like a liquid over long periods of time. Play with the variables in the recipe, and you'll learn more than if you simply follow the recipe exactly.

bRiNgiNg these PROJeCts iNto the ClASSROOM

THESE PROJECTS WERE ORIGINALLY done in Watsonville, California, with groups of 20 students from the third through eighth grades, once a week, in their after-school program. In fall 2007, we entered our fifth year with this program, serving around 400 students per week. Ours continues to be one of the most popular after-school activities in our district. Students love our projects because they are free to experiment and tinker with real stuff, and teachers love them because the students learn just by constructing the projects.

It is a tremendous irony that in this book we have mapped out these projects in a step-by-step, cookbooklike manner. When we teach the projects, we never give detailed instructions. We bring two working models for the students to study, and we explain only the basic gist of how to build a project. We then go over any very difficult or intricate parts and all safety issues. We also give a hint as to the science involved by asking two focus questions, though we do not discuss any answers at first. After an introduction of 10 minutes or so we pass out the materials and everyone starts building. We spend the bulk of our class time constructing the project.

Toward the end of the class, the students are (with great difficulty) drawn back to their seats for a short discussion on the content of the projects. We generally discuss answers to the focus questions, but often we also discuss other concepts that arose as the students completed their projects. Middle school students are also required to do a short write-up at the end, explaining what they have done and learned and writing answers to the focus questions.

We are careful never to do any part of the project for the student. The question asked most often is, "What do I do now?" to which the answer is "Go look at the model." To learn to follow a model as opposed to detailed directions is something rare and valuable in school culture. There are great benefits to this pedagogy: The teacher is not so necessary, which empowers the student toward lifelong self-learning and allows the teacher to focus on certain individual students' needs. Students can be creative and build the project according to their own tastes, and they can build at different paces as well, with those who finish first helping others or continuing to build more onto their project.

Tools and Materials

Each project uses many and varied materials. A great effort has been made to rely on free and recycled materials, such as plastic drink bottles and cans, film canisters, scrap wood, and paint-stirring paddles. Local sources for these materials can be found easily. Certain special materials—less than 5 percent—need to be acquired from specialty sources: electronics supply stores, science supply stores, and so forth. Nearly all of the parts can be found at the sources listed here:

Retail Sources

- Hardware or home improvement shops
- Office supply stores
- Grocery stores
- Craft shops
- Discount, dollar, or 99-cent stores
- Electronics shops such as Radio Shack (motors, battery snaps, magnets, audio plugs, wire, amplifiers)

Online Sources

- Air-Tite Products, Inc.; www.air-tite.com (syringes)
- Allmagnetics; www.allmagnetics.com (magnets)

- Discount School Supply; www.discountschoolsupply.com (paper, beads, glitter, paint, plastic eyes, craft sticks, pipe cleaners, craft pom-poms, liquid watercolor—much cheaper than common food coloring)
- Kelvin; www.kelvin.com (motors, battery snaps, magnets)
- Mouser Electronics; www.mouser.com (audio plugs, battery snaps)
- Oriental Trading Company; www.orientaltrading.com (magnifying glasses)
- Tap Plastics; www.tapplastics.com (mirrors)

Scrap and Donation Sources

- Bike shops (inner tubes)
- Cabinet shops or lumber yards (wood pieces)
- Photo shops (film canisters)
- Paint shops (paint paddles)
- Phone company yards (wire)
- Radio stations (CDs and CD cases)
- Recycling centers (bottles, cans)
- Restaurants (egg cartons, bottle caps, straws)
- Secondhand stores (wool, motorized toys for motors, wheels, and so forth)

A significant amount of time will be spent gathering and preparing these materials; therefore, it is far more efficient to gather many materials and deliver the projects to several different groups. If many students are to be served, good storage systems are important and a table saw is very useful for preparing small wood pieces from larger scraps of wood.

These toys have been used as the sole curriculum in our Students Teaching Project. We use the Watsonville Environmental Science Workshop to prepare and store the materials. Teams of three teach the projects: one lead teacher (college student or college graduate) and two high school students. These "Teacher-Students" meet once a week to learn the following week's project and prepare the materials. Naturally, more staff is better when doing hands-on projects with a group of students, but when high school helpers are not available, our lead teachers routinely teach the classes by themselves as well.

About the Watsonville Environmental Science Workshop

THE WATSONVILLE ENVIRONMENTAL SCIENCE Workshop is located within the Community Center at Marinovich Park in Watsonville, California. It was founded in 1997 with a seed grant from the National Science Foundation and is one of 12 such programs nationwide.

Our community science Workshop is not only an after-school program but also a unique community resource. Our Workshop complements the science and math education our students get from school and allows them to pursue the technical areas of their own interests. Our Workshop also gives community kids the opportunity to interact together in a rich, stimulating, and safe environment with adults present who care about their development in academics as well as their development as a whole person.

The core of our program is the open-structure, open-door Workshop hours. After school and on Saturdays, community kids and their families are free to come and construct the projects of their imaginations. While they are at the Workshop, they can peruse our exhibits and project models in addition to working on whatever project they choose to construct. They learn to use tools and a plethora of different materials. In this natural way, students can learn science, math, and engineering from direct experience. They get the opportunity to learn through inquiry, exploration, and peer consultation. The competence they gain builds true confidence. All the while, they are subconsciously defining "science" for themselves, and the definition involves fun and success. All of this is markedly different from what most of them get in school.

In addition to the core program, we take our most popular hands-on science projects to about 20 local school sites through our Students

Teaching program, in which adults and high school students team up to do the teaching. The S. H. Cowell Foundation has given us generous support for the Students Teaching Project. Three alternative high schools bring their classes to the Workshop once a week for a formal hands-on science lesson, complete with notes and write-up. Several field trips and camping trips each year get students out into the local environment. We work closely with the other environmental education programs of the City of Watsonville. Teachers frequent the Workshop for informal consultations on how to succeed with hands-on lessons for their classes, and we occasionally do mass teacher training as well.

Everything we do employs recycled, reclaimed, and scrap objects, so that students are made firmly aware of the value and potential of the materials around them. Conservation principles are conveyed, as is the presence of science in everyday life: students become aware that science is everywhere, not just in special labs and kits. In addition, this practice keeps our costs low and our Workshop sustainable. We are always on the lookout for donations of interesting junk.

For more information, please see our Web page: www.ci.watsonville.ca .us/scienceworkshop.

iNDeX

The Sacred Paths
of the West

SECOND EDITION

The Sacred Paths of the West

Theodore M. Ludwig

Valparaiso University

Prentice
Hall

Upper Saddle River, New Jersey 07458

Library of Congress Cataloging-in-Publication Data

Ludwig, Theodore M.
   The sacred paths of the West /
  Theodore M. Ludwig.—2nd ed.
     p. cm.
    Includes bibliographical references and index.
    ISBN 0-13-029355-5
    1. Religions. 2. Judaism. 3. Christianity. 4. Islam. 5. Monotheism. I. Title.
BL80.2.L83 2001
291—dc21
                                    00-057130

Editorial/Production Supervision: *Harriet Tellem*
Acquisitions Editor: *Ross Miller*
Editorial Assistant: *Carla Worner*
Prepress and Manufacturing Buyer: *Sherry Lewis*
Text Design: *Amy Rosen*
Cover Design: *Bruce Kenselaar*

This book was set in 10/12 Minion by Rosemary Ross, and was printed and
bound by RR Donnelley, Harrisonburg, VA. The cover was printed by Phoenix Color Corporation.

 © 2001 by Prentice-Hall, Inc.
A Division of Pearson Education
Upper Saddle River, New Jersey 07458

Printed in the United States of America
10 9 8 7 6 5 4 3 2 1

ISBN 0-13-029355-5

PEARSON EDUCATION (UK) LIMITED, *London*
PRENTICE-HALL OF AUSTRALIA PTY. LIMITED, *Sydney*
PRENTICE-HALL CANADA INC., *Toronto*
PRENTICE-HALL HISPANOAMERICANA, S.A., *Mexico*
PRENTICE-HALL OF INDIA PRIVATE LIMITED, *New Delhi*
PRENTICE-HALL OF JAPAN, INC., *Tokyo*
PEARSON EDUCATION PTE. LTD., *Singapore*
EDITORA PRENTICE-HALL DO BRASIL, LTDA., *Rio de Janeiro*

In Memory of My Parents

Paul Walter Ludwig

Thekla Friedrich Ludwig

Contents

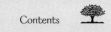

Preface to the Second Edition

This study of the religions of the West incorporates material from a larger volume on the whole range of the world's religious traditions, *The Sacred Paths: Understanding the Religions of the World,* third edition (Prentice Hall, 2001). The new edition has been revised to bring material up-to-date and to provide the reader with greater clarity in the discussions of complex historical and theoretical material.

Designed for those who want to concentrate on the religious traditions that have shaped Western culture, this volume focuses on the three Abrahamic religions—Judaism, Christianity, and Islam—in the context of the ancient traditions of Egypt, Mesopotamia, and Greece. To round out this context, a new chapter, on the important Zoroastrian tradition, has been added.

To serve the needs of people who are beginning their study of the world's religions, the basic approach in this volume is focused on the goal of understanding. And understanding begins with a sense of what a particular religion means for the people who practice it and live by it. It is important to realize that each religious tradition is a living and growing organism stretched out over time, and thus we pay attention to historical and cultural developments. But we also attempt to go beyond historical information and let readers find themselves in the place of the people who live by each religion—viewing the world through their sacred stories, their worldview, their rituals, and their notion of the good life.

The procedure used in this volume, then, combines the necessary discussion of historical matters with a thematic approach based on general issues that arise out of human experience—questions about personal identity, human existence and wholeness, and the right way to live. Since the reader can identify with such issues from personal experience, windows are opened toward an understanding of the meaning and guidance people find in their particular religious traditions. Further, this combination of historical and thematic approaches facilitates comparison among the religious traditions, highlighting the main motifs and concerns of that general dimension of human life we call religious experience.

Since this is a basic introduction for people who are beginning their exploration of the world's religious paths, the major focus is not on academic questions and theories about religion, nor on technical information about all the movements and historical developments that make up each religious tradition. Such theories and developments are important, of course, and this volume attempts to make readers aware of them in a beginning way. It is important that readers get the sense that each religious tradition is a highly complex living organism, with various movements arising at different points in history. Yet it is helpful for the beginning student to recognize first of all the general mainstream of each religious tradition in constructing an overall picture of the religious world of the West. The excitement and challenge of this venture will carry over, it is hoped, into a continuing engagement with understanding the complex religious traditions of the world and with the various issues raised in the academic study of these traditions.

It is particularly important that readers have some encounter with the sacred texts and scriptures of each particular religious tradition—yet the comprehension and appreciation of such sacred texts is notoriously difficult for an outsider. This volume incorporates extensive quotations from the sacred texts of each tradition, providing interpretation so the reader can see the significance of these texts and comprehend what they mean for people of that religious tradition. It will be helpful, of course, if this volume is supplemented with an additional collection of sacred texts, when that is feasible.

The inclusion of material on artistic expression in the different religious traditions helps the reader see that each religion or culture has its own unique aesthetic sense. Thus it is important, for understanding each tradition, to pay attention to the special artistic expressions growing out of that religious experience. Also, this volume gives particular attention to the role of women in each tradition. Greater awareness of women's experiences and leadership roles has made possible many new understandings and insights in all the religious traditions. Further, an important development in the modern Western world is the rise of new religious movements, and a special chapter is devoted to understanding some of these alternative movements.

Among the study features in this volume, the discussion questions for each chapter have been revised and expanded. These questions are designed to promote review of the material as well as further reflection on the character of each religious tradition. Other study features include maps, timelines, and a glossary of key terms. The suggestions for further reading for each religious tradition have incorporated many important books that have been published in the last few years.

Many have helped along the way in the development of this book and toward the completion of this second edition. And so I thank all those students and colleagues who have made so many helpful suggestions concerning ways in which this text can become a more helpful means for understanding the religious paths of the world.

The Sacred Paths
of the West

Exploring the Sacred Paths

INTRODUCTION

Beginning to explore the religious traditions of the Western world is an exciting, though somewhat daunting, venture. There is so much to see, to sort through, and to comprehend. We are dealing with the deepest hopes and dreams, the most careful thoughts and views, and the most cherished rituals and practices of countless generations of fellow humans. We are venturing onto the holy ground of others, and a humble, respectful, and grateful attitude is most appropriate.

As we begin this exploration, we need to be aware that we carry preconceived ideas and judgments with us. We may, perhaps, have a certain amount of knowledge about at least one religious tradition (our own, for example), and based on that, we have some notions about what religion is. One major hurdle in understanding the religious traditions of the world is getting beyond the normal tendency to look at the religious practices of others through our own filters of understanding, our own unchallenged views and experiences.

Another hurdle comes when we become inundated with the mass of detail and diversity of forms within the Western religions. It is easy to become confused and bewildered, losing any coherent sense of what religion is all about. What are we looking for? The answer to that question may seem very different with each new culture that we encounter.

To help get our bearings for this exploration in the sacred paths of the West, it will be beneficial, here at the beginning of our study, to stand back and reflect more generally on the nature of religious experience, on the main themes and forms through which religious experience typically finds expression. Such an exercise can broaden our narrow vision of religion and open new windows of understanding. Thus, in

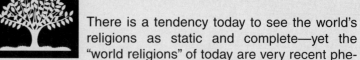

Chapter 1 we begin our exploration with some reflections on the nature of religion within human life. With a preliminary, working definition of religion we then take soundings from the various religious traditions to set up a collage of themes and forms of human religious experience. It is true, of course, that each particular human community has its own unique practices and meanings, and one should exercise great care in making cross-cultural comparisons. Yet we can recognize that humans through all times and places have always experienced similar life concerns related to birth and death, family and community, survival, and all the rest. And so their attempts to construct meaning through ideas and actions—that is, their religious expressions—can be linked together in a provisional way. In this manner, we can set up a tentative structure to guide our explorations into the sacred paths of the West.

Our look at prehistoric human religious developments is brief and tentative, and rightly so, since archaeological data from ancient sites, before any written records, do not give a clear picture of religious feelings and meanings. There may awaken a sense of adventure as we reflect on the immense ages during which humans lived on this planet, surviving, experimenting, and constructing meaning.

There is a tendency today to see the world's religions as static and complete—yet the "world religions" of today are very recent phenomena on the vast scale of humankind's religious history. Perhaps there will awaken in us a sense of indebtedness to our forebears who struggled to live, created religious meanings, and bequeathed their physical and spiritual powers to the world's human community of today.

It is true that many of the tribal, indigenous peoples of the world have faded from the picture as viable human communities in modern times. These peoples have been co-opted by modern societies and often incorporated into world religions. Yet the themes and structures of religious life can often be seen clearly in these tribal religious traditions and practices, for they tend to make little separation between religious activities and the other aspects of life. Encounters with the sacred is expected as part of the "normal" life experiences. Their sacred stories and their ritual practices still resonate as authentic human constructions of meaning. We can value the heritage of these tribal peoples, understand the struggles they have experienced, and sense the excitement of revitalization in some of these indigenous communities today.

CHAPTER 1

Perspectives
on Religious Experience

The human adventure can be viewed from many perspectives—and indeed there should be many perspectives, since there is not just one human story, but many stories. Common to these stories is a searching for meaning, for wholeness, for some connection to the larger continuity of human life. That searching has often been expressed in what we call religious structures, ideas, and experiences. In this book, we are setting out on a venture of **understanding**—understanding some of those religious traditions of humankind. To do this, we need to explore their main ideas and teachings, their rituals and art, their societal structures, their whole ways of life. In all of this, we want to get to know the people who practice these religions and live their lives by them.

As we study different religious traditions of the West, we will also be attempting to understand some fundamentals of religion itself as a key human dimension, with similar themes and structures across cultural lines—for all religion has to do with fundamental human issues and concerns. Who are we?—the basic question of identity—is crucial to our journey in life. What sense is there in life? How can we find the life that is real and fulfilling? Questions such as these reach to the depths of life concerns that are felt, vaguely or forcefully, by all human beings. They deal with the fundamental concern about the *meaning* of human existence. Does life actually have meaning—any **real** meaning—or do we just live and die in the small frame of a pointless, accidental cycle of the universe?

Of course, there are many dimensions of being human, many concerns that are not directly religious ones. We are concerned about our physical makeup, our biological structure, our reasoning capacities, our languages and forms of communication, our historical memories, our forms of society, our psychological makeup, and much more.

But no matter what aspect of human existence we happen to look at, deeper questions of meaning and purpose are close at hand: Is there any sense or direction in our history? Why have we evolved into reasoning animals? What is the meaning of sex? What responsibility do we have for fellow humans? In other words, the question of the *meaning* of human existence is confronted. And wrestling with that question of meaning in its deeper aspects involves us in religious thinking and experiencing.

Religion in this sense is not limited to any one dimension of human existence. Rather, it has to do with the overall meaning of human existence: Why is *everything* the way it is? What is the rhyme or reason behind all this? What is our purpose in living? Behind all such questions is a fundamental one: Where can we look for that which is ultimately real, that unlimited source, or sources, from which we derive life and meaning?

It is to that which they feel is ultimately real, the unlimited source, that people within the various religions direct themselves in their many different ways. We designate this focal point of the religions as the **sacred,** the ground of ultimate vitality, value, and meaning. The modes of experiencing the sacred, and the responses to this experience, are many and various; these are the forms and expressions that make up the religious traditions of the world.

SOME DIMENSIONS OF RELIGIOUS EXPERIENCE

The word *religion* of course has a variety of meanings as it is used in the modern world. It would be well at this point to suggest a working definition of what we mean by the term in this exploration. Here is a four-part description:

1. Religion is human involvement with what is considered to be the realm of the sacred.
2. It is expressed in thought, action, and social forms.
3. It constitutes a total system of symbols with deep meaning.
4. It is a path of ultimate transformation.

Human Involvement with the Realm of the Sacred The first part of the definition of religion suggests a relationship between two levels of experience: the limited human level and the level of that which is felt to be the sacred. Of course, we cannot examine the sacred as if it were an objective realm of reality; the sacred is not something to be proved or disproved. We must be clear that we are not attempting to define ultimate reality as an objective fact; we are simply exploring how people of different cultures have described their experiences of whatever it is that they consider the ultimate sacred. Still, it is the common experience of many people past and present that there is a sacred dimension of reality with ultimate significance, and, further, that the highest good in human life has to do with relating to that sacred.

Although the idea of the sacred is distinctive in each particular religious tradition, it is possible to discern some general outlines that resonate across religious boundaries. After all, if there are any common human life experiences throughout the different cultures of the world, we should expect some general similarities in the way people describe their experiences of what they consider to be the sacred. One suggestive perspective comes from Rudolph Otto, who studied various types of religious experience and put forth the view that basic to religious experience is a deep sense of the "numinous."[1] This is a term he coined from the Latin *numen* (holy, sacred) to express our basic response to experiencing the sacred even before we develop rational and moral notions about it. Experiencing the numinous as ulti-

mate mystery, people feel a strong sense of awe and reverence, at the same time being fascinated and drawn to the mysterious Other.

Drawing on Otto's perspective, let us make some observations about experiencing the sacred. First of all, bound up with the numinous is an unlimited, primordial, overpowering quality. The sacred is ultimate, the basis of everything else, and nothing can supersede or encompass it. It accounts for everything, and it holds everything together—but it is its own basis without depending on anything else. The sacred, whether expressed as God (Islam), Brahman (Hinduism), emptiness (Mahayana Buddhism), or some other formulation, is felt to be the universal foundation of all truth, reality, goodness, and value.

We encounter the sacred as Mystery, as the Wholly Other that remains completely "other" even when experienced within the human world. It cannot be completely held by humans, either with their hands or with their reason. Words can attempt to describe the sacred, but it is understood that words can only point to the mystery in a symbolic way. Every word refers to a conditioned human reality, but the sacred both encompasses and transcends human realities. For this reason, people express the experience of the sacred not only by words but also by a variety of other symbolic forms, such as sculpture, ritual actions, meditation, music, dance, silence, and so forth. On the Jewish festival of Simhat Torah, for example, dancing with the Torah scrolls provides a deep experience of the sacred, more than words can say. Bathing in "Mother Ganges" provides a direct, nonverbal sacred experience for Hindus. After the reception of the Eucharist in a Christian church, a moment of silence is often the most appropriate way of responding to the mystery. The stillness of Buddhist meditation brings one into direct touch with the ultimate truth in a way that words can never do.

Experience of the sacred is accompanied with awe and reverence. The sacred cannot be controlled by human design; it bursts the bounds of human understanding and overwhelms with energy and demand. The human response is awe, respect, and submission. For Muslims, for example, washing the body and prostrating oneself in prayer expresses the proper human relationship to the sacred. Rudolph Otto called this quality of the sacred the *mysterium tremendum* (terrifying mystery). For the ancient Israelites, the moun-

Experience of the sacred takes countless forms in the religions of the world. Here a Hindu man prepares a religious offering.

The Muslim pilgrim is drawn to Mecca and to the experience of the sacred there as by a powerful magnet. The Hindu worshiper lovingly performs *puja* to the image of the beloved god or goddess. A Christian writer, Augustine, said that the soul is restless until it finds rest in God.

Since the sacred is the source of ultimate value, the deepest need of human life is to have an ongoing relationship with the sacred. It is this need that is met in the various religious traditions of humankind. Each religious path, in its own way, provides the context so that the sacred is present to the human community, with the power, value structures, meaning, and purpose that fulfill the religious needs of human beings.

Expression in Thought, Action, and Social Forms
The second part of our description of religion suggests what goes into the making of that human involvement with the sacred. Since religion is, obviously, a human affair, it necessarily involves human forms or modes of expression. Joachim Wach, in his *Sociology of Religion*,[2] suggests there are three such modes of expression: theoretical (thinking, speaking), practical (doing, acting), and social (fellowship, community). These are the building blocks of religious expression, and they fit together to form a complex, unique universe of meaning, that is, a religious **tradition.**

The *theoretical* mode of expression comprises the verbal aspect of religion, what is told and described. The religious path sets forth a way of thinking about the most important, basic issues of life: how the sacred is experienced, where the world came from and where it is going, what the goal of human life is, and how we can achieve that. These things are talked about in two basic ways: narrative or story (**myth**) and theoretical statements about reality (**doctrine**). All religious traditions have stories or myths that put forth in narrative form the worldview and the important experiences of the sacred on which that religion is founded. Leading thinkers also express their basic perceptions in teachings or doctrines that generalize from the sacred stories to present the fundamental truths that they believe, providing intellectual guidance to the participants in that religious path.

The *practical* level of expression in religion has to do with its visible and performed side: **rituals, worship, ethics,** and so forth. Religion is not just mental but also physical, and the acting out, the performance, of the involvement

tain of Sinai was the awesome presence of the sacred; touching it could mean destruction. The image of a god or goddess in the Hindu tradition is full of power, so that one should not, for example, take pictures of it.

Experience of the sacred at the same time involves fascination and love; we are compelled and drawn to the ultimate origin of all that is good and true and beautiful, the source of meaning and purpose in life, the fountain of vitality and strength. The sacred is wondrous, marvelous, and compelling. Encounter with the sacred leads to the highest joy, rapture, and love. Buddhists who have experienced awakening describe it as ultimate bliss and rapture.

with the sacred is just as important as the stories and the doctrines. Prostrating oneself before the sacred presence, going on pilgrimages, sharing in a sacred meal, chanting texts and prayers, sitting in meditation, wearing colorful robes, burning incense, observing moral rules, and hundreds of other religious rituals and types of behavior represent the acting out or performance of the religious experience.

Religion is never simply an individual affair but always a group or communal experience involving *social forms.* It is the religious community that carries on the tradition, even before the individual was born and after he or she dies. And it is in identifying with the religious community that the individual finds personal identity. There are different structures of community depending on the type of religious experience, in family or clan, congregations, religious societies, and whole nations. And there are various types of religious leaders, such as queens, kings, priests, priestesses, sages, prophets, masters, nuns, monks, shamans, and many more. Participation in the social forms of the religious community is what gives continuity of religious experience.

A Total System of Symbols   Taken together, these modes of religious expression form a total worldview, a "map" of human involvement with the sacred, and this brings us to the third part of our definition. Religion guides and gives meaning by presenting a view of the whole order of existence. This religious map of human existence is made up of **symbols**—words, ideas, rituals, pictures, gestures, sounds, social groupings—that evoke the deepest feelings and most important meanings in our lives. These are the means by which a group of people express their perception of what life is all about. To live as part of this community is to share a whole way of knowing the world and one's place in it, a whole way of looking at life and death, and a whole set of assumptions about what is real and true and good. The system of symbols upholds deep-seated attitudes and motivations, providing a complete system of values for human life.

Let us consider a few examples of such symbols. In a Buddhist monastery an ordinary bowl for food becomes a "begging bowl," an important symbol of the spiritual status of the monk or nun on the path toward the ultimate goal of all people in the community. A rooster and a dove are two very common animals, but used by a priest in a Daoist ritual they embody the operational forces of yin and yang and create the balance of sacred power necessary for the well-

being of the human community. Common words can be powerful symbols. The words *blood* and *lamb* have ordinary straightforward meanings; but for a Christian to say "The blood of the Lamb has saved me" arouses deep religious feelings and meaning. Normal human activities often give rise to important symbolic meanings. For example, the act of eating a meal is one of the most common human activities and is often done without any particularly deep meaning. But a Jew sitting at the table celebrating the Passover seder with her family experiences deep religious meaning in that human activity. Similarly, washing oneself is an everyday human activity, but all religions have rituals that express sacred meaning in washing, such as baptism, bathing in a sacred river, or purifying oneself with water before entering a shrine.

We can envision the worldview of each religious tradition as a circle with a center. The circle suggests the totality of what the people understand as their existence in the world. It contains their universe of symbols that provides the pattern of life that is their religious path. Within the circle, then, we see the most important symbols of that religion. The meanings these symbols supply have been told in stories, painted and sculpted in art, sung and played by musicians, expressed in poems and dramas, acted out in rituals and worship, and argued and systematized by theologians and philosophers for centuries.

The various symbols fit together in a circle, for they are all related to each other in such a way as to present a comprehensive and persuasive outlook on life. Above all, the circle of symbols is centered—that is, there is a *central vision* that colors and permeates the whole circle in a pervasive way. We might suggest, for example, that for Muslims the center is the Holy Book, the Quran, whereas for Christians it is Christ. Buddhism centers on the path to nirvana, whereas the center for Shinto is the exhaustless life of the kami. Many Chinese would put the Dao at the center of their universe of symbols; other Chinese might center their world more on ancestors and family. The symbols closest to the center could be considered the *primary symbols,* those that are most essential to those of that religious path. Toward the outside of the circle appear somewhat more *secondary symbols,* those that are more inclined to change when new experiences and challenges arise, those that respond to the needs of the religious communities in different times and places. Of course, people do not always agree on whether a particular symbol is primary or secondary; diverse religious experiences lead to different emphases, even within one religious tradition.

We should therefore keep in mind that a religious tradition is not a static, unchanging affair but rather a living, dynamic organism. Changes and transformations do occur in response to new experiences, new stories, and new challenges. Sometimes what appeared to be a primary symbol to some at one time becomes less important in later ages, whereas a secondary symbol introduced by some new religious experience shifts into a primary position. For example, Indra was one of the most powerful gods for the ancient Aryans, but he shifts to a rather small role in later Hinduism. On the other hand, Vishnu was a minor god for the Aryans, but he rose dramatically to become one of the great gods in Hinduism. For traditional Jews, the idea of bodily resurrection after death was at one time a primary symbol, but in recent times it has faded to secondary importance for some modern Jewish thinkers. On the other hand, the Land of Israel, which was simply a spiritual idea during the medieval period, has become for many modern Jews a very primary symbol in concrete form. In spite of changes in the circle of symbols, however, there is an ongoing basic continuity, flowing outward from the central vision and maintaining the fundamental pattern of faith and life.

As we look at the issues of human life and focus on specific symbols from the religions, we must keep in mind that a particular symbol must always be viewed in its total context. Some of the symbols will, of course, appear quite similar in a family of religions, and rightly so, given the shared history and culture. The word *Dao* (the "way"), for example, is used by all three religious traditions in China—Confucianist, Daoist, and Buddhist traditions—but with significant differences of meaning. Our task is to see each symbol—each teaching, idea, story, ritual, practice, or community structure—in the light that is reflected from the central vision and from the total pattern of that particular system of symbols.

A Path of Ultimate Transformation   The fourth part of our definition points out that a religious tradition is not only a system of beliefs and expressions about the relation to the sacred; it is above all a path, a way of life. Each religious tradition offers something that many humans find

essential to human existence: a **path of transformation**, a path to ultimate meaning.

An important part of religious experience, it appears, is the realization of the defective or fractured nature of human involvement with the sacred, for from this arise the fundamental troubles and anxieties of existence. This awareness of the human problem is coupled with knowledge of the ideal, ultimate relationship to the sacred. One's religious practice provides a way of overcoming this fracture, of restoring the bridge to the sacred, of transforming oneself to attain the goal of life as expressed in that particular religious tradition. The path continues throughout one's lifetime, through rituals, symbols, disciplines, study, social relationships, and states of consciousness. Buddhists, for example, follow the Eightfold Path toward the ultimate attainment of nirvana. Christians follow the path of Christ to overcome sin and attain eternal life. For Hindus, the paths of action, worship, and knowledge lead toward spiritual realization and liberation from the cycle of birth and death. Following the life of Torah for Jews is the path toward spiritual perfection. The path is a way of life, a praxis designed to restore wholeness and ultimate meaning to human existence by involvement with the source of life, the sacred.

Grouping the Religious Traditions

It is a bit bewildering to look at the great variety of religions in the world, past and present. Each tribal group has its own distinctive way of life, which is its religion. And even the highly developed major religious traditions of the world are quite numerous, each with its unique ideas and practices—and there are significant divisions within many of these traditions. It is helpful to consider some ways of grouping the vast array of religions, so we do not get lost in the overwhelming variety of ideas, rituals, and structures found in them.

There are various ways of classifying and grouping the religious traditions, based on what we as observers consider significant and helpful. Each classification may well reveal and highlight important dimensions of those particular traditions; at the same time, other significant aspects may be obscured and overlooked. One might approach the religions with an historical scheme, for example, putting emphasis on the continuities and discontinuities as cultures developed

over time. Another simple framework would be to locate some religions as indigenous and ethnic, while others would be considered cross-cultural or universal. A genetic or family resemblance model is particularly helpful for comparing the religious traditions; one example of this would be putting religious traditions into family groupings depending on whether they emphasize **polytheism, monotheism,** or **monism.** Another possible taxonomy would group religious traditions into geographic cultural circles, such as those arising in India, those arising in East Asia, and those arising in the Mediterranean world. For a beginning exploration in the world's religions, it is helpful to draw on several such classification schemes, emphasizing a geographical frame and noting family resemblances within those groupings.

For example, religions arising in India share an historical development in the first millennium B.C.E. and a set of common perspectives on the world and the path to follow. These religions include the traditions known as Hinduism, Buddhism, and Jainism (Sikhism developed much later but shares some of the same perspectives). These religions tend to have a nondualistic (or monistic) worldview, the idea that somehow behind or within all the multiplicity of forms and forces in this universe there is one unified sacred reality. These religions do have gods that are important, but many thinkers go beyond the idea of a personal creator God, holding to the vision, for example, that the inner soul of reality or the truth of all reality itself is the sacred ultimate. They agree that human existence is part of the process of *samsara,* that is, birth and death over and over in an endless cycle. According to this perspective, the highest good for humans is to achieve awareness of ultimate reality through practices of meditation or devotion and to find liberation from the cycle of rebirths. Whereas Sikhism arose in India and contains many of these ideas, this religion also accepts some basic monotheistic perspectives.

On the other hand, the religions of East Asia, such as those of China and Japan, form a loose family grouping. There are many gods here, in Japanese Shinto and in the Chinese religions, Daoism and Confucianism, but at their center is an emphasis on harmony with the divine flow of nature and reverence for the ancestors and for family. Within that harmony, human existence is valued as positive and good. Chinese culture and religion have been influential throughout the lands of East Asia. In particular, the Mahayana form of Buddhism has adapted the Buddhist outlook to the East Asian perspective and thus plays a unifying role in the cultural grouping that makes up this East Asian family of religions.

The religions arising in the Mediterranean world arose historically from the context of cosmic, nature-oriented religions of the ancient civilizations (Egypt, Mesopotamia, and Greece). Yet the religious traditions that eventually developed—Zoroastrianism and the three "Abraham" religions (Judaism, Christianity, and Islam)—constitute a family of religions whose central perspective is basically monotheistic, that is, they envision one God who created everything. Since there is one God, this God must be almighty and in charge of everything in the created world. The highest good for the creation is to fulfill the will and design of this almighty creator, and to do this, humans need revelation from God through prophets. The three Abraham religions have a particularly close historical relationship, arising successively from the same Semitic society of the Near East, each tracing its roots in some manner to the ancestor Abraham.

We must keep in mind that any scheme such as this can only suggest the main historical and cultural connections within the different groupings of religions. It is also true that different perspectives can be found in the same religious tradition in varying degrees. Nondualistic Hindus, for example, know a great deal about worshiping the great God who created and sustains everything, with teachings and practices that resemble monotheism. Islam, for all its fierce monotheism, has long harbored the Sufi mystical movement, which has cultivated language that sounds much like the Hindu and Buddhist nondualist thinkers. Yet it is helpful to keep in mind a broad grouping of religious traditions, based on their historical and geographical connections and their dominant religious perspectives.

Comparison and Understanding   Since understanding also arises from comparison, it is part of our task to see how the perspectives of different religious traditions do have common presuppositions in their vision of human existence. In fact, seeing what is common sets the stage for

The Dome of the Rock in Jerusalem marks the spot from which Muhammad was taken on a journey to heaven. The mosque stands above the foundation of the Jewish temple, a spot sacred also to Christians.

reflecting on the unique characteristics of each of the approaches.

A word needs to be added about looking at the religions as we are doing here, studying them from the outside, as it were. Whereas many of us may have our own religious tradition, none of us belongs to all the religions. Therefore, we necessarily find ourselves in the position of being on the outside looking in at the intimate practice of someone else. In looking from the outside, we miss the inner compulsion of commitment and the special meaning the religion provides for the insider. Further, our view cannot be completely "objective," for our own personal beliefs and presuppositions stand in the way and color our perspective.

It is important, then, that we consciously make a deep effort to *understand* these religious traditions of others. To "under-stand" is to stand under what gives meaning to the other. It means to stand in her or his religious stance, to look at the universe of religious symbols from the perspec-

tive of being on the inside. This is not an easy task, and it is always an incomplete accomplishment. One cannot fully understand Hindu religious experience unless one is a Hindu, and the same is true of Buddhist and Shinto religious experience, as well as of all the others.

It is possible to understand, at least in an incomplete way, however, if a number of important measures are taken. First, an attitude of respect and openness is necessary, a recognition of the value and importance that the religion has for the other person. Second, a conscious effort must be made to become aware of our own presuppositions, since they color our views of the religions of others. By becoming aware of our presuppositions, we can "bracket" them to some extent so they do not hinder us from entering into the worldview of the other religion. Third, it is necessary to refrain, at first, from the important task of evaluation, that is, of asking the question of the "truth" of a particular religious idea. Each religious tradition by its very nature makes claims to truth and in doing so also passes an evaluation on the truth of other paths. There is a time and place for people from different religious traditions to engage in responsible investigation and evaluation, challenging themselves and each other in dialogue. But it is important first of all to understand, and a rush to evaluate and debate truth can stand in the way of understanding. Fourth, a willingness to learn from the religious experiences of others and even to grow in one's own understanding is an important component of the process of understanding.

There is also a certain value in being able to look at several religious traditions from the outside, as it were, if this is done sensitively and with understanding. By comparing various elements in different religions, and especially by comparing what is unfamiliar with elements familiar from one's own experience, it is possible to see universal structures of religion more clearly. We can see recurrent questions and concerns about life and death, and we can survey the persistent themes in the responses provided in different religious paths. We can see common practices that give structure to life and society and thus develop deeper understanding of the common human needs that give rise to the various religious traditions of humankind.

BASIC HUMAN CONCERNS AND RELIGIOUS RESPONSES

To help us in our exploration of the various religious traditions, our ground plan in this book is to take up a number of common questions and concerns about human existence in relation to the sacred and use them as windows into the fundamental views and practices of the people in each religious tradition. The goal is not to produce a synthesis of answers from all these religions, for each is unique and distinctive. We must be especially careful not to impose outside ideas on a particular religion. Rather, we must try sensitively to hear how the people of each religion frame their own concerns and responses. Still, if done judiciously, looking at common human questions provides opportunities to compare the religions while seeing clearly the unique characteristics of each.

Here is a description of some main questions and religious responses to think about as we find our way into the basic dimensions of religion. The questions and responses fall into three general areas:

1. **The Sacred Story.** The important question of identity—who are we?—finds its answer especially in the sacred stories of each religious path, as those stories originated and were passed on through various historical dynamics to the present community.

2. **Worlds of Meaning.** Questions of meaning and understanding are answered in the main theoretical teachings of the religious tradition. What's it *all* about? What sense is there in life? How can we start living *real* life? The answers point to teachings about the sacred reality, world origins and human existence, and the path of transformation.

3. **Ritual Practices and the Good Life.** Some questions relate to practical and social aspects of life: How can we find new power for life? How should we live? The answers point to ritual and worship, on the one hand, and to ethical life within the community, on the other.

It will be helpful to explore these questions and responses in a preliminary way, drawing on examples from across the religious traditions, in order to set the stage for our look at the religions of the West in the following chapters.

Sacred Story and Historical Context

One basic human concern is the question of identity: Who are we? Who am I? When a person tries to answer that question, she starts by telling the story of her life. Although there are many parts of her life story she might emphasize, one important aspect would be her religious identity: "I'm a Hindu." "My family is Buddhist." "I'm a Christian." "I'm Muslim." But what does that mean? It means that a person connects his or her own story with the sacred story, the master story, of his or her religious tradition—especially with those crucial events or realities of the founding of the tradition. To express his identity as a Buddhist, a person tells the story of the Buddha and the founding of Buddhism. To renew her Christian identity, a person looks to the sacred story of Christ, for that is the story—the master story—with which her own life story connects. To be a Sikh means to tie one's own life story into the master story of the Gurus who founded Sikhism. The story of the founding or the revealing of the religious path is of particular concern, because it provides the divine authority for one's religious identity. In this study of the religions we devote considerable attention to the master story and also the historical transformation of each religion.

Myth and Sacred Story   All religious traditions have master stories telling of decisive events and leaders through which the new truths and practices were inaugurated as the basis of the new way of life. These birth-giving events and leaders are told about in their stories, written about in their scriptures, sung about in their songs, depicted in their art, and remembered in their rituals. They form the central focus, the paradigm, by which the people express their self-identity.

These sacred stories, or "myths," have a very important function in religion, for they establish the basic outlook and the way of life of the people of that religion. They tell of the central encounters of the people with the sacred, those clear episodes that illumine all aspects of life. Thus these stories, even though they may seem in some cases to refer to distant mythological ages, are understood to be real and true, for they reveal the bridge to the sacred that is essential for human existence. Although they are presented in story form, they provide a kind of map for human life, a model that can be followed so life can be lived in the fullest way according to the design established by the sacred power. Knowing these stories means the people know how human life is to be lived in a meaningful way; not knowing the stories or forgetting them would be to live a chaotic, subhuman existence.

But knowing and remembering the sacred story are not just intellectual exercises. To perform the stories—repeating them in words and acting them out in rituals—is actually to become participants in the founding events. It is to reactualize the central happenings so they become real and powerful in human life today, just as they were in the special time told about in the sacred stories.

In sum, the story provides an answer to the question of identity by making it possible to identify with those events and beings that exemplify in a clear and powerful way the relationship with the sacred that undergirds human life. The master stories may be about human sages and leaders who founded the religious path, or they may be about gods and heroes in mythological ages—or both. But in all cases the stories tell about the beginnings, the origins, of the real, authentic way of human life. And thus they tell us who we really are.

Some of the religions are "founded" religions in the sense that their sacred history points to specific persons who had a role in the religion's origins. Buddhism, Jainism, Sikhism, Zoroastrianism, Judaism, Christianity, and Islam may be cited as examples, though the view of the founders may be quite different among these traditions. Since these religions focus on founders who lived in a particular age amid crucial events of human history, the stories tend to dwell more on actual historical events and human person-

alities than do the stories of religions that do not have central founding events and leaders.

Peoples of indigenous, tribal societies, even though they often do not remember a particular "founder," have their myths about the sacred beings and ancestors of the "time of the beginnings" who performed the crucial actions to create life the way it is. These myths are repeated in festivals so the power and vitality they tell about can become real once more for the people. Also, religions like Hinduism and Shinto, even though they have no particular founding events or leaders, have their stories about the gods and the cultural heroes, stories that provide the foundation of the authentic way of life.

In presenting and interpreting the stories of these communities, we rely on scholarly work that has clarified the origins and early history of each of the religions, providing a historical context for the stories. It is also our intention, however, to see each story as it is told and interpreted by that religious community. We are, after all, not dealing with history strictly speaking but with *sacred* history. And that sacred history is expressed not by archaeological finds or ancient history books but in the stories told in the worshiping communities.

Change and Transformation in the Religious Tradition
The history of the religious tradition does not end with the sacred story of the beginnings. Each religion is a living organism that changes and develops in new situations and experiences. Understanding this dynamic quality of religious tradition is important, for it is the "passing on" (*traditio*) of the story that finally shapes our religious identity. We receive and interact with the story through the tradition that has brought it to us.

For example, one cannot understand Buddhism in the world today without taking some account of the Mahayana developments and also the various developments in Southeast Asia and in East Asia. Judaism has been transformed by the teachings of the rabbis, the medieval persecutions, the emancipation, and most recently the experience of the Holocaust. To understand modern Christianity one must take into account the transformations brought about, for example, by the establishment of Christianity as the religion of the Roman Empire, the medieval synthesis of doctrine and life, and the Reformation and the Counter-Reformation. And it would be most difficult to understand Chinese religion without considering the rise of Daoism, the development of the state cult of Confucius, the importation of Buddhism, and so forth. So it is with each religious tradition. Although in this book we cannot focus extensively on the historical development of each religious tradition, it is important to become aware of the major transformations and the effect they have had on the understanding and practice of that tradition.

Worlds of Meaning: Theoretical Teachings

Sacred Reality   What's it *all* about? Confronted with the maze of human life in a mind-boggling universe, we wonder how we can make sense of everything that is. How does it all hold together? The answer presented in each religious tradition is the sacred, the ground of all, the ultimate reality. Each tradition has appropriate terms to point to this ultimate reality: God, Goddess, Brahman, nirvana, Dharmakaya, Dao, and many more. Without such a vision of sacred reality, religious people feel there would be no center, no order, only a chaos of things and events occurring haphazardly without rhyme or reason. And so since the beginning of human life on this planet, people have always sought after sacred reality as the source and support for this world and human existence within it.

What are some of the ways people think about the sacred? Some people, especially in the ancient world and among indigenous peoples of today, have understood the sacred to be experienced in numerous forms and powers. Some speak of an impersonal sacred power that penetrates and interacts with everything. Wherever we turn, in nature and in society, we encounter Power. Often the sacred is personified as gods and spirits, who are immanent in the various aspects of the world: One god shows power in the rain and storm, another in the healing and creating power of the sun, another in pregnancy and childbirth, and so forth. This view, often called polytheism, means power is shared, with no one sacred being having unlimited sway. Many of these religions do have a **supreme god** who is the primordial creator and has ultimate authority, but this god delegates the functions of the world to other gods and goddesses. This general vision of the sacred can also be found to be widespread in Asia, within the Hindu, Buddhist, Daoist, and Shinto traditions. It is generally understood, of course, that such divine beings are not ultimate in power or status.

Another view of the sacred is monotheism, the view that there is one sacred reality, a personal God who created and supports this world and everything in it, with no alternates, no competitors. There is one God and one world, the creation. However, God is not a part of this world. God is transcendent, that is, above and beyond the created world, holy and eternal. At the same time, God is present in a personal way to the created world. God encounters us especially in historical events, giving us guidance and challenging us to fulfill the divine will. The three Abrahamic religious traditions are strong advocates of this perspective on the sacred, but it can be found in modified forms in Zoroastrianism, Sikhism, and even special Hindu and Buddhist groups.

Still another conception of the sacred is sometimes called nondualism or monism, a broad category of thought and experience with an emphasis placed on the unity of all reality. Nondualism means that there is no real difference between the ultimate reality and the phenomenal world. Monism is the view that all reality is one unified divine reality. There may still be many personal gods, but they may all be understood as facets of the one sacred reality. Within these traditions, it may be emphasized that the sacred is our inner true self; it may be the suchness of reality; it may be the state of ultimate consciousness; it may be the principle that is found in all reality. This kind of perspective on the sacred ultimate is present in some forms of the Hindu, Buddhist, Daoist, and Neo-Confucianist traditions. Tendencies toward monism can also be found in certain mystical movements in Judaism, Christianity, and Islam, as well as in some philosophical thinkers in the Western tradition, such as Plotinus, Spinoza, and Hegel.

So the sacred can be experienced as many in nature, or one beyond nature, or one and many both in and beyond nature, and more. Depending on which vision is dominant, the religious path to the sacred has distinctive features in each particular religion. The crucial question is, how do we encounter the sacred? Is the sacred found in the forces of nature and society? Is the sacred encountered in history and events? Is the sacred met within as one's real self? Is the sacred experienced as a personal being or as impersonal reality? Is the sacred known as the ultimate truth of reality?

In each of the religions, people have opted for a particular vision of the sacred and thus each has a distinctive religious path. Yet people in each religion often explore the other possible perspectives as well in order to add depth to their own vision and experience.

Of course, religious perceptions change over time, and the modern secular worldview has influenced the view of the sacred in most religious communities. In ancient times, it was a common assumption of almost all peoples that this world and human life are supported by divine power or powers, although various peoples differed in their conception of the divine realm. In modern times, however, far-reaching questions have been raised in people's minds about the traditional beliefs concerning the sacred. As science and technology have developed all around the globe, notions of sacred reality have gradually been eased out of the picture. We live our lives in a very secular way, that is, without paying attention to the sacred in most aspects of our existence. Is there really a God? Are the kami really powerful forces? Do Vishnu and Shiva actually control the forces of the world? Is nirvana real? Is it true there is an underlying principle of all reality? These are pressing questions especially for those traditions most associated with Western culture—Judaism, Christianity, and Islam—but increasingly all religions are facing the challenge that modernity and secularity pose for the traditional concepts of the sacred.

In spite of these developments, adherents of the religions today still find meaning in the depth dimension of the sacred. There are, of course, questions and problems that have to be dealt with, and modern people cannot easily go back to conceptions of the sacred reality as a heavenly grandfather who watches lovingly over all his children, for example, or as gods, goddesses, and demons who cause all good and bad things to happen. It is the experience of many people of the different religions today that an important resource for retrieving the sense of the sacred is to be found in the tradition and practice of one's religious path. How can we find again a way to experience the sacred present and powerful in our lives? Take up the path and see, they would answer.

World Origins and Human Existence   What sense is there in life? And why are we here? Why is there so much evil and suffering in the world?

Questions like these are at the heart of all religious experience, for they pertain to the deepest needs of human life—the need to understand our own existence within the world and society, the need to feel a purpose or destiny, and the need to integrate evil and death into our view of life without despairing.

The religious traditions deal with questions like these, especially in their **cosmogonic** stories, that is, their stories about the creation and maintenance of the world and of humans within it. For it is in knowing the origins of the world that we know its real essence and character.

In the creation stories of the peoples of the world, the origin of the world is attributed to many causes. Often a variety of gods and divine helpers create the world, remaining as ongoing powers within the world. Sometimes the creation of the world is seen as a battle between the various divine forces, and humans get caught up in the conflict. The monotheistic religions insist that the entire creation results from the one creator God. Again, especially among the religions of India, the origin and the operation of the world may be viewed as an eternal recurring process, like waves on an ocean, emanating from the sacred reality.

The cosmogonic myths or stories telling of origins also provide important views about the nature of the world and the role of humans within it. Some of the ancient peoples and indigenous peoples teach that the world is controlled by many divine forces, expressing their wills in the functioning of nature; therefore the most important role of humans is to serve and propitiate these gods. People of the Abrahamic religions teach that because there is one God, the creator and preserver of all things, this world makes sense as a good and purposeful creation. And humans are to assist God in caring for this world, fulfilling God's design. Others, such as Hindus and Buddhists, teach that the world as we experience it is somewhat illusory and passing. The most important thing for humans to do is to get in touch with the ultimate reality rather than the changing and transitory world. Again, it is sometimes taught, as in the Chinese religions and in Hinduism, that there is a universal world order or harmony into which everything fits, and humans do best by living their lives according to this order.

It seems that all religions have some view of human failure and imperfection. This follows from their vision of what the ideal is. The ideal human existence is sometimes expressed in creation stories, in descriptions of the origins of the world and of humans. There was an age of innocence, for example, a paradisiacal state when people lived peacefully and in harmony. The original human state is looked to as a kind of standard of what we ought to be. And corresponding to that is the realistic view of how things actually are: fractured and estranged because of human imperfection and failure. Of course, the extent to which we are thought to be alienated from the good, ideal state differs in the various religions. But it is commonly accepted that humans are not what they can or ought to be. Of course, much evil happens without our choice. But in our experience we know that people sometimes do things that are destructive and violent. In our own lives, we recognize that we sometimes do things that are hateful and ugly, and we fail to do the things we ought to do—why? There is a big shadow of failure and imperfection cast over human existence.

The religious traditions of the world give differing reasons for human failure and evil. Some African tribal religions, for example, have myths of origin in which the first humans live in a paradisiacal state with the supreme god, represented by the heavens, close to them on earth. Because of some fault in the humans—like being too greedy for food—the supreme god moves far away, with the result that human life becomes full of pain, death, and evil. The three Abrahamic religions teach that God, although making humans as the crown of creation, also gave them, of all creatures, a dimension of freedom. And within that freedom comes the possibility and the reality of rebellion, unbelief, and fracturing of the loving relationship with God.

Another way of looking at the human problem is found in the Hindu and Buddhist traditions, where human existence is often seen as a kind of trap. Because of the fire of desire that leads us to cling to false ideas of self, we are trapped in an infinite cycle of material existences full of pain and suffering. We cling to the sensual ego-centered illusions, and by doing so we fall under the causal law of karma: We reap exactly what we sow, experiencing the fruits of our clinging actions. The general view among Confucianists, Daoists, and Shintoists is that the highest human good is to be in harmony with the universal order of the cosmos and the flow of sacred powers of the world. When we act in ways to cause disharmony, whether in society or in nature, we experience the resulting fractures and discords as evil and suffering.

Sometimes the problem is put in the form of a question: Is human nature fundamentally good or evil? If human nature is evil through and through, then what else can we expect except violence and destructive behavior any time that humans are free to act unchecked? But some would say that humans are basically good and peaceful by nature. Then the violence and evil must be the result of other forces, such as possession by evil spirits, the corrupting influence of society, or oppression by tyrants. Or human evil may arise from our human tendency to forgetfulness and ignorance.

Is human nature fundamentally good or evil? To put the question thus is certainly an oversimplification, for most religious thinkers emphasize human moral responsibility. Somehow humans must be free to make their own choices in decisions of behavior, or they would not be responsible for anything they do. The realities of human existence lead most people to conclude that there is within us a struggle concerning choices about good and evil. Outside forces perhaps influence us; perhaps there are inner inclinations toward good or evil. But finally—in the view of most religious teachers—the choice is authored by the person herself or himself, who bears the final responsibility for it.

What this unsettling state of imperfection, ignorance, discord, or sin does, when realized against the standard of sacred design and law for human existence, is to impel us toward some change: repentance, seeking help from sacred powers, or following a new path to transform our incomplete human existence.

The Path of Transformation and Wholeness   How can we start living *real* life? Where are meaning and peace to be found? How can we be healed?

Questions such as these arise when we come face to face with the existence of failure, imperfection, and evil in our lives, knowing at the same time that this is not the way things should be. These are questions about the possibility of **transformation** and salvation. "Salvation" in all religious paths means wholeness and health—a transformation away from the fragmentation, alienation, sin, and ignorance we feel in our lives, a movement toward peace, health, and perfection. Transformation as taught in a particular religious tradition responds to the way in which the human problem is understood and experienced. For example, sin must be transformed by forgiveness, pollution by purification, ignorance by knowledge, fracture by healing, and wandering by guidance on the straight path. All religions offer some means by which salvation or transformation can be possible.

Functioning as a means of transformation, a religious path provides methods of interaction with the realm of the sacred. This is the ultimate source of life and meaning, and the basic human problem arises when this source is cut off for one reason or another. The first need is for some kind of restoration of this contact so that sacred power can transform life.

Although people of all religions agree that it is the power of the sacred that transforms humans, there are different visions as to how this power arises and operates in restoring the relationship. People in some religions emphasize human depravity and helplessness; in this view, all power and salvation must come from a source outside oneself. A good example of such an approach is Japanese Pure Land Buddhism, which stresses the notion of complete human degeneracy and helplessness in this "age of the end of the Buddhist law." This means that the only hope for humans to escape an endless series of rebirths in the suffering realms is to rely totally on help from the compassionate Buddha, Amida. On the other hand, some religious teachers emphasize an approach to the means of transformation that relies on power within oneself. Also in Japanese Buddhism, Zen adherents say there is no need to look to Amida Buddha for help or salvation. Each person has the transcendent Buddha nature in herself or himself, and through the practice of meditation each person can awaken to that Buddha reality and reach enlightenment.

These two opposite extremes are from the same religious tradition, namely, Japanese Buddhism. This would suggest that even within one religion we might expect to find both the "outside power" and the "self power" emphases. And this is the case. In Hinduism, for example, one finds both a tradition of worshiping the gods and relying on their **grace,** and also a tradition of passing beyond the gods to pure realization of the sacred through discipline and meditation. It is true that people of some religions, like Christianity, speak more about "grace" (outside power); and people of other religions, such as Islam, place more emphasis on human responsibility for action (self-power). But the relation to the sacred is always a two-way relation. Even if salvation

Thai men light incense sticks from a candle during solemn rituals of ordination as Buddhist monks.

comes totally from the sacred power, still humans receive it and live it out in human religious structures. And even if the whole emphasis seems to be on one's own power in terms of performing disciplines, still these disciplines draw on deep sources of sacred power. One of the distinctive characteristics of each religious tradition, in fact, is its particular vision of the interaction between human practice and sacred gift.

The means of transformation or salvation that a religious tradition offers will involve all three levels of human expression: theoretical, practical, and social. On the theoretical level, the myths and doctrines are to be understood and accepted by faith and/or reason, so that the person's whole outlook on life can be transformed. On the practical level, ritual, discipline, and practice are means of transformation. Such activities would include things like praying, baptism, acts of repentance, sitting in meditation, studying, keeping rules of purity, acts of self-discipline, and the like. Means of transformation on the social level would include participating in social structures such as families, congregations, sacred peoples, priesthoods, monasteries, and the like, so that the new way of life can be lived fully as a lifelong practice.

Together, these various means of transformation make up a path to follow. This path of transformation is a dynamic process that goes on throughout life in greater and smaller rhythms. It continually involves a double movement: a distancing and separating from the situation that is fractured and wrong; and a restoration and renewal of the state of wholeness and harmony with the sacred. The movement of separation includes acts such as repentance, vows of abstinence, withdrawal of thoughts from outer things, and rituals of washing and purifying oneself. The movement of restoration and renewal comes through acts such as retelling sacred revelation, feelings of ecstasy in worshiping one's god, receiving assurance of forgiveness, and awakening the mind in enlightenment.

Further, the path of transformation is both a *means* and an *end* in itself. As a means it is a praxis, a method of moving toward a goal: transformation or salvation, restoration of the relationship with the sacred. In one sense, that goal is never fully reached within human life, for the problems of human failure and sin remain until death. For that reason, many religious traditions have ideas of the future human state in which the ideal goal is perfectly and completely consummated. There may be some model person who achieves that goal now, such as a savior, saint, prophet, buddha, arhat, or samnyasin. But for the rest of us, the path is a means toward a goal of salvation or transformation that will be a complete, perfect reality only in a transcendent state or a world or lifetime to come.

However, seen from another point of view, the path of transformation is itself the experience of transformation. There is an "already, even though not yet" quality to the experience in following the path. The path is itself the means we have of experiencing contact with the sacred. Zen Buddhism expresses this most strikingly. Master Dogen insisted that practice (sitting in meditation) and enlightenment (experiencing the Buddha nature) are the same thing, with no difference at all. Other religious teachers would perhaps not identify the path so closely with the transformation it brings. But all would agree that following the path is not just a means to reward in another world to come; the goal of transformation is already at least partially present right now as we follow the path.

Ritual Practices and the Good Life

Religion by its very nature is practical and social. Theoretical teachings about the sacred and about life need to be lived, not just believed. And the path provides a structure of life within a religious community. It is never just an individual affair but always involves the person in a larger community of people going on that religious path. The religious community provides daily life with a structure including both **sacred time** and sacred life. That is, the ordinary time of one's existence is punctuated by special times of ritual and festival. And the ordinary living of one's daily existence becomes the arena of the good life in fulfillment of the sacred design for the whole community.

Making Time Sacred through Ritual, Worship, and Art

Where can we find new power for life? How can we live more in touch with what is *real?* These questions and many more like them have to do with our need regularly to renew the meaning and purpose of our lives, day by day, year by year, in family and in community, through **worship** and **ritual.**

Mircea Eliade[3] has suggested that, looked at in a completely profane or secular way, human life would be a self-contained, closed system with intervention by sacred power logically excluded. There would be no "breaks" to the sacred, no special or strong (sacred) times that can provide centers of meaning and thus give structure and order to life.

Since humans cannot tolerate such a meaningless chaos of existing, we seek out special or strong times. In traditional religious contexts, these are the sacred celebrations, the festivals, holy days, and rituals that periodically punctuate and renew the ordinary day-by-day passage of our existence. Even modern, secularized people who have little use for traditional religious rituals have not transcended the need to have sacred times. Breaks in time, centers of meaning and renewal, are widely sought after in such forms as vacations, national holidays, parties, sports, entertainment, and the like. The purpose of such sacred times is "re-creation," that is, the renewal and enlivening of our otherwise humdrum routine of existing.

Religious communities have found that the power that motivates life needs constantly to be renewed. Life-power tends to run down, to become exhausted and weak. There is need regularly to move into sacred time, the time in which the realities of the sacred story are experienced as new and present once again. Ordinary time is transcended, and the people of *now* become contemporary with the gods and the founders and heroes of the Beginning Time. The rituals and festivals provide a rhythm of periodic renewal.

Rituals and festivals are also sources of orientation for life, centers around which all else makes sense. They establish a pattern of living, derived from the sacred story, that can extend out and sanctify the ordinary hours and days of existing. They make real again the identity shared by the community and the incorporation of the individual within it.

Ritual worship connects the sacred with the common elements of human life. Fundamental to religious ritual is the sense of sacred presence in the most vital areas of human experience: eating, sexuality, birth, death, working, play, family, community, water, earth, sun, and so forth. The materials for ritual celebration stem from these basic elements of the human context. A meal is a most universal form of religious ritual, for example. So also is washing by water, or burying in the earth, or dancing and singing, or offering products of one's labor—the list of religious rituals is as long and diverse as the vital aspects of human life.

Ritual worship not only incorporates the vital human aspects, but it also "returns" them, now sanctified, to life. By the offering of the first fruits of the harvest, all the harvest is sacred. Through the ritual uniting of a woman and a man, all their sexual life is consecrated. By means of the rites of puberty initiation, boys and girls are incorporated as men and women of the community. Ritual washing means all the body is pure and sanctified. Ritual worship thus transforms human life by lifting it up, connecting it with the sacred, and returning it, now sanctified and empowered, to daily existence.

Ritual celebration of sacred time, as an activity on the path of transformation, has a movement or structure for renewal. First of all there needs to be a **kenosis,** an "emptying out."[4] With the recognition that power has run down and become exhausted comes the need for an emptying out of the old situation, a distancing so that the renewal can take place. This kenosis takes many different forms in religious practice. Among the most common rituals would be those that symbolize washing or cleansing, removal of impurity, confession and repentance, separation from the usual state, returning to a condition of chaos or disorder, and dying.

Once the emptying out has been established, the **plerosis,** or "filling up," follows. Having been brought back to the original state, emptied of all exhausted powers, the renewing power of the sacred can be experienced. Rebirth and new life are symbolized by rituals such as emerging from the waters, putting on new clothes, sharing in a meal, receiving a new name, incorporation into a community, singing and dancing, and the like.

Very often the two movements of kenosis and plerosis are connected by an in-between **liminal** state (from **limen,** "threshold"). This liminal state can be seen, for example, in puberty initiations. Young boys and girls may be separated from their mothers and removed to the bush (kenosis) before being incorporated back into the community as young men and women (plerosis). During that time in the bush they experience a liminal, threshold state; they are "betwixt and between," having died to their childhood existence but not yet reborn as adults. In this liminal state, they return in a sense to a prebirth existence. Everything may be stripped from them; they may experience ritual death and receive sacred revelations. After this critical threshold experience, they are reincorporated into the community as new, reborn people.

Such a liminal experience can be observed in many rituals and festivals. The **New Year festivals** of many cultures, for example, typically have a time of cleansing and purifying (kenosis), which leads into a liminal condition of "antistructure" or chaos; finally renewed structure and order are created (plerosis). The Christian ritual of baptism involves a distancing from evil (renouncing the works of the devil), a liminal passage of symbolic death in the waters, and a renewal ritualized by a new name, white garment, and a burning candle. The ritual of pilgrimage, important in traditions as different as Hinduism and Islam, includes symbols of distancing through a long journey, vows, and a special garment. The liminal period covers several days full of intense rituals and experiences. And the pilgrim has a new spiritual and social status upon completion of the pilgrimage.

Festivals and Rituals of Passage   Among the most common rituals are those that occur periodically, such as seasonal festivals. They follow the rhythm of the year and celebrate different aspects of involvement with sacred power. Many of these seasonal festivals have some connection with the cycle of sacred power in nature: spring renewal festivals, fall harvest festivals, and the like. In some religious traditions, the seasonal festivals are associated with events in the sacred story. For example, the spring festival of Passover celebrates the deliverance of Israel from slavery in Egypt, the spring festival of Easter celebrates the resurrection of Jesus from the dead, and a spring festival in Buddhism commemorates the birth of the Buddha. All of these festivals, although they emphasize events in human history, retain symbolism of liberation of nature's forces from the captivity of winter.

Another very common type of festival occurring periodically is the holy day, a particular day singled out for commemorating and celebrating some aspect of sacred power. These may be lucky or unlucky days determined by the astrological calendar; they may commemorate the birth or death of some great saints or religious founders; they may be critical points in the transitions of the annual seasons, such as the winter solstice; or they may follow a repeating pattern, such as every seven days (Jews, Christians, and Muslims), every nineteen days (Baha'is), or bimonthly on the lunar pattern (Buddhists). Some rituals recur every day, such as morning devotions for Brahman Hindus, or even periodically throughout every day, such as the five daily periods of prayer in Islam.

Seasonal festivals and periodic holy days and rituals offer a plenitude of sacred centers in the living of human life, a rhythm of recurring renewal to sustain the identity of the community and of the individual within the community.

Another major type of ritual celebration is that associated with the vital passages of human life, especially birth, puberty, marriage, and death. These **rites of passage**[5] are focused on the individual within the context of the community, serving to transform the person into the new stage of life and to integrate her or him into the community at that new spiritual level. Each of these passages of life is liminal—that is, it involves crossing a threshold from one state of existence to another. Each passage is critical to the full human development of the person and to the welfare of the community, and therefore religious rituals accompany and actualize the passage.

To move from one stage of life to another means first of all to put an end to the old stage. Thus rituals of separation,

distancing, or dying are most appropriately used as the first movement in the celebration of passage. The end of an infant's prebirth state may be ritualized by burying the afterbirth, or washing the infant for the first time. Children to be initiated into adulthood are typically separated from their homes and parents as the beginning of their initiation. Carrying a bride-to-be away from her home to the marriage hall shows the end of her state of maidenhood. Funeral rituals typically include the removal of the body from the normal life surroundings.

Separated from the old stage, which is now completed and thus done away with, the person enters into a state of liminality, "betwixt and between." Having moved back to the precreation state, rituals of liminality bring the person into direct contact with sacred power. These include rituals of death and burial, suspension of time and identity, encounter with the ancestors, and so forth. Mother and newborn baby are often confined for a period of time during which various birth ceremonies take place. Children in indigenous societies die symbolic deaths during their initiation rituals, have their sexual organs cut, or engage in battles with mythical monsters. Marriage passage rites often include a period of betrothal during which the man and woman are neither single nor yet joined as one. In funeral rituals, the newly dead person is often felt to be in an in-between state, and the family and community observe a "wake" or sometimes a lengthy mourning period before the dead one is fully incorporated as an ancestor.

Finally, rituals of rebirth, filling up, empowering, and reincorporation into the community complete the passage. The person has left the previous state, passed over the threshold, and now is recognized and welcomed at the new level of life. The infant is named and thus incorporated into the community. The young people now speak a new language and take their places as adults. The marriage is consummated and rituals of establishing a new home take place. The dead one is welcomed back as an ancestor and is enshrined on the family altar.

Other rituals of passage have to do with spiritual rebirth; they follow the pattern of rites of passage but are not necessarily connected with the physical development of human life. Christian baptism, for example, is not simply a birth ritual but a ritualization of the death of the "old one" and the resurrection of the new spiritual being in whom Christ lives. In some traditions, initiation into secret religious societies follows the pattern of the rites of passage. Religious specialists such as shamans, yogins, priests, monks, or nuns enter into their new spiritual level of existence through passage rituals of ordination or consecration.

Artistic Expression and the Sacred　　In our discussion of sacred time and ritual, we need to include some consideration of the arts. In the broad sense, we can consider the arts as all human activities and creations that express the **aesthetic** sense of beauty and meaning, especially the visual, literary, and performing arts. Art is closely tied to celebration and ritual. Religious experience is expressed largely through aesthetic media, for our contact with the sacred must be grounded in our perception (*aesthesis*) of reality. People of the different religious traditions have always known that the sacred is experienced through the things of the world and of human existence. Although interior, direct contact with the sacred is also known, the outer forms through which the sacred is experienced have been lovingly cultivated into artistic forms.

As used in religious practice, art forms symbolize the sacred. That is, they point beyond themselves to some dimension of the sacred or of human relationship with the sacred. They are not mere signs or pointers, however. To symbolize the sacred means to share somehow in the sacred reality, to convey the power and the presence of the sacred. A statue of the Buddha on the altar is not itself, wood or stone, that to which Buddhists direct worship. But it conveys the presence of the Buddha to the worshipers and thus participates in the reality to which it points.

Some art is designed mainly to *represent* the sacred; other art intends actually to "present" the sacred. Art that represents the sacred may be instructional, bringing the sacred to the attention of the people. A drama acting out the story might have the goal of instructing the people. Images and statues on Hindu temples and Christian cathedrals function as a kind of visual narrative of the story of the religion.

Other art more directly *presents* the sacred for a worshipful, transformative religious experience. Use of the arts in worship and ritual is often of this more presentational type, evoking and creating the experience of the sacred. In Hindu puja (worship), the god is invoked into the image and worshiped. The artful ritual actions, objects, and chanting of the Shinto priest in a shrine festival present the blessing and power of the kami directly to the worshipers. Of course, art can combine both types. The dramatic Jewish Passover meal (seder), for example, educates by narrating the story, but it also creates the religious experience of being present at the great deliverance of the exodus from Egypt.

From the religious point of view, all aspects of human existence have the possibility of being open to the sacred. Therefore, the religious impulse is to involve all possible human arts, especially in worship and ritual. Since the arts are highly expressive, they can evoke experiences of the sacred at deeper levels than the rational and logical. For example, the various literary arts do, of course, make use of the logical, rational structure of language. But there is a difference between a precise philosophical proposition of faith that attempts to define (and thus limit) the sacred, and a liturgical poetic expression that makes the sacred powerfully present. The great power that people find in the scriptures of their religion is related to the artistic quality of the sacred literature. The aesthetic sound of mantras (sacred formulas) in Hinduism and Buddhism conveys power even if the literal meaning of the words is not understood.

Visual presentations of the sacred and of the sacred story are used in many religious practices, although there is also reluctance in some religious traditions to portray divine realities in representational visual form. Iconography (pictorial imagery) presents essential aspects of the sacred, but it also imbues the sacred with sensuous form—and thus limitations. Paintings, sculptures, small figurines, and symbolic abstract designs all serve to evoke senses of the sacred full of aesthetic power and beauty, with form, color, and texture.

The art of music has been found to be a powerful presenter of the sacred in almost all religions. The beautiful sounds of music—gripping rhythm, haunting melody, special qualities of different instruments—reach to deep levels of aesthetic sensibility and express many different aspects of the experience of the sacred. It is particularly powerful when words are wedded to music in sacred chants, mantras, hymns, and the like. The art of music, whether a solitary flute or the ringing "Hallelujah Chorus" of Handel's *Messiah,* gathers and directs spiritual emotions and evokes the sacred presence as no other art does.

Another art form widely cultivated in religious practice is dance, the aesthetic and spiritual expression of body movements. Closely associated with dance would be drama and liturgical rituals. The ritual actions of a Daoist priest very much involve arts of dance and drama, as do the Shinto kagura dances, the Muslim art of ritual prayer, and the Hindu dance-drama festivals.

The sense of sacred place is artistically expressed in different religious traditions by distinctive forms of architecture. **Temples** and shrines symbolize the *axis mundi,* the center of the world, providing a center of orientation for all the rest of space. The sacred building is often thought of as a microcosm of the cosmic world. The aesthetic quality of architectural forms expresses essential dimensions of the vision of the particular religious tradition. Soaring Gothic cathedrals reaching toward heaven, Muslim mosques filled with openness and light, Hindu temples with their dark and mysterious inner room, and simple wooden Shinto shrines in Japan—all give expression to particular spatial-local qualities of the experience of the sacred.

Since artistic forms can evoke deep feelings with powerful presentations of the sacred, occasionally they can be experienced as destructive or demonic. People can look to the art form itself as ultimate, a situation called idolatry ("worship of an idol") in some of the religious traditions. People in all religions know, however, that the art forms, no matter how beautiful or powerful, are *symbols* of the sacred. They point beyond themselves to the sacred, they convey and present the sacred; but they are not themselves the ultimate sacred. Still, many art forms have been resisted or banned in the history of the different religions. Poetry has been considered the work of demons. Music of certain types raises dangerous emotions. Dance can become too sensuous and ecstatic. Iconography—imaging the sacred in

Expression of the sacred in art. Paul Gauguin, French 1848–1903. "Christ on the Cross" ca. 1900. Woodcut, printed in brown ink (15 7/8 x 5 3/8 in.). The Metropolitan Museum of Art, NY. Harris Brisbane Dick Fund, 1929.

visual form—has been a controversial art in some religions, because people fear it leads to idolatry or to seeking to gain control over the sacred.

People of each religious tradition choose special aesthetic forms as the most appropriate, sometimes resisting others as useless, misleading, or even dangerous. We might say that each religion or culture has its own distinctive aesthetic sense, closely related to the deep insights of that spiritual vision. To really understand a culture, we must look at its literature, poetry, dance, visual portrayals, architecture, music, and the rest. For example, the Hindu experience of countless gods within an ultimate unity opens the way for the cultivation of all the arts. And the Muslim reluctance to link God together with likenesses of any thing has led to a restriction on representational visual arts and a flowering of decorative and verbal arts. Arts of some religious traditions are more conducive to meditation, others to celebration and ecstasy. In broad terms, the religious traditions of South and East Asia have stressed intuitional, meditative aesthetic experiences, whereas the traditions of the West have often emphasized an aesthetic sense connected with the word, intelligence, and logic. But these differences can easily be overstressed, for the shape of the aesthetic vision is often a matter of emphasis. Even within one religious tradition, significant differences can be found.

Sacred Life: Social Structure and the Good Life   How should we live? Where do we belong? What is our responsibility to human society? Religious experience carries with it an imperative to live in a way that conforms to one's religious identity. A person is always a part of a group, a community, and the good life is structured in that community context. Acting according to one's religious identity involves, in many religions, a sense of responsibility and mission to others in the world.

As we saw earlier, each religious tradition has a master story that gives identity and purpose to the religious community and the individual within it. The story tells about the original people, special and sacred. These people are set apart for special identity, for special life, and for a special role in the world. The Japanese Shinto myths, for example, tell how the Japanese islands and the Japanese people descended from the kami (the divine beings). The emperor descended from the most powerful kami, the sun kami Amaterasu. This mythology has supported the sense of the Japanese as a sacred people, with the emperor as the divine head of the nation. Buddhist stories tell how the Buddha, after his enlightenment, gathered a band of disciples into a monastic community of monks and nuns, the sangha. The lay people participate in this religious community by supporting and honoring the sangha. In traditional China, ancient teachings support the strong notion that the clan or extended family is the center of meaning for each individual, and beyond that there are the hierarchically organized village and state within which the individual finds religious identity.

The structure and organization of the religious community are grounded in the sacred history and traditions of the religion. Provision is made for some kind of religious leadership. Sometimes the religious leaders function by virtue of the power of their office, like kings and priests. In other cases, religious leaders are recognized by virtue of their personal charisma and power, as in the case of sages, prophets, shamans, healers, and diviners. The community also has social structures involving clan relationships, congregations, lay groups, secret societies, masters and disciples, apprentices, and the like.

Women in Religious Leadership   Every society has its traditional roles defined for women and men. Since almost all societies have been structured patriarchally, in almost all religious traditions women have been subordinated to men and have had limited access to leadership roles. Yet we know that women have always been deeply involved in religious activities and experiences in all the traditions. Unfortunately, their more intimate, private religious participation has generally been neglected or glossed over by the male-dominated

official stories and sacred writings. This makes it all the more important for us to search out material on women's lives in the different religions and to take note of their important roles.

Looking at the religious tradition from the point of view of women's experience leads to new understandings. This is not just a separate topic, to be dealt with under its own discrete heading. Rather, the significance of women's perspectives relates to all aspects of religious tradition—how the sacred history is told, the concept of the sacred, ethical precepts, and all else. For example, taking sensitive notice of women in the ancient Israelite tradition—seeing not just Abraham in the stories but also Sarah and Hagar—provides new questions for the sacred story (where was Sarah in the sacrifice of Isaac?), new maternal images for understanding God's presence, new relational perspectives for understanding the covenant relationship, and so forth. To realize that one strong and long-ruling Chinese emperor was a woman (Empress Wu), also a powerful Buddhist leader, forces us to rethink our usual images of the subordination and powerlessness of women in the Chinese religious traditions.

Further, we need to see the increasingly active leadership roles of modern women in these societies, as they make use of their religious tradition to break out of traditional limitations and help to renew and transform their societies. In traditional societies as widely different as Hindu, Muslim, Jewish, or Buddhist societies, women have emerged as strong political leaders, even heads of state. Women scholars, theologians, masters, and gurus are revitalizing their traditions, creating new models and possibilities for the future, not only for women, but for men at the same time.

Sacred Space, Sacred Land   The perspective about authentic life for the people is often tied together with stories about a sacred land or territory: the sacred islands for the Japanese, the tribal land and burial grounds for the African tribes, Jerusalem for Jews, the pilgrimage sites and sacred rivers in India, and the like. **Sacred space** is established by the presence of the sacred, and therefore it is experienced as the center of the world *(axis mundi)*, as Mircea Eliade has elucidated.[6] This center functions as the connecting point between the human realm and the divine realm. Once the center is established, it provides orientation and a sense of being at home in the world. Sacred space can be a whole land, or it may be a village, mountain, shrine, temple, altar, or even a house. This is the *real* space that provides meaning and identity. It gives a feeling of rootedness; cut off from it we feel lost in the chaos of foreign, meaningless space.

The Moral Pattern for Authentic Life   The moral pattern for the good life is usually presented in the sacred history, for there we learn what the gods did in the mythological age, or the rules laid down by the ancestors, or the examples provided by the founder.

It is the conviction of people of each religious tradition that this pattern for life is "natural" in a deep sense. It is the way of life that most fits our original nature, as we were intended to be before we turned away or forgot that pattern. Whereas rewards may be promised for living the moral life and punishments threatened for neglecting it, the fundamental motivation for following the ethical guidance of the religion is deeper. This is the model for *authentic* human life, that which harmonizes with the greater spiritual forces and patterns of the cosmos. To many indigenous peoples, real human life is to do what the gods did in the Time of the Beginning. According to Hindus, living according to the Code of Manu corresponds to the eternal Dharma (cosmic order), and that is right and brings happiness. The Five Classics, according to Confucianists, express the sacred pattern of life according to the will of Heaven, as exemplified by the ancient sages, and thus studying and following these Classics will bring peace and harmony. The Shari'ah law code, in Islamic thought, follows perfectly the universal pattern of God's creation, and thus it brings peace and harmony.

The ethical life has something to do with how we *should* be, and therefore it is based in the religious vision of creation and human nature. The law of morality is often thought to be an authority outside oneself, usually recorded in scripture and tradition, to which one submits. But the religious teachers also talk about how that law becomes internalized, transformed into the inner motivation for right living, so that one naturally does what is right—thus there occurs a sanctification of life.

It takes practice to live as one ought. Confucius taught that to transform ourselves into people of humanity *(ren)*,

it is most helpful to take up the discipline and practice of the principles of propriety *(li)*. Hindus believe that following the Path of Action, doing one's duty according to one's place in life without desire for reward, is a way of reaching higher spiritual perfection and better rebirths. The thing that makes Jews distinctive from others is their willingness to take up the discipline of the commandments *(mitzvot)*— not for the reward that this will bring, but because the very doing of the mitzvot is itself the good life. Even Christians and Pure Land Buddhists, with their basic mistrust of the idea of merit coming from good works, know of the sanctification of life, of the careful cultivation of the good tree that bears good fruit.

The religious tradition provides guidance in all areas of life. In personal behavior, often the stress falls on self-control and moderation. One should not be controlled by the passions and desires, but rather these passions and desires should be controlled and redirected toward transformation of self. The religious tradition also spells out the relation of the individual to others and indicates the right and wrong way of treating others in various situations. The ethical life is lived for the welfare of the community. In following the code of life, strife and competition are avoided and healing and harmony are promoted. The religious traditions usually teach motivations of compassion and sacrifice, giving oneself for the good of the community.

Technically speaking, "ethics" is the activity of thinking about moral decisions on the basis of the tradition. The religious tradition provides ethical guidance about many or most of the crucial questions in life. But the individual and the community, living in concrete situations with changing circumstances, also continually make ethical decisions about a variety of possible actions. In modern times, the ethical decisions have become increasingly numerous and difficult, involving such questions as abortion, serving in the military, adopting Western customs, and reforming social injustices. A great many burning questions today revolve around changing roles for women and men. Thousands of questions like these face people in all the religions today, and as they think about the possible decisions on the basis of the religious tradition, they are engaging in ethical thinking.

Some religions are tribal, which means the people have little opportunity to express solidarity with humans outside the tribe. People of tribal religious traditions do often have a sense of harmony with the natural world. They promote the welfare and continuation of the world that supports human society, made up of vegetation, animals, and the earth itself, in a kind of primal ecology. A feeling for the sacredness of all human life is also demonstrated among many indigenous, tribal peoples.

Within the world religions, there has developed more awareness of the universality of the human race and of the common human welfare in the world. Thus all the world religious traditions have some vision of the nature and purpose of all humankind and of their own role or mission in the world. In the context of world society, people of the religions have developed a sense of responsibility for the good of the larger world, especially in areas like social justice, education, and relief for the poor and hungry. In recent times, concern for reconciliation and peacemaking has come to the fore in many religions. Today people in all religious traditions see the need for peace and harmony between different cultures, especially in view of the drastic threat of modern warfare.

Inherent in every self-conscious religious tradition is the claim to be the truth and thus the ideal way of life. Whereas tribal peoples generally do not attempt to spread their religious practices beyond the borders of their own tribe, all religions that have a sense of universality also have some feeling of responsibility to bring the truth to the rest of the world. This does not necessarily mean trying to convince others to convert to this religion. This responsibility may simply be having a special role within the world that is of benefit to all, as is expressed in the Jewish idea of a special covenant history within the world. Others, such as Hindus, often have such a tolerant attitude toward truth embodied at different levels that they are usually not motivated to promote their religion to other cultures.

The concern that the truth must be shared with all peoples is especially strong in the so-called missionary religions: Christianity, Islam, and, to some extent, Buddhism, and also some newer branches of the older traditions, like Baha'i, Nichiren Shoshu, and the International Society for Krishna Consciousness. People of these religions feel a mission, for example, to Christianize all peoples, Islamicize the world, spread the Dharma, and so forth—for the ultimate welfare of all. For people of these religions, this kind of mission is also an important part of their self-understanding and identity. Apart from Buddhism and some of these new religious movements, the religious traditions of the East generally have not actively tried to convince others to convert to those religions. But as the world shrinks and communication between peoples of the globe increases, Hindus, Sikhs, Daoists, and Shintoists are increasingly presenting their visions of truth, to be heard and understood by the peoples of the world.

Concern for the welfare of the world, and the realization that people of other religions also have visions for the world and claims to truth, have led to conversation and cooperation among people from different religions. Many people today recognize that religions and ideologies have contributed a great deal to the conflicts in the world. In recent years, a new movement of dialogue among people from various religions has become a part of the religious happenings of the world. At the very least, there has developed a widespread sense that peoples of different religious traditions need to work together against the forces of exploitation and violence and secularization that threaten human society today in an unprecedented way.

Discussion Questions

1 Do you think questions such as "Who am I?" and "What is the purpose of life?" are universal human concerns, or are they the product of modern Western thought?
2 What are some aspects of the experience of the sacred that seem to be shared by people of different cultures and religious traditions?
3 Give some examples of how symbol systems change over time.
4 What is implied in calling religious practices a "path"?
5 How can a story or myth from ancient times still provide identity for people today? Give some examples.
6 What do cosmogonic stories reveal about the way a particular people look at the world and human existence?
7 What is meant by speaking of "transformation" or "salvation" in the various religious traditions?

8 How can participation in sacred times or festivals bring renewal of human life? What do the terms *kenosis, liminal,* and *plerosis* mean?

9 How does art represent and present the sacred?

10 Is the good ethical life something natural or unnatural?

11 Do you think a sense of universal truth and mission is something essential to a religion?

CHAPTER 2

Beginnings of the Human Religious Adventure

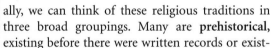

In this book, we are studying primarily the Western religions of today, seeing their roots in the past but concentrating on their present forms and practices. Among the families of humankind, these world religions, highly developed and encompassing large populations, are relatively modern phenomena. All of them have reached their classical form within the past three thousand years, even though their roots may reach earlier. That means we humans lived for hundreds of thousands and even millions of years—perhaps 99.9 percent of our human story in length of time—prior to the development of these world religions. While we have no way of knowing the mental and spiritual outlook of the earliest humans, we may at least assume that religious ideas and practices have been part of humankind's experience for as long as humans have had thinking, reflecting, and imagining capabilities. Further, up to the twentieth century at least, a large percentage of humankind in various parts of the world have remained outside the domain of our present world religions. Surely all of this accumulated religious experience is an important part of our human story. Our identity today as human beings is deeply indebted to these sacred experiences from other times and places.

It is far too much to suggest that all these religious activities of the past and present that fall outside the "world religions" form one unified family of religions. There is great diversity among them, and within their vast domains it is possible to find almost all symbols and forms of religion that come to expression also in the world religions. Gener-

ally, we can think of these religious traditions in three broad groupings. Many are **prehistorical,** existing before there were written records or existing in an ancient culture that had not yet developed writing, and thus we know only a small fraction of them through archaeological research. Other religions of the past are the *religious traditions of ancient civilizations;* these people did produce written records and texts so that, even though they no longer live, we can know about them through their literature and other artifacts. A third grouping contains the *religious paths of contemporary indigenous, tribal peoples,* those who have lived to the present day or at least to the recent past at a premodern level of tribal economy and society, having continued their archaic traditions for countless generations.

Perhaps one common characteristic among these religious traditions of prehistorical, ancient, and indigenous peoples is their tribal or ethnic character. The people do not envision their religious practices as universal, but as the mark of themselves as a particular people. However, certain thinkers in some of the ancient traditions, such as China, India, Greece, and Rome, did push toward a kind of intellectual universality. And religious ideas and practices often crossed ethnic and linguistic boundaries. Another common element among prehistoric, ancient, and indigenous peoples is the general acceptance of the plurality of sacred powers emanating from the cosmos—that vision we sometimes call "polytheism." Yet again we must qualify that statement. Some Greek and Roman thinkers articulated a vision of sacred unity encompassing all of nature (pantheism); there were stirrings of monotheism in ancient Egypt and Persia; some Vedic hymns from ancient India explore the one reality behind all the gods; and many indigenous peoples today have ways of speaking of the "One" behind all the plurality of sacred forces.

Ancient and contemporary indigenous peoples tend to have a very natural involvement with the sacred in their ordinary lives. They are open to the interweaving of the sacred within their social life, government, food-producing activities, birth, sickness, death, and all the rest. Mostly, these peoples do not even have a word for "religion," since it is identical with their traditional way of life. This is not to say that archaic and indigenous peoples are naive and sub-rational, for they are capable of sophisticated intellectual activity and often excel in practical wisdom. But they, unlike many of us who are drenched in modernity and secularity, are open to experiencing the sacred in the vital dimensions of life.

Unfortunately, it is not possible in this one volume to study these religious traditions of prehistoric, ancient, and contemporary indigenous peoples in extensive detail, culture by culture. The interested reader can consult many excellent studies of the prehistoric ages of human development, the ancient classical religions, and the indigenous cultures of more recent times. Here we provide a brief history of humankind's religious adventure. Then, in the next chapter we focus on how the religious paths of contemporary indigenous peoples exemplify the basic patterns and themes of religion. We will have occasion to explore some of the ancient civilizations and their religions later as we study the beginnings of the world religions arising in the Mediterranean world.

The Story of Humankind

With each of the major world religions, we begin by looking at the sacred story that gives identity to the people of the religious tradition. Here at the beginning, it is appropriate to sketch out a story of humankind, not as it is told in any religious tradition, of course, but as scholars have reconstructed the religious history of humanity. This is not really a *sacred* story, for we do not tell it through myth and ritual as the basis for our identity. But still we can feel respect and indebtedness to our human forebears who transmitted the

spirit of life and whose religious visions have somehow over millennia contributed to our own humanity.

The Origin of Religion: Theories   Scholars of religion have long been interested in the question of the "origin" of religion—how did religion begin and where did it come from? If we could answer the question of origins, they have felt, we would have some notion of the "original form" of religion and thus, presumably, we could explain why there is religion. In the late nineteenth and early twentieth centuries, many theories of the origin of religion were proposed, trying to explain why it would be that humans would somehow start having religious ideas and practices.[1]

One of the founders of the discipline of anthropology, Sir Edward B. Tylor, argued that religion originated in **animism** (from *anima,* "spirit"), from the experiences primitive peoples had of death and of dreams. They reflected on where life goes when a person dies and how deceased people can still be seen in dreams, and they came up with the notion that people and things have spirits that can leave their respective bodies and carry on a separate existence. People started worshiping the more powerful spirits, and religion was born. Sir James Frazer collected massive materials from the various ancient and indigenous cultures and argued that the earliest human response to the world was **magic,** the attempt to control and manipulate the forces of nature. Finding that magic did not deal effectively with the sacred forces, humans developed religious beliefs and rituals directed to personal gods. And Sigmund Freud constructed psychoanalytic theories about the origin and nature of religion, including the view that belief in God is a psychological projection of our father figure, growing out of the human need to feel protected and secure.

These theories, and many more, answer the question of where religion came from. Whereas this is a very interesting and thought-provoking issue, many scholars today think it is a misleading question. The interest in finding the origin of religion arose in the heyday of evolutionary theories of culture, and it suggests that we might find some particular point in human development at which religion began. The data necessary for such an investigation are simply not available. Further, since religious values and practices seem to form an essential human dimension, it may be supposed that religious feelings and experiences have been present as long as there have been human beings. So the really interest-

The Sphinx and the Chops Pyramid at Giza near Cairo provide colossal expression of the sacred from ancient times.

ing question of origins is "How long have there been human beings to express themselves through religious experience?"

Origins of Religion: Prehistorical Developments
The answer to how long human beings have expressed themselves through religious activities depends on the consensus of paleoanthropologists about recent discoveries. Many scholars feel that an early human species—as distinct from other animal species—existed two to three million years ago or even earlier in parts of Africa. These early hominids were of several types, but they shared the human characteristics of walking erect, using simple tools, and living in social groupings. A distinctly human type among these early hominids appears to have begun gathering and sharing food, living in campsites for periods of time. We, of course, know nothing about the feelings and ideas these early humans had about themselves and their world, but it is fascinating to sense our shared humanity across that vast stretch of time and imagine their spiritual needs and longings—not that different

from our own—in relation to food, companions, children, birth, and death.

Certainly, full humanity becomes recognizable with the type of humans that emerged about one million years ago in a variety of places in Africa, Europe, and China—a type that has been called **Homo erectus.** One of the outstanding discoveries of this human type was in a limestone-filled cave near Beijing, where skeletons of some fifteen individuals were found. By about half a million years ago these humans were exhibiting distinct human tendencies. Living in small communities in caves and rock shelters, they learned the use of fire for domestic purposes, for warmth, and for cooking food. They had many stone tools, cooperated in big hunts of animals like elephants, rhinoceroses, and deer, and probably had developed some form of human speech to communicate with each other. Unfortunately, the archaeological remains that have been discovered are still too scanty to provide much firm evidence of religious ideas and practices.

Clear archaeological evidence of religious ideas comes with the **Neanderthal** type of humans, living in parts of Europe, China, and Iraq in the Middle Paleolithic period, around 100,000 to 35,000 years ago. Neanderthal humans, contrary to popular prejudice, had developed a sensitive, complex culture, living in communities with many tools and some forms of art. A number of finds in their burials suggest they had religious ideas associated with death. For example, at one burial site, flint tools had been placed near the hands of the dead; at another, a skull was surrounded with a ring of stones; and in another burial, a group of skulls had been immersed in red ochre, perhaps a symbol of blood and life. Often bodies were laid on the right side with the head toward the east; in at least one burial the body was surrounded with flower blossoms. There is evidence here that death was looked upon as a passage to another kind of life—a basic religious belief.

Humans in the Upper Paleolithic Period

It is unclear whether Neanderthal humans are directly related to the line of descent of later humans, or whether they were a separate off-shoot of the human species. In any case, in the next cultural era, the Upper **Paleolithic** period (beginning about 35,000 years ago), the modern species of **Homo sapiens sapiens** developed, with communities now found in various places of the world—in Africa, of course, and in Europe, and even, by about 20,000 years ago, in Australia and North America. All we humans of the world today are descended from these human communities. Now there is abundant evidence of religious beliefs and practices. Many burials show careful treatment of the bodies: red ochre is sprinkled on the bones, probably symbolizing life-power; necklaces and other implements are buried with the body, showing that the dead live on in some way; some corpses are buried in a huddled-up position, symbolizing returning to the womb for rebirth; often bodies are lined up together in the same direction; and special treatment of the skulls is indicated. All of these things point toward the religious conception of death as a passage to new life and to ritual practices associated with death.

Other items from the late Paleolithic period show the fullness of religious concerns and practices. A great many female figurines have been found, many times more than male figurines, leading scholars to suppose widespread worship of goddesses among these peoples. One of the best known of these figurines is the so-called Willendorf Venus, from Willendorf in Austria. Made of soft limestone, this figurine is 4.4 inches high and is sculpted with ample body proportions and large breasts. Many other figurines appear conspicuously pregnant and have exaggerated breasts and buttocks. Most of the figures have no feet, but their arms display decorative bracelets, and often great care was taken in repre-

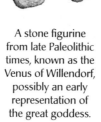

A stone figurine from late Paleolithic times, known as the Venus of Willendorf, possibly an early representation of the great goddess.

senting the style of hair or head covering. Many other finds include sculptured breasts and sculptured buttocks perhaps used as pendants, abstracted images of vulvas, female images painted on cave walls associated with animals, and a great variety of other drawings and markings that seem to reflect female symbolism. These figures almost always are found in connection with dwellings or camps.

Perhaps many of these finds were associated with religious ideas about a **great goddess,** the source of all life-power. Worship of a great goddess was probably one of the earliest and most widespread forms of religious practice. Of course, these numerous figurines and female symbols reflect the beliefs and practices of many different communities, with a great variety of cultural traditions, economic systems, and languages. So the meanings of goddess worship also no doubt have significant variety. The figurines may represent sacred female powers associated with pregnancy, birth, fertility, and the menstrual cycle; the goddess may be understood as the mother or mistress of animals, the goddess of the dead and the underworld, the mistress of the land, the protector of the dwelling, the goddess of the regenerative powers of nature, and more.

Religious concerns of our ancestors in the Upper Paleolithic era are also evident in impressive artistic drawings and paintings. While the last ice ages still held sway in much of Europe, in far recesses of caves in France and Spain people drew paintings on the walls, many having to do with animals and the hunt. Included are certain animal-human forms, which appear to be shamans or mythological figures such as the master or mistress of animals known from indigenous hunting cultures of today. Similar artistic motifs of animals and humans have also been found in Upper Paleolithic rock shelters in Africa. It seems clear that there were rituals connected with these paintings and drawings, promoting the continuance of life-power and the close connection felt between humans and animals, especially related to hunting activities. From these various archaeological remains, we can conclude that these prehistorical peoples, perhaps as early as 35,000 years ago, had religious ideas and practices not unlike those of the hunting peoples who have continued their traditional way of life into the twentieth century.

Religion in the Agricultural Revolution   Humans of the Upper Paleolithic era continued, like humans for hundreds of thousands of years before them, to live as hunters and gatherers, with their religious experience shaped by that kind of focus. By the end of the last ice age, around ten thousand years ago, human communities lived in virtually every part of the globe, although, of course, in many places the population was sparse. But now, in this **Neolithic** period, another great human development took place. Due perhaps to climatic changes as well as human cultural developments, people began to turn their attention to the earth, discovering how to assist the earth in producing plants for food, and finally how to cultivate plants for their own food. Soon, some of these peoples also domesticated herds of animals, such as sheep, goats, and cattle. This great **agricultural revolution** changed the shape of human life and religion forever.

Humans now became more attuned to the powers and cycles of the earth in producing vegetation, and religious interest focused directly on the great goddess identified as Mother Earth, the sacred power that gives birth to vegetation and thus all of life. In this Neolithic period, a large number of female figurines attests to the widespread worship of the life-giving powers of the goddesses associated with the cyclical death and rebirth of the vegetation. A society with particularly rich evidence of the centrality of goddess worship prospered in Anatolia (modern Turkey) during the sixth millennium B.C.E. This early urban center, thriving in crafts and trade, had a great many shrines, probably for extended family groups. In one shrine, the goddess is outlined in plaster on the wall of the shrine with her legs stretched wide in the posture of giving birth. There are rows of plaster breasts with nipples and animal skulls and horns. Goddess figurines found in grain storage areas show the goddess connected with agriculture. Some goddesses are shown as dancing maidens; others have abdomens swollen with pregnancy; still others are shown as mothers with a son or a daughter. Associated not only with fertility and life but also with death, some goddess statues are accompanied by vultures. Male gods are found only outside

shrines, usually associated with bulls or leopards. There was a priestly class devoted to the goddesses, apparently, including large numbers of women along with men. Other evidence suggests a society in which women played central roles not only in religious rites but also in other economic and social activities.

Producing their own food meant that people could settle down in villages and towns and lead a stable life. They could develop a society in which some people could produce the food while others could create arts and industry. Now some people had the incentive and leisure to invent writing and promote learning, to build temples and create elaborate cults of the gods and goddesses.

Religions of the Great Ancient Civilizations   After the great agricultural-urban revolution, the changes in human culture began to come much more rapidly, into the Bronze Age (ca. 3200–1200 B.C.E. in the eastern Mediterranean areas) and the Iron Age (starting ca. 1200 B.C.E.), and the great ancient empires developed with their city-state religions. Here the invention of writing begins to play a significant part, and we see the end of the prehistorical period and the beginning of the historical period of the human story. And in the midst of these developments, finally, come the beginning stirrings of the present-day world religions. In terms of total human history, the agricultural revolution, with the religious developments that have accompanied it, is a very recent event, one that still permeates our worldview today. Whether the present-day technological revolution will have an equally drastic effect on our culture and religion remains to be seen.

The depth and richness of humankind's story can be seen in the great religious systems of the ancient peoples of the world, associated especially with some of the classical civilizations. There are the ancient Egyptians, for example, and the peoples of Mesopotamia and ancient China. Many cultures stemmed from that original group of peoples called Indo-European, including the Iranians (Persians), Aryans (of India), Greeks, Romans, Celts, Germanic peoples, and more. Also to be included here are the ancient city-state peoples of the Americas: the Mayas, the Incas, and the Aztecs. These ancient civilizations generally became agriculture-based societies, most of which evolved complex city-state societies. They are characterized by belief in many great gods of nature, sacred kingship, strong priesthoods, and, in many cases, written texts. Most characteristic of these religions is the strong ritual component, for it is through the highly complex rituals that the society, the state, and even the cosmos are upheld.

Even though most of these religious cultures did not survive into the modern world, they made deep contributions to the human religious adventure. We see examples of ancient religions as we investigate the beginnings of some of the world religions of today. In the course of this book, for example, we will look briefly at the ancient Egyptian, Mesopotamian, and Greek peoples, the ancient Persians, and the ancient Hebrews.

Discussion Questions

1 Discuss the concept that the vast majority of our human ancestral history took place *before* the beginning of our world religions of today. What significance might that have for human self-understanding today?

2 Do the theories about the origin of religion put forth by Tylor, Frazer, and Freud make sense to you? What limitations do you see in these theories?

3 What is the nature of evidence for religious practices from the Lower and Middle Paleolithic periods (Homo erectus and Neanderthal humans)?

4 What major religious ideas and practices are known from our human ancestors of the Upper Paleolithic period (about 35,000 to 10,000 years ago)?

5 What kinds of changes in religious ideas and practices were occasioned by the Neolithic food-producing revolution?

6 What are some of the common characteristics of the religions of the ancient agricultural, city-state peoples?

CHAPTER 3

Sacred Paths
Among Indigenous Peoples

All the basic patterns and themes of religion are well illustrated among the contemporary tribal, indigenous peoples of the world. Many of these tribal groups survived with their culture relatively intact into the nineteenth and even the twentieth centuries, and so we still speak of them in the present tense in this chapter. We know, of course, that colonization and westernization of almost all parts of the globe in the past two centuries have destroyed many of these cultures and drastically changed conditions for those peoples who are still struggling to retain their traditional way of life. But even under these modern circumstances, there are indigenous peoples throughout the world who value their heritage and are seeking to recover at least some aspects of their traditional identity.

While these peoples exhibit a vast diversity of characteristics, some commonalities of religious expression can be noted. For example, such tribal, indigenous peoples often have a strong sense of the presence of the sacred in various forms, sometimes as spirits, ancestors, and gods, sometimes as a diffuse, impersonal power. Their myths and rituals are closely related to their life in hunting, farming, or herding, having to do with the fertility and vitality of the animals or plants that are necessary for existence. The tribe itself is the central social reality, and no distinction is made between "religion" and the traditional way of life in the tribe.

These indigenous peoples can be grouped into a number of cultural types that correspond to food-producing techniques. First of all, there are traditional **hunters** and gatherers, demonstrating the lifestyle of all our ancestors from the beginning of human history until the agricultural revolution. Included in this category are the gatherers and small game hunters, the peoples who carry on hunts of big game herds of animals, and those who live by fishing. Their religious ideas tend to focus on the sacred powers of the sky and on the gods associated with the life-power of the animals, such as the Animal Master. Important roles are played by **shamans,** people who can transcend their human limitations and communicate with the various spiritual beings; and much attention is directed toward the sacred relationship with the animals. Among the many hunters and gatherers of recent times are, for example, the Native Americans of the Plains with their buffalo hunt; the Eskimo (Inuit) of Greenland and North America and the Ainu of northern Japan who live by hunting the bear and by fishing; the Bushmen of southern Africa who gather plants and hunt small animals; and some groups of Aborigines of Australia's Western Desert who move about periodically in their hunting and gathering.

A second group includes traditional **planters,** those who cultivate the earth to raise food as did our ancestors in the Neolithic period. Their religious interests are directed toward Mother Earth as the life-producing source. The sense of close kinship with vegetation is expressed in planting and harvesting rituals. And there is emphasis on rituals symbolizing the necessity of death so that there can be new life and on sexual rituals to enhance the life-giving powers. Different types of planting, of course, provide the context for somewhat different religious emphases. But, broadly speaking, most planting peoples place their main attention either on tuberous root-crop plants, such as the yam and taro, or on cereal and grain plants, such as wheat, rice, millet, and maize (corn). Root-crop planters include many of the peoples of Melanesia and Polynesia, such as the Marind-anim and the Kiwai of New Guinea, the Ceramese Islanders in Indonesia, and the Maori of New Zealand. Cereal-grain planting peoples have been numerous in many parts of the world, including maize-growing Native Americans; the rice-growing Ngaju of Kalimantan; and many peoples of Africa who grow millet and wheat, such as the **Dogon,** the **Yoruba,** and the Ashanti. Of course, many of these planters raise a number of other plant foods in addition to what has traditionally been their staple food.

A third broad category of indigenous peoples is the **pastoralist** group, those who raise their own cattle or sheep. Pastoralists also often do some planting of food. Domestication of animals began as early as agriculture, and a number of important ancient civilizations were pastoralist, such as the Indo-Europeans and the ancient Hebrews. Religious ideas of pastoralists are often focused on sky gods and on the life-power of their herds of animals, expressed in rituals of sacrifice. Examples of pastoralists today or in the recent past can be found among African peoples, such as the Nuer, the Dinka, and the Zulu.

As we discuss the basic patterns of religion as illustrated among indigenous peoples, we do not attempt to cover all the great variety that have been and still are present in our world. Rather, we focus our discussion especially on the religious traditions of the Native American peoples, the African peoples, and the indigenous peoples of Melanesia and Australia.

IDENTITY THROUGH SACRED STORIES

Sometimes we suppose that anxiety about identity is one of the marks of modern human life, and we likely do not think of an African Bushman or a housewife in ancient Babylonia sitting around worrying about who he or she really is. But at the deepest levels the question of identity reflects an existential concern about how our little space of life fits into the greater life of the world, the ancestors, the family, and the sacred powers. The most drastic punishment imaginable in many tribal cultures is to make a wrongdoer an outcast, to withdraw name and social support so the person loses identity and becomes a nobody—no longer human, no longer a part of the sacred rhythms of life.

In order to provide the necessary context for human identity, each people has some kind of sacred history told in the form of stories. Some of these stories are very elaborate and sacred to everyone in the society, memorized by mythtellers as a kind of oral sacred literature. Other stories are local and disconnected, passed on family by family. But one mark of these stories is that they tell a sacred history about origins and foundings and developments that made the people what they are. Where did we come from? How did our ancestors learn from the sacred powers the real way of life? How did our rituals and social structures come about? By knowing this sacred history, the people know who they really are.

Indigenous peoples, with their openness to the involvement of sacred powers in all events and with their closeness to the rhythms of nature, are not as concerned about historical consciousness in their stories as are peoples of some of the world religions of today. This does not mean, as some have supposed, that they have no sense of history, for they do certainly remember important events, even long past. But purely "historical" events are not particularly significant apart from the involvement of sacred power in those events. The real story about who they are comes not from wars and disasters and victories and whatever else makes up "history," but from the action of the sacred powers and the ancestors in founding a way of life according to the sacred pattern. So the sacred history often takes the form of myths and stories about the sacred beings who created human existence and established the patterns that are still followed to live in the fullest human way. This is oral literature, expressed in many different forms, formulated by gifted shamans and storytellers, memorized and passed on by elders and bards. This is a living history, so the stories change over time and incorporate new happenings within the sacred pattern.

Recounting the Sacred History

The myths and other texts have to do with encounters with sacred power. The setting is often the Time of the Beginnings or at least has some connection with that sacred time, as experienced in ritual and festival. It is in these eruptions of sacred power into the world, as told in the myths, that the vital aspects of existence were created and still are sustained. Myths sometimes tell about the creation of the whole world and of humans, of course. But myths also tell of the creation of vital realities like animals and hunting, plants and planting, fishing, eating, sex and reproduction, death and ancestors, social structure, sacred land, rituals and festivals, medicine, and all the rest—all that makes our existence fully human according to the sacred pattern.

In modern usage, the word *myth* usually connotes something that is not true or real. But when used to designate the sacred stories of the religions, *myth* means that which is *really* the Truth, that which people live by, that which provides ultimate meaning for their existence. Myth tells the truth, the real Truth. "It is so because it is said that it is so," the Netsilik Eskimos say about their sacred stories. It is the Truth because it links us with the source of life and power, the Time of the Beginnings. "It was thus that the Nemu [mythical ancestors] did, and we do likewise," according to the Kai of New Guinea.[1]

One reason the myths, epics, and songs are so important is that they provide models and paradigms to follow in living the fully human life, that is, the life shaped by the sacred beings and ancestors. These oral traditions permeate every corner of life, whether having to do with ritual or festival, diet or marriage, work or play, war or art. They provide orientation to the world, define culture, and maintain basic values, molding people into the sacred patterns by instructing them and defining their activities and goals.

Perhaps it is important to note that indigenous peoples do not consider their oral traditions to be lacking or inferior simply because they are not written. A Carrier Indian in British Columbia is reported to have said, "The white man writes everything down in a book so that it might not be forgotten; but our ancestors married the animals, learned their ways, and passed on the knowledge from one generation to another."[2] In fact, the very orality of the myths, epics, and songs is what carries the power—passing them by word of mouth from one generation to the next, performing them in ritual and festival, transforming them, and adding to them as new experiences of the sacred are encountered. Let us consider several examples.

The **Hopi**, a maize-growing people living for centuries on the desert mesas of southwestern North America, think of themselves as the first inhabitants of America. Their vil-

lage of Oraibi may be the oldest continuously occupied settlement on the continent. Their sacred history about their emergence, wanderings, and settlement provides a sense of continuity and identity. The Hopi tell how this is the fourth world that humans have inhabited, the first three lower worlds having been destroyed. The first world was created very good and people were created wise, but gradually they forgot their origin and misused nature, so that conflict and war arose. The creator hid the people safe in an anthill while he destroyed the first world and created a second world for the people to live in. But eventually the people created conflict again, so the second world was destroyed, and then also the third world—and finally the fourth world, this present world, was created.

As they emerged into the fourth world, Masaw, guardian of the earth, told the people that, to fulfill the creation, the different clans should go separate ways and wander until they would settle together in the right place. Each clan should make four migrations—in the four directions—to the ends of the land, before coming back to the center again. So for many years the clans wandered about, leaving rock carvings, mounds, and broken pottery to record their migrations. Some peoples among them forgot the command of Masaw and settled in tempting places before finishing their migrations, building cities and civilizations that were to crumble. Some of the clans, however, finished the migrations properly and settled in the center of the world, the arid plateau between the Colorado and Rio Grande rivers, becoming the Hopi peoples. In their wanderings, they all had sacred experiences, and when they settled in their permanent villages, each clan contributed its special rituals and ceremonies to form the great ceremonial cycle of the year. Still today, after major ceremonies are concluded, the Hopi relate the history of their clans and their migrations, "so that we will always keep them deeply in our hearts. For the telling of our journeys is as much religious as the ceremonies themselves!"[3] These stories are not just tales for amusement. They tell of the sacred, creative events, and thus they present the structure of the world and its meaning. In these stories, the origins of all the present-day cultural forms and practices are seen. They present a special identity for the Hopi people, linking them to the ancestors of the beginning times and giving a model for life in this world. So they provide the basic orientation that gives meaning to the present community of Hopi.

Many peoples of Africa have mythic stories telling their sacred history and identity as a people. The sacred history of the **Lugbara** of eastern Africa provides identity for these people by telling how their society and clan relationships came about.[4] In the beginning phase, the world was the inverse of what it is now; there was no society, and the people were nonhumans living through magical means and practicing incest. Then a transitional phase began with the birth of the two Lugbara heroes, Jaki and Dribidu, who had both nonhuman and human characteristics. At first they lived as nonhumans outside normal social bounds, begetting offspring incestuously, even eating their own children. But they moved to Lugbaraland, and now they began to establish the social laws to be followed by their children, who are the founders of the present clans and the beginning of real human society in this present phase of the ordered, human Lugbara world.

This history shows how the Lugbara clans are the real people, living at the center as normal upright people with proper kinship relations, within a sacred world of meaning and order. Outside this center is a second large circle of related tribes in which the peoples are not entirely normal and practice sorcery. Beyond this is the third area entirely outside the bounds of humanity. These peoples (including the first Europeans the Lugbara met) are entirely inverted, walking on their heads, eating rotten meat, practicing cannibalism and sorcery. Thus, the Lugbara land and people form a sacred cosmos surrounded by progressively more chaotic and nonhuman spheres. As they remember their sacred history, telling the myths and performing the various rituals and practices based on them, the Lugbara can maintain the order of the cosmos and their own identity as real humans.

Identifying with the Culture Heroes   The sacred histories of the Hopi and Lugbara put forth an important role for the first ancestors and culture heroes of the people. It is by identifying with these first people in mythic times, by experiencing them as present in the telling of the stories and in the rituals that the people know their own place and role.

The story of the culture heroes is so important because they originated the real way of life. Aborigines of Australia have sacred histories about the heroes in the **Dreaming Time,** that time of the beginnings that overarches also the present time. These ancestor-heroes arose at the beginning of the world and traveled all over the surface of the land, shaping it and making it ready for humans. They are respon-

sible for all natural growth, the seasons, the replenishment of animal species, and the land's fertility. Their power and presence remain as "Dreaming" in the physical aspects of the world—rocks and stones, hills, tracks, tools, paintings, and much more. People today know and feel their presence in their sacred sites and in the stories and rituals.

There are a great number of these ancestor-heroes, and they are often linked to specific clans and to individuals. When a person is born, it is felt that the life-power comes from a particular ancestor-hero, so that person remains linked to that hero in a special way. The ancestor-heroes reside at various places, so the stories and rituals take on a larger, interlinked pattern, as different individuals and different clans cooperate in the necessary ceremonies and rituals for the renewal of the seasons and the land. An important function of the history about the heroes is to set the rules for behavior in the clan, providing the model for how to live in the full human way.

As another example of sacred history about culture heroes, we turn to the islanders of Ceram (Indonesia), just west of New Guinea. The Wemale of western Ceram are tropical yam cultivators much like peoples throughout Melanesia. Within their sacred history about the time of the beginnings is a myth about their first ancestors and about Maiden **Hainuwele,** a being full of extraordinary power. This myth, recorded by Adolf Jensen,[5] tells how the nine families of humankind emerged at Mt. Nunusaku and migrated to the Nine Dance Grounds. Among them was Ameta, who chased a wild pig into the water and, when he pulled it out, found a coconut on its tusk (though there were no cocopalms in the world). He put the coconut in his house, covered it with a cloth, and in a dream, a man told him, "The coconut which you have covered with a sarong there on the shelf, you must plant in the earth, for it is already starting to sprout."

So Ameta planted the coconut, and it quickly grew tall and carried blossoms. He cut some blossoms from the palm, but in doing so he cut his finger, and his blood dripped on the blossoms. Later he discovered that where his blood had mingled with the sap of the blossoms a little girl was developing. In his dream the man told him to wrap the girl in the cloth and bring her home, and so he did, calling her Hainuwele (Branch of the Cocopalm). Maiden Hainuwele grew up quickly and had extraordinary powers: When she relieved herself, her excrement consisted of precious articles such as Chinese plates and bells!

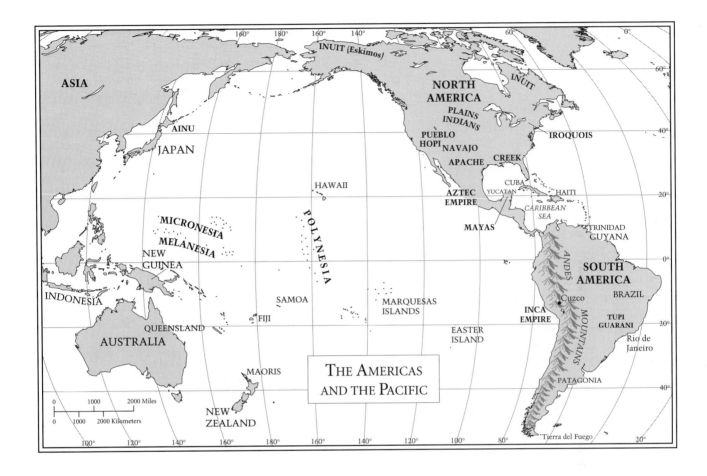

THE AMERICAS AND THE PACIFIC

The nine families of humankind held a great Maro Dance in the Nine Dance Grounds, the men dancing the large ninefold spiral, and the women handing out betel nut for them to chew on. In place of betel nut, Hainuwele handed out precious items such as coral, Chinese plates, bush knives, betel boxes, golden earrings, and beautiful bells, the value of the items increasing each night of the dance. The people got very envious of Hainuwele and decided to kill her. So on the ninth night of the great Maro Dance, they dug a deep pit and, in the slowly circling dance movement of the spiral, they pressed Maiden Hainuwele into the pit and trampled earth over her.

When she did not come home, her father Ameta performed divination to locate her body. Then he dug up her body and cut it up into many pieces, planting the pieces throughout the dance grounds. These pieces were transformed into things that had never existed before—above all, the tuberous fruit that has been the main food of the people ever since.

Ameta carried Hainuwele's two arms to Maiden Satene, who at that time still ruled over the people. Maiden Satene was angry at the people because they had killed. She built a large gate and, holding Hainuwele's two arms, summoned all humankind, saying to them: "I do not wish to live here any longer, since you have killed. Today I am going away from you. Now all of you must come to me by passing through the gate. Whoever makes it through the gate will remain people; whoever does not pass all the way through will experience something different." So whoever of the people did not pass all the way through was transformed into an animal or spirit—that is how there came to be pigs, deer, birds, fish, and many spirits in the world. Those who passed through the gate to Satene went on both sides; those on the left had to leap over five stalks of bamboo, and from these stem the Fivers; those going on the right had to leap over nine stalks, and from these stem the Niners. Then Satene left the people and went to dwell on the Mountain of the Dead, and whoever wants to go to her must first die.

This story tells of the first ancestors, the nine families of humankind, from whom the Wemale are descended. The actions of these ancestors shaped human life into the way it is now. The story relates the origin of many essential aspects of life: the cocopalm tree, the mystery of planting, the great Maro dance ceremony, death, rituals of divination, ritual killing and planting parts of the body, the journey to the realm of death, animals and spirits, and the main social divisions of the Wemale. Most important, the death of the powerful Maiden Hainuwele brings the great gift of yams that grow from her body. By telling and ritualizing the sacred story, the Wemale know who they are, how to live their lives, and how to relate to the culture heroes who are still present as they reenact the myths and rituals.

WORLDS OF MEANING OF INDIGENOUS PEOPLES

Religions of indigenous peoples do not have systematized doctrines or written scriptures. But that does not mean these peoples have ignored the theoretical side of religion. They reflect on the issues of life and express their ideas in a great variety of forms—in myths, epics, legends, songs, prayers, dirges, even dance, music, and art. All of these forms convey the perceptions and responses of these peoples to the deep questions of life, about knowing the truth, about ultimate reality, about the nature of this world and humans, and about the path toward living real life. If we know how to hear and "read" them, these myths, sacred stories, art forms, and the rest will help us see inside their worlds of meaning.

Sacred Reality in Sky and Earth

What's it *all* about? What is the source of sacred power? Since the beginnings of humankind people have wondered about questions like these, expressed in their own way. And the answers among the indigenous peoples are extremely diverse and complex. These people speak from their own

cultural experience, telling through their myths, rituals, and art how they envision what is ultimately real. What is typical of indigenous peoples is that they understand the modalities of the sacred reality in association with the structures of our world—sky, earth, storm, animals, vegetation, water, humans, and more. They live in a sacred cosmos, and they expect to encounter sacred power through the functioning of this cosmos.

Some years back, many scholars took an evolutionary view of religion, holding that very primitive peoples have only a vague conception of sacred power (dynamism) or spirits (animism). As their ideas advance they begin to believe in the great spirits and gods of nature (polytheism), and finally some peoples reach the point of seeing that one supreme God is in charge of all (monotheism). But field studies among indigenous peoples of today have clearly shown the error of such a view. Hunters and gatherers living at the most archaic level of subsistence often have a well-defined view of a supreme creator god. On the other hand, highly developed agricultural peoples with great gods of nature may also have a sense of impersonal forces within animals and trees and even inanimate objects. Overall, it has become clear that indigenous peoples have rather sophisticated and complex visions of sacred reality. Let us look first at the idea of supreme gods and then fill in the vast canvas of sacred reality with some of the other typical forms.

Supreme Gods For all the variety of religious systems, the ideas of supreme gods found in them have surprisingly similar features. Generally, such gods stand uniquely alone, transcending the other sacred beings and supreme over them. Very often the supreme god is associated with the sky, so that many of the qualities of the sky become expressions of the unique power of the supreme god. It is not that one should think of the sky itself as god; rather, the god's power and qualities are manifested especially in the sky.

What are the special qualities of the sky? The sky is above all; it is without beginning and end; it is present everywhere; and it is seemingly beyond and unaffected by the rest of this changing world. And so the god of the sky, the "high god," is above all and supreme, the final authority. The supreme god is primordial and eternal, existing from the earliest beginning and thus the source of all power and creation. The supreme god is present everywhere and therefore is all-seeing and all-knowing. But also the supreme god is often remote and inaccessible (like the sky), and therefore this god appears to be passive and indifferent in the daily affairs of human existence. This remoteness is compensated for by divine helpers, the gods and goddesses of nature that are much more involved in human existence.

The nomadic hunters of Tierra del Fuego have a supreme god called Temaukel, although they do not pronounce this holy name and call him instead "Dweller in the Sky." He is eternal, all-knowing, all-powerful, and the primordial creator—but he withdrew beyond the stars after creating the original ancestors, who then accomplished the rest of creation. There are no priests who worship this supreme god and no images of him, although in times of great drought or sickness people may make special prayers to him, for he is the judge and ultimately the master of all destinies.

The Zulu of South Africa look to Inkosi Yezulu (Chief of the Sky) as the supreme source of power. He shows himself especially in storms and rain, and the Zulu have specialists known as "heaven-herders" who shepherd the thunderstorms sent by the god of the sky. Ordinarily, people look to their ancestors for the various needs of daily life, but in times of dire need they will go to the hills to pray to the Chief of the Sky for help.

The Dinka of the Sudan in Africa look to Nhialic ("Above") as the one who created the sky divinities and the people, who still today creates people in the womb. Since the age of origins, Nhialic has moved far away in the sky, with the result that death and disease have come into the world. Since Nhialic is so remote, there are no temples, images, priests, or festivals dedicated to him. Yet Nhialic is still thought of as a father toward his children, as the source of order and justice, still present through leaders and prophets. Nhialic is the ultimate ground of divinity. Even though many other gods function to bring rain, sun, fertility, and so on, Nhialic is considered to be the unified supreme god who ultimately controls that total power.

Sometimes multiple spirits are conceived of as unified in the form of a supreme god supervising all others or taking on all the divine functions. Among the Lakota Sioux Native Americans, Wakan Tanka is the collective name for a whole set of gods and spirits of different functions. But Wakan Tanka is also conceived as the unity of sacred power, a supreme god who is personal in nature. Prayers are often addressed to Wakan Tanka as the supreme god.

Although the supreme gods of the sky are usually thought of as male, that is not always so. The Khasis people of Assam believe in a supreme goddess who is creator of all, who dwells

The Aztec Sun-God Tonatiuh, in a detail from the Codex Borbonicus. Neg./Transparency no. 332105, courtesy Dept. of Library Sciences, American Museum of Natural History.

in heaven and sees and hears all that happens on earth. And occasionally there are other gods and goddesses not necessarily associated with the sky whom we can recognize as supreme creator gods. The Kogi of Colombia, for example, have a supreme goddess, the Mother associated with the primordial sea, who gives birth to all the nine worlds, ruling the cycles of life, death, and rebirth for all creatures.

Gods and Goddesses of Nature   Since supreme gods are usually quite remote from daily affairs, indigenous peoples look to a variety of closer sacred beings, generally associated with forces of nature, for the ongoing needs of life. There are gods of the heavenly bodies and atmosphere, a great variety of gods of the earth, and gods and ancestors having to do with the social and cultural order. Each people has its own unique configuration of such sacred beings, all fitting together into a sophisticated vision of ultimate reality.

The great gods associated with the sun, moon, stars, and atmosphere are often considered to be manifestations or helpers of the supreme sky god. The characteristics of the natural phenomena are seen as qualities of the divine beings. For example, the sun-god epitomizes creativity, wisdom, omniscience, and constancy. Often considered a supreme god, the sun-god receives regular worship because of his crucial role in causing vegetation to grow. The god of the moon symbolizes mysterious power, death and rebirth, fertility and regeneration. Often considered female, she rules over the rhythms of life associated with water, vegetation, and fertility. Gods of storm and wind manifest strength and vitality, bursting open the clouds for rain and sending fertility to the fields, also sometimes causing destruction as well as bringing life-power.

First to list among gods of the earth is Terra Mater, the Earth Mother or great goddess known in some form in Upper Paleolithic times, long before the discovery of agriculture. The earth is the primary source and nurturer of all life, and it also receives all life back again, so all human cultures know the special qualities of sacred power through the earth. The Igbo of western Africa, for example, worship Ala, the source of fertility for the land and the family, the abode of the ancestors, and the guardian of laws; barren women pray to her for children and men ask her help for increase in livestock. To the Shoshoni Indians of Wyoming, among the various gods and spirits, one of the most respected is "Our Mother Earth" (Tam Sogobia). Our Mother Earth is the sacred power of the earth, nourishing plants and animals. Many prayers are addressed to her, and whenever there is a festival, offerings of tobacco or of water are poured on the ground in worship of Our Mother Earth.

Closely related to the earth are other gods and goddesses who promote fertility, prosperity, health, and well-being. Some of these are associated especially with the waters, experienced as a life-giving source. In Bambara land in West Africa, for example, the Niger River is said to be the body of Faro, the water spirit, who provides for the fertility and growth of all living things. The gods and goddesses associated with the waters are not only life-giving but can also become destructive. The Inuit (Eskimo) worship Sedna, a goddess who is the source of life from the sea as the mother of seals and other sea animals. But when humans break certain hunting, birth, and death tabus, Sedna withholds the sea animals and brings famine and destruction. Thus, shamans in trances journey to her deep-sea abode to placate her, so she will set the sea animals free and human life can prosper again.

As we see in the Sedna mythology, it is perhaps in securing and producing food that humans experience most deeply their close relationship with sacred powers. In hunting cultures it is expected that sacred beings will manifest themselves in animal form. To the Ainu of northern Japan, for example, the bear is really a "visitor" from the divine world. Many hunting cultures experience sacred power in the form of a **master (or mistress) of animals,** a god who protects the life of the herd, but who also provides boons to the humans by providing them the sacred life of the animals. The Northern Saulteaux of eastern Canada feel that the bears have a king or chief who watches over the bears and sends them into the people's traps; after killing a bear they dress it in fine clothing as an offering to the bear chief, who receives it back and regenerates its life again the next season.

Agricultural peoples learn the work of planting and harvesting from the gods and goddesses of vegetation, and it is the life-power of these sacred beings that humans receive by eating the plants. A Cherokee story tells of Corn Woman, who produces food by rubbing her body and is killed because the people think this is witchcraft. But before she dies, she instructs them to drag her bleeding body over a field seven times, and corn sprouts wherever the blood of Corn Woman moistens the soil.

Culture Heroes, Ancestors, and Spirits   Beyond the vast domain of gods of nature, sacred reality for indigenous peoples includes other spiritual powers. There are culture heroes, conceived in human or animal form, who were active in the Time of the Beginning to make the world fit for human habitation, give gifts of food, fire, and speech, and establish order and creativity in human life. Corn Woman of the Cherokee story would be this type of culture hero, as would Hainuwele of the Ceram islanders. The Dogon of West Africa have twin culture heroes who are credited with bringing the first millet seeds from heaven to earth and with teaching the arts of blacksmithing and pottery. Typically, a culture hero disappears after setting the world in order for humankind, returning to the sky, disappearing into the earth at a particular place, or being transformed into animals or plants.

For many indigenous peoples, human ancestors possess power and thus participate in sacred reality. Even though they inhabit the world of spirits, they are still present in the human community as guardians of the family traditions, providers of good fortune, and punishers of those who break accepted mores. They, unlike the supreme god, are closely involved in the details of daily life, powerful agents for blessing or punishment. Especially among peoples of Africa, the "Living Dead" are crucially important for the continued welfare of the family and the community.

The notion of sacred reality broadens out to include still other kinds of spiritual forces. There are nameless spirits that inhabit certain localities. And even inanimate objects can possess spiritual power. For some peoples, for example, objects of "medicine" are particularly potent sacred powers that can be used for good—or, in the wrong hands, for evil.

In this context, we can mention the concept of **mana**, a Polynesian word referring to the state in which certain places, people, and objects are especially strong and noble because they are filled with sacred power. For example, it may be believed that a particular noble family had great achievements and became the ruling family because of their intense mana. A related Polynesian concept is that of **tabu** *(tapu)*. Places, people, and objects that are full of sacred power in a contagious, volatile way are felt to be tabu, and contact with them is governed by strict rules and prohibitions. A festival takes place under a state of tabu, for example, when profane activities could disrupt sacred power with disastrous effects on the community.

Like the Polynesians and their concepts of mana and tabu, most indigenous peoples have the general notion that the world is full of power and that power can be confronted in special places, people, and things. But we should not consider notions like mana and tabu to be lower or more "primitive" forms of belief than the idea of a supreme god. Both mana and the supreme god—and all else in between— fit together in the complex worldview that sees all reality grounded in sacred power and open to various manifestations of that power.

The Yoruba Vision of Sacred Reality We must remember that beliefs about sacred reality arise out of the living experience of a particular people. So each religious

system makes sense in its own integral, complete way. As an example of one such religious system, let us look briefly at the view of sacred reality found among the Yoruba of Nigeria in Africa.[6]

Quite a bit of diversity exists in religious ideas among the five to ten million Yoruba, but the major gods and spirits are generally known among all Yoruba. There are three main sources of power: the supreme god called **Olorun,** the great divinities called **orisa,** and the ancestors. In addition, there are multitudes of spirits associated with natural phenomena.

The main source of power is the high god, Olorun, the owner of the sky, the originating power in the universe. All other powers, including the orisa and the ancestors, owe their being to him. Olorun is ever-living, omnipotent, and omniscient, the king and judge of all. Since he is unique and unlike anything else, the people make no images of him. Although Olorun is far away and has delegated many functions to the orisa and the ancestors, he is still approachable; people can call on him at any time without needing priests or shrines.

Most religious action and worship is directed to the orisa, for these are nearer gods that have more direct effect on day-to-day life. There are a great many orisa—perhaps as many as 1,700—but several important ones are mentioned here as examples. Orisa-nla was one of the first gods created by Olorun, and he was delegated to fashion the earth and to bring the first sixteen humans created by Olorun to earth. Orisa-nla then sculpted additional humans, including deformed people, who are specially sacred to him. He is known for giving children to barren women and for molding children in the womb.

Orunmila is a god closely associated with divination, for he was present at the creation of the human race and knows their destinies. Now he can be consulted about the future through rituals of divination. A rather complex god is Esu, who tests people to determine their character and even incites people to give offense to the other gods by failing to sacrifice to them. Since he contains both good and evil qualities in himself, he is a special mediator between divine and human power.

Yet another important god is Ogun, said to have been the first king of the holy city of Ife. He killed himself with his own sword and now is the god of metals, toolmaking, and war. He gives special guidance to hunters, blacksmiths,

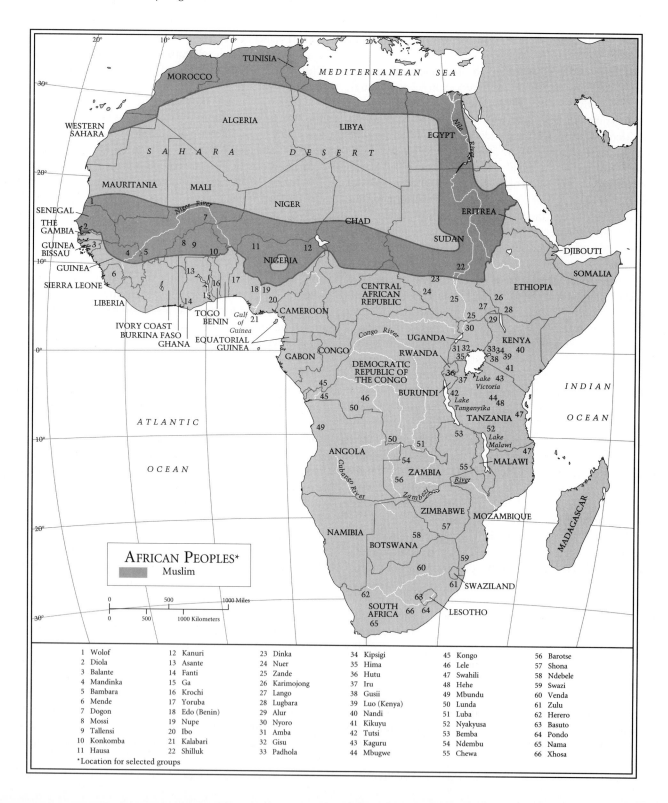

AFRICAN PEOPLES*

▨ Muslim

1 Wolof	12 Kanuri	23 Dinka	34 Kipsigi	45 Kongo	56 Barotse
2 Diola	13 Asante	24 Nuer	35 Hima	46 Lele	57 Shona
3 Balante	14 Fanti	25 Zande	36 Hutu	47 Swahili	58 Ndebele
4 Mandinka	15 Ga	26 Karimojong	37 Iru	48 Hehe	59 Swazi
5 Bambara	16 Krochi	27 Lango	38 Gusii	49 Mbundu	60 Venda
6 Mende	17 Yoruba	28 Lugbara	39 Luo (Kenya)	50 Lunda	61 Zulu
7 Dogon	18 Edo (Benin)	29 Alur	40 Nandi	51 Luba	62 Herero
8 Mossi	19 Nupe	30 Nyoro	41 Kikuyu	52 Nyakyusa	63 Basuto
9 Tallensi	20 Ibo	31 Amba	42 Tutsi	53 Bemba	64 Pondo
10 Konkomba	21 Kalabari	32 Gisu	43 Kaguru	54 Ndembu	65 Nama
11 Hausa	22 Shilluk	33 Padhola	44 Mbugwe	55 Chewa	66 Xhosa

*Location for selected groups

barbers, butchers, and (in modern times) mechanics and taxi drivers.

The Yoruba have two kinds of ancestors with power. Some are deified ancestors who, in effect, have become orisa and are worshiped widely. There is Shango, a tyrannical king with magical powers who, after his death, became associated with thunder and lightning, dealing out justice to the wicked. He is thus a guardian of social morality who punishes lying, stealing, and witchcraft. Oriso-oko was a leper who, with his wife, discovered agriculture, cured his leprosy, and taught others how to farm. So people worship Oriso-oko as the patron god of farmers. A popular goddess is Ayelala, a slave girl who was sacrificed in place of a man who had committed a wrong, as part of a covenant between two clans. Before she died she vowed she would punish those disregarding the covenant, and so she became the goddess who punishes all immorality and wickedness. These gods were once humans, but now everyone knows their divine powers and worships them.

Other ancestors are the family ancestors, and as the nearest sacred beings, they play an important part in Yoruba family life. Not all people who die become ancestors—only those who lived good moral lives and died well, who now are in closer contact with Olorun and the orisa. These ancestors are the guardians of family life and traditions, seeing all that happens; they bless well-doing and they punish those who break the family rules. They are the nearest intermediaries to the world of sacred reality.

Filling out the vision of the Yoruba, there are many more spirits associated with natural phenomena like the earth, rivers, mountains, trees, and wind. The spirit of the earth, for example, receives special sacrifices at the time of planting and harvesting. And the Yoruba feel there is a sacred energy (*ase*) directed toward generation and regeneration, experienced in the presence of the gods and the ancestors. All these sacred powers fit together in the dynamic spiritual universe of the Yoruba.

The World and Human Existence

What sense does our life have? Why are we here? Why is there suffering and death in the world?

These rather modern-sounding questions have actually been asked by humans for thousands of years, and indigenous peoples of today are quite familiar with them. In fact, many of the myths are direct responses to questions like these, telling of the origin of the world and of humans, including stories that describe the nature and role of humans. These peoples accept life the way it is given, including the rhythms of growth and death. Yet they also know of failure and wrongdoing, and such conditions form the background for the paths of transformation.

Cosmogonic myths of indigenous peoples provide a broad panorama of creative, imaginative perspectives on the origin of the world and of the basic conditions of life. Often the ultimate origin is a supreme god, but ideas of the world originating in chaos are also common. Even if there is a supreme creator god, typically other gods, goddesses, and culture heroes are involved in making the world the way it is today, fit for human habitation, but also full of the tensions and conflicts that characterize existence.

The Navajo Emergence Myth   One type of origin myth is the **emergence myth,** telling how living beings inhabited various worlds deep down in mother earth, eventually emerging to this world. Like other peoples of southwestern North America, the **Navajo** trace their origins from far beneath the present earth surface. They tell of four or more previous worlds stacked one on top of the other, each populated with animal and insect people that were eventually to evolve into the animals and people of this world. Already in the lowest world, First Man and First Woman were born, together with Coyote and other Holy People. But these lower worlds were small and dark, and the peoples grew numerous and fell into conflict and committed evil acts, so that each world was ruined and they had to climb upward to emerge into the next world.

Finally, the people emerged to the present world. First Man and First Woman began to whisper to each other, planning out how this world should be ordered for the people to live here. Then they performed ritual acts in a ceremonial hogan, a microcosmic building at the center of the world. First Man, using his medicine bundle, created the "inner forms" of all the natural phenomena. Pieces of jewel from the medicine bundle were put on the floor, forming a kind of painting of the life-forms that would be the sun, moon, mountains, plants, animals, and other physical features of this world. With prayers, creation songs, and smoke, these representations were then transported to their corresponding places on the earth's surface. The life-forms of dawn and evening twilight went on a tour of the new world, and they found everything in place, very beautiful. First Man and First Woman planned things carefully, but because Coyote and others interfered in their plans, things like unpredictable weather, sickness, and old age also became part of the order of things.

Finally **Changing Woman** was born, the Holy Person who grows old and then becomes young again, embodying the power of creation and sustenance. She gave birth to a set of twin sons, who prepared the earth for human habitation by slaying the monsters that had been produced by unnatural sex acts. To carry on the creative process, Changing Woman was given First Man's medicine bundle and created corn with it. She mixed cornmeal with balls of epidermal waste rubbed from her body and created the first Navajo people. After everything was created, the Holy People departed from the earth's surface, some living in lower worlds, others in mountains and other objects. Now they cannot be seen or heard with our ordinary senses, but through rituals, festivals, and prayer acts, their presence is known.[7]

The myth of the emergence provides the center of the world and the center of life for the Navajo. Most of their ceremonials are based on the era of emergence and reenact these powerful events, tapping into the creative power of Changing Woman and the other Holy People so that life can continue to be sustained. The myth reflects their attitudes about the world and their place in it. The beautiful, orderly world is filled with sacred beings that form the inner life of everything. All life thus is interconnected, and humans are part of the same life-power, brother and sister to the animals, the plants, the mountains, and all the rest. There is conflict and evil, but this is a good world, full of the restorative power of the Holy People, if humans know how to live in harmony with them.

The Earth-Diver and the Twins: An Iroquois Creation Myth   Widespread among Native Americans is the **earth-diver** cosmogonic **myth,** and it is often associated with the myth of antagonistic divine beings who created the world the way it is today. Typically an animal dives into the primordial waters and brings up the first particles of earth, which then grow into the whole world. But then, antagonism between divine beings who fashion the various aspects of the world results in the world as we know it, with its good and evil features. Whereas this type of cosmogonic myth is known in many parts of the world, it is especially popular among the Iroquois and other peoples of North America's eastern woodlands.

According to the Seneca version of the myth, in the beginning there was no earth, only a wide sea peopled by animals. But there was a world in the sky with a giant tree that radiated life. The sky-world people were told in a dream that the tree was to be pulled up so a new world could be created below. A hole resulted when the tree was pulled up, and a woman sitting at the rim of the hole was impregnated by wind from below and fell through the hole, to be mother for the new world below. A flock of birds broke her fall with their wings and placed her on the back of a turtle. The animals dived to the bottom of the water to find earth, and one of them brought back a small portion of earth, which was placed on the back of the turtle and soon greatly expanded to its present size.

The woman gave birth to a daughter, who in turn was impregnated with twins while playing in the water. They fought in the womb, and at birth one brother was born in the normal way but the other boisterously burst out his mother's side, killing her. When she was buried, corn and the other food plants grew from her body. When the twins were grown, the one called Good Spirit created human beings from dust and breathed life into them; he also made the good plants and animals of the world, lakes, and rivers with streams that run both ways to make travel easy. But his brother, Bad Spirit (who had burst his mother's side), created monstrous animals, pests, plant blight, disease, and death. He turned the currents in the streams so they would run only one way, and once even stole the sun. Finally the twins met in a duel in which Good Spirit won. Bad Spirit pleaded not to be killed and his wish was granted, but on the condition that he would henceforth help take care of humans. Another Iroquois version of the story tells that Bad Spirit was banished under the earth, but he still has helpers, half-human and half-beast, that he sends out to do his evil work.[8]

From this myth we learn of the origin of the earth from the waters, the coming of life-power from the world in the sky, and the animals' helpfulness in forming and supporting this world. And we see that the evil ways of Bad Spirit, just as the good ways of Good Spirit, shaped the world the way it is in its goodness and badness. Not only Good Spirit but also Bad Spirit continue to provide models for human behavior. The Seneca have a Society of Faces that uses masks to impersonate the many forms of Bad Spirit; they embrace those life-negating forces in order to cure disease, fight witchcraft, and remove disorder.

Origins in the Dreaming Time The role of the ancestors and the culture heroes in creating human existence is paramount in many myths of origins, as we saw earlier in the myth of Hainuwele, from the people of West Ceram in Indonesia. The Aborigines of Australia have a particularly strong feeling of relation to their culture heroes of the Dreaming, when humans and the present conditions of life were created. The Wulamba people of northeastern Arnhem land tell stories about the wondrous exploits of the **Djanggawul,** a brother and his two sisters, all of them bursting with fertility and creativity, who wandered all over creating plants, animals, and the ancestors of the Aborigines.

From a sacred island out to sea came the Djanggawul, their bark canoe loaded with Dreamings (sacred drawings and emblems) kept in a sacred mat. The Djanggawul brother had an elongated penis, and the sisters had elongated clitorises; these were so long that they dragged on the ground as they walked, leaving grooves that can be seen still today. Later they shortened the penis and clitorises, and the parts they cut off were transformed into poles. As they wandered about, they left Dreamings everywhere. For example, the brother left his hairbelt as a sandhill, and they made waterholes by inserting a sacred pole in the ground. Throughout the country they left trees, springs, plants, and special drawings.

When they came to Arnhem land, the brother said to the older sister, "I want to copulate with you." "Why?" said the sister. "I want to put a few people in this place," he said, and so they had intercourse. After she was pregnant, she was careful to open her legs only a little, for if she spread them out, children would have flowed from her, for she kept many people stored in her uterus. She gave birth to many male and female children. Then the Djanggawul brother and sisters left this place. The children they produced grew up and married and became the ancestors of the Aborigine people.[9]

The life-giving fertility of the culture heroes is celebrated in the rituals of the people, which reenact the major events during the wandering of the Djanggawul. On the sacred ground, a special hut representing a uterus is erected, and in it are stored sacred poles representing those used by the Djanggawul. In ritual dancing, these poles are removed from the hut and used to revitalize nature as in the myth. Women and children are covered with mats, representing the womb, and they emerge as the ancestors did from the wombs of the sisters. Human life comes from the sacred beings, their presence is felt all over the land, and by communing with them and repeating what they did, humans restore the world.

Myths of Origin in Africa African peoples have a great variety of myths about the creation of the world and of humans. In one way or another, the theme of primordial separation between the creator god and the world of humans plays a part in many of them, explaining the origin of suffering, evil, and death, but also showing humankind's responsibility for restoring order and life for the earth.

The Dogon of Mali in West Africa have a very sophisticated and complex myth of origins.[10] In the beginning, Amma, the supreme god, existed alone in the shape of an oval egg, which encompassed the whole universe by containing the four elements and the four directions. He designed the universe within himself and, after an initial unsuccessful attempt to create the world, transformed the world egg into a double placenta, each containing a pair of androgynous twins. But Ogo, one of the twins gestating in the egg, revolted and descended into the primordial darkness, taking a piece of the placenta, which became the earth. However, in copulating with the earth he committed incest (the placenta was his "mother"), and so the earth became defiled and sterile. Unable to restore complete order to his universe, Amma sacrificed the other twin, Nommo, scattering his body in the four directions to purify the universe, and the blood gave birth to various heavenly bodies, edible plants, and animals.

Now Amma restored Nommo to life and sent him and his other children, four pairs of heterosexual twins who are the ancestors of the human race, down to earth. They descended in a great ark lowered from the heavens by means of a copper chain; the ark contained everything needed to restore the earth and maintain human life, including all species of animals and plants and all elements of human culture. The first rains came, the sun rose for the first time, and the ancestors settled on the spot where they had landed. The people began to cultivate the land, and they were taught speech, weaving, blacksmithing, dance, and music. The rebellious twin, Ogo, was transformed into Pale Fox, who wanders the earth, by his tracks revealing mysteries that can be interpreted by diviners.

We know from the myth that this whole cosmos and everything in it emanates from the creator in the form of the cosmic egg. But the earth was created imperfect and fallen, only partially restored by the supreme god's sacrifice of one of his twin sons. The world still contains the elements of darkness and sterility resulting from the revolt and defilement of the other son of the supreme god. Humans, descended from Nommo who restored the world, are caught up in this tension, having the responsibility to promote order and creativity through their life and rituals in which they repeat the creative signs and words of the creator god.

A very common theme in African myths associates imperfection and evil in the world with a separation between earth and sky, the realm of the supreme god. Originally, earth and sky were very close together, and life was paradisiacal, with sufficient food and no sickness, sexuality, or death. But some wrongdoing on the part of the people, or some chance misfortune through no one's fault, caused the supreme god to move far away and resulted in the origin of sickness, deprivation, and death in this world. Since that time, human life has been full of conflict, struggle, and failure.

The Ashanti, for example, say that the supreme god originally lived in the sky close to earth. The mother of humans constantly went on knocking against him with her pestle while pounding out the traditional grain food, so the god moved high in the sky to get away from the constant knocking. The Mende tell how the first people used to go to the supreme god to ask for things so often that in irritation he finally moved away. The Yao tell that when the people first learned to make fire, they set everything alight, causing the supreme god to withdraw to heaven. Some peoples tell of rules that were broken, such as being forbidden to look at the supreme god, or to eat animals, or to disguise the fact of death, and breaking these rules resulted in the god moving far away.[11] Whatever the reason, the separation brought tragic consequences for humankind: conflict, famine, sickness, death, and all the other stark realities of human existence.

Human Existence in the World   With this large variety of cosmogonic myths, it is difficult to sum up the indigenous peoples' view of the nature of human existence, but a very general pattern is clear. The springs of life come from the sacred powers of the cosmos, the supreme god, the culture heroes, and the ancestors. Human life is one with the animals, the plants, and the rest of the world. And the highest good is to live in harmony with all these sacred forces, fulfilling the responsibility of maintaining order and bringing renewal to the earth by repeating the myths and rituals of the beginnings.

Humans are neither good nor evil by nature, but are from the same sacred reality as the whole cosmos. Evil and failure are built into our world, intertwined in the creative events of the Time of the Beginnings. On the human level, evil shows itself in many ways, especially in sickness—physical, mental, spiritual, and social sickness. But sickness takes many forms, such as disease, weakness, and death, of course—but also mental distress, possession by evil spirits, family disharmony, alienation of ancestors, disruption of community, and much more. Further, natural disasters, famine, tribal warfare, and other evidences of disharmony are often experienced in human life. Sacred power, abundant in the Time of the Beginnings, becomes exhausted, used up, out of harmony. What causes this? Magic, sorcery, evil spirits, and like causes play into the picture. But finally, it is a human question, for humans have a role in whatever it is that brings sickness, disharmony, and evil. So a human answer is needed. Humans need to take responsibility for living as they ought and fulfilling their role as humans.

Paths of Healing and Transformation

How can we start living *real* life? Where are healing and wholeness to be found? These are questions about the solution to life's failures and problems, as felt by all, including the indigenous, tribal peoples. The answers are embodied in the way of life learned from the myths and traditions. The path of transformation is a practical pursuit involving individual and community, worship, disciplines, and all the rest. Here we are interested in the theoretical basis of the path: How can the various rituals and practices *transform* exhausted life into real life, sickness into wholeness?

Restoring the Exhausted Sacred Power   Indigenous peoples do not seem to be primarily preoccupied with the afterlife, the destiny of the soul or life-force after death. Of course, death and what happens after are concerns, like other concerns, and they pay attention to death rituals, ensuring that one who dies becomes an ancestor and thus continues the health and harmony of the family. But they do not generally share the view of some world religions that only in a different state of life—heaven or paradise or nirvana—will there come the full authentic existence. Rather, the primary concern is with fullness and wholeness in human existence as it is given from the sacred powers and from the ancestors. And that means a life in harmony with these forces—a life in which the buffalo are plentiful and intimate with humans, the corn and yams come forth in abundance from mother earth, and the family lives in health and peace under the blessing of the ancestors.

As we have seen, visions of the human problem are manifold and complex. An underlying common theme among many of the indigenous peoples is the exhaustion of sacred power. In this world of good and evil, perfection and imperfection, the power that originated everything eventually gets used up. In the process arise sickness, disintegration, dry seasons, famines, death, and so forth. So the path of transformation is a way of life designed continually to retrieve and restore the sacred source of life. It is a path of healing and renewal. And that is possible through reestablishing contact and communion with the sacred beings, the ancestors, and the other sources of power. The primary way to do that is by repeating the myths, ceremonies, songs, and disciplines that have been given from the Time of the Beginnings. Through them it is possible to share again in the transforming events, and real life is restored.

The path is generally very concrete. It focuses on specific needs and concerns—someone is sick and needs healing; it is corn-planting time and good growth is needed; a wife is barren and children are needed. But the healing and renewal that come are of larger benefit than the immediate concern. Through the healing ritual or the corn-planting festival or the fertility-producing ceremony, the people of the community learn anew the traditions, they reestablish communion with the sacred powers, the bonds of the community are renewed, and personal life is more complete.

Some people in these societies pursue the path with great vigor and discipline and experience deep transformation in their lives. For example, there are religious specialists, like diviners or shamans, who may undergo long training and pass through an elaborate initiation in which they experience a spiritual rebirth. But even ordinary individuals may feel the need for deeper communion with the sacred powers and pursue special practices, as in the vision quest among Native Americans.

Navajo Blessingway Transformation Ceremonies
As an example of community practices on the path of transformation, we can look at the Navajo prayer ceremonials, especially the set that is called **Blessingway**. These Blessingway ceremonials were, according to Navajo tradition, first used at the time when First Man and First

A Navajo medicine man instructs his six-year-old son in the art of sacred sandpainting for healing purposes.

Woman built a hogan at the place of emergence and created the life-forms of this new world. Now Blessingway is used in ceremonial acts for many specific needs, such as blessing a new house, a girl's puberty rite, rain ceremonies, seed blessings, weddings, rituals for expectant mothers, and the like.[12] The overall effect of the Blessingway ceremonials is to make the primordial creative actions meaningful to specific life situations of today, so that the life of the community can be transformed and continue according to the sacred pattern.

At the emergence place, First Man and First Woman constructed a ceremonial hogan, and so Blessingway begins with purifying and blessing the hogan. This hogan becomes sacred space, a microcosm of the world and the center of the world where the Holy People who created the earth may again communicate with earth people and renew their acts of creation. A litany prayer follows by a singer, with responses by the person for whom the ceremony is being held, who carries a mountain soil bundle representing the medicine bundle of Changing Woman who first created humans. The bundle is pressed to various parts of the body, identifying the person with the creative powers of the bundle.

Next, the person sleeps in the hogan, performing a ritual bath the next day, reenacting the ritual bath performed by Changing Woman. The body is dried by ritual application of cornmeal. Then the whole night is spent singing Blessingway songs in a "no-sleep" ceremony. The night concludes with dawn songs and the person leaves the hogan and moves toward the east, "breathing in the dawn"—representing the final acts of creation in which the inner life-forms were transformed into the actual forms. The person thus departs from the sacred time of creation and returns to ordinary Navajo life—but now things are renewed and transformed.

When Changing Woman taught these Blessingway songs to the people, she said,

> Now it is known to me how from the very beginning itself songs came into being and how prayers came into being. These [songs and prayers] that were used to bring us all into being at the time, are known to me. . . . All of this will now be made known to you, all of it will be your ceremony, and all of it will be your songs, all of it will be your prayers. These will direct you as you live on in the future, and they will direct your mode of living. And should there be any mishap in things on which life depends, which enable you to live, all will be put in proper shape again by means of them, the body will be restored again by means of them.[13]

So, in reciting these prayers the original acts of creation are repeated, the world is recreated, and the person praying is made an integral part of that world by close association with the Holy People on whom all life depends. The creation put everything in its proper order, and that way is reinstated and maintained through the ritual. The source of life-power is directed to very specific needs, but the benefit is more general—the whole community participates in the renewal.

Native American Vision Quest As an example of individuals pursuing a path of discipline and heightened spiritual awareness, widely known among Native Americans is the **vision quest.** It was customary in some tribes that young boys—and sometimes girls also—as part of their puberty initiation began at a very young age to prac-

tice fasting and spending time in isolation pursuing the experience of a vision, receiving the power of a spiritual being. But the vision quest has been used more broadly also, in connection with special preparations at times of mourning, warfare, making important vows, meeting special needs, and acquiring a guardian spirit. Among some peoples it is felt that the visions come more or less spontaneously, without formal quests, but in most communities there is a need for special searching for spiritual vision and power.

It could be said that the vision quest stands at the core of the Native American religious path, for the basic idea is attaining spiritual powers essential to the successful fulfillment of human life. Through the vision quest, the individual finds identity, direction, guidance, protection, and destiny joined to the traditional way of life. People may go on vision quests a number of times, and the meaning of the experience is not always understood completely at first. After the vision experience, they examine it again and again, perhaps with the help of experienced holy men, reflect on it, consult it in different life situations, and live by its guidance.

Among the Plains Indians—for example, the Sioux—the vision quest attained important form and status, and today some Sioux people still try to restore their heritage and identity by following this path. Typically the vision quest begins by visiting an elder holy man and offering a sacred pipe, declaring one's intention to perform the "lamenting for a vision" for a number of days. Under the holy man's guidance, careful preparations are made. First comes an extensive purification in the **sweat lodge,** when the pipe is prepared to be used in the vision quest. The holy man offers many prayers to the spiritual powers to assist in the quest, such as this prayer directed to the supreme god: "O Wakan-Tanka, my Father and Grandfather, You are first, and always have been! Behold this young man here who has a troubled mind. He wishes to travel upon the sacred path; he will offer this pipe to You. Be merciful to him and help him!"[14]

After the purification ritual, the vision seeker is taken to a place on a mountain or hill where a sacred space is created by erecting four poles at the west, north, east, and south points. A bed of sage is placed in the center, and the sacred area may be enclosed with a tobacco rosary—a line with tiny tobacco pouches tied onto it. The seeker removes his clothes and remains in the sacred area for several days, offering his pipe to the spiritual powers, praying and communing with them, attentive to communication from them in the form of animals, storms, wind, and visions. The person performs many rounds of prayer, offering the pipe toward the powers of the west, the north, the east, the south, the sky, and the earth again and again. A modern Sioux, Arthur Amiotte, reports a small portion of his vision prayers this way:

> Facing the east, I asked these powers to hear me, and that the light which is the day that comes from the east should enter me and light my mind to its fullest power. I asked for the light of wisdom to see and understand what I must do and become so that my people may live. I asked for enlightenment for all the people, that they may discover the wisdom and peace of our religion as a light to guide them and bring day where there is so much darkness. I asked for the new life of spring to come to the people so that they may meet life with hope, as the earth greets spring in regeneration. . . .
>
> Pointing my pipe to the sky, I asked that the mystery of creation, reaching into infinity, bring together all of life in peace. I asked for wisdom to know and understand my part and place on this earth with other people. I asked to know humility and to become a better man so that my people may live better through my efforts and my work as a teacher. I asked for mercy and to be worthy to know the Spirit as it makes itself known to man.[15]

Fasting and praying for several days, the seeker hears communication from the various animals and objects, and perhaps experiences deeply moving visions. At the end of the quest he returns to the sweat lodge and relates the experiences to the holy man, who interprets them so the person can understand their meaning and their import for his life. Among the Sioux it is customary for the person to seek further clarification and guidance by going on a number of additional vision quests.

The vision quest exemplifies the path of transformation on the individual level. Through it a person restores communication with the sacred beings, receives spiritual powers, renews his or her identity with the tradition and the community, and attains understanding and guidance on life's path.

The Shaman's Path of Transformation   Indigenous societies have a great variety of religious specialists, set apart because they are following the path in a deeper or more focused way than are the ordinary people. Through

training, disciplines, rituals, and visionary experiences, their personal existence has been transformed, and so they not only show special power in their lives but are able to use that power for the benefit of the rest of the community. Let us look briefly at the way a person's life is transformed by following the shaman's path.

The word *shaman* comes from Siberia and refers to the religious specialist well known throughout Asia who can go into ecstatic trances to communicate with spiritual powers for healing and helping others. Scholars have used the word *shaman* to refer more broadly to all similar types of religious specialists found in the different cultures of the world, including some of those more commonly known as medicine men and healers. Mircea Eliade[16] has shown that the most basic definition of a shaman is one who has mastered techniques of ecstasy. That is, a shaman is able, through rituals, songs, dances, meditation, drugs, or other techniques, to enter a state of ecstasy ("standing outside" oneself), break beyond normal human limitations, and communicate with sacred powers in the other realms. The shaman attains knowledge and power through this and is able to use that knowledge and power to heal sicknesses, cause beneficial things to happen, lead the souls of the dead, provide guidance for hunting or planting, and much more.

How does a person get on the shaman's path? Typically persons become shamans either through hereditary transmission of the role or through a special sense of calling. Often shamans-to-be experience deep physical or mental crises that set them off from the other "normal" people. They have an overpowering sense of being called or possessed by sacred powers, a call that they cannot refuse, often experienced in dreams or visions. A Siberian shaman, for example, relates how he was made ill by the family spirits for many years and then, in a dream, was taken to the ancestral spirit at the center of the cosmic tree:

> In my dreams I had been taken to the ancestor and cut into pieces on a black table. They chopped me up and then threw me into the kettle and I was boiled. . . . While the pieces of my body were boiled, they found a bone around the ribs, which had a hole in the middle. This was the excess bone. This brought about my becoming a shaman. Because, only those men can become shamans in whose body such a bone can be found. One looks across the hole of this bone and begins to see all, to know all, and that is when one becomes a shaman.[17]

The person is chosen by the ancestors to be a shaman, and he or she experiences death and dismemberment, followed by a restoration in which special shamanic powers are received.

After the shaman has experienced a call of some kind, often there is a period of training in which master shamans provide instruction in the shamanic techniques and initiate the neophyte. During this period the new shaman might withdraw to solitude to learn the techniques and the traditions, the structure of the cosmos, the paths leading to the other worlds, ways of communicating with the gods, guardian spirits, demons of disease, and the dead, and so on.

The final stage in becoming a shaman would be public emergence and demonstration of the shamanic path. Among the Buriats in Siberia, for example, after many years of apprenticeship there will be a public demonstration and consecration of the candidate. A strong birch tree is set up in the tent, projecting through the smoke hole, and the candidate climbs to the top and shouts to summon the aid of the gods. Then the master shaman, the apprentice, and all the other shamans go to a sacred place where a goat is sacrificed and its blood is placed on the head, eyes, and ears of the candidate. The master shaman climbs a birch tree and cuts nine notches in the top of the trunk. Then the candidate and the other shamans all climb the birch and fall into ecstasy. Climbing the tree is a symbolic ascent into heaven; the new shaman is now recognized as one who is transformed and has the ability to communicate with the sacred beings and receive special power from them.[18]

The shamanic path typically lasts for one's whole lifetime. It is understood to be a special calling, in which a person sacrifices him- or herself for the greater spiritual realities. A Sioux holy man put it this way:

> You must know that a medicine man among our people is in possession of a special office. He is a servant of the people and of the gods. He enters upon a way that is sometimes not of his choosing, sometimes because he chose. . . . I did not ask for my office. My work was made for me and given to me by the other world, by the Thunder Beings. I am compelled to live this way that is not of my own choosing, because they chose me. I am a poor man; see how I dress and the house I live in. My whole life is to do the bidding of the Thunder Beings and of my people and to pay heed to what the Grandfathers tell me.[19]

RITUAL ACTIVITY AND THE GOOD LIFE

Sacred Time, Ritual, and Art

Where can we find new power for life? How can we live more in touch with what is *real?* Peoples of indigenous cultures, like all peoples, find the answers to concerns like these in experiences of sacred time, through worship, ritual, festivals, and sacred art.

As we have seen, indigenous peoples are open to sacred power and depend on it for meaningful and full human existence. One of the basic realities about power is that it runs down and becomes exhausted and therefore must continually be renewed. That renewal takes place in sacred time, when the ordinary run of time toward exhaustion and death is reversed and the sacred powers that created existence are made present once more in telling the myths and enacting the rituals. Since power runs down, there is need to establish a rhythm of periodic festivals and rituals, following the seasons and the life cycle, for regular and continual renewal of life.

So a major characteristic of sacred time, as indigenous peoples experience it, is that it is *reversible.*[20] Ordinary profane time is not reversible; once something is done, it cannot be done over again. For many people in the modern Western world, this relentless irreversibility of time is compensated for by a heavy stress on progress toward the future. We are working toward a future age that will be different from, and better than, the past. To indigenous peoples, this kind of abstract future is of little interest, for the source of being is the Time of the Beginnings, that is, sacred time, which does not slip relentlessly away but can be made present again in celebrating festivals and rituals. In that sense, sacred time is cyclical, not linear. In rituals and festivals, the people can go back and become contemporary with the sacred beings of the Time of the Beginnings.

Performance of the Myth in Ritual   Since the myths tell about the origins of the vital aspects of existence, in repeating them and using them in ritual, the people are reactualizing the mythic events and thus recreating and renewing those vital aspects of existence. Telling the myths and stories "performs" them. When it is time for the rice to sprout, for example, someone who knows the myths of the origin of rice may spend the night on the rice field, reciting the myths so the rice will come up as it appeared for the first time. In the deserts of southern Arizona, the Papago Indians, who depended for their survival on the growing of corn and squash during the short rainy season, would meet regularly at the council house during the summer to "sing up the corn." An old man who knew the myths of corn and squash would recite the story and the people would sing the songs. One version of the story tells how Corn was a man who seduced a Papago woman, and she lived with him a long time. When she returned to her husband she sang the songs Corn had taught her, passing on this important knowledge to the rest of the people. The song for when corn first appears goes like this:

> Songs begin.
> At the west they begin.
> Thereby the corn comes up.
> Upward its heart [the ear] is stretching.
> At the west they begin. . . .
> Songs are ending.
> At the east they are ending.
> Thereby squash come up.
> In a row its hearts [fruits] are standing
> At the east they are ending.

The Papago continue throughout the growing season to "sing up the corn" with the songs Corn taught the woman, as, for example, when the corn is one foot high:

> At the west, the red corn.
> See me!
> I come forth and grow tall.
> Yonder on the moist ground
> I come forth.
> At the east the white corn.
> See me! I come forth and grow tall.
> Yonder on the moist ground
> I come forth.[21]

The performative power of the sacred words sung by the people renews both the crops and the life of the people.

New Year's Festival: The Ngaju of Kalimantan Obviously there are countless ceremonies, rituals, and festivals among the indigenous peoples of the world, and we must be careful not to overgeneralize their common features and patterns. But certainly a prototype of renewal ceremonies is the New Year's festival that can be identified in many cultures—the time of the renewing of the crucial life-powers for the whole year. As an agricultural people of Kalimantan, Indonesia, the **Ngaju Dayak**[22] spend most the year cultivating rice as their main sustenance, clearing places in the forests for their rice fields, planting the rice, and tending it until it is harvested. When the harvest is complete, they celebrate the New Year's festival for an extended period.

This sacred time is called the "time between the years," and thus it is a period outside ordinary time; the year has run its course and been exhausted, and now there must be a return to sacred time to regenerate life-power. In the center of the village, a staff and banner are erected representing male and female powers, together making up the tree of life, which in the myths is the source of all life in the cosmos. The ordinary social divisions of the people are dissolved, social or moral rules are thrown out, and mass sexual intercourse occurs outside the normal relationships. The whole society returns to chaos and disorder. Toward the conclusion of the festival there is a great ritual battle in which the tree of life is destroyed. And a human slave is sacrificed, with all the people participating in the dance around the victim, stabbing him with spears and daggers, being smeared with his blood, and stamping dirt on the grave outside the village limits. In recent years, small animals have been used in place of slaves for this sacrificial ritual.

What does all this mean with its elements of disorder and chaos, breaking down of social structures, mass sexuality, and human sacrifice? We should note first that this festival is a liminal period, betwixt and between ordinary times. Separation from ordinary life is marked by the destruction of normal social forms; and at the conclusion of the festival a renewed social order is put into place again. But in this time and space in between, time is reversed and the people move back into the precreation chaos of mythical times. For in the beginning, according to the Ngaju myth of origins, Mahatala, the god of the upperworld, and Jata, the goddess of the underworld, made the earth, rivers, and first humans. The headdress of Mahatala became the tree of life, and from its leaves and fruit were made a rice tree, the source of rice. But the goddess's female hornbill and the god's male hornbill, feeding on the tree of life, got into a terrible fight and destroyed the tree of life and finally themselves. From the tree of life came forth various aspects of the world, like rivers and lakes. A maiden was born from the tree, and from the slain female hornbill came a youth; eventually they married and from them descended the humans of our world.

So the festival reactualizes the mythic events of the creation of the world, the origin of all plant and human life within the tree of life, the destruction of the tree so that creation can be renewed, and the marriage of the ancestors. The people of the village become contemporary with those events, and in repeating them make their power effective again in establishing a new year, renewed social order, new fields, and new crops.

Rituals of Food Renewal: Hunters and Planters
Many of the important festivals and rituals of indigenous peoples have to do with the seasonal or annual renewal of the food supply, as in the Ngaju example just cited, in the process, of course, renewing the whole life of the society. Two examples make this clear, one from a hunting people and the other from a planting people.

Spread across the arctic and subarctic regions of Asia and America are bear-hunting societies, and, like other hunters, they have rituals by which they maintain a sacred relationship with the animals they hunt. By performing these rituals they take responsibility for the maintenance and renewal of animal as well as human life. For example, the Ainu of Hokkaido and the other islands north of Japan have rich mythologies and rituals relating to the sacred life they share with the animals of their mountainous world, especially the bear.[23] They consider bears, like other animals, to be "visitors" from the world of the kamui (sacred beings) who have taken animal bodies to visit the Ainu world. By hunting them and using their bodies as food, the Ainu accept the gifts they have brought and return them to the kamui world.

The most important festival for an Ainu community is the **Bear Festival,** called Iyomante (sending-off). To hold a Bear Festival, an Ainu family or community captures a bear cub alive and rears it with care and affection; it is fed fish, millet, and even human milk. When the cub is grown, the people of the village are invited for the Bear Ceremony. They arrive in ceremonial dress, offering sacred wine, dances, and prayers to "entertain" the divine visitor, singing, "Today we

worship you as a god, therefore eat what we offer, and enjoy yourself." The people fast and abstain from sexual relations that night, in preparation for the main ceremony on the second day. After prayers, singing, and dancing, the bear is roped and led on a farewell walk, with the people making it run around to show its lusty and ferocious happiness. After it is strangled, the neck is cut and its blood drunk. Then it is skinned, and the carcass is carried into the hut through the special "kamui window" and set in the place of honor on a mat. Now the bear is the chief guest at the feast, and more entertainment and prayers are offered, such as this one recorded by John Batchelor:

> My beloved cub, pray listen to me. I have cared for thee for a long time and now present thee with wands and dumplings. . . . Ride thou upon these wands and carry with thee the good things presented to thee. Go to thy father and mother. Be happy. Cause them to rejoice. Upon arrival, call together multitudes of divine guests and make a great feast. Come again unto us that we may once more rear thee and enjoy another festival with thee.[24]

All parts of the bear's carcass are used for food and other items, and the skull is taken out and placed on a pole in the center of the sacred wands outside the house. After farewell prayers, the skull of the "departing kamui" is turned toward the east and the "arrow of sending away" is shot toward the eastern sky, after which the skull is quickly turned away from the east. The festival continues until all the flesh of the bear is eaten, and the skull of the bear is venerated as a guardian kamui.

So the Ainu celebrate their common life with the bear and renew that life-power—and in the process they tell the traditional myths, sing the songs, perform the dances, and in doing so bring about a renewal of the whole community.

Native American peoples of the North American eastern woodlands, such as the Creek, celebrate their most important festival, the **busk** (fasting), at the time of the first ripening of the corn in July or August, considering this the beginning of the year. No one is to eat the newly ripened green corn before this festival. The festival, lasting four days or so, takes place at a specially sanctified ceremonial ground outside the village. In preparation, the people clean their houses, repair their friendships, pardon sentenced criminals, and extinguish all their fires. Four logs are placed in the center of the ceremonial ground, pointing to the cardinal directions, and a new fire is lit by using a fire drill.

During the first three days of the festival, the men spend much time at the ceremonial grounds, fasting and purging themselves by drinking a purgative black drink. The whole community avoids certain foods, such as eating new corn or salt, and sexual relations are prohibited. Offerings of green corn and other items are made to the new fire, medicine specialists prepare new infusions of medicine on the fire, and women also come to receive the new fire for use in their homes. During these days many ritual events take place. For example, special dance rituals are performed, the men go to the river to perform a purification ritual, and young men and boys have their legs scraped so that the blood flows. On the last day, the fast is broken with the eating of the new corn, and there are many joyous dances.[25]

So the ripening of the corn is a special time when the sacred forces are present in a powerful way. The festival is referred to as "peace time"—peace within the community and peace with the sacred powers. In this period of crucial cosmic process, it is important for people to fast and purify themselves of used-up life-force, so they can participate in the renewal of life—the renewal of food, medicine, family, and social relations.

Rituals of the Passages of Life   Like the rhythms of nature, the rhythms of human life present special times for the individual and the community to renew power. In the critical passages of life—especially birth, puberty, marriage, and death—it is important to ritualize the separation from the previous state, the encounter with sacred power in the transitional liminal period, and the reincorporation into the community at the next level of human life. These rites of passage are exceedingly diverse and rich in symbolism among the indigenous peoples of the world, and much study has been devoted to them. Let us look briefly at two rites of initiation into adulthood.

The puberty ceremony for a girl who has experienced her first menstruation is the most elaborate ritual of the **Apaches** of southwestern North America.[26] Preparations for the four-day ceremony begin well in advance, planning and rehearsing the ceremony and preparing the ritual costumes and huge amounts of food for the hundreds of people who will come. The girl's main ritual implement is a wooden staff or cane, painted yellow and decorated, which

she will keep all her life; and a small pendant of abalone shell is tied to her hair to identify her with Changing Woman, the creatress. During the four days of the ceremony, the power of Changing Woman will reside in her.

The first morning as the sun begins to rise, she walks in ceremonial dress to the dancing ground, carrying the sacred cane, and, facing the rising sun, dances to songs that tell the story of Changing Woman. She prays, "Long life, no trouble, Changing Woman," as she receives the powers of Changing Woman and is transformed from a girl into an Apache woman. A second set of songs recalls how Changing Woman was impregnated by the sun to give birth to Slayer of Monsters, the foremost Western Apache **culture hero.** So the initiate kneels and faces the sun, raising her hands and swaying from side to side, to ritualize receiving the fertilizing rays of the sun as Changing Woman did. In another ritual, her sponsor massages the girl as she lies on a buckskin, giving her the shape of a woman. A medicine man explains, "Changing Woman's power is in the girl and makes her soft, like a lump of wet clay. Like clay, she can be put into different shapes. [Her sponsor] puts her in the right shape and Changing Woman's power in the girl makes her grow up that way, in that same shape." Then the girl runs to the east, encircles her cane, and runs back again, four times, symbolizing health and long life through the stages of life.

The ceremonies continue for three more days, as the ways of womanhood are revealed to her and she takes on the power and creativity of Changing Woman, able to cure the sick and bring rain. Some ceremonies occur to disseminate this special power for the benefit of the whole Apache community. For example, basketfuls of candy are poured over her head, and because of contact with her these candies can bring healing, a good crop, and other benefits to the people who receive them. The girl has now become a woman, she is ready for marriage and a fruitful life—and the whole community has been renewed through the powerful presence of Changing Woman in myth and ritual.

Initiation rituals for boys are very widespread and tend more often to take place for groups of boys rather than individually. Among the **Ndembu** of Zambia in central Africa,[27] when a group of boys from a cluster of villages is approaching puberty, the leaders of the villages decide to hold a rite of **circumcision.** Without being circumcised, a man is considered polluting and cannot marry and have normal social relations with the people. A senior circumciser is chosen, and other recognized circumcisers are invited. A camp is set up where the parents of the boys will live during the ceremonies, and a fire is lit that will burn for the length of the rituals and on which the mothers will prepare all food for the novices during their seclusion. After dark, drums start to beat, and a wild dance follows in which the boys have to be carried so they do not touch the earth. Suddenly the circumcisers enter in the procession with their apparatus and lead the wild dancing, which continues on and off throughout most of the night, the sleepy boys being roused to take part. Next morning the boys are fed a big meal, each mother feeding her son by hand as though he were an infant. Suddenly the drums begin to beat frantically, and the fathers and guardians of the boys grab them, strip off their clothes, and dash off into the woods down a newly cut path to the site of the circumcision, known as "the place of dying." The mothers are chased back to the camp, wailing as at the announcement of a death. The boys are carried off to the circumcisers for the brief operation, then herbal medicine is applied so that healing occurs. The men feed the boys and give them beer, and then the men go back to the camp and dance in a circle with the women.

There follows a period of several months in which the boys live secluded in a hastily erected lodge. During this whole period, until the wounds are healed, their parents must refrain from sexual intercourse or eating salt. The boys are forbidden to speak while eating and have to refrain from certain foods. During this period of seclusion in the lodge, they are taught the various things they need to know as adults in the society. When their circumcision wounds are healed, masked dancers come to beat the boys with sticks, and they are washed in a stream and sent into the bush to trap animals. The masked dancers go to the camp and dance for the women, also bringing salt for them to use. That night the parents of the boys, and also the circumcisers and their wives, are expected to have sexual intercourse. Not long afterward the boys are painted and dressed up and brought back to the parents' camp, so decorated that their mothers are not supposed to recognize them as the same children as before. There follows a joyful night dance with a huge crowd participating, climaxing in the burning of the seclusion lodge. The next morning, closing rituals put an end to the rite of circumcision, and the

boys return to their villages to continue to grow up and begin to participate in adult life.

Art Among Indigenous Peoples   Most museums have sections devoted to "primitive art," and the strange statues, masks, and other artifacts seem to grow out of a vision from another world. Modern Western people puzzle over what kind of reflection of reality is expressed in these art objects, what symbolic statements these are about the meaning of life.

But to indigenous peoples, as to all people who express their religious vision in art, art is not a matter of art objects. Rather, art is a living process, very much a part of life, vitally connected with the myths, rituals, and festivals of the people. Much of the art is presentational, that is, it presents sacred reality in living, creative events. Art is performed, and the objects that remain may only be the by-products and leftovers of these creative events. Indigenous peoples tend not to set their religious beliefs and feelings into systematized doctrines or even in enduring art objects; rather they sing out and paint out and dance out their religious vision.

In almost all nonliterate cultures, sound is paramount, for through spoken or sung words the myths are presented, prayers are offered, incantations chanted. Through the vibrations of human words—and the words of birds, thunder beings, bullroarers, and drums—the sacred powers are present to create life again. In these oral cultures, songs and poems are as common as the air we breathe—and as essential. In fact, in one Eskimo language, the Amassalik, the expression meaning "to breathe" is the same expression that means "to make poetry." And a great Eskimo shaman, who could, through the power of his songs, call caribou to come to him, said:

> How many songs I have I cannot tell you. I keep no count of such things. There are so many occasions in one's life when a joy or a sorrow is felt in such a way that the desire comes to sing; and so I only know that I have many songs. All my being is song, and I sing as I draw breath.[28]

The art of words is especially creative when wedded with music and dance, for it is not the informational content of the words but the *performative* quality that is important— spoken, sung, and danced, the words bring about the renewal of life according to the sacred pattern.

Widespread throughout indigenous cultures is the carving of images, statues, symbols, and masks that present the sacred beings or powers. The process of making these sacred objects often is considered a religious process, with appropriate rituals of purification and dedication. These images, masks, and so forth are important insofar as they are alive with the power they present. The masks become alive when used in ritual by properly prepared and attired dancers. Outside of that living ritual context, these objects are of little use or interest to the people. Among the Yoruba, the masked dancers *(egungun)* that perform at festivals and rituals wear special masks that have been handed down for generations in their families. These masks possess great power, and special rites must be performed by the men who wear them—for in wearing them the dancers actually become the embodiment of the family ancestors, present among the people in living form.

Elaborate mask to be worn by a Yoruba secret society dancer; the carved head of the mask supports a chief's hut filled with performing musicians.

Other visual creations, such as drawings, paintings, and engravings, also serve to present the sacred for particular rituals and events. In Arnhem Land in Australia, the Aborigines perform their sacred art not only by the activity of painting, carving, and engraving, but they at the same time sing and chant the designs on, in this way empowering them to become "Dreaming." Creating the art is the same as ritually performing it—the painting, the chanting, the dancing are all visible signs of the Dreaming made present and powerful again.

Aborigines of Kimberley in western Australia look to ancestors of the beginning time called Wandjina, whose power is present in paintings on walls of caves. These spectacular paintings are larger than human size, with figures painted in red ochre and black charcoal against a whitened background. These painted figures are the Wandjina, the sacred beings associated with the sky, rain, spirit children,

and the fertility of nature. When their wanderings in the beginning time were over, their bodies became paintings and their spirits went into spirit-homes nearby, ready to be reactivated when their "bodies" are repainted. So when their paintings are touched up again with the proper ritual, these beings are made present again to send life-spirits for humans and bring fertilizing rain for the land.

The Wandjina paintings are retouched and maintained over generations, but often drawings and paintings are not considered to have a long duration; a painting may, for example, be painted over for each new ceremonial use. From ancient times, Pueblo peoples of southwestern North America have painted murals on the walls of their *kivas,* the ceremonial chambers in which many of their rituals are performed. But these beautiful intricate murals are not preserved indefinitely. Rather, with the changing of the seasons and the ceremonial cycles, the old murals are whitewashed over and new ones are painted, to provide the appropriate setting for the new ceremonial cycle.

Sandpainting is a well-known art among the Navajo of North America, and art appreciators bemoan the fact that each sandpainting must be destroyed on the day it was made. Made on the floor of a ceremonial hogan, sandpaintings are done in the context of various Navajo ceremonial ways, explicitly for the purpose of curing illnesses. They depict Holy Persons according to a pattern known only in the memory of the painter, and these Holy Persons become present when corn pollen is sprinkled on the painting and on the sick person. In the ritual, the sick person then sits in the middle of the painting, and by taking sands from the figures on the painting and pressing them onto the body of the person, he or she is identified with the Holy Persons and their power serves to set the world in order again. The singer then completes the destruction of the painting and the sands are returned to nature. Here religion and art are one and the same; the paintings are created to make the Holy People present, and apart from that process they have no separate function. The destruction of the picture shows that these realities have become one with the sick person, to bring renewed life and health. The whole sandpainting process, then, is a ritual performance of re-creation, modeled on the Navajo story of the creation of the world. It provides healing by setting the ailing person right with the life-giving powers of the Holy Persons.

Society and the Good Life

How should we live? What is our responsibility to the world and to society? Far from being untamed savages, as early explorers thought, indigenous tribal peoples often have highly structured societies and complex codes of behavior and rules for living the right kind of life. And within their limited world they feel a responsibility for the continued peace, order, and health of their society and their environment.

Sacred People: Communal Identity   John Mbiti reports an African saying that reflects the relation between the individual and the community: "I am, because we are; and since we are, therefore I am."[29] Of course, indigenous peoples have a conception of the individual person, and there are many religious rituals designed to enhance individual well-being and personhood, as, for example, the vision quest noted earlier. But the individual is always rooted in a social nexus, consisting of the family, the clan, the village, and the larger community. Apart from that social nexus, the individual loses meaning and identity, thus becoming a non-person, less than a human being. The real fulfillment of personhood comes within the network of communal relations grounded in the traditions of the people.

Tribal societies often have very complicated social structures. Typically there are a number of clans or extended families that together make up the whole people, but the relationships between these clans take different forms. There may, for example, be a moiety arrangement between two clans that make up a tribe, as is common among Australian Aborigines. In these cases, marriages are usually exogamous (outside of one's own clan), and the two clans have different ritual responsibilities and duties. Within clans the relationships may also be complicated. The kinship system extends very broadly horizontally and means that, in one way or another, everyone is related to everyone else. In some African tribes it is possible an individual has literally hundreds of "uncles," "brothers," or "sons and daughters."

Sacred leadership within indigenous societies shows great diversity, of course, but some common types and functions can be recognized. Among leaders that have an official or "given" status are the head of the family or clan, the headman of the village, the chief or king of the tribe, and sometimes the priests who perform the official rituals. These are leaders who have power simply because of their position, and either their position is hereditary or they are chosen in some way by the people. But most leaders have their functions by virtue of personal power that is simply recognized by the people. There are shamans of various types, including medicine men who use shamanic trances. There are other healers who practice herbal medicine, diviners (who interpret communications from the sacred powers), and mediums (people through whom the spirits communicate). Some societies also have prophets who speak for the gods and lead the people according to the divine will. There may be rainmakers, singers, and more. And, of course, many societies have those who use power for evil purposes, namely, sorcerers, who may be much like shamans or diviners but use their power to hurt others.

Women in Religious Leadership   Women in these indigenous, tribal societies generally do not have roles of public power, and often participate in women's religious rituals and activities apart and hidden. Yet individual women frequently are recognized by the whole community for their personal religious charisma, functioning as mediums, diviners, shamans, and healers of various types. Among the Kaata people of Andean Bolivia, for example, there are more women diviners than men diviners. Women diviners play their roles in rituals concerned with misfortune, to remove bodily and social ills, while men diviners focus on rituals of good fortune. Among the Iroquois in North America, women often have roles associated with knowing and validating the traditions of the tribe. For example, the woman selected as the "chief's matron" holds the set of wampum beads that validates a chief's position. Many indigenous societies think of male and female power not in terms of superior-inferior but in terms of balance and mutual interdependence. While there is much ritual separation between men's and women's groups in traditional Australian societies, for example, there is also essential ritual coparticipation—performing different aspects of a ritual together at the same time and in the same ritual space. Among the Iroquois, women's societies play essential roles in the rituals of the ceremonial cycle, along with men's societies. Women are not subjected to men in these roles; both men's and women's roles are woven together in a traditional system of balance and interdependence.

Religious Leadership Among the Yoruba Let us look at a typical example of social structure and religious leadership among indigenous peoples. The Yoruba[30] of West Africa are a farming people divided into a number of social groups, each with a specific urban center. A fundamental social unit is the family, where the family head performs the important religious functions, supervising the family ancestral shrine, giving names to the children, leading funerals, and so on. But at the level of the town or city, the oba (chief) assumes responsibility for ritual leadership. In the Yoruba view, the chiefs rule their subjects on behalf of Olorun, the supreme god, and so the chiefs are below only the gods in power and respect. Because of their status, their bodies are sacred; an assault on a chief is regarded as an act of sacrilege. The chief of the holy city of Ife has superior position, for the gods established the world and the first kingship there.

Another important group of Yoruba religious leaders are the priests, associated with the many shrines throughout Yorubaland. The Yoruba have many gods (orisa), as discussed previously, and each god is attended by a special priesthood. These priests are guardians of the shrines and of the objects of worship. They act as intermediaries, offering sacrifice, leading devotion, and declaring the gods' will. One priesthood stands out with special importance for all Yoruba: the babalawo (father of secrets), who are priests of Orunmila, the god who knows the future and communicates through a special system of divination called Ifa. These priests, who go through long years of training, perform divination rituals and draw on a rich oral tradition of poems and legends to interpret the will of Orunmila. By this means they are able to give advice on what can be done to secure the most favorable outcome with regard to the basic concerns and needs of life.

In addition to the priests, there are mediums—people who become possessed by sacred powers during worship. In the ecstasy of possession, the person acts and speaks in a strange fashion, making utterances that the other worshipers understand as communications from the god that is possessing the person. Another recognized group of religious leaders are the medicine specialists, who are experts in identifying the causes for various illnesses and prescribing cures. Medicine specialists may use divination or work with a babalawo divination priest, but they have thorough knowledge of the incantations and the various traditional medicines, such as herbs, plants, leaves, roots, barks, animals, skins, bones, brooms, needles, minerals, and much more. Their medicine has power that comes from the gods.

The Yoruba recognize that specialists in power can also use that power for evil, and so there are sorcerers who use their powers to help people gain advantage over others or do harm to them. And few doubt that witches exist. These are mostly women but also a few men who meet regularly at night in spiritual form (their physical bodies are at home on their beds). At these meetings, they contribute their human victims whose life-blood they have sucked out. Witchcraft is done secretly, yet many Yoruba believe there are such evil people, and they take measures to protect themselves.

Sacred Land and Sacred Space The good life includes not only a sense of belonging to a community but also of belonging to a place, and indigenous peoples have a strong sense of spatial orientation in their world. Their myths tell of the creation of the world and of the original ancestors starting right here on the sacred land. Navajoland is the place of emergence, where First Man and First Woman and Changing Woman created the world and the people. The mountains and valleys of Cherokeeland originated when the earth was first brought up from the water and was still soft. Great Buzzard flew close to the land, and where his wings struck the ground and turned up again, the valleys and mountains were formed. For almost all indigenous peoples, the sacred history that gives identity for the people is tied up with their sacred land, and once they are torn away from their traditional land (as has happened very frequently in modern times) they experience great trauma.

There are, of course, many dimensions of sacred space—land, village, shrines, burial grounds, home. An important

Impressive images on Easter Island, a timeless presence of sacred beings.

macrocosm). Houses, shrines, temples, and ceremonial halls are often built as symbolic miniatures of the world, to connect with those greater sacred forces.

For example, the sweat lodge constructed for Native American purification ceremonies is full of symbolic representations of the cosmos, as explained by Black Elk, a Sioux holy man.[32] The frame of the lodge, made from young willows, is set up so as to mark the four quarters of the universe, and the round altar at the center of the lodge is considered the center of the universe, full of the power of Wakan-Tanka, the supreme god. The door is to the east, from which wisdom comes, and the path leading to the east is covered with dirt taken from the center of the lodge. The fireplace, used to heat the rocks, is at the end of the path outside to the east, the fire representing power from the sun. Heated rocks are brought in to be placed in the round altar, one in the center, one at each of the directions, and then the hole is filled up with the rest of the rocks to represent everything in the universe.

In the ritual, the water poured on the hot rocks to make the steam represents the thunder beings. Tobacco and smoke are used, and also sage and sweet grass, representing fruits of mother earth. The sacred pipe is placed with its stem pointing toward the west, and the power of the west is invoked, then the powers of the north, east, and south, as prayers are said to all the sacred powers of the universe. A portion of these prayers, as reported by Black Elk, says:

> We shall burn the sweet grass as an offering to *Wakan-Tanka,* and the fragrance of this will spread throughout heaven and earth; it will make the four-leggeds, the wingeds, the star peoples of the heavens, and all things as relatives. From you, O Grandmother earth, who are lowly, and who support us as does a mother, this fragrance will go forth; may its power be felt

characteristic of sacred space, differentiating it from other "profane" space, is that it is founded around a center where manifestations of the sacred powers are experienced. The Achilpa of Australia are nomadic gatherers and small game hunters who move about from place to place. They believe that when Numbakula created the world and the ancestors, he lived with them for a while to establish their way of life. Then he made a sacred pole, anointed it with blood, and climbed it to disappear in the sky. The Achilpa have kept the pole as their most sacred possession, using it to direct their movements from one place to the next. At their new camp, they set it up once again so they can again live in a meaningful world of sacred space. The pole is the center point of their world, the *axis mundi,* through which they can communicate with Numbakula in the sky. It is reported that once, when the sacred pole was broken, they were extremely disturbed, wandered about aimlessly, and lay down on the ground to await the death they thought was to come.[31] Without this center, their sacred world had become chaos again.

Another element in sacred space is the sense that the small space is a microcosm of the entire sacred world (the throughout the universe, and may it purify the feet and hands of the two-leggeds, that they may walk forward upon the sacred earth, raising their heads to *Wakan-Tanka!* [33]

In the small confines of the sweat lodge, this small world is felt to be one with the sacred universe.

Morality and the Ancestors   There are many spiritual agents in the world that can cause suffering and evil. Even the supreme god sends natural calamities, destruction, and death. But at the bottom of it all, it is humans who initiate evil happenings, out of greed, ignorance, or vengeance on someone else. It is humans who use the spiritual powers toward bad ends. On the other hand, it is the responsibility of humans to maintain order and peace in the family and the community, and this is promoted by right, harmonious relationship with the spiritual powers. So morality is really human-centered, though it has links to the sacred powers, to the ancestors, and to nature.

Of course, the ultimate sanction for morality resides in sacred authority, and this is generally conceived in a hierarchical pattern. The supreme god or gods have ultimate authority over all morality, executing justice with impartiality, and when punishment for evil comes from this divine source, nothing can be done to change it. However, the supreme gods or sacred powers or culture heroes generally do not interfere in the ordinary life of the people; here morality is governed by the family ancestors and the family and community elders.

The standards of morality governing offenses generally are not absolute and universal but are *situational,* related to the results of the action. It is not actions in themselves that are considered good or evil, but the beneficial or damaging results that flow from them. A sin committed in secret does damage to no one and therefore is not "evil," for example, but if that action becomes public and results in shame and retribution, then it is evil. There are, of course, many laws, rules, customs, set forms of behaviors, and prohibitions that constitute the moral code of any given community, and often these are thought to be ordained in the events of the Time of the Beginnings. Breaching this code constitutes a threat to the established order and to the welfare of the community, and thus it must be punished in some way.

So what is the good life? It is to recognize one's place in the order of things, in family and community, and to live according to the traditions that promote the welfare of all.

It means to honor the ancestors, consult them about important decisions, and not offend them. It means to worship the gods and spirits and to see to it that the important rituals and festivals are observed. The moral code obliges each person to avoid anything that upsets the sacred balances and causes harm to family and community, and on the other hand to work at mediating and reconciling whenever there is division within the community.

All of this calls for ethical reflection, for even in an indigenous tribal community there are constantly changing patterns of relationship and obligation, and situational decisions have to be made. Such ethical decisions come about through consensus, for the most part, arrived at through a complex web of consultation and advice, through elders, priests, headmen, diviners, friends, relatives, and especially the ancestors.

Responsibility for Society and the World   Almost by definition "tribal" societies are family- and clan-centered, and individuals find their highest good in promoting the welfare of their immediate group. This does not mean that indigenous peoples have no sense of a greater human environment in nature and in society. First of all, most origin myths recognize that all other humans were created along with the tribal ancestors, and so there is a notion of common humanity even across tribal lines.

Further, responsibility for the environment of nature is keenly felt by indigenous peoples. There is an ecological balance, created by the sacred powers of the beginning. Human life can be sustained only within the larger womb of the natural environment. And it is particularly the human responsibility—since humans know the myths and rituals that renew power—to ensure the continuance of nature's life and harmony. The good life means living in communication and peace with all the "peoples" of the earth—the animal, bird, plant, and other peoples. Perhaps this sense of responsibility toward the whole environment can be caught in the words of Smohalla, a holy man from the Wanapum tribe in the present-day state of Washington. He led a Native revival movement called the Dreamers in the second part of the nineteenth century, resisting attempts by government authorities to make his people become homesteaders.

[God] commanded that the lands and fisheries should be common to all who lived upon them. That they were never to be marked off or divided, but that the people should enjoy the fruits that God planted in the land and the animals that lived upon it, and the fishes in the water. God said he was the father, and the earth was the mother of mankind; that nature was the law; that the animals and fish and plants obeyed nature, and that man only was sinful. This is the old law. . . .

It is a bad word that comes from Washington. It is not a good law that would take my people away from me to make them sin against the laws of God. You ask me to plow the ground! Shall I take a knife and tear my mother's bosom? Then when I die she will not take me into her bosom to rest.

You ask me to dig for stone! Shall I dig under her skin for her bones? Then when I die I can not enter her body to be born again.

You ask me to cut grass and make hay and sell it, and be rich like white men, but how dare I cut off my mother's hair?

It is a bad law, and my people can not obey it. I want my people to stay with me here. All the dead men will come to life again; their spirits will come to their bodies again. We must wait here, in the homes of our fathers, and be ready to meet them in the bosom of our mother.[34]

Many tribal societies have traditions of warfare, for the preservation and continuation of one's own people is of paramount importance. And in situations of limited space and resources, there necessarily will come conflict with other tribes and the need to preserve one's people through warfare. But most tribal societies, in emphasizing loyalty and bravery, do not inculcate violence and aggressiveness toward other humans. There is a contentment to live according to the patterns and level of life inherited from the ancestors, without the drive of modern westernized people to make "progress" and achieve ever greater wealth and luxuries.

In the modern world, as peoples of indigenous tribal heritage have become aware of the international dimension of human life today, some of them have drawn from their own traditions to offer hope and encouragement to their own people and to the others in the world willing to listen to them. Lame Deer, a modern-day holy man of the Sioux, tells how White Buffalo Woman gave the sacred pipe to her people, the pipe that contains the whole universe, that binds all, even enemies, together in peace. Lame Deer looks to the day when those sacred pipes will again be used in purification and prayer, for peace in the whole world:

We Indians hold the pipe of peace, but the white man's religious book speaks of war, and we have stood by while the white man supposedly improved the world. Now we Indians must show how to live with our brothers, not use them, kill them or maim them. With the pipe, which is a living part of us, we shall be praying for peace, peace in Vietnam and in our own country. We Indians say "our country" because it is still ours even if all other races are now in physical possession of it, for land does not belong to any single man but to all people and to the future generations.

We must try to use the pipe for mankind, which is on the road to self-destruction. We must try to get back on the red road of the pipe, the road of life. We must try to save the white man from himself. This can be done only if all of us, Indians and non-Indians alike, can again see ourselves as part of this earth, not as an enemy from the outside who tries to impose its will on it. Because we, who know the meaning of the pipe, also know that, being a living part of the earth, we cannot harm any part of her without hurting ourselves. Maybe through this sacred pipe we can teach each other again to see through that cloud of pollution which politicians, industrialists and technical experts hold up to us as "reality." Through this pipe, maybe, we can make peace with our greatest enemy who dwells deep within ourselves. With this pipe we could all form again the circle without end.[35]

Perhaps the message that indigenous peoples have for the rest of today's world will prove more important than has generally been thought.

Modern Transformations of Indigenous Societies

The modern century has brought great stress and change to the indigenous peoples of the world, to the extent that for many of them the traditional way of life is a thing of the past. Education into Western ways, exploitation and suppression, being uprooted from their sacred lands and forced to live in urban areas, conversion to one of the world religions—these factors and others have caused the religious vision of indigenous peoples to fade along with the way of life that supported it, bringing about a profound identity crisis for these peoples.

But there is still a vitality among the traditional religions, as shown by certain creative responses to European encroachment and modernization. Even the story of Hainuwele (pp. 34–36), though it echoes from the past, responds to modern civilization. For what makes Hainuwele's powers so special that the people conspire to kill her is that she is able to produce fabulous *foreign* items—knives, earrings, bells. In fact, one modern scholar has argued that the real point of the Hainuwele story as recorded in 1937 was to respond to Western colonization, which had suppressed tradition and imposed taxes. This disrupted the traditional system of values based on equivalence, where prestige depends on giving and receiving in equal proportion. So the story deals with this incongruity in traditional terms, through killing and cannibalism.[36] Even if this interpretation is accepted, the modern version of the story certainly has deep roots in Wemale tradition, and it is an example of the vitality that oral stories have in meeting current issues through traditional modes of thought.

Of course, groups of archaic, indigenous peoples do still exist in the world today, protected from outside forces of modernization either by governments or by remote location. The numbers of these peoples, however, have shrunk rapidly and will continue to shrink; probably most of these peoples eventually will disappear. But that does not mean the end of their religious visions. Among the traditional religious groups that have responded in vital, creative ways to the challenge of the modern secular world, two important directions of response can be seen. One response is to graft elements of Western culture and religion onto the traditional base and thus create new religious movements. The other response is to reaffirm the traditional identity and vision as an authentic and viable posture even within the modern world.

Religions of the Oppressed: Blending of the New and the Old   One particular response of the indigenous peoples of Melanesia to the invasion of modern Western forces was the development of **Cargo Cults.** During the twentieth century, these societies were forced out of the Neolithic period directly into the world of great cargo ships, cash, radios, beer, and all the rest, as Australian and Dutch colonizers, and American troops during World War II, arrived with their bizarre new culture. A significant response to this was a series of millenarian movements, looking for a new age in which the ancestors from the other world would come on great white ships laden with cash and goods of the Western world. The arrival of ships from the white world evoked memories of their own traditions about the ancestors living in the land of the dead across the sea, returning annually to visit at the end of the harvest season. These modern ships were really gifts from the ances-

tors that had been stolen by the whites; but now the ancestors would liberate them and a great age of prosperity would begin. After seeing airplanes land for the first time, the natives of the highlands of New Guinea began to anticipate the arrival of their ancestors in an airplane laden with gifts. In some places they even cleared an area for the planes to land and built storehouses to store the food.

The Cargo Cults could not survive, of course, though they kept surfacing off and on into the 1950s. Prophet after prophet would arise in different parts of Melanesia and fan the hopes of liberation and prosperity, but the revival would end in disappointment and despair. These movements symbolize the wrenching of traditional societies forced into the modern world of exploitation and cash, and they also show how people respond to new situations by drawing on their own spiritual resources.

Native Americans, devastated by the advance of white people through their sacred lands and by their forced moves to reservations, produced a series of prophetic leaders in the late eighteenth and nineteenth centuries. For example, in 1799 Handsome Lake received new revelations and founded a movement that spread widely among the Iroquois, combining the traditional belief in the Great Spirit with the beliefs of the Christian Quakers, among whom Handsome Lake had been raised.

But the crisis in Native American identity boiled over toward the end of the nineteenth century, and starting around 1870 a series of antiwhite, Native revival movements swept the West and the Plains areas. The best known of these was the **Ghost Dance** movement, which reached a climax with the Sioux uprising and the tragic massacre by the U.S. Army of several hundred men, women, and children at Wounded Knee in 1890. One of the leaders of the Ghost Dance movement was a prophetic figure called Wovoka, preaching something new in the Native American vision: the cataclysmic end of this world age and the creation of a new age in which Native American culture and religion would be restored. All whites would be carried away by high winds, leaving their possessions to the Native Americans. The ancestors would return from the dead, the buffalo herds would be restored, and sickness and death would be eliminated.

In his visions, Wovoka was told by God that the people should work hard, love one another, and live in peace with the whites. They should replace their old rituals with the Ghost Dance, a ritual of collective exaltation and trance.

The dance would usually last four or five days, with people painting their bodies and wearing a decorated white garment called the Ghost Shirt. The men and women would arrange themselves in concentric circles, the arms of each resting on the shoulders of both neighbors, and in the vibrant rhythms of the dance they would sing laments for the dead and raise their arms to the Great Spirit. In ecstatic trance they would call out, "Father, I come! Mother, I come! Brother, I come! Father, give me arrows!,"[37] and fall on the ground unconscious in exhaustion, only to revive and continue. The Ghost Dance movement was in part protest and challenge to white oppression, in part apocalyptic vision taken over from Christianity, and in part a revival of tradition and identity. It spread through all the tribes of the Plains and the West; only the Navajo were not drawn into this Native revival. But with the Sioux tragedy at Wounded Knee and deteriorating conditions everywhere, active agitation for liberation and restoration could not be sustained.

Some of the Ghost Dance energy and vision was channeled into the rise of another movement, the **peyote religion,** which reflects the desire of Native Americans to retain their own religious roots even while being assimilated into modern white society. Spreading rapidly through most tribes, this movement was incorporated in 1918 and, in spite of legal harassments over the use of peyote in early years, continues to be influential today as the Native American Church. The leaders follow a course of peaceful coexistence with white people and have adopted many elements from Christianity while reasserting Native American values and traditions. For example, God the Father is the Great Spirit, Jesus is the Guardian Spirit of the Natives, and the Holy Spirit is enveloped in the peyote. Many Native traditions are maintained, centering on visions, spirits, and healing. The peyote cactus button, with its quality of producing visual and auditory hallucinations, had earlier been used ritually for healing, but in the Native American Church it becomes a communal sacrament eaten in a nighttime ceremony complete with prayers, drums, and visions. The movement follows a strict code of morality, and it offers to some Native Americans a religion that maintains their traditional identity within a modern setting.

The continuing exploitations of Africans by Western nations and industrialists beginning with the slave trade, the advance of modern education and urban industry, and the missionary growth of Christianity and Islam have combined to fracture drastically and in many cases destroy the traditional African societies and their way of life. One response has been new religious movements that combine Christianity (or Islam) with native African ideas and practices. An example from outside Africa is Haiti, where the slaves brought from Africa retained many of their traditions. Today many Haitians still practice Voodoo (Vodou), consisting of various beliefs and rituals of African origin under a veneer of Christianity. In Muslim parts of Africa, the people often retain most of their traditions and practices while adopting Islam. And many Christianized Africans have broken away from the mainline mission church bodies to join separatist or independent churches that have revived traditional African practices. In general, these groups emphasize freedom from white control, possession by the Holy Spirit, experience of visions and dreams, and healing.

As an example of the many movements that mix Christian and traditional practices, consider the **Zionist churches** of South Africa. These are prophetic and healing churches that draw on biblical notions of Zion as the realm of salvation and actualize that salvation in very concrete, African form. This Christian-African movement provides a community identity for uprooted and oppressed people. Zionists sing hymns and chants with melodies from the Bantu and Zulu traditions, practice washing of feet, and focus attention on healing. Worshipers come forward to be vigorously shaken and stroked to expel demons from the body and bring wellness. Many rules govern life, especially prohibitions against eating pork or taking European medicines.

Many of the independent churches were founded by charismatic prophets who received new revelations, and among them the Zulu prophet Isaiah Shembe (1870–1935) stands out. Influenced by Christian ideas in his youth, he received a series of remarkable visions through lightning and thunder, and in obedience he gave up his wives and became a wandering prophet and faith-healer, eventually ordained in the African Native Baptist Church. Shembe went about as a kind of Zulu diviner-seer, inspired by the Spirit, preaching, healing, and casting out evil spirits. Convinced that keeping the Sabbath rather than Sunday as the holy day was an essential divine commandment, in 1911 he founded his own church, the Nazareth Baptist Church. Shembe drew many other practices from Old Testament law and ritual, such as refraining from eating pork, not cutting his hair, and removing shoes when worshiping. He also drew on many Zulu customs that had parallels with Old Testament practices, such as circumcision, polygamy, and dancing in spiritual ecstasy. Responding to a revelation from Jehova (as he called God), Shembe founded a mountain religious center called Ekuphakameni ("High Place"), where heaven has come down to earth and the presence of Jehova is felt. The strength of the Nazarite movement has been in linking biblical ideas and practices together with traditional Zulu customs—holy places in Zululand to go to for festivals, rituals with the people arrayed in traditional Zulu dress, hymns and melodies that echo traditional Zulu songs, and Shembe himself considered as a new Moses and Jesus for the Zulu nation in his role as prophet and healer. Today Nazarites still find meaning in the story of Isaiah Shembe, the servant sent by God to the Zulu nation.

Revival of Traditional Religious Identity   The traditional religions of indigenous peoples of today have faded largely because these peoples have suddenly been forced to become modernized, and these revivalistic movements have attempted to combine the two factors of tradition and westernization, creating something new in the process. Another sort of response, still small and uncertain but potentially powerful, is the attempt to recover the authentic traditional identity in its wholeness and integrity and live it in a viable way in the modern world. So there are groups today in many of the North American tribes who are taking a new pride in their tradition, seeking to restore the rituals and ceremonies and to live by the spiritual disciplines of their heritage. Some Plains Native Americans, for example, have renewed the ritual of sweat lodge purification and go on vision quests, and some tribes cooperate in staging the great Sun Dance each year. A common native spirituality and identity is being forged among some Native Americans, drawing on traditional perspectives and practices that cut across tribal boundaries.

Among the Australian Aborigines there is also an upsurge of interest in their unique heritage and in their religious linkage to their traditional land, with some success in creating a common sense of identity among Aborigines and Torres Strait Islanders. Polynesians and Melanesians are taking renewed interest and pride in their specific cultural heritages and in their common "Pacific Way." And modern Africans and African-Americans have for some time been experimenting with ways to retrieve their rich spiritual heritage as a resource for life in today's changing world. What will come of these new movements and revivals is difficult to predict, but the story of religion in our world today will be enlivened by the new adventures of these fellow humans who are renewing their traditional religious heritage.

Discussion Questions

1   What are some basic characteristics of the myths of indigenous peoples? In what sense can we say that myths tell what is *really* the truth?

2   What does the myth about Hainuwele reveal to the Wemale about their existence?

3   If they believe in a supreme god, why do indigenous peoples often find greater significance in gods of the atmosphere and the earth?

4   What perspective on sacred reality is denoted by the terms *mana* and *tabu*?

5   Why do indigenous peoples generally not place great emphasis on a better state of life after death? Do they have any ideas of "transformation" or "salvation"?

6   What connections are there between the healing of an individual and the wholeness of the community?

7   In what sense is the vision quest a path of transformation?

8   What does it mean to say sacred time is "reversible"? Contrast this with modern secular conceptions of time.

9   Interpret the religious significance of the breaking down of social structure, mass sexual activity, and human sacrifice in New Year rituals.

10   What elements of "death" and "rebirth" are there in the Ndembu boys' initiation rituals?

11   How are religion and art united in Navajo sandpainting? Why is the painting destroyed in the process of the ritual?

12   In ideas about the moral life among indigenous peoples, why is the role of the ancestors particularly important?

13   What are two directions of response to modern Western civilization among traditional indigenous peoples? Which do you think will prove more effective?

PART TWO

Religions Arising in the Mediterranean World

INTRODUCTION

The three closely related religious groups that look to Abraham as ancestor—Jews, Christians, and Muslims—grew up in the eastern Mediterranean world before spreading throughout the globe. They were deeply influenced by the many great civilizations present in this world from ancient times on, such as ancient Egypt, Mesopotamia, Greece, Rome, Persia, and others. Most of these religions and cultures eventually disappeared, although the ancient Persian religion taught by the prophet Zarathustra survives today in small communities of Zoroastrians in Iran and Parsis in India. While our focus will be on understanding the religious paths followed by Jews, Christians, and Muslims, we will look more briefly at the ancient religions of Egypt, Mesopotamia, and Greece, as well as the religious path of the Zoroastrians.

From the Bronze Age onward, the dominant cultures of the ancient Mediterranean world, in Egypt, Mesopotamia, and Greece, were city–state cultures, and their religious systems reflected their social and political orders. Typically they featured a cosmic type of religion, with a pantheon of gods who controlled the various functions of nature and society. Sacred kingship reflected the divine order itself. And highly developed worship and ritual were led by priests and priestesses, revolving around temples, festivals, oracles and revelation from the gods, wisdom concerning the good life, and rituals to prepare for the afterlife. Thinkers in these cultures did considerable speculation about the gods and the role of humans, and that wisdom was often expressed in stories, proverbs, prayers, and poems.

The Zoroastrian religion and the religion of ancient Israel, and later, Judaism, Christianity, and Islam, developed in this cultural milieu, absorbing many of its features and transforming others. The ancient Persians were Indo-Europeans (like the Aryans who settled in India), and Zoroastrianism arose as a reform movement within Persia. Zarathustra taught ideas about a supreme God and prophetic revelation. Zoroastrians perceived a cosmic struggle between good and evil forces, with ideas about ethical life, the judgment of the soul, resurrection of all from the dead, a final cosmic battle, and the restoration of the world. They developed a rich religious life, with scriptures, priests, fire rituals, and more.

Judaism, Christianity, and Islam are clearly a closely related group of religions, sometimes called the "families of Abraham." To mention Abraham is to set our discussion in a certain historical and cultural context related to the Abraham who is mentioned in the sacred writings of all three religions. Abraham presumably lived around 2000 B.C.E. in Syria and Palestine, representing one of the numerous bedouin clans of the semidesert regions. In what sense could such a legendary character be a unifying figure for religions as separate in time and place as Judaism, Christianity, and Islam?

The common relationship of these three religious traditions is two-fold, both an historical-cultural continuity and a religious relationship. In the sacred history, Abraham is understood to be the ancestor of the Hebrews who escaped from Egypt and constituted themselves as the people of Israel. Judaism, rising from the roots of Israel after the Babylonian exile, continues the line of Abraham. Christianity, though it arose two thousand years after Abraham, grew out of the stock of Judaism, as Jesus himself and all his early followers were Jews. Even though Christianity rapidly spread to non-Jews throughout the Roman world—so that Christians, of course, can no longer claim to be physical descendants of Abraham—they represent a continuation of the history and culture of the Hebrews. Their way of thinking and their outlook on the world were highly influenced and shaped by the tradition of Judaism. Islam arose six hundred years after Christianity. Yet the bedouin/Semitic culture of Arabia was related in a general way to that culture represented by the Jewish people. Further, Muhammad and his companions were strongly influenced by the history and culture both of the Jews and the Christians through their sacred writings and their presence in Mecca and Medina.

Thus in terms of historical traditions and cultural continuities, it might be said that Christianity grew out of Judaism, and Islam grew out of both Judaism and Christianity. Without Judaism there would not have been either a Christianity or an Islam. And laying aside the question of how the earlier religions influenced and shaped the later ones, a general unity of culture can be postulated in the Semitic tradition of the Syro-Palestino-Arabian area during the formation of these three religions. They do make up one family of religions, based on a continuity of historical and cultural traditions.

But even apart from considerations of history and culture, each of the three religions looks to Abraham as a special ancestor in a religious way. For Jews to call Abraham "our father" is to repeat the biblical assertions that God, seeking to carry out the divine will for the world, called Abraham and Sarah and covenanted with them, promising that their descendants would be great and would bring a blessing to the world. The covenant of God with Israel that forms the basis of the Jewish religion was seen as the fulfillment of the promises made to Abraham and Sarah. Similarly, the Christian scriptures call Abraham "our father," making it clear that this fatherhood is not "according to the flesh" by natural descent, but "according to the spirit"; God's promise to Abraham and Sarah and God's plan for the world are being

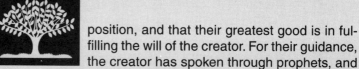

carried on by the followers of Jesus the Christ. The Muslim scriptures also look to Abraham as one of the great prophets of God, and further believe that Abraham and Hagar are the father and mother of all faithful Muslims. Tradition holds that the Meccans are descendants of Abraham and Hagar through their son Ishmael, and that Abraham even built the great shrine in Mecca, the Ka'bah. Thus the religious experience of Jews, Christians, and Muslims can be expressed in a symbolic way by pointing to the relationship with ancestors Abraham and Sarah/Hagar.

But what is that common vision that can be appealed to by reference to the common ancestors? One of the most central ideas, shared to some extent with Zoroastrianism, is the insistence on *monotheism.* There is one God, the creator of all that exists. In rejecting all forms of polytheism or plurality of gods that control this world, these religions share a common vision both of God and of the world. God is the almighty creator, for no other divine power controls any aspect of the created world. But God is also *transcendent,* beyond creation, not a part of it. Thus the perspective of monism or nondualism is also rejected: Everything is not God; the world is not divine but the good creation of God. At the same time, God is *personal,* acting in relation to humans as a partner working through people and events in love and compassion to carry out the sacred design for the world.

These religions share the common view that this world is God's good creation, though Zoroastrians suggest a pervading presence of evil powers within the creation. All agree that humans are given a high position, and that their greatest good is in fulfilling the will of the creator. For their guidance, the creator has spoken through prophets, and that revelation has been written down as holy scripture, providing the truth that is necessary for humans to live as God intends for them. This revelation is not in the form of timeless myths or secret knowledge, but it is based on God's own actions in human history, and it guides humans in how they are to live in obedience.

These religions share a vision of human history moving in a linear fashion from a creation at the beginning to an end of history when God will bring the divine design to completion. Involved in that end of history is God's evaluation in judgment and the appropriate reward or punishment in the life of the world to come. Thus in contrast to some of the other religions of the world, Zoroastrians, Jews, Christians, and Muslims share a sense of movement toward the future, when God's design will be completed and creation will be brought to its fulfillment.

Zoroastrians, Jews, Christians, and Muslims will read the previous paragraphs about the common vision they all share and say, "Yes, but there is more. . . ." And there *is* more to each religion's vision of the world, more distinctive and vital assertions and commitments. To sketch out the common vision shared by these religions is only to set the stage, the general plan onto which each weaves its own characteristic experiences and understandings of God and human existence. In the following chapters we attend to the various facets of the worldview of each of these religions, starting with their roots in the religions of the ancient Mediterranean world.

Religions of Ancient Egypt, Mesopotamia, and Greece

ANCIENT EGYPTIAN RELIGION

For three millennia, from the first dynasty around 3100 B.C.E. to the first centuries of the Common Era, when Egypt converted to Christianity, the rich and diverse elements of Egyptian religion were practiced. With settled agricultural life in tune with the regular inundations of the Nile River, the Egyptians developed city-states, each with its own religious traditions. During much of their history these city-states were unified under a succession of dynasties. The tradition of **divine kingship**—in which the human social order centered on the king is seen as a reflection of the divine cosmic order—had already begun when King Narmer (Menes) united the Two Lands (upper and lower Egypt) around 3100 B.C.E., founding the capital Memphis with its temple to the god Ptah. Ancient Egypt remained remarkably stable through the Early Dynasties (3100–2700) and the Old Kingdom (2700–2200). The building of the great pyramids reflected the continuing potency of divine kingship. Toward the end of the Old Kingdom, society started to become more open, and people not of the royal family could rise to high office and share in the afterlife.

A time of chaos, the First Intermediate Period (2200–2050 B.C.E.), ensued, and then Egypt was reunited with its capital at Thebes during the Middle Kingdom period (2050–1800). After a time of foreign rule of much of the delta by warrior rulers from Asia called Hyksos, Egyptian rule expanded in the New Kingdom period (1570–1165), with Thutmose I (ca. 1509–1497) leading expeditions as far as Syria. Ramses I of the Nineteenth Dynasty was a particularly significant king in the history of Egyptian religion; in his time there was widespread growth of temples and royal tombs containing texts about the afterlife and paintings of judgment scenes. Finally Egyptian power and influence faded with the Persian conquest in the sixth century and the triumphs of Alexander the Great in the fourth century B.C.E.

Cosmic Harmony and Human Existence

Extending through this long cultural history, Egyptian religion is a vast panorama of cosmic integration. The whole world of nature is seen to be filled with sacred power in the form of gods and goddesses, with an overarching sense of order and rightness (**maat**), all forces working together harmoniously through the mediation of the king and priests.

The gods and goddesses of ancient Egypt were very numerous, and with the amalgamation of city-states different gods were identified with one another or took over one another's functions. One system of myths puts forth an original group of nine gods (the **Ennead**, revered especially at Heliopolis). Atum, the creator, rose from the primal ocean and, perched on the primeval hillock, created Shu, god of air, and Tefnut, goddess of moisture. They produced Geb, the earth god, and Nut, the sky goddess, who in turn became parents of Osiris and Isis, forces of life and regeneration. Further, Geb and Nut produced Set, the destroyer of life, and Nephthys, a protector of the dead. Osiris and Isis, for their part, became the parents of Horus, with whom the human kings of Egypt are identified in their divine status.

There were a number of cosmogonic myths in ancient Egypt, and the different perspectives often merged or influenced one another. One important mythological system, at home especially in ancient Hermopolis, tells how Ptah, god of Memphis, sprang forth from primeval chaos that was represented by four pairs of gods: Amun and Amaunet (hiddenness), Kuk and Kauket (darkness), Huh and Hauhet (formlessness), and Nun and Naunet (watery abyss). Ptah, arising from these divine forces of chaos, conceived the creator god Atum in his heart and brought him forth on his tongue by speaking his name.

Throughout most of Egyptian history there was a notion of the supreme god associated with the sun, called Atum, Re, Amun, or a combination of these names, as city-states fused their myths. For one brief period, under **Akhenaton** (r. ca. 1360–1344 B.C.E.), the "heretic" king, a form of monotheism was established by royal decree: Only Aton, the **sun-god,** was to be worshiped as king of the entire world, embodying all the attributes of the other gods. This policy ended with the death of Akhenaton, but it shows the tendency in Egyptian religion to fuse the gods and elevate the sun-god to supremacy.

What is the real nature of the world and of humans? In picturing the structure of the cosmos, ancient Egyptians generally thought of the goddess Nut stretched out, her body spanning the heavens from east to west. Sometimes the sky was thought of as a giant cow goddess (Hathor) whose four legs are supported by four gods, while other gods (stars) sail on small boats on her belly. The sun-god is thought to be born from the goddess Nut, crossing her body during the day. But the sun is swallowed by her at night, passing through her body to be born anew in the morning, dispelling the darkness of chaos once again in the dependable rhythm of nature.

In ancient Egyptian thinking, humans are created in the image of the gods. It is said they were generated from the weeping of Re's eye, or they were conceived in Ptah's heart and spoken by his tongue, or they were made on the divine potter's wheel. Humans can enjoy success and happiness in this life, as a gift of the gods; yet death inevitably comes, when the soul *(ba)* leaves the body and must journey through the underworld. The *ba* was sometimes represented in burial scenes as a small bird, leaving the body and flying up to the sky. The Egyptians' view of the afterlife was rather complex. In addition to the *ba* soul, it was thought that at a person's birth the gods fashioned a body-replica, the *ka,* which is reunited at death to live on in the tomb. In addition, the Egyptians were concerned about the human personality or spirit, the *akh,* that personal identity which remains apart from the body after death. With all these concerns, ancient

Ancient Egyptian tablet with hieroglyphic writing depicts Queen Nefertiti and King Akhenaton making offerings to the sun god Aton. Photographic Services, The Metropolitan Museum of Art.

Egyptians felt it was important to give attention to preparing for the afterlife and preserving their bodies to live on, and there were many religious rituals, spells, and other preparations to ensure their well-being after death.

So the path of transformation, including the worship of the gods and other duties of life, focused especially on the afterlife. In earliest times, the idea of continued life after death seems to have been reserved for the royal family and gradually extended to other nobility. But eventually all Egyptians became fascinated with the cult of the dead, as various ideas from early cults merged together. Especially important was the cult of **Osiris,** permeating much of Egyptian history and culture. Osiris, as the god of the Nile, embodies the powers of death and resurrection. An important myth tells how he, as king of Egypt in a golden age, civilized the Egyptians and taught them to cultivate grains and worship the gods. But his envious brother Seth murdered him and scattered his body all over Egypt. His sorrowing queen Isis recovered the parts of his body and revived him sufficiently to conceive a son, Horus, by him. Horus waged a fierce war against Seth and ultimately reigned as king over Egypt, while Osiris became the lord of the underworld, the one who bestows immortality. Kings, when they died, would be identified with Osiris, while the new king would rule as the divine Horus.

The cult of Osiris grew dramatically during the Middle and New Kingdom eras. Even the common people could participate, hoping for a blessed afterlife. The soul, they believed, entered the underworld through a series of gates for which special passwords were needed. In the hall of judgment the deceased needed to recite a lengthy negative confession, and the heart was weighed on a great set of scales. Those passing the test would be led before the throne of Osiris, who allowed them to enter the hall of the blessed.

Ritual and Ethical Life

A key to Egyptian society was the divine king. Identified with Horus, in this life he was thought to be a "good god," to become a "great god" in the afterlife. He is the mediator between the realm of the gods and the human realm, acting as the high priest in carrying out the essential rituals to keep the world functioning. He is the one who causes *maat* (justice) to continue on earth. Maat was a goddess, daughter of Re, symbol of truth, justice, and order in the cosmos and in society. She was personified especially in the king and in the king's rule.

In addition to the king, there were many priests and priestesses—a high percentage of the population—to assist the king in worshiping the gods. Among them were high priests, temple scribes to interpret omens and dreams, even common people as helpers, servers, porters, watchmen, and attendants. Women shared in these ritual responsibilities, sometimes as priestesses of the gods, singers, musicians, and mourners.

Worship at the great temples was very elaborate and required many functionaries, aiming to maintain the world order by strengthening the gods. The temple was considered the mansion of the god, with the statue of the god kept in an innermost chamber, and daily rituals at the temple included washing and clothing the god and making meal offerings. At festival times the god would be taken out of the temple and carried in procession for all to see. Other important rituals were those associated with the cult of the dead, including prayers, incantations, and rituals of the "opening of the mouth," to bring life back into mummies and other representations of people.

The culture of Egypt attained a high state of development in religious ideas and also in artistic expression. A vast array of art forms flowered, including sculptures, reliefs, paintings, temple architecture, amulets, stelae (inscription stones), jewelry, and much more. And in their religious interests the ancient Egyptians created a vast literature. Since they developed hieroglyphic writing at an early period, important sacred texts were written on temple and tomb walls as well as on papyrus. Their very large sacred literature included mythological texts, guides for the dead, prayers, hymns, formulas for spells and omens, ritual directions, lists of kings, and philosophical wisdom texts.

Many texts lay out a pious, moral vision of how to live the good life; passing successfully to the next world requires making a "negative confession" before Osiris's tribunal, vouching for the good life one has lived. The ideal life is to uphold *maat,* justice and order, and thus live happily in this life. But always the reality of death is present. A fine literary composition gives a dialogue between a man and his soul about the man's wish to commit suicide. The soul can give no satisfactory argument against it, although it tries to persuade him to forget his cares and seek sensual enjoyment. Over against the unrewarding and weary life of seeking pleasure and facing the evils of society, death can be contemplated as a blessed release, as the man argues:

> Death is in my sight today
> (Like) the recovery of a sick man,
> Like going out into the open after a confinement. . . .
> Death is in my sight today
> Like the longing of a man to see his house (again),
> After he has spent many years held in captivity.[1]

Not all Egyptian thought is that pessimistic, but this dialogue shows the depth in which ancient Egyptians reflected on the questions of life and death. The wisdom of Egypt influenced the Israelite religion as well as Greek philosophers.

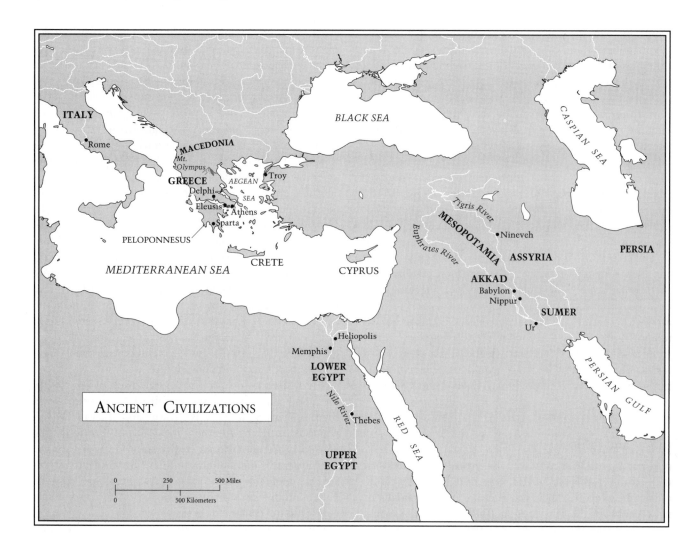

ANCIENT CIVILIZATIONS

RELIGION IN ANCIENT MESOPOTAMIA

Civilization in ancient Mesopotamia (roughly the territory of present-day Iraq) developed at about the same time as in Egypt, starting around the middle of the fourth millennium B.C.E. First the Sumerians created a great empire made up of city-states like Eridu, Ur, and Uruk, based in the delta of the Tigris and Euphrates rivers. The ancient Sumerians were creative people, inventing things like cuneiform writing, the potter's wheel, and ox-drawn plows. Eventually, around 2300 B.C.E., Sargon of Akkad, an area of Semitic peoples north of Sumeria, established rule over the area. By

around 1800, most of the area was unified as the Babylonian Empire, though other invaders ruled from time to time, including the Hittites and the Kassites. Starting in about the tenth century B.C.E. came the rise of the Assyrians in northern Mesopotamia to become a great empire. After a brief Babylonian revival in the sixth century, traditional Mesopotamian civilization and religion began to fade when the Persians took over around 540 B.C.E.

Despite these shifts, Mesopotamian religion remained remarkably constant in the interplay between Sumerian and Semitic cultural traditions. The whole area was dependent on agriculture, with irrigation already being used in ancient times, and the society was centered on a number of city-states. Cuneiform writing was invented by the Sumerians around 3500 B.C.E., and a large sacred literature of myths, ritual directions, prayers, hymns, and wisdom texts developed, first in Sumerian and then in Akkadian (the Semitic language of Babylon). Fortunately, a goodly number of these texts, written on clay tablets, have been discovered in the ruins of ancient libraries.

Cosmic State and Human Service

In contrast to Egypt, with its regular rhythms of Nile River inundations, life in ancient Mesopotamia was more unpredictable, with droughts and floods and invasions of peoples from the surrounding plateaus, and perhaps for that reason the religion of Mesopotamia is less trusting of the cosmic order. Order and fertility are not given through the regular operation of sacred powers, but they continually need to be achieved by integrating and harmonizing the many powerful sacred beings. The universe is rather like a **cosmic state,** with a hierarchy of individual powers that are often in conflict and thus need to be controlled and integrated into a functioning cosmos.

These sacred powers are immanent within the forces of nature—sky, storm, sun, moon, waters, earth, and the rest; all these natural phenomena have within themselves a will and power. And all together make up the divine cosmic state, governed by the great gods of the universe. The leader of the divine assembly is the sky god Anu, father of the gods and the one who maintains order in the cosmos through his command. Other leading gods are Enlil, god of the storm, exercising force for the gods; Enki (Ea), god of earth-waters and of wisdom; Ninhursaga, the earth mother-goddess; the moon-god Nanna (Sin); the sun-god Utu (Shamash); and many more. The "Great List of the Gods" from Assurbanipal's library (ca. 650 B.C.E.) includes no fewer than two thousand names of gods! A widely popular goddess is Inanna (Ishtar), a sky goddess who functions as both the goddess of warfare and the goddess of love and fertility. The husband of Inanna is the fertility god Dumuzi (Tammuz), who dies and descends to the underworld, to be brought back to life in the spring. **Marduk,** the god of the city-state Babylon, reached supremacy among the Babylonians, ruling as king of the cosmos.

According to the Mesopotamian creation myths, the gods themselves arose out of divine chaos and shaped the cosmos from that chaos. The Babylonian version of the creation myth, called *Enuma Elish*, begins with the mingling together of sacred chaos, personified as the great dragons Tiamat (symbolizing the great salt waters) and Apsu (the sweet waters). From this chaotic mingling arise the gods—young, active, and boisterous. When Tiamat and Apsu try to kill their offspring, the gods rally and defeat Apsu and contain him as the underground waters. The gods choose the young hero Marduk (god of Babylon) as their champion, and Marduk enters into battle with Tiamat, kills her, splits her body in two, and from the two parts structures the whole cosmos. And to make the cosmos work and function, Marduk places the gods at their various stations, in the heavens and in the earth, to be immanent in the forces of nature.

Humans, according to the *Enuma Elish* and other texts, are created to be servants of the gods, to sacrifice to them and fulfill their needs. For the cosmic forces need to be maintained; otherwise conflict and disaster may erupt, as when the gods decided once to destroy humankind by sending a great flood. Humans long for immortality, like the gods, but finally they are limited and must accept their fate in the cosmos. These themes of human existence are summed up remarkably in the famous epic of Gilgamesh, legendary king of Uruk in Sumer. After great adventures with his heroic friend Enkidu, Gilgamesh rebuffs the amorous advances of the goddess Ishtar, and he and Enkidu kill the monstrous bull of heaven that Ishtar unleashes in her rage. And Enkidu further enrages Ishtar by flinging the bull's shank at the goddess—and is sentenced to death by the gods. After his friend's death, the despondent Gilgamesh starts on a search for immortality, traveling to the end of the earth to seek out the ancient Utnapishtim, who once won eternal life from the gods. Utnapishtim tells Gilgamesh how he received eternal life in ancient times when the gods rashly tried to destroy humankind through a great flood. The wise god Ea, knowing that the gods depended on humans for sacrifices, warned Utnapishtim to save his family and animals by building an ark, and the grateful gods conferred the gift of eternal life on him. Utnapishtim finally tells Gilgamesh where to find a plant of immortality, but as Gilgamesh pauses to bathe, a snake steals the plant and obtains immortality instead. Gilgamesh thus returns home, having learned reluctantly to accept his limitations as a mortal human.

So the path for humans is to serve the gods, determine their will through divination, and assist in maintaining cosmic order through rituals and festivals. These human

Sumerian statuettes from Tell Asmar, dating from ca. 3000–2500 B.C.E., depict gods, priests, and worshipers. The tallest figure represents the god Abu, lord of vegetation. Courtesy of the Oriental Institute Museum of the University of Chicago. Photo by Victor J. Boswell.

responsibilities rested especially on the king of the city-state, who was the special servant of the city-god and a vessel of sacred power. In important rituals, the king would play the part of the great god, and it was his rule that maintained order, fertility, and well-being for the people. One important ritual, for example, was the sacred marriage in which the king and a temple priestess would have sexual union, playing the parts of the fertility god and goddess so that the fertility of plants and animals would be restored. Many priests and priestesses assisted in the worship of the gods and the performance of the sacrifices, rituals, incantations, and divinations.

Ritual and Ethical Life

In Babylon the new year's festival, **Akitu,** was a particularly significant festival, lasting nearly two weeks with many important ritual events. On the fourth day of the festival, the epic of creation, *Enuma Elish*, was read, telling how the city-god Marduk defeated the dragon Tiamat and created the world. On the fifth day, the temple of Marduk was purified, and the king of Babylon was divested of his royal insignia and slapped by the priest; then he made a confession as he knelt before the statue of Marduk and was reinvested with his insignia. Gods from the other city-states (represented by their statues) arrived on the sixth day, and on the eighth day the king "took Marduk by the hand" and led him to the Shrine of Destinies, where Marduk was proclaimed king over the assembled gods. Then the king led Marduk and the gods in a great victory procession along the street to the River Euphrates, where they all boarded boats and proceeded to the Akitu house. There a great banquet of the gods took place, and perhaps there was also a reenactment of the battle between Marduk and Tiamat and a sacred marriage between Marduk and his spouse. On the eleventh day, the gods returned to Babylon and held a solemn assembly to fix the destinies of the land, and the new year's festival ended with another great banquet.

The ancient Mesopotamians did a lot of reflecting about the good and ethical life. A famous attempt to create a just society is found in the law-code promulgated by King Hammurabi of Babylon (fl. 1792–1750 B.C.E.) and inscribed on a stele. The preface to the code says that Hammurabi was called by the gods "to cause justice to prevail in the land, to destroy the wicked and the evil, that the strong might not oppress the weak."[2] Many prayers addressed to the gods, recorded on clay tablets, included confessions of sins and statements of repentance. Questions about why the gods sent suffering and death were discussed, as in the remarkable hymn called "I Will Praise the Lord of Wisdom." The author, like Job of the Hebrew Bible, is an official of high rank who, in spite of his piety, suffers misfortune and disease and raises questions about the moral governance of the world. "What is good in one's sight is evil for a god. What is bad in one's own mind is good for his god. Who can understand the counsel of the gods in the midst of heaven?"[3] There was no conception of reward in the gloomy world of the dead, so the good ethical life was focused entirely on the present existence, in serving the gods and maintaining justice and rightness in human society.

RELIGION IN ANCIENT GREECE

The peoples of classical Greece made tremendous contributions to the world in religion, philosophy, literature, politics, science, and art. The Greek peoples, like the Romans and other early Europeans, were heirs of the Indo-Europeans who migrated into Europe in the second millennium B.C.E., assimilating many of the traits of the indigenous peoples of the Aegean area. Living by agriculture, eventually the Greeks created various city-states, governed by kings, tyrants, powerful nobles, or democracies. Two city-states came to have special power, Athens and Sparta, and under Athenian leadership a brilliant classical period (ca. 500–338 B.C.E.) saw rich developments in art, philosophy, politics, and science. But the struggle between Athens and Sparta weakened the country, and in 338 B.C.E. Philip of Macedonia (north of Greece) gained rulership, followed by his son Alexander the Great. Alexander conquered far and wide in the eastern Mediterranean and the Near East, spreading Greek culture in an international form known as Hellenism. Finally, in the second century B.C.E., Greece was incorporated into the rising Roman Empire, and Hellenism continued to be a powerful cultural force for many centuries.

Worlds of Meaning in Ancient Greece

Although the Greeks did not have sacred scriptures as such, they did have a rich repertoire of myths (muthoi) about the gods, and these were passed on and added to by countless bards, singers, and poets, forming the basis of the broad Greek way of understanding the world. In the ninth and eighth centuries B.C.E., several literary works were composed, providing a grand view of the gods: Homer's *Iliad* and *Odyssey,* and Hesiod's *Theogony* (Birth of the Gods). Most of the myths presented in these works had already become literary tales, no longer living myths associated with rituals, but they provide us a vast panorama of the Greek sacred vision.

The ruins of the circular Temple of Athena at Delphi in Greece, in a mountainous setting.

An outstanding feature of the Greek gods is their humanity. They are like humans in many ways—but at the same time immortal, powerful, perfectly beautiful, and above suffering. The Greeks considered the gods to be of two kinds: the **Olympian gods** living on Mt. Olympus, full of power and ruling the world; and the Chthonian ("earthly") gods associated with earth-fertility and the realm of death. Among the twelve Olympians, **Zeus** (Jupiter to the Romans) is the father of the gods and the ruler of the universe, and his jealous wife is Hera (Roman Juno), goddess of women, marriage, and childbirth. Apollo, son of Zeus and a mortal woman, is the god of archery, prophecy, and music. And Hermes (Roman Mercury) is the messenger of Zeus and patron of travelers and thieves, as well as the god of animals. Other Olympian gods are Poseidon (Neptune), god of the sea; Artemis (Diana), the virgin goddess and mistress of wild animals; Athena (Minerva), goddess of wisdom; Demeter (Ceres), goddess of grain; Ares (Mars), god of war; Aphrodite (Venus), goddess of love and beauty; Hephaestus (Vulcan), god of fire; and Hestia (Vesta), goddess of the hearth. Not included among the Olympians but still of great significance is Dionysus, god of fertility and ecstatic rapture. Dionysus represents the mystical and ecstatic aspect of Greek religion, whereas Apollo represents the rational and orderly aspect. Important among the Chthonic gods are the Heroes, such as Heracles, a man who achieved divinity by his great labors, and gods of the underworld such as Hades.

Greek mythology tells how Gaia (earth) sprang from chaos and then gave birth to Uranus (sky); Uranus and Gaia gave birth to the Titans, among them Kronus, who castrated his father Uranus and became sovereign. Kronus was a cruel father who swallowed his offspring, but Zeus, the sixth child, escaped this fate and overthrew Kronus and the Titans, himself to become sovereign over the gods.

According to Hesiod, the Greeks believed there have been four ages of the world, each one more degenerate than the previous. The humans Zeus created to live in our present world are burdened with cares and troubles; but still Zeus and the other gods watch over them, observing their just and unjust deeds. The gods intervene in human life, even taking different sides in wars and fighting among themselves. Still, humans live at a great distance from the gods; we are mortal, destined to journey to Hades to exist as vague shadows. A major sin bringing severe punishment is *hubris* (pride), being unwilling to bow to the gods and what they have ordained, not accepting the lot of mortal humans. The path to follow for the blessed life, accordingly, is to give the gods their due through worship and respect, and to live human life in moderation and justice.

Ritual Activities and the Good Life

Public worship of the gods took place for the welfare of the whole community, led by ruling officials, priests, and priestesses, at official temples and shrines. Sacrifices were made of animals and other foods, to be consumed both by the gods and the worshipers. There were many great festivals throughout the year. For example, in Athens a major festival took place almost every month, such as a festival in honor of Demeter at the time of the sowing of corn, a cele-

bration of the sacred marriage of Zeus and Athena, a wine festival in honor of Dionysus, a harvest festival in honor of Apollo, and many more.

Key to the Greek notion of the good ethical life is the acceptance of one's place with regard to the gods, and with that the practice of moderation. In a play by Sophocles, Odysseus is warned:

> Look well at this, and speak no towering word
> Yourself against the gods, nor walk too grandly
> Because your hand is weightier than another's,
> Or your great wealth deeper founded. One short day
> Inclines the balance of all human things
> To sink or rise again. Know that the gods
> Love men of steady sense and hate the proud.[4]

A characteristic development in Greek religion was the opportunity for individuals to experience forms of mystical union with the gods. This took place in a number of movements usually called **mysteries,** since the rituals were done secretly by initiates. In the Dionysus cult, the divine forces hidden in nature and in humans were roused by rituals that led into frenzied ecstasy, wild dancing, and drunkenness, the experience of being possessed by Dionysus. Again, people could be initiated into the mysteries at Eleusis, associated with Demeter, goddess of vegetation, and her daughter Kore, resurrected from Hades. In highly secretive rituals enacting the rebirth of life, the initiates experienced union with Demeter and the promise of a happy life after death. Another movement was Orphism, also based on a myth about revival from the underworld that can be shared by the worshipers. Orphism taught that by purification and a strict moral code, such as abstaining from eating the flesh of living creatures, one can so purify the soul that it will live a blessed life in Elysium after death. These ideas about personal salvation and immortality continued to develop in the Hellenistic Roman period, as, for example, in the mysteries associated with Isis, the great goddess who resurrected Osiris and can thus give new life.

Of great significance for Western civilization was the development of humanistic and philosophical thinking among the ancient Greeks. The early philosophical schools were devoted to studying the nature of the universe, and they developed naturalistic, rational theories. The philosophers came to question the old mythologies about the gods and their immoral actions, and a new era of thinking began that directed itself to human, secular concerns on the basis of rational thought rather than mythology. Socrates (ca. 470–399 B.C.E.) quoted an inscription on the Apollo temple at Delphi, "Know yourself," and taught the young people of Athens to think critically about everything—and was condemned to death as one who spoke against religion and corrupted youth. Socrates' disciple Plato (427–347 B.C.E.) taught that reality consists of universal ideas or forms; human reason can discover or "remember" the ultimate principles of reality from which human reason is derived. And Plato's disciple Aristotle (384–322 B.C.E.) carried philosophy far into the investigation of the natural world, setting forth some of the basic categories of **philosophy** and science that guided the development of Western thought for many centuries.

Discussion Questions

1 Discuss the ancient Egyptian concern about the afterlife and the role of the cult of Osiris.

2 What are some basic contrasts between ancient Egyptian and Mesopotamian perspectives on the world and human existence?

3 Explain the suggestion that the gods of ancient Mesopotamia form a "cosmic state."

4 What was the ancient Babylonian perspective on creation and the role and purpose of humans?

5 What is the ancient Greek notion of *hubris?* How is this related to their view of the nature and role of humans?

6 What do you think was the relation between ancient Greek religion and the development of philosophical thought?

The Zoroastrian Tradition

The religion founded by the prophet **Zarathustra** is one of the most ancient of today's living religions, and it was once the religion of the great Persian empire. The ancient roots of Zoroastrianism are connected to the Aryan tradition, the same Indo-European grouping of people who contributed to the development of Hinduism in India. But in the historical context of ancient Persia, interacting with the Mediterranean world, the Zoroastrian way eventually exerted significant influence on Jewish, Christian, and Muslim thought and practice. Ideas and beliefs of the Persians included notions of one God (**Ahura Mazda**) together with a dualism of good and evil divine powers, an emphasis on ethical life for humans, judgment for the soul, heaven and hell, the coming of world savior figures, the resurrection of all, and world-transforming cosmic events.

The vicissitudes of history were harsh on Zoroastrians, and today there are fewer than 200,000 members of this ancient religion living mostly in Iran, India, and the West. But the religious ideas and historical influence of this religious tradition have a significance far beyond the relatively small numbers of adherents in the world today.

SACRED STORY AND HISTORICAL CONTEXT

Whether in Iran, Bombay, or New York, Zoroastrians today have a clear sense of their identity based in the ethical teachings and ritual practices of their religious tradition. These teachings and practices have been shaped in a great variety of historical circumstances over the past three thousand years. Zoroastrians believe their religion goes back originally to the teaching of the great prophet Zarathustra, also known in the West as **Zoroaster,** following Greek usage.

Zarathustra's Life and Teachings

There is little doubt as to the existence and seminal influence of Zarathustra. But when did he live? There are widely divergent answers to this question. Ancient Zoroastrian tradition was indifferent to worldly chronology, but later Greek sources suggest a number of widely differing dates, from around 500 B.C.E. to as far back as 6000 B.C.E. Scholars today acknowledge the complex problem of locating Zarathustra historically, but there is some consensus that a date around 1000 B.C.E. may be tentatively accepted, given various historical considerations.

Zarathustra is held to be the author of the **Gathas,** sacred hymns which make up the earliest part in the collection of sacred texts, the *Avesta*. Apart from allusions in the Gathas, very little documentation exists about the life of Zarathustra. Apparently he lived in eastern Iran, and he was deeply religious. The dominant religious practices of his time were those of the Indo-Aryan tradition, similar to the Vedic religion of India. There were a great many gods, such as Vayu (the wind god), Mithra (the god of the covenant), Atar (the fire god), and so on, as well as innumerable good and evil spirits. There were important sacrificial rituals, especially the sacrifice of a bull or ox, the libation sacrifice involving the fermented haoma drink, and the great fire sacrifice. Priests performed these sacrifices, and they also foretold events, interpreting omens and dreams.

According to Zoroastrian tradition, Zarathustra was trained as a priest *(zaotar)*, and after some years of marriage with children, at about the age of thirty he experienced a transformative vision. Returning from a river with water for the haoma ritual at the spring festival, he was led by divine being Vohu Manah (Good Purpose) into the presence of Ahura Mazda and the other Immortals. Here he was taught the basic elements of the true religion, and moreover he was commissioned to proclaim this to the people.

The new vision was a reformation of the traditional religion. As central to his new vision, Zarathustra now taught that Ahura Mazda is the supreme God, eternal and uncreated, omniscient and the creator of all that is good. All the other gods are subordinate, incorporated into the powers and attributes of Ahura Mazda. Special place is given to the **Holy Immortals (Amesha Spentas)**, divine beings created by Ahura Mazda to aid him. Their names reflect various moral and spiritual forces and qualities: Good Purpose, Truth, Dominion, Devotion, Perfection, and Immortality. Over and over in the Gathas, Zarathustra gives praise to Ahura Mazda as the creator, working through the Holy Immortals: "Truly I recognised Thee with my thought, O Mazda, to be First . . . , when with my eyes I perceived Thee to be Father of Good Purpose, real Creator of Truth, by Thy acts Lord of existence" (*Yasna* 31.8). And again, "By virtue of His abounding authority of power over Wholeness and Immortality and Truth, Lord Mazda will give perpetuity of communion with Good Purpose to him who is His ally in spirit and acts" (31.21).[1]

Another key point that Zarathustra emphasized was fundamental conflict between good and evil in the spiritual sphere as well as the material sphere. While holding to the supremacy of Ahura Mazda, Zarathustra also posited an Evil Spirit **(Angra Mainyu)**, who like Ahura Mazda was uncreated and self-existing. Evil Spirit, followed by demonic gods (daevas), upholds the Lie **(druj)** rather than Truth **(asha)**— and this leads to the universal conflict in human history between the truth-followers *(ashavan)* and the followers of the lie *(dregvant)*. Yet Zarathustra felt that each person has freedom of will to choose between good and evil. Consequently, he taught that good deeds and evil deeds will have their own consequences in terms of happiness and misery,

and his hymns often refer to a final consummation in which the souls of humans will be judged at the Chinvat Bridge. The righteous will receive their eternal reward in heaven, while the followers of evil will fall into the abyss of torment.

Because he condemned many of the ideas and practices of his times, Zarathustra come into sharp conflict with many priestly groups, and in the first ten years of his mission he converted only one person, his cousin. His inner anguish during this period is reflected in his hymn to Ahura Mazda: "To what land to flee? Whither shall I go to flee? They thrust me from family and clan. The community with which I have kept company has not shown me hospitality, nor those who are the wicked rulers of the land. How then shall I propitiate Thee, Lord Mazda? . . . Whom, Mazda, hast Thou appointed protector for one like me, if the Wicked One shall dare to harm me?" (*Yasna* 46:1, 7).[2] This hostility caused Zarathustra to flee his own region to seek refuge at the court of King Vishtaspa in northwest Iran. Although his enemies had him imprisoned for a time, eventually King Vishtaspa, his queen, and his whole court accepted Zarathustra's teachings, and the true religion taught by Zarathustra began to spread widely. The prophet Zarathustra, it is said, was a family man, having a son and three daughters with his first wife, as well as two more sons with his second wife. According to tradition, Zarathustra lived to age seventy-seven, firmly establishing the true religion among his followers.

Development of the Zoroastrian Tradition

Just as it is difficult to articulate the historical context of the prophet Zarathustra, the scarcity of sources leaves the further developments of the Zoroastrian tradition somewhat unclear. Yet there is no doubt that over some time the teachings of Zarathustra spread and thrived, eventually becoming very influential in the Persian empire. Zoroastrianism functioned as Persia's state religion up through the Sassanid period (227–651 C.E.)—until the rise of Islam eventually led to the diminishment of Zoroastrian communities in Iran and their establishment in India.

Becoming the Religion of the Persian Empire   Were the kings of the Achaemenid dynasty (550–330 B.C.E.), such as Cyrus, Darius, and Artaxerxes, followers of Zoroastrianism, or were they rather still adherents of the ancient Indo-Aryan beliefs? The predominant evidence from this period suggests that these kings had indeed accepted Zarathustra's teachings by this point. We might note that it was during this period that Jewish exiles in Babylon came under Persian rule. King Cyrus permitted and assisted a group of Jewish exiles to return to Jerusalem; this Cyrus is mentioned by name as God's "messiah" in the writings of the Jewish prophet known as Second Isaiah (*Isaiah* 45:1). And, according to the Jewish scriptures, the lawyer Ezra journeyed from the Babylonian Jewish community to Jerusalem, with a special commission from King Artaxerxes giving him authority as "the scribe of the law of the God of heaven" to restore pure Judaism (*Ezra* 7:12–26). It is intriguing to link these Jewish interpretations with Zoroastrian ideas of the supreme God and the coming of world saviors. In any case, it may be that there was a complex mixture of Zoroastrian teachings and earlier Indo-Iranian religious practices coexisting in Persia during this time.

The cultural impact of Hellenism was strong during the next period in Persia, controlled by Alexander the Great and, subsequently, by his generals. This Seleucid period (330–227 B.C.E.) is remembered as a disaster in Zoroastrian tradition, since Alexander burned the royal capital at Persepolis and many priests, the custodians of the religious tradition, were killed. This posed a distinct threat to the continuance of the Zoroastrian tradition, as much of the oral literature was in danger of being lost. It is remarkable that, in spite of this severe crisis, Zarathustra's Gathas continued to be handed on by word of mouth during this whole time, an unbroken transmission from the prophet's own period until the *Avesta* was first written down in Sassanian times. The Zoroastrian tradition regained its strength in Persia during the rule of the Parthian kings (ca. 247 B.C.E.–227 C.E.) and, with support from the kings, the scattered oral texts of the *Avesta* were collected and transmitted once again.

During the Sassanid period (227–651), the Zoroastrian tradition flourished again as the state religion of Persia— only to be severely diminished later as Islam was accepted by most Persians. The Zoroastrian tradition was challenged in this period by numerous religious forces—the persistence of Judaism, the rise of Christianity, and the challenge of Hinduism and Buddhism. Another factor was the popular appeal of Manichaeism, a cosmic dualism taught by a new prophet, Mani (216–276), who drew on elements from Christianity and Buddhism in addition to Zoroastrianism. In the face of all this, the Zoroastrian religion took on Iran-

ian nationalistic overtones and was strictly enforced by the rulers as the official Persian religion. The priesthood became a powerful body supported by the government, and those who deviated from the prescribed religious practices were at times persecuted. The authoritative Avestan scriptures were gathered and compiled during this period, and numerous additional theological works were set down in Pahlavi, the official language of the time. Among these writings, the *Bundahishn* (Original Creation) is especially important, structuring time from the creation to the final judgment in four 3,000-year eras. The cosmic struggle between Ahura Mazda (Ohrmazd in Pahlavi) and the Evil Spirit Angra Mainyu (**Ahriman** in Pahlavi) is a particularly prevalent theme in these theological writings.

Decline and Survival of the Zoroastrians   The last Sassanian king suffered defeat in 642 and was assassinated in 651, and the whole Persian Empire fell to the Arab Muslims. Little is known about the process by which the majority of Iranians converted to Islam, but eventually Zoroastrians were reduced to a small minority in Iran. Theoretically, Muslims considered the Zoroastrians, like the Christians and Jews, to be monotheists and "People of the Book," meaning they respected Ahura Mazda as the one God, the *Avesta* as scripture, and Zarathustra as a prophet. In practice, however, it seems the Zoroastrians were mocked as fire worshipers and called by the derogatory term *gabars,* that is, unbelievers. Because of ongoing persecution, the Zoroastrians who remained in Iran tended to migrate to remote places in south-central Iran. In spite of numerous difficulties, these small communities have kept the Zoroastrian faith alive in Iran to the present. For a time in the twentieth century there seemed to be a revival of Zoroastrian fortunes, as Shah Pahlavi (r. 1941–1979) emphasized the ancient cultural heritage of Iran, of which Zoroastrianism was a major component. But with the fall of the Shah in the Islamic revolution of 1979, this era ended, and some Zoroastrians, particularly those who had some ties with the Shah's establishment, emigrated to the West.

Some time after the Muslim conquest in Iran in the seventh century, groups of Zoroastrians migrated out of Iran to western India, to the coastal region of Gujarat north of Bombay. Here they became known as **Parsis** ("Persians") and maintained their separate identity as a closed ethnic group. Functioning similarly to a caste in India, they made

A Parsi fire temple in Bombay, India. Above the entrance is an ancient Zoroastrian symbol. The two guardian figures flanking the entrance reflect Zoroastrianism's Persian background.

no attempt to spread their religion to others. Parsis did eventually adopt certain cultural features of India, including typical foods, wearing of saris by women, and using garlands of flowers to adorn pictures of Zarathustra. In modern times, Parsis tended to migrate to Bombay, where they became very successful especially in trade and industry. Widely known for their honesty and loyalty, they were given responsibilities by the British and showed leadership in government, education for women, and philanthropy.

Today the Parsis of India still make up the majority of the world's Zoroastrian community. Ties have been reestablished with the Zoroastrians of Iran, through international conferences and symposia in Tehran and in Bombay. And overseas communities of Zoroastrians have begun to flourish in places like Toronto, New York, Los Angeles, and Sydney. At first, these overseas communities were mainly Parsis from India, but since the Shah's demise in 1979, these communities have been augmented with Zoroastrians who have emigrated from Iran.

ZOROASTRIAN WORLDS OF MEANING

Supreme God and Lesser Divine Powers

Zarathustra was one of the earliest religious leaders to emphasize the supremacy of one God, as he raised Ahura Mazda above all the other gods worshiped by the ancient Iranians. It is unclear whether he taught monotheism in the strict sense, since he spoke of the working of Ahura Mazda through the other divine powers, the Holy Immortals or Amesha Spentas. Yet there is no doubt that in early Zoroastrian teachings Ahura Mazda was considered supreme as the good creator and ruler. The Gathas give praise to Ahura Mazda as the first over all, eternal, good, and bountiful, the creator of all good things, who gives life and wisdom to every good living thing. Zarathustra dedicated himself to this highest Lord: "Truly I shall vow myself and be, O Mazda, Your praiser as long as I shall have force and strength, O Truth! May the Creator of life accomplish through Good Purpose the true fulfillment of what is most wonderful, according to wish (*Yasna* 50.11)."[3]

In a famous passage, Zarathustra explores with powerful rhetoric his conviction that Ahura Mazda is the supreme creator of the world and of human civilization:

> This I ask Thee, tell me truly, Lord. Who in the beginning, at creation, was Father of Order (Asha)? Who established the course of sun and stars? Through whom does the moon wax, then wane? This and yet more, O Mazda, I seek to know. This I ask Thee, tell me truly, Lord. Who has upheld the earth from below, and the heavens from falling? Who (sustains) the waters and plants? Who harnessed swift steeds to wind and clouds? Who, O Mazda, is Creator of Good Purpose? This I ask Thee, tell me truly, Lord. What craftsman created light and darkness? What craftsman created both sleep and activity? Through whom exist dawn, noon and eve, which remind the worshipper of his duty? . . . This I ask Thee, tell me truly, Lord. Who fashioned honoured Devotion together with Power? Who made the son respectful in heed to the father? By these (questions), O Mazda, I help (men) to discern Thee as Creator of all things through the Holy Spirit.

(*Yasna* 44.3–7)[4]

Though clearly Ahura Mazda is supreme, this passage and many others in the Gathas amplify the divine reality by including additional divine powers that were created by Ahura Mazda, or perhaps emanate from Ahura Mazda, as assistants or subordinates in divine functioning. While no systematized listing of these powers is given in the Gathas, later Zoroastrian thinkers set their number at seven, speaking of them as the "Holy Immortals," the Amesha Spentas. They are personified forces or qualities: Good Purpose (Vohu

Manah), Truth (Asha), Dominion (Khshathra), Devotion (Armaiti), Perfection (Haurvatat), Immortality (Ameretat), and Holy Spirit (Spenta Mainyu). Holy Spirit is often identified very closely with Ahura Mazda, as the divine creative essence. The members of this divine Heptad are traditionally associated with aspects of creation. For example, Vohu Manah is associated with cattle, Armaiti with earth, Asha with fire, etc. And the powers represented by these Holy Immortals are immanent in the world, indwelling within just people and thus providing a basis for spirituality and ethics.

As Zoroastrian theology developed, other elements from the earlier Indo-Iranian and other traditions were incorporated. In the section of the *Avesta* called the *Yashts*, there are many hymns devoted to other divine powers or **Yazata** that no doubt stem from ancient traditions. For example, many rituals were directed to Haoma, the god manifested in a stimulating beverage prepared by the priests. And Anahita, goddess of water and fertility, was widely worshiped. A most popular god was Mithra, guardian of light, giver of wealth, and protector of truth. A great hymn to Mithra states:

> We worship Mithra of wide pastures, who bestows peaceful dwellings, good dwellings on Iranian lands. . . . May he come to us for victory, may he come to us for happiness, may he come to us for justice, he the strong, the powerful. . . . We worship Mithra of wide pastures, right-speaking, eloquent, possessing a thousand ears, well formed, possessing ten thousand eyes, tall, with wide look-out, strong, unsleeping, wakeful, . . . who ascends, the first invisible god, over Hara, before the life-giving, swift-horsed sun which first touches the beautiful, gold-tinted mountain tops. From there he, the most strong, surveys all lands dwelt in by Iranians. . . . We worship Mithra of wide pastures, . . . who stands erect and watchful, the espier, mighty, eloquent, replenishing the waters, having heard the invocation, causing rain to fall and plants to grow, drawing the boundary line, eloquent, perceptive, undeceived.
>
> (*Yasht* 10.4–5, 7, 12, 61)[5]

Mithra, a god of covenants, took on aspects of a solar deity with royal and militaristic attributes. From Iran, the cult of Mithra was widely diffused through the Roman empire, becoming a popular mystery religion.

How all these Yazatas were related to Ahura Mazda in the different periods of Zoroastrian history is not entirely clear. Today many Zoroastrian thinkers emphasize Ahura Mazda

as the supreme God, with the Amesha Spentas and other Yazatas as subordinate helper beings. Other more traditional Zoroastrians continue to worship the Yazatas as divine powers in their own right.

Divine Dualism: Good and Evil Forces   Zarathustra envisioned the supreme God Ahura Mazda presiding over a dynamic process of existence that involved good and evil forces, both in the spiritual realm and in the material-historical realm. In the Gathas, Zarathustra often spoke of the twin forces of good and evil that are locked in conflict.

> Truly there are two primal Spirits, twins renowned to be in conflict. In thought and word, in act they are two: the better and the bad. . . . Of these two Spirits the Wicked One chose achieving the worst things. The Most Holy Spirit, who is clad in hardest stone, chose right, and (so do those) who shall satisfy Lord Mazda continually with rightful acts.
>
> (*Yasna* 44.3, 5)[6]

Holy Spirit, Spenta Mainyu, upholds truth and rightness *(asha),* but Evil Spirit, Angra Mainyu (Ahriman in Pahlavi), upholds the lie or falsehood *(druj).* Other gods, called Daevas by Zarathustra, also joined with Evil Spirit, leading humans into deception and falsehood.

Zarathustra maintained the supremacy but not the omnipotence of Ahura Mazda, in the cosmic process in which forces of good and forces of evil engaged in conflict, pointing toward the ultimate triumph of the good. Later in the Sassanian period, this process was described more like a cosmic dualism. Pahlavi texts suggest that Ahriman (the Pahlavi form of Angra Mainyu) is almost of equal status with Ahura Mazda himself.

> It is thus revealed in the Good Religion that Ohrmazd [Ahura Mazda] was on high in omniscience and goodness. For boundless time He was ever in the light. That light is the space and place of Ohrmazd. Some call it Endless Light. . . . Ahriman was abased in slowness of knowledge and the lust to smite. The lust to smite was his sheath and darkness his place. Some call it Endless Darkness. And between them was emptiness.
>
> (*Greater Bundahishn* 1.1– 5)[7]

Ahriman is the direct opposite of Ahura Mazda. Ahriman is the source of all evil: falsehood, misfortune, disaster, war, sickness, and death. Yet even the strongest traditions of cosmic dualism in Zoroastrianism always gave the edge to Ahura Mazda, ensuring the ultimate triumph of goodness. Thus many Zoroastrians today emphasize that their religious vision is monotheistic, one God presiding over a cosmic and historical process in which forces of good and evil clash, with God's will directed to the final triumph of the forces of good.

Creation and Human History

Zoroastrian tradition presents the creation of the world and the sweep of history in three general phases: the creation of the world, the mingling together of the two opposing spirits, and the final separation and transfiguration.

The ancient Indo-Iranian traditions, reflected in the Avesta, commonly envisioned the gods creating the world in stages, starting with the sky made of stone and rock crystal, as a huge round shell to enclose the world. Then they formed water and the lower part of this shell, then earth resting on the water. At the center of earth they formed a huge plant, then a primordial bull, then a primordial human, and finally fire as the vital force to give warmth and life to the world. From the divine sacrifice of the plant, the bull, and the human, the continuing generation of plants, animals, and humans began. In this ancient cosmology, the earth itself is envisioned as surrounded by a great mountain range, and at the center of the earth is Mount Hara, around which the sun circles. The mighty river Aredvi flows down from Mount Hara into the sea Vourukasha, supplying all the waters of the earth. And in this sea grows the Tree of all Seeds, from which the rain scatters seeds over the earth each year.

Zarathustra built on these ancient notions by teaching that behind the creation of the world there was the one God Ahura Mazda, eternal and uncreated, who was the source of all the other beneficent deities. Ahura Mazda created the world through the Holy Spirit Spenta Mainyu—who is his active agent and yet in some sense one with him. And Ahura Mazda made this whole world with the help of the lesser gods, the Holy Immortals (Amesha Spentas), whom he brought into existence to aid in the task of creating the world. After creating the world, the Holy Immortals entered into their separate creations as guardians. Thus, they are both transcendent, as aspects or emanations of Ahura Mazda's own nature; and they are also immanent as the inner reality of their material creations.

Indeed, it seems that a key aspect of Zoroastrian thought about creation is the concept that everything exists in a double state, both spiritual and physical. The spiritual aspect is seen as the embryonic state, and the physical aspect is the fruit or realization of this. Thus Zoroastrians do not view the material world as evil in itself, in contrast to Gnostic or Manichaean views that set up a dualism between good spirit and evil matter. Both spirit and matter are good, though they can be taken over by Evil Spirit and all those forces, spiritual and material, that join his camp.

Historical Eras and Eschatology   Zoroastrian tradition after Zarathustra developed a grand vision of the whole sweep of creation, history, and consummation, as represented, for example, in the Pahlavi text *Bundahishn*. In general outline, all of time is divided into four eras of 3,000 years each. During the first trimillennium, Ahura Mazda originated the primordial elements of good creation in their spiritual form. But at the close of this era, Ahriman the Evil Spirit began to stir and created a great host of demons and creatures of darkness for an assault on the celestial realm. In the face of this attack, Ahura Mazda then made a treaty with Ahriman that would last three more eras. The world would be ruled by Ahura Mazda for a 3,000-year period, then by Ahriman for the next 3,000-year period, and during the final trimillennium the two divine antagonists would struggle for victory.

During Ahura Mazda's 3,000-year rule, he transformed all good creation from the spiritual state to the physical state. And to ensure ultimate victory over Ahriman, Ahura Mazda created the spiritual body of Zarathustra, who would eventually be incarnated and bring the Good Religion into the world to bring about final transformation. But when Ahriman took over as ruler in the next 3,000-year era, he created great evil on the earth, generating storms and earthquakes, creating hordes of destructive beasts, and digging a great hole for the fires of hell. He created wicked thoughts and corrupt desires in humans, seeking to doom them to everlasting suffering in the infernal regions of hell.

Just before the end of Ahriman's era of rule, Ahura Mazda created Zarathustra's physical form and sent him to teach the Good Religion, calling on humans to follow Ahura Mazda's goodness and prepare for the crucial events of the final era. During this final period of the world, according to Zoroastrian tradition, people will become evil, deception and hatred will rise, and great battles will take place. Yet Ahura Mazda will send a savior at the end of each 1,000-year period, three saviors in all, each a descendent of Zarathustra, to reconstitute the Good Religion among humankind. A final great battle will take place between the vast forces of Ahriman and Ahura Mazda, resulting in the ultimate triumph of Ahura Mazda, the resurrection of all dead, the final judgment, the conflagration of the world including Ahriman and all his followers, and the creation of a new, transformed universe. This is the time of *Frasho-kereti*, restoration, when the world will reach perfection.

The Path of Human Transformation

The cosmic drama of good and evil is reflected in human experience, according to Zoroastrian thinking. Humans, created by Ahura Mazda and his helpers as good creation, are bombarded and deceived by evil forces. Yet humans are not determined by forces beyond their control. As they have been given the divine gifts of body, soul, and mind, humans have the freedom to choose between good and evil and thus determine their ultimate destiny.

Zarathustra talks of the two groups of humankind: *asha-van*, the followers of Asha (Truth), and *dregvant*, the followers of Druj (Lie). "Since, O Mazda, Thou didst fashion for us in the beginning, by Thy thought, creatures and inner selves and intentions, since Thou didst create corporeal life, and acts and words through which he who has free will expresses choices, then each lifts up his voice, be he false-speaking or right-speaking, with knowledge or without knowledge, according to his heart and mind" (*Yasna* 31.11–12).[8] The moral choices that people make demonstrate whether they are *dregvant* or whether they are included among the *asha-van*. Zarathustra felt that Ahura Mazda gave revelations to him to provide guidance and encouragement to people in their moral struggle. The Good Religion empowers those who hear and accept to transform their minds and their hearts. One who possesses Asha, Truth, is separated from evil in a state of spiritual purity, and this is the basis of spiritual realization, in which increasing enlightenment and intellectual vision result. And they can demonstrate this spiritual state by good thoughts, good words, and good deeds.

The moral choices that people make, according to Zarathustra, determine their future destiny, when judgment and retribution will take place for all.

> This I ask, Lord: what punishment shall be for him who promotes power for a wicked man of evil actions? . . . The healer of life, having knowledge, Lord, has hearkened, he who has thought upon truth, ruling his tongue at will for the right speaking of words, when the distribution in good shall take place for both parties by Thy bright-blazing fire, O Mazda. Heavenly glory shall be the future possession of him who comes (to the help of) the just man. A long life of darkness, foul food, the crying of woe—to that existence, O wicked ones, your Inner Self shall lead you by her actions.

(*Yasna* 31.15, 19–20)[9]

As suggested in this hymn by Zarathustra, Zoroastrian theology developed an expressive vision of the journey of the soul after death. After staying with the body for three days, the soul is conducted to the Chinvat Bridge, the separator that spans the abyss of hell and leads to paradise on the other side. The bridge is like a sword, with a broad flat side. For the soul with wicked deeds, the bridge turns the sharp edge up so that the soul teeters and falls into the abyss of hell. But the soul with an accumulation of good thoughts and words and deeds walks easily over the broad, flat bridge and enters into paradise—a place of eternal bliss, beauty, and light.

In the Zoroastrian vision, there will be an ultimate ending of time, with a general resurrection of all dead. The final cosmic battle will lead to the banishment of evil forces forever, the earth will be purified in a great conflagration, and a restored world will endure forever under the rulership of Ahura Mazda. Zarathustra taught that the moral undertakings of good people will contribute to this restoration. He prayed, "And then may we be those who transfigure this world. O Mazda (and you other) Lords, be present to me with support and truth" (*Yasna* 30.9).[10]

RITUAL AND THE GOOD LIFE FOR ZOROASTRIANS

Prayer, Rituals, and Art

Prayer and Purification   For making time sacred and for renewing life, Zoroastrians have many rituals, festivals, and other spiritual activities. Zarathustra criticized the priests of his time for their excessive ritualism and absence of ethical virtue. Yet Zarathustra was a highly spiritual

Prayer is central to Zoroastrian spiritual life. Five times a day a Zoroastrian says prayers, standing in the presence of fire (actual fire, or else sun or moon). He or she should first perform purification, washing face, hands, and feet. A central ritual in these acts of prayer is the untying and tying again of the sacred cord, the **kusti.** All Zoroastrians receive the kusti together with the sacred shirt at the time of their initiation into the Zoroastrian community as young boys and girls. The sacred cord passes three times around the waist, over the sacred shirt. The worshiper first unties the cord, reciting a formula of protection: "Protect us from the foe, O Mazda and Spenta Armaiti! . . . Begone, O Drug [variant of Druj]! Crawl away, O Drug, disappear, O Drug!" He or she shakes the kusti to dispel all evil and negative thoughts. Then in retying the cord the worshiper recites another formula of exorcism and strong personal repentance:

> Ohrmazd [Ahura Mazda] is Lord! Ahriman he keeps at bay, he holds him back. May Ahriman be struck and defeated, with devs and drujs, sorcerers and sinners, kayags and karbs, tyrants, wrongdoers and heretics, sinners, enemies and witches! May they all be struck and defeated! . . . O Ohrmazd, Lord! I am contrite for all sins and I desist from them, from all bad thoughts, bad words and bad acts for which I have thought, spoken or done in the world, or which have happened through me, or have originated with me. For those sins of thinking, speaking and acting, of body and soul, worldly or spiritual, O Ohrmazd! I am contrite, I renounce them.[12]

Through this ritual and these prayers, Zoroastrians daily strengthen their resolve to follow the path of Ahura Mazda.

Along with prayer, rituals of purification play an important role in Zoroastrian daily life. Pollution enters daily life in many ways, especially from dead and putrefying matter cast off from human and animal bodies. The simplest ritual of purification is *padyab,* ablution with water several times a day. The faithful may dip their fingers in water and apply it to their foreheads and eyes while praying to Ahura Mazda. On special occasions, such as after childbirth or in preparing for major religious rituals, a ritual bath *(nahn)* of purification is performed. A special kind of purification is *bareshnum,* used especially for initiation of priests. This complicated ritual takes place over several days and includes, among other rituals, the use of consecrated bull's urine, following ancient Indo-Iranian traditions.

A Zoroastrian priest performs a fire ceremony in the fire temple. The mask is worn to keep from contaminating the pure fire by his breath.

person, and the hymns he composed (the Gathas) have been the mainstay of Zoroastrian prayer life, recited as part of the daily liturgy. Today these hymns are still recited in the ancient Avestan language. With them, other brief prayers are frequently used, such as these two ancient, powerful prayers:

> As the Master, so is the Judge to be chosen in accord with truth. Establish the power of acts arising from a life lived with good purpose, for Mazda and for the lord whom they made pastor for the poor.
> Asha [Truth] is good, it is best. According to wish it is, according to wish it shall be for us. Asha belongs to Asha Vahishta.[11]

Fire Temples and Rituals   Fire has always been a central symbol in Zoroastrianism, and no religious ceremony is complete without the presence of this powerful spiritual force. The ritual use of fire goes back far into the ancient Indo-Iranian tradition, continuing as a central focus also in the Vedic practices in India. Fire, along with sky, water, and earth, was part of the original pure creation. Zoroastrian tradition speaks of five natural expressions of fire; these exist, respectively, in front of Ahura Mazda, in clouds, in the earth, in human and animal bodies, and in plants. Thus fire is a constituent, vital element present in all of nature.

The traditional sanctuary for Zoroastrians is the **Fire Temple.** On a stone platform in the central chamber a sacred fire burns continuously on a bed of sand or ash in a large metal urn. Priests maintain the fire, performing the proper rituals and saying the prayers during the day. Priests wear cloth masks over their mouths so that they do not pollute the sacred fire through their breaths. Lay worshipers often come to pray at the temple, bringing offerings such as sweet-smelling sandalwood, to be added to the fire. Several fire temples in India and Iran have maintained fires that are especially sacred, combined from many different sources and maintained for many years. The sacred fire at Udvada north of Bombay is said to have burned continuously for over a thousand years.

Fires are also maintained outside the temples, especially in the homes of adherents. Prayers are made regularly before the house fire, including the ancient *Atash Niyayesh* (fire litany), in which fire is invoked with the words, "Worthy of worship are you, worthy of prayer! Worthy of worship may you be, worthy of prayer, in the dwellings of men!"[13] Many Zoroastrians consider it a grave wrong to allow the sacred fire to be extinguished. Occasionally Zoroastrians use fire rituals in thanksgiving services *(jashan),* for times such as communal anniversaries, special events in the family, and the like. In these services, priests recite prayers before the urn with the sacred fire, and then members of the congregation file by, each placing a bit of incense in the fire in a communal act of worship.

Festivals and Life Passage Rituals   From ancient times Zoroastrians have had an extensive calendar year consisting of twelve months of thirty days each, with each day and month dedicated to a divine being. Later, five extra days were added to make a 365-day year; these five days,

called Gatha days, are a time of prayer for deceased ancestors. The beginning of the New Year is especially important, a time for renewal of creation and of life, as it occurs at the time of the vernal equinox in spring. Additional celebrations include midspring, midsummer, early autumn, midautumn, and midwinter festivals. During these seasonal festivals, Zoroastrians gather to worship and feast together. Due to the separation of Zoroastrian communities in Iran and India, over time three different calendars have come into existence, leading to some differences in the celebration of these festivals. Some communities, for example, celebrate the New Year festival in August rather than in mid-March.

Zoroastrians have special rituals for the passages of life, especially for puberty, marriage, and death. All children between the ages of seven and ten, boys and girls alike, go through the **Naojote** (New Birth) ceremony. First comes a ceremonial bath, then there are prayers and declarations spoken by the child together with a priest. Then the priest invests the child with two sacred objects that are to be worn throughout life. One is the *sudreh,* a sacred shirt with a small pocket (to be filled with good deeds). The other is the *kusti,* a woolen cord about fifteen feet long, tied three times around the waist, knotted in back and in front. The Naojote ceremony concludes with a recital of the Zoroastrian faith and a final benediction. The sacred objects received in this ritual serve as constant reminders for spiritual life. Throughout one's life, the kusti is untied and tied again in connection with prayers during the day, as well as when dressing. With the completion of this ceremony, the young person is prepared for a life in keeping with Zoroastrian ideals and responsibilities.

Marriage is an extremely important event in the Zoroastrian community, and all young people are strongly encouraged to marry within the Zoroastrian faith. Since orthodox Zoroastrian communities do not accept converts, even through marriage, the Zoroastrian faith can continue in the future only through young Zoroastrians marrying each other and bringing new generations of children into the community. Moreover, through marriage the souls of the husband and wife provide spiritual nourishment for each other, even after death. Thus to marry a non-Zoroastrian means both to damage the future of the community and to hinder the spiritual progress of one's soul. Since marriage is an important spiritual event, the couple prepares by performing the purification ceremony *(nahn).* Marriage rituals

The *kusti* (sacred cord) is being tied around this boy's waist in the *Naojote* (New Birth) ceremony.

in the Zoroastrian tradition are often performed at fire temples, the community gathering with the bride and bridegroom in the open courtyard. Priests recite appropriate scriptures and pass a long string around the couple again and again, symbolically binding them together. After the marriage ritual, it is customary to have a banquet of traditional food to celebrate the new Zoroastrian household.

Funerals in Zoroastrian communities have distinctive rituals. The body is purified with water and invested with the sudreh and kusti. Since a corpse is highly polluting, it is handled by specially purified corpse-bearers, who place it on a marble stone slab, since stone absorbs less pollution than other materials. A traditional practice is to bring in a dog into the presence of the dead person, following ancient notions that a dog has special divine sight and can keep evil spirits away. The body is kept in the home for three days, as Zoroastrians believe that the soul remains with the body

for three days after death before journeying to the Chinvat Bridge for judgment. On the fourth day, the corpse-bearers bring the body to a massive tower called a **dakhma, a Tower of Silence.** The tower is constructed with a circular stone platform on top, inclined toward a well in the center. The dead body is placed here, stripped of clothing and exposed to the elements and the vultures. The vultures quickly strip the body of flesh and the bones are dried and bleached by the sun, after which they are swept into the central well to disintegrate. In this way, Zoroastrians believe, the polluting effects of the decaying body on the air, fire, earth, and water are avoided. This practice also emphasizes equality of all people, as the mighty and lowly alike are exposed without clothing, and their bones crumble together into dust.

In modern times, some Zoroastrians have come to think the use of these Towers of Silence is no longer practical, especially in crowded urban areas. While Towers of Silence continue to be used by many Parsis in India, Zoroastrians in Iran have shifted toward burials in the earth, and Zoroastrians living in the West have adopted burial or cremation.

Ceremonial Art and Symbolism in Zoroastrian Practice
There are some indications, from Greek sources, that the ancient Zoroastrians did not use statues, temples, and altars for their religious rituals, and later practices show a reluctance to use anthropomorphic representations of divine figures. One ancient Iranian symbol that is widely used by Zoroastrians today is a winged disk with a tail and two leg-like projections; a bearded figure is emerging from the disk wearing a loose-sleeved robe and holding a large ring in his left hand. This is a very ancient symbol, attested as early as the reign of King Darius (522–486 B.C.E.). Many scholars think this ancient symbol is a representation of Ahura Mazda, although modern Parsis believe that Ahura Mazda cannot be represented iconographically.[14] A popular interpretation among modern Zoroastrians is that this symbol is a depiction of the soul progressing spiritually to union with Ahura Mazda. The soul, represented by the disk, has two wings for its spiritual journey. The two curved legs represent the opposing forces of Spenta Mainyu and Angra Mainyu that pull the soul from side to side. The soul has a rudder in the form of a tail to balance itself between these forces, and the tail has three layers of feathers, representing good thoughts, good words, and good deeds. The ring held in the figure's hand

represents the cycles of life on different planes through which the soul will progress; and the figure's head expresses the truth that Ahura Mazda has given each soul intelligence and free will to choose obedience or disobedience to the universal divine laws.

With respect to Zarathustra, in recent centuries a tradition has developed of portraying him with full beard and long wavy hair descending from a turban, wearing white robe and trousers, with a cape over the robe. A staff is in his right hand, and behind his head appear the sun's rays—indicating, perhaps, his inspiration from the Lord Ahura Mazda.

Fire itself is an important Zoroastrian symbol, of course, and the artistic representation of a fire burning in an urn on a stand or an altar is a frequent decoration. Such a representation, with the flame sculpted in stone and painted in gold, might be placed, for example, on the roof of a fire temple.

Architecture has tended to be simple in Zoroastrian tradition. Fire temples generally have been unpretentious and functional, constructed as rectangular, one-roomed buildings. The roof has a vent for the smoke from the fire to escape. Sometimes, in larger temples, the urn that contains the fire is enclosed in a metal grillwork structure. In more modern times, temples have been built to resemble some of the architectural details of the ancient ruins of Persepolis, from the glorious Achaemenian period in Iran. Thus, columns are used, and human-headed, winged bulls flank the entrance. Such architecture provides modern Zoroastrians a sense of connection with the ancient roots of their religion.

Community and Ethical Ideals

The Zoroastrian Community   While Zoroastrians typically have a tolerant attitude toward people of other religions, the sense of identity as members of the Zoroastrian community has been strict and uncompromising. Zarathustra arose as a prophet with a mission for humans, and in those ancient times Zoroastrians engaged in spreading their faith. However, since the conquest of Persia by Muslims there has been little impulse among the small Zoroastrian communities to incorporate new converts into their faith. Rather, the Zoroastrian community is determined largely by heredity. This concept of the community has been true especially among the Parsis in India, where the community functions almost as a caste, with marriage only within the community and no incorporation of outsiders as converts. But the situation in Iran also encouraged a closed sense of community, especially as the Zoroastrians have often been considered to be "fire worshipers" or infidels by their Muslim neighbors.

This restricted sense of community shows itself in the signs often posted at the entrances of fire temples in India: "No admission except Parsees." Such restrictions are explained in terms of purity; it is feared that the purity of the temple fire may be polluted by the presence of nonbelievers. Orthodox Zoroastrians explain that people of other religions will reach their spiritual goal through their own religions; the Zoroastrian path was revealed exclusively for the Indo-Iranians and their descendants. Converts to the faith are not accepted, and a Parsi woman who marries a non-Parsi is effectually excluded from the Parsi religious rituals. It is true that, in the face of today's pluralism of religions, some western Zoroastrians are rethinking this traditional exclusivity, teaching the universalism implicit in Zoroastrianism and supporting intermarriage in some circumstances. Orthodox Zoroastrians protest such liberal reinterpretations and insist that the Zoroastrian community is the heritage and the responsibility of each one born into this faith.

The primary religious leaders among Zoroastrians are the priests. Zarathustra was a priest, and although he criticized many priestly practices, the major prayers and rituals have always been led and performed by priests. The priesthood has traditionally been passed on in certain families, and it is restricted to males. Training begins at a young age, and after passing examinations, serving as an acolyte, and mastering the scriptures and rituals, the person becomes a *mobed,* the first rank as a priest. Upon being appointed to serve in a temple, he attains a higher priestly rank, *dastur.* Priests are usually not salaried, but they are supported by laypeople as they say prayers and perform rituals on their behalf. Traditionally the priests are intermediaries for the people rather than being teachers or counselors. And so they chant the prayers in the ancient Avestan language, perform the fire rituals in the temple, and officiate at the other rituals and ceremonies according to the needs of the people.

Although the priestly role is important in ritual activities, given the emphasis placed on individual responsibility in the Zoroastrian tradition, it follows that laypeople are also knowledgeable and able to function as leaders in their faith. Education has been stressed in the Zoroastrian communities; the Parsis have been known as leaders in education in India. So it is not surprising that some of the widely used interpretations of Zoroastrian teaching have been written by laypeople.

The status and role of women in Zoroastrian communities presents a mixed picture, as is often the case in other religious traditions. Women cannot be priests—and this creates a large gender gap. Zoroastrian notions of purity and pollution enter the picture, and menstruating women are to be secluded in another room when prayers and rituals are performed. On the other side of the gender ledger, however, it should be mentioned that in the fundamental ceremony of Naojote (New Birth), girls as well as boys are initiated with the sacred shirt and the sacred cord to take their place as responsible bearers of the faith. In India, Parsis gained renown for their leadership in education for women.

Ethical Life and Social Responsibility   Zoroastrians, small in number today, have been much respected for their high ethical ideals and practices. The religion is based on the notion of individual free choice and responsibility, set in the cosmic drama of good and evil forces. The fundamental choice that is called for goes deep to the roots of motivation—one must choose whether to be a follower of the Truth or of the Lie, and that choice involves a transformation of one's very being, setting forth on the path of Ahura Mazda that leads ultimately to victory over evil and the transfiguration of the world.

Zarathustra called for people to show their commitment to Ahura Mazda not only by fighting against evil as such, but positively through good thoughts *(humata),* good words *(hukhta),* and good deeds *(hvarshta).* And that involves demonstrating and encouraging the virtues of truthfulness, honesty, justice, and wisdom as one lives in the world. That means, for example, that one should strive for economic justice; hoarding one's wealth or extracting usury from others is condemned. Contracts should be kept; a salary that has been promised should be paid, said Zarathustra. Being generous and charitable to those in need is especially meritorious. Zarathustra quotes words from Ahura Mazda, "He who will give (to a faithful one) a quantity of meat equal to

this bird of mine Parodarsh, I shall not question him twice on his entering Paradise."[15]

In the struggle for good, against evil, Zoroastrian tradition does not call for withdrawal from the world into some ascetic frame of life. The world itself, in both its spiritual and physical aspects, is not evil, and believers are enjoined to participate fully in the maintenance of life. People are encouraged to become married and have families; the celibate ideal fostered in some other religions finds no place in Zoroastrianism. Healthy engagement in the world, in the family, in the workplace, in the community, are proper expression of good thoughts, good words, and good deeds.

Zoroastrians today point out that their religion has long advocated a strong environmental ethic. Highly respected are the seven primal aspects of creation: sky, water, earth, fire, plants, animals, and humans. Polluting activities that degrade any of these aspects of creation are considered evils that must be striven against. For example, one motivation for placing the dead in Towers of Silence to is avoid pollution of air, water, earth, and fire. Zoroastrians speak strongly about their determination to avoid polluting rivers, air, or the earth itself through careless activities. Animals too share life energy with humans and are to be respected. Domestic animals should be fed properly so that their health and well-being can be maintained. Even plant life should be considered a gift and treated with respect and reverence.

Zoroastrians today quietly maintain their own separate religious identity, carrying on in their own way the prophet Zarathustra's ancient mission, to live and work toward the ultimate transfiguration of the world.

Discussion Questions

1   Discuss the key innovations and reforms that Zarathustra brought to the Indo-Iranian religious practices of his day. Would you call him a "prophet"?

2   What appears to be the relationship between Ahura Mazda and the Holy Immortals? Between Ahura Mazda and Angra Mainyu? Is this a "monotheism" as you understand it?

3   Explain the Zoroastrian vision of cosmic history in the four 3,000-year eras. Do you think this history is to be understood literally?

4   How are humans affected by the cosmic dualism of good and evil? What seems to be the goal of human life, in Zoroastrian thinking?

5   Discuss the significance of fire in Zoroastrian ritual and worship. How do other elements (earth, water, air, etc.) also play into Zoroastrian ritual?

6   What do you think are the key reasons for the Zoroastrian practice of exposing their dead on Towers of Silence?

7   Discuss the reasons why orthodox Zoroastrians do not accept converts into their faith. Do you think this shows an intolerant attitude? What is their feeling about people of other religions?

CHAPTER 6

Jewish Sacred Story
and Historical Context

For a special portion of people in the world today, the question of identity is linked with being Jewish. To be Jewish means in some way to identify with the sacred story of the People of the Covenant.

The religion of Judaism has a long and complex history. Unlike both Christianity and Islam, which became full-formed religions within the generation of their founders, Judaism reached its classical form more than a millennium after the foundational sacred history associated with Moses and the covenant at Sinai. Through many vicissitudes during its long history, Judaism has developed and been transformed. Yet Judaism today still retains the essential characteristics it acquired as it was shaped during the Rabbinic period—it still is the "Way of Torah."

the descendants of Abraham are contained in both the Tanakh and the Talmud.

Thanks to an enormous amount of scholarly investigation, both in archaeology and in the ancient texts, the history of the people of Israel within the world of the ancient Near East can be seen with a certain amount of clarity. That history, beginning with the ancestors of the Israelites as seminomads on the fringes of the Arabian desert around 2000 B.C.E., is a remarkable story of an obscure tribe experiencing a moment of royal glory before fading from the world scene once more. Whereas the political history of Israel may have been relatively insignificant, its sacred history has been of momentous consequence for a good part of the human race. We can use the scholarly reconstruction of Israel's history to help in understanding, but most important is seeing the Jewish story as Jews themselves interpreted it.

FOUNDATIONS
OF THE JEWISH STORY

To simplify the complex history of Judaism, we may speak of two foundings: the founding of the Israelite religion under the leadership of **Moses,** and the founding of Judaism after the Babylonian exile, beginning under the leadership of Ezra and culminating in what is known as "Rabbinic Judaism." The religion of *Israel* is that known from the pages of the Hebrew bible, the **Tanakh.** The religion of *Judaism,* grown from the Israelite religion, reached final form in the teaching of the rabbis as set down in the **Talmud.** However, to Jewish thinking, the Israelite religion and the Jewish religion are not two religions but one and the same. And the full sacred writings of this one religion of

Beginnings: Israel,
People of the Covenant

According to the story, the people of Israel were created when YHWH (the special name of Israel's God, probably pronounced **Yahweh**), the God of their ancestors, heard their cries in slavery in Egypt and brought them out, taking them as a special people by making a covenant with them and giving them the **Torah** (law). This is the founding of the religion of Israel. It should be noted that Jews of later times (and still today) adopted the practice of not pronouncing the sacred name Yahweh, substituting a word like Adonai (Lord) instead. We will use the name Yahweh in this part of the story to reflect the usage in ancient Israel.

Prologue: All Humankind and Abraham   When the Israelite singers and scribes told their national story, they reached back to the story of creation and the early history of universal humankind. According to the first chapters of *Genesis,* God created a good world and created humankind within it to take care of it and live the good life of serving God. But people turned away from God, following the evil inclination of their hearts. The first man and woman disobeyed God and were expelled from God's special garden; one of their sons (Cain) murdered the other (Abel) and was cursed to become a wanderer on the earth. Evil and violence filled the earth. When humans sought to glorify themselves by building a great tower to heaven, God confounded their languages and scattered them throughout the earth—and human history as we know it began.

This failure and scattering of humankind on earth, in spite of God's good intentions for them, set the stage for God's great plan of intervention in human history. The story introduces the family of Abraham. We know from archaeological material from ancient Mesopotamia that the stories about the clans of Abraham, Isaac, and Jacob fit into the general cultural milieu around the beginning of the second millennium B.C.E. These clans were seminomadic herders on the fringes of the Arabian desert, caught up in the general movement of similar Semitic people from southern Mesopotamia toward Syria and the land of Palestine. But, according to the story, this particular movement was more than a mere land-seeking migration of clans; it was directed by Yahweh, the God of the later Israelites.

> Now Yahweh said to Abram, "Go forth from your own land, your kindred, and your father's house, to a land that I will show you, for I will make you into a great nation. I will bless you and make your name so great that there will be a blessing. Those who bless you I will bless, but I will curse those who curse you. And in you all the families of the earth will be blessed."
>
> (*Genesis* 12:1–3)

In this story, God took steps to initiate in human history a new design, focused on Abraham and Sarah and their descendants as a great nation with a land given to them by God, who would bring a blessing to all the families of the earth through them.

Abraham and the clans associated with him were pastoralists, wandering from pastureland to pastureland. Wor-

ship focused on the clan God, called "the God of Abraham." And they also built altars to the supreme God El, who was worshiped in different places under names such as El 'Elyon (Exalted God), El Roi (Seeing God), and El Shaddai (Mighty God). But in the view of the Israelite story, the God the ancestors worshiped was none other than Yahweh, the personal God of the Israelites (even though, according to the story, Yahweh revealed that name for the first time to Moses). God made a covenant with Abraham, giving him children in his old age. First Hagar, servant of his wife Sarah, bore him Ishmael, and then Isaac was born from Sarah, the ancestress of the people of Israel. As the sign of the covenant, God instituted the ritual of circumcision for Abraham and his descendants. Showing faithfulness, God continually renewed the promises to Abraham even when Abraham faltered in his faith, as when he passed off his wife Sarah as his sister so the Egyptians would not kill him to possess her (*Genesis* 12:10–20).

In the end, Abraham stood the test of faithfulness. When God commanded him to sacrifice his beloved son Isaac, Abraham obeyed, and God spoke through an angel: "Do not lay your hand against the boy or do anything to him, for now I know that you are God-fearing, because you have not withheld your son, your only son, from me" (*Genesis* 22:12). God provided a ram to be sacrificed in place of Isaac. Since then, Abraham has been the model of Jewish faithfulness to God in all situations.

The story traces God's covenant through Abraham and Sarah's son Isaac and his wife Rebekah, to Jacob, Isaac's younger son. The sacred history does not present these ancestors as perfect heroes. Jacob, for example, cheated his brother, and by his cunning he established himself as a wealthy man with twelve sons. A key story tells how Jacob wrestled with God one whole night, refusing to let go until he received God's blessing. With the blessing Jacob also received a new name: "No longer shall your name be called Jacob, but **Israel,** because you have striven with God and with men, and you have prevailed" (*Genesis* 32:28). The name *Israel* means "he strives with God," and it became the name of Jacob's descendants in a very expressive way: They are God's people who always struggle with God.

The story reaches the end of the prologue by describing how Jacob (Israel) and his family found their way down into Egypt during a drastic famine and how Joseph (one of the sons, who had been sold into slavery by his brothers) rose to great power in Egypt. This took place during the

Obeying God's command, Abraham prepares to sacrifice his son Isaac, but an angel of the Lord stops him. "Abraham's Sacrifice of Isaac," by Caravaggio. Uffizi Gallery, Florence, Italy.

time that lower Egypt was ruled by the Hyksos, Asiatic people who wrested control from the Egyptians for a time (ca. 1750–1550 B.C.E.). During this period the **Hebrews,** as Jacob's descendants were called, prospered in Egypt. But eventually the Hyksos were driven out by the Egyptians, and the Hebrews consequently fell upon bad times under Egyptian domination. The sacred story tells how there arose a king of Egypt "who knew not Joseph" (*Exodus* 1:8), who enslaved and oppressed the Hebrews. Here was the deepest crisis of all: The children of Abraham were in bondage, with the God of their fathers and the covenant with Abraham forgotten.

Exodus from Egypt   The people cried out in their slavery, and "God heard their groaning, and God remembered his covenant with Abraham, with Isaac, and with Jacob" (*Exodus* 2:24). Now the great drama of redemption begins, as God called Moses to deliver this people.

As told in the book of **Exodus,** the birth of Moses took place under foreboding circumstances, for the Egyptians were killing all Hebrew infant boys to control the Hebrew population. But Moses' mother placed her infant son in a basket among the reeds at the brink of the river Nile, and he was found and adopted by a daughter of the king. Given an Egyptian name, Moses was brought up at the Egyptian court, but he became a fugitive because he murdered an Egyptian who was beating a Hebrew. He fled to the desert east of Egypt, where he lived with Jethro, the priest of the Midianites, a clan related to the Hebrews. He stayed there for years and even married Zipporah, the daughter of the Midianite priest.

While Moses was tending the sheep of his father-in-law on the holy mountain of Midian, God, manifested in a burning bush, encountered him and told him to go to the pharaoh of Egypt and demand that he let the Hebrews go free. When Moses asked who this God was, God revealed the special name, "Yahweh," interpreting it to mean, "I Am"—associating the name Yahweh with the verb *hayah,* "to be." At the same time Yahweh identified with the God worshiped by the ancestors of the Hebrews:

> You shall speak thus to the people of Israel, "Yahweh, the God of your fathers, the God of Abraham, the God of Isaac, and the God of Jacob, has sent me to you." This is my name for ever, my memorial throughout all generations.

(*Exodus* 3:15)

Then Yahweh commanded Moses, with his brother Aaron, to deliver the Hebrews from Egypt and to bring them back to worship at this wilderness mountain after they escaped from Egypt.

When the pharaoh resisted Moses' demands, the story continues, God brought a series of terrible plagues, ending with the destruction of all the firstborn of the Egyptians, after which the pharaoh and the Egyptians finally relented. This "night of watching," described in Exodus 12, has ever since been celebrated in the Passover (Pesach) festival. Each Israelite family was to slaughter an unblemished lamb, paint the doorposts with its blood, and roast and eat it with unleavened cakes and bitter herbs. They were to eat it with belt fastened, sandals on their feet, and staff in hand, in a posture of haste. This was to be a day of remembrance, a festival to be kept from generation to generation for all time—so all future generations could reexperience the great deliverance of the Exodus.

When finally the Hebrews, brought together under the leadership of Moses, escaped from Egypt, the Egyptians pursued. But God safely brought the Hebrews through the Red Sea (literally, the sea of reeds), but then routed and utterly destroyed the army of the Egyptians in that same sea. God led the Hebrews through the wilderness with signs and wonders, finally bringing them back to the holy mountain in the wilderness, Mt. Sinai.

Torah and Covenant at Mt. Sinai   Here at Mt. Sinai, according to the Jewish story, the greatest miracle of all took place:

> Moses brought the people out from the camp to meet God, and they took their stand at the foot of the mountain. Because Yahweh descended upon it in fire, all of Mt. Sinai was smoking. . . . And Yahweh came down upon the top of Mt. Sinai, and he summoned Moses to the mountain-top. Then Moses went up. . . . And God spoke all these words: "I am Yahweh your God who brought you out of Egypt, out of the house of slavery. You shall have no other gods before me."
>
> (*Exodus* 19:17–20:3)

Thus God spoke to Moses, and through Moses to the people of Israel, the whole Torah, the laws and commandments that would form the basis of life for the people.

The revelation of the Torah on Mt. Sinai climaxed with the making of the **covenant** with the people of Israel. The covenant God made with them was a two-way contract: God would be their God, bringing them to the promised land, protecting them; they would be a holy people, serving only Yahweh of all gods and obeying the commandments.

After Moses told the people all the words of God and wrote them down, they sacrificed bulls as offerings. Moses took half the blood in basins and threw it against the altar; then he read the book of the covenant to the people. They said, "We will do all that Yahweh has spoken, and we will obey." And Moses flung the blood over the people, ratifying the covenant God had made with them on the basis of the Torah (*Exodus* 24:3–8). Here on Mt. Sinai came the self-revelation of God, and by it God created both Torah (the law) and Israel (the covenant people).

To understand the centrality and the uniqueness of this covenant relationship between Yahweh and the people of Israel, it is helpful to see how the Israelite story contrasts it with the religions of the other peoples of the ancient Near East. Among the agricultural city-states of Egypt, Mesopotamia, and Palestine, a cosmic type of religion prevailed, with many gods in charge of the different forces of nature. It was the power of these gods that made the cosmos a functioning world, and the role of humans was to serve the gods, responding to their will, entreating them to act favorably, and empowering their vitality by periodic rituals and festivals. In this organic or biological view of the functioning of the universe, humans played an important role. When the vitality of the gods would run down (as, for example, when vegetation dies in the winter), it was necessary for the people by ritual means to expunge the used-up forces and restore the life-power of the gods.

Among the Canaanites, Israel's neighbors in Palestine, particular importance was attached to the storm-fertility god, **Ba'al,** and the fertility goddess, Asherah. To the Canaanite farmers, the powers of these gods of vegetation were of vital importance. Rituals aimed at awakening them so the crops would grow included sexual rituals at the local shrines in which all the people had the duty to participate. The people felt bound to the gods in the recurring cycles of the forces of nature, and serving the gods meant participating in those natural fertility cycles so the power of the gods would continually be replenished.

Contrasting the religion of Israel to this cosmic type of religion, which characterized the great civilizations of neighboring peoples, the Israelite story emphasizes over and again that the people of Israel are bound to their God Yahweh in a covenant relationship, based on law given by God. A covenant *(berith)* is a contract, a treaty between two parties, which binds them together with mutual promises and obligations. Rather than a cosmic or biological relationship, the Israelites were related to God in a political contract, with Yahweh as a personal partner who responded to them in the give-and-take of personal decisions and actions. Rather than focusing on the rhythm of the seasons of nature, their religion focused on encounters with Yahweh in the events of their historical life. Rather than being bound by the laws of the natural processes of death and life, they were bound by the mutual obligations of the covenant, based on the covenant law mediated to them by Moses.

Israel's covenant law was communal law, containing stipulations both in relation to God and to fellow Israelites. Yahweh alone was to be worshiped, not with graven images and fertility rituals like the Canaanite gods, but with prayer and praise, with repentance and sacrificial gifts. Fellow Israelites were to be treated with equality and justice, to be loved as oneself. Israel's whole life, whether concerned with worship of God or with human conduct in society, was structured by Yahweh's covenant demand: "You shall be holy, for I Yahweh your God am holy" (*Leviticus* 19:2). It was by the keeping of the covenant that they retained their identity as "Israel, the people of Yahweh."

The Promised Land and the Kingdom

After the exodus and the making of the covenant at Mt. Sinai, Israel's story continues with a movement toward the fulfillment of their destiny as Yahweh's people: the possession of the Holy Land and the establishing of the Kingdom of Israel. Characteristically intertwined in the story is the tension of the covenant, the "tug of war" between God and Israel symbolically portrayed by Jacob wrestling with God. God promises and demands and pushes Israel onward. Israel responds sometimes faithfully, sometimes unfaithfully. Yahweh punishes but restores in love. And the covenant relationship goes on between the two partners.

After setting out from Mt. Sinai to possess the promised land, according to the story, the people frequently murmured and rebelled against Yahweh. They even accused Moses and Yahweh of dragging them out to the desert to die. Yahweh punished—a whole generation died in the wilderness, including even Moses—but Yahweh also fulfilled the promise by bringing their descendants into the land of Canaan and giving them victory and possession under the leadership of Joshua. The actual conquest was, as we know from archaeology and other historical sources, a long process of infiltrating, conquering, and assimilating. It is described in the sacred history as a "holy war," with Yahweh at their head conquering the enemies with a divine terror. They would move onward with the portable shrine called the "Ark of Yahweh's Covenant" leading the way. When the ark began to move, Moses chanted, "Arise, O Yahweh, and may your enemies be scattered." And when the ark stopped, he intoned, "Rest, O Yahweh of the ten thousand thousands of Israel" (*Numbers* 10:35–36). These wars of conquest had religious meaning in that taking the land of Canaan was a covenant duty. The Holy Land was their promised inheritance, and by taking possession of it they were glorifying Yahweh's name before the nations. In retelling this story, then, the identity of the people of Israel has always been bound up with the Holy Land.

The people of Israel established themselves in Palestine by about 1200 B.C.E., and for the next two centuries they maintained a loose tribal confederation, adapting themselves to an agricultural rather than pastoral way of life, and rallying around tribal leaders (judges) to fight off hostile peoples. Eventually there came about two very important transformations of their destiny: They settled down as farmers, building cities to dwell in; and they became a kingdom, the Kingdom of David. Both these developments have central significance in the telling of the story, for both involved the relation of Israel to their covenant God.

Struggle with Canaanite Culture   The first transformation involved the relationship of the newly arrived Israelites with the agricultural religion of the Canaanites, which centered on the fertility god Ba'al, together with the goddess Asherah and other gods and goddesses. The Israelites had been seminomadic pastoralists, wandering with their herds in the semiarid regions of the area. They had met their God Yahweh in the desert, and as they wandered Yahweh went with them, the divine presence symbolized by the portable shrine, the Ark of the Covenant.

But now that they settled down, their way of life changed drastically. They became farmers, and, influenced by their Canaanite agriculturalist neighbors, they were strongly attracted to the gods of the land. To some Israelites, Yahweh seemed to be the god only of the desert; but Ba'al and Asherah's powers were important for the vitality of the land, so they became worshipers of these fertility deities.

Many Israelites tried to remain faithful to Yahweh, but they introduced fertility rituals and ideas into their worship of Yahweh. According to the prophet Jeremiah, upon every high hill and under every green tree the people were sprawling like harlots, participating in fertility rituals at Ba'al shrines (*Jeremiah* 2:20).

This struggle between faithfulness to Yahweh and the need to worship the gods of the land went on for many centuries, providing much of the drama of the Hebrew scriptures. The key question was powerfully articulated by the early prophet Elijah, in a day when the queen of Israel was none other then Jezebel, a Ba'al worshiper from Tyre and a fierce persecutor of the worshipers of Yahweh. The story tells how Elijah challenged the people, "How long will you keep on limping on two different opinions? If Yahweh is God, follow him; but if Ba'al, follow him." So Elijah challenged the 450 prophets of Ba'al to a contest, to see which god would answer their invocations by sending fire to consume the sacrifice. The prophets of Ba'al danced wildly, prophesying and crying out to Ba'al to no avail all day. Elijah indulged in ridicule: "Cry louder, for he is a god. Perhaps he is musing or engaged, or he is on a journey, or maybe he is sleeping and must be awakened." Finally it was Elijah's turn, and he prayed: "O Yahweh, God of Abraham, Isaac, and Israel, today may it be known that you are God in Israel and that I am your servant." The fire of Yahweh fell, consuming the offering and the whole altar; and the people fell on their faces and cried, "Yahweh is God! Yahweh is God!" As a final emphatic gesture, Elijah seized the prophets of Ba'al and Asherah and slaughtered them all (*I Kings* 18:17–40).

Such stories tell how the Israelites, struggling and faltering, finally came to know Yahweh as the one God of all, even of the rain and the land and the crops. The upshot of the whole dramatic struggle of Israel with Canaanite culture is the overwhelming monotheistic commitment emphasized in the psalms and prayers and prophetic writings of the Hebrew scriptures, echoed in the rabbinic writings and the liturgies of the Jewish synagogues.

The Kingdom of Israel The other great transformation that the story brings to center stage is the creation of the Kingdom of Israel. The story delights in the struggle between Israel and Yahweh. The initial impulse toward kingship in Israel was the desire to have "a king to rule over us, like all the nations" (*I Samuel* 8:5), and this was understood by the tribal

leader Samuel to be a rejection of Yahweh, who had always been their king in the covenant relationship.

In the characteristic double action of warning and promise, Yahweh warned them through Samuel of the tragedies and failures that lay ahead in becoming a kingdom ruled by a powerful king, warnings that are abundantly illustrated in the stories of the sins and rebellions of the kings over the next five hundred years in Israel. But Yahweh also responded positively to the request for a king, and the symbol of Yahweh ruling through the agency of the king of Israel became a primary element of the religion of Israel. First Saul was anointed as a tribal king, but it was really David (ruled ca. 1000–960 B.C.E.) who consolidated all the tribes into the Kingdom of Israel and established the religious model of the king, adopted son of Yahweh, with whom Yahweh has made an everlasting covenant to rule over the sacred people. The Davidic kingship thus was integrated into the covenant relationship between Yahweh and the chosen people. This was celebrated in one of the psalms:

> Your love, O Yahweh, I will sing forever! . . .
> Of old you declared in a vision
>   and spoke to your faithful one:
> "I have endowed a warrior with strength,
>   I have exalted a chosen one from the people.
> I have found David my servant,
>   with my holy oil I have anointed him. . . .
> He will cry to me, 'You are my father,
>   my God, my saving rock.'
> And I will make him first-born,
>   highest among the kings of the earth.
> Forever I will maintain for him my love,
>   and my covenant will stand firm for him.
> I will establish his posterity forever,
>   and his throne as the duration of the heavens."
>
> (*Psalm* 89:1, 19–29)

A king must have a royal city, according to the divine kingship ideology of Israel's surrounding cultures, with the god of the kingdom dwelling in the royal temple. Therefore in Israel there was established the holy city of Jerusalem and the temple on Mt. Zion—extremely important symbols in the Jewish religious tradition. David was originally king only over the tribe of Judah, ruling from the Judean city of Hebron. But when the elders of all the tribes of Israel made a covenant with David before Yahweh and anointed him king of Israel, David needed a new capital city outside tribal territory to symbolize the unity of all the tribes. So he and his personal army attacked the Canaanite city of Jerusalem and took it. David took up residence in the stronghold of Zion, now renamed the City of David, and built his palace there. Prior to this time the Ark of Yahweh's Covenant had been moved around to different sanctuaries among the tribes, but now David wanted to bring this shrine of Yahweh's presence to his royal city to symbolize the religious unity of the new kingdom. So in a great festive procession, the ark was brought up to Zion, the City of David, and placed in a tent sanctuary there (*II Samuel* 6). Now Yahweh was present in Zion, the holy city.

But this new interpretation of Israel's relation to their God was not accomplished without the characteristic struggle symbolized by the name of "Israel." When David decided to build a temple for Yahweh in place of the tent on Zion, the prophet Nathan brought word from Yahweh that the tradition of Yahweh dwelling in a tent should be maintained. From the religions of the surrounding peoples, the Israelites knew that the god of the land, Ba'al, was housed in temples rooted in the earth; to build a temple for Yahweh seemed to some a rejection of their God who had delivered them from Egypt and dwelt among them in the holy tent.

Yet David's son Solomon, in a time of peace and prosperity, accomplished what had been denied to David. With the help of Canaanite architects and workers, he constructed a magnificent temple, thirteen years in the building. In a great festival, the priests brought the Ark of the Covenant to the inner shrine, the Most Holy Place of the temple, and "the glory of Yahweh filled the house of Yahweh" (*I Kings* 8:11).

The Idea of the Messiah   It is from the role of the king as the deliverer of Israel that the notion of the "messiah" arose in Israel. Originally the term **messiah**, which means "anointed one," applied to the king as the one anointed to lead Yahweh's people. But eventually the kingship was swept away in the destructions from foreign invasions. Yet the kingship had become an important part of the religious vision of Israel, and the expectation arose that God would not abandon the promises to King David, that one day the Kingdom of David would be restored and made great in the earth once more. Thus when the kingship fell on bad times, the hope arose that God would sometime in the future send a new son of David, a messiah, to restore the house of David. The idea of the messiah has undergone many developments in Jewish thought, but the basis of this important expectation was established when Israel chose, and Yahweh accepted, a king over the people Israel.

With the establishment of the Kingdom of Israel, the king ruling over Yahweh's people, and the temple as Yahweh's presence in the holy city of Jerusalem, the promised destiny of the people of Israel might seem to have been reached. And in a certain sense that is true, for most of the primary symbols of the Jewish tradition had by now been created: Abraham, Exodus, covenant and Torah, holy people, Yahweh as Lord of all the earth, the king, the messiah,

and the holy city of Jerusalem with its temple. But the religion of Israel was based on a continuing covenantal tug of war with Yahweh, and that struggle went on in episodes of faithfulness and unfaithfulness, punishment and restoration, according to the sacred story.

Decline of the Kingdom: The Prophets

The story presents the history of kingship in Israel in dark colors. Even the glorious reigns of David and Solomon were marred by sin and serving other gods. The story reports that David's lust for the woman Bathsheba led him to have her husband murdered so he could have her. Solomon loved women so much that he had seven hundred wives, all princesses, and three hundred concubines; these foreign women enticed him to worship other gods. Finally, as punishment, God tore the kingdom from Solomon's son's hand, leaving only the tribe of Judah as the Kingdom of David, the other tribes breaking away to form the northern Kingdom of Israel.

The judgment passed on many of the kings of Judah and of North Israel is scathing. The great majority of them, according to the later story, turned away to serve other gods, oppressed the poor, and generally broke covenant with Yahweh, all this leading to the destruction and exile of both North Israel and Judah. The northern Kingdom of Israel was destroyed and the population scattered by the Assyrians in 721 B.C.E. And the final night descended with the destruction of the Kingdom of Judah in 587 B.C.E. by the Babylonians and the exile of the few Jewish survivors in Babylon—the sole remaining heirs of the briefly glorious history of the covenant people of Yahweh. But in this struggle with darkness, a remarkable new religious phenomenon appeared—the **prophets** of Israel, providing yet another important element in the making of the Jewish religious tradition.

The early prophets in Israel were groups of seers who entered into visionary, ecstatic trances, like shamans, and gave out the word of Yahweh for a particular situation. Both Kings Saul and David, for example, were caught up in the ecstatic contagion of these bands of prophets (*I Samuel* 10:5–13; 19:18–24). Somewhat later, individual prophets began to speak forth God's word, as when the prophet Nathan brought God's judgment against King David for

having taken Bathsheba. Elijah and Elisha thundered God's words against the Baʿal worshipers of their day.

Beginning with the prophet Amos in the middle of the eighth century B.C.E., there arose a series of individuals known as the "classical" prophets, those whose words were recorded in the scrolls of the prophets. The prophets were spokespersons for Yahweh. They received a word from Yahweh for a particular situation, and they proclaimed and interpreted it to the king and the people, no matter what the consequences, be it a word of promise and hope or a word of warning and judgment. Sometimes they acted out the "word" of Yahweh, as when Hosea married a sacred prostitute from one of the fertility shrines to demonstrate how God kept loving Israel even as they went after other gods (*Hosea* 1–3). Again, Isaiah walked naked through the streets of Jerusalem for three years as a visual warning that the Israelites would be led away naked as prisoners of war (*Isaiah* 20:1–4).

The prophets interpreted the word of Yahweh for the people, showing them how Yahweh had acted in the history of Israel and would continue to act in the future. They proclaimed that Yahweh had a plan, a design for the covenant people. The unfaithfulness of the people would lead Yahweh to punish and destroy them. But God would continue to love the people even in destroying them; eventually, the prophets envisioned, God would restore them anew as the covenant people.

The prophets strongly emphasized the ethical consequences of being the people of Yahweh, proclaiming the wrath of Yahweh when they did not live up to the covenant. Amos, for example, lashed out against the women of the nobility: "Listen to this word, you cows of Bashan who are on Mt. Samaria, you who oppress the poor, who crush the destitute" (*Amos* 4:1). He uttered unthinkable words against the official religion, which he said masked the covenant demand for justice and morality. Through the prophet Amos the word of Yahweh sounded forth:

> I hate, I despise your pilgrim-festivals,
>   and I do not delight in your sacred assemblies.
> Even if you offer me your burnt offerings and cereal
>   offerings,
>   I will not accept them,
>   nor will I look on the peace offerings of your fatted
>   animals.

Remove the noise of your songs from me;
    the music of your harps I will not hear,
Rather, let justice roll on like the waters,
    and righteousness like an everflowing river.

(*Amos* 5:21–24)

To be chosen people of Yahweh, the creator of the world, meant, according to the prophets, both a great rejoicing and a heavy responsibility to glorify God's name by demonstrating justice and righteousness in the world. And when they did not live up to their covenant commitment, they would receive special punishment from God. God's word came through Amos: "Hear this word that Yahweh speaks against you, O Israelites, against the whole family which he brought up from Egypt: 'Only you have I known among all the families of the earth; therefore will I punish you for all your iniquities'" (*Amos* 3:1–2).

In their prediction of doom and destruction, the prophets insisted it was Yahweh, the God of Israel, who was bringing the destruction, not the various powers of the world. When the Assyrians came against Israel, the prophet Isaiah said the Assyrians, in spite of their arrogance, were merely the tool of Yahweh, the rod of God's anger (*Isaiah* 10:5). And Jeremiah interpreted the destruction of Jerusalem by the Babylonians as part of God's plan. He spoke the word of Yahweh: "I am the one who made the earth, humankind, and animals on the earth with my great power and my outstretched arm, and I give it to whomever I will. Now I give all these lands into the hand of Nebuchadnezzar, king of Babylon, my servant" (*Jeremiah* 27:5–6).

But precisely because the prophets saw the invasion and destruction of Israel by foreign foes as God's own doing, they had hope, for they knew God would never abandon the divine plan and the promises to the chosen people. Through this same Jeremiah, God spoke again:

I will gather them from all the lands to which I banished them in my anger, wrath, and great fury, and I will return them to this place and cause them to dwell in safety. Then they will be my people and I will be their God. And I will give them one heart and one way of life, to fear me forever, for their good and their children's good after them. I will make an eternal covenant with them, not to turn away from doing them good. And I will place the fear of me in their hearts so they will not turn away from

me. I will rejoice over them to do them good, and I will plant them in this land in faithfulness with my whole heart and soul.

(*Jeremiah* 32:37–41)

Yahweh would not let the people go, the prophets said. God would make a new covenant with them and restore them to their land, so they could go on living as the sacred people.

So what would seem to be merely a tragic fate in the cruel movement of world history—a tiny nation perishing like countless others—becomes in the eyes of the prophets a part of God's own design. God is involved in human history through the chosen servant, Israel; as they suffer punishment, God suffers with them (*Isaiah* 63:9). A deeply moving image in the prophetic writings is that of the Suffering Servant. The great prophet who wrote the words contained in the second part of the scroll of Isaiah (*Isaiah* 40ff.) lived in Babylonian exile. To answer the question of why Israel was suffering so much, this prophet, whom we call Second Isaiah, spoke of God's plan to lay all the sins and burdens of the world on the chosen servant Israel (*Isaiah* 53). To Jews, this picture of Israel as God's Suffering Servant, bringing justice and righteousness into the world even as they suffer with God the pains and the rejections of the world, has been a sustaining force in times of suffering and persecution.

The Founding of Judaism

The Babylonian **Exile** (beginning in 587 B.C.E.) brought a drastic crisis in the sacred history of the Jews. In a sense, the story of Israelite religion came to an end, for the Kingdom of Israel was no more, and the Kingdom of Judah was destroyed never to reappear as a kingdom, with its survivors as exiles in a strange land far from Jerusalem. The story relates that God intervened again to deliver the chosen people from Babylon through the work of King Cyrus of Persia, who conquered the Babylonians and established the Persian Empire. As part of his enlightened policy, in about 538 B.C.E. Cyrus permitted and even assisted Jewish exiles to return to Jerusalem (*II Chronicles* 36:22–23; *Ezra* 1:1–4). But the few exiles who returned found Jerusalem devastated and the surrounding population hostile. The glorious Kingdom of David was forever gone. Something new had to be created, a Jewish community that could remain faithful to the covenant under these difficult circumstances. Here Ezra the scribe enters the story with what we may call the second founding of Judaism.

Ezra and the Early Jewish Community   Ezra was a priest and scribe among the Jewish exiles still living in Babylon a century after the first groups of exiles returned to Jerusalem. The religious life of the Jews in Jerusalem was in disarray. The temple was used for secular purposes, inter-marriage was producing children who could not even speak Hebrew (even the high priest had married a non-Jewish Samaritan), and businesses ran as usual on the **Sabbath.** Ezra arrived in Jerusalem from Babylon with an unusual commission from the Persian king giving him religious authority over all Jews in and around Judea. His official title was Secretary for the Law of the God of Heaven (*Ezra* 7:12). Ezra was learned in the Torah of Moses, and apparently he brought with him a copy of the Torah that had been edited by Jewish scholars in Babylon (*Nehemiah* 8:1).

Ezra's great task was to make the whole Jewish people renew their covenant obligations to their God; he argued that it was because they had broken the covenant that the disastrous destructions had occurred. He read the Torah publicly to the assembled people from early morning until noon. The reading and study of the Torah continued day after day, and the Jews renewed the covenant by swearing to obey all the law given by God through Moses. The purifica-tion of the people called for drastic action, for the reality of mixed marriages (Jews with non-Jews) had become such a deep problem that it threatened the very identity of the Jewish community. Ezra stood before Yahweh, weeping and confessing the sin of the people in marrying foreign wives and thus turning away from God. Drawn by this public dis-play of emotional repentance, a great crowd gathered round and became convinced that the only hope lay in divorcing their foreign wives. A commission was set up to see that all mixed marriages were dissolved, and three months later the Jewish people were again pure (*Ezra* 9–10).

An important part of Ezra's purpose was to transform the lives of the people so they would keep the covenant in all aspects of their daily lives, and this went beyond the dis-solving of mixed marriages. He brought the people together day by day to study the Torah—and in the process, Judaism was transformed into a religion centered on the study of the Torah. Ezra probably drew on his own experience in Babylon. Since there was no temple there, the Jews met at the abode of religious leaders on the Sabbath, and there they read the

Torah, studied it, and applied it to their lives. It is from these kinds of meetings that over the course of the next centuries the important institution of the **synagogue** stemmed. While the word *synagogue* came to mean a building, the Greek word originally referred to a religious meeting. Since these meet-ings took place apart from the temple, the focus was not on priestly sacrifice but on prayer and study of the Torah. To lead in studying the Torah, there developed a group of scribes capable of reading, interpreting, and applying the Torah—the teachers of Torah who later were called **rabbis.**

With these developments, Judaism, while remaining faithful to the ideals of Israel, the people of God, took on a new look. A transition had been made from a militarized kingdom to a community based on the Law of Moses. Now Judaism could exist with or without statehood, even scat-tered throughout the world. Central to life in the Jewish community was study of the Torah, and synagogues even-tually developed wherever Jewish communities lived. Teachers of Torah became the key religious leaders, even though official religious and political power remained with the priests for a number of centuries.

The Maccabean Revolt and Roman Dominance   The next centuries were stormy years for the Jews. Great events took place, such as the war of independence against the Seleucids of Syria. Climaxing long years of Seleucid rule over Palestine, Antiochus IV, who called himself Epiphanes (The Manifest [God]), tried to Hellenize the Jews—make them accept Greek culture and religion—and thus break and destroy the Jewish religion. Around 167 B.C.E., he set up an altar of Zeus in the temple and issued laws prohibiting the distinctive Jewish practices. Led in revolution by the Maccabean family, Jewish fighters managed to drive out the Seleucids and create an independent state that lasted for the next century. Their victory culminated in the cleansing of the desecrated temple in 165 B.C.E., an event celebrated in the festival of **Hanukkah.** But the Romans took over Palestine in 63 B.C.E., and Jewish national independence came to an end until about two thousand years later.

In spite of the Maccabean resistance, Hellenization did affect the Jews, especially those large numbers who lived in cities like Alexandria in Egypt, speaking Greek and follow-ing Hellenistic culture. For Jews such as these, a translation of the Hebrew scriptures into Greek was made, called the Septuagint (because seventy Jewish scholars were said to have made the translation).

A central figure among Hellenistic Jews was Philo of Alexandria (ca. 20 B.C.E.–ca. 45 C.E.). Committed to the Jewish faith, he attempted to show its correlation with the major teachings of Hellenistic philosophy. He accepted Greek philosophical ideas such as the dualism of material and spirit, and he taught that through reason the soul can be illumined by God. In order to reconcile biblical ideas with Greek philosophy, Philo made use of allegory in interpreting the Bible; the biblical stories showed the human path in overcoming the passions and seeking spiritual illumination. Abraham's journey to Palestine, for example, is an allegory of the soul's journey toward God.

The Western (Wailing) Wall, a most sacred site for Jews, is part of the foundation of the ancient temple. Above on the temple mount is the Muslim Dome of the Rock mosque.

During the Roman period in Palestine, Jewish groups developed that pursued different ways to live according to the Law of Moses. There were the **Sadducees** who made up the ruling class, the priests, and the nobility, who cooperated with the Romans and lived conservatively according to the Law. Activists called **Zealots** agitated for the violent overthrow of Roman dominion and the establishing of a new independent Jewish state. Separatists called **Essenes** withdrew from Jewish society because they considered it too corrupt; they lived in the desert near the Dead Sea and attempted to practice a "pure" Judaism. There was a group known as the **Pharisees,** including many scribes and teachers (rabbis), who reinterpreted the Torah in such a way as to apply it to all aspects of Jewish life. It was these Pharisees who were the forerunners of what is known as **Rabbinic Judaism.** And some Jews looked to Jesus of Nazareth, one of these rabbis, as the messiah (the Christ) and called themselves "Christians"; these messianists eventually parted company with Judaism.

The Development of Rabbinic Judaism　An important event for the development of Rabbinic Judaism was the destruction of Jerusalem and the temple by the Romans in 70 C.E. and the scattering of the Jews. This event initiated what is known as the Great **Diaspora,** or "scattering" of the

Jews. It destroyed what had been the heart of Judaism: the temple and the Jewish community in Jerusalem. The establishment represented by the Sadducees, centered on the temple and its institutions, came to a final end. The Zealots held out at the mountain fortress **Masada,** near the Dead Sea, for several years; finally the whole group committed suicide rather than submit to the Romans, providing for all Jews a symbol of bravery and zeal. But this was the end of the Zealot aspiration. The Essenes were destroyed in the general upheaval. But the Pharisees scattered to other places, taking their Torah scrolls with them, setting up synagogues and schools to study the Torah. It is this branch of Jews—the rabbis of the Pharisees and their followers—who continued the religion of Judaism in Palestine and beyond, structuring it as we know it today.

And so the sacred history of the Jewish people includes stories about the rabbis. A story about an important rabbi, Yohanan ben Zakkai, and his disciple, Joshua ben Hananiah, takes this view of the destruction of the temple:

Once as Rabban Johanan ben Zakkai was coming forth from Jerusalem, Rabbi Joshua followed after him and beheld the Temple in ruins. "Woe unto us!," Rabbi Joshua cried, "that this, the place where the iniquities of Israel were atoned for, is laid waste!" "My son," Rabban Johanan said to him, "be not grieved: we have another atonement as effective as this. And what is it?

It is acts of loving-kindness, as it is said, 'For I desire mercy and not sacrifice.' "

(*Avot de Rabbi Natan*, ch. 6)[1]

The rabbis taught that the temple was everywhere, in the home and in the heart; Jewish life has sacrifices greater than those of the temple. The Torah had commanded, "You shall be a kingdom of priests and a holy nation" (*Exodus* 19:6). Therefore the laws of the Torah about purity, thought by some to apply only to the temple, were to be extended to the life of every Jew in the home. The other realities of the life of Israel, God's people, were gone—the kingship, the Holy Land, and the temple. But the Torah remained. And in keeping the Torah, the Jewish community, wherever it might be, was fulfilling all the hopes and dreams of Israel, the people of God.

The Making of the Talmud   But how can the obscure, arcane, and difficult rules and commandments scattered throughout the Hebrew Torah, given in an ancient age for use in temple rituals, be "kept" by Jews living in a totally removed age and place? We can end our brief look at the essentials of the story of the founding of Judaism by hearing the rabbis on that: God has given the "oral Torah," which interprets the written Torah in practical, everyday settings. According to the rabbis, at Sinai God handed down a two-part revelation: the part Moses wrote down and passed on publicly in Israel as the Torah; and the oral part, preserved by the great heroes and prophets of the past and handed on to the rabbis who finally wrote it down (the Talmud). The *whole* Torah thus consists of both parts, the written Torah and the oral Torah. And by studying and living according to the whole Torah, one is conforming to the very will and the way of God.

A striking Jewish notion is that the oral Torah is open-ended; new things can be discovered in the Torah. Whatever the most recent rabbi learns through proper study of the Torah can be considered as much a part of the Torah revealed to Moses as is a sentence of the Hebrew scripture itself. In that sense, learned Jews actually participate with God in the giving of the Torah. For Rabbinic Judaism, keeping the Torah becomes the key element in God's design for the world. It is said, for example, that if all Israel would properly keep a single Sabbath, the messiah would come. If Israel would fully and completely keep Torah, all pagan rule would end.

Because of this central importance of keeping the Torah, the Jewish sacred history tells also about the great rabbis who participated in the creation and writing down of the "oral Torah" (the Talmud) as the essential guide to keeping Torah. There are, for example, the famous rabbis Hillel and Shammai in the early days of Herod's rule, who founded two houses that debated the law. Rabbi Akiba ben Joseph, tortured and martyred under the Romans for teaching the Torah, gathered much of this rabbinic material, and his disciple, Rabbi Meir, elaborated it. Eventually the material was classified and written down under the direction of the Patriarch Judah I (135–217 C.E.) and was called the *Mishnah* (repetition).

But the rabbinic teaching and discussion went on among rabbis in Babylon and in Palestine. These additional discussions produced many further teachings and commentaries on the *Mishnah* known collectively as the *Gemara* (completion) or Talmud (instruction). By the end of the fifth century C.E., the *Gemara* was also written down and added to the *Mishnah*. Eventually the whole set of writings became known as the Talmud (existing in both a Babylonian and a Palestinan version). The creation of the Talmud, the "oral Torah," is one of the essential elements in the story that provides identity for Jews. In fact, it is the oral Torah, the Talmud, as interpretation of the written Torah, that lays out the complete Jewish way of life.

FURTHER TRANSFORMATIONS OF JUDAISM

Not long after the Babylonian Talmud was completed, providing a complete structure for Jewish life, the Islamic revolution burst onto the scene. For quite a few centuries, the centers of Jewish life were in Muslim lands: Baghdad (in Babylonia), Egypt, North Africa, and Spain. The Middle Ages were full of suffering and persecution, although Jewish life continued to develop and flourish. With the Enlightenment came the beginnings of Jewish emancipation, and Judaism developed in new ways to meet the challenges of the modern age.

Jewish Life and Thought in Islamic Contexts

Muhammad respected the Jews as a "people of the book," seeing himself as the last of the line of prophets. Few Jews followed Muhammad's new revelation, but generally, Muslims allowed Jews to live peacefully within the vast territories taken over by the rapid Islamic expansion. As Muhammad and his successors were establishing dominion over all of western Asia, North Africa, and Spain, Jews in these lands continued to look to the Jewish academies in Babylonia for leadership. As new situations arose, they submitted questions to the rabbinic leaders (Geonim) of these academies, who provided answers *(responsa)* with new interpretations of the Talmud. Through their *responsa,* these scholars fixed the pattern of Jewish worship and life.

During this time, Islamic scholars held the intellectual leadership of the Mediterranean world, translating the whole corpus of Greek scientific and philosophical thought into Arabic. A number of Jewish thinkers were attracted to this new learning, but there were also reactions against it. For several centuries Jewish thinkers struggled with the problem of faith and reason: Is truth acquired by one's own reason and judgment, or simply from the authoritative revelation of the Torah?

The Challenge of the Karaites   A crisis appeared in the eighth century when a group arose to challenge the whole conception of the Talmud as the oral Torah. The **Karaites** (scripturalists) demanded that scripture alone be the guide for life, rejecting the centuries of accumulated rabbinic interpretation. In part, the Karaites were rebelling against the authority of the Geonim, reflecting the feeling of some that the rabbinic scholars had grown distant and unresponsive. Operating in Arabic rather than Aramaic (the Talmudic language), they also were influenced by groups in the Islamic community that emphasized reason rather than established authority.

The Karaites appealed to the individual's reasoned interpretation rather than to rabbinic authority, offering simple, direct understandings of the injunctions of the Torah. For example, since *Exodus* 35:3 prohibited the kindling of fires on the Sabbath, the Karaites held that Jews should spend the whole Sabbath in the cold and darkness—against the rabbinic interpretation that fires can be used (although not kindled) on the Sabbath. They rejected ritual objects such as phylacteries and festivals such as Hanukkah, because they were not mentioned in scripture but rather constructed by the rabbis. Trying to break away from the Talmudic rabbis, they set up a community in Jerusalem, and their influence spread throughout the Jewish communities, posing a threat to Rabbinic Judaism.

The challenge of the Karaites was met by thinkers like Saadia ben Joseph (882–942), head of the Sura academy in Babylonia. Trained in Hebrew and Arabic learning, he provided an Arabic translation of the Hebrew Bible. He was also learned in philosophy and was able to assure Jews there was no conflict between revelation and the kind of reasoning used by the rabbis. God has endowed humans with the ability to reach truth through reason, he taught, although revelation contained a higher, uncorrupted form of truth. Saadia's counterattack was successful; the influence of the Karaites waned rapidly, and the Talmudic tradition held sway.

Jewish Philosophy: Maimonides   Troubled times came to the Muslim lands in Asia, and when some Muslims conquered Spain and established the Umayyad dynasty of Cordova, the center of Jewish life gravitated westward from Babylon to Spain. There, a brilliant Jewish culture developed under a tolerant Muslim rule. The golden age of Spanish Jewry, from about the ninth to the eleventh centuries, included substantial contact with the Arab philosophical schools, and Jewish thinkers took up philosophical questions seriously for the first time since Philo. There was considerable resistance in some quarters to the use of such Greek philosophical rationalism, for the work of the Talmudic thinkers had always been considered the highest form of reasoning. The great writer Judah Halevi (1075–1141), for example, used his considerable literary powers to provide a lyrical defense of traditional Jewish piety. He insisted that Aristotle's speculative God is not the same as the God of Abraham; religious truth is to be found in the words of those who stood at Mt. Sinai rather than in speculative philosophy.

Moses **Maimonides** (Moses ben Maimon, 1135–1204) was born in Spain as times were becoming more troubled for Jews there. Muslims were rousing themselves to meet the challenge of the Christian crusades, and Jews were being forced to convert to Islam. So Maimonides' family migrated to Morocco, then to Palestine, and eventually to Egypt, where he became a brilliant Talmudic scholar and also physician to the Egyptian ruler. His great work was to attempt to reconcile the revealed scriptures of Judaism and the intellectual basis of Aristotelian philosophy. In fact, he felt that philosophical reason could provide the key to understanding the revealed scripture.

His influential book, *Guide for the Perplexed,* written in Arabic, gave a rational definition of the essential faith of Judaism, unlike the traditional rabbinic teachings that emphasized conduct rather than rationalized doctrines. His famous thirteen principles of the Jewish faith, although not attaining the status of a creed in Judaism, have been enormously influential and are included in the standard prayer books. They are as follows:

1 The existence of God, the creator.

2 God's unity.

3 God's incorporeality.

4 God's eternity.

5 The obligation to worship God alone.

6 The truth of the words of the prophets.

7 The superiority of the prophecy of Moses.

8 The Torah as God's revelation to Moses.

9 The immutability of the Torah.

10 God's omniscience.

11 Retribution in this world and the next.

12 The coming of the Messiah.

13 The resurrection of the dead.

In his view of the relationship between reason and revelation, Maimonides held that the scriptural prophecy consisted of a harmonious flow of reason and inspiration from God to the human mind. The prophecy of Moses was different in kind from the rest, for it was a perfect expression of God's will. Maimonides accepted Aristotle's proof for the existence of God, and he was particularly interested to show God's incorporeality; God could not be one if he occupied a body. He dealt with the problem of biblical anthropomorphisms (descriptions of God in human form) by allegorizing them; for example, God's "voice" is not to be taken literally but as a symbol of rational prophetic understanding. But he rejected Aristotle's idea of the eternity of the world, for that went against the biblical idea of creation.

As to the various laws of the Torah, Maimonides saw much practical benefit in them. The laws prescribing animal sacrifice weaned the Jews away from worshiping pagan gods; the **dietary laws** kept people from gluttony; and **circumcision** was a way of keeping sexual desire under control. Keeping the Torah, for Maimonides, contributed toward a decent, humane society. He thought of the messianic age as a time when humans could devote themselves to philosophical study, drawing closer to the knowledge of God.

Maimonides was very influential in his own times and ever since, even though his kind of rationalism did not win wide acceptance. His God of the philosophers was too rational for intimate relationship, and he was criticized for not including the idea of love in his philosophical system. A different kind of Jewish response to the increasingly rigid Talmudic structures and the challenge of rationalism had been building up for some time, with emphasis on the religious experience of the heart, and this burst forth in the form of Jewish mysticism.

Mysticism and the Kabbalah   Close communion with God based on inner experience was integral to Judaism from the beginning. Moses on Mt. Sinai, face to face with

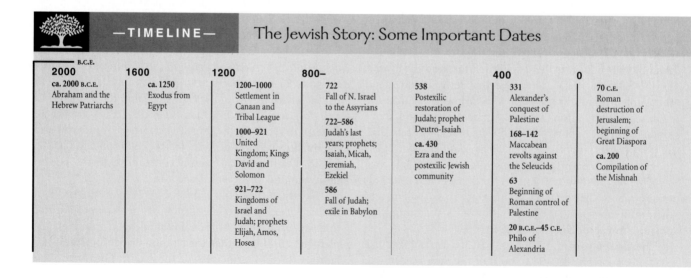

—TIMELINE—   The Jewish Story: Some Important Dates

B.C.E. 2000	1600	1200	800–		400	0
ca. 2000 B.C.E. Abraham and the Hebrew Patriarchs	ca. 1250 Exodus from Egypt	1200–1000 Settlement in Canaan and Tribal League	722 Fall of N. Israel to the Assyrians	538 Postexilic restoration of Judah; prophet Deutro-Isaiah	331 Alexander's conquest of Palestine	70 C.E. Roman destruction of Jerusalem; beginning of Great Diaspora
		1000–921 United Kingdom; Kings David and Solomon	722–586 Judah's last years; prophets; Isaiah, Micah, Jeremiah, Ezekiel	ca. 430 Ezra and the postexilic Jewish community	168–142 Maccabean revolts against the Seleucids	ca. 200 Compilation of the Mishnah
		921–722 Kingdoms of Israel and Judah; prophets Elijah, Amos, Hosea	586 Fall of Judah; exile in Babylon		63 Beginning of Roman control of Palestine	
					20 B.C.E.–45 C.E. Philo of Alexandria	

God as he received the Torah, is a primary example of the inner mystical experience of closeness to God. Further, there are poets like David in psalmic ecstasy and prophets like Jeremiah caught up in intimate communion with God's will. Ezekiel's vision of the chariot on which was enthroned the "appearance of the likeness of the glory of the Lord" (*Ezekiel* 1:4–29) was especially considered the paradigm of the inner mystical experience of God.

In the medieval period, Jewish mysticism spread and took the form of the **Kabbalah** (tradition). Mysticism had developed together with the Talmud, in the form of popular oral traditions, and it held an important place in Judaism from the twelfth to the seventeenth centuries. Advocates of the Kabbalah considered it equal to the Torah, but its meaning was open only to initiates. The Kabbalah was an esoteric (inner) form of biblical interpretation that looked for the inner, secretive meaning of the text. Based on the notion that the Hebrew scriptures contained all divine truth, it found every word, letter, number, and accent of the Hebrew text to have some spiritual significance.

The central work of the Kabbalah was called the *Zohar* (splendor), written as a mystical commentary on the Torah. Using an esoteric method of interpretation, the Zohar portrays a grand vision of God's relation to the world. God as the ultimate reality is En Sof, completely transcendent and beyond all human thought. But from the En Sof come ten emanations (*sefirot*), and these represent God's presence within the created spheres. Something of

God is in every human, and therefore by living pious lives according to the Torah, Jews can assist in restoring the fullness of God and of the whole universe. Such a vision, which took a variety of forms, fascinated many Jewish mystics and left an important imprint on Judaism. It also had a strong influence on certain medieval Christian thinkers. The mystics dealt with the same issues as the philosophers: the nature of God, creation, exile and restoration, good and evil. Their vision had a wide appeal, and they stimulated expectation of the restoration through the messiah, providing meaning and hope to many who lived in difficult circumstances.

Tragedy and Response in Christian Medieval Europe

At the same time that Jewish culture flourished under Muslim rule, Jewish settlements were slowly spreading into Christian Europe. As early as the Roman period, Jews were brought to Italy, Greece, and other parts of Europe. With the triumph of Christianity, Jews came under certain restrictions, but Charlemagne (crowned emperor of the Holy Roman Empire in 800 C.E.) saw the important contribution that Jews could make to the economic and scholarly life of the empire and encouraged their immigration. These Jews of Germany and France eventually became known as Ashkenazim, whereas the Jews of Spain and the Mediterranean areas became known as Sephardim.

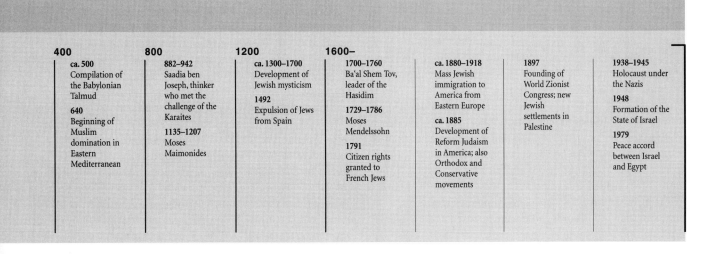

400	800	1200	1600–			
ca. 500 Compilation of the Babylonian Talmud	**882–942** Saadia ben Joseph, thinker who met the challenge of the Karaites	**ca. 1300–1700** Development of Jewish mysticism	**1700–1760** Ba'al Shem Tov, leader of the Hasidim	**ca. 1880–1918** Mass Jewish immigration to America from Eastern Europe	**1897** Founding of World Zionist Congress; new Jewish settlements in Palestine	**1938–1945** Holocaust under the Nazis
640 Beginning of Muslim domination in Eastern Mediterranean	**1135–1207** Moses Maimonides	**1492** Expulsion of Jews from Spain	**1729–1786** Moses Mendelssohn	**ca. 1885** Development of Reform Judaism in America; also Orthodox and Conservative movements		**1948** Formation of the State of Israel
			1791 Citizen rights granted to French Jews			**1979** Peace accord between Israel and Egypt

Crusades and Persecutions   Jewish life and scholarship flourished in France and Germany. But a fateful day, November 26, 1095, brought a change that colored Jewish life indelibly. On that day, Pope Urban II preached a sermon calling on Christians to recover the Holy Land from the infidel (the Muslim Turks). For the next two centuries, a series of crusades aroused Christian religious passions and nearly always led to attacks on and massacres of Jews in communities throughout Europe—initiating a long, tragic period of Jewish persecution that went on for many centuries and was revived even in the twentieth century.

Aroused by the crusades, popular religious passions flared up against the Jews under a variety of pretexts. They were frequently accused of the ritual murder of a Christian, using the blood to bake unleavened bread for Passover—this blood-libel charge continued into the twentieth century. Another accusation was that of desecrating the sacred host (the consecrated bread, which was understood to be transformed into the body of Christ in the celebration of the Mass); Jews were often charged with stealing the sacred bread and tormenting Christ by piercing and pounding it. In times of plague, Jews were accused of poisoning wells of Christians or performing other forms of evil sorcery. If there were no other pretext, people could always be aroused against the Jews by the reminder that they were the killers of Christ. Beginning with Pope Inocent III and the Fourth Lateran Council in 1215, Jews were forced to wear distinctive badges and endure many other indignities. From the fourteenth through the sixteenth centuries, Jews were expelled from almost every European nation, sometimes a number of times.

The Story of the Marranos   The story of Spanish Jewry is especially tragic. When massacres broke out in 1391, many Spanish Jews, unlike Jews throughout the rest of Europe, accepted Christian baptism and thus came to be accepted as equals of the Christian people. These "New Christians," called **Marranos** (pigs), often remained Jewish at heart and kept Jewish practices secretly as much as possible. As they thrived amid their Christian neighbors, new outbreaks of hostility occurred, and Queen Isabella set up a special tribunal for hunting out and punishing heretic Christians—the dreaded Inquisition. The first *auto da fe* (Act of Faith) in 1481 burned six men and women of Jewish extraction, and many thousands more were tortured and executed

over the next few decades. Jews who had not become Christian still lived in Spain—but in 1492 Isabella and Ferdinand signed a decree expelling all Jews from Spain, a crowning tragedy for Spanish Jewry. Many went to neighboring Portugal, where again they were forced to become Christian by the brutal means of their children being seized and baptized. Great massacres occurred, such as the killing of two thousand New Christians in Lisbon in April 1506.

The Marranos and other Spanish Jews, fleeing these persecutions, made their way to many parts of the world, taking their special Jewish culture with them, including their language, Ladino (Hebraeo-Spanish). They went to Italy, England, France, the Netherlands, and Germany. Other Marranos went to Turkey, Palestine, and Syria. Some migrated to the New World—to Brazil, Mexico, and Peru (followed even there by the Inquisition). In 1654, some Marranos from Brazil became the first Jews to immigrate to North America.

Renaissance and Ghetto   The Renaissance in Germany and Italy included the active participation of many Jews as scientists and scholars. There was a Hebrew renaissance that strongly influenced Christian thinkers such as Pico della Mirandola, Martin Luther, and John Calvin. As the leader of the Christian Reformation in its initial stage, Luther was at first attracted to the Jews, but twenty years later he turned against them with savage verbal attacks, just as he also castigated the Turks and the Papists.

The Counter-Reformation of the Roman Catholic Church, with the church on the defensive, revived the old anti-Jewish laws, including the wearing of the badge. In 1555, Pope Paul IV forced Jews to live in Jewish quarters on certain streets, surrounded by high walls with the gates closed at night. These quarters were called **ghettos,** named after the Jewish quarter in Venice, the *Ghetto Nuovo* (new foundry). Of course, living in the ghetto afforded some protection to Jews from hostile people outside. And the ghetto acted as a conserver of Jewish solidarity and culture.

There was hardly any limit to the indignities the Jews were forced to bear. Their costume was regulated and their children were snatched away for baptism. They were forbidden to ride in carriages or employ Christian servants, and they were often denied the right to marry. They were forced to pay special tolls, take degrading oaths in court, attend conversionist sermons, and run stripped nearly naked in carnival races. But in the midst of this demeaning ghetto life, Jewish culture was shaped and even flourished.

Vibrant Jewish Life in Eastern Europe   Jews had been living in eastern Europe for many centuries, but with the expansion of German communities into Poland came many more Jews. In the late Middle Ages, the persecutions in Germany and western Europe brought hundreds of thousands of Ashkenazic Jews to Poland and the surrounding Slavonic territories. It was there in eastern Europe that the heart of Jewish civilization was nurtured for a number of centuries up to the modern age. The Jewish community usually lived in towns or villages (shtetls), complete with synagogues, rabbis, holy days and festivals, weddings and funerals—everything that makes up the complete Jewish way of life. Self-governing, autonomous, with uneasy arrangements with peasant Christian neighbors, Jews were able to preserve their own values, language (Yiddish), institutions, and culture in full vigor, without being integrated into the Polish or Russian community at large. Jewish learning and scholarship were vigorously cultivated, especially the method of Talmudic interpretation called *pilpul*—special mental gymnastics centered on the text. Every town had an academy and distinguished scholars, and the town prided itself on the number of young men devoted to the study of the Torah and the Talmud.

But tragedy followed the Jews of eastern Europe also. Beginning with the Cossack rebellion of 1648–1651, when some 200,000 Jews were slaughtered, Jews of Poland and the Ukraine underwent centuries of persecution, leading up to the pogroms of the 1880s and finally the Nazi **Holocaust.** The tide of refugees began to swell again, this time westward into the German states—and finally also to Palestine and to America.

A significant response to life in eastern Europe was the popular mystical revivalist movement of the **Hasidim,** founded by Israel ben Eliezer (1700–1760), known as the BESHT or Ba'al Shem Tov (Master of the Good Name). He taught that religious feeling and piety were more important than scholarship, and that each individual, no matter how poor or ignorant, could commune with God by spiritual exaltation and abandonment of self. There are certain Zaddikim (Righteous Ones), he taught, who are very close to God and carry on the leadership of the Hasidim (pious ones), as the disciples of the BESHT called themselves.

They held large gatherings devoted to song and ecstatic dancing and feasting, spreading this revivalist movement throughout the Jewish communities of eastern Europe, attracting many Jews who were disillusioned with the rigid intellectualism of the Talmudic rabbis. In reaction, the traditional rabbinic leaders tried to expel those of the Hasidic movement. But gradually both sides became more moderate and tolerant, and the Hasidim, now numbered by the hundreds of thousands, took their place as a legitimate part of the Jewish way of life. Through the Hasidim, the emotional, poetic, and mystical dimension of religion was reinforced within Judaism and has strongly influenced many down to the present day.

Emancipation, Enlightenment, and the Modern Age

The emancipation of the Jews throughout Europe was the great development of the early modern age, ushered in by the Enlightenment of the eighteenth century. Enlightenment thinkers considered differences of race and religion to be mere accidents, thus opening the way to emancipation of the Jews and their full participation in society. Of course, age-old prejudices could not be swept away by mere ideas. It took drastic changes like the French Revolution of 1789 to make the decisive breach and bring down the walls of the ghetto.

Jewish Involvement in the Enlightenment   The Enlightenment (Haskalah) form of Judaism emerged in the eighteenth century, alongside traditional Talmudic Judaism and Hasidism, and it is well represented by **Moses Mendelssohn** (1729–1786). Born at Dessau in Germany in a medieval Jewish ghetto, he paid the special Jewish toll to enter the gate of Berlin and thus symbolically brought the Jewish community into the modern world. After studying in Berlin, he won a prize from the Prussian Academy of Sciences for the best philosophical essay, and immediately he was accepted and courted by the enlightened intellectuals of Prussian society. The writer Gotthold Ephraim Lessing, for example, was a close friend and modeled his *Nathan der Weise* after Mendelssohn. This enlightened, modern Jewish thinker brought together two strands that had heretofore been totally separate: traditional Jewish life and ritual, on the one hand, and enlightened scientific thought, on the other. Mendelssohn attempted to build a bridge between

Judaism and Christian Germany by providing an interpretation of Judaism as a rational system of ethics thoroughly compatible with modern scientific thought. Moving away from Yiddish, he made a translation of the Torah in excellent German, with a commentary in pure Hebrew. Thus he provided an impetus for Jews to pursue both Germanic studies and modern Hebrew letters, transcending the ghetto boundaries of Yiddish (Hebraeo-German).

The Jews of the Enlightenment, like Mendelssohn, had to perform a balancing act. Mendelssohn remained a loyal Jew practicing his religion, but he also participated fully in the intellectual life of the Enlightenment. His fellow Jews wondered about his rationalism and rejection of everything mystical, and his philosophical colleagues wondered about his continued practice of Jewish tradition. As the age of the Enlightenment ended with pressures of reaction and nationalism, Jews increasingly had to make a decisive choice, as exemplified by Mendelssohn's own children— either as Jews, or baptized as Christians, or as free thinkers.

Many Jews of the nineteenth century participated in the revolutionary movements sweeping Europe, which established constitutional governments, and with this they were granted full emancipation as citizens. This, however, was accompanied by ever more vicious reactions and new outbreaks of hostility from their fellow citizens. Now that the religious basis of persecution became less persuasive, the prejudices were transferred to other grounds—national, ethnic, or "racial"—culminating in the anti-Semitism of the late nineteenth and twentieth centuries with its tragic, shattering consequences.

A woman rabbi reads from the Torah scroll in a synagogue service.

Reform, Orthodox, Conservative, Reconstructionist
Many Jews, especially in eastern Europe, retained the traditional Jewish life with little substantial change or question. But in western Europe and later in America, leading Jewish thinkers responded to the Enlightenment, scientific progress, and the industrial revolution with new proposals for change in the traditional Jewish way of life—or impassioned defenses of that life. Their proposals and responses created the main forms of Judaism today.

The movement called **Reform Judaism** started in Germany as Jewish thinkers, influenced by Mendelssohn, attempted to modify traditional Jewish practice in keeping with the ideas and realities of modern scientific, secular life. With Abraham Geiger (1810–1874) taking the lead, these Jews advocated changes such as using German in the syna-

gogue, men and women sitting together, organ music, and modification of dietary restrictions to better fit the modern age. Dropping or modifying practices that had ancient roots but did not fit the sensitivities of the modern age would allow the eternal meaning and message of Judaism to shine through for modern people. Geiger argued that Judaism changes with each age, reflecting God's progressive revelation in history. What was appropriate for one age might no longer fit in another. These Reform Jews emphasized the ethical dimensions of Judaism more than the ritualistic aspects, and they rejected the idea that the messianic age would mean a return to Zion. Rather, the goal of peace and harmony should be pursued in the European nations to which these emancipated Jews had dedicated themselves.

As German immigrants to America swelled in the mid-nineteenth century, Reform Judaism was firmly established. An early Reform document, the Pittsburgh Platform of 1885, stated that only the moral laws of Judaism were binding, and only those ceremonies that elevate life in modern civilization should be retained. Thus most dietary laws went out, and the traditional prayer shawl and head covering became obsolete. In recent decades, Reform Judaism has moved to recover more of the traditional Jewish liturgies and practices, in keeping with the need of Jews today to establish their Jewish identity in our thoroughly secularized society. Since 1972, Reform Judaism has been extending rabbinic ordination to women.

Some Jews in Europe were uneasy with the radical changes brought about in Reform Judaism and the arguments based on enlightened, rational grounds. This moderate movement, later known in America as **Conservative Judaism,** was led especially by Zecharias Frankel (1801–1875) in Germany and later in America by Solomon Schechter (1847–1915). Judaism has indeed changed over the centuries, they acknowledged, but such changes have always developed from the living experience of the Jewish people as they centered their lives on the traditional rituals, which, Frankel argued, form the very soul of Judaism.

In America, the Conservative movement was swelled by the arrival of a large wave of immigrants from Russia at the end of the nineteenth century. These immigrants shied away from the modernized Reform synagogues and were attracted to the Conservative congregations, which kept many of the traditional rituals but opened doors for the newly arrived Jews to begin the move into American society. In recent years, Conservative Judaism has addressed the issue of women's rights, first by allowing women to read the Torah from the pulpit and by counting women toward a *minyan* (quorum of ten). In 1985, the Conservative Rabbinical Assembly began to accept women into membership.

A Jewish movement born in America grew from Conservative Judaism. From the distinctive teachings of Mordecai Kaplan, professor at Conservative Judaism's Jewish Theological Seminary, came **Reconstructionist Judaism.** Kaplan construed Judaism as a civilization that evolved to serve the needs of the Jewish people. The rituals, laws, literature, art, folkways, values, and ideals of Judaism should be "reconstructed" to provide the highest degree of Jewish self-realization. Whereas the Reconstructionist movement is small, its ideals have influenced Reform and Conservative

Jews considerably. Women are also being ordained as rabbis in the Reconstructionist movement.

The challenge of modern, enlightened Judaism both in its Reform and Conservative forms called forth a strong reaction in Europe and America in the form of the **Orthodox** movement, led especially by Rabbi Samson Raphael Hirsch (1808–1888) in Germany, who believed Jews had to retain their total adherence to Jewish law even as they participated in the life of secular society. Hirsch and the other Orthodox leaders attempted to interpret the tradition so it would be more attractive to enlightened modern people, but they insisted on the divine authority of the entire Torah and the necessity of observing all the traditional rituals. This, Hirsch argued, was the way God had revealed for the training of the authentic Jewish person, and abandoning any part of the traditional practices amounted to a betrayal of Judaism.

In America, the arrival of hundreds of thousands of Jewish immigrants from eastern Europe at the beginning of the twentieth century, with whole communities in New York speaking Yiddish and carrying on the traditional Jewish way of life, augmented the Orthodox movement. Small communities of Hasidic Jews are also considered part of Orthodoxy in America. Orthodox Judaism is especially strong in the state of Israel.

Zionism, Holocaust, and State of Israel   Toward the end of the nineteenth century, the modern movement of **Zionism** arose with the goal of Jewish national liberation. The pogroms of Russia caused many Jews to look for respite in a Jewish homeland, and in western Europe emancipated Jews became disillusioned over the continuation of persecutions and discrimination. One sobering event was the Dreyfus trial in 1894. Alfred Dreyfus, a Jew in the French Army, was falsely convicted of treason in a blatantly anti-Semitic court proceeding, showing dramatically the precarious position of Jews even in a modern European society. Theodore Herzl (1860–1904) of Vienna provided an impetus for Zionism by writing an influential book, *The Jewish State,* and organizing the World Zionist Congress (1897). He and others felt that only in a state with Jewish sovereignty could Jews finally end their homelessness and shape their own destiny.

Some Jews (like Herzl himself) were indifferent to the location of the Jewish state. But many Jews, especially those from eastern Europe, began to advocate Palestine as the only place for the Jewish homeland, where the historic Jewish way of life, steeped in the biblical values and ethos, could be preserved and cultivated. Jews began immigrating to Palestine, helped by the Jewish National Fund with contributions from Zionist Jews through the world. Not all Jews at this time were Zionists. Reform Jews tended to prefer assimilation within the national societies, and some Orthodox groups felt the restoration of Zion could take place only with the coming of the Messiah. But history itself gave the answer to the problem, with the Nazi Holocaust destroying European Jewry and providing the definitive answer for almost all Jews of today: The Jewish homeland is essential so that this will never again happen to the Jewish people.

The Holocaust, as the great modern example of humanity gone amuck, has evoked a number of responses among Jews of today. Some have spoken of the eclipse of God, the hiding of God's face in these tragic events. More radical thinkers speak of the death of God and hold that it is no longer possible to believe in God "after Auschwitz" (one of the Nazi death camps). Still others attempt to reinterpret divine providence in the face of this modern outburst of evil. One survivor of the Holocaust, Elie Wiesel, says it is better to keep silent than to try to explain the unexplainable; he simply tells the story so humankind will not forget. For many, both Jews and non-Jews, the Holocaust has become a symbol for the unthinkable inhumanity that can be unleashed by humans, a portent of other holocausts that could erupt through nuclear conflict, military struggle, ethnic cleansing, or other brutalities of our modern age.

One immediate effect of the Holocaust was the impetus given to the creation of the state of Israel. Jewish refugees fled the devastation of Europe and migrated in increasing numbers to Palestine, joining Jewish communities established there in the earlier phases of the Zionist movement. Supported by Jews all over the world, these Jews declared Israel to be an independent state in 1948, a Jewish state that would forever be a homeland for all Jews. The Jewish state has had a troubled history since that time, with many clashes with the Palestinians and surrounding Arab states. But in the biblical land Jewish identity has been forged anew. The biblical language of Hebrew is heard again, now as a modern language. The age-old festivals are celebrated, and the full Talmudic way of life is made possible once

again. Of course, many Israeli Jews have become secularized, and the majority of Jews live elsewhere in the world. But for all of them, the state of Israel helps provide a link with the traditions of Judaism and a guarantee that the Jewish people have survived and will continue to exist as the people of God in the eternal covenant.

Discussion Questions

1   In what way are the ancient figures of Abraham and Sarah important for the Jewish sacred story?
2   Describe the Exodus and the covenant at Mt. Sinai. How do these events of long ago still provide identity for Jews today?
3   How was the covenant relationship between Israel and their God different from the way other peoples of the ancient Near East understood their relationship to their gods?
4   In what ways does the history of ancient Israel reflect the sense of a covenant "struggle" between Israel and God?
5   Explain how the development of Israel into a kingdom brought about religious changes. What was the significance of the idea of the messiah?
6   Explain the role of the prophets in Israel. What was the special message of the prophet we call Second Isaiah?
7   Why may Ezra be called the "founder" of Judaism?
8   What is the origin of the oral Torah (the Mishnah and Talmud), and what is its significance in Judaism?
9   Describe important developments in Jewish life under Muslim rule.
10   Do you think there is any relationship between Christian treatment of the Jews in the medieval period and the Holocaust in the Nazi era? What is it?
11   In the midst of persecutions, in what ways did Jewish life flourish in Eastern Europe?
12   What are the strong points of each of the modern American Jewish movements for presenting a viable and strong Judaism for the modern age?
13   Why do Jews living throughout the world think preserving the state of Israel is an essential mission for Judaism today?

CHAPTER 7

Jewish Worlds of Meaning

ONE GOD AS CREATOR, REVEALER, AND REDEEMER

What's it *all* about? Most characteristic of Jewish religious thought is the commitment to monotheism, one God as the creator and master of all. Modern historical study of the Tanakh has outlined the development of monotheism in the religion of ancient Israel. Jewish tradition, of course, accepts monotheism as a basic tenet of the Torah. However, the religion of Abraham and the ancestors of Israel was not monotheistic, according to the stories in Genesis, but a distinctive practice was the worship of the clan God, the "God of the Father"; later Yahweh, the God of Israel, was identified with "the God of the Fathers."

But even Yahweh, as discussed in the previous chapter, was not at first known as the only God of all. Other gods of the land were also important for life and growth, so Israelite devotion was split between Yahweh and the fertility gods, Ba'al and Asherah. From another perspective, the religion of many early Israelites was henotheistic: Yahweh was their God to whom they must be loyal, avoiding the gods of other peoples. Since other nations had their own gods, at first the Israelites did not think of Yahweh as powerful over all peoples; those other peoples with their gods were hostile to Yahweh and Yahweh's people.

The Development of Monotheism

Through this struggle with other peoples and their gods, and through their own conflict over worshiping Yahweh and the fertility gods, the people of Israel came to under-

stand the extent of Yahweh's power and presence in the world. They ultimately came to the conviction that their covenant God, Yahweh, was the one God of all nature and of all peoples.

Yahweh versus Ba'al   The stories of the prophet Elijah (*I Kings* 17–22), who lived in the northern kingdom of Israel in the ninth century B.C.E., highlight the struggle between allegiance to Yahweh and worship of Ba'al, the god of the land. Since Ba'al was believed to be the god in charge of life-giving rain, Elijah issued a challenge right on Ba'al's front doorstep: "As Yahweh the God of Israel lives, whose servant I am, I swear that there will be neither dew nor rain these years unless I give the word" (*I Kings* 17:1). The drought lasted three years, until finally Elijah showed Ba'al up to be powerless in his great contest with the prophets of Ba'al on Mt. Carmel—and only then did Yahweh send rain. The story tells dramatically that Yahweh, not Ba'al, has the power to withhold rain and to grant it for the growth of the crops.

The prophet Hosea provides another viewing of the struggle between Yahweh and Ba'al in Israel's religious practices. From Hosea we learn that many Israelites participated in worship at Ba'al shrines, involving sexual religious rituals, offering raisin cakes to images of Ba'al, and the like—fertility rituals to promote the growth of the crops and the well-being of the people. Hosea himself, on orders from Yahweh, married a cult prostitute and had children by her to dramatize the relation between Yahweh and the covenant people. Through him it was forcefully demonstrated that Israel had broken the covenant with Yahweh, saying instead, "Let me go after my lovers, who provide me my bread and my water, my wool and my flax, my oil and my drink" (*Hosea* 2:5). Hosea portrays Yahweh lamenting over Israel like a rejected lover: "She does not know that I am the one who gave her the grain, the new wine, and the oil, that I lavished silver upon her and gold which they used for Ba'al" (2:8). But Yahweh does not give up on Israel, planning to punish them in order to turn them back. Through Hosea, Yahweh says:

> I will punish her for the days of the Ba'als,
>   in which she burned incense to them,
>   and decked herself with her rings and her jewelry.
> For she ran after her lovers,
>   but she forgot me, says Yahweh.
> But now, listen, I will allure her,
>   I will go into the wilderness with her
>   and speak lovingly to her.
> And I will give vineyards to her there,
>   the Valley of Achor becoming a gateway of hope.
> Then she will respond there as in the time of her youth,
>   as when she went up out of Egypt.
> And on that day, says Yahweh, you shall call me "My Husband";
>   you will no more call me "My Ba'al."
>
> (2:10–16)

Through the prophets, by such poignant images and actions as these, a new, deeper understanding of Yahweh grew in Israel. The realm of nature, fertility, and growth was not controlled by the Ba'als, or even shared by Yahweh and other gods of nature. Rather, the exclusive power and presence of Yahweh, Israel's covenant God, was felt in all areas of their existence. It was Yahweh who sent the corn at the harvest, the wine at the vintage; the Ba'als should be forgotten and never mentioned again.

Yahweh, God of All the Nations   As Israel began to understand that Yahweh has power over all aspects of human existence, so also they struggled to overcome the limitations of a henotheistic view. At one time it was accepted that one could not worship Yahweh outside the land of Israel: "How can we sing the song of Yahweh in a foreign land?" asks one of the psalms used among the exiles in Babylon (*Psalm* 137:4). As late as the Babylonian exile, some Jewish exiles lost heart because they believed this catastrophe had proved that Marduk, the god of Babylon, was more powerful and had defeated Yahweh. But the prophets drew out the implications of their faith, extending the sphere of Yahweh's power to all nations. Amos insisted that Yahweh had brought not only Israel from Egypt, but also the Philistines from Caphtor and the Aramaeans from Kir; and when any of these peoples commit crimes, it is Yahweh who punishes them (*Amos* 9:7; 1:3–2:3). The prophet Isaiah saw the invading armies of the Assyrians as Yahweh's "rod of anger" sent against the Israelites (*Isaiah* 10:5). And Second Isaiah, the prophet of the Babylonian exile, went so far as to describe mighty King Cyrus of the Persians as "the anointed one of Yahweh," whom Yahweh had taken by the hand to subdue nations before him (*Isaiah* 45:1).

In the vision of these prophets, Yahweh is no tribal God sharing power with other divine beings. The God of the covenant has universal power as the only God. Second Isaiah in particular stated eloquently the vision of a full-blown monotheism, ridiculing images of the gods that are powerless, insisting over and over that Yahweh is the one God, the creator and director of all:

> To whom can you liken God,
>   or what sort of likeness can you compare to him? . . .
> He is the one who sits throned on the vault of earth,
>   with its inhabitants like grasshoppers.
> He is the one who stretches out the heavens like a curtain,
>   and he spreads them out like a tent to live in.
> He is the one who reduces the princes to nothing,
>   he makes the earth's rulers as nought.
>
> (*Isaiah* 40:18, 22–23)

> Thus says Yahweh, the king of Israel,
>   their redeemer, Yahweh of hosts:
> I am the first, and I am the last,
>   and beside me there is no God!
>
> (*Isaiah* 44:6)

Not only Jews but also Christians and Muslims draw from this fundamental ancient Israelite vision of the Lord of Israel as the one God of all the earth, as expressed in the stories and the prophetic oracles of the Tanakh.

Jewish Vision of the One God

For over two thousand years devout Jews have twice daily recited the **Shema:** "Hear, O Israel! The Lord our God, the Lord is One" (*Deuteronomy* 6:4). Nothing in Jewish life is more hallowed than the saying of these words. These are the last words to come from the lips of the dying Jew and from the lips of those Jews who are present at that moment. This short credal statement shows it is the *unity* of God that is the fundamental Jewish theological assertion. By and large, Jews have not tended to develop systematic theology, that is, rational ideas and doctrines about God. Rather than defining God, they relate to God through worship and through life. But they know the most important doctrine about God is that God is One.

God as One and Unique   The Shema means, first of all, that God is not many. All forms of polytheism are rejected, for that tears God apart and thus also tears the world and humankind apart. Since God is one, all of reality is also a unified order, and there can be one universal law of righteousness that holds sway over all. No one is excluded from the rule of God, for there are no other gods.

The Shema also means that God is one, not two or three. At the time Rabbinic Judaism was developing, the Persian religion of Zoroastrianism was powerful, with a somewhat dualistic conception of reality: Ahura Mazda (Ohrmazd) is the God of goodness and light, but the realm of evil and darkness is controlled by the spirit Angra Mainyu (Ahriman). Such a theory is a handy explanation for the existence of evil in the world, and it was attractive also to some Jews and Christians. But the rabbis insisted that any thought of a divine power in competition with God had to be squelched. Further, of course, Jews cannot accept the Christian idea that God is triune, Father, Son, and Spirit. The problem is not so much different aspects of the one God, but the Christian insistence on the incarnation of God in the man Jesus.

It is true that Jews have some sense of different aspects or modes of operation of God. The Tanakh often speaks of God's "spirit," "presence," "angel," or "glory" being present with the people. In the Middle Ages, Jewish mystics worked out a vision of God that contained both unity and diversity. God purely in Godself is *En Sof,* absolute and without limit. But the pure Godhead cannot be known to humans, so God is manifested in ten emanations known as the sefirot; God emerges from concealment in such a way that creatures can experience the divine reality. Some Jews have been uncomfortable with this Kabbalistic idea of God, but it does show that humans experience the one hidden God through various modes of God's self-revelation.

But saying that God is one is not just a matter of arithmetic. The Hebrew word for "one" *(ehad)* also means "unique," the one who is unlike any other. God is different from anything humans might name as gods or create as gods. From this sense of God's uniqueness arose the strict prohibition in Judaism against making any images or likenesses of God—for God is not like anything else. All else is made; God is not. All else changes; God does not. All else has rivals and comparables; God does not.

God as Transcendent and as Immanent   Another way of putting this is to say that God is *transcendent,* that is, far above and beyond the created world. In total contrast to everything that has been created in time and space, God is eternal, with no beginning or end. God has no limitations of space or knowledge or power, being present everywhere, all-knowing, and all-powerful. Using terms like these, Jews point to the complete *otherness* of God.

But to say that God is transcendent is only half the story. Jews also hold firmly to the conviction that God is not just a God far off, but a God near as well. God is *immanent,* near and present to all creatures. The Tanakh tells how God's "spirit" or "presence" went with the people on their wanderings. Though the highest heaven cannot contain God, still the Israelites concretely felt the presence of God dwelling in their midst in the temple at Jerusalem. The rabbis spoke especially of God's Shekhinah (from the root *shakhan,* to dwell), that is, the divine Presence that filled the Israelite tent of meeting and that fills all the world as well.

Thus God, the almighty creator, is immanent and at work within the processes of creation. The ongoing creator and sustainer of all continues at work, knowing when even a sparrow falls, giving food to each and every living thing. As creator, God is also the lawgiver, the source of natural law to which the world conforms and also of the moral law that guides human life. God is the director of history, unfolding the eternal will in the drama of the history of the sacred people and the whole world.

But God is also present in a *personal* way, according to Jews. While the human idea of person is inadequate to describe God, we have no better word to designate the

The Yad Vashem Holocaust Memorial in Israel, honoring the millions of Jews and others who perished under the Nazis.

experience of meeting God as a helper, a redeemer, and a friend. God is one who loves the chosen people, as taught in countless ways by the rabbis. One of the favorite names for God that Jews use is "Our Father" *(abenu).* A Talmudic passage emphasizes the personal presence of God:

> Come and see how beloved Israel is before God; for wherever they went into exile the Shekhinah went with them. When they were exiled to Egypt, the Shekhinah went with them; in Babylon the Shekhinah was with them; and in the future, when Israel will be redeemed, the Shekhinah will be with them.
>
> *(Meg.* 29a)[1]

God and the Puzzle of Evil   The puzzle of evil casts a long shadow in the world, and Jews have known a large share of persecution and suffering. If there is one God, and God is both the almighty creator and a present loving father, what sense can be made of evil and suffering?

Since the times of Israel of old, Jews have struggled with this question, refusing to give up these beliefs that God is one, almighty, and loving. A variety of partial solutions to the problem of evil have been offered by Jews of different eras. For example, in some ways evil can be seen as the result of a previous sin of an individual or the community.

Or it may be discipline or testing from God so that humans will learn to choose the good. If it seems too much now, it may be compensated in the life to come. What seems to be evil may result from a partial view of things, or it can be understood as the absence of good. But another kind of answer in the Jewish tradition is that of Job: "I lay my hand on my mouth," Job said. "I have uttered things that I do not understand, things too wonderful for me to know" (*Job* 40:4; 42:3). In discussions of the perplexities of evil and suffering, the rabbis like to quote a text from the Torah: "And Aaron was silent" (*Leviticus* 10:3). Once, according to a rabbinic story, Moses was transported to Rabbi Akiba's lecture hall and was granted a vision of Akiba's martyrdom—his flesh being weighed in the meat market. Moses protested, "Such is his knowledge of the Law, and such is his reward?" But God said, "Silence, so it has seemed good to me" (*Men.* 29b).[2] Theologizing about God is after all not the central focus in the Jewish tradition. To be a Jew is to experience God by living the life of Torah, not by rationalizing about God.

Since the Nazi Holocaust, however, there has been a great deal of discussion about God and evil among some Jewish thinkers. Some go so far as to say that it is impossible to believe in a God of the covenant after Auschwitz. Others hold that, whereas the Holocaust destroys all traditional categories of thinking about God, the experience of the covenant people with God goes on. Some feel that the main task of Jews today is to keep remembering the Holocaust; others say it cannot be spoken of today. In all, recognizing the breach in our thinking caused by this great outpouring of evil, Jews, like Israel of old, continue to struggle with God and refuse to let go.

THE WORLD AND HUMAN EXISTENCE

What sense is there in life? Why is there so much evil and suffering? What is the world all about? A sixteenth-century Jewish creed gives as the first principle of the Jewish faith: "I believe with perfect faith that the Creator, blessed be His name, is the Author and Guide of everything that has been created, and that He alone has made, does make, and will make all things."[3] Jews see creation from the point at the center: God's giving of the Torah to the covenant people. According to a well-known rabbinic teaching, God first looked into the Torah and then created the world, following the design spelled out in the Torah.

Creation and Preservation of the World

The Jewish tradition, as the root of the Abrahamic tradition, first contributed the fundamental idea of God as the one creator, with the world as God's good creation. At the very beginning of the Torah, the ancient scribes placed a priestly liturgy about cosmic creation (*Genesis* 1:1–2:4). According to this hymn, God first of all called forth the world from a dark, watery chaos, and by divine command made it a good, purposeful world. God, completely separate and sovereign, created the world as an orderly, functioning cosmos. The creator separated the light from the darkness, created a firmament to hold back the waters of chaos above, and placed lights in the heavens to rule the day and night and the seasons. God gave the earth the power to bring forth plants, each according to its kind, and creative powers were also given to earth and sea to bring forth every kind of animal and fish. Day by day, the creation liturgy goes on, God created and then rejoiced in what was made: "It is good!" Finally the poem has all of nature in place, from the seas and the dry land to the stars and plants and animals. Then God said, "Let us make *'adam* (humankind) in our image, after our likeness, and let them rule over the fish in the sea, the birds of the heavens, the cattle, over all the earth, and all reptiles that crawl upon the earth" (1:26). After creating humankind male and female in the divine image, finally God completed creation and rejoiced, "It is very good!" Resting on the seventh day, God instituted the Sabbath day as a day of rest and rejoicing in the good creation.

The Genesis story emphasizes the prior existence of God, transcendent and apart from the world. God has a design, a purpose for the world. But God is in no way mingled together with the creation; with a divine command all is called to be and to function. Later Jewish thinkers said that God created everything out of nothing, to emphasize that only God is eternal. The creation reflects the glory of God, but God is not within the creation. The world is God's creature, functioning according to the divine will and command.

God the creator is the ongoing preserver and guide of all creation. A Jewish morning prayer says,

> Praised are You, O Lord our God, King of the universe.
> You fix the cycles of light and darkness;
> > You ordain the order of all creation.
> You cause light to shine over the earth;
> > Your radiant mercy is upon its inhabitants.

> In Your goodness the world of creation
> > is continually renewed day by day.[4]

God is the personal, merciful creator who continually preserves and watches over the world, giving life and breath and food to all, returning living beings to the dust in their term, sending forth the divine spirit to replenish the earth. There is no place to flee from God's presence, no time or place of life when God is absent.

The Nature and Role of Humans   The role of humans within God's orderly and purposeful creation is to serve the creator and fulfill God's will in the world. The creation story says humans are created "in the image" of God, and that is explained to mean serving as God's representative in ruling over creation. A hymn from ancient Israel puts it in lyrical terms:

> O Lord our Lord, how majestic is your name in all the
> > earth! . . .
> When I look at your heavens, the work of your hands,
> > moon and stars which you established—
> What is humankind, that you should remember them,
> > humanity, that you should care for them?
> Still you have made them but little less than God,
> > crowning them with glory and honour.
> You give them rule over all the works of your hands;
> > all things you have put under their feet.

> (*Psalm* 8)

The power of this vision of the nature and role of humans can be seen by comparing this Jewish view with the commonly accepted notion of the role of humans in the ancient Near East. Creation texts from Babylon, for example, say that Marduk, the creator God, made humans from the blood of a demon, mixed with clay, to be slaves to the needs and demands of the gods. But the Jewish view elevates humans to "little less than God," cared for and loved by God, and given the great responsibility of being master over all God's creatures. Humans are to serve God, but they are at the same time partners with God in the ongoing creating and preserving of the creation, working to fulfill the purpose and destiny of all. The rabbis taught that humans are co-partners with God in the work of creation, by causing the earth to be inhabited and not desolate and by using human

Blowing the shofar (ram's horn) on Rosh Hashanah is a symbol of God the creator summoning the people to new life.

skills to further God's creative purpose. A judge who judges justly, for example, is given credit with being a partner with God in the work of creation (*Sanh.* 10a).

Although humans are the high point of creation, the other creatures also have a role and purpose. In the traditional rabbinic scheme, humans are midway between the animals who have no moral sense, on the one hand, and the angels who cannot do evil and the demons who can do only evil, on the other. Animals are to be respected and treated fairly and humanely; inflicting unnecessary pain on animals is particularly to be avoided. One rabbi ruled that one must not eat before giving food to one's animals (*Ber.* 40a).

Serving God means a life of wholeness, faithfulness, and obedience. To the Jews has been given the Torah, so that God's whole design for the good life can be followed. But to all humans God has provided guidance, through nature itself and through the human conscience. All humans know and can follow the basic principles of God's law, sometimes called the Seven Commandments of the Children of Noah:

1 Not to worship idols,
2 Not to commit murder,
3 Not to commit adultery and incest,
4 Not to eat a limb torn from a living animal,
5 Not to blaspheme,
6 Not to steal, and
7 To have an adequate system of law and justice.

In the Jewish view, human reason and understanding are not necessarily in conflict with serving and obeying God. Reason can lead astray when followed blindly, but used wisely and prudently, human reason can discern the basic principles of God's law and thus assist in living the good life.

The Shadow of Sin

The Jewish tradition values humans highly, but it has no delusions about human nature. Stories at the beginning of the Torah provide a realistic assessment of the human capacity for evil. Within the first human family, Cain rose up and murdered his brother Abel out of anger and jealousy, and God warned him—and all humans—that "sin is lying in wait at the door" (*Genesis* 4:7). Humankind became so evil that God sent a great flood to destroy them. But even righteous Noah's family and descendants demonstrated the same inclinations. These stories of rebellion and violence among the peoples of God's earth have strongly influenced the view of human nature found in Christianity and Islam also. Throughout the Jewish Tanakh there is abundant evidence of the human capacity for wickedness and for causing great suffering and destruction in God's good world.

In the teaching of the rabbis, human sin is *averah,* from *avar,* meaning "to pass over" or transgress God's will. Jews have a definite idea of what the good life is: following the commandments of the Torah. And sin is to transgress all this. Milton Steinberg explains the rabbinic view: Sin is "any act or attitude whether of omission or commission which nullifies God's will, obscures His glory, profanes His name, opposes His Kingdom, or transgresses the *Mitzvoth* [commandments] of the Torah."[5]

Struggle to Control the Evil Inclination   In the Jewish tradition there is no idea of an evil or "fallen" human nature that inevitably drives humans to sin. Rather, the rabbis taught that there are two basic inclinations or drives in everyone: the *yetzer hatov,* the good inclination, and the *yetzer hara',* the evil inclination. Sin results when a person lets the evil inclination get the upper hand.

But why did God create humans with the evil inclination? This is the inclination that drives humans to gratify their instincts and wants; it has to do with ambitions and appetites, including especially the sex drive. Thus this "evil inclination" is really essential in providing motivating power for life. Commenting on God's words in the creation story, "It was very good," Rabbi Nahman ben Samuel said, "That is the evil inclination. But is the evil inclination very good? Yes, for if it were not for the evil inclination, man would not build a house, or take a wife, or beget a child, or engage in business" (*Gen. R., Bereshit,* 9:7).[6] Another rabbinic story tells that Ezra and his associates once wanted to kill the evil inclination. But the evil inclination (personified in this story) warned them that the whole world would go down if they did this. They imprisoned the evil inclination, but then they found that throughout the world there could be found no newly laid egg. Finally they put out his eyes so he could not tempt people to incest (*Yoma* 69.b).

Thus the Jewish tradition has the realistic view that life is a continuing struggle, but we can control the evil inclination and even use it in a positive, life-affirming way. The most important help in mastering the evil inclination is, of course, the Torah. A well-known rabbinic parable tells of a king who inflicted a big wound on his son but then counseled his son to keep a plaster on the wound. As long as the wound was protected by the plaster, his son could eat and drink whatever he wanted without any ill effects; but if the plaster was removed, the wound would fester (*Kidd.* 30b). So also God has in a sense "wounded" humans by giving them the evil inclination; but he has also given them the Torah as the antidote, allowing them to live their lives without fearing that the evil within them will drag them down to ruin. Another rabbinic parable says the evil inclination is like iron that one holds in a flame in order to make a tool of it; so, too, the evil inclination is to be held in the fire of the Torah (*Avot de Rabbi Natan,* ch.16).

Sometimes it is said that, unlike Christianity, which holds that a person sins because of being a sinner by nature, in the Jewish view a person is a sinner simply because he or she sins. That is, sin is an action of transgressing God's laws, not a state of being that is twisted and alienated from God. But this does not mean that Jews are unduly optimistic about human nature. The scriptures describe bounteous human evil, and Jews have seen sufficient evidence of that in their long history as a people. Saints do struggle and master the evil inclination; but even Moses, our rabbi, sinned and was punished.

The Results of Sin   Sin has consequences. The rabbis point out that when Cain killed his brother Abel, he also killed all Abel's unborn children. So there is punishment for sin, just punishment, because sin arises from the free will of humans. Traditional Judaism knows the idea of Satan, the accuser who tests people and tries to lead them astray (*Job* 1–2). But Jews strongly affirm that we humans have free choice and do have the capability, with the help of the Torah, of mastering the evil inclination. Therefore we are justly punished as the recompense for our sin.

But there are different kinds of sin, and therefore different kinds of punishment, depending on whether the sin is against God or against one's fellow humans. In one sense, the rabbis say, the sin itself is the recompense of sin (*Avot* 4:2). The guilt and sorrow and alienation caused by doing a sin is surely retribution for the sin. Some recompense for sin comes in this life, both in terms of punishment by society and also punishment by God. Disease, war, and slavery can be divine punishment, as when God sent Assyrian armies against Israel or caused a plague to punish wrongdoers. But Jews are also aware of the problems involved in explaining misfortune and suffering as punishment for sin. The story of Job's innocent sufferings leads the rabbis to say that finally we do not know why the righteous suffer; even Moses did not know (*Ber.* 7a).

In traditional Judaism, it is emphasized that final recompense for sin is given by God in the life to come. The rabbis used this teaching to explain why the wicked could be prosperous in this life in seeming defiance of God's just laws; their recompense will come with torments and sufferings in Gehinnom. Some rabbis did teach that even those suffering in hell will rest every Sabbath, or that the punishment would last for only twelve months. Many Jews today feel uncomfortable with traditional descriptions of punishments in the world to come. But the main point of these descriptions is that sin is hateful in God's eyes. It is better to live the good life, and God has given sufficient guidance and help for that.

FOLLOWING THE PATH OF TORAH

How can we start living *real* life? Where is meaning and healing to be found? The Jewish tradition recognizes the tension between what humans are supposed to do according to God's design of creation and what humans actually do in their daily lives. Humans inevitably fall short of what God asks of them. Jews know from the biblical history that time after time human failure brings forth divine punishment. So what can one do to find whole life, to transform this human situation?

God as Redeemer

Jews first of all look to God not only as the creator but also as the redeemer, who forgives and restores and thus makes it possible for humans to turn back to the life God intended for them. In the traditional daily prayer, after praising God as the creator and the revealer of Torah, Jews call upon God as the redeemer, the one who saves and delivers them:

> You are our King and our father's King,
> our redeemer and our father's redeemer. . . .
> You, O Lord our God, rescued us from Egypt;
> You redeemed us from the house of bondage. . . .
> [God] humbles the proud and raises the lowly;
> He helps the needy and answers His people's call. . . .
> Fulfill your promise to deliver Judah and Israel.
> Our redeemer is the Holy One of Israel.[7]

In this prayer, Jews look to the great redemption of Israel in the past, and they look ahead to the redemption in the time to come. But redemption also takes place in the present—whenever God humbles the proud and raises the lowly, whenever God helps the needy and hears the people's call. Redemption or salvation takes place in common everyday events.

How does God redeem? Not through an intermediary who stands between God and humans to save them, as in Christian views. Between God and humans stands no one. As Steinberg writes, "As nothing comes between soul and body, father and child, potter and vessel, so nothing separates man from God, Soul of his soul, his Father and Fashioner."[8] God redeems and saves by being God for humans. That is, God continually searches and calls for humans to become partners as they were created to be.

In this search of God for humans, Jews identify a number of important movements on God's part. God intervenes in human history to redeem the sacred people by mighty acts. God reveals the Torah as the total design for the good life. And God answers humans when they repent by showing them mercy and forgiveness. Yet God does not take away human freedom and initiative. The searching and calling come from God, but ultimately each person must take the first step of responding to God's call.

The Jewish sacred story is full of God's mighty acts of salvation. God delivered them from slavery in Egypt with a mighty arm. God brought them to the holy mountain and entered into a covenant with them, giving them the Torah. God led them into the promised land and gave it to them as an inheritance, raising up the house of David to save Israel from its enemies. Even God's acts of punishment were intended as a means of redeeming the people from their sins and turning them back to the right path. In the midst of the great catastrophe of the Babylonian exile, the prophet known as Second Isaiah spoke these words about the destruction of Israel and God's intentions for them:

> Comfort, oh comfort my people, says your God.
> Speak tenderly to Jerusalem, and call to her
>   that her time of service is fulfilled,
>   that her iniquity is satisfied,
>   that she has received from the Lord double for all her
>   sins. . . .
> See, the Lord God comes with might, with his arm ruling for
>   him;
> indeed, his reward comes with him,
>   and his recompense is before him.
> Like a shepherd he will pasture his flock,
>   he will gather them in his arm;
> he will carry the lambs in his bosom,
>   and lead the ewes to water.
>
> (*Isaiah* 40:1–2, 10–11)

Through mighty deeds of salvation, God has always been the redeemer of the people, and will continue so in the present and in the future.

The Jewish tradition also stresses the guidance that God has given to make it possible for humans to turn and lead the good life. This is the Torah, the great gift of God's grace for the welfare of humankind. In a sense, giving the Torah is the one great act of God's salvation for humankind. The Jewish daily prayer celebrates this blessing from God:

> Deep is Your love for us, O Lord our God;
> Bounteous is Your compassion and tenderness.
> You taught our fathers the laws of life.
> And they trusted in You, Father and King.
> For their sake be gracious to us, and teach us,
> That we may learn Your laws and trust in You.
> Father, merciful Father, have compassion upon us;
> Endow us with discernment and understanding.
> Grant us the will to study Your Torah,
> To heed its words and to teach its precepts. . . .
> Enlighten our eyes to Your Torah,
> Open our hearts to Your commandments. . . .
> You have drawn us close to You.[9]

As God has taught and guided the people of old in the laws of life, so Jews believe God continues to teach and guide, giving the will to study the Torah, the mind to understand it, and the heart to follow it.

The Human Movement of Repentance

So far it does sound as though salvation comes mainly from God's side. And in a sense it does, for God is the redeemer. But Jews also insist that the human partner in this relationship likewise has an active role in this process of salvation and transformation. God created humans with an important realm of free will within the various conditions of life over which we have no control. And in this realm of moral freedom the drama of faithfulness or faithlessness is played out. A rabbi taught that before a human is conceived in his mother's womb, God has already ordained concerning him whether he be strong or weak, intelligent or dull, rich or poor. But God has not predetermined whether he will be wicked or virtuous, since everything is in the hand of Heaven except the fear of Heaven (*Ber.* 33b).[10] God is in search for humans; but it is up to humans to seek God. Jews believe that the initiative in seeking God must come from the human side. Abraham Heschel, quoting the saying, "Whoever sets out to purify himself is assisted from above"

(*Yoma* 38b), comments simply: "God concludes but we commence."[11] God gives grace, calls us, searches for us— but God expects us to take the first step in responding to the call.

Within the human life of imperfection and sin, that first step toward God has to be repentance. The Hebrew word for repentance, *teshuvah,* literally means to "turn around," to make a complete change in one's direction of life. To turn to God means to answer the call, to respond to God's search and set out on the path of the good life of Torah. Through the prophet Malachi comes God's call: "Since your fathers' days you have turned aside from my statutes and have not kept them. Return to me, and I will return to you" (*Malachi* 3:7).

Repentance is a human act, not a mysterious sacrament that works even without our efforts. This human undertaking of repentance involves four concrete steps, according to the rabbis. First comes the readiness to acknowledge a wrongdoing. Second, the person does acts of compensation for the injury inflicted on others by what she has done, when it is a sin against others. Third, the person makes a genuine resolve to avoid a repetition of the same sinful deed. Only then is the person ready to take the fourth and final step of praying for forgiveness from God, knowing that she will receive God's mercy.[12]

Repentance is the highest of the virtues in Judaism. The rabbis taught that when a person repents out of love, his sins are converted into merits, and that in the place where a repentant sinner stands, even the righteous who have never sinned cannot stand (*Ber.* 34b). Reflecting on this philosophical puzzle, Joseph Albo (d. 1444) pointed out that if justice were to be the determining factor there could be no repentance at all, for justice demands that, once done, a wrong cannot be righted and the sinner must be punished. But repentance is based on God's infinite grace. When a person sincerely repents and turns to God in love, the person is really demonstrating that the sin was not committed voluntarily but in error, for the sinner would erase it if he or she could. This repentance out of love brings God's grace into play, which flows in love to the person and converts his or her sins into merits.[13]

One of the most holy days in Judaism, **Yom Kippur** (the Day of Atonement), is set aside for repentance. The liturgy used on this day in the Jewish synagogue strikingly expresses

A Jewish family prays at the Western Wall in Jerusalem.

the deep Jewish sense of sin, repentance, and forgiveness, as in these few excerpts:

> Our God and God of our fathers, hear our prayers; do not ignore our plea.
> We are neither so brazen nor so arrogant to claim that we are righteous, without sin, for indeed we have sinned.
> We abuse, we betray, we are cruel.
> We destroy, we embitter, we falsify.
> We gossip, we hate, we insult.
> We jeer, we kill, we lie.
> We mock, we neglect, we oppress.
> We pervert, we quarrel, we rebel.
> We steal, we transgress, we are unkind.
> We are violent, we are wicked, we are xenophobic.
> We yield to evil, we are zealots for bad causes. . . .
> We have sinned against You unwillingly and willingly.
>   And we have sinned against You by misusing our minds.
> We have sinned against You through sexual immorality,
>   And we have sinned against You knowingly and deceitfully. . . .

> For all these sins, forgiving God, forgive us, pardon us, grant us atonement. . . .
> May it be Your will, Lord my God and God of my fathers, to help me abstain from further sin. With Your great compassion wipe away the sins I have committed against You.[14]

To say this prayer with conviction and sincerity means turning back to God and following God's way; it is a prayer of transformation.

On the Path of Transformation

Repentance is only the first step. The path of transformation for Jews is really the whole life of Torah. This means following the *mitzvot* (commandments), which God has given through the Torah as the discipline by which to purify oneself and shape one's life ever more closely to God's design. There are many mitzvot, 613 of them by traditional count, made up of 365 negative commandments corresponding to the number of days in the year, and 248 positive commandments corresponding to the number of members of a person's body. How these mitzvot apply to life is set forth in the Jewish **Halakhah,** the "way," the code of life spelled out in the Talmud. The Halakhah determines the way a person lives, how one shapes the daily routine into a pattern of holiness. The Halakhah governs every aspect of daily life, all the way from birth to death. It includes prescriptions about how to relate to God in prayer and in worship, what foods to eat and how to prepare them, how to marry and have children and die and bury the dead, how to treat others, and all the rest. We look more closely at some of the specifics of the Halakhah in the following chapter. Here it is important to see that the Halakhah makes up a path of transformation for Jews, a discipline which involves a practice of outward behavior that brings about an inner transformation of the heart.

It is a misunderstanding of outsiders to think Jews are interested only in the outward performance of all these mitzvot. Commenting on the rabbinic saying, "God asks for the heart," Heschel writes,

> The true goal for man is *to be* what he *does*. . . . A mitzvah, therefore, is not mere doing but an act that embraces both the doer and the deed. The means may be external, but the end is

personal. . . . It is a distortion to say that Judaism consists exclusively of performing ritual or moral deeds, and to forget that the goal of all performing is in *transforming* the soul. Even before Israel was told in the Ten Commandments what *to do* it was told what *to be: a holy people.* To perform deeds of holiness is to absorb the holiness of deeds. . . . Man is not for the sake of good deeds; the good deeds are for the sake of man. . . . The goal is not that a ceremony be *performed;* the goal is that man be *transformed;* to worship the Holy in order to be holy. The purpose of the mitzvot is *to sanctify* man.[15]

In this understanding of the Jewish performance of mitzvot, it is clear that this is indeed a path of spiritual transformation. Looked at from the outside, the observance of all the minutiae of the Jewish law might seem to be mere outer show with little real spiritual depth or meaning. Indeed, a traditional Christian understanding of Judaism sees it as a religion of "works," in which humans strive by their good deeds to be rewarded with salvation. To Jews, however, this is not a matter of "salvation by works." Rather, the Halakhah provides a structure of life divinely given for the benefit of humans, a discipline based in real human action that transforms the heart in love for God. By walking in the way of God, humans can become Godlike. So Jews take on the discipline of the mitzvot with thankfulness and with joy.

Of the various mitzvot, we should single out the study of the Torah as the supreme obligation for Jews on the path of transformation. The study of the Torah is not just an intellectual exercise but a means for perfecting the human spirit that has been made in the image of God. Rabbi Meir said,

Whosoever labours in the Torah for its own sake merits many things; and not only so, but the whole world is indebted to him: he is called friend, beloved, a lover of the All-present, a lover of mankind; it clothes him in meekness and reverence: it fits him to become just, pious, upright and faithful; it keeps him far from sin, and brings him near to virtue.

(*Aboth* 6:1:2)[16]

The very act of study, memorization, and commentary on the Torah is a holy act and in fact the central ritual of Judaism. It is through study of the Torah that one comes to know God and therefore to love God with the whole heart.

If the Torah reveals God's complete pattern for the sanctification of human life, the first and most important response is to study and learn the Torah so it becomes a part of one's very nature.

Universal Blessing, Now and Hereafter

A striking factor in the Jewish path of transformation is its seemingly limited application within the whole human race. Unlike Christianity and Islam, which are missionary religions seeking to bring their respective paths of transformation to all people, the Jewish tradition has always considered the path of Torah to apply only to the Jewish people. There is, of course, a repeated rabbinic tradition that God did intend the Torah for all peoples, but only the Jews accepted it. The path of Torah is closely linked to the covenant that God made with Israel, the chosen people. Jews have never felt they have the mission of bringing other peoples of the world into Judaism. Rather, Jews hold that, whereas anyone who wants to can become a Jew, no one has to do so in order to be saved in this world or in the next. Rabbi Joshua said that the righteous of all nations will have a share in the world to come (*Tosefta Sanh.* 13:2). Non-Jews can turn and follow God's way simply by keeping the seven commandments of the children of Noah. But for Jews, who have taken on the responsibility and the joy of the covenant, the path of Torah is the fulfillment of human potential and the way of salvation.

Following the path of Torah brings blessing, in this world and in the world to come. In this life, keeping the Torah is itself its own reward. For it is the divine pattern of life, and to live it is to become Godlike—which is the highest possible reward and blessing. One who lives the life of Torah becomes a channel of blessing in the world; in that way he or she receives the reward of the good life.

It is obvious, however, that many times righteous people undergo frequent sufferings in this life—just as the wicked may have wealth and success. So the Jewish tradition also teaches recompense for the righteous in the world to come, when the immortal souls of the righteous will be rewarded in Gan Eden (paradise), sharing the joys of their closeness to the divine glory. Traditional Jews also believe in the resurrection of the body, when the body will be reunited with the soul in the joy and bliss of paradise. Many modern Jews have reinterpreted these traditional beliefs in recompense, immortality, and resurrection so that they are not understood in a literal sense. Yet even Jewish modernists generally believe that some essence of the person lives on after death, and that there is a setting right of the scales of justice in terms of blessing and reward for those who have followed the path of Torah. In any case, we should always connect the world to come with how we live in this world. Rabbi Jacob said,

> This world is like a vestibule before the world to come; prepare thyself in the vestibule, that thou mayest enter into the hall. He used to say, "Better is one hour of repentance and good deeds in this world than the whole life of the world to come; and better is one hour of blissfulness of spirit in the world to come than the whole life of this world."

(*Aboth* 4:21, 22)[17]

Discussion Questions

1   In what ways was the religion of some of the ancient Israelites polytheistic and henotheistic? Outline the development of monotheism.

2   What is the Shema, and why is it so important for Jews?

3   Discuss how, in Jewish experience, God is both transcendent and immanent in the world.

4   What are some responses to the problem of evil and suffering according to Jewish thought? What is the impact of the Holocaust on this question?

5   What does the creation liturgy of Genesis I reveal about the nature of the world and of humans?

6   Is the Torah universal truth? What is the traditional idea about the seven commandments of the children of Noah?

7   What is the rabbinic tradition about the good and evil inclinations? What perspective does this place on the question of the sinfulness of humans?

8   In the Jewish path of transformation, what are the roles of God and of humans?

9   Describe the four steps of repentance, as taught by the rabbis.

10   Abraham Heschel says that "the true goal for man is *to be* what he *does*." What does he mean by this, and how does this relate to the discipline of Halakhah?

CHAPTER 8

Ritual Practices and the Good Life for Jews

JEWISH RITUALS AND WORSHIP

How can we find new power for life? How can we stay in touch with the divine? For Jews, the Torah provides the basis for making human life sacred. There are mitzvot (commandments) dealing with both ritual–ceremonial actions and with ethical behavior, creating sacred times and sacred living. Traditional Jews keep both types of mitzvot; modern Jews sometimes tend to keep the spirit of ethical directives but not all the ritual and ceremonial laws.

Only the basic mitzvot are mentioned in the written Torah. On the basis of the oral Torah, the Talmud, with its interpretations and applications of the written Torah, rabbis over many centuries have compiled the Halakhah, the "path" or code that provides the blueprint for everything about life, daily, seasonally, from cradle to grave. Since the Halakhah is so all-encompassing, it is difficult to make a sharp division between worship and the good life. Jews have, however, made a general distinction between ritual–ceremonial laws, on the one hand, and ethical laws, on the other. First we focus on the rituals and ceremonies of Judaism.

Sabbaths for Rest, Festivals for Rejoicing

Jews have a rich tradition of sacred times. The rituals and festivals provide a rhythm of return to the source of sacred power, daily, weekly, and seasonally.

Queen Sabbath   At the very center of Jewish life is Shabbat (Sabbath), the only festival prescribed in the Ten Commandments. Sabbath has been extremely important to Jewish life and identity. The Sabbath, say Jews, has kept Israel more than Israel has kept the Sabbath. It is the supreme symbol of the covenant relationship with God.

The Torah provides two important interpretations of the Sabbath, in the two listings of the Ten Commandments. According to *Exodus* 20, Jews are commanded to rest on the Sabbath because God rested on the seventh day after finishing the creation. In *Deuteronomy* 5, resting on the Sabbath day is a reminder of the deliverance from slavery in Egypt. Thus the Sabbath means rejoicing with God in the creation; and it means celebrating freedom in human society. Because of this, Sabbath has always been considered a joyous time by the Jews, a time of worship, prayer, and study, but also a time of family gathering, festive meal, rest from labor and worry, and giving rest to animals also. It is a festival of worshiping God and respecting human values.

The Sabbath begins at sundown on Friday evening and ends at sundown on Saturday evening. Jews prepare for the Sabbath celebration by cleaning house and getting the meals ready—for such work is not permitted on the Sabbath. At sundown the mother of the family lights two candles, says the Sabbath prayer, and "Queen Shabbat" comes. Friday evening is the time for the Sabbath family meal, often with a special guest or two. During the meal the special Sabbath prayer (Kiddush) is said over a glass of wine. In modern times, Friday evening is the occasion for a communal Sabbath service at the synagogue. Jews traditionally spent Saturday morning at the synagogue worshiping and studying the Torah. Nowadays, Saturday is spent in rest and quiet with family and friends. As the end of Sabbath approaches on Saturday evening, Jews use special prayers and rituals to bid farewell to Queen Sabbath.

The Days of Awe: Rosh Hashanah and Yom Kippur
The Jewish year begins with the Days of Awe, also called the High Holy Days. They start with **Rosh Hashanah,** New Year, on the first of Tishri, coming in early autumn in the modern calendar. These are considered the most solemn days of the year. They symbolize death and renewal—the old is swept away and the new is put into place. Sins are forgiven, relationships mended, and people are sealed in God's books of life. Jewish tradition has it that everything a person does is recorded in God's books, and these are opened for examination at the beginning of the New Year to be weighed and judged and the verdict inscribed. One book is for the just, and another book is for the hopeless sinners. But the third book—for those who are in between—is not sealed until Yom Kippur, giving people a chance to repent.

The solemn liturgy of the Rosh Hashanah synagogue service has the main theme of God as King, the one who created the world: "This is the day the world was born." God the King continues to renew the creation, and is also coming to judge all things. A special ritual is the blowing of the *shofar,* the ram's horn, a number of times in the service. The stirring sound is interpreted as a call to arouse our sleeping souls for war against sin. People are greeted, "*Leshanah tovah tikateivu*" (May you be inscribed for a good year). At home with family and friends, people dip apples in honey, expressing the hope for a sweet year. In the afternoon, it is customary to walk to a body of flowing water and throw bread crumbs in, symbolically casting sins away. Orthodox and Conservative Jews observe Rosh Hashanah for two days, repeating the rituals on the second day.

The ten days between Rosh Hashanah and Yom Kippur (on the tenth of Tishri) are days of repentance, preparing for the most solemn holy day of all: Yom Kippur, the Day of Atonement. Superseding even the Sabbath in importance, it is called "the Sabbath of Sabbaths." Traditional Jews spend almost the whole day at the synagogue, fasting and praying. The interior of the synagogue is decorated with white, symbolizing purity. The Yom Kippur eve service begins with the famous *Kol Nidre* prayer, set to a haunting melody that symbolizes the longing of the soul for God. During the day of Yom Kippur, Jews individually and communally confess sins to God and ask for forgiveness. This is the only time of the year (besides once on Rosh Hashanah) that Jews prostrate themselves, in memory of the ancient temple service. The concluding service on Yom Kippur is called Neilah (closing), referring to the closing of the gates of heaven, a reminder that time for repentance is running out. The ark holding the Torah scrolls is left open to the end of the service, and people stand throughout the service—heightening the sense of urgency of reaching God with prayers. The service concludes dramatically with a final blast of the shofar signaling passage from sin to forgiveness, from death to life.

Sukkot: The Festival of Booths   Just five days after Yom Kippur, on the fifteenth of Tishri, **Sukkot** represents a quick shift in mood to a holiday of celebration. The Festival of Booths lasts for seven days, during which Jews build a hut *(sukkah)* and make it their home, at least symbolically. Sukkot was the festival of ingathering of harvest, and appropriately, the festival includes the ritual use of citron, palm branches, myrtle, and willow. The frail temporary hut in which the family dines reminds Jews of the wandering in the wilderness; it also reminds them that physical possessions are unreliable and the simple, natural life is desirable. Guests are invited to share meals in the hut, and the mood is one of rejoicing and thankfulness.

Following the last day of Sukkot is a holy day of assembly in the synagogue; Reform Jews combine this with the last day of Sukkot. The celebration on this day is called Simhat Torah (rejoicing in the Torah), for on this day the annual cycle of reading the Torah scroll is completed, followed immediately by reading the opening verses of the Torah. In this service, the whole congregation processes and even dances seven times around the sanctuary with the Torah scrolls to express their joy over God's revelation. Children are especially encouraged to join in the rejoicing.

Minor Festivals: Hanukkah and Purim   Hanukkah, the Feast of Lights, is a popular minor festival occurring at the winter solstice. This eight-day festival recalls the victory of Judah Maccabeus and the Jews over the Seleucids in 165

B.C.E. The Seleucids under Antioches Epiphanes had humiliated the Jews, outlawing their religious practices and desecrating the temple with worship of Greek gods and pig sacrifices. When the Jews rededicated the temple, they found only a small cruse of oil, enough to last one day. But when they lit the temple menorah (candelabra) with it, it burned for eight days. Hanukkah celebrates this miracle of oil and the Jewish fight for independence. Jews light the eight candles successively on the eight nights of Hanukkah. It is a season of joy, games, special foods, and gift-giving. The festival symbolizes the sanctity of the individual's conscience and the right of everyone to choose his or her own religious practices.

A Jewish family celebrates Passover through the ritual of the seder, a liturgy telling the story of the Israelites' deliverance from slavery in Egypt.

Purim, coming in early spring, commemorates the survival of the Jewish people told in the story of Esther. The wicked Haman of the Persians masterminded the extermination of the Jews, but Mordecai and his grandniece Esther risked their lives to save their people. Purim has a carnival atmosphere as the story of the wicked Haman and the heroes Mordecai and Esther is told and acted out. The festival includes plays, masquerades, and games of chance, and even some social drinking is permissible. Purim is also a time for acts of righteousness.

Pesach (Passover)   Passover (**Pesach**) is one of the high points of the Jewish year, coming at the beginning of spring (in March or April). Since it celebrates Israel's deliverance from slavery in Egypt, it is "the festival of our freedom." It has elements that were originally connected with spring festivals of both pastoralists and agriculturalists, but most importantly it is the festival by which Jews are commanded to remember God's intervention in Egypt and the deliverance of the people from bondage. As a spring festival, it also symbolizes the deliverance of all nature from the bondage of winter. A major message of the festival is that the Jews were delivered

from Egypt not just for their own sake but for the sake of promoting freedom for all enslaved peoples. There is thus a note of anticipation in the Passover celebration, looking to the future deliverance of Israel and all peoples.

Preparing for Passover involves a thorough cleaning and purifying of the house, getting rid of all traces of *hametz* (leaven) and storing all utensils used for the rest of the year. Only matzoh (unleavened bread) and other unleavened food can be eaten for the seven-day festival, for the Israelites fled in haste from Egypt and ate unleavened bread for seven days.

Passover is primarily a family festival. The focus is on the ritual meal called the seder (order), celebrated in the evenings of the first two days, during which the story of the Exodus from Egypt is told in word, song, and ritual. The procedure for the seder is written in a guide called the Haggadah (story). The seder includes four cups of wine to remember the redemption of Israel; a special cup for Elijah, the herald of the future redemption; salt water to remember the tears of the ancestors; drops of wine spilt in sorrow over the plagues the Egyptians experienced; and four questions to be asked by the youngest child present. Passover is a celebration of new life and freedom, a season of rebirth and renewal.

Shavuot, the Festival of Weeks (Pentecost)   The final major festival, **Shavuot,** seven weeks after Passover, originated as a celebration of abundant spring harvest. It remembers especially the giving of the Torah on Mt. Sinai, God's great gift to Israel, the heart of the covenant bond between God and people. Shavuot is a festival of reconsecration to the teaching of the Torah and to the covenant. A beautiful metaphor used on Shavuot is that of marriage between God and people: Passover is the time of courting, Shavuot celebrates the marriage, and Sukkot is the setting up of the household.

For Shavuot, Jews often decorate the synagogue and home with green plants, branches, and trees. The story about the giving of the Torah on Mt. Sinai is read. Some Jews stand at the reading of the Ten Commandments and even read them in a special chant. In Israel, the recent custom of bringing the first fruits of the harvest in joyful processions is performed on Shavuot. And many synagogues, especially Reform and Conservative ones, have confirmation ceremonies on Shavuot, celebrating graduating from religious school and attesting to the covenant given at Sinai.

There are other Jewish holy days, fast days, and celebrations, of course. An important recent addition is Yom Hashoah, Holocaust Memorial Day, observed in April as a memorial to the six million Jewish martyrs of the Nazi era. Significantly, some Christian churches also observe Yom Hashoah.

Mitzvot of Ritual and Worship

The performance of the ritual duties is not limited to the holy days and festivals in Judaism. Since all of life is to be made holy, ceremonial observances in worship of God extend to all of life. They include worship and prayer, daily rituals at home, observance of dietary laws, and ceremonies associated with the passages of life.

Worship, Prayer, and Study   The duty of worshiping God is at the heart of the Jewish tradition, as it is also for Christianity and Islam. In ancient times, worship at the temple included prayer and rituals of sacrifice, but since the destruction of the temple, the focus has been on prayer. Traditional Jews live their lives constantly aware of the pres-

ence of God, always ready to utter words of praise and blessing to God. Jewish prayer can be spontaneous, arising from the longings of the heart. But the rabbis, knowing that we can easily forget a parent who is absent, specified periods during the day for worship. They created a tradition of prayer that blends together a fixed liturgy and the spontaneous offerings of the heart.

Important to Jews is the prayer book, a composite of Jewish worship experience from ancient times up to the present. The prayer book specifies the exact times for prayer and even provides the prayers to use on all important occasions. In recent times, prayer books have been translated into the vernacular languages. The Reform movement in particular has modernized the prayers and provided translations. Yet the general shape of liturgical prayer remains.

Jewish prayers presuppose a community. The plural form is used, and prayer ideally is said in a congregational setting where there is a *minyan,* a quorum of ten. Each prays by himself or herself but is fully aware of the community. Traditional congregational prayer would involve a group of men in a room, each standing by himself yet close to others, some swaying this way and that, whispering or speaking in a low tone to God. Standing before God the king, they do not shuffle their feet unseemingly. They bend their knees when they begin and when they end in honor of God's presence.

Respect for God also requires proper attire for worship. Orthodox and Conservative men wear a *kipah* or *yarmulke* (cap) during prayer. For festival worship, many wear a *tallith* (prayer shawl), and some very pious ones wear a special undergarment with fringes on the four corners. Observant Jewish men will also wear *tefillin* (phylacteries), small black boxes containing words of the Torah, attached to the forehead and arm with leather bands.

Important among these prayers are the Eighteen Benedictions, to be said in the morning, noon, and evening prayers. They have to do with themes of repentance, redemption, healing and blessing, gathering of the exiles, redemption of Jerusalem and Israel, thankfulness, and the like.

The act of studying the Torah is also an important ritual for Jews—in fact, it has been said that it is the central ritual of the Jewish tradition. Whereas Jews, of course, study the Torah to gain intellectual knowledge, the act itself of studying is a holy ritual in which one is united with the rabbis and even with God in studying Torah.

Daily Rituals and the Dietary Laws   From awakening in the morning until sleeping at night, the traditional Jew speaks words of thankfulness to God. There are blessings to be said when dressing, washing, attending to bodily needs, eating, seeing lightning, tasting a new fruit of the season, hearing good or bad news, and for almost every conceivable occasion. The three formal prayer services during the day require considerable time, and one is further expected to devote a portion of each day to study of the Torah. Women are generally exempted from such obligations, for the reason that their role as homemaker does not allow the time required for these ceremonial observances.

The Jewish idea of "kosher" food is widely known. The dietary laws go under the term **kashrut** (ritual fitness), although this term also refers to other ritual objects as well. The basis for kashrut is the Torah's injunction about prohibited and permitted foods in *Leviticus* 11 and *Deuteronomy* 14. All vegetables and fruits are permitted, but the flesh of horses, pigs, and birds of prey is prohibited, as are all shellfish. The permitted foods must be slaughtered in a carefully prescribed manner by a *shochet* (ritual slaughterer), who drains the animal of blood. Further, meat products and dairy products may not be prepared or eaten together, and the utensils used for preparing each must be kept separate.

These dietary laws from ancient Israel, as has often been pointed out, show an early awareness of sanitation and cleanliness. Some of them also possibly relate to ancient tabus or cultic practices involving other gods. But to Jews, the most important reason for observing these dietary laws is religious; they are divine laws, and for whatever reason God gave them, obeying them is a sign of keeping the covenant. They have preserved the uniqueness of the Jewish people throughout their tumultuous history, keeping them from being assimilated into other peoples. Keeping kashrut is a ritual that preserves the Jew's sense of communal identity with other Jews.

The question of the observance of the dietary laws is, of course, answered quite differently by various groups of Jews today. Traditional Jews observe all the laws without compromising and with rejoicing. Others observe kashrut at home but not outside. Some observe the laws selectively, avoiding pork and shellfish, for example. Still others argue that, whereas these laws may have applied in ancient times, they no longer have literal relevance today.

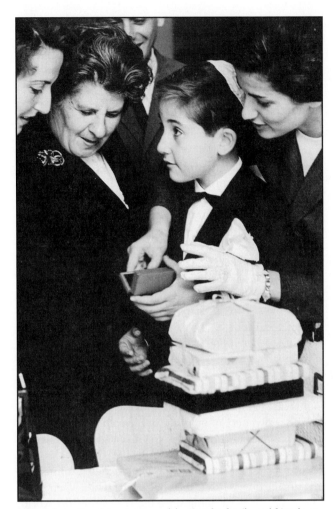

A boy's bar mitzvah is a joyous celebration for family and friends, as the boy becomes an adult member of the Jewish people. Here the thirteen-year-old boy opens presents.

From Cradle to Grave   Like all religions, Jews have rituals that sanctify the important, critical moments in an individual's lifetime: birth, puberty, marriage, and death. These are passages from one stage of life to the next, and the rituals associated with them express the death–rebirth symbolism that establishes the ending of the old stage and the beginning of the new. While the rituals pertain to individuals, they always involve the community of which the individual is a part.

The covenant between God and Israel is literally engraved on the flesh of all male Jewish infants through the covenant of circumcision, **brit milah,** done on the eighth day after birth. Circumcision is performed by a *mohel,* a circumcision specialist, in the presence of a quorum of ten men. An empty chair is left for Elijah, the guardian of the covenant. Over a cup of wine this blessing is said: "Praised are You, Lord our God, who sanctified the beloved from the womb and set a statute into his very flesh, and his parts sealed with the sign of the holy covenant."[1] Male infants are named at their circumcision, but traditionally female infants are named in the synagogue by the father when he is called up to read the Torah.

The passage through puberty is sanctified by the **bar mitzvah** (son of the commandment) ritual. The young Jewish boy is expected to progress in studying the Torah and Talmud up to his thirteenth birthday, and then he will be called up in the synagogue to recite blessings and lead part of the service, perhaps also giving a talk on the message of the Torah. A joyous social celebration follows the bar mitzvah ceremony, in recognition that the boy has now taken his place as a responsible adult in the Jewish people. Recently in Reform and Conservative congregations this puberty ritual has also been extended to girls, being called in this case **bat mitzvah,** daughter of the commandment.

The sacred duty of marriage in Judaism is spelled out in many passages of the Talmud, for it is a supreme mitzvah for the survival of the covenant people. Indeed it is suggested in the Talmud that one who remains unmarried impairs the divine image (*Yeb.* 63b). One rabbi, when asked what God has been doing since the creation of the world, replied that God has been sitting on the divine throne and making matches, assigning this man to that woman, this woman to that man, and so on (*Gen. Rabbah* 68:4). The wedding ritual sanctifies the marriage, which is performed under a *huppah* (canopy). There are blessings over two goblets of wine, and the groom places a ring on the bride's finger with the words, "Be consecrated to me with this ring as my wife, according to the law of Moses and the faith of Israel." The marriage contract is read, seven wedding benedictions are chanted, and the bridegroom breaks a glass with his foot in memory of the destruction of Jerusalem—a reminder of sorrow on this occasion of joy. With shouts of "Mazel tov!" (good luck), the wedding celebration begins for this new household in Israel.

The rituals of death focus realistically on this common end of all mortal life, rejoicing in the life that God had granted and reflecting hope for the world to come. Orthodox Jews believe in the bodily resurrection of the dead in the world to come, whereas more modern Jews take an agnostic view of the life beyond. In any case, great importance is placed on the respectful burial of the dead. In traditional Jewish communities, the burial society is a most highly respected group. Members sit with the dying person, offering prayers and reciting the Shema, the last mitzvah for a dying Jew. Jewish law forbids embalming the body; it should return quickly to the dust. The body is thoroughly washed and dressed in a white shroud. Before the burial service, the mourners tear their garments. The service concludes with the recitation of the Kaddish, a doxology sanctifying God's name. The initial period of mourning is the *shivah* (seven days), followed by another period of mourning until thirty days after the burial. Special prayers are also said on the annual anniversary of the death.

Artistic Expression in Jewish Religious Life

Basic Jewish sensitivities about God, the world, and human life are evident in the art created in Jewish communities the world over, from ancient times to the present. The Jewish aesthetic sense was strongly influenced by the Torah's prohibition against making images of any living thing, a corollary of the oneness and uniqueness of God. Because of this, Jews have generally avoided any representations of God and saintly personages, and traditionally they have given little attention to representational art in general. Instead, the literary and decorative art forms have flourished.

This reservation about representational art has not been a monolithic, unchanging attitude, however. There is evidence of some Jewish pictorial art using human figures in certain periods of Jewish history, especially in the Hellenistic era and in manuscript decorations during the medieval period. The synagogue at Dura-Europos in Syria, dating from about 245 C.E., is most striking in its lavish artistic portrayals, including human faces and forms. Five horizontal bands of decorative and figural paintings entirely cover the inside wall of the synagogue. Besides decorations of animals and theater masks, the paintings include scenes of well-known biblical episodes, such as the exodus from

Egypt, the finding of Moses, the anointing of David, and so forth. The art of book illumination with beautiful decorations and figures reached high form during the later medieval period, with artists showing great creativity in decorating and drawing scenes for books, especially for the Passover Haggadah.

In the modern period, of course, there have been and are well-known Jewish painters who create art based on Jewish themes. Many famous Jewish artists in the nineteenth century included painters like Camille Pissarro, Jozef Israels, and Leopold Horowitz, and in the twentieth century the well-known Paris School of Art included a large number of Jewish painters. To sense the vibrancy of modern Jewish art, one need only mention Marc Chagall, who has expressed the spiritual themes of the Jewish tradition in many of his paintings and stained glass windows. In Israel today, a kind of Jewish national art has developed, reflecting in some sense the new Jewish identity in the holy land.

Although they traditionally steered away from representational art, the other arts have been fully developed in the Jewish tradition. Jews have devoted much artistic energy to what might very generally be called the aesthetics of the word: literature, poetry, prayers, psalms, liturgies, calligraphy, and manuscript decoration. An impressive Jewish literature has developed, in Hebrew and the Hebraeo dialects like Yiddish and Ladino, and also in the various other languages of the world. Jewish writers in every century created stories and parables, poetry, short stories, novels, plays, mystical treatises, and philosophical essays, to give diverse expression to the experience of being part of the long Jewish story.

The Talmud states that the glorification of God should use all the finest objects for worship. In keeping with that attitude, in all historical ages Jewish artists have devoted much time, expense, and artistic creativity to making various ritual objects to use in worshiping God. Besides manuscripts and Torah scrolls written in beautiful calligraphy and exquisitely decorated, Jewish artists have created beautiful ornaments and crowns for Torah scrolls, kiddush cups, seder plates, Sabbath lamps, embroidered brocades for ark curtains or wrappings for Torah scrolls, and much more.

The Psalms say that everything that has breath should praise the Lord, and Jews have excelled in the arts of music, songs, dancing, and the like. It is true that, after the destruction of the temple, rabbinic custom excluded the use of musical instruments in synagogue worship, except for the shofar (ram's horn). The exclusion of musical instruments served to heighten the emphasis on the text, for which forms of chanting were developed. Dancing was also avoided in some periods, but in traditional places like Yemen, religious dancing is a part of festivals like Simhat Torah, circumcision, weddings, and the like. In modern time, however, choreographers have created dance and ballet inspired by Jewish history, ritual, and music. And many of the most recognized performing musicians, composers, and conductors today are of Jewish heritage, drawing deeply from their Jewish tradition as they interpret and help to create the musical arts of the modern world.

The ancient temple in Jerusalem was a magnificent architectural creation, designed according to a heavenly divine model; its function was to be a sacred place of divine presence, a meeting point between God and humans. In the Jewish tradition, the architecture of the synagogue, the primary meeting place for prayer and study, has been cultivated in keeping with its meaning and function. Unlike temples of ancient times or in other religions, the synagogue is designed to contain all the worshipers, not just the priests. And the focus is not outward from the center of divine power toward the people, but inward toward the center of prayer and study. The synagogue took different forms in different parts of the world, but everywhere the architecture expresses the centrality of the bimah, the altar with the Torah scrolls—the center of Judaism.

THE LIFE OF TORAH: JEWISH COMMUNITY AND ETHICS

How should we live? To the Jew this question has never been difficult to answer. A Jew should live as one who belongs to the *kelal yisra'el*, the total community of Israel, following the laws given by God in the Torah. The sense of Jewish peoplehood has remained strong since ancient times. Though difficult to define or explain, belonging to the Jewish people still provides deep identity and meaning today for traditional practicing Jews and modern secular Jews alike.

The Jewish People

How does one become a member of the Jewish people? Basically, one is a member of the Jewish people either by birth or by conversion. According to Jewish law, a person is a Jew by birth if his or her mother is Jewish. Recently, Reform Judaism has extended this provision to include either parent, so long as the family shows the intention to raise their children in the Jewish religion. One who is a Jew by birth can never be deprived of that identity, even if he or she completely abandons Jewish practices. The symbolic entry into the Jewish people for boys born in a Jewish home is the ritual of circumcision, performed on the eighth day after birth as the sign of the covenant.

Even though Jews do not seek to gain converts, in every age there have been persons who by their own choice have become Jewish. Such a person, traditionally called a "proselyte," is welcomed into the Jewish community by rituals of circumcision (for males) and a ritual bath (mikveh). When a non-Jew becomes convinced that she or he wants to be Jewish and persists in doing so (Jewish tradition says the rabbi is to discourage potential proselytes and yield only if they persist), they become of equal rank and status as a Jew by birth.

It is not an easy matter, then, to answer the question, "Who is a Jew?" It does not depend on race, color, or nationality, for among Jews may be found people of all races, colors, and nationalities, and none is excluded. It may perhaps be said that a Jew is one who, whether by birth or by conversion, has taken on the identity of the covenant people of God, choosing to be different from all other peoples of the world by this unique role.

As a sacred people, Jews do not have any tight structure or organization. Rather, the people of God function as a kind of extended family, gathered into communities in various parts of the world, helping and encouraging one another to live the life of Torah. Wherever they live, Jews form congregations, gathering in local synagogues for study and worship. The congregation is governed by the people, especially those recognized as elders and scholars. Ever since the destruction of the temple in Jerusalem by the Romans in about 70 C.E., Jews have had no priests as religious leaders. Rather, religious leaders are those who are most learned in the Torah and Talmud, that is, the rabbis. Traditionally, a rabbi is one who has received ordination from other rabbis in recognition of his knowledge of the Law, qualifying him to be a leader and judge for a community of Jews.

There is no worldwide organization that governs the whole Jewish people. Rather, Jews in various lands tend to develop their own structures of organization, including both religious organizations and philanthropic groups. In the state of Israel, the Ministry of Religious Affairs recognizes the Orthodox chief rabbinate as the authority in matters of Jewish religious law. In America, there are four organizations that set the standards for Jewish rabbis and the congregations they serve: the Reform, Conservative, Orthodox, and Reconstructionist groups. Orthodox Jews try as much as possible to maintain Jewish life and ritual according to the traditional Jewish Law, whereas Conservative Jews have adapted somewhat more to the demands of modern life. Reform and Reconstructionist Jews have changed or replaced certain elements of the Jewish Law to meet the needs of modern times; for example, they ordain women as rabbis—a practice that Conservative Jews have also finally adopted.

Women in Religious Leadership   The ordination of women in some of the modern Jewish groups in America is a significant moment in the long story of women in Judaism. Although women have always been highly esteemed in the Jewish community, they have seldom played leadership roles and traditionally were limited to activities in the home—a role that was accepted as important and not inferior to men's roles. But Judaism has always been a patriarchal religion, back to father Abraham, and women are little represented in the sacred texts and in the significant historical events as these were preserved in Jewish memory. Some images of women in the Bible and in Jewish tradition are clearly negative and subordinate to men. Biblical laws, for example, presume women to be property of their fathers and husbands. The rabbis talked of women as inferior to men, not permitted to be judges, rabbis, or cantors. Women were segregated from men in synagogues, not counted toward the religious quorum (minyan), not expected to study Torah, and unacceptable as witnesses in court. In the traditional daily prayer, a Jewish man would pray, "I thank Thee, God, for not having made me a woman."

But that is only one side of the picture. The Hebrew Bible also presents surprisingly strong women in leadership roles, models that Jewish women are recovering today. There is Sarah, ancestress of Israel, powerfully present in the sacred story with Abraham even when the patriarchal memory glosses over her role. Miriam, sister of Moses, was called "the prophetess" and led the Israelite women in a bold dance of victory after the crossing of the Red Sea (*Exodus* 15:20). Deborah was a prophetess who judged Israel, accompanied Barak to battle against a king of the Canaanites, and is said to have sung a mighty victory song that is recognized as one of the oldest surviving examples of Hebrew poetry (*Judges* 4:4–14). The Book of Ruth tells the heartwarming story of two women, Ruth (a non-Israelite) and her mother-in-law Naomi, who carry on their family line, with Ruth becoming an ancestress of King David. The Jewish woman Esther became queen of Ahasuerus, king of Persia, and heroically saved her Jewish people from destruction (*Book of Esther*).

Even in medieval times, countless Jewish women, untold but always there, took on strong family responsibilities in trade, financial management, and travel, while Jewish men were often occupied with duties of study and ritual. That inner strength started to become more public in modern times. Henrietta Szold, for example, lobbied for equality for Jewish women in the 1890s, studied at Jewish Theological Seminary in New York, and helped to found the network that became the Hadassah Medical Organization in Israel. Internationally known was Golda Meir, strong political leader and premier of Israel in the 1970s. Today many Jewish women are in the forefront of religious leadership, and Jewish women are developing new interpretations of traditional practices as well as finding ways to break out of the old patriarchal system altogether.[2]

The Life of Halakhah

What is the good life that we should live? Jews use the term *Halakhah* to designate that code of laws that prescribes how a Jew should live every aspect of life. Halakhah literally means "way," and it is a total way of life, drawn from the Torah and the Talmud. In traditional Jewish thinking, the Halakhah is the revealed will of God and therefore the ultimate criterion for all human conduct. A number of collections and systematizations of the Halakhah exist, but a most famous and influential one is the *Shulhan Aruk (The Set Table)* made by Rabbi Joseph Caro (1488–1575). This brief four-part code of Jewish law has been expanded through commentaries and supercommentaries, but even today is the place Jewish discussions of law begin. The opening sentence, elaborated by commentators, is famous:

> A man should make himself strong and brave as a lion to rise in the morning for the service of his Creator, so that he should "awake the dawn" (*Psalm* 57:9). . . . "I have set the Lord always before me" (*Psalm* 16:8). This is a cardinal principle in the Torah and in the perfect ways of the righteous who walk before God.[3]

That is, all our actions should be infused with the radical awareness that we are in every moment acting in the presence of God and therefore that every detail of our actions is important.

The Discipline of Halakhah   The Jewish tradition speaks of reward and punishment for deeds, but it would be a misunderstanding to see the performance of the mitzvot in this light. The commandments are to be performed for their own sake, not for the sake of reward. There are, of course, resulting benefits to self and others in doing the commandments, but fundamentally it is the act itself that carries value and goodness. Abraham Heschel has likened the Halakhah to artistic creation; works of piety are like works of art, serving a functional purpose but carrying the most important value intrinsically.[4]

A way of understanding the significance of performing the Halakhah is to see that, in Heschel's words, "the true goal for man is *to be* what he *does*."[5] We are what we do. The law provides a structure of life and a discipline, in harmony with God's design, and it is in following that structure and practicing that discipline, with its required rituals and actions, that people express their identity as Jews and as humans.

A basic idea of Jewish ethics is that what God has made is good—but not perfect. The distinction and obligation of humans are that they can improve what God has made. The divine image is in humans, and therefore they can, if they will, transform this world. For that they need the guidance and the discipline of the Halakhah.

The Halakhah is not understood to be a burden; rather, it is a great joy. To Jews, the mitzvot of God's law are gifts and a sign of God's great love. The law submits all human faculties and passions to God's will, but it suppresses none. Even the passions are beneficial when controlled under God's law. In fact, God connects law with everything God loves—and the distinguishing mark of God's people of Israel is that there is not a single thing in their lives that God, through the Torah, has not connected with a commandment.

Enjoy the Good, Struggle Against the Evil   The Halakhah is based on a positive, optimistic view of human life. Since God created all things good, humans have the obligation to enjoy and enhance life. Good food, wealth, and sexual pleasure are all gifts of God and should be enjoyed in the rightful way. It is a mitzvah, for example, to get married and raise children—Jewish law does not condone celibacy or asceticism. In general, we are commanded always to do what enhances life, for others and for ourselves, such as acts of kindness to others, keeping our body clean, feeding animals, and burying the dead—all these are acts of ethical distinction.

On the other hand, we are forbidden to do that which degrades life. Overindulgence in food and drink, lack of cleanliness, and the like degrade one's own life. Exploiting and using other people or humiliating them degrades their life together with one's own. The Halakhah contains many laws against theft, which includes underpaying the laborer, interrupting his work, deceiving by making something old look new, and the like. Further common sins against others, prohibited by the law, include things like taunting, insulting, misleading, slandering, hating or being angry, and nursing revenge.

Jewish law follows a middle way, advocating neither complete self-denial nor selfish indulgence. Even the so-called evil tendency, as we saw earlier, is a gift of God for the promotion of human good; without the passions we would not eat, marry, or work toward success. Even selfishness and competitiveness, controlled under God's law, can be beneficial. It is good and right that one should desire good food and eat it with relish. But it should be for more than just assuaging hunger. It should be done with thankfulness to God, serving as the occasion for strengthening the bonds of family and friends.

Sexual pleasure, too, is a duty in Judaism, sanctified in a marriage marked by love. Marrying and having children is a duty, but marriage is not only for the purpose of producing children. Rather the sexual act between husband and wife is the culmination of the loving relationship between the two. Abstinence from marriage is a triple sin, against the health of the body, the fulfillment of the soul, and the welfare of society. Divorce is allowed in Jewish law when the partners no longer love or care for each other—though, of course, moral and social pressure is exerted against divorce. A wife can dissolve the marriage, for example, if it took place under false pretenses, if the husband is immoral, if his profession is intolerable to her, if they are sexually incompatible, if he has blemished her reputation, if he has embarrassed or insulted her, and so forth. The husband can dissolve the marriage for similar reasons. Marriage is holy, but is not meant to be a lifetime of suffering.

Among the various principles of the Halakhah is the important principle of *tzedakah*. This is sometimes translated as "charity," since it has to do with the duty of giving to those in need. But the Hebrew word means "justice" or "righteousness"; giving to those in need is not just an emotional matter of compassion, but it is something that is just and right. It is on the basis of justice that the Torah commanded the ancient Israelites to leave a small portion of their fields unharvested for the poor to glean. An important aspect of *tzedakah* is to guarantee the dignity and honor of those in need, even to restore independence and an honorable living to them. And, the rabbis taught, the poor man really does more for the rich man than the rich man does for the poor man (*Ruth Rabbah* 5:9). Special concern should be shown for those who cannot help themselves. A rabbinic exhortation says,

> In the future world, man will be asked, "What was your occupation?" If he reply, "I fed the hungry," then they reply, "This is the gate of the Lord; he who feeds the hungry, let him enter" (*Psalm* 118:20). So with giving drink to the thirsty, clothing the naked, with those who look after orphans, and with those, generally, who do deeds of loving kindness. All these are gates of the Lord, and those who do such deeds shall enter within them.

(*Midr. Ps.* on 118.19)[6]

Another important principle is to seek and pursue peace among members of the community. Shalom, the Hebrew word for peace, is thought of as the highest ethical imperative. It is so important that a person may even lie or suffer humiliation to preserve it—something not permitted under other circumstances. Patriarch Judah I said, "Great is peace, for even if the Israelites worship idols and there is peace among them, God says, 'I have no power, as it were, over them, seeing that peace is among them'" (*Gen. Rabbah, Noah*, 38:6).[7] Astonishingly, shalom takes precedence even over the most basic of all the commandments.

Whereas the outsider may be overwhelmed with the number and complexity of the Jewish commandments,

Jews have often pointed out that they all boil down to love: love for God and love for one's fellow humans. A famous story tells that a heathen once came to Rabbi Shammai and told him he would become a proselyte to Judaism if the rabbi could teach him the whole law while he stood on one foot. Rabbi Shammai drove him away. Then the heathen went to Rabbi Hillel, who received him and taught him, "What is hateful to you do not to your fellow: that is the whole Law; all the rest is explanation; go and learn" (*Sab.* 31a).[8] The Jewish path of Halakhah is an elaborate system embracing every aspect of human life, sanctifying it all and infusing it all with God's blessing, putting into concrete operation love for God and love for fellow humans.

In modern-day Jerusalem, orthodox rabbis engage in discussion.

The Missions of Peoplehood

The Chosen People of the Covenant   Ever since the ancient Israelites gathered at Sinai and concluded a covenant with their God there, the term *chosen people* has been central to Jewish identity. God entered into the covenant relationship with them and gave them the gift of the Torah.

God chose Israel. But Jews know that this can be easily misunderstood by others and even by Jews. The idea is not that of a tribal God protecting and blessing the chosen people no matter what. Nor is this the idea of one people chosen to rule all others, or a people superior to all others. Again, the idea of Jews as the chosen people does not mean Jews have special rank and privileges before God that other peoples do not have. The sacred scriptures emphasize several important things about Israel's election as God's people. First of all, Jews were not chosen because they are better than others:

> The Lord loved you and chose you not because you are more numerous than all the nations, for you are the smallest of all nations. It is because the Lord loved you and was keeping his oath which he swore to your forefathers, that the Lord brought you with a strong hand and redeemed you from the house of slavery.
>
> (*Deuteronomy* 7:7–8)

Second, this choice was a two-way affair: God chose Israel, but Israel chose to be chosen: "Moses came and related to the people all the words of the Lord, all his laws. And the whole people answered with one voice and said, 'All the things that the Lord told us, we will do'" (*Exodus* 24:3). The rabbis told how God offered the Torah to all the other nations, but all refused it. Then God gave it to Israel, who accepted it joyfully (*Sifre to Dt.* 33:2). Israel thus became the chosen people not simply because God chose them, but because they themselves chose to be God's people through their readiness to accept the Torah and to struggle for its truths.

Third, being the chosen people of God means that greater responsibility and higher standards of performance are demanded of the Jewish people compared to other peoples. The prophet Amos listed the punishments that will befall

all the nations of the world for their particular transgressions, but he saved the harshest judgment for the chosen people: God says to Israel, "Only you have I known among all the families of the earth; therefore I will punish you for all your iniquities" (*Amos* 3:2). To be God's chosen people is not something lightly to boast about; it involves heavy responsibility. God expects much more from the chosen people than from the other peoples.

The term chosen people really means "treasured people" (*'am segullah*). Jews are God's treasure because their primary task is to be God's witness in the world, testifying that there is one God and that all people are God's children. The prophet called Second Isaiah gives this word from God:

> I am the Lord. I have called you in righteousness;
>   I have taken you by the hand and I have kept you.
> Now I have given you as a covenant to the people,
>   a light to the nations,
> to open the eyes of the blind,
> to bring out the prisoners from the dungeons,
>   those who sit in darkness from the prison.
>
> (*Isaiah* 42:6–7)

The Jewish people are to be God's instrument for activating the conscience of all humans to serve God in truth and justice. In *Zacheriah* 2:6 God says, "I have spread you abroad as the four winds of the heavens." One rabbi pointed out that this passage does not say that Israel is spread "upon" the four winds but rather "as" the four winds; this means that, just as no place in the world is without wind, so also the world cannot exist without the people of God present everywhere (*Ta'an.* 3b).

Holy Land and State of Israel   During their long history of being oppressed and scattered throughout the earth, Jews have retained a strong sense of "peoplehood." The unity and mutual responsibility of Jews is often expressed in the Talmud: "Israel's reconciliation with God can be achieved only when they are all one brotherhood" (*Men.* 27a).[9] In fact, the people of Israel form one unity through all generations; one rabbinic teaching said that when Moses summoned the people before God to make the covenant, all souls were present then, though their bodies were not yet created (*Tanh. B., Nizzabim,* 8,25b). Especially since the great Holocaust of World War II, during which

more than six million Jews were deliberately exterminated by the Nazis while much of the rest of the world did very little to come to their aid, the centrality of peoplehood for Jews has taken on new and urgent significance. Only if they care for each other, Jews feel, and take responsibility for the survival of the Jewish people will they ensure that such a Holocaust will not happen again.

The relatively recent experience of the Holocaust is part of the reason that Jews throughout the world feel such a strong commitment to the state of Israel today. The Holy Land has always been an important symbol in the Jewish identity, ever since the promises God made to Abraham and the gift of that land to the Israelite people of old. After World War II, the dream of a Jewish homeland in the Holy Land became a reality with the establishing of the state of Israel. Today, Jews in every land feel the mitzvah (commandment) to guard and protect the survival of the Jewish people by maintaining the existence of the state of Israel as a Jewish state in the Holy Land.

Responsibility to the World   Why should there be the Jewish people among the peoples of the world? Do Jews have any kind of responsibility toward the welfare of others? The distinctiveness and uniqueness of the Jews does not abolish the universality of God's love and design for the creation. Jews do not feel compelled to try to convert others to the Jewish religion. Yet they see the ethical life of the Torah as a design that reaches out also to the non-Jews of world society. The commandments about enhancing life rather than degrading it, for example, apply to all people, not just Jews. The moral principles of the Torah are to govern societies as well as individuals.

The personal mitzvah of *tzedakah* is translated into philanthropy, devising creative ways to provide for the needs of the poor and help them regain independence and dignity. The resources of nature and of society make up a gift from God that should enhance the welfare of all people. This does not mean abolition of private property, for the law guarantees the individual the right to own what she or he has worked for and to enjoy its fruits. But no one, including governments, has the right to withhold wealth from use, to destroy it by wastefulness, or to use it selfishly against the communal interest.

Where evil rises in the society, Jews are required not only to avoid it passively but to defy and actively protest it. The rabbis taught that a person who can protest and prevent his household from committing a sin and does not is accountable for the sins of his household. Further, if he could protest and prevent his fellow citizens but fails to do so, he is accountable for the sins of the fellow citizens; and if he could keep the whole world from sinning but does not, he is accountable for the whole world (*Sab.* 54b). On the basis of their ethical principles, many Jews have been in the forefront of protesting slavery and injustice in society, advocating freedom and equality, compulsory education, rights of workers, improvement in the status of women, and other humanitarian moral changes for society.

The important mitzvah of pursuing peace (shalom) is extended to conflict and warfare between peoples and nations. The Hebrew scriptures' description of holy war in the early period, commanded by God, can perhaps be interpreted to mean that such warfare is in accordance with the divine will. But it should be remembered that those passages are balanced with other sections in the scriptures that emphasize shalom. A famous passage in *Isaiah* 2 says that, in the messianic age, all nations will flow to Jerusalem and beat their swords into plowshares, learning war no more (*Isaiah* 2:4). The rabbis pointed out that the command to "seek peace and pursue it" (*Psalm* 34:14), unlike many other commandments, does not begin with "if" or "when," to be fulfilled only on the appropriate occasion. Rather, you should seek peace wherever you happen to be, and you should run after it if it is elsewhere (*Num. Rabbah, Hukkat,* 19:27). Shalom does not just mean the absence of war, however; it expresses the health and wholeness of humans who experience equality and justice. Therefore, the Jewish approach to war and conflict has emphasized the connection between peace and justice. Noting that God told Moses to make war on Sihon, but Moses sent messengers of peace instead (*Deuteronomy* 2:24ff.), the Talmud says, "How great, then, must be words of peace, if Israel disobeyed God for peace's sake, and yet He was not wrath with them" (*Tanh. B., Debarim,* 3b).[10]

The Jewish tradition does not, however, advocate pacifism. The rabbis distinguished between optional war and obligatory war, which is a just war in defense against attack from outside. The right of a person to preserve his or her own life is paramount, and thus a war of self-defense is justified. However, the rabbis taught that destructive action should be avoided if a lesser action suffices. The theme of making peace, balanced with the requirement of justice, is still characteristic of the Jewish approach today. The massive atrocities of the twentieth century require an active resistance to evil. But the threat of nuclear destruction leads some modern Jewish thinkers to conclude that ancient ideas about justified warfare are, in the modern context, a contradiction in terms.

Basic to the Jewish ethical vision, though shaken a bit by the events of the Holocaust, is the optimistic idea of transforming the world. Only humans can transform and perfect the world that God has made. Particularly in Reform Judaism, the pursuit of social justice and human fulfillment has been made into a central emphasis; Judaism's mission is to be an irresistible force for freedom and human improvement in the world. Orthodox Jews resist this kind of focus, but they also hold to the traditional teaching that, when humans repent and perform righteousness, then the messiah will come and bring in the ideal age. There is a sense in the Jewish tradition that deeds of righteousness sustain the world and keep it from disaster. Rabbi Jonathan played with the passage from *Psalm* 36:6, "Thy righteousness is like the mountains of God; thy judgments are a great deep," transposing it to read, "Thy righteousness is over thy judgments as the mountains of God are over the great deep"; then he explained, "As these mountains press down the deep, that it should not rise and engulf the world, so the deeds of the righteous force down the punishments that they should not come upon the world" (*Pes.K.* 73b).[11]

Bringing Truth to the World   As noted, the Jewish mission to the world is not conceived in terms of converting all others to Judaism. Jews certainly believe their way of Halakhah is supreme and God-given, but their mission is to work with God toward a transformation of the world, a purifying and perfecting of human society.

One of the most characteristic Jewish ideas is that of the coming of the messiah, sent by God to redeem Israel and usher in a new era in which all people will worship the one true God. Traditional Jews have always held that this will be a personal Messiah; others have thought more in terms of a messianic age of restoration that God will bring about sometime in the future. Here, we quote Louis Jacobs on this complicated topic; he writes that the basic affirmation of the expectation of the messiah is that human history will find its culmination and fulfillment here on earth. "Ultimately, the doctrine declares, God will not abandon His world to Moral chaos. Eventually He will intercede directly in order to call a halt to tyranny, oppression and the pursuit of evil so as to restore mankind to the state of bliss here on earth. . . ." We must admit we simply do not know what will happen in the messianic age, Jacobs writes;

> we affirm our belief that God will one day intervene, that no good deed goes to waste, that the human drama will somehow find its fulfillment here on earth, that we do right to long and pray for God's direct intervention. More than this we cannot say. We must leave it to God who alone knows all secrets.[12]

Some modern Jews have found deep meaning in the teaching of the medieval Kabbalists about the "breaking of the vessels." Isaac Luria's (1534–1572) mystical vision of the creation of the world involved the idea that God withdrew into Godself to make room for the world, then sent out divine light into this space. The light was to be preserved in special "bowls" *(sefirot),* which had been emanated from God for this purpose. But the divine light was too much for the lower vessels; they burst and were hurled down with some of the divine light. From these shards, the dark forces of gross matter took substance. Now all the worlds had sunk to lower levels. But immediately after the disaster the process of restoration *(tikkun)* began, which means the restitution and reintegration of the original whole. The restoration has been almost completed by the supernal lights, but certain concluding actions have been reserved for humans. It is the human historical process and particularly its innermost soul, the religious actions of the Jews,

which prepare the way for the final restitution of all the scattered and exiled lights and sparks.

For all the intricacies and strangeness of this medieval vision, it does supply a mystic model for a Jewish mission in the world: to assist God in restoring this imperfect world into the transformed world of God's purpose.

Discussion Questions

1   What is meant by the Jewish saying that the Sabbath has kept the Jews more than the Jews have kept the Sabbath? Describe how Jews keep the Sabbath.
2   What are the main themes of the High Holy Days (Rosh Hashanah and Yom Kippur)?
3   What freedoms does Pesach celebrate?
4   Explain the meaning of *kashrut.* What sense do the dietary laws make for modern Jews?
5   Describe the main Jewish rites of passage, at birth, puberty, marriage, and death.
6   How has the prohibition of making images affected Jewish art?
7   How might one best answer the question, "Who is a Jew?"
8   Describe the role of women in traditional Jewish religious life. What models are there of strong women leaders?
9   Describe some of the key principles of Jewish ethical life, according to the Halakhah.
10   What is the "whole law" that Rabbi Hillel taught to a heathen person while he stood on one foot? What do you think is the significance of this story?
11   What are the central meanings of the Jews being called the "chosen people"?

CHAPTER 9

Christian Sacred Story and Historical Context

FOUNDATIONS OF THE CHRISTIAN STORY

Who is a Christian? A Christian is one who is baptized in the name of Jesus Christ and identifies with the Christian sacred story. The sacred story as told by Christians centers on the life of Jesus, as related in the Christian writings called the gospels. But it encompasses much more than just the story of Jesus' life. It reaches back to the sacred history of Israel as God's preparation for the fulfillment in Jesus; it includes the gathering of the Christian church after the death and resurrection of **Christ;** and it extends to the decisions and clarifications about Christian faith and life given in the New Testament writings and even in the decisions of the early councils of the Christian church.

Jewish Roots of the Christian Way

Jesus was a Jew. Born into a Jewish family, he lived his life practicing the Jewish way; he died and was buried a Jew. Those who followed him and formed the Christian church after his death were Jews. Thus the Christian story begins with Judaism, with those Jews living in Palestine in the Roman occupation and looking for the way to live according to God's covenant.

The times in which Jesus lived were confused and violent. The Jewish people under oppressive Roman rule feared for their religious identity, and they developed different forms of Jewish life under these circumstances. There was a group of Jewish revolutionaries, some of them called Zealots, who were agitating for a Jewish state independent of Rome and were causing uprisings. For example, about the year 4 B.C.E., a certain Judas of Galilee led a bloody revolt against the puppet ruler Herod, king of Galilee, over the question of tribute money being paid to the Romans. They were defeated and some two thousand savagely crucified, but their revolutionary sentiments continued to be felt widely among the Jewish people.

Other Jews felt differently. The Pharisees believed that a return to the full keeping of the whole Torah would purify the Jewish people, for the kingdom of God would come by keeping the Torah, not by violence and force. The Sadducees, made up of established leaders among Jews, considered it essential to preserve the temple and traditional way of life, so they worked together with the Romans to maintain a degree of security and stability. The Essenes felt the majority of the Jews to be hopelessly impure and so withdrew to the shores of the Dead Sea to live a life of purity and await the coming of the messianic age. Many Jews felt a sense of expectancy, of a time soon when God would intervene to restore the sacred people and establish the kingdom of God. But the ideas about how that kingdom would be established differed from group to group.

In this setting, Jesus was born about 4 B.C.E. (the traditional dating is slightly incorrect) and grew up in Nazareth of Galilee, just a few miles from the city of Sepphoris where the Zealots revolted. He was born into a poor family, helped his father as a carpenter, became a wandering preacher and healer and teacher, claimed to present a new message about God and God's kingdom, presented a threat to the authorities, and was executed by crucifixion by the Romans when he was about thirty-three years of age. His was a short, tragic life. But the Christian story sees it differently. Christians see in this short, tragic life the presence of the messiah, the Son of God, the savior of the world.

The Jewish Scriptures as the "Old Testament"   The Gospel of Matthew, standing first in the Christian collection of writings known as the New Testament, begins with a genealogy of Jesus: "A book of the descent of Jesus Christ, son of David, son of Abraham" (*Matthew* 1:1). Thus, the Christian story begins by firmly linking Jesus with the history of God's covenant people Israel. As Jews, the first Christians read and interpreted the Torah in much the same way as did their fellow Jews—with one crucial difference: Everything in the Torah and in the whole Hebrew scriptures was understood to point symbolically to Jesus as the messiah.

According to the Christian story, then, God the loving parent created humans to live in fellowship and happiness with their creator. But humans fell into sin, rebelling against God and thus creating an estrangement from God that will continue for all generations. Because of this estrangement, humans live in evil and suffering and death, with eternal punishment the only prospect for the future. God, although a righteous judge, is also a loving parent. So God set about on a plan of salvation, a plan to overcome the sin and evil of humankind and reconcile them to God. For that purpose, God called Abraham and his descendants, made a covenant with them, set up the Kingdom of David, and sent prophets to proclaim the divine word. In all of these events, people, and words, God was revealing the plan for the salvation of the world, promising Israel that one day this plan would be fulfilled in a complete and final way. The faithful people of Israel believed in God's promises, and it was counted to them as righteousness. Thus, the Christian story looks upon the **Old Testament** (the Hebrew scriptures) as the gradual unfolding of God's plan of salvation, foreshadowing and preparing for the culmination of this salvation through God's work in Jesus Christ. In this sense, everything in the Old Testament points ahead to Christ: The high priest foreshadows Christ's priestly role; the king points to Christ's royal office as Son of God; the blood shed at the covenant ceremony prefigures the shedding of Christ's blood to establish a new covenant; and so forth. The Christian story stresses the incomplete character of the Old Testament. It is understood to be open-ended, reveal-

ing the nature of God and the plan of salvation but ending before that salvation has been fully accomplished. In the Old Testament there are key prophecies, in which God reveals the divine intentions, given to encourage the faithful people to trust the promises and look to the future salvation. In particular, the prophecies about the coming of the messiah and the establishing of the messianic age are important. For example, *Isaiah* 61:1–2 presents a vision of the messianic age, according to the Christian understanding:

> The spirit of the Lord God is upon me,
>   because the Lord has anointed me;
> he has sent me to proclaim good news to the poor,
>   to bind up the broken-hearted,
> to proclaim liberty to the captives
>   and release to those who are bound;
> to proclaim the year of the Lord's favor.

According to the Christian story, Jesus read this passage at a synagogue meeting, and as he explained it he said, "Today this scripture is fulfilled in your ears" (*Luke* 4:16–21).

Therefore, as the gospel writers introduce Jesus and describe his life and death, they carefully link him to God's plan of salvation as it has been unfolded in the story of the Old Testament. The expectation of the messiah is in the foreground, and the key question is that one asked by disciples of John the baptizer: "Are you the one who is coming, or do we look for another?" (*Luke* 7:20). The stories chosen and narrated about Jesus by the writers of the **gospels** answer that question with a clear, "Yes, this is the one!"

Life and Teachings of Jesus

The focal point of Jesus' story is his death on the cross and his **resurrection,** understood by Christians as the climax and fulfillment of God's plan of salvation. To the story of his death and resurrection, however, are affixed stories of Jesus' birth and youth, his teachings about God, and the deeds by which he was witness to God's power of salvation. These stories point to the identity of Jesus as the Christ, the one in whom God's presence comes into the human world.

The Birth and Baptism of Jesus   The birth of Jesus, as told in *Matthew* and *Luke,* came when God intervened once again in the course of human history to redeem the sacred people, as at the time of Moses. "The birth of Jesus Christ was in this way," wrote Matthew. "Mary his mother was betrothed to Joseph, but before they came together she was found with child by the Holy Spirit." When honorable Joseph was about to set aside the marriage, an angel of the Lord appeared to him and told him this child was conceived by the Holy Spirit. "She will bear a son, and you shall give him the name Jesus [savior], for he will save his people from their sins" (*Matthew* 1:18–25). According to the story as told by Luke, while Joseph and Mary were in Bethlehem to enroll in the census at their ancestral town, the baby Jesus was born, an event accompanied by hosts of angels singing the praises of God to shepherds in the fields. Wise men from the east came to offer gifts to the newborn king of the Jews. All these events symbolized the fulfilling of God's plan and prophecies of old. When Jesus was a grown man, he began teaching and healing. The gospels first introduce John the baptizer, an ascetic Jew living in the wilderness and preaching repentance and **baptism** for the remission of sins. This is the man of whom the prophet Isaiah had written, "The voice of one crying in the wilderness, 'Prepare the way of the Lord'" (*Mark* 1:2). John pointed to Jesus as the one who was to come after him, the lamb of God; and Jesus went out to be baptized by John in the river Jordan. Again God intervened with a sign: As Jesus came up out of the water, he saw the heavens open and the Spirit descending like a dove on him; a voice spoke from heaven, "You are my beloved son, with you I am well pleased" (*Mark* 1:9–11). Then Jesus, now knowing he was God's chosen one, went out to the wilderness to be tested for forty days, thus repeating in his own life the story of God's people Israel (who were tested forty years in the wilderness).

Preaching and Doing the Kingdom of God   Attested by divine signs as the messiah, the chosen one of God, Jesus began preaching in his home area of Galilee, proclaiming the "good news of God" and saying: "The time is fulfilled, and the kingdom of God is come near! Repent, and believe the good news!" (*Mark* 1:15). Jesus, in his preaching as presented in the gospels, told that the decisive age had now come for human history. The long period of preparation was over, the "time" was fulfilled. What was bursting upon the people was the long-awaited **kingdom of God,** when God would intervene in human history to bring about a new age of

Christ sits between two apostles in this high-relief from the upper panel of the sarcophagus of a Roman prefect who died in 359 C.E.

divine rule. And the proper response to this astounding revelation was to repent and believe the good news.

Shortly after Jesus began preaching the coming of the kingdom of God, he started to gather a community of disciples around himself. Walking by the sea of Galilee he saw two fishermen who were brothers, Simon Peter and Andrew. The story reports that Jesus said to them, "Come with me, and I will make you to be fishers of people." At once they left their nets and followed him (*Mark* 1:16–17). He called two more fishermen who were brothers, James and John; eventually twelve disciples gathered around him. Although the number twelve seems important to the story, symbolizing as it does the twelve tribes of Israel, many more people also followed Jesus as he went about Galilee as a wandering preacher and healer: "He went about the whole of Galilee, teaching in their synagogues, preaching the good news of the kingdom, and healing every disease and infirmity among the people. . . . And great crowds followed him" (*Matthew* 4:23–25). These disciples came from various social groups, although many appear to have been poor and uneducated. He associated with known sinners and tax collectors (whom many Jews condemned as collaborators with the Romans). And there were also women among his followers, including Mary Magdalen, thought to be a prostitute, and Mary and Martha of Bethany. The numbers of disciples and followers fluctuated, and many deserted him when times got bad. But here was the kernel of the new community, following Jesus as their master.

Jesus' work over the short period (traditionally thought to be three years) from the beginning of his preaching in Galilee to his trial in Jerusalem is rehearsed somewhat differently in each of the four gospels. But each describes a combination of teaching and deeds of helping and healing, all of which was to make the kingdom of God present among the people. Jesus' teaching about the kingdom of God described it as a new order in which the love of God and the love of the neighbor would be the ruling motivation. In contrast to nationalistic expectations of a revival of the grand kingdom of David, Jesus taught about an inner kingdom, shared by all those who do God's will.

Much of Jesus' teaching about the kingdom took the form of **parables,** that is, short stories from everyday life that suggest the reality and the quality of the kingdom. He taught that the kingdom of God is like a wedding feast to which people are invited (*Matthew* 22:2–10). Or again, the kingdom is like a mustard seed growing silently to become a large shrub (*Mark* 4:30–32). The kingdom is not political, nor is it just a future event. The kingdom is already at hand, working in a mysterious and quiet manner, having to do with the community of those who follow Jesus.

That the new era was breaking upon them was vividly demonstrated in Jesus' actions. At Capernaum, where Jesus was teaching in the synagogue, a man possessed by an unclean spirit shrieked: "What do you have to do with us, O Jesus of Nazareth? Have you come to destroy us? I know who you are—the Holy One of God!" Jesus exorcised the unclean spirit with a command, and all the people said, "What is this? A new kind of teaching with authority! He commands even the unclean spirits, and they obey him" (*Mark* 1:21–28). The gospels recount many such incidents where Jesus performed deeds of healing, exorcism of evil

spirits, multiplying food and wine, even raising the dead— as signs that the new age of God's kingdom had dawned.

A Radical New Way of Life   Corresponding to the new age of the kingdom, Jesus taught a new way of life. As a practicing Jew himself, he emphasized two main tenets of the Jewish Torah: to love God with all one's heart, soul, and mind; and to love one's neighbor as oneself (*Matthew* 22:35–40; cf. *Deuteronomy* 6:5; *Leviticus* 19:18). However, he taught a more radical approach to loving God and one's neighbor than most of his fellow Jewish teachers did. In the homily called the Sermon on the Mount, he contrasted his teaching with the accepted tradition:

> You have heard that it was said to our forefathers, "You shall not kill; anyone who kills will be liable to judgment." But I say to you, anyone who nurses anger against his brother will be liable to judgment. . . . You have heard that it was said, "Do not commit adultery." But I say to you that everyone who looks on a woman lustfully has already committed adultery with her in his heart.
>
> (*Matthew* 5:21–28)

Much of Jesus' teaching overturned the usual notions of behavior and God's rewards for it. Again from the Sermon on the Mount:

> Blessed are those of gentle spirit, for they shall inherit the earth.
> Blessed are those who hunger and thirst for righteousness, for they shall be satisfied.
> Blessed are those who show mercy, for mercy shall be shown to them.
> Blessed are those whose hearts are pure, for they shall see God.
> Blessed are the peacemakers, for they shall be called children of God.
> Blessed are those persecuted for the cause of righteousness, for theirs is the kingdom of heaven.
>
> (*Matthew* 5:3–10)

So radical is the demand for a new kind of life in the new age that Jesus said, "You have heard that it was said [to your fathers], 'Love your neighbor, and hate your enemy.' But I say to you, love your enemies and pray on behalf of your persecutors. . . . You therefore shall be perfect, as your heavenly father is perfect" (*Matthew* 5:43–48).

Throughout these teachings and deeds there is the ring of a strong sense of authority, of speaking for God, of sensing God's presence in a powerful way. In his prayers to God, Jesus (who spoke Aramaic, the common language of Palestine at this time) used the Aramaic term **Abba,** a familiar and endearing word for "father." It is true that many of Jesus' sayings about his relationship with God are shot through with mystery and ambivalence. In the earliest gospel, that of *Mark,* Jesus is not reported to have claimed to be the messiah or the Son of God—though others speak of him that way. But the gospel writers, telling the story at least a generation after the time of Jesus, certainly knew the belief of the earliest Christians that Jesus in fact was the messiah. The *Gospel of John,* for example, has Jesus clearly revealing his identity as the Son of God through whom the Father is working. In any case, Jesus' actions and words were so radical and so full of the claim to God's authority that he was bound to come into conflict with the accepted Jewish interpretations.

Conflict over Authority   The gospels and epistles of the New Testament—the new Christian scriptures—were written some years after Jesus' death, and they reflect to some extent the conflicts that developed later between the Jewish and Christian communities. But the Christian story pinpoints the heart of the conflict especially in Jesus' new interpretations of the Jewish Torah. On the one hand, he made the requirements much more stringent and radical. But, on the other hand, he acted as if he were above the Torah. For example, when he and his disciples walked along the road on a sabbath, they picked grain in the fields to prepare some food. When confronted by the Pharisees over this unnecessary breaking of the sabbath law, Jesus stated, "The sabbath was made for the sake of humans and not humans for the sake of the sabbath; therefore the son of man is master even of the sabbath" (*Mark* 2:27–28). He healed people on the sabbath. He forgave sins in his own name, leaving some lawyers to say, "Blasphemy! Who but God alone can forgive sin?" (*Mark* 2:7).

Possibly the biggest scandal Jesus caused resulted from his attitude toward sinners, toward those who consistently broke the Torah. He associated with such people and became known as a "friend of sinners." He sat at table with them, extending the intimacy of table-fellowship to those who had put themselves outside the covenant people of God. And he taught that God forgives such people—in defiance of the traditional perception that God rewards those who do the divine will and punishes those who willingly break laws of the Torah and refuse to repent. Further, he suggested that even the presumed righteousness of the religious teachers was no real righteousness at all. In words reminiscent of the prophets of old, Jesus castigated them: "Woe to you, scribes and Pharisees, hypocrites! For while you give tithes of mint and dill and cumin, you have neglected the more important demands of the Law, namely, justice, mercy, and faith. These you should do while not neglecting the others. O blind guides, you strain the gnat out, but you drink down the camel!" (*Matthew* 23:13–24). The parable of the wedding feast summed up this upside-down view of God and the covenant people. Those good people invited to the wedding, who found various excuses not to come, will find themselves shut out, while the bridegroom will send out to the highways and hedges to bring in the poor, the maimed, the blind, and the lame (*Luke* 14:15–24).

What Jesus was teaching about the Torah and about God went beyond the covenant notion of the life of Torah as the highest good for humans and of God as a partner who rewards those who are faithful and punishes those who break the Torah. Jesus said that he came not to destroy the Torah but to fulfill it (*Matthew* 5:17); but he radicalized the demands of the Torah so that the most pious people in Israel fell far short of keeping the Torah in his eyes. And he taught that God is a friend to sinners, searching out the outcasts and rejected of the people. The whole notion of God as one who rewards and punishes based on covenant law was rejected in Jesus' teaching. Rather, God forgives and accepts sinners—even the woman caught in adultery, even the tax collector.

These teachings and acts of Jesus seemed to some to be extremely arrogant and boastful—after all, Jesus was putting himself above the Torah; he was presuming to give radical new interpretations of the commandments. He claimed to be "master of the sabbath." Above all, he claimed to have a special close relationship with God as "Abba," which gave him authority to teach things about God that seemed to contradict the Torah given through Moses. In the traditional view, such rash words and deeds were "blasphemy," that is, dishonoring God, putting oneself in place of God.

Crucifixion and Resurrection

The historical facts of Jesus' arrest, trial, and execution cannot be clearly and accurately reconstructed, for the Christian story is more interested in the theological meaning of this happening than in historical detail. Jesus certainly did antagonize some of the leaders of his Jewish community, and it is possible they brought religious charges against him. But he also posed a political threat to the Roman occupational government; large groups of people acclaiming him as the messiah, the "king of the Jews," could easily turn into a violent, nationalistic uprising. So it was the Roman government that arrested him, condemned him hastily to death, and executed him by crucifixion. It is true that there are elements of anti-Jewish feeling in the stories of Jesus' trial as recorded in the gospels—probably reflecting the sour relations between Christians and Jews in a later generation when the gospels were written. It is also true that in later centuries Christians sometimes rashly charged Jews with the death of Jesus. But Christians today have come to realize that such anti-Jewish elements are not an authentic part of the story of Jesus. He did no doubt have conflicts with some Jewish teachers and leaders. But, as the Apostles' Creed insists, he "was crucified under Pontius Pilate," the Roman governor.

The Meaning of Jesus' Death   But the Christian story really is not interested in the question of who killed Jesus. Much more important is the question of why Jesus died. The gospels present his death as having a meaning and purpose, indeed of happening in accordance with God's will and design. From early in his public career, Jesus began to predict he would have to follow God's plan and suffer and die at Jerusalem. The story says that, after Peter had just stated he believed Jesus to be the Christ, the messiah, "he [Jesus] began to teach them that the son of man must suffer many things, be rejected by the elders, chief priests, and scribes, be put to death, and after three days rise again" (*Mark* 8:27–32). Why did this have to happen? Jesus taught that "the son of man goes as it is written of him" (*Matthew* 26:24)—that is, in the scriptures God's plan had been revealed, and by Jesus' suffering and death, this plan of salvation would be accomplished.

The disciples, of course, did not understand such talk, and Peter rebuked Jesus for saying this. Their idea of the messiah was still that of a royal hero who would set up a great kingdom and place them at his right hand and his left in positions of power (*Mark* 10:37). Only after his death did his followers begin to understand that God's plan for the salvation of humankind involved taking all the sins and burdens of the world on Godself through the righteous servant. God's **plan of salvation** was to take the form of a *suffering* messiah. They looked to the great prophetic passage from *Isaiah* 53 as the key to understanding why the son of man must be given up to suffer and die:

> He was despised and rejected by men,
>   a man of sorrows and acquainted with grief;
> and as one from whom people hide their faces
>   he was despised, and we had no esteem for him.
> Surely he himself has borne our griefs,
>   and our sorrows he carried;
> yet we counted him stricken,
>   smitten by God, and afflicted.
> But he was wounded for our transgressions,
>   tortured for our iniquities;
> the chastisement upon him made us whole,
>   and by his stripes we are healed.
> All of us strayed like sheep,
>   each of us turned to his own way.
> But the Lord laid upon him the iniquity of us all. . . .
> Therefore I will allot him a portion with the great,
>   and with the mighty he will share the spoil,
> because he poured out his soul to death,
>   and with the transgressors he was numbered.
> Yet he bore the sin of many,
>   and for the transgressors he interceded.

(*Isaiah* 55:3–6, 12)

Jesus' role as the messiah was to follow the path of the suffering servant. Telling his disciples to be servants of one another, Jesus said, "For even the son of man did not come to be served but to serve, and to give up his life a ransom for many" (*Mark* 10:45).

Holy Week in Jerusalem   Because of this conviction that he was carrying out God's plan, Jesus turned with his disciples from Galilee and made his way up to Jerusalem to confront the religious leaders there. The gospels concentrate on this **passion** [suffering] **story,** the events from Jesus'

Jesus' agony in the Garden of Gethsemane. Painting by El Greco.

During supper Jesus took bread, and, saying the blessing, broke it and gave it to the disciples with the words: "Take and eat; this is my body." Then, taking a cup and giving thanks, he gave it to them saying: "Drink from it, all of you, for this is my blood of the covenant, poured out for many for the forgiveness of sins."

(*Matthew* 26:26–28)

The early Christians understood this act as the institution of the sacred meal of the Christians, the Lord's Supper or **Eucharist.** Paul wrote that Jesus told them to "do this in remembrance of me," and then Paul added, "As often as you eat this bread and drink this cup, you proclaim the death of the Lord, until he comes" (*I Corinthians* 11:23–26).

triumphal entry into Jerusalem until his death. He rode into Jerusalem as a king, seated on a donkey, with great crowds before and after singing the old chant of tribute to the king: "Hosanna to the son of David! Blessed is the one who comes in the name of the Lord!" (*Matthew* 21:9). He confronted the authority of the religious leaders directly with his own charismatic authority. He went into the temple, the symbol of priestly authority, and overturned the tables of those who exchanged money and sold pigeons for sacrifices; and he healed blind men and cripples in the temple, refusing to answer the elders when they asked him, "By what authority are you doing these things?" (*Matthew* 21:23).

In Jerusalem, Jesus went to an upper room where he celebrated the Passover meal together with his community of disciples. Teaching them again about his coming death, Jesus used the wine and the bread of the Passover meal to symbolize his own body and blood, which would be sacrificed, as reported by Matthew:

The gospel accounts tell the next part of the story in detail, leading to the fulfillment of Jesus' mission. After the Passover meal, Jesus and his disciples went out into the Garden of Gethsemane to pray. Jesus was in agony, and he prayed, "My father, if it is possible, let this cup pass from me. Yet not as I will, but as you will" (*Matthew* 26:39). One of his disciples, Judas, had betrayed his whereabouts to those looking to arrest him; when he was seized, all his disciples deserted him and fled. He was first brought to the house of the high priest, where various charges were brought against him. Finally the high priest put him under oath and demanded, "Tell us if you are the messiah, the son of God." Jesus answered, "You have said. But I tell you this: Hereafter you will see the son of man seated at the right hand of Power, coming on the clouds of heaven." At this, the high priest and council decided he was indeed guilty of blasphemy, and they handed him over to Pilate, the Roman governor (*Matthew* 26:59–66). In the meantime, Peter was denying he even knew Jesus, and Judas was in remorse for what he had done and hanged himself.

Jesus refused to answer Pilate's questions during the trial, and finally Pilate, washing his hands to signify his innocence in the matter, had Jesus flogged and handed him over to his soldiers to be crucified. Taking him to Golgotha, the hill of execution, they crucified him between two criminals. Suffering on the cross, Jesus asked forgiveness for his tormentors and, in his torment of suffering, cried out the words of *Psalm* 22, "My God, my God, why have you forsaken me?" Finally, with the words, "It is finished!," he died. The gospels tell how his death was accompanied with divine signs: three hours of darkness came first; then, when he died, the curtain partitioning off the Holy of Holies in the temple was torn in two from top to bottom. And the Roman centurion watching this all was moved to say, "Truly this was a son of God" (*Mark* 15:39).

The Christian story tells how Jesus' body was taken and buried in a tomb by a respected Jew, Joseph of Arimathaea, and how a guard was set so Jesus' followers would not steal the body. The next day was the sabbath, so early on the day after the sabbath several women who were followers of Jesus came to the tomb to anoint his body with oils—but they found the tomb was empty, and a youth sitting there in a white robe told them, "Do not fear! You are looking for Jesus of Nazareth, who was crucified. He is risen, he is not here" (*Mark* 16:6).

Other disciples at first refused to believe this news, according to the gospel accounts; but Jesus, risen from the dead, appeared to them a number of times—while several of them were walking on the road, and again while the eleven disciples were sitting at table. He had told them to meet him on a mountain in Galilee, and they made their way there. Before he finally left them, he gave them a **great commission** to go out into all the world and bring the good news of salvation to all. Luke reports that after Jesus had given them this commission, he was lifted up, and a cloud removed him out of their sight (*Acts* 1:9).

Thus ends the story of the earthly Jesus—and begins the story of the risen Christ, Lord of the church, reigning at God's right hand and present in the world wherever his followers are. For this story of Jesus is a *sacred* story; in it Christians see revealed God's own son, the messiah, the savior of the world. When Christians gather together, they tell this story to one another as the Gospel, the Good News of God acting in Jesus Christ to bring salvation for all the world. Christians identify with this story, taking inspiration from it and modeling their lives on Jesus' own life.

Beginnings of the Christian Church

The four gospels are followed in the Christian scriptures by a writing called *The Acts of the Apostles,* written by Luke to continue the gospel story with the story of the risen Christ and the gathering of his followers into the "Christian church"—that is, the real founding of Christianity as a religion.

Pentecost and the Birth of the Church   The story tells how the disciples were confused and afraid after Jesus' death, and that only seeing the risen Christ kindled their courage. But before Jesus left them he told them to wait in Jerusalem to be baptized by the Holy Spirit. So on the Jewish festival of Shavuot (**Pentecost**), they were all together, when suddenly a great wind filled the house and tongues like flames of fire rested on each one. They were filled with the Spirit and began to speak in other tongues so that Jewish pilgrims from various parts of the world could understand them, each in his own language. Peter, assuming a leadership role, stood up and preached the first Christian sermon, explaining that this happening was the promised pouring out of God's Spirit (*Joel* 2:28–32), which was to take place on the great day of the Lord. The new age had come! Peter explained how this Jesus, who was crucified, had been chosen by God; in God's plan he had been killed, but God raised him to life. "Let all the house of Israel then know for certain that God has made him both Lord and messiah, this Jesus you crucified!" When the people asked what they should now do, Peter said, "Repent and be baptized, every one of you, in the name of Jesus Christ, for the forgiveness of your sins; then you will receive the gift of the Holy Spirit" (*Acts* 2:1–39).

Those who accepted Peter's words were baptized (some three thousand that day, the story says), and the Christian **church** came into being. They continued to practice baptism, to meet together to hear the apostles teach, to celebrate the Lord's Supper, to pray, and to share the common life. At first they sold their property and had everything in common. When disagreements arose concerning distribution of food to widows, the whole group selected seven deacons to handle the needs of food and clothing of the community, while the apostles devoted themselves to prayer and the ministry of preaching the gospel. With that began the earliest forms of ministry in the church.

Persecutions and the Conversion of Paul   The Christian sacred story tells of the trials of the early church in Jerusalem. Those following Christ still considered themselves Jews and attended the temple; but other Jews, considering them to be an erring sect worshiping a false messiah, persecuted them, scattering many of them to the country districts of Judea and Samaria, where they continued to convert and baptize many. The first martyr was Stephen, one of the deacons, whose testimony to Jesus so enraged a crowd that they stoned him.

A witness to the stoning was a young Jew named Saul, who was born as a Roman citizen in Tarsus of Asia Minor but came to Jerusalem to learn better the Jewish way of life. Saul joined in the persecution of the Jewish Christians with great zeal until, on the road to Damascus, a light flashed from the sky and Saul heard a voice saying, "Saul, Saul, why do you persecute me?" It was the risen Jesus, who gave Saul the mission to proclaim his name before nations and kings (*Acts* 9:1–16). Saul, later known as **Paul,** became the great missionary for Christ, making trips throughout the Greek-speaking world—Asia Minor, Greece, and Italy—preaching the gospel of Christ and establishing Christian congregations wherever he went. Other apostles and leaders also went out in mission, to Samaria, Syria, Ethiopia, Arabia, and other places, and many people believed in the gospel about Jesus Christ and were baptized. Christians were carrying out the commission given by Jesus: "You shall be my witnesses in Jerusalem and in all Judea and Samaria and to the end of the earth" (*Acts* 1:8).

In this Christian story of the people of God gathered around Jesus Christ, two developments were particularly crucial on the way to the universal Christian church. One arose from the tension within the early Christian community between the Jewish heritage and the mission to bring the gospel to all the world. The other development arose from the need to translate the Jewish Christian gospel into language and concepts understandable to people in the Hellenistic (Greek-speaking) world of the Roman Empire. Both of these developments involved a great deal of thinking and struggling with the meaning of faith in Jesus as the Christ. This was the beginning of *theologizing,* that is, creating Christian doctrines of faith to guide people and pre-

serve the good news about Jesus. These developments arose out of specific situations in the different Christian communities. It was in response to such situations that the gospels and the letters that make up the New Testament were written. Paul, whose letters responding to problems in different congregations are the earliest writings in the New Testament, had a particularly profound influence on the development of Christian **theology.** The Johannine writings (the *Gospel of John* and the *Letters of John*), traditionally attributed to Jesus' disciple but of uncertain authorship, have also had a deep impact on theological perspectives.

Jews and Gentiles in the Christian Church   After Paul's conversion, he returned to Tarsus, and then with his colleague Barnabas he set up work in Antioch. He felt himself called especially to bring the gospel to the gentiles (non-Jews), so with Antioch as a base he launched out into the Greek world. At first, he regularly went to the Jewish synagogues to proclaim to the Jewish communities, scattered throughout the Roman world, that the fulfillment of their hopes was in Jesus as the messiah. Usually, he had limited success among the Jewish people, so more and more he began to take the message about Christ to the non-Jewish population. Thus there arose many Christian congregations that were made up of both Jewish and gentile Christians. And the question arose: Should the non-Jewish Christians be compelled to follow the rules of the Torah, like circumcision and the dietary laws? Some Jewish Christians were insisting that they must, since these were laws given by God; others apparently advocated separating into two churches, one comprised of Torah-observing Christians and the other of gentiles who did not observe the laws of the Torah.

The basic question was discussed in a meeting of the apostles in Jerusalem. They decided to impose no "irksome burdens" on the gentile Christians, except for these essentials: to abstain from meat offered to idols, from blood, from anything strangled, and from fornication (*Acts* 15:6–29). It was their view, thus, that it is not necessary for Christians to observe all the Torah of Moses. The problem kept arising, however. In Galatia, some Jewish Christians tried to insist that the gentiles must be circumcised and obey the dietary laws in addition to faith in Christ, and Paul responded with the Letter to the Galatians in which he wrote what became the classic defense of Christian liberty. He insisted that a person is made right with God only by trust in the promise about Christ, not by any works or ritual observances. Here he articulated the central Christian doctrine of salvation simply by faith, and he further showed how this would lead Christians to live their lives freely motivated by the promptings of the Spirit of God. And in the Letter to the Ephesian congregations, Paul showed how there can be but one Christian church. Although Christians come from various races and nationalities, they are one because they are part of the one "body of Christ." The Johannine writings likewise emphasize that, within the different communities, there is "one flock and one shepherd" (*John* 10:16).

Bringing the Gospel to the Hellenistic World   The other major development in the Christian sacred history of the earliest church was the translation and interpretation of the good news about Jesus for the peoples of the Hellenistic world. For the early Jewish Christians, the good news of Jesus could be told almost entirely in terms and concepts drawn from the Jewish scriptures, as Peter did in his first sermon on the day of Pentecost (*Acts* 2). Jesus was the fulfillment of God's promises through the Old Testament prophets; he was the messiah, the son of David, the suffering servant on whom God places sins, the sacrificial lamb of atonement; God chose him at the fullness of time, to establish the long-awaited kingdom of God through him. Jews who heard this message would understand it, even if they were not inclined to accept Jesus as the messiah. But the non-Jewish peoples of the Hellenistic world knew nothing of the Old Testament, of the expectation of the kingdom of God and the messiah. They looked at the world and human existence in a different way, in ideas shaped by Greek thinking, mystery religions, and a pervasive religious perspective known as **Gnosticism.** Thus, it was the delicate task of early Christian theologians to translate the good news about Jesus into ideas that these people could understand and believe, without losing what the good news was all about.

In a general way, the picture of the world in the Hellenistic religions was more vertical, without the Jewish sense of history moving horizontally toward a fulfillment in the new age of the kingdom of God. People pictured two realms, the divine realm of light above, and the material realm of darkness beneath, which was held by demonic forces. The human soul is a spark of light from above, whereas the body is a prison of material from which the soul has to be liberated. In the Hellenistic mystery religions, this salvation

took place by initiation into the worship of a personal divine redeemer through whom liberation could be experienced. In the Gnostic groups, it was felt that a divine redeemer from the world of light would impart secret knowledge to people, teaching them how their souls could be delivered from the prison of the world and their bodies.

Struggling to communicate the gospel of Christ to people with these kinds of ideas, Paul, the Johannine author, and other early theologians began to plumb the depths of the doctrine of **Christology,** that is, thinking about the nature of Christ. They argued that to call Jesus the messiah, the savior on whom God laid the sins of the world, was to say at the same time that God was somehow present in a special and powerful way in Jesus the messiah. It was to say that God "came down" and became the redeemer of the world in Jesus. It was to say, then, that Jesus was God. One way of putting it was this:

> [Christ Jesus], being in the form of God, did not think to grasp at equality with God but emptied himself, taking the form of a slave, being born in human likeness. And being found in human shape, he humbled himself, being obedient even to death—death on a cross. Therefore God exalted him highly and gave to him the name which is above all names, that at the name of Jesus every knee should bow—in heaven, on earth, and under the earth—and every tongue confess, "Jesus Christ is Lord," to the glory of God the Father.

(*Philippians* 2:5–11)

Again, the early Christians confessed that "He [Jesus] is the image of the invisible God. . . . All the fulness of God was pleased to dwell in him, through him reconciling everything to himself, making peace through the blood of his cross" (*Colossians* 1:15–20).

The early theologians rejected the Gnostic ideas about the material world and the body being an evil prison. Rather, they talked about the **incarnation** of God in Jesus Christ: God became flesh in the person of Jesus and thus was united with the flesh of all humanity (*John* 1:14). Further, they continued the Jewish belief in the resurrection of the body, rejecting the Greek idea that only the soul was immortal and would be delivered from the evil prison of the body.

In communicating the gospel to the Hellenistic world, the early Christian church came to incorporate in its story the ongoing encounter with God through the worship of the risen Christ, the Son of God who is present in a real way in his body, the church. The Christian story in the Hellenistic world also continued the Jewish perspective of history moving toward a consummation. Christ will come again at the end of this world, and then will be the resurrection and the judgment and the full establishing of the kingdom of this world as the kingdom of God. These teachings about the last things, called **eschatology,** play an important role in Christian theology.

In telling the story of Jesus and of his church, then, Christians are telling their own identity. For they identify with Christ, living as Christ's body present in the world.

FURTHER TRANSFORMATIONS OF THE CHRISTIAN WAY

At the close of the New Testament period, around the end of the first century C.E., the church had been established in many parts of the Roman world. But there were many challenges that it faced over the next several centuries, as Christians created a church that transcended the decline and fall of the Roman Empire. The medieval synthesis of culture produced Christendom, but that was shaken and torn apart in the Reformation and the Enlightenment. Much of the modern history of Christianity has been tied up with the rise of science and industrialization, introducing problems that the Christian churches are still trying to meet. Christian identity today has been shaped by all these historical transformations.

The Early Christian Church in the Roman World

Because Christians had been closely tied to Judaism, severing that relationship was a painful process. Further, leaving the security of being a Jewish sect that was permitted by the Roman authorities, the Christian church found itself an illicit religion in the Roman Empire, and at times its members suffered persecution and had to practice their religion secretly and underground. This "church of the catacombs" continued to grow, however, and the blood of the martyrs became the seed of the church.

The Challenge of Gnosticism   Continuing challenges to faith and doctrine came in the form of Hellenistic cults and philosophies. Gnosticism especially proved to be a per-

sistent influence in shaping beliefs of the Christians, providing as it did an answer to the question of evil and how one can be freed from it. The world of matter is evil and unreal, but humans are essentially spiritual, Gnosticism taught; salvation means escape from this worldly prison. These ideas led to new pictures of Jesus as the great Spirit descended from the world of light, spreading his secret teaching to liberate the souls of his followers from the prison of this material world.

A leading Christian thinker with Gnostic tendencies was Marcion (died ca. 160). He taught that love is the central element in Christianity, and that Christ's salvation is of the spirit, not the body. Since the Old Testament is based on law and justice, Marcion concluded that the God of the Old Testament was an evil creator who had made physical sex the means of reproduction. Marcion rejected the Old Testament completely, and he carefully edited Christian writings to exclude anything contrary to his Gnostic ideas. He rejected marriage, wine, and anything to do with the body. Only celibates could be baptized.

Many Christian thinkers entered the lists to defend Christian faith against Gnosticism and Marcionism. For example, Irenaeus (ca. 130–202) defended the authority of the Old Testament, arguing that God created all matter and form. Humans are created in the image of God, even though they have become bogged down in sin. Christ, eternal with the Father, truly became man, exhibiting what humans should be in growing to their full stature; the divine entered this life to show us how to recover the image of God.

Canon, Creed, Clergy   In order to resolve the questions raised by Gnostics and others, the early church needed to do several things: declare what its authentic scriptures were, formulate its beliefs clearly, and establish the continuity of a recognized leadership. The result was the canon (accepted sacred writings) of the New Testament, the **Apostles' Creed,** and the structure of clergy leadership.

Between the second and fourth centuries, Christian leaders came to agreement on which sacred writings should make up the Christian scriptures of the New Testament. Copies of various gospels and letters of the apostles had been circulating in the churches, but now an effort was made to determine which ones should be considered authoritative for all Christians. The major test was that they should have been authored by an apostle. Further, the

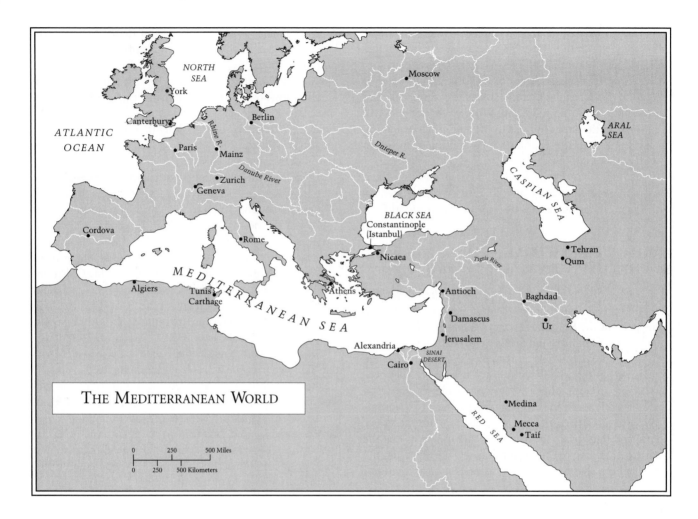

THE MEDITERRANEAN WORLD

content should correspond to the faith that was handed down by the apostles. By these tests, eventually the Gnostic and other questionable writings were excluded, and the New Testament was narrowed down to the generally accepted canon of twenty-seven writings.

The Apostles' Creed was the earliest confession of faith that widely circulated in the early church, having been composed around the year 150. It emphasized doctrines especially against Gnostic ideas, asserting the creation of the world by God, Christ as true man who suffered and died, the resurrection of the body, and the final judgment.

To combat the misguided teachings and maintain unity and order, the early church devised a structure for ecclesias-tical leadership. Paul had already adopted the practice of appointing bishops (overseers) to guide the congregations of Christians that he founded. Now the office of bishop became the church's bulwark of unity and defense against heresy. To assist the bishop in leading communities of Christians, presbyters (elders) and deacons were also ordained, the presbyter to preside over worship and the deacon to minister to the people's needs.

Philosophy and Theology   As more and more edu-cated people of the Roman world converted to the Christi-ian way, the fertile challenge of Greek philosophy became more pressing. Up to now, Christian thinkers had responded to challenges on an ad hoc basis, with letters, specific defenses (apologies), sermons, and manuals of ethics. But the serious confrontation with philosophical worldviews called for more comprehensive theological systems. The big question increasingly raised itself: How does Christian belief about the world stand up to the systematic understanding of the philosophers and scientists of the Graeco-Roman tradition?

Some Christian thinkers, trained in philosophy but now convinced of the truth of Christianity, answered this by arguing the truth of scripture and the apostolic tradition over against the uncertainties of human reason. Tertullian (ca. 145–220), for example, argued that God's revelation was found in the scriptures and apostolic testimony, not in philosophical speculation: "What has Christ to do with Plato, Jerusalem with Athens?" Still, Tertullian began to devise a theological system explaining the Triune God—the **Trinity**—as Father, Son, and Holy Spirit.

Others, like Justin Martyr (ca. 100–166) and Clement of Alexandria (150–215), saw Greek philosophy as an authentic expression of God's truth. Justin felt that the same Logos (Word, *John* 1:1) that had inspired the prophets of the Old Testament and became manifest in Christ had also inspired the Greek philosophers. He did hold, however, that the truth of philosophy is incomplete apart from its completion in Christ. Clement also held that all truth comes from the universal Logos, and thus philosophical speculation and prophetic revelation are compatible. Clement even suggested that theologians could look to the thinkers of ancient Persia, India, and other places to find truth that comes from the eternal Logos and that is fully expressed in the Christian scriptures and in Christ.

Emperor Constantine and Imperial Christianity Christians steadily increased in the Roman Empire. But as an illicit religion, they continued to suffer periodic persecutions. The last persecution was the most vicious—that under Emperor Diocletian (r. 284–305). But in 312, one of his generals, **Constantine,** was victorious over the other generals in gaining control of Rome, and a new day began. Perhaps seeing the trends, Constantine began to side with the Christians (although he himself was not baptized as a Christian until he was on his deathbed). In 313, the Edict of Milan granted toleration to Christianity, and Constantine did much to strengthen and unify the church. Although anti-Christian policies were briefly revived under Emperor

Julian (the Apostate, r. 361–363), by 380 Emperor Theodosius I made Christianity the *only* religion allowed in the Roman Empire.

Now the situation of the Christian church changed—it was established, an integral part of Roman culture, joined with the political structures of the Roman Empire. Its destiny was, for the time at least, intertwined with Rome. Christianity clearly had become a world religion.

With the growth of the church in the Roman Empire, church structures gradually became consolidated as bishops of important regions took on dominant leadership roles. From early times, the role of the bishop of Rome was especially respected because of the traditional links that Peter and Paul had with the church in Rome. By the fourth and fifth centuries, the bishops or "popes" of Rome were asserting primacy over the whole church. The primacy of the papacy—that is, the pope of Rome looked to as the leader of the whole church—was resisted in the Eastern regions of the church, for the bishop of Constantinople was considered an equal office. But, at least throughout the Western church, the institution of the papacy came to dominate church leadership for many centuries.

Counterculture: Monasticism   Judaism had placed little importance on asceticism, that is, withdrawal from the social and sensuous aspects of life. But from early on, groups of Christians devoted themselves to fasting, prayer, contemplation, and a life of poverty. Many followed Paul in considering virginity and celibacy to be superior to marriage, and martyrdom was seen as the supreme way to heaven.

As the Christian church moved into partnership with the political structure and culture of the Roman state, the monastic movement created a kind of counterculture of withdrawal. And, although **monasticism** began as a rigorous discipline practiced in isolation, later the monasteries became important socializing forces in the development of Christendom, as most church leaders underwent training and discipline in the monasteries.

Already in the third century there appeared the two basic types of monasticism. The eremitical (hermit) monk was an individual seeking salvation in isolation, and the cenobitic (communal) monks practiced their disciplines in small communities. In the fourth and fifth centuries, thousands of Christians withdrew from society and took to monasticism. Some went to extremes, doing things like living in caves or tombs, fasting frequently, not bathing, waking every three minutes to praise God, avoiding contact with the opposite sex, and generally outdoing each other in the extremes of physical deprivation. One well-known but extreme eremitic monk was Simeon Stylites (d. ca. 454), who sat for thirty-six years on top of a 60-foot pillar!

Two important leaders of monasticism were Basil of Caesarea (ca. 330–379) and Jerome (ca. 347–420). Basil created a monastic *Rule* that provided structure for the monks within the larger church order. He set forth an ideal of perfect service to God and communal obedience, emphasizing poverty, chastity, prayer, study, and labor. Basil's *Rule* formed the basis of monasticism in the eastern section of the Christian church. In the western part of the Roman Empire, Jerome combined his scholarly pursuits (such as translating the Bible into Latin) with the promotion of monasticism. Under his influence, even rich women of Rome joined monasteries or turned their homes into monasteries. One widow, Paula, traveled with Jerome to Syria and Palestine, founding monasteries and convents and a hospice for travelers.

Theological Controversies and Church Councils   As Christianity became a world religion, it spread through the Roman Empire and beyond it to the East—to Edessa, Armenia, Mesopotamia, Persia, Arabia, perhaps even to India and China. Growing and maturing in these different environments, with challenges from Gnosticism, philoso-phy, and a variety of eastern spiritual influences, some basic differences of belief and thought arose within the church.

Many of the major controversies concerned the doctrine of God, especially the Trinity and the person of Christ. These Trinitarian and Christological controversies took place in the fourth and fifth centuries, giving rise to a number of important ecumenical (worldwide) councils—gatherings of bishops from all over the church to debate and decide on orthodox doctrine. Through these debates and the resolutions decided by the councils, the catholic (universal) Christian faith was defined and the dissenting beliefs rejected as "heresies" (beliefs dividing the church).

The Arian controversy erupted in the eastern churches of the Roman Empire and caused a great rift. Arius, a priest from Egypt, put forth the view that the Son was created by the Father in time. This created Logos took the form of the earthly Jesus to bring saving knowledge. Thus, "there was when he was not," and only the Father is truly eternal God. This Arian view (**Arianism**) was widely accepted, for it was based on biblical statements, and it seemed to solve the problem of the Trinity appearing to be three Gods. Here appeared to be a simple, strong monotheism.

But Bishop Athanasius (ca. 296–373) and other Christian thinkers recognized a danger to the Christian faith in this popular Arian view. To worship Christ as a being created in time would be to worship a divine being other than the one God! Emperor Constantine, anxious to settle this

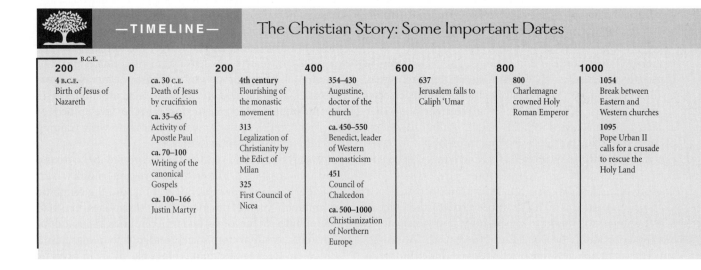

—TIMELINE—   The Christian Story: Some Important Dates

B.C.E. 200	0	200	400	600	800	1000
4 B.C.E. Birth of Jesus of Nazareth	ca. 30 C.E. Death of Jesus by crucifixion	4th century Flourishing of the monastic movement	354–430 Augustine, doctor of the church	637 Jerusalem falls to Caliph 'Umar	800 Charlemagne crowned Holy Roman Emperor	1054 Break between Eastern and Western churches
	ca. 35–65 Activity of Apostle Paul	313 Legalization of Christianity by the Edict of Milan	ca. 450–550 Benedict, leader of Western monasticism			1095 Pope Urban II calls for a crusade to rescue the Holy Land
	ca. 70–100 Writing of the canonical Gospels	325 First Council of Nicea	451 Council of Chalcedon			
	ca. 100–166 Justin Martyr		ca. 500–1000 Christianization of Northern Europe			

dispute and unify his realm, convened an ecumenical council at Nicea in Asia Minor in 325. The **Council of Nicea** solved the problem by deciding that the Son is "true God from true God, begotten, not made, one in being with the Father." The catholic position was that there is one God who nevertheless consists of three "persons"—Father, Son, and Holy Spirit. Some years later, the Council of Constantinople arrived at a final formulation for this Trinitarian view: the Trinity is an eternal unity, the Father eternally ingenerate, the Son eternally begotten of the Father, the Holy Spirit eternally proceeding from the Father.

While these councils settled the issue of the Son as fully divine, another controversy arose concerning the nature of Christ himself: Did he have a split personality? Did his divine nature replace his human nature? What part of him was divine and what part human? Nestorius of Syria held that Christ was two persons, one divine and the other human; but only the human person was born from Mary's womb. Another group called Monophysites (single nature) took an opposite view, insisting that Christ has only a single divine nature. Finally, the Council of Chalcedon in 451 formulated the orthodox position: The incarnated Christ has two natures, divine and human, united in a single person. He is

one and the same Christ, Son, Lord, Only-begotten, recognized in two natures, without confusion, without change, without division, without separation; the distinction of natures being in no way annulled by the union, but rather the characteristics of each nature being preserved and coming together to form one person and subsistence.[1]

Augustine, Bishop of Hippo   Emperor Constantine moved his capital eastward to Constantinople, and the Greek-speaking Christians of the East began drifting away from the West. The northern barbarians were closing in on Rome. The church, now identified with the Roman Empire, was wracked with new controversies in place of those that had been settled. For example, Manicheism, a mixture of Zoroastrianism, Christianity, and Buddhism, presented a strong rival to Christianity. It taught a dualism of light and darkness and advocated a severe asceticism to liberate the divine particles of light. Within the Christian church, Pelagius was teaching that every person is free, as Adam was, to sin or not to sin; thus there was not a universal need for Christ's work of redemption.

In these intercrossings of history and controversy, **Augustine** (354–430) stood forth as one of the greatest theologians of the early church. In his *Confessions* (an autobiographical masterpiece of Latin literature), Augustine says the soul is restless until it finds rest in God. He did much searching before he found his resting point. He lived with a mistress for fifteen years, had a son, and searched for the truth in Manicheism for many years. He reports his own

1200	1400–			1600	1800–	
13th century Rise of the Franciscan and Dominican orders; founding of many universities	**15th and 16th centuries** Renaissance in Italy; moves to Northern Europe	**1534** Henry VIII as head of the Anglican church	**1549** Jesuit priest Francis Xavier arrives in Japan	**1648** Peace of Augsburg ends wars of religion	**1859** Darwin's *The Origin of Species*	**1962–1965** Second Vatican Council
1225–1274 Thomas Aquinas, theologian	**1515–1582** Teresa of Avila, mystic	**1536** John Calvin's *Institutes of the Christian Religion*	**1582** Matteo Ricci arrives in China	**1703–1791** John Wesley, leader of the Methodist revival movement	**1909** American Fundamentalist movement	**2nd half of Twentieth century:** Flourishing of ecumenical movements; development of liberation theology, feminist theology
ca. 1260–1327 Meister Eckhart, leader of the mystical movement	**1517** Posting of 95 Theses by Martin Luther	**1545–1563** Council of Trent		**1781** Immanuel Kant's *Critique of Pure Reason*	**1919** Karl Barth's *Epistle to the Romans*	
					1948 Founding of the World Council of Churches	

prayer during this time: "Give me chastity and continence, but not yet." Then he studied Neo-Platonism, heard the preaching of Ambrose, bishop of Milan, and found his way back to the Christian faith (the religion of his mother). While he still was struggling with his attachments to his sensual way of life, he heard a child's voice from over a garden wall crying, "Tolle lege, tolle lege" (Take up and read, take up and read). He opened at random a copy of Paul's *Letter to the Romans* and read: "Let us walk becomingly, as in daytime, not in rioting and drunkenness, not in lust and wantonness, not in strife and rivalry. Rather, arm yourself with the Lord Jesus Christ, and give no thought to the flesh for its desires" (*Romans* 13:13–14). Augustine felt that this was an oracle from God; his doubts were resolved, and he soon was baptized. He practiced the monastic life, became a priest, and finally was made bishop of Hippo in north Africa.

Arguing against Pelagius, Augustine insisted that the fall into sin caused a basic change in human nature. Sin lodges in the will, consisting of the attempt to usurp the place of God. We are not able not to sin, and hence we cannot help toward our salvation but must depend entirely on God's grace in Christ.

Augustine, like others, was deeply affected by the sack of Rome by Alaric and the pagan Goths in 410—eternal Rome had fallen! To show that this was not the fault of Christianity, Augustine wrote his monumental *City of God,* finishing it just four years before his death, when his city of Hippo was under siege by the Vandals. Augustine argued that there are two cities, the earthly city and the heavenly city. Those who belong to the city of God are the elect, although they are compelled to live in the earthly city. Because humans have fallen, God has provided governmental institutions to regulate sinful society. The two cities intermingle throughout history—but in the church the city of God has begun its fulfillment. Since the earthly city does give relative peace and order, Augustine argued Christians should participate and seek at least to mitigate violence and injustice in the world.

Medieval Christianity: The Age of Faith

With the invasions of the barbarians of northern Europe and the decline of the Roman Empire, the Christian church faced an uncertain future. Having finally Christianized the Roman Empire and become established as its state religion, Christians now faced hordes of non-Christian invaders and the threat of being swept away with the Roman Empire. The challenge was met; the invaders were Christianized and carried the new religion to new regions north and east. The period of Christendom was ushered in, to last for the next thousand years until the Renaissance.

Christendom   Germanic tribes repeatedly invaded the western part of the Roman Empire. But as the nature of the empire changed under their influence, they gradually adopted the culture and religion of the people they were conquering. A particularly significant event took place near the Rhine River in 496. Clovis, king of the Franks, was a worshiper of tribal gods; but, under the influence of his Christian wife, Clovis appealed to Christ in a battle against another Germanic tribe. Clovis won the battle, and afterward he and many of the Franks were baptized. Clovis remained a cruel tribal chieftain, and the Christianization of the morals and societal values of the Germanic peoples was a long process. But the result was a new construction: Christendom, arising from the fusion of the religion of the Roman Empire with the culture of the northern barbarians.

As the power of the Roman political state declined, the church in the West especially cultivated the monastic life. Benedict (ca. 480–550) became the fountainhead of Western monasticism by establishing a Rule at Monte Cassino, which became the pattern followed widely. Promoting a moderate asceticism, the Rule called for the communal life to revolve around the Divine Office of prayer at fixed times throughout the day. Prayer was to be balanced by work and study, and these monasteries, following Benedict's Rule, became major centers of social work, evangelism, and scholarship during the Middle Ages.

Some of the monastic orders were especially devoted to missionary work among the barbarians. The old Celtic Christian church in Britain fell into disarray with the incursion of the Anglo-Saxons. But the Benedictine monk Augustine of Canterbury (d. 604) was sent as missionary to these pagan invaders and initiated a new era of Christian growth in England. Augustine followed a principle of accommodation as he evangelized the Anglo-Saxons: Shrines and holy days dedicated to the pagan gods could be taken over and Christianized, thus making the conversion of the pagans less traumatic and more enriching for Christianity.

Before long, the monasteries of England were sending missionaries to Germany.

As the Germanic peoples were taken into the Christian fold, they often in turn became strong missionaries to other Germanic tribes. Frequently such "evangelizing" turned more to force than to persuasion, as in the Christian conquest of the north German Saxons or the exploits of King Olaf in Christianizing Norway. The great Charlemagne (ca. 742–814) led the way in converting the north German Saxons, as he established an empire stretching from northern Spain to Bavaria. Pope Leo III crowned him Holy Roman Emperor on Christmas Day, 800. The result was the creation of a more stable, unified Christendom including also the northern Germanic tribes.

In the East, two brothers, Cyril (826–869) and Methodius (ca. 815–885), were sent out as missionaries to the Slavs of Moravia. The conversion of Prince Vladimir of Kiev in the tenth century led to the "baptism of Russia," and the Eastern **Orthodox church** flourished there. After the fall of Constantinople to the Turkish Muslims, Moscow became the center of Eastern Orthodoxy and was considered the "Third Rome" of Christianity.

When the pope crowned Charlemagne as Holy Roman Emperor, the idea was born of a unified Christendom with even the secular rulers under the authority of the pope. The church was a part of Europe's feudal structure, with church officials serving as vassals of great nobles. Often the rulers and the popes came into conflict, especially when the German emperors interfered in church affairs. After a confrontation, Pope Gregory VII (r. 1073–1085) excommunicated Emperor Henry IV. Relenting, Henry stood barefoot in the snow for three days outside the castle of Canossa, in submission to the authority of the pope. But three years later, balking at a second excommunication, Henry marched on Rome and deposed Gregory. Thereafter, a compromise of sorts was reached between the cross and the crown, as spelled out in the Concordat of Worms (1122). Secular rulers were to recognize the local bishops' loyalty to the pope, and the pope was supposed to appoint bishops acceptable to the emperor.

Eastern Orthodoxy: Split with the West   During the period of the early church councils, much of the theological leadership of the church had been in the eastern Greek-speaking regions. The theology and liturgy of the Eastern church continued to cultivate accents different from the Western Latin churches. The Western church, following Augustine, emphasized the utter sinfulness of human nature and Jesus' death as the key to God's redeeming activity. But the tendency in the East was to focus on the restoration of God's image in humans through the incarnation of Christ. Christ united the Godhead to human nature; by sharing in Christ's perfect humanity, humans could be raised up to God. The Eastern church kept a "high" Christology, in which the divine nature of Christ was the focus, for this is what, in union with humankind, makes it possible for humans to rise to God.

Eastern Christianity was also developing the sacred **liturgy** as a solemn celebration recapitulating the whole drama of salvation, unifying worshipers on earth and in heaven. The solemn ritual, beautiful chanting, rich vestments, and colorful icons combined to provide a powerful expression of the Christian faith in ritual. The liturgy spread over into mystical practices in the monasteries, where cultivation of interior contemplation focused on illumination of the soul with the divine Light.

The invasions of the barbarians effectively cut the Eastern church off from the Western, and gradually they lost touch with each other. Often Rome and Constantinople found themselves in political conflict, and ecclesiastical rivalry also became more bitter, as the Roman popes pressed their claims to papal authority. The Eastern bishops were willing to recognize the Roman bishop as *primus unter pares* (first among equals) because of the tradition of Paul and Peter at Rome; but they refused to accept the universal jurisdiction claimed by the Roman popes.

A symbolic crowning touch to the East–West split was the little Latin word *filioque* (and the son). Already in the sixth century, some Western churches began adding to the *Nicene Creed* the phrase that the Holy Spirit proceeds from the Father "and the Son." Eastern theologians feared that this clause would impair the unity of the Trinity, for they saw the Father as the foundational source of the Trinity, with the Son eternally begotten of Him and the Spirit eternally proceeding from Him. The squabble was symptomatic of deeper rifts, and neither side would give in. An Eastern council condemned the Roman pope for heresy because of the *filioque* clause. Finally in 1054, the pope in turn excommunicated the patriarch of Constantinople, putting the finishing touch on a schism that had been developing over several centuries.

Islamic Pressure and the Crusades   Medieval Christendom gradually absorbed and Christianized such foreign invaders as the Vikings from Scandinavia and the Magyars (the later Hungarians) from Asia. But the eruption of Islam into the Christian world was a different story. Five years after the Prophet Muhammad's death, Jerusalem fell (637) to 'Umar, the second caliph. The new religious wave devastated Christian Palestine, Syria, Egypt, and North Africa, as Muslim armies overthrew the Byzantine overlords and the peasant population happily accepted the new religion of equality and justice. The Muslim tide advanced into Spain and even across the Pyrenees into France, stopped finally by Charles Martel at Poitiers (732). Later, across Asia Minor (Turkey) the Muslims went, and finally in 1453 Constantinople fell to the Muslim Turks, putting an end to the Byzantine Empire.

Since the Muslims recognized Christians and Jews as monotheists, "people of the Book," they were not forced to become Muslim, although many did. Christian communities continued to live and thrive in Muslim lands, paying a special tribute tax to the rulers in return for security and autonomy. Christian pilgrims were still permitted to visit the holy places of Jerusalem. But when the more intolerant Seljuk Turks gained control of Jerusalem in the latter part of the eleventh century, Europeans feared they would suppress pilgrimage and destroy the Christian shrines. The Byzantine emperor was also under pressure from the Turks, and in 1095 he appealed to Pope Urban II for assistance.

Urban II preached a remarkable sermon at the Council of Clermont in France (1095). He described the desecration of Jerusalem, portrayed Christ himself as leading any army that went to the rescue, and promised cancellation of debts, exemption from taxes, possession of new lands, and a reward of eternal life to any who joined the holy war against the Muslims. Crying "Deus vult!" (God wills it!), knights from Germany, France, and Italy set out for the Holy Land. Many claimed new land for themselves and settled along the way, but in 1099 a small band reached Jerusalem. On Good Friday they breached the walls and instigated a great massacre, unmoved by the tears of women and children.

Their victims included Christians who happened to look like their Muslim neighbors.

Despite the "success" of the first Christian crusade, the Muslims continued to fight back, and a series of **crusades** followed. The second crusade was promoted especially by the saintly, peace-loving man of God, Bernard of Clairvaux—but it failed miserably because of quarrels among the leaders. The third crusade also failed, and the fourth crusade (1201–1204) went out of control and attacked Christian Constantinople. There were other crusades, like the Children's Crusade of 1212 led by a shepherd boy, whose most tangible result was a host of slave boys for Mediterranean ship captains. The spiritual energy that had promoted this crusading effort cooled, and what was left was desire for booty and control of trade routes. Three new orders of knighthood to protect the Holy Land emerged: the Hospitalers, the Templars, and the Order of Teutonic Knights. But the Holy Land was not won, Islam was not driven back, and the church was not purified.

Reformers, Scholastics, and Mystics   Even before the crusades there was a growing desire for reform of the church and especially its monasteries and clerics, many of whom had become infected with worldly concerns. Two new monastic orders in particular brought new life to the church in the Middle Ages. Dominic (1170–1221) realized that to win the masses it was necessary to live simply and preach the Word clearly. In 1214 he founded the Dominican Order, dedicated exclusively to preaching and scholarship. They lived by begging and were called the Black Friars because of their simple black habit. One rule was that no one could preach without three years of theological training. The Dominicans established themselves in the fast-growing universities and produced one of the greatest Christian thinkers of the times, Thomas Aquinas, and also the great mystic Meister Eckhart.

Francis of Assisi (1182–1226) revolted against his own youthful indulgence in riches and sensuality to devote his life to the ideal of poverty. He begged for his livelihood, working only to serve, storing nothing and owning nothing. He wandered about preaching and tending lepers, and even made a trip to Egypt to preach to the Muslims. His followers were organized into the Franciscan Order.

The pressure for learning was mounting. Between 1200 and 1250, many new universities were started in Europe, with professors and students coming from all over western Europe, communicating in the Latin of the day. Scholars began to rediscover Greek philosophical thought, especially through the commentaries of Muslim scholars like Avicenna and Averoes. In the thirteenth century, Christian scholasticism thrived especially through the work of Thomas Aquinas (1225/7–1274).

Aquinas, who taught at the universities of Paris and Naples, used a synthesis of Plato and Aristotle to create a systematized theology, which has remained widely influential down to the twentieth century. He held that philosophy examines the natural order by means of reason, whereas theology examines the supernatural by means of revelation. Philosophy cannot contradict theology because both are forms of truth. Theology perfects philosophy, taking it to realms it cannot penetrate on its own. Aquinas felt that humans can discover the existence of God through observation and reflection. Philosophy is available to all, even Jews and Muslims, and so it provides a universal basis for reflection and discussion. His magnum opus, written during the last two years of his life, is the *Summa Theologica* (left incomplete), a massive, systematized statement of the Christian faith.

An important movement, which was at one and the same time an expression of medieval spirituality and an alternative to the intermediary function of the church, was mysticism. The mystics sought direct contact with God rather than relying only on ecclesiastical machinery, sacraments, and satisfactions.

A leading mystic in Germany was Meister Eckhart (ca. 1260–1327), who chose to talk of God in essentially negative terms. Thinking in Neo-Platonic concepts, he felt God to be beyond being and nonbeing but also present as the divine spark in the world and in the soul. The mystical goal is complete union of the divine spark in us with God, which is the loss of individuality and immersion in God's reality. It is through negating the empirical self, leading a life of poverty and stillness and contemplation, that creatureliness can be transcended in union with God.

Eckhart's disciple Johann Tauler (ca. 1300–1361) emphasized the life of sacrifice and charity that the mystical experience of God promotes. When the plague of the Black Death struck (1348), Tauler expended himself ministering to the sick and dying. Eckhart and Tauler inspired thousands of clergy and laypeople to practice this kind of simple mysticism, dedicated to the inner life of contemplation and

piety. Another mystically inclined movement that emphasized practical love and included both clergy and laity was the Brethren of the Common Life. They lived in houses with a rule like monks but did not take permanent vows. Practicing the "new devotion" of a simple, undogmatic faith, they established schools and gave free instruction. One of them, Thomas a Kempis (ca. 1380–1471), produced Christianity's most widely used devotional book, *The Imitation of Christ*.

Thus, mysticism moved beyond ecclesiastical structures and caught the imagination of common people who desired intense religious experience within their ordinary vocations. It appealed also to women, such as Catherine of Siena (1347–1380), who spoke of her mystic experience as a "spiritual marriage with God" and devoted herself to helping victims of the Black Death. Two centuries later another woman mystic, Teresa of Avila (1515–1582), became very influential. St. Teresa balanced her mystical experiences with periods of intense activity in reforming her own monastic order, the Carmelites, calling it back to its original ideal of poverty. Struggling against antagonism and harassment from opponents, St. Teresa was guided by her visions and inner knowing, producing very influential spiritual writings describing her mystical marriage to Christ. In her best known writing, *The Interior Castle,* she uses the image of a transparent crystal castle complete with seven mansions to describe the seven levels of prayer and the experience of the soul. The innermost mansion is Jesus Christ, and the closer one moves to this inner mansion the stronger the light of union with Christ becomes.

Renaissance and Reformation

The need for continual reformation and renewal is felt in most world religions. As an established part of culture and society, religion can easily become fossilized or used for nonspiritual ends. From time to time movements of renewal arise, calling the religion back to the original experience and purpose.

Renewal and Renaissance   In the later Middle Ages, as the feudal structure of society was weakening and the grand system of the medieval church was starting to unravel, new voices for reform began to be heard, leading to the Protestant Reformation and drastic changes in church

An engraving depicting Martin Luther, leader of the Reformation.

as the Renaissance, which contained the seeds of many aspects of modernity: individualism, secularism, rationalism, nationalism, urbanization, and industrialization. Interest in the culture of ancient Greece and Rome increased, and Christian scholars learned the biblical languages. The spread of printing presses made for the rapid dissemination of the new learning. The Renaissance scholars dedicated themselves to a humanistic philosophy not necessarily centered on religious concerns, sometimes even questioning the basis of religious beliefs and practices. Christian humanists, like Johannes Reuchlin (1455–1522) and Desiderius Erasmus (ca. 1466–1536), attempted to reconcile the new learning with traditional Christian faith. But the popes of the Renaissance were not up to the challenge of the times, giving themselves to corruption or consolidating their political power.

Martin Luther and the Reformation   The spark that ignited the **Reformation** was an ironic piece of the Renaissance. In the wave of enthusiasm for the new classicism in architecture, Pope Julius II developed some ambitious plans for a new and magnificent St. Peter's Basilica in Rome and laid the first stone in 1506. The project dragged on at enormous cost, and Pope Leo X (1475–1521) began to raise money through the traditional practice of selling indulgences. The church had long claimed the right to grant indulgences—that is, remission of punishment in purgatory due for sins—drawing on the great store of merit gained by Christ and the saints. Although it was the question of indulgences that first sparked Luther's protest, actually the whole medieval synthesis of Christendom was being called into question.

Martin Luther (1483–1546), of peasant stock, went to the University of Erfurt to get a law degree. A crisis in his life led him to join the Augustinian Order and study theology, after which he was assigned to teach at the new university of Wittenberg in Saxony. In 1510, his order sent him to Rome, but his experience of the ignorance and corruption of the Holy City left him with doubt and despair. He wrestled with his own sense of unworthiness and inability to find relief through the monastic practices. But a momentous experience changed his life: his so-called tower experience. Preparing for lectures on the *Psalms,* he was bothered by the references to God's righteousness. Turning to *Romans* 3:21–24, he read:

and society. An English scholar, John Wycliffe (ca. 1329–1384), promoted translating the Bible into English and became a critic of many aspects of the medieval church, including the papacy. The availability of the Bible in the vernacular proved to be a revolutionary force. In Czechoslovakia, John Hus, rector of the University of Prague (ca. 1373–1415), led a religious rebellion, appealing to scripture to attack abuses of the church that were out of line with the injunctions of the New Testament—and was burned at the stake in Constance as a heretic. The influence of Wycliffe, Hus, and other reformers reverberated across Europe, setting the stage for more widespread reformation and transformation of society.

Some of these reforming movements were influenced by the larger movement of cultural and social change known

Now God's righteousness is revealed apart from the law, testified to by the Law and the Prophets, God's righteousness which is through faith in Jesus Christ unto all who believe. For there is no difference; all have sinned and fall short of the glory of God, being justified as a gift by his grace through the redemption that is in Christ Jesus.

Raging at God over the impossibility of living up to the righteousness of God, Luther suddenly saw a totally different meaning: The righteousness of God is a *forgiving* righteousness, by which God makes us righteous through Christ. This theology of "justification through faith by grace" henceforth became the heart of Luther's theology, leading him ultimately to reject all ideas of justification through one's own monastic practices or through the works of the church: penance, the **sacraments,** absolution, and the like.

Confronted by the sale of indulgences—which many German priests and rulers found objectionable—by the pope's legate, John Tetzel, Luther was provoked into action. Following the custom of academic disputation, he composed ninety-five theses for discussion, setting forth a variety of arguments against the practice of indulgences. His protest hit especially at the papal claim to control the treasure of merits generated by the saints out of which credits could be drawn to cover sinners' debts. But the protest was really much broader, calling into question the whole structure of papal authority and the intermediary practice of the church. The ninety-five theses circulated rapidly, thanks to the newly invented printing press and the general discontent in Germany with papal rule.

Before long the pope condemned Luther for heresy, and Luther responded with additional protests and writings in which he rejected papal supremacy and the infallibility of the church councils. The pope finally excommunicated Luther. But in the rising tide of German nationalism, the Elector of Saxony took Luther under his protection, even when Emperor Charles V put Luther under the ban of the empire in 1521.

Luther's doctrine of justification by faith through God's grace meant that humans can do nothing to merit salvation—thus undercutting the ecclesiastical penitential system. It also called into question the monastic ideal—and thousands of men and women in Germany left the monasteries for secular life. Luther himself married a former nun,

Katherine von Bora, and established the model of married clergy. A second important teaching, that scripture is the sole authority, led Luther to translate the Bible into German and, with the help of the printing press, make it available to all people (in the process creating a standard for the German literary language). This principle undercut the authority of the pope and the bishops to decide on matters of faith. His third important principle, the priesthood of all believers, put laypeople on a par with monks and priests and elevated the worth of secular vocations for Christians.

The Reformation Spreads Many others joined Luther in the protest (becoming known as Protestants), and the result was a drastic restructuring of the church throughout Christendom. Another important reformer was John Calvin (1509–1564), who provided a systematic presentation of Protestant thought in his landmark *Institutes of the Christian Religion.* Calvin started from the premise of the absolute sovereignty and glory of God, stressing also its corollary, the complete pervasiveness of sin in human nature. Salvation is by grace alone, although it is limited to those whom God has elected for salvation. Calvin carried the emphasis on God's sovereignty into the order of society, establishing a theocracy at Geneva in which the order of God governed all aspects of human society. Strict regulations were enforced: People could be punished for missing church or for adultery. Some holding unorthodox views, such as Michael Servetus, were burned at the stake for heresy. The Calvinist teachings spread to France, Germany, the Netherlands, England, and Scotland, where it became known as Presbyterianism. From these places, Calvinism also spread to America and became an important force in American **Protestantism.**

A more radical form of reformation found a representative in the fiery Ulrich Zwingli (1484–1531) of Zurich in Switzerland. He abolished the mass completely and removed pictures and images from the churches. He later died in battle leading a Protestant army in a civil war against the Catholics. After his death, some carried the movement to a still more radical phase, promoting a church based strictly on the New Testament and specifically denying the validity of infant baptism (hence their name, Anabaptists). Since they insisted that every Christian should believe and be baptized for him- or herself, they posed a threat to the union of church and state, which still existed even in Lutheran and Calvinist regions. So they were fiercely persecuted and nearly all the early leaders were put to death—an estimated fifty thousand martyrs by 1535. With their radical emphasis on individual faith, they were the forerunners of Baptists and Congregationalists in England who wanted to separate church and state functions. A portion of the Anabaptists were committed to pacifism, following teachings of Jesus. From these have derived the Mennonites, the Hutterites, and the Society of Friends, all deeply committed to peace and works of service.

In England, the ideas of the Reformation fanned the dissatisfaction with Rome that already existed. Henry VIII (r. 1509–1547) broke with Rome over the pope's refusal to annul his marriage, and in 1534 he declared himself supreme head of the Anglican church. He dissolved the monasteries, seized church property, and executed those who refused to recognize him as head of the church. Soon a new liturgical order, *The Book of Common Prayer,* was produced. There were also dissenters who wanted to completely purify the Anglican church from all rituals left over from the Catholic church. These Puritans, as they were called, followed Calvinistic teachings; the community was ruled by the elect saints and a strict moral code was enforced. Puritans achieved political power during the Cromwellian period, but with the Restoration and the reestablishing of the *Book of Common Prayer,* the Puritans joined the Baptists, Quakers, and other nonconformists outside the Church of England.

The Reformation movement also reached to the Roman Catholic church, with reforming popes who corrected abuses and corruptions in the Roman church. Scandals such as the sale of indulgences were checked, and great care was taken to appoint men of high caliber to posts of bishops and abbots. The impact of the Protestant Reformation was so great and raised so many questions about traditional doctrines and practices that a general church council was needed to clarify Catholic teaching and discipline. The **Council of Trent** met in three sessions between 1545 and 1563, carefully spelling out the Catholic teaching on a great number of questions. Although there were hopes of reconciliation with Protestant reformers, the Council basically held firm on all the traditional teachings regarding the authority of the popes, the celebration of the mass in Latin, reverence for the Virgin Mary and the saints, celibacy for the priests, and other such contested doctrines and practices. The pope was empowered to draw up an Index of Forbidden Books (to stop the spread of Protestant ideas). Positions on both sides of the Reformation were now solidified and all hope of reconciliation was gone.

The Catholic Reformation brought about a great renewal of faith and piety among the Catholic Christians. New religious societies were founded, among them the influential Society of Jesus (the Jesuits). Ignatius Loyola (ca. 1491–1556), a former Spanish military officer, founded the Jesuits for the purpose of propagating the Catholic faith, both in far-flung mission fields and at home in resistance to Protestantism. It was first of all through the Jesuits, for example, that the Christian faith was planted in East Asia. Among them, Francis Xavier (1506–1552) first brought Christianity to Japan in 1549, and Matteo Ricci (1552–1610) had a remarkable career as a missionary in China. Other Catholic orders also sent out missionaries and planted the Catholic church firmly in India, the Philippines, and Central and South America. What the Catholic church lost in Europe was gained in the mission fields.

State Churches and Denominations   With the Reformation, medieval Christendom came apart at the seams. Conflict erupted into open religious warfare. The Peace of Augsburg in 1555 brought temporary peace with an influential principle: *cuius regio, cuius religio*—that is, the religion of the ruler became the religion of the realm. After more religious wars, the Peace of Westphalia (1648) drew the religious map of Europe, setting up the state churches of Catholicism, Lutheranism, and Calvinism, which have remained substantially the same ever since.

In the Eastern churches, the Reformation changes did not have as much immediate effect as in the West. The Greek Orthodox church was still struggling to hold back the Muslim-Turkish expansion. A reformation did take place in the Russian church under the great Patriarch Nikon (1605–1681), who worked to develop an educated clergy and to simplify the elaborate liturgy. These reforms, however, led to state interference in church affairs, and later Peter the Great (1676–1725) had the state take over the administration of the church. A further repercussion of the reform was a faction of "Old Believers" who refused to accept the reforms and split off from the main church.

In the immigrations to the New World, all these state and dissenting churches were represented, so that a central characteristic of American Christianity is its multiplicity of **denominations.** In the American development, groups from the different state churches of Europe have sometimes united, sometimes further subdivided, to add to the complexity of the denominational structure. Further, the American experience has created new denominations more on the fringes, such as the Church of the Latter Day Saints (Mormons), the Jehovah's Witnesses, the Seventh-Day Adventists, and the Christian Scientists.

An important development in the American Christian experiment is the practice of separation of church and state. The Pilgrims who came to America were from the dissenting Congregationalists of England, bringing the idea of separating church and state functions, both still under divine law. Eventually, a separation of state and religion was written into the Constitution and has been a powerful influence in the development of American Christianity and of American law and politics.

Nuns carry palm branches and recite prayers in this Palm Sunday procession on the Mount of Olives. They are marking the beginning of Holy Week, commemorating the passion, death, and resurrection of Jesus.

Christians in the Modern Period

Responses to the Scientific Revolution and the Enlightenment   Christendom, disrupted by the various Reformation movements, now was confronted with the scientific revolution and the Enlightenment. The discoveries of Galileo and Copernicus, scientists working in the heartland of Christianity, shook the traditional Christian views of God and the world. Questions were raised about the authority of the church and its tradition, humans no longer seemed at the center of things, and skepticism began to spread about miracles and supernatural events.

The Enlightenment brought in a new emphasis on reason and philosophy. Attempts to develop a rational religion independent of revelation resulted in Deism, a philosophy that held that religion could be based on certain innate rational principles, such as the existence of a God and the certainty of reward or punishment for ethical or unethical deeds. The philosopher Immanuel Kant (1724–1804) proved, by the use of reason, that the existence of God cannot be proved by reason; he did hold, however, that religion belongs in the realm of morality, not reason.

Reacting against the sterile rationalism that was developing even in the Reformation churches, a revival of **pietism** began among the Bohemians and Moravians. Influenced by them, John Wesley (1703–1791) began preaching a revival of religious experience in England, emphasizing the need for an inner experience of Christ and a feeling of certainty of salvation. His movement, called Methodism, appealed widely to peoples recently moved to the cities in the Industrial Revolution. In great open-air meetings, Wesley eloquently preached about the dominion of sin and the warmth of God's love. Once a person was born again through the experience of salvation, she was assured she would never fall away and be damned. The Methodist movement spread rapidly, bringing a whole new repertoire of pietistic hymns and emotional experience across England and over to America.

Biblical Scholarship, Liberal Theology, and Fundamentalism   One fruit of the new scientific, enlightened view of the world was scientific biblical scholarship, giving rise to a dramatic intellectual crisis in Christianity. The Bible had always simply been accepted as the inspired Word of God, providing the source of God's direct revelation. But inevitably, the methods of critical historical research were turned to the biblical literature, and the results threw up questions about many cherished beliefs: the literal truth of miracle accounts, the veracity of historical descriptions in the Bible, the Mosaic authorship of the Pentateuch, and even the reliability of the portrait of Jesus in the New Testament. Biblical scholars were investigating the holy writings just as they investigated other books, showing that the Bible contains legends, errors of fact, and later events read back into earlier periods.

Adding to the threat was another fruit of the scientific approach to human history: Charles Darwin's *Origin of Species* (1859). The new evolutionary theory of the development of the species seemed to reject the whole biblical account of creation and, moreover, suggest that humans were simply highly evolved beasts.

The force of this new scholarship and scientific perspective was powerful, and many Christian thinkers tried to deal with it positively. The Catholic Modernist movement attempted to reconcile biblical critical scholarship with traditional Catholic teaching. And Protestant thinkers constructed a liberal theology that advocated a humanitarian ethic built on progress and social concern, at the same time reviving a piety that centered on Jesus as the ideal human life.

But other Christians reacted strongly against the perceived threat, finding these products of science to be in deep conflict with their traditional faith. They insisted on holding firmly to their fundamental tenets. They interpreted the Bible literally, including all its supernatural elements. Christians of this persuasion were found in all denominations. In an encyclical in 1907, Pope Pius X ruled against those who applied the new methods of research to the scriptures or theology, and among Protestants the **Fundamentalist** movement was dedicated to a literal interpretation of the Bible. The large and sometimes bitter gap between liberal Christians and Fundamentalists has been an important factor in modern Christian history and is still very real today, particularly in American Christianity.

Modern Theologies: Neo-Orthodoxy, Correlation, Aggiornamento   In the present century, numerous challenges have confronted the Christian churches, focusing the direction of Christian thinking and action today. The rapid increase of industrialization, two catastrophic world wars, worldwide instant communication, the nuclear age, the growing disparity of rich and poor nations, liberation movements—such developments have set much of the church's agenda in modern times.

Liberal ideas of progress and humaneness were shattered by World War I, and Christian thinkers responded with **neo-orthodox** theologies centering on human sinful failure and the radical message of salvation, which comes from the transcendent God. Karl Barth (1886–1968), a Swiss Calvinistic theologian, used the methods of biblical scholarship to focus on the essential biblical message, which brings the self-revelation of God. Human reason is incapable of reaching out to God, but God through biblical self-revelation does the work of salvation for humans. All religions, including Christianity as a human institution, are man-made and stand under God's judgment. Only God's revelation in Christ brings renewal and salvation, Barth taught.

Paul Tillich (1886–1965), a German Protestant theologian, although agreeing with some of the concerns of Barth, taught that theology must practice a method of correlation: The modern world frames questions, and the theologian uses the resources of the Christian tradition to construct an "answering theology." Modern science, philosophy, art, and even the religions of the world become resources for Christian theology in this method of correlation.

Roman Catholic theologians like Karl Rahner likewise have constructed methods of relating Christian faith to the intellectual and social trends of the modern world. Pope John XXIII, sensing the moment of renewal, called the Second Vatican Council (1962–1965) to carry through a visionary program of *aggiornamento*—bringing Catholic tradition and practice up to date while retaining their vitality and commitment. Liturgical reforms brought the use of the vernacular into worship in place of Latin. The Council expressed concern and hope for peace in the world, asked for cooperation with other Christians, and spelled out a theology of respect for other religions.

Missions, Social Renewal, and the Ecumenical Movement   Although the Roman Catholic church, through its religious orders, was engaging in widespread missionary activity as early as the sixteenth century, the nineteenth and twentieth centuries saw a surge of missionary activity by Protestant denominations as well. Missionaries went out to India, China, Africa, and throughout the world in a great march onward of Christian soldiers. Mission societies were formed in Europe and America to support foreign missionaries. It is true that some of this earlier missionary activity carried a flavor of Western superiority and sometimes accompanied political and economical exploitation. But

Western Christians have learned from non-Western Christians, and today the mission outreach of the Christian churches is generally associated with service, partnership, and respect.

Christian awareness of oppression and poverty in the societies of the world today has grown in modern times. Today many Christians work for liberation: liberation of people from the tyranny of racism, liberation of women from roles of subjugation, liberation of oppressed and poverty-stricken peoples in countries throughout the world. Social concern is high on the agenda of many of today's Christian churches. Other Christian groups, of course, resist what they see as too much involvement of the church in worldly affairs.

Experiences in the missionary movement and in social concerns have led many Christians of today to promote Christian unity. The fragmentation of the church that occurred over the past several centuries is finally being reversed as Christians from many denominations work together in closer harmony. Growing out of this **ecumenical** (worldwide) **movement** was the World Council of Churches, founded in 1948 at Amsterdam, representing a degree of cooperation between most of the Protestant churches. And the Second Vatican Council of the Roman Catholic church also set up a Secretariat for the Promotion of Christian Unity.

As Christians work together more closely throughout the world, new attitudes have begun to prevail concerning the links that hold all humankind together. The peace movement, transcending national boundaries, is promoted by many Christians in the East and West. Christians work together with secular agencies and institutions to promote the welfare of human society. And a new attitude of respect and dialogue with peoples of other religions is evident, at least among many Christian groups.

Discussion Questions

1 How does the Christian view of the scriptural story of God working through the people of Israel differ from the Jewish view?

2 What was the main content of Jesus' preaching of the coming of the Kingdom of God? By what actions did he demonstrate the presence of the Kingdom?

3 Outline some of the areas in which, according to the Gospels, Jesus differed from the understanding of the Jewish tradition held by his fellow Jewish teachers.

4 Why is the Christian story so interested in the question of *why* Jesus died? What answers does it give to this question?

5 What were some of the problems that developed between Jewish Christians and Gentile Christians? What answers did Paul and others provide for these problems?

6 How did Paul and others translate the gospel of Jesus from the Jewish context into the Greek-Hellenistic context?

7 How did Christianity become the religion of the Roman Empire? In what sense was monasticism a countercultural movement?

8 What were some of the basic issues in the theological controversies of the fourth and fifth centuries? What were some of the main doctrines settled on by the church councils, such as the ones at Nicea and Chalcedon?

9 Describe some differences in emphasis between the Eastern and Western churches.

10 What were the main issues involved in the Reformation movement in the sixteenth century? What were some of Martin Luther's key teachings?

11 How did state churches and denominations develop? How did the United States come to have its constitutional policy of separation of church and state?

12 What were some of the effects of the Enlightenment and the rise of science on Christianity? What particular threat did some Christians feel in the scientific study of the Bible?

13 Explain the ecumenical movement among the Christian churches today.

CHAPTER 10

Christian Worlds of Meaning

LOVING PARENT AND TRIUNE GOD

What is really ultimate? The Christian tradition, growing out of Judaism, has much the same view of God as that held by the Jews, up to a certain point. God is the one God of all peoples and ages, both transcendent and immanent, both lawgiver and merciful parent. Christians place a great deal of stress on the mercy and compassion of God: "God is love," according to a well-known text (*I John* 4:8). Jews also have this conception of God, so the difference is one of emphasis. Like Jews, Christians also see God as the judge who upholds standards of justice and punishes wrongdoing.

Seeing God's Face in Christ

The essential difference in the Christian vision comes at the point where the real heart and mind of God are revealed. For Jews, the way to really know God is in the covenant relationship, especially in the Torah, given by God in love. For Christians, the way to really know what God is like is through the revelation in Jesus Christ; here God's divine face is shown for all to see. Apart from Christ, God remains the almighty, righteous creator beyond human knowledge or contact; in Christ, the mystery has come to dwell among humans, so they can experience God's own glory and truth and love. Thus what is distinctive about the Christian vision of God is that the eternal brilliance of God's mystery is reflected through the "image" of God, Jesus Christ. The same scriptural writings used by the Jews now take on new meaning, for God's design and purpose can be seen in them in a new way.

Thus, Christian thinking about God starts from Jesus' own experience of God as revealed in the New Testament. One of Jesus' favorite terms for God was "Abba," by which he showed both his closeness to God and also God's character as the near and loving "father." This does not take away from the transcendence of God or the demands of the divine law. God is still the judge and evaluator of all, and one of Jesus' parables paints a vivid picture of the final judgment when God rewards the righteous with the eternal joys of heaven but consigns the wicked to everlasting punishment (*Matthew* 25:31–46). God does uphold justice. But what Jesus reveals about "Abba" is that God's *real* intention for all creatures is mercy, and that God is involved in the dirt and grime of human existence to see to it that the design of mercy wins out.

God as the Loving Parent Among Jesus' many stories telling about God's real nature, the parable of the prodigal son stands out. Once there was a man, Jesus told, who had two sons; on the younger son's insistence, he gave him his inheritance. The younger son left home and squandered all in reckless living. Finally, starving and wishing he could eat with the pigs he was tending, he came to his senses, resolving to return home and confess to his father his sins, begging to be treated like a servant.

> So he set off and came to his father. But while he was still at a distance, his father saw him, and his heart went out to him. Running out, he flung his arms around him and kissed him. Then the son said to him, "Father, I have sinned against

Heaven and against you; no longer am I fit to be called your son." But the father said to his servants, "Quick! get the best robe and put it on him, and put a ring on his hand and shoes on his feet. Then bring the fatted calf, kill it, and let us feast and make merry."

The older son was angry that the younger son was rewarded for his riotous, sinful living whereas he himself got no special rewards for his years of dedicated service to his father. "Dear son, you are always with me," said the father, "and all my possessions are yours. It is fitting to celebrate and be glad, for your brother here was dead and has come alive, he was lost and is found" (*Luke* 15:11–32). This picture of God as a waiting father, standing on tiptoe, straining to see in the distance a glimpse of his wayward son returning, has colored the Christian view of God from beginning to end.

Christians therefore see God as the loving father and mother, wanting to create humans in order to be able to show love to them. They understand God as pained and hurt in the face of human rejection. As the righteous judge, God punishes them in anger, never, however, letting them go. As loving parent, God waits for the wayward children to return, sends warners and prophets, and finally goes out to bring them back, so the divine love may be fulfilled. God, who was present in so many ways through the people of Israel, finally became concretely present in human history in Jesus Christ as the forgiving parent who welcomes even sinners. One time, as Luke tells, the tax collectors and other bad characters were all crowding in to listen to Jesus, and the Pharisees and scribes grumbled: "This fellow receives sinners and eats with them." And Jesus answered them with this parable:

Which one of you having a hundred sheep and losing one of them, does not leave the ninety-nine in the wilderness and go after the lost one until he finds it? And finding it, he lifts it on to his shoulders rejoicing, and coming home he calls together his friends and neighbors, saying, "Rejoice with me, for I have found my lost sheep."

(*Luke* 15:1–7)

And that is what God is really like.

Because they see God present in Jesus, Christians understand the suffering and death of Jesus as God's way of becoming the "friend of sinners" in a complete way. Just as God has been present to the world through the servant people Israel, now God is present to the world in the new servant Jesus, through him receiving all the evil and sin of the world and absorbing it in Godself, so that finally both divine justice *and* mercy might prevail.

One God, Three Persons: The Trinity

Because Christians believe they have seen God's true nature revealed in Jesus Christ, they call Jesus the "Son of God." Since God was present in the world in a powerful and saving way in Jesus, Christians say God was "incarnated" in Jesus: God "became flesh and dwelt among us" (*John* 1:14). Whereas this teaching arose out of the early Christians' experience of Jesus' death and resurrection, it took several centuries of experiencing and reflecting for Christians to be able to explain what they meant by calling Jesus the "Son of God." It was not until the church councils of the fourth and fifth centuries C.E. that satisfactory formulations were devised to say what needed to be said to guard from error and misunderstanding, but at the same time not to say too much about the mystery of God. It was partly this need to understand and preserve the experience of God's presence in Christ that Christians, much more than Jews, started theologizing, thinking and reasoning about God and God's work. Out of this theologizing came the doctrine of the Trinity: God is one God in three persons.

In all of this thinking, Christians tried carefully to insist on the unity of God. But their experience had taught them that God, eternally unified in self, is present and works in the created world in a number of aspects or modes or "persons" (from the Latin *persona*, the masks worn by actors playing roles on the stage). Using biblical terms, Christians called these aspects or persons by the names of Father, Son, and Holy Spirit. But what do these words designate about the one God? The words of the *Nicene Creed*, formulated in the early church councils, guide Christians in understanding the mystery of the Triune God.

The Nicene Creed   The first statement in the *Nicene Creed* emphasizes the unity of God: "We believe in one God." Then the creed goes on to specify the several faces of God: first, "the Father, the Almighty, maker of heaven and earth, of all things seen and unseen." The Father is God's face as creator, almighty and transcendent, Lord of the

The soaring gothic arches and vaults of the National Cathedral in Washington draw attention heavenward, symbolizing the presence of God.

became incarnate from the Holy Spirit and the Virgin Mary, and was made man. He was crucified for us under Pontius Pilate; he suffered death and was buried. On the third day he rose again in accordance with the scriptures, and he ascended into heaven and is seated at the right hand of the Father. He will come again with glory to judge the living and the dead. His kingdom will have no end.

What is this statement saying about the one God? It insists very carefully that the Son of God is totally and completely one with God: He was not created at a certain time but has always been God, not of a different being from the Father. The Son is also, as was said of the Father, the creator of all. But in this face of God we see the incarnation: "For us" God came down and was born a human and died on the cross. God became the redeemer, not solely in the form of the transcendent God but in the person of humanity. In Christ, the Son of God, the divine nature and the human nature were united, so God could redeem the human race. The Son rose in victory and now rules the world with the Father. With the Father, the Son will be the judge of all to fulfill justice and mercy completely.

But the Bible tells of another face of God's presence in the world, the "Spirit." So the third article of the *Nicene Creed* specifies:

> We believe in the Holy Spirit, the Lord and the giver of life, who proceeds from the Father (and the Son), who with the Father and the Son is worshipped and glorified, who has spoken through the prophets. We believe in one holy catholic and apostolic church. We acknowledge one baptism for the forgiveness of sins. We look for the resurrection of the dead and the life of the world to come.

whole universe. God created everything in the world, and God's purpose is justice and mercy for all.

The second article of the *Nicene Creed* goes on to specify the face of God as it is reflected in the Son:

> We believe in one Lord Jesus Christ, the only Son of God, begotten of his Father before all worlds, God from God, Light from Light, true God from true God, begotten, not made, one in being with the Father, through whom all things were made. For us humans and our salvation he came down from heaven and

Whereas the Father represents God as the creator and sustainer, and the Son represents God as the redeemer, the Holy Spirit represents God's ongoing spiritual presence in the world and in humans. Through the Spirit comes life; through the Spirit comes revelation and guidance. This is the presence of God that prompts human longings and prayers, that sustains them in their doubts, that cleanses and renews them. The Spirit guides and unifies the church, works through baptism and forgiveness, and sustains the faithful in hope. And so the Spirit is worshiped together with the Father and the Son—one God in three persons.

Christians do not find it easy to explain the meaning of the doctrine of the Triune God, for these terms, many of them derived from Greek philosophy, are limited in their appropriateness to describe the mystery of God's own being. But Christians have found this idea of one God in three persons a helpful and necessary one to express the way in which they have experienced the mystery of God—and that helpfulness is not so much in rational thought as in worship and praise of God.

The Problem of Evil in the World   As to the problem of how God could allow evil and suffering in this world, which God created and loves, Christians use many of the same responses as Jews. Out of love God disciplines, punishing so people will repent. God tests people to refine their faith. Evil is but the absence of good. The sufferings of the moment will cause the eternal rewards to shine more brilliantly. Evil comes as a result of the freedom that God has allowed. But there is one more specifically Christian response to pain and suffering: In all our suffering, God suffers. Through the cross of Christ, evil is overcome by God's own submission to the evil that works so much suffering and ruin in creation. This answer does not explain evil away or give a reason for its existence. But it does help Christians to bear it, trusting that even at this point God is with them as their loving father—and as their loving mother, Christians say, becoming more aware of the rich feminine images of God in the Bible as well as the traditional masculine ones.

CREATION AND HUMAN EXISTENCE

What is the meaning of life? Why is there so much suffering in the world? Christians, as they think about creation and the role of humans in the world, largely take over the Jewish view put forth in the Hebrew scriptures as in *Genesis* 1 and *Psalm* 8. That is, the one God created the universe in an orderly fashion, determined it all to be good, and placed humans as the crown of creation, to play the role of God's representative within this good world.

The Nature of Creation

The Christian view of creation is succinctly summed up by Paul when he writes, "From him [God] and through him and to him are all things; to him be glory forever" (*Romans* 11:36).

Creation had a beginning "from" God, out of nothing. God is the only being who is necessary, existing self-sufficiently; all other things are contingent and could easily not exist. This world is entirely God's creature, dependent on God for the gift of being and life. Creation is "through" God, continuing through God every day. Every instant the whole universe exists in the power of God's activity as the preserver. And creation is "to" God; it has a goal, a future that centers in God. There is a design or purpose to this universe inherent in the will of the creator who brought it into existence. But that means there is a demand, a law built into creation, which leads it to fulfill the design of the creator.

Creation in Christ   What is most distinctive about the Christian view of creation, as compared to the Jewish view with which it shares many points, is that Christians understand creation from the point at the center of their faith: the revelation of God's love and mercy in Christ. Why is there something and not nothing? What caused God to create? Love, Christians answer, the love that is seen in Jesus Christ. The Letter to the Colossians emphasizes this Christocentric view so strongly that it says, "Everything has been created through him [Christ] and for him. He exists before everything, and everything holds together in him" (*Colossians* 1:16–17).

Therefore, Christians read back from Christ to understand God's creation of the world and of humans. They understand the stories about creation in the book of Genesis from this point of view, emphasizing above all God's parental love. God wanted a world. God wanted humans as children to respond to the divine love in personal trust and fellowship. So God's great love overflowed in creativity, and the world and all that is in it came into being. All of God's creatures are special, but humans were made as very special creatures, so God could express love by entering into a close personal relationship with them. God lovingly created the first human, as told in *Genesis* 2, of the dust of the ground, breathing "spirit" or breath into him, making a woman as a fellow human, and thus choosing humans of all the creatures to be special partners in a loving relationship.

Since Christ is the focus of God's revelation and reveals God's deepest design and intention, Christians see all God's law or design summed up in Christ, who is the "end" or fulfillment of both God's love and justice. In answer to a lawyer's question about what the greatest commandment was, Jesus said, quoting the Torah, that loving God with one's whole being and loving one's neighbor as one's self sum up all the teaching of the law and the prophets (*Matthew* 22:35–40). This means that the law of creation is the law of love. For it is finally love that moves people to be fruitful, helpful, and creative, to invest themselves in their families, their work, and their art. Whatever is valuable and creative derives from such personal investment and love—and that is first and foremost true of God and the creation that was lovingly brought into existence.

A Good and Right Creation   God the creator has a design and purpose for creation, Christians believe, and humans play a central role in that design, as God works through human history to accomplish that purpose. That means that this is a moral universe, for it is fashioned according to God's design. God's love is balanced with justice or rightness throughout creation. That law of creation is known and felt by humans in their natural experience, so that all have a knowledge of God's will. The good life according to God's design, then, includes both love and justice, as lived by humans in loving and serving God in faith and obedience.

Christians affirm with *Genesis* 1 the essential "all-rightness" of the world. God gives the world not only its existence but also its value. This universe is ultimately right and moral, not just accidental and neutral. God's creatures—especially humans—are intrinsically valuable. And life within this created, material world is meaningful and full of value and significance. "Glory be to God for dappled things," wrote Gerald Manley Hopkins, expressing the Christian's delight in all aspects of God's good creation. "God saw everything that he had made," *Genesis* 1 reports, "and it was very good." That includes matter, food, drink, play, and bodily appetites, including sex.

Humans are children of God. As creatures they are to love and serve God, fulfilling the design of creation in human fellowship and in harmony with all God's creatures. All this existence is valuable, because the creator has given it value. This means, for one thing, that there is no person, and no aspect of a person's life, that is insignificant or trivial. For another thing, it means that no earthly being or institution can claim absolute value—all persons are created equally valuable. Further, the world of nature has been given its own value, not to be tyrannized or ruinously exploited by humans.

Christians affirm that reason is a special gift from God. Since humans know from their own nature and conscience

what God's basic design (law) is, they ought to be able reasonably to fulfill that design, living in love and justice with fellow creatures. But human reason is also driven by other factors, especially by the will that turns a person back upon oneself in pride and selfishness—the condition that Christians call sin. Therefore, human reason is an ambiguous guide to living the good life and fulfilling God's real design in creation. A minimal kind of justice and order can perhaps be created by humans at their best, using their reason and effort—but the real meaning of creation, the wholeness of existence full of both justice *and* love in relation to the creator and also to the fellow creatures, is beyond the reach of human striving on the basis of reason. Something more is needed, and that must come as grace from God's side.

Sin and Separation from God

Why do people do evil and destructive things? In spite of the strong feeling that humans were created in the image of God, perfect and good as God wanted them to be, most Christians emphasize the sinfulness of human *nature* more forcefully than do Jews or Muslims. It is not just a matter of an evil tendency, which can be controlled or mastered by one who has the mind to do so. Rather, there is a deep, complete fracture in the very nature of humans, causing separation from God and inevitable sinfulness in human existence. Sin for Christians is not just an act done by a person; sin is the very being of humans, the state of alienation from God and God's design.

Paradise and the Fall into Sin   The story of origins in *Genesis* 2 and 3 is especially important for Christians, and they read it somewhat differently from Jews. God created humans to be partners, perfect and in full harmony with all of creation, serving God and taking care of creation. God provided all that is needed for a full, happy life: a garden of delight, work to fulfill human existence, animals to be named by humans, a fellow human for companionship—above all, close fellowship with God. God did give a command to the man and the woman in the garden: "You may freely eat from every tree in the garden, but from the tree of the knowledge of good and evil you may not eat" (*Genesis* 2:16–17). Why? God gave no reason. But clearly this is important in the human relation to God: A command sets a limit, and it requires a response on the humans' part. No longer can they maintain their dreaming innocence—God wants real partners. The command is the opening of the way for humans to transcend their own inner limits and relate to the power outside themselves. God stands over against us humans as "you," so that we can no longer only think incessantly of "me." Now, with God's command inserted into human life, the humans become aware both of God and of themselves as free agents making decisions, acting on them, and taking responsibility.

This story is told about the first man and the first woman, but in the Christian view it really is the story of all humans. God encounters them as personal Lord, and they are faced with a decision: to obey or to disobey the divine will. Humans are always confronted with this decision: whether to respond to God as personal Lord and Master in their role as creatures, or to turn to their own way in defiance of God's will. That they are free to decide shows that God has entered into a personal relationship with them. That they consistently turn to their own way shows their inevitable human sin and rebellion against the creator.

This inevitable human sin and rebellion is depicted in *Genesis* 3 in the well-known story of the "fall." Some Christians take this story literally as an account of the first human pair and their fall into a sinful state. Most understand it as a symbolic description of the natural state of humans: created to be partners of God but always choosing the selfish and rebellious course. Whether read literally or symbolically, the story in *Genesis* 3 presents a powerful portrait of human existence as seen in the Christian view.

The man and the woman were roused out of their dreaming innocence by the snake, the "wisest" of all the creatures God had made. Whereas the man and the woman had not done any thinking or deciding yet, just taking care of the garden, cleaving to each other unashamedly, and taking walks with God in the garden, the snake had been thinking: "Did God really say that you shall not eat from any tree of the garden?" (3:1). The snake exaggerates, and the woman exaggerates also in her answer. But the crucial step is made: The humans begin to think and to desire and to exercise their freedom—in rebellion against God's command.

This decision in rebellion against God disrupted the human situation with God in every area of human existence, since God is the basis of all that makes for human existence. If the relation to God the creator is disrupted, all else is also shattered. When God comes to walk in the garden in the cool of the day, the humans hide in their shame. Now enmity breaks out with the animals, nature no longer cooperates with the man in producing food, and the woman experiences great pain and risk of death in the natural function of childbirth. The man and the woman are alienated from each other: they cover themselves with clothes, they blame each other, and the man usurps the rule over the woman in this disrupted state. Finally, the humans are driven from God's presence out into the ruptured world of human existence, with no way back to the garden.

Originating Sin   The Christian interpretation of this story sees in it the "fall" of humankind into a sinful state, blotting out or distorting the image of God in which they were created. Paul writes that "sin came into the world through one man"; now, however, "there is no difference, for all have sinned and come short of the glory of God" (*Romans* 5:12; 3:23). Augustine interpreted this state of humankind as **original sin,** the condition of all humans of not being able not to sin.

There has been considerable disagreement among Christians about the nature of "original sin." Some Christians have followed Augustine in thinking of original sin in terms of a fallen nature passed on physically through birth from one generation to the next, starting from the first human parents. Again, some Christians tend to say sin originates with the devil, who tempted the first parents and who still goes about as a roaring lion seeking people to devour. Most Christians today try to find ways of thinking about sin that do not blame our sinfulness on Adam and Eve or on the devil—sin is something that belongs to our own nature and we must take responsibility for it.

One way to understand original sin would be as "originating" sin, that is, the fundamental tendency in all human nature to follow one's self-will, placing oneself as creature in the place of God the creator. The originating sin thus produces a kind of idolatry, worshiping oneself instead of God. The human will is in bondage, curved in upon itself.

The Christian idea of sin is not easy to understand, but it tries to uphold a number of important meanings. For one thing, to say that sin is original means that sin is inborn, a condition all humans share without exception. There is no one who is perfect and sinless in this view.

This means, at the same time, that there are no persons who are worse sinners than others. Of course, there are some who do more hurtful, destructive actions than others; the sins people commit do have varying gravity and consequences. But all are equal in sharing the same sinful human nature. And therefore if one can be redeemed, all can equally be redeemed. There is no human, even the worst murderer and rapist, who is so despicable as to be nonredeemable. In fact, sometimes one who has obviously committed a lot of sins is more aware of his or her predicament and need for God's help than one who has lived a "good" life and feels confident of personal merit before God. Jesus told a story about a Pharisee and a tax collector, to give a lesson to some who trusted in themselves that they were righteous and despised others. Both went to the temple to pray. The Pharisee thanked God that he was not like evil men, especially this tax collector. But the tax collector stood far off, eyes cast down, beating his breast, and said, "O God, be merciful to me, a sinner." Jesus said, "I tell you, this man went home justified rather than the other" (*Luke* 18:9–14). Whereas there may be differences of sins in terms of evil effects, there is no difference in sinful nature: All have an equal share of original sin.

The idea of original sin also means that sin involves the whole person, originating from the center of one's being. It is not that sin comes from certain animal drives and lusts, or that it has to do mainly with one's lower members below the belt. All members, faculties, hearts, minds, wills, and whatever it is that makes humans what they are, all share in the sinful nature. There is nothing humans can do, then, no matter how noble or intellectual or creative, that is not at the same time contaminated by human sin.

The Christian view of sin sounds pessimistic and gloomy—and so it is, pointing to the condition of humans separated from God. But it should be noted that this idea places the big emphasis on humans' sinful nature, not so much on the various things humans do. Therefore, this is a freeing and positive idea as well. It frees a person to live courageously in this world amid the ambiguities of human existence. Acknowledging one's sinful nature—and therefore the need to turn to God for help and mercy—a person can live with courage and hope in the ups and downs of human existence, knowing that pleasure and drink and sex and wealth and everything else are not bad in themselves. It is our sinful nature, Christians believe, that originates sin—and the only help for that comes from God.

The Wages of Sin   God does hate sin, however, demanding that humans be perfect as God is perfect. So, Christians believe, the sin that humans share calls forth God's wrath and punishment. Every individual sin, of course, has its own consequences. But by tracing sins back to a sinful nature, it is possible for Christians to talk of consequences that all humans share equally. These consequences are spiritual "death" or separation from God, a fragmented and warped human life, and ultimately eternal death and punishment.

Paul writes that "through one man sin came into the world, and through sin came death, and so death spread to all people, because all have sinned." Again, he says that "the wage for sin is death" (*Romans* 5:12; 6:23). This does not mean creaturely finitude is punishment for sin—only God is eternal, and all creatures are limited by beginning and end. But Christians use the image of "death" to refer to the separation and estrangement from God that sin causes. Adam and Eve had to leave the Garden; people, by worshiping themselves instead of God, separate themselves from the source of all life and love and wholeness. Cutting the lifeline to God—which is what sin does—means spiritual death.

And such spiritual death, in the Christian view, affects everything we are and do as humans. Cut off from God, we become hurtful and hateful in our relations with each other. People abuse and exploit the wonderful world of nature that God created good and gave over to them to take care of. They find no harmony and peace in their fragmented lives. Their creaturely limits, symbolized by death, cause great anxiety, suffering, and a feeling of hopelessness.

Christians believe that death is not the end of human existence, but that the consequences of sin will continue in the world to come. God is the judge of all, and God's evaluation of sinfulness will bring about the final consequence: eternal death and punishment. Christians of earlier times depicted the horrors and everlasting torments of the damned in hell by graphic words and pictures (read Book 21 of Augustine's *City of God*). Many Christians today have problems with these grotesque portraits. But what they do show is the seriousness of sin in God's sight—and the need for humans to receive help and forgiveness from God.

THE PATH: SALVATION BY GRACE

The question of salvation is a central question for Christians, who see all human nature enslaved to sinfulness. God has a high design for humans; they are to be perfect in love and fellowship with the creator. But in the face of human rebellion and idolatry, this design becomes a demand that is beyond the human possibility. Humans are lost and helpless, cut off from God, without hope in the world. And so the most important question becomes, How can we be saved from this sin and punishment?

Saved by Jesus Christ

The story of the jailer at Philippi is a familiar one to Christians. With Paul and Silas bound in his prison at Philippi, the jailer experienced great terror when an earthquake occurred, which he thought had allowed his prisoners to escape. There was nothing left for him to do except to take his own life. But Paul and Silas stopped him, for none of them had tried to escape. Trembling with fear, the jailer fell down before them and asked, "Men, what must I do in order to be saved?" And they answered simply, "Believe on the Lord Jesus, and you will be saved, both you and your household." He believed, and he and all his family were baptized. Then he took them up to his house, washed their wounds, set a meal before them, and rejoiced with all his household (*Acts* 16:25–34).

The starting point in the Christian vision of salvation is the recognition that ultimately humans cannot attain salvation by themselves; they cannot on their own restore the relationship with God that has been disrupted through sin. To say this is not to deny that there are good things that people can do, in the sense of righteousness and justice in relationship with fellow humans. God's law is sufficiently in our nature that we do by nature know justice from injustice, and even our self-interest will lead us to try and establish a society of order and fairness. But to be in the right relationship with God is the key to salvation, and this, most Christians believe, is beyond our human possibilities because of our fundamental sinful nature.

It is at this point that the Christian tradition diverges significantly from both Judaism and Islam. For Jews, as we have seen, the divinely given path of Torah is the path of transformation; following it and performing its mitzvot bring blessing, joy, and salvation. For Muslims likewise, as discussed later, following God's law is the path of transformation that brings felicity in this world and the next. But in

Jan Van Eyck, "The Last Judgment." Tempera and oil on canvas, transferred from wood, 22 1/4 x 7 3/4 in. The Metropolitan Museum of Art, Fletcher Fund, 1933.

Christian understanding, the law (God's demands on humans, as revealed in the Torah) cannot be a path of salvation, for it demands of us what we cannot do. "You shall be holy, as I the Lord your God am holy" is the demand of God's law. But no human is or can be holy, and so following the way of the law cannot restore the relationship with God; it cannot bring salvation. In fact, Paul argued that the law becomes an accuser, showing us our sin every time we fail to keep a precept perfectly.

Most Christians believe that God's law does have the function of maintaining some form of order and justice in human society, curbing people's wickedness and guiding them toward God's design of justice. But more importantly with respect to the path of salvation, the law shows the depths of the estrangement from God. Whereas in Jesus' parable the Pharisee praying in the temple thought about his merits in keeping the Torah, the tax collector thought of that same divine law and could only beat his breast, saying, "God, be merciful to me a sinner." And Jesus says the tax collector is the one who went home justified by God—that is, recognition of sinfulness is the first step in turning toward the redemption that comes from God. For as long as a person tries to justify herself—that is, tries to claim worth and merit before God on the basis of what she does—she remains trapped in a no-win situation. It is a tendency of human nature to try and claim worth in oneself, to justify one's existence—whether through work, determining self-worth by how much one earns, or through one's social standing among friends, or through some other accomplishment. God's law breaks through all this and shows us how futile it is to try and justify ourselves by our performance in life.

When we abandon our attempts at self-justification and turn to God, Christians believe, we find we are justified and saved through Jesus Christ. But how does this happen? How does Jesus save us? To understand this mystery of salvation, Christians start from the testimony of the scriptures. "God was in Christ, reconciling the world to himself" (*II Corinthians* 5:19). Just as Jews look back to many acts of salvation by which God delivered the sacred people, so Christians believe that God was also at work through Jesus Christ to bring salvation for all peoples.

This means first of all that whatever happened in Jesus Christ is the fulfillment of God's whole plan and design to restore humankind to the relationship of love and fellowship with God. Of all of the images in the scriptures about God saving the people, the Jewish image of sacrificing a lamb to make **atonement** for the sins of the people has appeared to many Christians to set the pattern by which God brings salvation. Symbolically the sins of the people were placed on the lamb; the lamb became a substitute, bearing and thus abolishing the sins of the people. Christians look to the prophecy of Second Isaiah (*Isaiah* 53), telling of the suffering servant of God, on whom God will place the sins and the burdens of all to make atonement for them. This pattern of atonement reaches its fulfillment in Jesus Christ, atoning for the sins of all humankind by his sacrifice on the cross, and by this atonement bringing about the restoration of the loving relationship between God and humans.

But even this image of the atonement does not really explain *how* this salvation takes place. In trying to understand it further, Christians have used additional metaphors and images. For example, Christ can be envisioned as a victorious king, triumphing over the powers of hell by his cross. Or he can be viewed as the sinless one who paid the debt of sin that we all owe before God the judge, whose scales of justice must be balanced. Or, again, Jesus Christ can be understood as the mediator who reconciled the two parties at war with each other, God and humans. These and other images of the atonement are all attempts to explain the same reality, the experience of salvation and restoration through Jesus Christ.

Every metaphor or human analogy has its limitations when used to understand a divine mystery. Are we to think that in some magical way the sins all people have committed are somehow heaped on Christ's shoulders as he died on the cross? Are we really to think there are evil powers of hell that the Son of God had to do battle with and defeat in order to free humans from their grasp? Are we really to think of God as an angry judge, insisting on someone paying the debt all people owe so the scales of justice can be balanced? Are we really to think of a war between God and humans that has to be settled by a mediator? Taking any one of these images in a strict literal fashion can lead to some less than Christian ideas about God and God's relation to humans. Yet such human images are helpful, and Christians have found much meaning in all these images by which to understand the atonement.

God So Loved the World   The basic motif behind all these ways of understanding the atonement is God's love demonstrated concretely in Christ. God is holy and hates sin—for sin ruins God's good creation, and it destroys fellowship and love. It causes suffering, pain, and death, and that not just in this present existence but also in the world to come. Something has to be done from God's side, Christians believe. God has to intervene as God really is, as both holy judge and as lover of all creation. But to be a real lover of humankind, God becomes vulnerable, as all lovers do.

How does God, the transcendent creator, become a lover for humans? In the Christian experience, it is by God taking a body in the created world with which to bear the sin of the world. The demands of justice and judgment are met, according to the truth that sin has consequences. But the Christian good news is that God took these consequences on Godself in Jesus Christ, replacing the demand and punishment of the law with the power of love. That means God's love must be a suffering love; God suffers for the sins of the world in the servant, Jesus Christ. It is God's love that does not allow giving up humankind to judgment and condemnation, for

> God is love. In this the love of God was manifested to us, that God sent his only son into the world, so that we might have life through him. In this is love, not that we have loved God but that he has loved us and sent his son as an expiation for our sins.
> (*I John* 4.8–10)

Jesus Christ is thus the means through which God brings the divine love into the world for the salvation of humankind.

In the end, all the consequences of sin are summed up in death: "The wage of sin is death." So the atonement made by Christ also brings triumph over the fear of death. Jesus Christ is raised from the dead! In the perspective of the Bible, a resurrection from the dead is not utterly amazing, where God's power is concerned. There are scriptural stories of people who escaped death or were raised from the dead; Jesus himself raised people from the dead. But the resurrection of Jesus Christ is unique in that this is the first fruit, the foretaste of the world to come in which death is abolished. It is God's stamp of approval on the redemption worked out through the life, sufferings, and death of Jesus Christ.

Who Is Christ? So who was or is this Jesus Christ? Together with the doctrine of the atonement, Christian theology stresses the doctrine of the incarnation, with its classic expression in the *Gospel of John:* "And the Word became flesh and lived among us, and we have seen his glory, glory as of the only Son from the Father, full of grace and truth" (*John* 1:14). More than any other teaching of Christianity, this teaching of the incarnation of God in the human being Jesus has caused lines of defense and objection to be established by both Jews and Muslims. How can God become a human? How can God have a son? What does this teaching of the incarnation mean?

This is a question faced by the early Christians, and by Christians ever since. Is this Jesus Christ a human, or is he God, or is he a God-human mixture, or what? The answer to this question is the Christian doctrine of Christology, thinking about the nature of Christ. The important thing, in the Christian view, is to see this question in relation to the doctrine of **soteriology,** the belief in salvation through Jesus Christ. That is where Christians start in their religious experience; through Jesus Christ they experience the love of God in its fullness, meeting God present with saving power. And therefore they think of Jesus Christ as the Son of God, through whom God's love and salvation are experienced within creaturely existence in this world.

For several hundred years, Christian thinkers struggled with the need—and the difficulty—of expressing clearly just who Jesus Christ is in both the divine and the human dimensions. The need was to keep the good news of salvation from becoming something else—another law or demand, a magical story, or the like. The difficulty was the uniqueness of this mystery: How does one even begin to talk about God taking human sin on Godself? Finally, Christians decided that in order to maintain the good news of salvation, it is necessary to teach that Jesus Christ is both fully and completely God and fully and completely human.

There were other options, of course. Some Christians (led by Arius and thus called Arians) were teaching that Jesus was really human, created to be God's son and savior of the world. But Christians found that to restrict Jesus from being fully God causes problems for soteriology; how could the suffering and death of a mere human, no matter how noble, make atonement for the sin of the whole world? Only if God makes this atonement could it bring to all people the promise of forgiveness and salvation. Another group of Christians approached the question from the other side from the Arians; the Docetists (from the Greek word *dokeo,* meaning to "seem" or to "appear") taught that Jesus Christ was fully God but just "seemed" to be a human with the mask of flesh and blood (**Docetism**). But Christians found that if this view were followed, the whole notion of Jesus Christ sharing human sufferings and bearing human burdens and sins would become meaningless. For only one who is truly human can experience the suffering and death that humans must experience.

So Christian thinkers decided that the only way to preserve the good news of salvation through Christ is to talk of Jesus Christ as fully God and fully human, two natures united in the one person. Most Christians do not pretend to be able to explain rationally how this can be so. But they believe it because it is the good news of salvation. Christ took human sin, suffering, and death on himself as the human brother, making atonement for the sin of the whole world as the divine Lord. And still today, Christians believe, Christ lives and rules as fully God and fully human. He sympathizes with human weaknesses because he knows human nature; and he intercedes for humans and declares them righteous by virtue of his divine power.

The Way of Faith

The path for salvation is necessarily a two-way affair, even in Christianity, and in the Christian vision the appropriate human response is faith, which is the accepting of the grace that comes from God in Christ. It is not a "work" in the sense of fulfilling God's law and demand, or justifying oneself by some worthwhile deeds. Rather, faith is saying yes to God's love, accepting the divine promise that we have been reconciled to God. This is what Christians call the doctrine of **justification by faith.** Faith is not primarily an intellectual act, although it does involve mind and reason. It is the movement of the will in response to God's love, trusting that God has made all things whole again.

There is an objective, intellectual side to faith, having to do with ideas and doctrines about God and humans. But the primary meaning of having faith, Christians believe, is coming into a personal relationship with Jesus Christ as Lord. For Jesus said, "I am the Way, the Truth, and the Life; no one comes to the Father except through me." And again, he said, "If someone loves me, he will keep my word, and my Father will love him, and we will come to him and make our abode with him" (*John* 14: 6, 23). When the good news of Jesus Christ is told, God is promising, "I love you, and I have saved you." Faith is accepting that promise and getting in on the story of Christ, making that story one's own story. As a person responds in faith and trust, Christ makes his

home with her. Her life is filled with Christ's love, and her death is shared with him, trusting Christ's promise that she will also share his resurrection and eternal life. This personal relation with Christ is the overcoming of the fracture of sin. It is reconciliation with God.

Salvation through faith is a lifelong process, and Christians, like Jews and Muslims, make use of prayer and worship as the means toward this transformation. Baptism is an important ritual for Christians, for it symbolizes the inclusion of the new person in the family of God. Through baptism the person dies to the sinful nature and is reborn with a Christlike nature, for Christ dwells in him. Throughout one's lifetime the knowledge that "I have been baptized" provides comfort and hope whenever doubts and anxieties arise. Hearing the word of the gospel is a reminder over and over of the story of Christ that has become each Christian's story. Sharing in the Eucharist (Lord's Supper) is a concrete experience of being united with Christ through this sacred meal. And prayer in the name of Christ keeps the new relationship with God alive and well. Christians speak of these practices as the "means of grace," believing that as one participates in them, the Holy Spirit is at work in her heart, continually transforming her sinful nature so her faith and love become more perfect.

The struggle of life continues, however. Christians realize that until the end of life a person will always be *both* a sinful human being *and* a redeemed human being. But though sin continues, God's forgiveness continues. So we can live courageously, Christians believe, not having constantly to prove our worth before God, and thus free to live in the world and show love to one another as God loved us.

It is at this point in the path of transformation that Christians talk of the value of work and actions. Works grow out of faith. People who have experienced God's love and grace will be inwardly motivated to demonstrate that kind of love and grace also in their lives—freely, not for sake of reward. Christians speak of the process of the "sanctification" or making holy of our lives. Through the power of the Holy Spirit, our faith and our experience of God's love shape and mold our hearts, minds, and wills, so that more and more we live Christlike lives in the world. "We become what we are," Christians might say: By faith we *are* saved, and now we go about becoming the kind of persons who demonstrate in their lives what that salvation means.

The Life of the World to Come

Like Jews and Muslims, Christians also believe in the world to come: resurrection, judgment, and eternal life in heaven. The eternal life that begins now through faith in Christ is not something that death can snuff out. Christ died, but he broke the power of death and rose again on the other side of death. Now he rules as the Lord over all. All who are united with him in faith already experience that resurrected life in this world, through worship of the risen Lord. But Christ has promised that he will come again to judge all people. Christians understand this as a word of promise rather than of threat, for the judge is none other than the Savior, the friend of sinners and our brother. And he has promised that he will say, "Come, you blessed ones of my Father, inherit the kingdom which has been prepared for you since the world was founded" (*Matthew* 25:34).

Traditional Christian piety has constructed many imaginative descriptions of paradise in heaven and the bliss of eternal life, descriptions that are still meaningful to modern Christians even though the cosmology underlying them is no longer held. Many modern Christians have problems with the notion of heaven as an exclusionary place, from which the vast majority of God's human race will forever be banned. They ask, could the loving parent of all peoples allow heaven for only that small part of humankind who had the good fortune to hear about Christ and believe in him, while consigning all other peoples who have lived on this earth to eternal punishment? And so some Christians believe that God, in ultimate divine mercy, will not allow anyone to be lost, even as other Christians hold to the traditional view that large numbers of unbelievers will be excluded from eternal salvation.

This is a difficult question. The attitude of many Christians is to leave these things up to God's eternal love and mercy. God will judge; and the judge will be none other than the Savior. The important point remains that eternal life comes by God's grace, not on account of one's deserving merit. And this means that life in heaven, too, is a gift of grace, not a reward. The prospect of life in heaven is not to be the motivation for becoming a Christian. It is God's love that stirs one to the life of faith, and heaven is simply the last image in the process of salvation. Just as God at the beginning said the creation is "very good," so at the end the promise of eternal life in heaven is God's way of saying that the new creation of salvation is very good.

Discussion Questions

1 What key aspects of God do Christians believe are revealed in Jesus Christ as the "image" of God?

2 Discuss how Christians can believe in the unity of God and still talk about the Trinity.

3 Explain what the *Nicene Creed* states about each of the three "persons" of God.

4 Why did God create the world, in the Christian view? What is the role of humans?

5 How can the world be a good world created by God, and yet a world full of sin and evil? Is God's love or God's justice predominant?

6 What sort of theological interpretation do Christians typically give to the story of Adam and Eve in the Garden of Eden?

7 Explain the Christian doctrine of sin (called by some "original sin").

8 How does the Christian view of God's Law differ from that of Jews and Muslims?

9 What are some of the things Christians mean when they talk about being "saved" by Christ? Explain the idea of "atonement."

10 What were the views of the Docetists and the Arians about the nature of Christ? What is the traditional orthodox doctrine?

11 On the Christian path, what is the role of faith? Of works?

12 Discuss the question of whether some people will be excluded from heaven. Why is this a troubling question for Christians? How is it answered differently, and why?

CHAPTER 11

Ritual Practices and the Good Life for Christians

CHRISTIAN WORSHIP AND RITUAL

How can we find new power for life? Christians, like Jews, believe that all life is to be worship of God. How Christians live is based on the teachings and the example of Jesus, focusing on love. God is to be worshiped and praised, both in acts of love toward God and in good deeds of love toward others. Jesus, quoting the Torah, said there are two great commandments: to love God with all one's heart, strength, and mind; and to love one's neighbor as oneself. Of course, God is worshiped not because this has been commanded, but out of love and gratitude. Christ lives within, and this provides the motivation and power to live a life in worship of God.

Breaking Bread and Praising God

We are told that the earliest Christians "day by day, both attending the temple together and breaking bread in their homes, partook of food with joyous and simple hearts, praising God and enjoying favor with all the people" (*Acts* 2:46–47). From the beginning, Christians followed the Jewish tradition of assembling together to pray and praise God, also "breaking bread" in their homes, that is, observing the Lord's Supper, which Jesus instituted during his last Passover meal with his disciples. From these earliest practices evolved the distinctive Christian forms of communal worship, including the Sunday service of prayer and Eucharist and the cycle of holy days and festivals throughout the year.

It should be noted that Christian groups in the modern world differ significantly from one another in their attitudes and practices regarding worship and rituals. Christians do not have a commonly accepted pattern set down by divine law, as is the case in Judaism and Islam. Even those rituals and ceremonies of worship mentioned in the New Testament have been interpreted differently in the various Christian communions. Some groups do have "canon law," which governs the conduct of public worship. Other groups take an approach of freedom and spontaneity, following, of course, their own accepted pattern of worship. It is possible to speak of "liturgical" and "nonliturgical" church bodies. Those that are liturgical place a good deal of emphasis on the traditional liturgy (order of public worship), properly ordained clergy, and use of sacred rituals or sacraments. The nonliturgical denominations emphasize a free and spontaneous approach to prayer, reading the Bible, testifying to faith, and exhorting others in worship together. Liturgical denominations include the **Roman Catholic,** Orthodox, Anglican, and Lutheran churches; nonliturgical groups would be Baptists, Quakers, and the variety of free evangelical churches. Somewhere in between are such groups as the Methodists and the Calvinist (Presbyterian, Reformed) churches, who do not emphasize the traditional liturgies and sacraments but do follow commonly accepted forms of worship. Of course, there is variety even within one denomination, between those who are "high church" (more liturgical emphasis) and those who are "low."

In recent times, the so-called liturgical renewal has affected most church groups, bringing a higher appreciation of the traditional forms of worship even in the nonliturgical churches. In the following description, we look in a general way at the broadly based, traditional practice of Christian worship, noting significant variances where appropriate. It should also be said, of course, that many modern Christians, just like many modernists of other religions, participate only marginally in the sacred rituals of the church, though they still consider themselves Christian and live generally in keeping with Christian morality.

Sunday Worship   Just as Jews consider the Sabbath the heart and soul of Judaism, so also Christians observe the central practice of communal worship each week, the day being Sunday, the day of Christ's resurrection. Worship takes place on other days, too, but the Sunday worship service is the most distinctive Christian sacred time. The service itself developed from the Jewish synagogue service of praise, prayer, scripture readings, and exposition of scripture. To this service focused on God's word, the early Christians added the liturgy of the Eucharist (Thanksgiving), that is, the celebration of the Lord's Supper instituted by Christ. Thus, the complete Sunday worship service in many liturgical churches consists of two parts, the Liturgy of the Word and the Liturgy of the Eucharist, although some may at times use only one part.

Often an Entrance Rite begins the service, with a call to worship, communal confession of sins, hymns, and prayers. The Liturgy of the Word includes readings of the scriptures: Old Testament, Gospels, and Epistles. A minister expounds the scripture in a sermon or homily, and the people respond with hymns, psalms, and the saying of the creed. They offer common prayer for all Christians and for all people according to their need. The Liturgy of the Eucharist may begin with the people greeting one another with peace and bringing offerings to God, including the bread and wine to be used in the Eucharist. There follows the Great Thanksgiving prayer narrating Christ's institution of the sacred meal, asking for the Holy Spirit, and establishing unity with all Christians everywhere. After the bread is symbolically broken, the people commune with Christ and with each other by eating and drinking the bread and wine, believing that in this ritual Christ is pre-

sent among them. At the conclusion of the service, the minister blesses the people and may say, "Go in peace, serve the Lord," an indication that the people carry the renewed spiritual blessings into their daily life. Nonliturgical churches, of course, have many variations of the Sunday worship service, with more emphasis on reading the Bible, preaching, songs, and prayer.

The Sacraments   The Eucharist is considered by many Christians to be a "sacrament," that is, a sacred ritual through which God's saving power comes to the believers. Most Christian denominations perform some sacraments, although they do not all use that term or agree on what it means. Some of the ceremonies were mentioned or authorized in the New Testament, and others were added. Ceremonies called sacraments include baptism, the Eucharist (Lord's Supper), confession and forgiveness, anointing the sick, **confirmation** of the baptized, ordination of clergy, and the rite of marriage. Roman Catholics and some Anglicans refer to all seven of these ceremonies as sacraments; Lutherans and some Reformed traditions retain most of these ceremonies but reserve the term *sacrament* for baptism, the Eucharist, and (sometimes) confession and forgiveness. Other denominations avoid sacramental language altogether, although virtually all Christian groups practice baptism. The important symbolism of the sacraments is that God's power and presence are connected with ordinary human activities like washing, eating, drinking, and so forth. Participating in the sacrament, people dedicate their total being to God and receive divine forgiveness and power, thus sanctifying all of life.

The Eucharist (also called the Lord's Supper, Holy Communion, the Mass, or the Divine Liturgy) has been the central sacrament of the Sunday service from the beginning, although Christians have not been unified in interpreting its meaning. One long-standing view, traditionally accepted by Roman Catholics, is the doctrine of "transubstantiation," a miraculous change of the bread and wine into the body and blood of Christ. In the Reformation, thinkers like Luther reacted against the idea that each mass was a new sacrifice of Christ, holding rather that Christ was "truly present" in, with, and under the bread and wine. More radical reformers like Zwingli held that the bread and wine only symbolize the body and blood of Christ. These basic interpretations are still held in the Christian denominations of today, so that the Christian church experiences division precisely in this sacrament of unity. Ecumenical discussions today are attempting to reach some kind of consensus or at least better mutual understanding of the alternative positions on the meaning of the Eucharist.

Festivals and Holy Days

Christians, like people of other religions, celebrate sacred times throughout the cycle of the year. Most Christians agree in setting aside as sacred time the spring celebration of Christ's death and resurrection on Good Friday and Easter, the winter celebration of his birth at Christmas, and also the coming of the Spirit and the beginning of the church on Pentecost. Many churches expand these with times of preparation and extended celebration, and many additional holy days are observed throughout the year.

Lent and Easter   The most obvious holy season from the very beginning was the Paschal (Passover) season when Christ's death and resurrection occurred. Eventually this Paschal season was extended by celebrating the events of Holy Week: Christ's entry into Jerusalem, the last supper, the crucifixion, and the entombment—all leading up to the climactic event of the resurrection. In further developments, the preparation for remembering Christ's death began six weeks earlier with the Lenten season, and the **Easter** celebration itself extended six weeks after Easter.

Starting from Ash Wednesday, when traditional Christians put ashes on their foreheads, the season of **Lent** is devoted to special disciplines of prayer, repentance, fasting, or voluntarily giving up certain pleasures. Holy Week begins with Palm Sunday, remembering the triumphal entry into Jerusalem and the beginning of Jesus' passion week. Maundy Thursday celebrates Christ's last supper with his disciples when he used the bread and the wine of the Passover meal to institute the Lord's Supper. Good Friday is an especially solemn day for Christians, remembering Christ's three hours of agony on the cross and his death and entombment. Saturday night may be given over to a service of vigil. And early Sunday morning, with the rising of the sun, Christians begin to celebrate the resurrection of the Lord in a joyous festival service. Such an Easter service may have a colorful procession of clergy and people, trum-

pets sounding, and choir singing. People greet one another, "Today Christ is risen!" "He is risen indeed!" This joyous mood continues for the next six weeks, including the celebration of Christ's ascension into heaven forty days later on Ascension Day.

Advent, Christmas, and Epiphany   Christmas, the Feast of the Nativity, began to be observed widely in Christian churches about the fourth century, when December 25 was set in the Western churches. Of course, the actual time of year when Jesus was born is not known. Many Christians observe the season of **Advent** for four weeks before Christmas and the season of **Epiphany** for some weeks after Christmas. This is the time of the celebration of God's love in the incarnation of Christ.

Advent is the beginning of the Christian year, commencing also the half-year cycle in which events from Christ's life are celebrated. Advent is a season of preparation, and the worship services bring Christians back to Old Testament times, hearing the voices of the prophets, preparing their hearts for the coming of the messiah. Some Christians place an advent wreath with four candles in their homes, lighting one additional candle each week in preparation for the nativity of Christ.

Christmas is a highly joyous festival, with songs, plays, nativity scenes, and other rituals celebrating God's great love in becoming one with humanity as a baby born in a manger. It is a time especially dear to children, who are given special roles in telling of the Christ-child. Symbolic of God's great gift is the tradition of exchanging gifts and greeting cards at Christmas time, and decorating an evergreen tree with lights symbolizes Christ's light shining in the darkness of this world.

The Feast of the Epiphany (showing forth) comes on January 6. This feast originated in the East as a commemoration of Christ's birth and baptism, and still today the Eastern churches have a ritual of blessing the baptismal waters. In the Western churches, Epiphany has become associated with the story of the wise men from the East coming to Bethlehem to present gifts to the newborn King.

Pentecost and the Season of the Church   Pentecost, some fifty days after the resurrection of Christ, is the celebration of the outpouring of the Spirit on Christ's disciples after his ascension into heaven. Its roots lie in the Jewish festival of Shavuot, the celebration of the giving of the Torah on Mt. Sinai. In the Christian view, instead of the Torah, God gave the Spirit to give guidance to the church, so Pentecost, the feast of the Holy Spirit, is also the birthday of the church.

Beginning with Pentecost, the next half year is considered the season of the church, since it contains no major festivals from Christ's life. Feast days in this period observed by many Christians are All Saints' Day on November 1, set aside to commemorate the saints and heroes of the faith, and All Souls' Day (Commemoration of the Faithful Departed) on November 2, remembering all those who have kept the faith and gone on to their reward. In the more liturgical churches, holy days in honor of the apostles and saints are scattered throughout the whole year—devoted, for example, to St. Luke the Evangelist, St. Peter and St. Paul the Apostles, St. Michael and All Angels, St. Mary Mother of Our Lord, and many, many more.

Worship in Daily Life

How does one sanctify daily life? Christians, like Jews and Muslims, find the practice of daily prayer and study of the scriptures to be important in keeping a close relationship with God in ordinary life. And there are Christian rituals surrounding the main events and passages of life.

Prayer and Meditation The early Christians took over from Judaism the practice of daily prayers at certain times of the day. The apostles prayed at the third, sixth, and ninth hours (9 A.M., 12 noon, and 3 P.M.). Later, the tradition of daily prayers developed into a cycle of public worship throughout the day, the "Daily Office," followed especially in the monastic setting, with laypeople also attending. Prime, mattins, lauds, terce, sext, none, vespers, and compline are names that have been used for these short services throughout the day, which included psalms, hymns, scripture readings, and prayers. The churches of the Reformation simplified these services. Some churches abolished the daily office in favor of more informal devotions, whereas the Lutherans and Anglicans retained at least mattins (morning prayer) and vespers (evensong).

Apart from these daily services, which are little observed in modern hectic life, many Christian families have a time set aside daily, usually in the evening, for scripture reading and prayer. Groups may meet together occasionally for Bible study. Some Christians make the sign of the cross on themselves with a brief prayer upon rising in the morning and going to bed at night. Prayers of thanksgiving at mealtime are customary, but there are no prescribed dietary laws to follow as in Judaism. In times of sickness, there is intercession to God and perhaps a pastoral visit from a congregational leader who prays with the sick. In some denominations, Christians periodically confess their daily sins to a priest and receive forgiveness—confession (or penance) is one of the sacraments in some of the liturgical churches.

Rituals of the Passages of Life Whereas some Christians have taken over from the Jews the practice of circumcision of newborn male children, this does not have any special religious significance. The universally practiced rite of initiation into the Christian community is baptism, for male and female alike, and for most Christian denominations this occurs shortly after birth. Some Protestant denominations, especially those in the Baptist tradition, reserve baptism until the child is old enough to understand the meaning of this ritual. Baptism uses the universal water symbolism of cleansing and purifying. Most Christians believe the child is born with sin, like all humans, and the ritual of baptism signifies the washing away of sin through Christ's merit. The child is said to be "born again," having participated in the death and resurrection of Christ. Now the child is united with Christ and with Christ's body, the church, for the rest of life.

The ritual of washing in baptism may be done by complete immersion in water—a vivid experience of death and resurrection preferred by groups who practice adult baptism only—or by a symbolic washing with a small amount of water, the general custom for infant baptism. The baptizer reads about baptism from the New Testament and asks the child to profess the faith and vow to be faithful to Christ. In the case of infants, family and friends (godparents) speak on behalf of the infant, underscoring the communal character of this ritual. Administering the washing with water, the baptizer says, "I baptize you in the name of the Father, Son, and Holy Spirit." Some churches follow the early Christian practice of anointing with oil, and in the Eastern Orthodox churches the infant receives Holy Communion as a full member of the church.

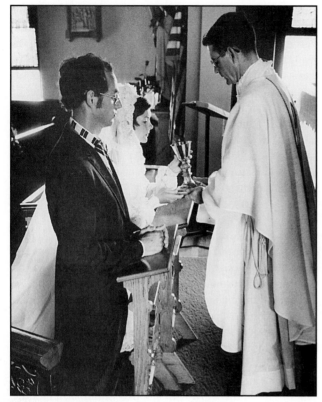

A Roman Catholic nuptial mass, with the bride and groom receiving the sacrament of the Eucharist.

The Western churches that baptize infants have established the practice of confirmation for both boys and girls, at an age roughly corresponding to puberty. This ritual, a sacrament in some churches, is seen as a confirmation of the vows that were made at baptism and an entrance into full membership in the church. It is thus a kind of passage to adulthood in the religious community. Confirmation is performed in a group before the congregation. The bishop or minister may lay hands on the head of each candidate or give the right hand of fellowship to symbolize full incorporation into the church. Confirmation, like bar mitzvah, is a time for family and friends to celebrate the new spiritual status of the youth.

Some Christian churches see marriage as a sacrament, but virtually all groups provide a ritual to accompany this important passage of life. In the history of Christianity, there has been some feeling that marriage is not as high a spiritual state as celibacy. But Christians are unanimous in considering marriage a great blessing from God, resulting in the family as the heart of the human community and the church. Marriage is considered a lifelong commitment of faithfulness to one's spouse, intended so by God.

The wedding ritual differs widely in the various churches. Usually performed in a church sanctuary, it is always a festive occasion for family and community. A traditional form of the ritual, followed by many (with modernizations), is that of the Anglican *Book of Common Prayer*. After scripture readings, songs, and prayer, the priest asks each,

> Wilt thou have this woman [man] to thy wedded wife [husband], to live together after God's ordinance in the holy estate of Matrimony? Wilt thou love her, comfort her, honour, and keep her, in sickness and in health; and, forsaking all other, keep thee only unto her, so long as ye both shall live?

Answering, "I will," both now give their troth to each other, holding their right hands together:

> I, _____, take thee, _____, to my wedded wife [husband], to have and to hold from this day forward, for better for worse, for richer for poorer, in sickness and in health, to love and to cherish [and to obey], till death us do part, according to God's holy ordinance; and thereto I plight thee my troth.

Finally the minister says,

> Those whom God hath joined together let no man put asunder. Forasmuch as _____ and _____ have consented together in holy wedlock, and have witnessed the same before God and this company, and thereto have given and pledged their troth to each other, and have declared the same by giving and receiving of a ring, and by joining of hands; I pronounce that they be man and wife together, In the Name of the Father, and of the Son, and of the Holy Ghost. Amen.

These pledges and vows of lifelong faithfulness and love are considered the heart of the wedding ritual. Many local customs attend the celebration, such as throwing rice on the newlyweds, giving gifts, and a joyous party in honor of the new family.

Death is considered by Christians as a passage to the life promised and won by Christ, so death rituals combine the sense of loss and sadness with the mood of joy and confidence. The reality of the saints—the faithful who have gone before—has always been strong in the Christian tradition, and a funeral is a time to commend the departed one to the company of saints awaiting the resurrection and eternal life in heaven. A funeral is a time to reflect on the brevity of life and the destiny that awaits all. It is a time to renew hope and confidence in God's mercy and promises. Johannes Brahms' musical composition *German Requiem* combines these two moods in a sublime way: There is the funeral march with its driving drumbeat to the text, "All flesh is grass"; and there is the moving chorale portrait of the heavenly dwelling place.

Like weddings, death rituals differ widely among various groups of Christians. For some, the sacrament of extreme unction—anointing the dying person with oil—is practiced; for others, prayer accompanies the passage into death. The church bell tolls mournfully, informing the congregation of the death. Chosen mourners carry the body in a casket into the church for a service of scripture reading and prayer. The procession then goes to the church cemetery, where the body is placed in the grave in the earth. Throwing earth upon the casket, the priest may say,

> Forasmuch as it hath pleased Almighty God of his great mercy to take unto himself the soul of our dear brother [sister] here departed: we therefore commit his body to the ground; earth to earth, ashes to ashes, dust to dust; in sure and certain hope of the Resurrection to eternal life, through our Lord Jesus Christ; who shall change our vile body, that it may be like unto his glorious body, according to the mighty working, whereby he is able to subdue all things to himself.
>
> *(Book of Common Prayer)*

Whereas no specific periods of mourning are followed, most Christians remember the dead in various ways, such as lighting a candle or saying prayers on their behalf.

Art in Christian Worship and Ritual

Fundamental to Christian teaching, in contrast to Judaism and Islam, is the incarnation: God became human; the divine is manifested within the created world. Thus the Christian aesthetic sense has generally encouraged full use of all the arts in the worship of God: sculpture and painting, architecture, music, literature, poetry, drama, and dance.

It is true that Christians inherited the Jewish aesthetic sense, including the prohibition of images, and for the first centuries Christians continued the Jewish emphasis on the word rather than on pictorial art. As Christianity spread throughout the Roman Empire, however, the tradition of representational art developed, especially for portraying Jesus and the saints. Christian iconography was preoccupied with the person and role of Jesus and his followers, portraying Jesus both as the earthly founder of the church and as the heavenly savior. Many symbolic expressions developed, such as portraying Jesus as the Good Shepherd. In the different cultural areas and times, portrayals of Jesus and the saints have taken many different styles. Whereas in the early centuries the crucifixion scene seems to have been avoided, later this became a central theme of Christian art, presenting both the victorious Christ on the cross and, especially in the medieval period, the suffering savior.

In the eighth century, there was a serious controversy regarding the use of icons—flat, two-dimensioned paintings of the saints. Some felt these icons were receiving too much worship and miraculous powers were being attributed to them. But a theology of icons developed and won the day: since Christ consented to become a man, theologians argued, it is permissible to portray Christ in visible human form. Artists in the Middle Ages and the Renaissance created countless paintings and sculptures with Christian themes, some to be used on altars in churches. In keeping with the medieval trend toward devotionalism, painting expressed warm, loving attitudes toward Christ and the saints. In the Renaissance period, monumental and vigorous expressions of humanity's relationship to God were painted. For example, Michelangelo's paintings on the ceiling of the Sistine Chapel focus on God reaching forth the gift of life to Adam; Leonardo da Vinci's *The Last Supper* shows Christ as master surrounded by his disciples, portrayed as real human personalities.

But in Reformation times an iconoclastic movement developed among the more radical reformers, who reacted against "papist" imagery and ritual, destroying iconographic imagery and liturgical furnishing. They established the tradition in Reformed and Baptist churches of little art, ornamentation, and liturgy. The liturgical churches have continued the tradition of using all the arts, with color, ornamentation, paintings, statues, poetic liturgies, music, and the like.

Religious drama in the Christian tradition grew from the liturgical mass, which itself was presented as a kind of historical drama. Important for the education and edification of the common people were the mystery and morality plays put on in the Middle Ages. The literary arts in general flourished in Christians circles, based on the biblical narratives and poetry as the great spiritual source and literary model. Widely influential has been *The Divine Comedy* by Dante (1265–1321), in which Dante guides the reader through Hell, Purgatory, the earthly paradise, the Limbo of good pagans, and finally Heaven. Later the epic *Paradise Lost* by Milton (1608–1674) presents the Christian universe in Puritan tones. Writers like William Blake, W.H. Auden, Fyodor Dostoevsky, Emily Dickinson, Flannery O'Connor, and many more, in poetry, novels, and dramas, have given artistic expression to Christian themes, ideas, and values.

The art of music has always played a great role in most parts of the Christian church. Medieval plainsong chants developed into Renaissance polyphonic masses, in the hands of composers like Palestrina and Gabrieli. In the baroque era came the great oratorios and chorales of composers like Handel, J.S. Bach, and many others. Musical expressions have continued in Christian communities with great variety up to the modern-day folk masses and various musical forms in the different non-Western cultures. Christian musical artists have excelled in cultivating the possibilities of music as artistic expression of Christian theology and inspiration for faith and life.

Christian architecture, influenced by the synagogue, started with house churches and developed into the basilica, a structure that set aside sacred space with the altar, the symbol of Christ, as the center of action. In the medieval period, cathedrals developed where bishops presided with many priests and monks. There would be rood screens fencing off the area for the monks to chant the daily offices, together with many altars for celebrating daily masses. Particularly expressive of Christian medieval ideas is the Gothic cathedral, soaring to heaven but planted on earth. With its ribbed vaulting, pointed arches, and flying buttresses, the gothic cathedral gives a strong sense of lightness and soaring spaces; the overall effect is to express verticality with a sense of heavenward movement. The baroque cathedral became a kind of divine theater, with a light and airy quality, giving the worshipers a sense of being in contact with heaven above. Eastern Orthodox Christians have favored the dome as a representation of heaven, with space radiating downward to the earth, giving architectural expression to the incarnation.

In the Protestant Reformation, the reformers destroyed the rood screens and brought the pulpit to the center, or they put the pulpit, altar, and baptismal font together at the east end, creating space in which all worshipers present could hear and see all that goes on, focused on the word of God.

THE LIFE OF LOVE: SOCIETY AND ETHICS

How should we live? To be a Christian means to live as befits a member of the Christian church, the new "people of God" gathered around the worship of Jesus Christ, living the life of love as Jesus lived.

The Society of the Church

The Greek word for church is *ekklesia*, from the word meaning "called out." The church is made up of the people "called out" by the Spirit of God to form the new people of God in fulfillment of God's plan of salvation. Christians think of the church as the continuation of the chosen people of God, gathered around the Christ who is the fulfillment of God's whole design. Peter uses many Old Testament images of the people of Israel to describe this new people of God:

> For you are a chosen family, a royal priesthood, a holy nation, and a people of God's possession, that you should proclaim the triumphs of the one who has called you out of darkness into his wondrous light. Once you were no people, but you are now the people of God. You were outside his mercy once, but now you have received his mercy.
>
> (*I Peter* 2:9–10)

According to the Christian perspective, once the people of God were the Jewish people with whom God covenanted, and the gentiles were on the outside. But now in Christ, gentiles are also made a part of God's family, the church.

Who Makes Up the Church?   The church is not like other voluntary human societies that people choose to join or not to join. It is not a club or interest group. The church exists wherever there are believers in Christ who share their commitment to Christ and live Christian lives. Jesus said, "Wherever two or three are gathered together in my name, I am there in the midst of them" (*Matthew* 18:20). That means that the church is constituted by the worship of Christ.

How does one become a part of this new people of God? One does not become a Christian by birth. Rather, one chooses to belong by believing and being baptized. Of course, being born into a Christian family is an important way in which the family of God continues. Most Christians practice infant baptism as a sign that children as well as the rest of the family share in the family of God. A significant number of Christians prefer to wait until the children are old enough to choose for themselves to be baptized. In either case, the emphasis is on faith and choice. A person baptized as an infant chooses to remain in that baptismal identity. He or she is instructed and guided in faith and life and typically reaffirms the baptismal identity in the ritual of confirmation when grown up. An adult who has not been a part of the church may come to believe in Christ, and the profession of faith and reception of baptism testify that he or she has been called by the Spirit to be part of the new people of God.

Churches, Congregations, Ministry The catholic (universal) church, like Christ, is incarnated; it is embodied in concrete form in Christian communities or "churches" everywhere on earth. Although there were periods in earlier church history when many Christians were under one ecclesiastical structure, in modern times there are numerous world churches, state churches, denominations, and sects that make up the body of Christ. The body of Christ, Christians believe, must be present in concrete form within the diverse cultures and ethnic groups of the world. In this real, living church of Christ, there sometimes appears to be little unity, and many Christians are troubled by these divisions. One of the most significant developments today is the ecumenical movement, in which Christians are trying to make real the unity of the whole *oikumene* (world) of diverse Christian communities.

On the local level, Christians typically gather together into communities called congregations, centering usually in a church building in which the believers assemble for worship on Sundays and other important times. Congregations in turn are usually associated together in larger structures, whether that is a worldwide organization like the Roman Catholic church, a state organization like the Anglican church of England, a denomination like the Methodist church in the United States, or the like. For all the trauma caused by competing associations of Christians, the various

Many Protestant denominations ordain women as ministers. (Courtesy of Pastor Jean Holmes, Nauraushaun Presbyterian Church, Pearl River, NY)

churches and denominations of the world do represent the concrete, human embodiment of the universal church, the body of Christ.

Christians as Christ's presence in the world share in common the responsibility for the ministry of the gospel and the worship of God. In order to provide for the ongoing function of the ministry of preaching the word and celebrating the rituals, most Christians believe that Christ instituted a "ministry" within the church to guide and carry out this work for the benefit of all. In the early Christian church, a three-part ministry developed. A bishop was appointed for each Christian community, having responsibility for the ministry of worship and for serving the well-being of the believers. As the communities grew, the responsibility for worship was entrusted to presbyters (elders or priests), and the responsibility for service and caring for the family of believers was given over to deacons.

Today the various Christian communities have many versions of this ministry of bishop, priest, and deacon, ordained to lead and guide the family of believers in their worship of Christ and their ministry to the world. One of the stumbling blocks to the unification of the church is the great variety of understandings and practices related to the ordained ministry. Some churches, like the Roman Catholic and the Anglican church, have hierarchically structured church leadership, starting with the pope or the archbishop of Canterbury and moving down to the levels of parish priests. Other churches, like the Southern Baptists or the Quakers, operate with a church polity from below, with each congregation of believers responsible for designating leaders in the ministry of the church. Many of the church bodies, such as Methodists, Presbyterians, Lutherans, and the United Church of Christ, have begun the practice of ordaining women to all the offices of the ministry. But others, such as the Roman Catholic and Orthodox churches, have strongly resisted this inclusion of women within the ordained ministry.

Women in Religious Leadership   The checkered portrait of women in the history of Christianity is reflected in the disagreement among some denominations today about ordaining women to full ministry. The traditional Christian views about the role of women have been strongly influenced first of all by Jewish culture (there were no women among Jesus' twelve disciples). Extremely influential has been the interpretation of the creation and fall story in *I Timothy* 2:11–14 (probably written by a disciple of Paul):

> A woman should learn in silence with due submission. I do not permit a woman to teach or to have authority over men; she should keep silent. For Adam was created first, then Eve; and it was not Adam who was deceived, but the woman who, being led into deception, became a transgressor.

The arguments here—that the man was created first in the order of creation and should therefore be dominant, that the woman was the one who first fell into sin, and the conclusion that women should not teach men but should remain silent in the church—have characterized the view of women in the Christian church up to modern times. The patriarchal struc-

ture of the early Christian society is seen in the judgment of early theologians that flesh and desire were especially associated with women's sensuality, leading to the view that virginity and celibacy are superior to married life. Women were often described in despicable terms as temptresses, the "gateway of the devil," storehouses of filth and evil.

Like men, women too consecrated themselves to God by entering the monastic life, but even there they were under the rule of men—the male members of the order, the local bishop, the patriarch or pope. Throughout the medieval period, most women in Christian communities had few rights, found their role only in the home, and received no formal education. There were strong women—probably more than we know—who broke out of these restraints, but such women could be stigmatized and even burned as witches. Influenced by the church's theology about women, Western societies, even those developing modern democratic or representative governments (e.g., the U.S. Constitution, the French Declaration of Human Rights) still subordinated women to men. Suffrage for women in Christian churches and in Christian nations is a very recent development.

Yet feminist biblical scholars and theologians today (both women and men) have recovered many positive images of women already in the scriptures. The creation story in Genesis actually reflects a mutuality and equality of men and women, many scholars have pointed out. God created humans in God's own image, "male and female God created them" (*Genesis* 1:27). Jesus showed a high positive regard for women and for their abilities and religious capacities. He had warm relations with women such as Mary and Martha, and he assumed that women—even those with reputations as prostitutes—could learn and thus be among his disciples (see, for example, *John* 11:5ff.; *Luke* 7:37–50). And Paul's pronouncement of equality is powerful: "There is neither Jew nor Greek, there is neither slave nor freeperson, there is neither male nor female; for all of you are one in Christ Jesus" (*Galatians* 3:28). Many women were active in leadership roles in the early church. For example, Priscilla is frequently mentioned as equally active with her husband Aquila in missionary travels, in teaching the way of God, even in "risking their necks" for Paul's life (*Acts* 18:1–3, 18, 26; *Romans* 16:3). Monica, mother of St. Augustine, was known widely for her piety and prayers, but also for her wisdom and mystical experiences. In fact, a great many women in the medieval period became renowned for their wisdom, their mystical experiences, and their activities to help the poor and suffering—earlier we noted Catherine of Siena and Teresa of Avila.

Drawing on images and models such as these, today there are many strong, capable Christian women as leaders, ministers, theologians, even bishops in some church bodies. Feminist theologians emphasize not only women's equality in value and competency with men, but they also explore women's ways of knowing and experiencing as a resource in the ongoing need to rethink and reconstruct theology to meet the needs of Christians and the world today.[1] Thus more emphasis is given to the feminine qualities of God, to inclusive language in worship, to metaphors and practices that emphasize mutuality, personhood, and community rather than conflict, hierarchy, and individuality. "Feminist theology" remains controversial in some Christian circles, but to many Christians it is bringing dramatic new breakthroughs in understanding the Christian gospel for these times.

Sanctification of Life in Ethics

How should we live? Christians, like Jews and Muslims, believe that all of life should be worship of God, whether these are acts of love for God expressed in ritual and prayer or acts of love toward others. In understanding how to live the life of love, Christians look to the Ten Commandments and especially to Jesus' new commandment of love. However, Christians do not live the ethical life because it is "commanded." Rather, it is because of love and gratitude to God. Faith and the experience of forgiveness create a new being in place of the old. The new person lives in union with Christ. "It is no longer I who live but Christ who lives in me," Paul said (*Galatians* 2:20). Since the springs of motivation are touched by Christ, ethical behavior is not so much a discipline leading *to* transformation as an expression *of* transformation.

Love Fulfilling Law in Liberty　　From earliest times in the Christian tradition, there has been considerable thinking about the basis of ethical actions. Certainly the early Christians agreed that the heart of Jesus' ethical teaching was love. But how does one put that love into action? The discussion was at first (and still is, for that matter) couched

in terms of law versus liberty. Should we do the right, loving things in life because it is God's will (law)? Or, as forgiven and restored children of God, are we free to do what we ourselves find to be best and most loving (liberty)?

Since the first Christians were Jews, it was natural that they held the Jewish Torah in high esteem as the great gift of God. So, as they sought guidance in how to love God and their neighbors, they turned to the commandments given by God. Surely the Torah would provide the best definition of God's will of love, for God is the supreme evaluator of good and evil. Following God's law without question is the sure guide to the loving ethical life, without falling into rationalized, self-serving decisions about how to act.

Whereas this legalistic approach to ethics has much merit in terms of order and confidence, there are drawbacks, as Christians discovered. As new situations arise, it is not always clear what the law would have one do, especially since Christians look to the New Testament more directly than to the Old Testament for ethical guidance. Often a person has either to rely on the authority of the church to tell what one should do, or to resort to arbitrary interpretations of the law. God's law prohibits all killing, but what about state-ordered killing (war or capital punishment)? Are women permitted to be priests and ministers or not? What about abortion? Christians disagree on what God's law actually says about such matters. But the biggest weakness in the legalistic approach is the feeling that, once one has done what the law stipulates, he or she has fulfilled God's will of love. We keep the Ten Commandments—so why should we worry about housing discrimination or people starving?

In counteracting notions of Jewish Christians about the necessity for Christians to keep the Torah, Paul placed a great stress on freedom: "Christ has freed us for freedom; stand firm, then, and do not again submit to a yoke of slavery" (*Galatians* 5:1). Paul was concerned first of all about faith rather than works of the law as the basis for salvation. But Christians have applied this "freedom" approach to the ethics of love also. Christ has abolished the law. Love cannot be coerced, love must be freely given. Since we have been redeemed and made new creatures, with Christ living in us, we should rely on that motivation to love freely and truly. Those who stress the freedom of love often quote Augustine's saying, "Love, and do what you will. . . . Let love's root be within you, and from that root nothing but good can spring."[2] If one truly loves God, one's love will always find the best way to act toward others also.

This "freedom" ethical approach brings out important dimensions of Christian love, especially in contrast to the legalistic approach. But there are serious drawbacks here as well. In some early Christian congregations, there arose "antinomians" (people against the law), who taught that, since Christ has abolished the law, Christians are free to do whatever they please. Some held that Christians have been perfected by Christ and thus can do no wrong; others held that, since God forgives all sins through Christ, it doesn't matter that one sins. In either view, freedom is the style and law is out as a guide to love. But it quickly became clear to Paul—as it has been to Christians ever since—that total liberty as a moral principle easily degenerates into selfish license and some very unloving behavior toward others.

Paul said there is "a more excellent way" (*I Corinthians* 12:31), the way of love as a transformation of both law and liberty. "Indeed, love is the fulfilling of the law," Paul wrote (*Romans* 13:10), showing that God's will as revealed in the law is brought to fulfillment through the practice of love. The law of God is not just a written code, to be fulfilled by slavish adherence to all its details. It is a revelation of God's fundamental intention for humans. Paul wrote, "All the law is fulfilled in one word, in this: 'You shall love your neighbor as yourself'" (*Galatians* 5:14). This means freedom from the literal form of the law, but not freedom to do whatever one pleases. People need God's will for guidance—with the understanding that loving and caring for the neighbor is what God's will is all about. As to who the neighbor is, Jesus himself had much to say on that, identifying the neighbor as anyone in need: the sick, prisoners, those hungry and thirsty, strangers, and orphans. Whatever we do in caring for the least of these our brethren, Jesus tells us, we do for him (*Matthew* 25:40).

So law is transformed by love in freedom, and freedom is transformed by love in God's will (law) of caring for the neighbor. With the Corinthian congregation, Paul took up a specific question of Christian freedom, namely, whether it is lawful for Christians to eat food that has been sacrificed to idols. His answer sums up the relation between law, liberty, and love: "All things are allowed, but not all things are beneficial. All things are allowed, but not all things build others up. No one should seek his own good but that of the other" (*I Corinthians* 10:23–24). On the one hand, Christians

are free to follow their own consciences; on the other hand, the welfare of their neighbors is dear to God. Christian love is the way to bring both together in an ethical Christian life.

One more word from Paul: "For you, brethren, were called to freedom; only do not use your freedom as an occasion for the flesh, but through love be servants of one another" (*Galatians* 5:13). In love, Christians are truly free and truly servants. How can one be free and slave at the same time? It is through love. Of course, there are different kinds of love. What is meant here is God's kind of love shown in Christ, that is, *agape,* which is unconditional, nondiscriminatory, self-giving love. Other kinds of love—important for full human life—are based on mutual friendship *(philia)* or passionate attraction *(eros).* But agape is love with no strings attached, based in God's grace for all. Friendship and passionate love certainly have their place in Christian ethics; but it is in showing God's kind of love, agape, that Christians can both be free and be servants of all.

Justice and Mercy Toward One's Neighbor   The ethic of love is not just a theory but a matter of practical action. How do I love my neighbor as myself? Does loving mean never punishing but always forgiving? In this imperfect world with evils in every choice, don't we always wind up doing some harm as we try to do the good? Questions like these abound as Christians attempt to live real life in love. From the many commandments in the Torah, Christians have singled out especially the so-called "Ten Commandments" as an indication of how love works in action. Interpreting the Ten Commandments through the perspective of the New Testament, Christians see that these commandments provide the ideal combination of both God's justice and God's mercy. There must be justice in order for all God's creatures to live with integrity and value; there must be mercy in order that the failures of our human freedom might be transformed.

Taken from *Exodus* 20, in the traditional numbering used in some Christian churches (e.g., in the *Book of Common Prayer*), these are the Ten Commandments:

1 You shall have no other gods before me.

2 You shall not make for yourselves any graven image.

3 You shall not take the name of the Lord your God in vain.

Mother Teresa, champion of the poor in India and winner of the Nobel Peace Prize, talks with a small boy after church services in San Francisco.

4 Remember the Sabbath day, to keep it holy.

5 Honor your father and your mother.

6 You shall not kill.

7 You shall not commit adultery.

8 You shall not steal.

9 You shall not bear false witness against your neighbor.

10 You shall not covet your neighbor's house; you shall not covet your neighbor's wife, or his manservant, or

his maidservant, or his ox, or his ass, or anything that is his.

These Ten Commandments may be divided into two "tables": the first four have to do primarily with loving God, and the last six have to do with loving one's neighbor. But, as has often been pointed out, keeping the first four requires loving one's neighbor—for we live in human communities, not as solitary individuals. And, of course, keeping the last six requires loving God. Another important aspect of these Ten Commandments is that each has a positive as well as negative quality. To have God alone as the center and source of life (first commandment) means to treat all other people as creatures loved by God. Not to steal and not to kill require promoting the just wealth and the well-being of others. In this way, the Ten Commandments become for Christians not just a law code but a basic guide to the freedom and service of Christian love.

In practice, Christians do not always agree about personal ethical decisions. Christian love does not translate directly and unequivocally into positions on abortion, taxes, homosexuality, warfare, or capitalism, and faithful Christians often disagree on such questions. But some traditional Christian ethical positions might be briefly sketched out.

Christians have always viewed marriage—and thus human sexuality—as one of God's great gifts, and some Christians even consider marriage a sacrament. There has been a certain tendency to view sexual passion itself as tainted by the fall into sin, and thus arose the Christian tradition of celibacy as a higher spiritual life. Most Christians feel, however, that sex within marriage is a healthful, positive human activity. It provides for procreation and thus creates the family, and it gives love and companionship. Some churches, it is true, have held that the only purpose of sex in marriage is for procreation.

One thing the great majority of Christians agree on is that marriage should be monogamous: God intends one woman and one man to be wed for life as the best way of fulfilling the divine loving design. As for the other questions, in modern times there tends to be a general division between "liberal" and "conservative" positions on questions of marital and sexual ethics. Such a division often exists even within the same denomination. One position would hold that premarital sex, abortion, divorce, and homosexuality, for example, are always absolutely wrong. The other position would find the same situations to be wrong or right depending on whether caring love is expressed within them.

Christians agree on the value and dignity of human life, labor, and happiness. Therefore, private property and freedom to accumulate wealth and possessions have generally been supported by Christians. There is a certain suspicion about unbridled human greed and a concern to ensure fairness and equal opportunity for the downtrodden in the face of human selfish competition. Some have gone to vows of poverty; others have advocated a kind of socialism as the ideal type of society. There are indeed Christian socialists as well as Christian capitalists.

The Christian ethic of love from the very first created an attitude of pacifism toward violence and war. Jesus' own example and teaching lent strong support for this: "If any one strikes you on the cheek, offer him the other one also" (*Luke* 6:29), "love your enemies" (*Luke* 6:35), and so forth. Christian pacifism was the rule for the first centuries, until the Roman Empire became Christian and the need arose for Christian political leaders to take responsibility for maintaining order and justice in society. At that point, the doctrine of the "just war" was developed by theologians like Augustine. In this theory, Christian participation in violence or war is held to be justified if it meets certain requirements. The war must be entered into only as a last resort, for a just cause of defense or protection, declared by a lawful authority, and with a reasonable prospect of success. The war must be conducted justly without excess violence or harming of noncombatants, the means used must be proportional to the end result, and mercy must be shown to the vanquished. Throughout the medieval period and until recently, most Christian denominations have supported the basic outline of the just war theory, although groups like the Mennonites and the Quakers developed a strong position of nonviolence and pacifism.

In the face of modern warfare, however, many Christians find the whole idea of a "just war" to be untenable, since the necessary requirements could never be met, certainly not in nuclear warfare. So Christian churches are struggling anew with the problem of the love ethic: how to establish both justice and mercy in the volatile world of today, with the enormous problems of nation-states and huge arsenals. Some still advocate a kind of just security ethic, reasoning that the welfare of the human race depends on a balance of military power in the world. Other Christians are finding new meaning in pacifism, not as a passive resignation but as active nonviolent pursuit of justice and peace. As a result, many Christians are active in peace movements in the East and in the West.

Responsibility and Mission in the World

The Christian church is made up of real communities of Christians throughout the world. But just as the Jewish people do, so also these people of God transcend particular space and time. The church is "catholic," that is, universal, extended through all the world and all time, past, present, and future. It represents all humankind. At the same time, Christians believe the church is one, just as Christ is one. In spite of various divisions, in spite of different races and nationalities, all believers in Christ are united in one family of God.

A favorite image used by the New Testament writers to refer to the church is "the body of Christ." This emphasizes the oneness of the church, even though it encompasses a great variety of Christians. Just as a person's body has many members that work together for the good of the one body, so the diverse communities of Christians all live and work for the oneness and well-being of the body of Christ (*Romans* 12:4–5).

To say the church is the body of Christ is also to evoke the idea that Christ is still present in the world in this "body." All those who make up the church are Christ's ongoing presence within the world. Jesus commissioned his disciples: "Peace be to you! As the Father has sent me, so send I you" (*John* 20:21). In this way, the church is defined by its role or mission—to be about loving, healing, forgiving, and reconciling the peoples of the world by being the continuing presence of Jesus Christ in the midst of human society. Generally, Christians speak of this mission both as a social responsibility and as a saving mission: both seeking the welfare of the world's people and bringing the saving gospel of Christ to them so they can believe and share the Christian hope.

In the World But Not of the World   The world is God's good world, but it is also a fallen world, and therefore participation in the life of the world is an ambiguous thing.

Jesus left Christians with a rule of thumb: They should be *in* the world but not *of* the world (*John* 17:11, 16). Being of the world, in the language of the times, meant to have the fallen, lust-driven world as one's source of being. Christians, rather, are born of the Spirit. Yet they are to be in the world, for it is still the world that God has redeemed, and Christians are to continue the presence of Christ in the world for that purpose.

Christians agree on the mission to bring the gospel to the world. But what does this mean in relation to the cultural and societal existence of people? What about government, economics, art and literature, oppression, poverty, and all the rest? Christians have not completely agreed on what the church's responsibility is toward the concrete problems and possibilities of this world. For some Christians, the only possibility is total withdrawal and renunciation of the world as hopelessly evil. For others, the coming of God's kingdom is understood to be identical with social improvement and the perfecting of this world's potentials. Both of these are radical positions: either Christianity is in total opposition to this world's culture or it is totally identical with the best of it. Most Christians have not accepted either of these radical positions but have sought some middle ground to live out the role of being in but not of the world.

Among these various approaches, a dualist view and a transformationist view have been particularly dominant. The dualist view would understand this world to be primarily a preparation for the next, with the conclusion that Christians have no special role to play in the social, political, economic, and cultural arenas. As human beings, of course, Christians should be good citizens and work to the extent of their abilities for the betterment of life. But Christ came, they say, not as a social worker but as the savior. Therefore the church's mission is not primarily to change the effects of original sin (poverty, oppression, and violence) but to bring people to eternal salvation.

The transformationist approach sees things a bit differently. To be sent as Christ was sent means being involved in loving one's neighbors, easing people's sufferings, and actively seeking to transform the structures that control this world. This approach does not deny the fallenness of the world or the mission of spiritual salvation. But God is still active in the creation. If Jesus Christ is indeed the first fruits of the new creation, and Christians are his presence in the world, then it is a high priority for Christians to be involved in whatever it takes to transform human society and culture so that it more completely reflects God's will and design. Motivated by this vision, many Christians of today are actively involved in movements of liberation, peacemaking, betterment of education and the arts, enhancing the dignity of women and minorities, and the like.

Mission to the World   The identity of the Christian church has been deeply shaped by the charge that Christ gave to his disciples before his ascension into heaven:

> Go forth and make disciples of all the nations, baptizing them in the name of the Father and of the Son and of the Holy Spirit, teaching them to observe all that I have commanded you. And, lo, I am with you always, until the end of the age.

(*Matthew* 28:19–20)

The missionary emphasis in the "great commission" is not just on being in the world or bettering the world, but teaching and making disciples of all peoples. So evangelism, sharing the good news of Christ in order to bring others to faith in Christ, has always been a central activity of Christians.

Carrying out this mission of witnessing has had its high and low points in the history of the church. Many early Christians traveled widely, spent their lives learning new cultures, debated and argued, performed great works of love, and even sacrificed their lives in witnessing the good news of Christ. After Christianity became dominant in the Roman Empire, missionary activity tended to become tied to imperialistic goals, and that has been a special burden for the Christian mission down to the present century. The need to integrate Christian witnessing with an attitude that values and respects those of other religions has become much more urgent in the modern global village. Many Christians today are rediscovering that, in its origins, Christianity was a religion of humility and love. Being Christ's presence in the world means sharing one's deepest beliefs and hopes with others, but it also means listening to them and learning from them in dialogue.

Discussion Questions

1   What are main elements of the Sunday worship service? What differences might there be between liturgical and nonliturgical churches?

2   What are "sacraments"? Discuss the main sacraments in the liturgical churches.

3   Describe the main movement of Christian festivals throughout the year, especially the Advent-Christmas-Epiphany season and the Lent-Easter season.

4   Discuss the rituals associated with the main passages of life for Christians.

5   How does the Christian emphasis on God's incarnation relate to Christian artistic expression? What arts seem important for Christians?

6   Discuss the meaning of the "church." How can it be both universal and local, both one and many?

7   Discuss the role of women in Christian religious leadership, both historically and in the present.

8   What is the relationship between law, freedom, and love in Christian ethics? How might these elements come into play in difficult ethical decisions today?

9   Is there a Christian position on ethical issues such as pre-marital sex, abortion, and homosexuality? Explain why or why not.

10   Pacifism has been an important tradition from earliest times in Christianity—why? What is meant by the "just war" doctrine? What is the stand of major church groups today?

11   What are some main Christian attitudes toward involvement in social concerns?

CHAPTER 12

Muslim Sacred Story and Historical Context

For about one-fifth of the people of the world today, personal identity is somehow connected with being **Muslim.** And to be Muslim means to find one's identity in the sacred story of the prophet Muhammad, the giving of the **Quran,** and the founding of the worldwide Islamic community, the **ummah.** Like Jews and Christians, Muslims also look to a historical figure who is the founder of their religion. But Muhammad is the founder in a different way than either Moses or Jesus were founders. Moses transmitted God's Torah—but he died before entering the promised land and thus could not himself put the laws into practice in the life of the nation of Israel. Jesus transmitted God's revelation, but more importantly, he himself became God's revelation; he died before there was a Christian church, and he is worshiped as the divine Lord. Muhammad also transmitted God's revelation. But he himself also founded the Muslim community and put the laws of the revelation into total effect in the lives of the people. To Muslims, Muhammad is the final agent of God's revelation, the seal of the prophets. And the story of the Muslims is focused on the miracle of that revelation through Muhammad and the establishing of the community of Islam based on God's revelation.

THE STORY OF THE PROPHET AND THE BOOK

The Jewish scriptures and the Christian scriptures contain much material about Moses and Jesus, as well as narratives about the other important founders and events. In con-

trast, the Muslim scripture, the *Holy Quran,* is predominantly God's message to humans and thus contains very little narration about Muhammad and the events that led to the founding of Islam. Whereas some of the suras of the Quran can be placed in the context of events in Muhammad's life, for the most part the Muslim story of the founding of Islam relies on reports *(hadiths)* from Muhammad's companions, material that has become known as the **Hadith.** Based on material from the Hadith, there are many early Muslim biographies of Muhammad's life; the best known is by Ibn Ishaq[1] in the middle of the eighth century C.E., about 120 years after Muhammad's death.

The Times Before Muhammad

As in the case of Christianity, the Islamic sacred history links itself clearly with the religions that preceded it, Judaism and Christianity. Muhammad, of course, was not a Jew or a Christian, but the Muslim tradition considers him to be the legitimate successor of and fulfillment of the founders of both previous religions. The Muslim story joins the Jewish and Christian stories in telling of God's work: God created the world and Adam and Eve, and from them all peoples. God sent **prophets** such as Abraham, Moses, and David to guide humankind. And God worked through Mary and made her son Jesus a great prophet. Of course, the Muslim story interprets these events and prophets somewhat differently than do the Jewish and Christian stories, but it is important that the link is made. The revelation in Islam is the fulfillment and the end of the

Bedouin in the Arabian desert pause for the ritual of prayer to Allah.

revelations that God has been giving since Adam and the beginning of the human race.

The Prophet Abraham   One specific link with the past religious history is of particular significance for the Muslim story: Muslims are not Jewish, but Abraham is also their ancestor. Abraham, the Quran says, lived before there was a Jewish or Christian religion; he surrendered himself to God in practicing the pure religion, the same revelation that God gave to all the prophets and to Muhammad. Abraham was the father of both Isaac, who was the ancestor of the Jews, and **Ishmael,** who became the ancestor of the Muslims. Ishmael was actually the firstborn of Abraham; in her barrenness, Abraham's wife Sarah gave her maid **Hagar** to Abraham for a wife, and Abraham had Ishmael by her. When God asked Abraham to sacrifice his son Ishmael, he proved faithful; both he and his son submitted to God, and God blessed them (*Quran* 37:103). Abraham practiced the true religion of Islam (*islam* means "submission" to God) and thus he was a muslim (submitter).

Muslim tradition says that, when Sarah forced Abraham to send Hagar and Ishmael away, Abraham brought them to Mecca and later visited Ishmael there. According to the Quran, God commanded Abraham and Ishmael to purify God's house in Mecca, the **Ka'bah,** which had been destroyed

by the flood. So Abraham and Ishmael submitted to God and rebuilt the house, purifying it and making it a refuge and a place of pilgrimage (2:124–127). The stone on which Abraham stood is still seen in the great mosque at Mecca, a constant reminder to pilgrims that Islam continues the pure religion of Abraham the muslim. The Quran states that Abraham prayed, "My Lord, make this land secure, and turn me and my sons away from serving idols. . . . Our Lord, I have made some of my seed to dwell in a valley where is no sown land by Thy Holy House; Our Lord, let them perform the prayer" (14:35–37).[2]

Abraham and Ishmael prayed that **Allah** would raise up a messenger in the midst of their descendants who would declare God's revelations to them and instruct them in the scriptures and in wisdom (2:129). Thus it was among the descendants of Abraham and Ishmael in Mecca that the pure worship of the one God was preserved, and, when it was forgotten, from their midst God raised up a new prophet and a new community of Muslims.

The Times of Ignorance   According to the Muslim story, the world of 1,500 years ago had become exceedingly dark, and humanity was steeped in ignorance and superstition. The religions revealed through Moses and Jesus, though they had originally been pure Islam, had been distorted by Jews and Christians. A new religion was needed that would be for the whole human race. At such a crucial stage of human civilization, God raised up a prophet in Arabia for the whole world. The religion God gave him to propagate was Islam, like all the prophets before; but now it was in the form of a complete and full-fledged system, covering all aspects of human life.

Arabia was the best-suited country for the birth of the much-needed world religion, according to the Muslim story. It was situated right between two great civilizations, the Byzantine and the Persian empires, and the Arabs were a fresh and energetic people, not affected by the artificial and decadent social systems of the great civilizations. And their language was the human language most suited to express the high ideals and subtle aspects of divine knowledge, the one that could most powerfully move humans to submit to God. These desert people had developed important ethical values and virtues, such as loyalty, bravery, the art of poetry, and a pervading sense of hospitality and generosity.

But the people of Arabia were still in deep spiritual darkness. As there was no unified government, each tribe was an independent unit and a law unto itself. Life was violent, murder and robbery were common, and the most trivial incidents often set off prolonged blood wars between the tribes. Their ignorance extended to morality; they indulged in adultery, gambling, and drinking. Because daughters were considered a burden, they even practiced infanticide of infant daughters.

Although they had a vague idea that Abraham and Ishmael were their forefathers, the people of Arabia knew little about the teaching of the prophets of old. The Jews and Christians who lived in Arabia had passed on some of their teachings, but their ideas about the prophets were distorted and filled with figments of their own imagination. The Arabs worshiped many gods and divine forces. Trees and springs were venerated; sacred stones were rubbed or kissed to derive power from them; other spirits of the desert and the oasis played important roles. There was the high God called Al-Lah (the God) who was thought to be creator of the world. There were also three special goddesses spoken of as the daughters of Al-Lah: Al-Lat, a mother goddess associated with the moon; Al-'Uzza, the goddess of the planet Venus; and the mysterious goddess of fate called Manat. These three goddesses are mentioned in the Quran (53:19–20). Al-'Uzza in particular was worshiped by sacrifice (perhaps human sacrifice), and she was associated with stone pillars, symbolic of generative power. There were shrines for these gods and goddesses in various places.

The city of Mecca was a special sacred area, with its ancient shrine called the Ka'bah (which contained many images of gods), a sacred well called Zamzam, two holy mountains, and many sacred stones and pillars. During part of the year, a truce from fighting was observed by the desert tribes so that they could make pilgrimages to Mecca to worship the gods and goddesses and participate in festivals.

Rituals included circling around the Ka'bah (sometimes naked) and running back and forth between the two hills.

This was "the age of ignorance" (al-jahiliyyah), according to the Muslim story.

Muhammad as the Final Prophet

By the time Muhammad was born in 570 C.E., Mecca had become a cosmopolitan city. Some of the desert tribes had given up bedouin life and settled in Mecca, tending the sacred sites and participating in the active caravan trade that crisscrossed the desert. There was some rivalry among the tribes that made up the Quraysh, as these tribes of Mecca were called. Muhammad's grandfather 'Abd al-Muttalib of the Banu Hashim family seems to have been prominent among the Quraysh about the time Muhammad was born, but soon the **Umayyad** family came to dominate and the Hashim fell on bad times. 'Abd al-Muttalib had a number of wives from different clans who gave him ten sons and six daughters (Muhammad's father and his uncles and aunts). For his son 'Abdallah he obtained as a bride Amina bint Wahb, and their first and only child was Muhammad.

'Abdallah died either during Amina's pregnancy or shortly thereafter, leaving his wife impoverished. According to custom, the infant Muhammad was given over to a nurse from a bedouin clan so that he might be filled with the culture of the desert. He was reunited with his mother Amina when he was about five, but she died soon after. Muhammad, orphaned from both parents, lived with his grandfather, who died when he was eight, and then with his uncle Abu Talib, who now was the head of the Hashim clan. Abu Talib brought Muhammad up, at least once taking him along on a caravan trip to Syria. As a young man, Muhammad began to work for the caravan company of a wealthy widow named **Khadija**; she was impressed by him and soon they were married. He was twenty-five at the time, and she was fifteen years older; yet she still bore him six children, four daughters and two sons who died in infancy. Now Muhammad had become a secure, respected member of Meccan society.

The Light of Prophecy Rests on Muhammad   Such is the bare outline of the first part of Muhammad's life. But the Muslim sacred history makes it clear that, from the very beginning, God had designs for this man, and this is indicated by extraordinary events reported in the traditional biographies. For example, a story about Muhammad's conception relates that 'Abdallah had a white blaze between his eyes when he went in to Amina, but the light disappeared when Muhammad was conceived; the light of prophecy had been passed on in the conception of Muhammad. And while Amina was pregnant the light shone from her so that she could see as far as Syria. Another story tells that Muhammad saw two angels come to open his breast and clean his heart. Then they put him on scales, putting on the other side of the scales first ten of his people, then a hundred, then a thousand, and he outweighed them all. Then one angel said, "Leave him alone, for by God, if you weighed him against all his people he would outweigh them." Yet another story is told about a trip to Syria with his uncle, where a Christian monk named Bahira recognized Muhammad as the envoy of God, in accordance with the Christian writings. Bahira then examined Muhammad's back and found the seal of prophecy between his shoulders.[3] Thus even a learned holy man of the Christians recognized that Muhammad was to be the prophet of God.

As a young man, Muhammad showed himself to be honest, moral, and wise, even though he was unschooled. He tended to the sick and organized a movement to protect the weak and fight for the rights of the oppressed in the violent society of Mecca. He became known as Al-Amin, the trusted one. At one time, the people of Mecca were rebuilding the Ka'bah, but leaders of the four main clans fell into a bitter dispute over who would have the honor of putting the revered Black Stone back in its position. They appealed to Muhammad as an arbitrator, and he placed the Black Stone in the middle of a cloak and had the clan leaders lift the stone by the corners of the cloak, himself putting it back into its place in the wall of the Ka'bah. During these years, the story holds, Muhammad held himself apart from the pagan religious practices of the Quraysh, even though he had not yet received the revelation of monotheism from God.

The Night of Power   Muhammad, now a respected man among the Quraysh, was not yet content, for he was troubled about the religious practices of the Meccans. He felt the need to find solitude and meditate, so he started retiring for days at a time to a cave in the mountain of Hira nearby. One day, when he was about forty, he came home from the cave greatly agitated and cried out, "Cover me, Khadija,

cover me!" as he lay prostrate on the floor. After a while he told her about a vision of the angel Gabriel in the cave:

> He came to me while I was asleep, with a coverlet of brocade whereon was some writing, and said, "Read!" I said, "What shall I read?" He pressed me with it so tightly that I thought it was death; then he let me go and said, "Read!" I said, "What shall I read?" He pressed me with it again so that I thought it was death; then he let me go and said "Read!" I said, "What shall I read?" He pressed me with it the third time so that I thought it was death and said "Read." I said, "What shall I read?"—and this I said only to deliver myself from him, lest he should do the same to me again. He said:
>
> Read in the name of thy Lord who created,
> Who created man of blood coagulated.
> Read! Thy Lord is the most beneficent,
> Who taught by the pen,
> Taught that which they knew not unto men.
>
> (*Quran* 96:1–5)[4]

As reported in the Quran, in a vivid vision he saw a glorious being standing erect high up in the sky near the horizon; then the angel moved down until he was only two bow-shots from Muhammad (*Quran* 53:1–18). It is said that Muhammad, in his panic over this visionary experience, thought to throw himself over a precipice—but then he heard a voice from heaven hailing him: "O Muhammad, you are the Messenger of God!"[5] Khadija comforted Muhammad and told him to rejoice, since God would not forsake him. She sent him to her cousin Waraqa, a monotheist who was versed in Jewish and Christian writings, and Waraqa told him this was truly a revelation from God. This night of the first revelation, believed by many to be the night of the 26th of Ramadan, was later to be called "the night of power," a night that was worth a thousand months (*Quran* 97:1–5). God had sent down divine revelation through the angel Gabriel upon Muhammad.

For many days after this, the revelation did not come again, although Muhammad secluded himself in the cave, thirsting after the glorious vision he had seen. But then the revelations came again; the angel appeared again and spoke, "O thou wrapped in thy mantle, arise, and warn!" (74:1–2). And the revelations continued to come over the next years, now causing less surprise and terror, though these were still deep spiritual experiences for Muhammad.

Proclaiming the Revelation in Mecca Khadija was the first one in Mecca to accept Muhammad's words as true revelation from God. Soon afterward, Muhammad's friend **Abu Bakr,** his cousin 'Ali (son of Abu Talib), and Zayd, a slave freed by Muhammad, submitted to the new revelation. Thus began the new religion that would be known as Islam. At first Muhammad preached quietly and secretively to people who would listen about the new revelations, and in three years there were about forty followers for this new faith, mostly young men and some outside the clan system. But after that three-year period, revelations came from God telling him to preach openly to all the Meccans.

As Muhammad now began openly to proclaim the revelations he was receiving from God, more converts were made, but the vast majority of the Meccans became angry and grew hostile to him. The revelation from God warned them to give up their false gods and worship only the one God, to abstain from promiscuity and lust, to live in virtue, and to treat one another with kindness and equality. This was a message that they found threatening to their way of life. It would mean giving up their tribal gods and rituals, the way of life of their fathers; it would mean abandoning many of the luxuries and pleasures of the kind of life they were accustomed to; it would mean reforming Meccan society and thus threatening the position of the wealthy merchants; it would mean giving up the lucrative pilgrimage trade.

Muhammad continued to proclaim his message whenever he could, at fairs, during the pilgrimages, in the marketplace. At first the opposing Meccans mocked and jeered at him, and even his uncle Abu Lahab called him a madman. The Meccans would throw dirt and excrement on him as he passed by. They demanded that he produce some sign to testify that he was a prophet or perform some miracle. Muhammad simply insisted that the only miracle was the revelation sent by God, and he challenged them to produce a writing like it—which they could not do.

Some of those who converted and became Muslims were treated violently by the Meccans. But Muhammad's own Hashimite clan, headed by his uncle Abu Talib, stood by its obligation to protect Muhammad as a member of the clan, even though Abu Talib and most of the Hashim refused to become Muslims. At one point, the other Mec-

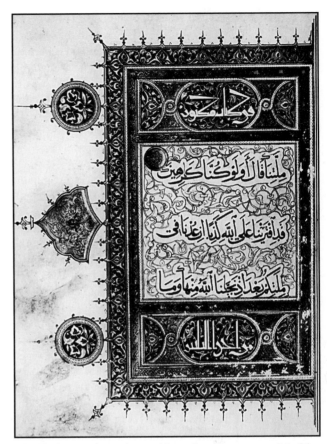

A highly decorated page from a thirteenth-century manuscript of the Quran.

cans sent a delegation to Abu Talib demanding that he withdraw his protection, but the uncle was resolute. Another time they offered to give Muhammad anything he wanted if he would stop his persistent preaching—money, honor, kingship, even a cure from the spirit possessing him. But Muhammad insisted that he wanted neither money, honor, nor power; God had simply sent him as a messenger, revealed a book to him, and commanded him to be an announcer and a warner. They challenged him to remove the mountains that shut Mecca in and open up rivers or to resurrect their fathers—then they would believe. Muhammad simply persisted: He had brought God's message to them, and they could either accept it or reject it and await God's judgment.

Since they could neither get Muhammad to give in nor get his clan to repudiate him, the other clans of the Quraysh tried a political move; they ordered a social and economic boycott of the Hashim clan: No one should have any dealings with them, sell food to them, visit or converse with them. The boycott lasted for several years, causing a good deal of suffering and hardship. But Abu Talib and the Hashim maintained the clan's obligation to protect Muhammad, and eventually the boycott was ended.

Crisis in Mecca   During these difficult years, Muhammad continued to receive revelations from God. One night, the story relates, Muhammad was sleeping next to the Ka'bah, when the angel Gabriel came to him. Mounted on the wondrous steed Buraq, Muhammad rode through the sky to Jerusalem, where he prayed at the "farthest mosque" (the site of the temple; *Quran* 17:1). Then Gabriel led Muhammad through the seven heavens into the presence of God. This great spiritual experience of Muhammad has always been a model for Muslims of the mystical experience of God's presence.

Conversions to Islam also continued during these years, in spite of the difficulties. One important convert was 'Umar ibn al-Khattab, who had been an active opponent and even struck his sister when she became a Muslim. But when he listened to the Quran being recited he was so moved that he professed submission to God. **'Umar,** who later became the second caliph, was strong and active and contributed much to the growth of the Islamic community.

But the year 619 C.E. brought new trials for Muhammad and the Muslims. The death of his wife was a deep personal loss, for she had been a strong support for him. Also, his uncle Abu Talib died, and he was succeeded as head of the Hashim clan by Abu Lahab, another uncle of Muhammad's who had already been strongly antagonistic. At first Abu Lahab appeared reluctant to withdraw the traditional protection of the clan, but Muhammad's continued attacks on the clan as unbelievers provoked the uncle to look for some way to reject him. He asked Muhammad point-blank whether Abu Talib, who never became a Muslim, and his grandfather 'Abd al-Muttalib (who died when Muhammad was a young boy) were condemned to hell as unbelievers. When Muhammad answered that they were, Abu Lahab angrily considered this a grave insult to the leaders of the clan and withdrew his protection.

Establishing the Ummah in Medina

Unable to preach safely in Mecca, Muhammad went to the neighboring city of Ta'if and preached for ten days, but the people there only ridiculed him. Back in Mecca the situation grew dangerous. However, about this time (620 C.E.) six men from Medina, an oasis settlement 200 miles north of Mecca, came to Mecca for the religious fair, and they were impressed with Muhammad's personality and his message. Medina was made up of about a dozen different tribes, including some Jewish tribes, and a long-standing blood feud was causing much difficulty. An even-handed mediator was urgently needed. The next year these Medinans came back with others, representing most of the tribes; they made a promise to Muhammad to accept him as prophet. Muhammad sent a trusty Muslim back with them to instruct them, and by June of 622 a representative party of seventy-five people from Medina made the pilgrimage to Mecca. They met secretly with Muhammad and pledged to fight on behalf of God and God's messenger Muhammad.

Hijra: Immigration to Medina and Founding of the Ummah   In small groups over the next months, Muhammad's followers in Mecca began slipping out and migrating to Medina. Muhammad himself, together with Abu Bakr and 'Ali, remained until the last minute, to detract attention from this escape. The enemies of the prophet grew alarmed at the prospect of a power base for Muslims in Medina and decided to seize and kill him, with a member of each clan striking together so that all would share the responsibility for his blood. On the night they came, 'Ali lay in Muhammad's bed while Muhammad and Abu Bakr escaped and hid in a cave for three days. Finally they reached Medina on September 24, 622, to the great joy of the Muslims in Medina. Upon their offer of quarters, Muhammad loosened his camel, and when she stopped in an empty lot in the quarter of the Banu Najjar, Muhammad chose that as the site to build his house, which was also to be used as a **mosque** (masjid) (hall of prayer). This immigration of the Muslim community from Mecca to Medina is called the **Hijra;** with it began a new age in the Islamic movement, and in honor of that, Muslims date their calendar from the first day of this lunar year. The year 622 C.E. is Hijra year 1 in the Islamic calendar, for now for the first time, the community of Muslims could put the whole Islamic system of life into full practice.

The Muslims from Mecca who migrated to Medina were known as the Emigrants (Muhajirun), and those people of Medina who received the Emigrants were known as the Helpers (Ansar). Together they made up the community of Islam, the ummah. The ummah is a community based on a common faith, a community of prayer and worship as well as a community with its own government, economy, and military force. The basis of this ummah is recorded in the Constitution of Medina, which states that any serious dispute between parties in Medina must be referred to God and the prophet Muhammad.

Whereas most of the tribes of Medina submitted to Muhammad's religious authority, the Jewish tribes refused to recognize him as the new prophet from God, and eventually most of these Jewish tribes were expelled from Medina. There were also tensions among the Muslims: The Helpers suspected they were being treated unfairly by the Emigrants; and some Medinans only superficially accepted Islam and subsequently became known as the Hypocrites. In spite of these tensions, the ummah thrived and grew, and Muhammad's role as both their religious leader and their political leader became stronger.

During these years at Medina, Muhammad continued to receive revelations from God, so that by the time of his death in 632 C.E. the entire content of the Quran had been revealed. The basic rituals and duties of Muslims were established: confessing the oneness of God and Muhammad as God's prophet, ritual washing and prayer, giving alms, fasting, and pilgrimage. The regulations on matters of religious law were either revealed to Muhammad or stipulated by him on the basis of the revelation in the Quran. One important revelation was the change in direction in which the Muslims should face to say their prayers. Previously they had faced Jerusalem in prayer, but now God revealed that they should face the Ka'bah in Mecca (2:142–150).

In these revelations, the crucial role of Muhammad as the last of the whole line of prophets was established. God had been sending prophets ever since the beginning of the human race—some twenty-five are mentioned by name in the Quran, including Adam, Abraham, Ishmael, Isaac, Moses, David, Solomon, Job, and others. Jesus is mentioned many times in the Quran as an important prophet in the sacred story, and thus the prophet Jesus is highly regarded by Muslims. Conceived in Mary's womb by God's command, Jesus was sent as the messiah to the Jewish people to bring God's

revelation. He healed the sick and raised the dead by God's power. Some charged him with crimes and attempted to crucify him, but God took Jesus to paradise, from where he will return before **Judgment Day.** Muhammad continues this line of prophets, but he is the "seal of the prophets," through whom God has sent down the final, perfect revelation.

Muhammad's own family played an important role in the formation of the community of Islam. After his wife Khadija died in 619, he married numerous other wives and established the model of an active, dedicated Muslim household. Almost all of these wives were widows of Muslims killed in battles with the Meccans and other hostile tribes. For example, Hafsah, daughter of 'Umar, had been widowed by the age of twenty. Among Muhammad's wives, she had the distinction of being one who could read and write and, according to some Muslim traditions, helped to collate the separate leaves of the Holy Book, the Quran. One wife who was not a widow was 'Aisha, the young daughter of Abu Bakr; she was especially lively and caught the interest of the community. She lived some fifty years after Muhammad's death and left more reports *(hadiths)* about Muhammad than anyone else did. Collectively the wives of the prophet were highly respected and were known as the "Mothers of the Believers."

Submission of Mecca   With the development of the ummah at Medina, the new religion was now fully in place, and the age of ignorance was over—except that the holy city of Mecca was still in the hands of unbelievers. In 624, two years after the Hijra, a Meccan army headed for Medina. Outnumbered three to one, the Muslims were uncertain whether God wanted them to defend themselves, that is, to fight in the name of their religion. God revealed to Muhammad in a sura, perhaps at this time:

> Assuredly God will defend those who believe; surely God loves not any ungrateful traitor. Leave is given to those who fight because they were wronged—surely God is able to help them—who were expelled from their habitations without right, except that they say "Our Lord is God."

(22:38–40)

In this battle at Badr, God gave victory to the Muslims, the army "fighting in the way of God" (3:13). The victory was a turning point for the Muslim community, for it established the conviction that God would see to it that the divine will would be carried out in historical events. The Meccans made two more major assaults. In 625, they nearly killed Muhammad at the battle of Uhud. And in 627, a Jewish tribe and the Hypocrites joined the Meccans in an assault on Medina. This serious threat was met when the Muslims, on the advice of a Persian convert, dug a trench around the city, frustrating the tribal war tactics of the Meccans. After this, Muhammad consolidated the Muslim position in Medina and the surrounding area, and the time came to end the problem of Mecca.

Although Muhammad now had the strength to assault Mecca, he turned to conciliation instead. He made a ten-year peace truce with the Meccans, and in 629 (Hijrah 7), Muhammad and a host of Muslims went on a pilgrimage to Mecca. In keeping with the peace truce, the city was vacated of its inhabitants during the Muslims' three-day visit. But soon the Meccans again instigated hostility, and on January 1, 630 (Hijrah 8), Muhammad set off with a force of ten thousand men toward Mecca. While they were still a day's journey from the city, a delegation of Meccans met them and offered to submit to the new faith. Muhammad entered the city in peace, treating the Meccans with great magnanimity and giving them a general clemency. And he personally entered the Ka'bah and destroyed the 360 idols, proclaiming, "God is great! Truth has come. Falsehood has vanished" (17:81).[6] Henceforth this was to be the shrine of Allah alone, and it was to be tended and visited only by Muslims. And the former unbelievers of Mecca submitted to Allah and became Muslims.

Muhammad soon dispatched emissaries to all parts of Arabia to preach Islam to the tribes and tear down pagan temples. Several tribes had to be subdued by force, but in 631 (Hijrah 9), the "year of delegations," many former pagan tribes of Arabia sent representatives to Mecca to offer their submission to God and their fighting men to Muhammad. Now they entered God's religion in crowds, as God said to the prophet: "When comes the help of God, and victory, and thou seest men entering God's religion in throngs, then proclaim the praise of thy Lord, and see His forgiveness; for he turns again unto men" (sura 110). And Muhammad sent out teachers to teach the precepts of Islam to these tribes, telling them to deal gently with the people. Christian and Jewish tribes in Arabia reached agreements with Muhammad, paying a tax in return for protected status.

Muhammad had fulfilled his mission: much of Arabia had submitted—a land and a people that had never before been united under any set of ideals. Idolatry was destroyed;

superstition and vice were replaced by faith and virtue. Blood kinship, for the first time, was subordinated to a community based on faith that offered equal rights and justice for all. Laws from Allah regarding charity, acting justly, observing peace, worshipping God, and the like were now commonly accepted by all, even across tribal lines. In the short period of twenty years since his first revelation, Muhammad had realized a goal of Islam: the whole people of Arabia united in one brotherhood, fulfilling in their lives the total design of the one God.

Muhammad's Final Pilgrimage   Muhammad returned once more to Mecca with a large group of followers in March of 632 (Hijra 10) to make what turned out to be his "farewell pilgrimage." The city had been purified of all traces of idolatry, and now Muhammad established the model for the pilgrimage ritual (**Hajj**), which, he decreed, could only be performed by Muslims. He retained many of the earlier pilgrimage traditions, such as circling the Ka'bah seven times, kissing the Black Stone, running between the two hills, drinking water from the well of Zamzam, and throwing pebbles at the stone pillars. But these rituals were now completely disassociated from polytheistic ideas and restored to their meaning as acts of submission to the one God. Ever since that final pilgrimage, Muslims have participated in Muhammad's story by retracing his steps and repeating the rituals of the pilgrimage as he did.

During the closing rituals of the pilgrimage, astride his camel atop Mt. Arafat, Muhammad spoke his "farewell" sermon to the assembled multitudes, saying:

> O men, listen to my words. I do not know whether I shall ever meet you in this place again after this year. Your blood and your property are sacrosanct until you meet your Lord, as this day and this month are holy. You will surely meet your Lord and He will ask you of your works. . . . I have left with you something which if you will hold fast to it you will never fall into error—a plain indication, the book of God and the practice of His prophet, so give good heed to what I say. Know that every Muslim is a Muslim's brother, and that the Muslims are brethren.

Muhammad's sermon ended with this statement: "O God, have I not told you?" And the assembled multitude echoed, "O God, yes!" And the prophet said, "O God, bear witness!"[7]

Not long afterward the prophet fell ill in Medina. Though weak and feeble, he continued to lead the faithful in public prayer up to the third day prior to his death. In his last exhortation to the faithful assembled at prayer he said, "O men, the fire is kindled, and rebellions come like the darkness of the night. By God, you can lay nothing to my charge. I allow only what the Quran allows and forbid only what the Quran forbids."[8] He died a few hours later in the arms of his young wife 'Aisha, in June 632 (Hijrah 10). And he was buried in 'Aisha's home, on the spot where later a mosque was erected.

There was concern and confusion among the Muslims during the days of Muhammad's illness, and when he died there were some who claimed that the apostle of God was not dead but would return. But Abu Bakr went into the house and kissed Muhammad, saying, "You are dearer than my father and mother. You have tasted the death which God had decreed: a second death will never overtake you." Then he went out and cried to the people: "O men, if anyone worships Muhammad, Muhammad is dead; if anyone worships God, God is alive, immortal!" Then Abu Bakr recited this verse from the Quran, which the Muslims had forgotten: "Muhammad is nothing but an apostle. Apostles have passed away before him. Can it be that if he were to die or be killed you would turn back on your heels? He who turns back does no harm to God and God will reward the grateful" (3:144). 'Umar, who had been saying Muhammad was not dead, now said, "By God, when I heard Abu Bakr recite these words I was dumfounded so that my legs would not bear me up and I fell to the ground knowing that the apostle was indeed dead."[9] Thus it was that an extremely important point was established in Islam: Muhammad is the prophet of God, but God alone is to be worshiped.

Because he was the prophet through whom God gave the Quran, however, Muhammad was looked to as the model for what a Muslim is to be, and therefore his own story became the central story for Muslims to model their own lives after. His words and his actions, passed on by his companions in the traditions of the Hadith, provided the paradigm for interpreting the stipulations of the Quran and applying them to the various situations of life. In this sense the story of Muhammad is the story of every Muslim.

A Religion for All Peoples: Expansion of Islam

The story goes on, for until this point Islam had become the religion of the peoples of Arabia, but not yet a universal religion beyond this limited area. Under the first four caliphs (deputies of Muhammad), the religion of Islam expanded to become a religion for peoples far beyond Arabia. These first four successors of Muhammad are called the "rightly guided caliphs."

Successors to Muhammad: The Caliphs Muhammad did not designate who should be his successor as leader of Islam, but after his death the Muslim leaders quickly decided that Abu Bakr, Muhammad's trusted friend, father-in-law, and one of the first converts to Islam, should be caliph. The role of caliph combined the offices of chief executive, commander-in-chief, chief justice, and leader (imam) of public worship—but not that of prophet, since Muhammad was the final prophet. Abu Bakr (r. 632–634 C.E.) was honest and deeply committed; it was said that he wept whenever he recited verses of the Quran. In the two years he was caliph before he died, he consolidated the unity of Islam among the tribes of Arabia, dealing resolutely with tribes that apostatized after the death of Muhammad, with those who refused to pay the alms tax, and with false prophets that arose. He also began the task of assembling and collating the scattered suras of the Quran, which were memorized and recited by many but not written down in one volume.

The next two caliphs, 'Umar (r. 634–644) and 'Uthman (r. 644–656), had also been early converts to Islam, and it was their contribution, in only about twenty years, to make Islam a world religion through great waves of Islamic expansion far beyond the Arabian peninsula: to Palestine (Jerusalem fell to 'Umar in 637), Syria, Persia, and Asia Minor, to Egypt and across north Africa. Although this expansion was accompanied by military battles in a "holy war" for Allah, many of these people willingly accepted Islam as a liberation from their former oppressive rulers and religions. 'Umar adopted fair means of treating the Jews and Christians who fell subject to Islamic rulers; they were "people of the Book" and were guaranteed basic rights and freedom of worship in exchange for the head tax paid to the Muslims. 'Umar began the process of putting the guidance of the Quran into public law throughout the Muslim world, and 'Uthman had the official final recension of the Quran produced.

The fourth rightly guided caliph was 'Ali (r. 656–661), Muhammad's cousin (son of Abu Talib), one of the first converts to Islam, who married Muhammad's daughter Fatima. 'Ali was a widely respected Muslim, a very close companion of the prophet. But a tragic period of internal fighting becomes part of the Muslim story at this point. The last part of 'Uthman's reign was marred by dissension between his own Umayyad family and the other Muslims, leading to 'Uthman's assassination. After 'Ali was chosen as the fourth caliph, Mu'awiya, as leader of the Umayyad family, disputed his leadership. After an indecisive battle, arbitration was decided in favor of Mu'awiya, and soon after that 'Ali was assassinated by fanatics (661). Mu'awiya then established the Umayyad Caliphate, which ruled the Islamic world from its capital at Damascus for the next century.

'Ali was Muhammad's cousin and son-in-law, and Hasan and **Husayn,** the sons of 'Ali and Muhammad's daughter Fatima, were the surviving male heirs of Muhammad. Because of special interest in the family of Muhammad, there had long been a "faction *(shi'a)* of 'Ali" that felt 'Ali was the obvious successor to Muhammad. 'Ali was tragically assassinated, as were his son Husayn and others of the family—but these martyrdoms only gave impetus to the feeling among his faction, the **Shi'ites,** that the family of

Muhammad, through 'Ali, Hasan, Husayn, and their descendants, should be the real spiritual leaders of Islam. The Shi'ites call these leaders **imams** rather than caliphs, tracing them down through a number of generations from Imam 'Ali. Most Shi'ites hold that there were twelve imams before the final one disappeared, to return sometime in the future. Shi'ites look to these imams for special guidance, since the light of Muhammad was passed on to Imam 'Ali and on to the rest of the imams. Thus the imams also have become part of the story for Shi'ites. In all the other important respects, however, the Shi'ites share the same story with the **Sunnites,** the majority group in Islam that looks to the four rightly guided caliphs as the proper successors to Muhammad.

The story culminates, then, in the rule of Islam as a unified, worldwide ummah, whether that is called the caliphate or the imamate. This is, of course, an ideal that has never been completely achieved. But it is the goal set forth in the Muslim story: that the ummah become the

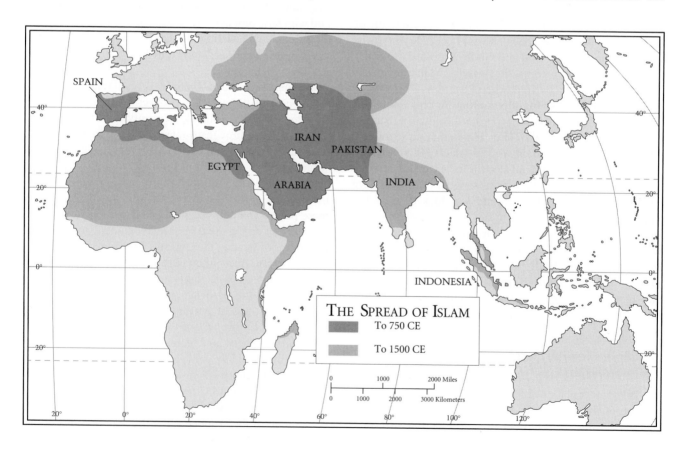

ideal human society, in which Muslims as representatives of true humanity submit their lives totally in accordance with God's will as revealed through the prophet Muhammad. The best way to achieve this goal is in the establishment of the Islamic state, as Muhammad and the early caliphs did, in which all the laws that govern life, in both the public and the private domain, are based on God's revelation in the Quran.

To be a Muslim means to identify with this sacred story, seeing the revelation that God gave through Muhammad in the Quran as the final truth for all human society, and looking to the model of Muhammad and his companions for guidance in living the full human life.

THE ISLAMIC UMMAH IN HISTORY

After the founding period of the prophet and the four rightly guided caliphs, the Muslim movement continued to expand rapidly. The territory under control of Muslim rulers was called the **Dar al-Islam,** the "abode of Islam," in contrast to the **Dar al-Harb,** the "abode of war" controlled by unbelievers. In the Dar al-Islam, it was possible to conduct all aspects of life, spiritual, political, cultural, and social, in accordance with the law of Islam, and this provided opportunities for great achievements in Islamic thought and culture. The classical period of Islam included the Umayyad and the **Abbasid** caliphates, up to the chaos caused by the invasion of the Mongols in the thirteenth century.

The Classical Period of Islam

The Umayyad Dynasty   With the assassination of 'Ali, the fourth caliph, in 661, Mu'awiya of the Umayyad family was able to gain consensus throughout the Muslim world for his caliphate, establishing a family dynasty centered in Damascus. There was a brief challenge to Umayyad rule in 680 posed by the revolt of Husayn, 'Ali's younger son, but this was put down ruthlessly in a great massacre at Karbalah in Iraq. Although this gave the Shi'ites a rallying point and helped establish the permanent existence of the Shi'ite movement within Islam, effective political resistance to rule by the Umayyad family was stopped for the time being.

Mu'awiya was a brilliant leader at Damascus, ruling consensually as the first shaykh among shaykhs. The Umayyad rulers called themselves caliphs, even though later Muslim historians sometimes refer to this dynasty as the "Arab kingdom," implying that the Umayyad dynasty was more like an oriental kingdom than deputies of Muhammad. Under the Umayyads, Islam continued its rapid expansion all the way across north Africa and up into Spain. The Islamic tide even crossed the Pyrenees into France, turned back finally by Charles Martel at Poitiers in 732. Expansion also continued eastward in central Asia up to the borders of India. Islamic art and architecture entered into a creative phase; an outstanding artistic achievement was the building of the Dome of the Rock mosque in Jerusalem by 'Abd al-Malik (691).

The Abbasid Dynasty: Golden Age of Islam   As Islam expanded, the numbers of mawali (non-Arabs "adopted" into Islam) who joined the ummah rapidly increased. These mawali found themselves in a kind of second-class status under the Umayyads; for that reason, many of them were attracted toward the more egalitarian policies of the Shi'ites. Finally, a group of Arabs from Khurasan in the northeast rallied the opposition to the Umayyads. Calling themselves Abbasids, after Muhammad's paternal uncle al-'Abbas, they proposed restoring rule to caliphs who were of the house of the prophet—thus attracting the support of the Shi'ites. The mawali also joined them, their army including many soldiers from Iran.

The Abbasid rulers brought Islam to its golden age. It was multicultural and international, and scholarship, literature, and the arts flourished as never before. Shortly after taking rule in about 750, the Abbasids removed the capital to a new Madinat al-Salam (City of Peace) on the Tigris River called Baghdad. There the caliphs ruled much in the style of Persian oriental kings, enjoying such titles as "the Presence" and "the Caliph of God." The fabulous culture of Baghdad under these caliphs is reflected in some of the stories of the *Arabian Nights,* at the time of the famous caliph Harun al-Rashid (786–809). Baghdad society here seems worlds away from the Arabic culture of the Quran. In Baghdad, the caliph of God had absolute power of life and death. It is said that officials going into the inner rooms of the Presence routinely carried their shroud on their arms in case they should displease the caliph and meet instantaneous execution. Here were viziers (ministers) with lavish palaces, poets, slaves, eunuchs and harems, exotic travel, and great wealth and luxury.

But important for Islamic history was the surge of scholarship that took place under the Abbasids. A great library was built in Baghdad, and scholars translated Greek and Syriac works into Arabic. Now Aristotle and Plato became known to Muslim scholars, and they turned their attention to questions of reason and revelation, and of divine power and human will. Muslim culture and learning flourished in other areas as well. In Muslim Spain, with its capital at Cordova, a rival caliphate ruled, a remnant of the Umayyad family, under which a brilliant Islamic scholarly culture was cultivated. And in Egypt, a Shi'ite dynasty managed to establish itself as another rival to the Abbasids. Calling themselves Fatimids (after Fatima, daughter of Muhammad and wife of 'Ali), they founded the city of Cairo and established the famous university Al-Azhar.

But the classical golden age of Islam came to an end with the difficulties in the Abbasid realm in the eleventh and twelfth centuries. Turkish tribes from central Asia surged into Iran and Iraq and gradually assumed power. In Baghdad, the new Turkish leader, the "Prince of Princes," took over real power and the caliph became merely a figurehead. When the Seljuk Turks became dominant in Palestine and threatened Christian pilgrimage access to Jerusalem, Christian leaders of Europe initiated the crusades to drive the Muslim infidels from the Holy Land. Jerusalem fell to the crusaders in 1099, although it was recaptured in 1187 by Salah-al-Din (Saladin). The end of the classical period of Islam was signaled by the eruption of the Mongols into the Islamic lands in the thirteenth century. In 1258, the Mongols attacked Baghdad, burning it to the ground and executing the last caliph. For a couple of centuries, Muslim rule was in disarray, until new dynasties established themselves in various part of the Muslim world.

Development of Shari'ah (Law) and Theology   This golden age of Islam under the Umayyads and the Abbasids proved very fruitful in religious and cultural expressions. It produced brilliant new discoveries of science and established the canons of Islamic art, as calligraphy, architecture, and poetry flourished. Most important developments came in the systematic working out of Islamic law, the **Shari'ah,** and in the creation of *kalam,* rational theology.

Since the Quran is understood as God's perfect and final guidance, from early on Muslims attended to the question of how to apply it to every aspect of life. The example *(sun-nah)* of the Prophet himself, as reported in the Hadith, provided the primary sources for interpreting the law of the Quran. In the centuries following Muhammad, these *hadiths* were assembled and evaluated, and scholars were hard at work formulating the Islamic Law, striving (**ijtihad**) to work out applications to all areas of life.

Since this process took place in different localities, the shape of the Shari'ah differed slightly from place to place. Eventually four schools of law emerged among the Sunni Muslims: the Hanafi, Maliki, Shafi'i, and Hanbali schools. There are no fundamental differences between them, and each regards the others as fully orthodox. The Shi'ites developed three schools of their own, the most prominent one being the Ja'fari. Shi'ite law shares its main aspects with Sunnite law, differing principally in the conception of divine authority, which comes through the imam, the perfect leader and successor Muhammad.

The development of the law in Islam was the culmination of the fundamental Quranic principle that all of life is governed by God's decrees. Although the law was organized and systematized by the legal scholars, it was not created by them. It grew out of the ummah's striving to bring all aspects of life into accordance with God's design. By the tenth century, most of this legal design was fixed, at least in Sunnite Islam, and the principal function of the legal scholars changed from formulating law to passing on the decisions of the past. This fixation of the law was known as the "closing of the gate of *ijtihad*," and from then down to the modern era, scholars have passed on the legal formulations of the past. Shi'ite scholars, with their conception of divine guidance from the imam, have generally not considered the gate of *ijtihad* to be closed.

At first, disputes about faith in Islam were settled simply by appeal to the Quran itself or to the testimony of the Prophet's companions. Increasing contact with Greek philosophical thought during the classical period opened new possibilities of exploring the basic doctrines of faith and drawing further implications from them.

There were some early disputes about how to understand certain points of faith. The relation between believing in God and performing the required actions—between faith and works—was interpreted in a radical way by the **Kharijites.** They rejected the idea that a grave sinner could still be considered a believer. They taught a perfectionist ethic and ruthlessly purged their own community of those guilty of grave sins. It was some radical Kharijites who assassinated Caliph 'Ali because he did not take a firm stand in God's cause against Mu'awiya. The view that prevailed among Muslims, however, was that judgment about sinners should be suspended and left to God, thus avoiding the wrenching of the Muslim community that would be caused by the constant searching out and punishing of those guilty of sinning.

Another early doctrinal discussion concerned human freedom and divine predestination. Those who emphasized free will came to be known as Qadarites (those who discuss determination), holding that humans have the power and capability to act and thus should be held responsible for their actions. The Qadarites (like the earlier Kharijites) tended to oppose the Umayyad dynasty, which they held was not according to God's decree but a result of the misuse of human freedom. In reaction, the Umayyad supporters took a more deterministic stand, insisting that God had decreed the Umayyads to rule as caliphs. The prevailing view that matured in Islam stood strongly on the side of divine predestination, putting more emphasis on the unity and almighty character of God than on human freedom.

In spite of these controversies, a spirit of tolerance developed concerning the boundaries of the ummah. Diverse and dissident groups generally were considered part of the ummah, as long as they believed in the oneness of God and the prophethood of Muhammad, performed the prayer, and fulfilled the requirement of sharing wealth.

While the earlier controversies were settled in a kind of ad hoc fashion, with the overall welfare of the ummah in mind, the intellectual climate heightened during the Abbasid period. Now Muslims were spread across Asia, northern Africa, and Spain, and they came into direct contact with Greek philosophical thought. The need became urgent for more rational, systematic expressions of the faith.

One group that used philosophic argumentation in developing rational theology *(kalam)* was the **Mu'tazilite** movement. The Mu'tazilites (withdrawers) got their name by "withdrawing" to an intermediate position on the question of whether believers can commit grave sins. But they went on to apply rational speculation to questions about revelation, the nature of God, and divine justice.

In some respects, the Mu'tazilites were conservative orthodox thinkers; they held firmly to two basic Islamic beliefs: the unity of God and absolute divine justice. With rigorous logic they attacked some questionable popular ideas. For example, most traditional Muslims interpreted the Quran literally even when it described God in anthropomorphic (humanlike) terms, such as God sitting on a throne, people seeing God's face in the resurrection, and so forth. The Mu'tazilites, holding tenaciously to the unity of God, insisted that such ideas were only metaphors and were not to be taken literally—God cannot be described in terms of human qualities.

Further, Muslims traditionally said that the Quran was eternal and uncreated. But the Mu'tazilites argued that this could not be so; such a view would amount to **shirk,** associating another eternal divine essence with God. The Quran, they said, is not divine and eternal but was created in time by God to give guidance to humans.

The Mu'tazilites also felt compelled to defend God's justice by declaring that God's predetermination is not absolute; humans have freedom to choose between good and evil. It would be accusing God of gross injustice to say that people are punished or rewarded for actions that God had predetermined!

Mu'tazilite thought flourished for a century before being pushed aside by more traditional positions, but in the process, it stimulated the further development of rational theology. Orthodox Sunni thinkers worked with reason and logic to meet the Mu'tazilite challenge, up to the limits of human reason, while remaining in submission to the authority of revelation. The great theologian al-Ash'ari (d. ca. 935) combined reason and revelation in a way that has found acceptance by orthodox Muslims. He held that when the Quran speaks of God in human terms, such as describing God's hand, this was to be accepted as accurate, even though the mode in which God possesses this quality is unknown to humans. Believers accept this truth literally, "without asking how and without likening [to humans]."

The Quran, al-Ash'ari and other orthodox thinkers held, is eternal. But a set of distinctions exists between the eternal attributes of God's word and the physical written or recited Quran, which is created. As to divine determinism and human free will, they argued that God indeed causes all events in the universe; but not being limited by the divine law, God is beyond ideas of evil and injustice. Although God causes all things, humans through their actions "acquire" responsibility for them. By such argumentation, the orthodox theologians used reason and turned it against the Mu'tazilites.

Even after the defeat of the Mu'tazilites, Muslim thinkers continued to try to square Islamic faith with Greek philosophy (falsafa). One such philosopher was Ibn Sina (d. 1037), widely known in the West as Avicenna. But the theologian-mystic **al-Ghazali** (1058–1111), one of the greatest thinkers in the history of Islam, blasted such dependence on reason with his book, *The Confusion of the Philosophers*. Some Muslim intellectuals continued to work with rational speculation, like Ibn Rushd (d. 1198), known in the West as Averroes. Against al-Ghazali's attack he defended rational theology with his book, *The Confusion of the Confusion*. But generally, orthodox theology backed off from speculative philosophy, even while keeping the method of Aristotelean logic. In fact, the greatest impact of thinkers like Avicenna and Averroes was on Jewish and Christian thinkers such as Maimonides and Aquinas. Islamic theology, like Islamic law, solidified in orthodox form, to remain largely unchanged until the modern era.

Islamic Mysticism: The Sufis   At the same time that Islamic legal scholars were solidifying the law and Greek philosophy was having strong influence on Muslim thinkers, other Muslims were being attracted to mysticism—the interior contemplation and experience of union with God. Like similar developments in Judaism and Christianity, the mystical movement in Islam came to clash with orthodox beliefs and practices.

Sufism, as the Islamic mystical movement is generally called, began as an ascetic movement. The Umayyad and Abbasid rulers had made the house of Islam into "the Arab Kingdom," with the lure of wealth and power too much for many to resist. In reaction, some Muslims went back to the model of Muhammad and the four rightly guided caliphs, who lived lives of honesty and simplicity in their devotion to God. In spite of his great authority, Muhammad had a very frugal lifestyle; 'Umar's shabby garments were legendary; and 'Ali gave away everything to the point of poverty for himself. The Muslim ascetics who distanced themselves from sensuous life and luxury took coarse woolen garments as their symbol, probably receiving the name **Sufi** from the Arabic word *suf* (wool). Since they aspired to a life of poverty, the term *faqir* (poor one) was also used to refer to them.

The Sufi movement soon incorporated additional elements. The legal discussions of the day focused on outer conformity to the Islamic law—but what about inner emotional submission to God in love? Love (*mahabbah*) became a central theme for the mystics. The rationalist strove for intellectual knowledge of God—what about interior, contemplative, experiential knowledge? Such interior knowledge of God (*ma'rifa*) likewise became a central theme for the Sufis.

The Sufis looked to evidences in the Quran and Hadith for their emphasis on love and inner union with God. God is our friend, who will have "a people He loves, and who love Him" (5:57–59). God is nearer to us than the jugular vein (50:16); and wherever we turn, "there is the Face of God" (2:115). Muhammad was the intimate friend of God, having his consciousness transformed through long vigils, contemplations, and direct revelations from God. His night journey to heaven and his face-to-face communion with God were seen as a mystical paradigm that could be repeated in the Sufi path. In their interpretation of the Quran, the Sufis used, in addition to the literal meaning, also an allegorical and symbolic meaning that guided their mystical practices.

The emphasis on love of God can be seen, for example, in the poetry of the great woman Sufi saint, Rabi'ah (d. 801), who lived a life of rapture and joy amid her austerities. She expressed her mystical thirst for God in a prayer: "O God, if I worship thee for fear of Hell, burn me in Hell, and if I worship Thee in hope of Paradise, exclude me from Paradise; but if I worship Thee for Thine own sake, grudge me not Thy everlasting beauty."[10] A famous poem defines the kind of love she had for God:

> I have loved Thee with two loves, a selfish love and a love
>   that is worthy (of Thee).
> As for the love that is selfish, I occupy myself therein with
>   remembrance of Thee to the exclusion of all others.
> As for that which is worthy of Thee, therein Thou raisest the
>   veil that I may see Thee.
> Yet there is no praise to me in this or that,
> But the praise is to Thee, whether in that or in this.[11]

Sufis felt that, whereas other Muslims follow the Shari'ah as the outer path to God, there was also an inner way beyond the outer path, and they called this the Tariqa. The Sufi path begins by following the outer path in order to break attachment to earthly things. But at its higher levels, the Tariqa becomes a way of inner meditation, leading finally to freedom from attachment to self and a "passing away" *(fana)* into God. The method of the inner path involves techniques of **dhikr,** the "remembering" of God, which the Quran says should be often done (33:41). By remembering God both aloud and silently in the heart, Sufis advanced on the inner path through the "stations" and "states" of spiritual attainment toward inner knowledge and experience of union with God.

Some Sufis became so intoxicated with the inner path that clashes with orthodox teaching set in. One group of Sufis felt themselves beyond the Shari'ah to the point where they could willfully reject and transgress the law. Some Sufis focused on achieving the intoxicating union with God at any cost. An early Sufi, Abu Yazid (d. 875), experienced God deeply in his soul and shocked orthodox Muslims by exclaiming, "Glory to Me! How great is My Majesty!" Another intoxicated mystic, still controversial among Muslims to this day, was al-Hallaj (d. 922). He had a deep knowledge of Christianity, in addition to Hinduism and Buddhism. Al-Hallaj described the mystical union with God by the famous allegory of a moth that circles ever closer to the candle's flame and is finally united with it by being consumed by it—an allegory of the soul and God. He bothered orthodox Muslims especially by his public pronouncements of his experience of union with God, such as his famous utterance, *ana al-Haqq* (I am the Truth, i.e., God). Refusing to take back such a blasphemous statement, al-Hallaj accepted death so as to be one with God. Taken to be crucified, al-Hallaj approached the gallows laughing, thanking God for showing him the mysterious vision of God's face. Perhaps knowing his resemblance to Jesus, al-Hallaj prayed:

> And these Thy servants who are gathered to slay me, in zeal for Thy Religion, longing to win Thy favor, forgive them, Lord. Have mercy on them. Surely if Thou hadst shown them what Thou hast shown me, they would never have done what they have done. . . . Whatsoever Thou dost will, I praise Thee![12]

In later centuries, some Muslims have pointed out that al-Hallaj, in saying *ana al-Haqq,* was surrendering his own existence and testifying that God is all. Yet his public flaunting of his mystical experiences gave offense to many Muslims.

Al-Ghazali and the Acceptance of Sufism   In the radical mysticism of Sufis such as al-Hallaj, the Sufi Tariqa seemed to have become incompatible with the orthodox Shari'ah. But in the experience and teaching of the great Al-Ghazali (1058–1111), a reconciliation was effected between the Sufi way and the orthodox law, making it possible for Sufism to become thought of as the "heartbeat of Islam." Al-Ghazali lived as the Muslim ummah was approaching its five hundredth anniversary (he died in the year 505 of the Hijrah), and his life of devotion and work of renewal have led many to consider him the second greatest Muslim after Muhammad. At thirty-three years of age, he started teaching in the new Islamic institute in Baghdad, becoming a master of rational theology and philosophy. But a spiritual crisis affected him, as he realized he was mired in his comfortable and rewarding position. In his spiritual autobiography, *Deliverance from Error,* he wrote:

> I considered the circumstances of my life, and realized that I was caught in a veritable thicket of attachments. I also considered my activities, of which the best was my teaching and lecturing, and realized that in them I was dealing with sciences that were unimportant and contributed nothing to the attainment of eternal life. After that I examined my motive in my work of teaching, and realized that it was not a pure desire for the things of God, but that the impulse moving me was the desire for an influential position and public recognition. . . . One day I would form the resolution to quit Baghdad and get rid of these adverse circumstances; the next day I would abandon my resolution. I put one foot forward and drew the other back. . . . Worldly desires were striving to keep me by their chains just where I was, while the voice of faith was calling, "To the road! To the road!"[13]

Falling into a physical ailment in which he could barely eat and could not talk, al-Ghazali finally took to the road and lived as a Sufi for the next eleven years in Syria, Palestine, and Arabia. Eventually he returned to teaching for a while, and then he founded a Sufi retreat center in his native Persia. In his many works, he was able to bring about a synthesis between Sufism and the orthodox tradition of law and theology. He lived by the law, but he provided for it a deep spiritual sensitivity. In his teaching and especially in his own example, he brought Sufism back into the orthodox Islamic path.

Sufi membership, which before al-Ghazali had been small, elite groups, now became more representative of all levels of society. Following al-Ghazali's example, other orders or brotherhoods were established. Each was based on a spiritual master (shaykh) who had perfected a distinctive path or Tariqa and gathered disciples around himself. The disciples (faqirs) lived with the master and practiced the path communally. Among the distinctive practices of the different brotherhoods were chanting of certain divine phrases, breath control while chanting, communal recitation, ecstatic dancing, and the like.

One particularly well-known Sufi brotherhood was founded by the great Sufi poet, Jalal al-Din al-Rumi (d. 1273). Rumi, born in Afghanistan, moved to Anatolia and became a master of Sufism. An intense friendship that ended in a tragic death inspired him to put his deep love for God into poetry—and the result is some of the most inspired Sufi poetry of all time. Rumi founded the order of the Mawlawiya, often called the "whirling dervishes" because of their distinctive ecstatic dance: With the shaykh

in the center, the dancers with flowing robes spin and circle around to the accompaniment of plaintive music.

A Sufi thinker who went far beyond the bounds set by al-Ghazali but who had much influence on Islamic thinkers was Ibn 'Arabi of Spain (1165–1240). Trained in all the religious sciences, Ibn 'Arabi focused on the twin points of unity of being and love. Feeling his thinking led by an inner light from God, he taught that all created things are manifestations of God—external to God but having emanated from the divine mind. In stressing the unity of being, Ibn 'Arabi also exalted the feminine principle, declaring that to see God in woman is more perfect than seeing the divine one in any other forms. Love was at the heart of his vision of the universe, and on that basis he was tolerant of all religions as reflections of the unity of being.

Religious Ideas of the Shi'ites   During the classical period, the one major division in the worldwide Islamic community developed: the Shi'a movement, which today comprises about 15 percent of the world population of

---

—TIMELINE—   The Muslim Story: Some Important Dates

C.E.

500	600	700	800	900	1000	1100
570 C.E. Birth of Muhammad	**ca. 609–610** First sending down of revelations from God	**711–713** Muslims enter Spain and India	**9th century** Flourishing of Mu'tazilite thought	**909–1171** Fatimid dynasty in Egypt	**1058–1111** Al-Ghazali, leading Muslim thinker	**1187** Recapture of Jerusalem by Salah-al-Din
	622 The Hijira; emigration to Medina	**ca. 750–1000** Development of religious law and schools of law	**ca. 878** Occultation (concealment) of 12th Shi'ite Imam	**912** Execution of Al-Hallaj, Persian Sufi	**1099** Capture of Jerusalem by Christian Crusaders	
	630 Submission of Mecca	**750–1258** Abbasid dynasty at Baghdad		**935** Death of Al-Ash'ari, thinker who met the Mu'tazilite challenge		
	632 Death of Muhammad	**786–809** Caliph Harun al-Rashid				
	632–661 Expansion of Islam under first four caliphs					
	661–750 Umayyad dynasty at Damascus					
	680 Martyrdom of Husayn at Karbala					

Muslims. The split between the Shi'ites and the Sunnites (the orthodox Muslims) began as a political division but later led to some divergent religious emphases.

From the time of Muhammad's death there had existed a *shi'at 'Ali*, a "faction of 'Ali" who thought Muhammad's cousin and son-in-law 'Ali was destined to be the successor of Muhammad. Although 'Ali was passed over in the choice of the first three caliphs and died tragically after his brief frustrated time as fourth caliph, his followers continued to hold that he and his descendants were the proper successors to Muhammad in God's design. 'Ali had married Muhammad's daughter Fatima, and their sons Hasan and Husayn were the male descendants of Muhammad—and the Shi'ites felt that the successors of Muhammad should come from the "people of the house," that is, Muhammad's house. Shi'ites report *hadiths* which indicate that Muhammad did at various times indicate that 'Ali and the "people of the house" were to be his successors. A particularly significant incident took place at the pool of Ghadir al-Khumm as Muhammad was on his way back to Medina from his farewell pilgrim-

age. There, before the assembled Muslims, Muhammad publicly designated 'Ali as his successor, according to the Shi'ites, saying that whoever has Muhammad as his master has 'Ali as his master.[14] Whereas Sunnites hold that this incident simply shows the affection Muhammad had for 'Ali, Shi'ites see it as proof that 'Ali is the divinely designated imam or successor of Muhammad. Yet 'Ali, sensing the importance of maintaining the unity of the ummah, did not press the claim when the first three caliphs were chosen, and his own delayed and brief rule as caliph was marked by division and tragedy.

After 'Ali's death and Mu'awiya's takeover of the caliphate for the Umayyad family, 'Ali's son Hasan gave up any claim as successor of Muhammad. But in 680, 'Ali's younger son Husayn put forth the claim to be the rightful successor. On his way to Iraq, where he had many supporters, Husayn and his whole family were ambushed at Karbalah; the men were massacred and the women taken in chains to Damascus. But what appeared to be a great defeat became a religious rallying point for the Shi'ites. They interpreted Husayn's

1200	1400	1500	1700	1800	1900	
1258 Destruction of Baghdad by Mongols	1453 Capture of Constantinople by Ottoman Turks	1502–1736 Safavid Shi'ite dynasty in Iran	ca. 1760 Beginnings of the Wahhabi reform movement	ca. 1800 Beginnings of Western domination over Muslim lands	1916 Hashemite rebellion against Ottoman Empire	1947 Partition of India and creation of Pakistan
		1517 Beginning of Ottoman caliphate			1924 Secularization of Turkey	1978–1979 Revolution in Iran and creation of the Islamic Republic of Iran
		1520–1566 Sulayman the Magnificent			1928 Founding of the Muslim Brotherhood	
		1526 Founding of Mughal Empire in India			1932 Rise of the Sa'ud family to rule in Arabia	
		1556–1605 Rule of Akbar in India				

death as a martyrdom in God's cause, showing that God provides blessings through the sufferings of the people of the prophet's house. Muhammad's own death, the death of his infant sons, the death of the youthful Fatima, 'Ali's assassination, Hasan's death by poisoning, Husayn's martyrdom at Karbalah, plus the tragic deaths of succeeding imams, all show God's redemptive design. Annually on the tenth of Muharram, Shi'ites remember the massacre at Karbalah with processions, passion plays, and intensified spiritual discipline.

Besides their view of the proper successor of Muhammad and their inclination to view the suffering and deaths of the imams as having deep spiritual meaning, the Shi'ites differed with the Sunnites in a number of ways. Sunnites viewed the caliphate in a contractual way, the caliph ruling by consensus as the deputy of Muhammad. But the Shi'ites developed a more vertical, intrinsicalist view of the imamate: The highest spiritual authority of Muhammad was passed on to 'Ali and then to each of the succeeding imams. Just as Muhammad was kept sinless and perfect, so also the imams, possessing the "light of Muhammad," are kept by God from error in interpreting God's revelation. All true interpretation therefore comes from the imam, not from the consensus of other scholars.

Further, Shi'ites held the idea of the **hidden imam.** In particular, the twelfth imam Muhammad disappeared and went into a state of hiding or occultation *(ghaybah),* from which he will return one day to destroy evil and establish a new perfect age of Islam. Meanwhile, this hidden imam illumines and guides the religious scholars *(mujtahids)* as they interpret the Quran and establish law for Muslims. The largest group of Shi'ites accepts this idea about the twelfth imam, earning thereby the name **Twelvers** *(Ithna 'Ashariyah).* The Twelvers became dominant in Iran during the sixteenth century and still today make up the vast majority of Muslims in Iran, with large numbers also in Iraq.

A smaller group differs from the Twelvers on the identity of the fourth imam, holding him to be Zayd, a grandson of Husayn; the Zaydis, living in Yemen today, are very close to Sunnites in their practices. Still another group claims the proper seventh imam was Isma'il; since they consider him to be the last imam, the Isma'ilites are often called Seveners. From the Isma'ilites have come some splinter groups of a more radical nature, such as the order of the Assassins, who used the art of the dagger, combined with taking hashish, to accomplish their purposes. Small groups stemming from the Isma'ilites, such as the Druze of Lebanon and the 'Alawites of Syria, developed radical, secretive teachings and practices to the extent that many other Muslims no longer recognize them within Islam.

It should be emphasized that the Shi'ites agree with the Sunnites on all the major points of Islamic faith and practice, with the exceptions noted here. They have their own schools of law.

Medieval Empires: Stability and Flourishing Muslim Culture

After the disruptions caused by the Mongol invasions, new Muslim empires eventually were established in the sixteenth century, to restore some order and stability in the Muslim world. And they succeeded well. Spread abroad, especially by traders and Sufi brotherhoods, Muslim civilization was extended through much of the world by a whole series of dynamic sultanates. Eventually, these sultanates developed into three empires that were especially important: the **Safavid** Empire in Iran, the **Mughal** Empire in India, and the **Ottoman** Turkish Empire bridging western Asia, northern Africa, and eastern Europe.

From the fifteenth century on, the West was moving into the Renaissance, followed by the great explorations and discoveries, the rise of science, and the Enlightenment. But most of this bypassed Islam. The Muslim world, having had its golden age earlier, entered into a period of stagnation and retreat. Although the disruption caused by the Mongols was overcome in the new Muslim empires, the scientific revolution and the Enlightenment did not reach into Muslim society until the Western powers began to encroach upon Muslim lands in the nineteenth century. Still, there was continued expansion of Muslim rule, both into eastern Europe and into all of India. And although modernity did not emerge, there was a great flourishing of traditional Muslim culture in the Middle East, India, and the Malaysian-Indonesian archipelago. In fact, areas under Muslim rule had never been greater than during the medieval empires.

Late in the thirteenth century, the Turk Osman (d. 1326) is said to have founded the Osmali or Ottoman dynasty in Asia Minor. The Ottomans reconquered most of the old area of the Islamic ummah, subjugating the smaller Muslim principalities and taking over guardianship of the holy cities of Mecca and Medina. They combined the traditional Mongol-Turkish warrior heritage with the Islamic missionary impulse, setting themselves forth as the defenders and propagators of Islam. Before long they also made deep inroads into Christian Europe: in 1453 Constantinople fell to the Ottoman Sultan Mehmet II, and by 1550 the Ottomans controlled the Balkans, most of Hungary, and parts of southern Russia. Some of the panic of European Christianity at the time of the Reformation reflects this surge of Islam. Yet Christian communities generally fared well in Turkish Muslim lands, and Jews fleeing persecution in Europe found safe haven under Ottoman rule. The Ottoman caliphate was proclaimed in 1517 as the supposed head of the Muslim ummah, and it continued, with a long period of decline, until it was terminated by the Turkish people themselves in 1924.

Some have felt that the reign of Sulayman the Magnificent (1520–1566) was the most glorious in all the annals of Islam. He was a great warrior and statesman, effected a massive codification of law, built many architectural glories throughout Istanbul (formerly Constantinople), and promoted music, poetry, and the arts at his lavish court. Religious scholars (**'ulama**) played a very important role in the Sunnite Ottoman Empire with its close fusion of religion and state, but they lost their independent standing and became a clerical bureaucracy within the Ottoman system.

East of the Ottomans, a new empire came into being in Iran (Persia). The Safavids had been a Sufi brotherhood working for the purifying of Islam, eventually taking on Shi'ite messianic aspirations and engaging in armed struggle. In 1501, Shah Ismail (1487–1524), head of the Safavid family, invaded and occupied Tabriz, proclaiming himself shah of Iran and setting up the Safavid dynasty. He claimed to be a descendant of the twelfth imam, a divinely guided reformer, and he forged a new religious-political identity for Iran with Shi'ism as the religion of the realm, and it has remained so in Iran down to the present.

Among the great cultural achievements of the shahs of Iran was the capital city Isfahan, created by Shah 'Abbas (r. 1588–1629), most famous of the Safavid sultans. Full of beautiful gardens, monuments, mosques, and Islamic schools, Isfahan attracted travelers and Muslim scholars from all over the world.

As early as the tenth century, Muslim warriors invaded India, and the sultanate of Delhi was set up to control northern India. These first Muslim invaders looked upon Hindus and Buddhists as polytheists, with their elaborate temples and devotion to gods, Buddhas, and bodhisattvas. So they looted the temples and destroyed the monasteries.

The Mongols were converted to Islam, and early in the sixteenth century, an army led by Babur (d. 1530), a descendant of Genghis Khan, invaded India and founded the Mughal Empire in northern India. The famous ruler Akbar (r. 1556–1605), grandson of Babur, extended his rule to include most of India. Akbar was a Muslim, but he developed a very tolerant attitude toward Hindus, marrying a Hindu princess and revoking all Muslim laws that discriminated against them. He set up a policy of universal religious toleration and encouraged discussions at his court between Muslims, Hindus, Zoroastrians, Jains, and even Christians. Eventually, in the second half of his reign, Akbar tried to establish a new religion, the Divine Wisdom, a kind of synthesis of all these religions.

But Akbar's successors recognized that Akbar had gone beyond the boundaries of Islam, so they restored the Muslim faith. One of these successors, Shah Jahan (r. 1628–1658), achieved enduring fame by building the Taj Mahal as a crowning glory of Islamic art. But Mughal power disintegrated rapidly, and when British forces became dominant in the eighteenth century, they took over effective administration of its remnants. At the time when political unity was disintegrating, a Sufi leader, Shah Wali Allah (1703–1762), founded a Muslim revival movement, which sought to unify the Muslim community and revitalize its religious practice. He attempted to revive early forms of Islamic belief and practice rather than simply relying on the four schools of law. He even translated the Quran into Persian to make it more available to the people. The legacy of the Mughal Empire in India is the largest single group of Muslims in the world—now divided in India, Pakistan, and Bangladesh.

Reform Movements and the Modern World

While Islamic society was flourishing in traditional modes in these wide-flung empires, in Europe, dramatic changes in learning, science, and technology were taking place. By the beginning of the nineteenth century, the forces of European colonization were felt on all sides, and Islam was pushed and shoved into the modern era with all its religious problems and opportunities.

The Wahhabi Reform Movement   Just as the first rumblings of Western intervention were striking the Ottomans, a different kind of challenge erupted from central Arabia.

The Taj Mahal, a grand Muslim building from the Mughal period in India.

Mecca in 1806. Although the Ottomans eventually recaptured Mecca, a century later the Sa'ud family succeeded in reconquering Arabia, and they reinstituted the Wahhabi policies. Still today, the Wahhabi influence is dominant in Saudi Arabia, where the ancient form of Islamic law remains in force as the law of the land. The Wahhabis also provided a strong stimulus to Muslim reform outside Arabia. At the beginning of the nineteenth century, Muslims in India and West Africa moved with the same zeal to purify the dominant Muslim establishments.

Challenge from Western Culture and Muslim Response

As the Western world moved gradually into the modern era, the Muslim sultanates were overpowered by new Western advances in naval power, the steam engine, and other developments of the scientific age. The symbolic beginning of the modern period in the Islamic world was in about 1800, when Napoleon and his forces came to Egypt and opened this Muslim land up to Western dominance and exploitation. The same pattern was followed in other Muslim lands throughout the nineteenth century and even up to the mid-twentieth century. The Dutch took control of Indonesia, the British ruled Malaya, Russia moved into central Asia, Iran was divided between the British and the Russians, and north Africa became a group of European colonies. In 1876, the British Christian Queen Victoria was proclaimed Empress of India!

Such events shook the Muslim world deeply, bringing both a loss of independence and a loss of confidence in the face of the modern achievements of the West. The pattern of Muslim rule in the various empires that had evolved in the medieval period no longer was viable. One of the first responses to the onslaught of the modern era was a new nationalism in some of the Muslim lands.

Muhammad ibn 'Abd al-Wahhab (1703–1792) founded a reform movement that attempted to purify Islam of centuries-long accumulations of beliefs and practices, returning to the original purity of the Quran and the Sunnah of the Prophet. The reform movement was premodern in that it was not a protest against traditionalism in the name of modernity, nor was it a reaction against modernization. The Wahhabis were traditionalists who attacked innovations like those of the rationalistic and esoteric interpretations of the Quran, the Sufi blurring of the distinction between God and humans, the cult of saints that had developed, and the like. They held that the clear words of the Quran and the tradition of the Prophet should be literally understood as direct guidance for life. The Wahhabis destroyed tombs and shrines dedicated to saints, and they initiated religious education and enforced Islamic morality.

The **Wahhabi** movement spread rapidly and became a highly disciplined group of Muslims practicing a purified Islam. They struck up an alliance with the house of Sa'ud in Arabia and managed to gain control of the holy city of

In the nineteenth and early twentieth centuries, the Ottoman Empire was in the process of disintegrating. People of the Balkans expelled their Muslim overlords and created independent nations. As the world lurched into World War I, the Ottomans took the side of the central powers. With British encouragement, this provided the chance for the Hashemite Arabs of the Hejaz, under the leadership of Husayn ibn 'Ali, to revolt against their hated Turkish overloads. The British guaranteed the Arabs autonomy once the war was ended, but after the war the British and French retained mandates over most of the Arab lands in the Middle East. Husayn's sons were appointed hereditary rulers of Iraq and Transjordon. But Britain reserved Palestine with the intent of creating a homeland for the Jews in accord with the secret Balfour Declaration of 1917—a policy the Arabs considered a betrayal by the British. The Hashemite leader Husayn ibn 'Ali was driven out of the Hejaz by the Sa'udis, who established the kingdom of Saudi Arabia. Under pressure from the rapidly increasing Jewish immigration into Palestine, Arab nationalism rose to a high pitch. However, the divisions in the Arab world were such that Arab nationalism did not result in unified actions or goals. The complicated Arab–Israeli political conflicts have spilled over into tensions between Muslims and Jews.

Nationalism prevailed also in Turkey—but of a different sort. The last effective ruler of the Ottoman Empire, al-Hamid II (r. 1876–1909), had tried to reassert his role as true caliph for all the Muslim world. But the defeat suffered in World War I and the threatened dismemberment of the Turkish homeland itself created a nationalist revolution led by Mustafa Kemal (1881–1939). This revolution ushered in a modern Turkish state and a national identity based on distinctively Turkish culture, history, and language. Islam was included merely as one of the elements of this national identity, and the Ottoman caliphate was declared ended. To throw off the shackles of traditionalism, the Islamic scholars ('ulama) were excluded from any public role, and secular law replaced Islamic law. Religion became a personal, voluntary matter, and women were emancipated from the traditional family codes. The Turkish leaders insisted this was not an antireligious movement but rather a reform of religion; freed from the authority of the religious scholars, men and women could turn to the religion of the Quran to meet their religious needs.

In India, nationalism took the form of an Indo-Muslim movement. Thinkers like Muhammad Iqbal (1876–1938), seeing that Muslims in India were faced with being a perpetual minority within a secularized Hindu state, advocated the partitioning of India and the creation of a separate, independent Muslim state. A poet and philosopher of Islam, Iqbal saw Western secular influences as destructive because the West had no spiritual roots in service to God. In order for a Muslim to live life in submission to God, it was necessary to have a Muslim state. At the same time, Iqbal advocated liberal values for society and the creation of an Islamic League of Nations. India was partitioned in 1947, with great suffering and displacement of populations, and the Muslim state of Pakistan was created. Later, East Pakistan rebelled and established the separate state of Bangladesh. For many Indian Muslims, the creation of Pakistan was a great new day for Islam; others regretted it deeply and chose to remain in India.

Although the changes have not been so dramatic elsewhere in the world, in the last half century most of the Muslim lands have been restored politically to Muslims. The British, French, and Dutch have gone, and Muslims generally have been free to choose their own method of self-rule. One price of this nationalism has been the breakup of the worldwide unity of Islam. Now a Muslim is a "citizen" of a particular state rather than a "believer" within the ummah. There have been Muslim thinkers in the modern era who proposed and fought for a pan-Islamic unity that transcends nationalism, and there still exists a sense of worldwide Islamic brotherhood. But Islam needs to be fulfilled in concrete religious, social, and political forms; and in the modern world, it has not been possible to transcend the political barriers of the nation state.

Modern Thinkers: Muhammad 'Abduh and Amir 'Ali One important Muslim response to modernization influences has been to rethink the bases of Islam. Some Muslim thinkers have tried to show that the Muslim tradition is compatible with modern science and progress; in fact, Islam has contributed a great deal to the modern spirit. Muhammad 'Abduh (1849–1905) of Egypt wanted to strengthen Islam and push out Western influences and power, but he saw no basic conflicts between religion and modern science. He pointed out that the Muslim tradition has always advocated

Muslim women praying during the fasting month of Ramadan.

progress in science, researching and understanding the natural law that operates according to God's design. In Egypt, 'Abduh supported educational reform and tried to modernize the curriculum of the famous university al-Azhar, so that Islamic scholars would become grounded in modern thought as well as in the religious sciences. In his view, Christianity as an other-worldly religion was less suited to the modern spirit than was Islam with its long tradition of scientific investigation.

Another influential modern thinker was Amir 'Ali (1849–1928), an Indian Shi'ite lawyer who advocated the goals of the brotherhood of all Muslims, respect for women, and government for the people. In his widely read book, *The Spirit of Islam,* Amir 'Ali portrayed Muhammad as a political liberator for the people of his day, and he asserted that Islam today should return to that kind of vision. Muhammad allowed plural marriage because, in the society of his day, it was the best way of protecting women from destitution and exploitation; and secluding them was the way of showing them respect. But it is only traditionalism that has rigidly perpetuated these practices in modern times. Amir 'Ali thus argued that the Muslim tradition

really offers modern people a liberating spiritual base. In the process, Amir 'Ali interpreted the Quran in the light of its historical context; the laws it prescribes are the best for its day but are not to be considered unchangeable edicts for all time. To many Muslims, however, this is an unacceptable form of modernization.

The Modern Resurgence of Islam   While many Muslims today live in very secularized societies, the weight of Islamic tradition goes against accepting such secularization of life with all its accompanying effects on the individual and on society. In response to the ever-increasing pervasiveness of secular Western influences in every part of the world, the last few decades have seen new Islamic revival movements. One such militant revival is the Muslim Brotherhood, which was founded in Egypt in 1928 and spread to north Africa, Syria, and Iraq. The Brotherhood holds that all efforts toward modernization have to be purged of their Western influences and adjusted to the pure teaching of Islam. Even modern Islamic regimes should be swept away if they perpetuate a secular society or one that is imperfectly Islamic. The primary nation of Muslims is the ummah, and allegiance cannot be given to Western-style nation-states that do not promote the ummah.

Another example of the revival of Islam to meet the threat of Westernization is the Islamic Republic of Iran. During the 1960s and 1970s, Shah Reza Pahlavi strongly promoted the modernization of Iran's economy, education, military, and culture. Western-style recreation, consumer goods, and social life prevailed. Women in the cities, for example, went about in short dresses without covering hair or arms. In addition to the shah's rejection of traditional Islamic values and customs, he enforced harsh repressive security measures against his opponents. Finally, in 1978–1979 Shi'ite religious leaders, inspired by the exiled Ayatollah Khomeini, overthrew the shah and established an Islamic republic. The constitution of Iran makes it clear that, while it is a modern state with full protection and rights for all its citizens, the fundamental law of the state is Islamic law, and the final authorities in the interpretation of that law are the religious scholars. Iran is perhaps the clearest example of the attempt to wed complete submission to God's law with the demands and opportunities of modern civilization.

There are many other examples of Muslim resurgence throughout the world today. Muslims in Pakistan have attempted to create a Muslim state while still guaranteeing political and religious freedom to non-Muslims. In Nigeria, Muslims are hoping to bring social and political life in their country more in conformity with the Islamic Shari'ah. And Muslims in Indonesia are seeking ways to express their Islamic way of life while maintaining harmony and national

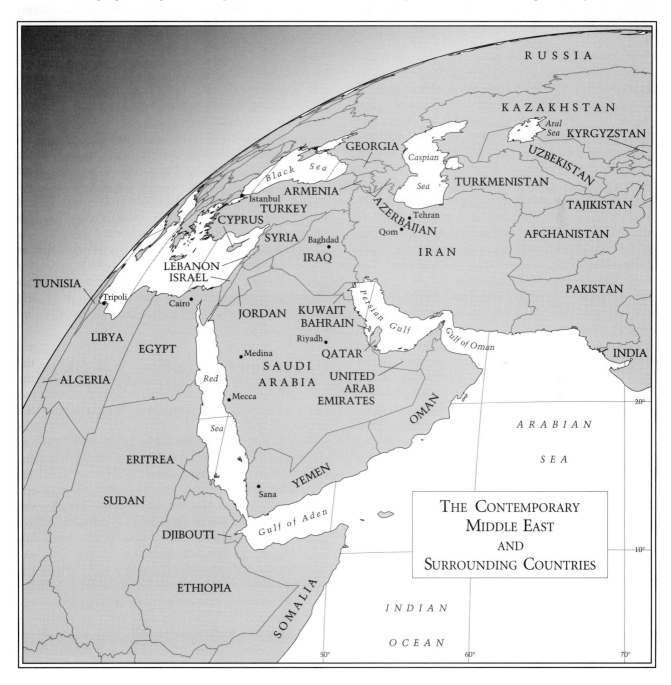

THE CONTEMPORARY
MIDDLE EAST
AND
SURROUNDING COUNTRIES

unity in their pluralistic society. To many Muslims, in countries across the Muslim world, the Islamic resurgence is an expression of their desire to live in the modern world by drawing on their own Islamic spiritual sources rather than simply accepting Western secular models.

Islam in the West   A new factor in modern Islam is the increasing numbers of Muslims living in Western societies. There are more than 18 million Muslims in Europe, for example, about half of them in the southeastern regions, with the other half in western parts of Europe. France alone is home to over five million Muslims. And the numbers of Muslims who have immigrated to America or are studying in America have increased dramatically, so that Islam is the fastest growing religion in the Americas. Along with the traditional capitals and major cities of Islam like Cairo, Istanbul, Damascus, Islamabad, and Jakarta, today are included cities like Paris, London, New York, Detroit, and Chicago. The problems and opportunities of these Muslim communities living in non-Muslim societies have been increasingly discussed by Islamic leaders.

A particularly important Muslim movement in America has been the so-called Black Muslim movement, which has attracted many African-Americans. Some of the first Muslims in America were slaves from Africa, although their Islamic identity was suppressed under conditions of slavery. While there were a number of attempts by African-Americans to foster Islamic identity, the most prominent and lasting movement was the Nation of Islam, founded by Elijah Muhammad (1897–1975), who was born in Georgia as Elijah Poole. Elijah Muhammad identified himself as the messenger of God, and he founded Nation of Islam communities in many major cities, providing identity, status, and a strict moral way of life for many living in difficult situations in the inner cities. Elijah Muhammad's preaching included a racial mythology that fostered black nationalism and excluded integration with whites. A Nation of Islam leader who moved away from this racial mythology was Malcolm X, founder of the Organization of Afro-American Unity, which supported black nationalism but rejected black separation. Malcolm X was assassinated, but eventually Elijah Muhammad's son, Warith Deen Muhammad, took over leadership of the main Black Muslim group and transformed it into the American Muslim Mission, a nonracist, authentic Islamic community in America. The central organization was dissolved in 1985, and these mosques have forged close links with the other Muslim communities while continuing to serve African-Americans of the urban neighborhoods. Another charismatic leader, Louis Farrakhan, broke with Warith Deen Muhammad and revived the Nation of Islam, eloquently denouncing the causes of racism and poverty and sponsoring popular events such as the 1995 Million Man march on Washington. But even the smaller Nation of Islam has moved closer to orthodox Islamic practices and has ties with leaders in the Muslim world.

Because of the increasing presence of Muslims in the Western world, and also because of crucial situations involving Muslims and non-Muslims in parts of the world such as Palestine and India, in recent years some Muslims have shown an interest in establishing dialogue with people of other religions, particularly Christians and Jews. Whereas Christians and Jews have been engaging in dialogue for some years, these "trialogues" are fairly new developments. Muslims in the West are increasingly seeing the importance of imparting an authentic understanding of Islamic religion to non-Muslims and creating strategies and opportunities for interfaith cooperation.

Discussion Questions

1   What was cultural and religious life like in Arabia before Muhammad brought the new teachings of Islam?

2   Describe how Muhammad began receiving revelations from God. What was his own reaction? Were there any who believed him?

3   What kind of reaction was there among the people of Mecca when Muhammad began publicly proclaiming his new revelations?

4   Why was the Hijra such an important event that the Muslim calendar dates from it?

5   Discuss Muhammad's relationship with the whole line of prophets sent by God in earlier times. What is the Islamic understanding of the prophet Jesus?

6   What was the role of the caliph? What was accomplished by the first four caliphs?

7 Describe the classical period of Islam, under the rule of the Umayyads and the Abbasids. What great achievements came about during these times?

8 What did the Mu'tazilites argue for, and what was the response of al-Ash'ari and other orthodox thinkers?

9 Describe the main aspects of the Sufi movement. Why was al-Hallaj executed? What was the contribution of al-Ghazali?

10 What were the main Shi'ite religious ideas that differed from those of the Sunnites?

11 What were the three great Muslim empires that flourished beginning in the sixteenth century? Describe some of their achievements.

12 Describe the intent and results of the Wahhabi reform movement.

13 What have been the major forms of Muslim revival and renewal during the twentieth century?

CHAPTER 13

Muslim Worlds of Meaning

ALLAH, LORD OF THE WORLDS

What's it *all* about? To Muslims, the assertion of the oneness (**tawhid**) of God is the bedrock of all life and truth. The Muslim confession of faith is brief and focused: "There is no God but God, and Muhammad is the messenger of God." This is called the **Shahadah** (Confession), and it is the basic statement of faith for all Muslims. Reciting this confession with faith and true intention is what makes one a Muslim. These are the first words recited in a baby's ear at birth, and they are the last words on the lips of a dying Muslim. Recited in prayers many times each day, the confession epitomizes the spirit of Islam.

Life Centered in One God

"There is no God but Allah"—*la ilaha illa Allah.* There is no reluctance among Muslims to pronounce the divine term *Allah* (God) such as Jews feel about pronouncing the divine name of Yahweh. Rather, the feeling is that this confession, with its sonorous, liquid syllables, should perpetually be heard. Indeed, the very mention of Allah brings blessings, and so it is the most repeated word in the Muslim vocabulary. Friends are greeted with the name of Allah. After any favorable action a Muslim voices, "Praise be to Allah" *(alhamduli-llah).* Referring to intentions for the future, the Muslim adds, "If Allah wills" *(insha allah).* Every sura of the Quran (except sura 9) begins with the *bismillah,* "In the name of Allah." And in the call to prayers five times every day, and on countless other occasions, the cry goes out, *Allahu akbar,* "God is Greater!"

The Unity of God   When Muslims say, "There is no God but Allah," the emphasis is not particularly on the existence of a divine reality or on the name that one calls this divine reality. The Arab tribes of Muhammad's time did not doubt the existence of gods, and they also knew and believed in Allah as the supreme God, the creator. What Muhammad proclaimed that was new and radical was the sole existence of Allah, to the exclusion of any other divine beings. The word *Allah* in Arabic simply means "the God" *(al-ilah).* It is not a personal name known only by devotees of a particular religion, like the name Yahweh or Jesus Christ or Krishna. It is the word universally used in the Arabic language to designate "the God."

What the confession stresses above all is the unity of God, the doctrine of *tawhid.* God is one. Whereas this sounds deceptively simple, to Muslims the whole experience of God is concentrated in these words.

God is one. That means, first of all, that God completely fills up the divine realm to the total exclusion of any other divinity. God cannot be divided into many parts, or even two or three parts. It is not possible for there to be competitors to Allah in the divine realm. There are no associates, no divine helpers or enemies of God. Muslims do believe in the existence of angels, messengers of God who carry out God's will in the world. But these angels are creatures of God, belonging to the created space-time world. Only God is God.

The unity of God further means that God is transcendent, that is, far beyond and separate from the created world. Emphasizing the transcendence of God in stronger tones than do Jews or Christians, Muslims insist on a total separation of the two realms, the divine and the created, with no overlapping and no mixing together. To mix God together with the created realm would be to compromise God's oneness and uniqueness. It would be to elevate something created to the status of divinity, thus positing a competitor to the one God. The greatest sin, according to the Quran, is *shirk,* associating something else with God. This is the great sin of polytheism, which looks on created things such as sun and moon, mountains and trees, spirits and angels, as fellow divinities with God. But this is also the fallacy of Christians, who say that God has a son, thus mixing God together with human flesh and imagining that there are thus two gods, the Father in the divine realm and the Son in the created realm. "It is not for God to take a son unto Him. Glory be to Him!" (19:35).

The oneness of God means, therefore, that all power belongs to God. There is no other source of power, since God has no competitors. It follows, then, since God is the only creator of the world, that everything that takes place in the created world results from God's will. The Quran says, "No female bears or brings forth, save with His knowledge; and none is given long life who is given long life neither is any diminished in his life, but it is in a Book" (35:11). Again, "No affliction befalls in the earth or in yourselves, but it is in a Book, before We create it" (57:22). God does, within the structure of almighty governance, allow a certain measure of freedom to creatures, thus giving them moral responsibility for their actions. But the fact that God is almighty means most importantly that no other divine power rules and directs our lives.

The Unity of All Human Knowledge　Since God is one, it follows that the created world is also one. It is not enslaved to a variety of supernatural powers but is totally under the dominion of the one God. In an eloquent passage, the Quran celebrates the unity of God's power:

> What, is God better, or that they associate [gods with Him]? He who created the heavens and earth, and sent down for you out of heaven water; and We caused to grow therewith gardens full of loveliness whose trees you could never grow. Is there a god with God? Nay, but they are a people who assign to Him equals! He who made the earth a fixed place and set amidst it

rivers and appointed for it firm mountains and placed a partition between the two seas. Is there a god with God? Nay, but the most of them have no knowledge.

(27:60–61)

The Quran says that if there were in heaven and earth other gods besides God, surely the heaven and earth would dissolve into chaos (21:22). Thus belief in the oneness of God is an affirmation of the unity and dignity of the created world. The creature knows that God alone is the possessor of all power, and that none besides God can bless or harm, give or take away life. This belief thus frees humans from fearing any other power in the created world. It makes it possible to live life to the fullest as God intends, not overawed by the greatness of another, not putting oneself above another. Knowing that all power, blessing, and wealth come from God makes it possible to treat all other creatures fairly, to have a humble and modest attitude, and above all to strive in everything to obey and observe the law that God has given as the guide for all creatures. Associating God's power and authority with created beings would take away the dignity, unity, and value of God's creatures.

So God is not like anything, for anything else is part of the created realm, and God is beyond all this. To liken God to anything created raises the danger of compromising God's oneness. Therefore, the Muslim tradition strictly prohibits the use of pictures or images of God. Even words and verbal images that compare God with anything else are to be avoided. "God is Greater!"

So can we know or say anything at all about God? God has given self-revelation to humans, and it is that revelation that is the source of knowledge of God—the Quran. What the Quran says about God we are to believe and submit to, recognizing that words of human language are limited in expressing the reality of God. But since God is the only divine power, all of the knowledge we derive from this created world is also, in essence, knowledge of God the one creator. Thus knowledge encompassed in the sciences and humanities, insofar as it is not contaminated by human error, leads to the same truth about God as that found in the Quran. There is no other divine power to be discovered with human reason, through science and humanities; all knowledge must lead to the one God. The unity of God thus means the unity of human knowledge.

God Is Present and Merciful
Even while stressing God's transcendence and almighty power, Muslims express a strong experience of the real presence of God, that is, God's immanence. God is not present as part of the created world, but the divine reality is present everywhere nonetheless. "To God belong the East and the West; whithersoever you turn, there is the Face of God," says the Quran (2:115). Or again, the Quran says that no three people meet together but God is their fourth; nor five people but God is their sixth; no matter how many, God is with them wherever they may be (58:7).

God as present to us is known by many names, which express the various divine attributes.

> He is God; there is no god but He.
> He is the King, the All-holy, the All-peaceable, the All-faithful, the All-preserver, the All-mighty, the All-compeller, the All-sublime. Glory be to God, above that they associate! He is God, the Creator, the Maker, the Shaper. To Him belong the Names Most Beautiful. All that is in the heavens and the earth magnifies Him; He is the All-mighty, the All-wise.

(59:22–24)

One of the attributes of God most stressed in Islam is mercy. The *bismillah,* a statement that begins all but one sura of the Quran, emphasizes this with a double force: "In the name of Allah, the Most Merciful, the Most Compassionate." Thus Muslims know that God's ultimate design for creation is one of love and mercy.

God and the Problem of Evil   The problem of evil and suffering in the world is understood by Muslims within the context of God's almighty power and mercy. In one sense, God is the cause behind everything, and therefore even what appears to be evil and suffering is also caused by God.

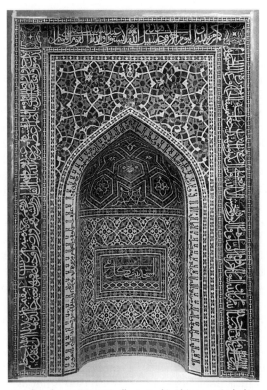

Muslim decorative art is illustrated in this mosaic-laden mihrab (prayer niche), built in the thirteenth century in Isfahan, Iran. The Metropolitan Museum of Art, Harris Brisbane Fund, 1939.

Oftentimes suffering can, for example, be understood as testing or discipline from God. At the same time, the Quran teaches that within the overall structure of the divine design God gives freedom and responsibility to all creatures, rewarding them for good and punishing them for disobeying. In this sense, we bring evil and suffering on ourselves by our unbelief and disobedience.

Beyond these kinds of explanations Muslims do not go. For it is not proper to inquire too inquisitively into the divine character; rather one should worship and submit to God. "God is our Enough," Muslims say when faced with a puzzle of life, for it is the reality of God rather than our understanding that comes first and foremost. Characteristically, Muslims end all inquiries about God and God's ways with the words, "God knows." And that is sufficient.

NATURE OF THE WORLD AND HUMANS

The World as God's Creation

What is life all about anyway? The *Fatihah* or "Opening" of the Quran states, "In the name of God, the Merciful, the Compassionate. Praise belongs to God, the Master of the Worlds!" *(rabb al-'alamin).* And so God is, in Islam as in Judaism and Christianity, the master and designer of all that exists. Much that is said by Jews and Christians about the creator and about the world and humans as the creation has familiar echoes in the Islamic affirmations. But the Muslim view has its own distinctive colorations, for Muslims start from the center of their faith to understand creation—from the Quran, with its rhapsodic revelations about God as the creator and master, and the world as servant and sign of God's power and design. Moving out from the revelation of the Quran, Muslims believe they can see the signs of God the creator in everything, for all exists and operates according to God's design and purpose.

God as the Master Creator   God is the Master of the Worlds. This means two important things for Muslims: God is transcendent with no associates in the created realm; and creation fulfills its worth and dignity in serving God.

God is the Master *(rabb)*. The Quran says, "That then is God your Lord; there is no god but He, the Creator of everything. So serve Him, for He is Guardian over everything" (6:102). God does not share creative power with anything; God has no associates in the created realm who assist in the divine powers. Unbelievers often mistake elements of the created world to be associates with God, such as forces of nature, angels, or divine-human beings. But this is *shirk,* that great sin of compromising the unity of God. Throughout the Quran the rhapsody goes on, changing color and tone but presenting the same essential message:

> In the Name of God, the Merciful, the Compassionate
> All that is in the heavens and the earth magnifies God;
> He is the All-mighty, the All-wise.
> To Him belongs the Kingdom of the heavens and the earth;
> He gives life, and He makes to die, and He is powerful over
>   everything.
> He is the First and the Last, the Outward and the Inward;
> He has knowledge of everything.
> It is He that created the heavens and the earth in six days
>   then seated Himself upon the Throne.
> He knows what penetrates into the earth, and what comes
>   forth from it,
> what comes down from heaven, and what goes up unto
>   it. . . .
> To Him belongs the Kingdom of the heavens and the earth;
>   and unto Him all matters are returned.
> He makes the night to enter into the day and makes the
>   day to enter into the night.
> He knows the thoughts within the breasts.
>
> (57:1–6)

The Quran speaks of God creating the world in six days, although there is no day-by-day narrative account as in *Genesis* 1. But as to how God created, there can be no compromising God's transcendence: Creation comes through the mighty word. God simply commands, "Be," and it is (36:82). Even the idea that God rested on the sev-

enth day is avoided. After the six days of creation, God sat on the throne, regulating the world (10:3). For God to rest might imply weariness, and therefore the Quran states emphatically that God was not wearied by the act of creation (50:15). For this reason, perhaps, the notion of a sabbath rest is not a part of Islamic worship; the communal day of prayer (Friday) is not considered to be a day of rest from work.

Dignity and Value of Creation   Since God is Master of the worlds, this means all creation has been given dignity and value as creature. Those who mix God's divinity with created things actually undermine and denigrate the worth of the created realm. All creation finds its worth in being servant *('abd)* of the master creator. God created everything in the universe with a design. In the Quran God says, "We have not created the heavens and earth, and what between them is, for vanity" (38:27), nor as "playing" (21:16). Rather, everything in the orderly universe is assigned a place in a grand scheme, all knit together by the Master of the Worlds to follow that design and purpose.

And it is in following that design and purpose that all things find their true value and dignity. God created everything for one overarching purpose: to serve God. "To Him has surrendered whoso is in the heavens and the earth, willingly or unwillingly" (3:83). All things by nature follow the cosmic law of creation—the law of the Master—and that means the whole of nature is in some sense "muslim." There is a natural, cosmic "islam," in which stars and rain, molecules and plants, minerals and animals all worship and serve God by conforming to the law of their being. Since all follow God's design, all things must have dignity and value, for God "has created all things well" (32:7).

Humankind: Caliph and Servant   Like the Torah, the Quran singles out humans as God's special creation, some passages bringing together both the original creation of humans from dust and clay, and God's continuing creation of humans in the womb:

> Surely We created you of dust,
>   then of a sperm-drop,
>   then of a blood clot,
> then of a lump of flesh, formed and unformed
>   that We may make clear to you.
> And We establish in the wombs

what We will, till a stated term,
then We deliver you as infants,
then that you may come of age.

(22:5)

Whereas the Quran nowhere talks of humans made in the "image" of God (which might be misunderstood as being "like" God), it does state that God breathed the "spirit" into humans, providing the breath of life, the animating spirit. And humans were created male and female: "Mankind, fear your Lord, who created you of a single soul, and from it created its mate, and from the pair of them scattered abroad many men and women" (4:1).

Among all the created things, humans are singled out for a special role, designated as the *khalifa* (caliph) of God. The Quran states:

And when Thy Lord said to the angels,
"I am setting in the earth a viceroy *(khalifa)*."
They said, "What, will you set therein one
who will do corruption there, and shed blood,
while We proclaim Thy praise and call Thee Holy?"
He said, "Assuredly I know
    that you know not."
And He taught Adam the names, all of them;
then He presented them unto the angels
and said, "Now tell Me the names of these,
    if you speak truly."
They said, "Glory be to Thee! We know not
save what Thou hast taught us. Surely Thou art
    the All-knowing, the All-wise."
He said, "Adam, tell them their names. . . ."
And when We said to the angels, "Bow yourselves to
    Adam";
    so they bowed themselves, save Iblis; he
        refused . . .

(2:30–34)

The word *khalifa* means deputy or representative, indicating that humans have a preeminent status and role, to exercise dominion over the rest of creation as the caliph of God. God teaches humans the names—this establishes human competence in identifying, naming, and managing creation, and it is something even the angels cannot attain. In another dramatic passage, the Quran reports that God offered the divine trust to the heavens and the earth and the mountains, but they refused to carry it, being afraid of it—but humankind carried it (33:72).

But even as humans are God's caliph over the rest of creation, the proper relation to God the Master is to be servant. "Praise belongs to God, the Lord of all worlds. . . . Thee only we serve," states the opening sura of the Quran. Humans share this servanthood with all creation—indeed, human life largely submits to God's law by nature: genetic patterns, heartbeat and breathing, growth in youth, and decline in old age. But humans differ from all other creatures in three divine qualities: an intelligence that can discern between the true and the false; a will freely to choose; and the power of speech to worship God.[1] God possesses these qualities perfectly, and God has given them in trust to humans. It is in this arena that the real drama of humans serving the Master is played out. One who achieves completeness by using reason, free will, and speech to follow God's design is a perfect "muslim," with not only her body but also her reason, judgment, and speech submitted to God. Now she is at peace with the whole universe, serving the one whom the whole universe serves—and thus she is fit to be God's caliph within creation.

To be God's caliph and servant, humans need guidance. "Guide us in the straight path," says sura 1. And this is what is provided in the Quran and in the Law taken from it—a detailed blueprint of the Islamic order for human life. Such guidance does not contradict or demean human reason. In fact, Muslims feel that God endowed humans with the capacity to reason and acquire knowledge, and by using this correctly humans will choose the truth of the Master. Guidance comes from the Quran—but through human reason this same truth can be uncovered in all the human arts and sciences for human welfare.

Negligence and Unbelief

Why do people do evil and destructive things? The Muslim answer is quite different from the Christian answer to that question. There is no idea of a fundamentally sinful human nature in Islam, as there is in Christianity. The Islamic view is more similar to the Jewish answer but still has its own shape. What is perhaps most distinctive in the Muslim view is the idea that it is forgetfulness and negligence of what we really are that lie behind human sin and evil-doing.

By Nature Muslim, but Forgetful   As we saw, all people are "muslim" by nature, according to the law of God's creation. Just as a stone falls and a tree grows and a fire burns in accordance with the law of nature, so humans involuntarily follow God's natural law in most of their various mental and physical functions. But God created humans for a special role among all creation, expecting them to be God's viceroy on earth. Yet only God is perfect. Humans are limited and imperfect, and there are obstacles in the way of using intelligence, will, and speech in submission to God's law. Humans by nature are negligent, not paying attention to the true nature of things and to their own true nature. And they are forgetful, allowing the guidance given by prophets in the past gradually to slip out of active remembrance. Though humans were created as God's caliph and though they made a covenant with God to accept the divine trust, they are always forgetting who they really are and neglecting the natural law of submission to God as the way of fulfilling their true nature. Humans have the tendency to fall asleep, as it were, and live in a kind of dream world, unaware of who they are and what they should be doing in this world.

Thus, looked at in the ordinary human state, people are weak and negligent, subservient to their surroundings and prisoners of their own needs and passions. It is not that their needs and passions are evil. God created humans with passions and drives as part of the design for a full, useful human life. Without passions, humans would never be motivated to strive for success and well-being in family and society. Some Muslims, like Jews, talk of two inclinations that God created in humans: the spiritual inclination that directs the intelligence and will to follow God's law; and the inclination to fulfill the desires and passions with which God has endowed humans. Both inclinations are necessary and good, when followed in harmony with God's law for human nature and fulfillment. But one who is asleep to his true nature unknowingly becomes a slave to the inclination of the passions. And this means becoming a slave of the creaturely surroundings of human life—a slave of other humans needed to gratify one's lusts, and a slave of the material world needed to satisfy one's cravings for wealth and pleasure.

Muslims emphasize that sin is not of the essence of human nature. There is no such thing as "original sin," which would mean that the human will is fatally warped and inevitably leads to evil deeds. Rather, sin arises from forgetting and neglecting what we really are, failing to use our intellect and will to recognize the Lord and Creator. This leads us to misuse our reason and our freedom of choice by choosing to deny God and surrendering to our needs and passions.

A Kafir: Concealing One's Muslim Nature   A person who out of forgetfulness and neglect denies God is called a **kafir,** an unbeliever. In Arabic, *kufr* means to cover or conceal. The one who denies God is really concealing what is real and true in the whole universe and in his own life and nature. An unbeliever thinks she has true knowledge and understanding, having the illusion that she is following her reason and choosing that which is true. Yet an unbeliever is really blinded by ignorance, for she sees the intricate working and design of the whole universe, but she is blind as to the Designer of it all. She experiences the marvelous working of her own body, but she understands nothing of the Maker of her body. Such a one participates in the human race, to whom God has given the divine trust and the divine qualities of intellect, will, and speech—yet she denies the Source of this all. Like a person who has rented a house but refuses to pay the rent, she as one of humankind has accepted the trust that God gave to humans but refuses to acknowledge the Creator or live up to her part of the bargain.

What an unbeliever does, really, is to rebel against the very course of nature, the law that God has ordained for all things. He sets up creaturely things as worthy of the love and reverence he should show only to God. Thus the *kafir* always becomes a *mushrik,* one who associates other things with God and thus commits the great sin of denying the unity of God *(shirk).* An unbeliever bows his head to other powers, whether these are sun and moon, angels, human heroes or powerful tyrants, or the person's own wants and passions. Thus he commits the greatest injustice and treason possible: He uses God's bountiful gifts, at the same time denying and disobeying his real Lord and Master.

The Struggle Within   Since sin is not of the essence of humans, it is possible to live in total submission to God's law—that is, it is possible for humans to be perfect Muslims, since God does not require anything of us that is beyond our capabilities. Muslims believe that the prophets through whom God has sent revelation have all been perfect humans, completely fulfilling God's will. However, Muslims recognize that prophets are rare individuals, and that most humans have the tendency of forgetfulness and neglect. Even for believers who sincerely desire to live according to God's law, there are internal drives and desires that seek to get the upper hand. Muslims do take sin seriously; to master one's forgetfulness and the dominating drives of one's nature is the great war or struggle in human life.

In the Muslim view, any act of doing what God has prohibited or failing to do what is commanded is a sin. But there are some sins that are more serious and damaging than others. Here is a list of some of the acts that are major sins and thus liable for severe punishment:

1 To believe that there are partners of God.
2 To disbelieve in God, God's prophets, or God's books, or to deny any of the fundamental principles of Islam.
3 To lie.
4 To commit adultery or other illegal sex.
5 To steal.
6 To cheat or deceive anyone.
7 To bear false witness.
8 To bring false charge against anyone.
9 To backbite.
10 To do damage to anybody or injure anyone's feelings.

As in Judaism and Christianity, so also in Islam, unbelief and sin have consequences. Of course, the unbeliever cannot do harm to God, the Master of the worlds. But by *kufr*, humans bring about their own disgrace and failure, both in this life and in the world to come.

By going against the natural law given by God, unbelievers destroy all harmony and peace in their own lives, and in every part of the world they bring infection and abuse with their unbelief. So unbelievers will not find peace and well-being in life. Having destroyed the natural order, they will meet failure in everything they do. Their selfishness and treason against God will infect their family life, business, and relations to others. They will cause war and bloodshed

in human society. And they will abuse and disrupt the harmony of nature. In one way or another, all the evils and troubles of the world have their origin in human unbelief.

On the day of judgment, God will make an accounting of what each person has done. Each person's deeds will be weighed in a balance, and, in the case of an unbeliever, the evil deeds will far outweigh the good deeds. Everything the unbeliever has done will testify against him or her. Then God will consign the traitor to the horrors of the eternal Fire. In this way, the laws that had been so disrupted and twisted by the unbeliever will finally be set back in order.

> All this; but for the insolent awaits an ill resort, Gehenna, wherein they are roasted—an evil cradling! All this; so let them taste it—boiling water and pus, and other torments of the like kind coupled together.
>
> (*Quran* 38:55–58)

In the Muslim view, there is no excuse for being an unbeliever. God's design in the world, and the gifts of intelligence and will, should lead all people to acknowledge and submit to the Creator. To awaken humans out of forgetfulness, God has always and to all peoples been sending prophets with reminders. So all who sin in unbelief are justly punished by God.

The warning of the coming punishment for unbelief should lead us to repent, to ask God for mercy. In God's gracious design, it is possible for us to repent, be forgiven, and turn our efforts anew to living our lives as God would have us.

GUIDANCE ON THE STRAIGHT PATH

How can we start living *real* life? How can we be transformed? It should be noted from the outset that the Muslim tradition has no word that is properly translated as "be saved" or "salvation." Muslims consider the idea of "salvation" to be appropriate to religions like Christianity, where the stress is on God's action while humans have a passive role. In the Muslim's view, as we have seen, humans have a divinely designed nature that has the capacity of realizing God's design. Rather than asking, "How can I be saved?," Muslims would rather ask, "How can I achieve the life of felicity?" The Muslim word "felicity" (*falah*) or the verb "to become felicitous" denotes a thoroughly active concept of the human path toward the ideal life. There is action from God, the Merciful and Compassionate, of course. God guides, forgives, and inspires. But fundamentally, the path is an active one of human self-transformation in harmony with God's design of felicity.

As we have seen, Muslims see humans as not essentially sinful or wicked; rather, God created them good and endowed them with divine attributes by which humans can realize the divine trust. But humans are imperfect, and this shows itself especially in forgetfulness and negligence, from which derive all acts of sin and unbelief with their disastrous consequences. The path of transformation then is a "reminding" to counter human forgetfulness and an "inspiring" to counter negligence. And the practice of the path will be directed toward the divine qualities of intelligence, free will, and speech. The path fills one with knowledge, brings about willing submission, and provides the practice of prayer and worship.

Islam as a Path of Knowledge

The path of Islam is fundamentally a path of knowledge. Although the central concept is that of *islam* or submission, this is not where the path begins. As we have seen, there is a cosmic islam in which the whole creation submits to God's design in following the natural law, and to a large extent also in human life we share in this natural submission. But in the distinctly human realm, that constituted by the divine qualities of intelligence, free will, and speech, submission to God does not take place naturally according to the law of creation. For this is the realm in which humans are called upon to take up the divine qualities and fulfill the divine trust by submitting to God out of free will.

Faith and Submission   But what is it that leads to islam, submission to God, in the distinctively human realm? The Muslim answer is **iman.** This is the Muslim word for "faith," but its meaning is somewhat different from the Christian notion of faith. Muslims point out that Christians often see "faith" as a believing without knowing why, an accepting without rational certainty, a "leap of faith" even against the testimony of reason. But iman in the Muslim path is faith on the basis of rational certainty arrived at through the use of our intelligence. This is the highest form of knowledge. It goes beyond the pseudo-knowledge of rational thinking

Muslims in Cairo observing the ritual of prayer.

without God's guidance, on the one hand, and the superstition of believing without reason, on the other. It is this iman, which we can translate as "certain knowledge," which then leads one freely to islam or submission.

How do we arrive at this iman or certain knowledge? It is true that God's whole creation is like a book full of signs that speak to our intelligence and should bring about certain knowledge on our part. But because humans are forgetful and negligent, these signs alone are usually not sufficient to arouse us out of our dreaming. Therefore, starting with Adam, God has sent reminders through the prophets for guidance on the path toward certain knowledge and submission. This is the role of all the revelations that God has sent to all peoples of all times and places. These revelations have included the Torah brought through Moses and the Gospel brought through Jesus, culminating in the Quran as the final, perfect reminder. The Quran, in Muslim teaching, is the eternal, uncreated Book, authored by God and sent down through the prophet Muhammad. It is the perfect, incomparable Book containing the complete truth for all peoples of all times and places. God's revelation arouses our intellect from its dreaming state and challenges us to use our reason to ascertain the truth about existence.

Recite: In the Name of thy Lord who created,
    created Man of a blood-clot.
Recite: And thy Lord is the Most Generous,
    who taught by the Pen,
        taught Man that he knew not.

(96:1–5)

Although this guidance in the Quran comes from God, no one is compelled to accept and follow it. "No compulsion is there in religion," the Quran states (2:256). Rather, humans are to hear the revelation, study, examine, test, and inquire of it, until finally their reason leads them to iman, certain knowledge of the truth. This is possible because the same God both created human reason and sent down the Quran as guidance. If we truly and freely follow our intellect, Muslims believe, we will arrive at the certain knowledge that the truth presented in the Quran is the ultimate truth and highest knowledge. And—following our intellect further—we will find that everywhere in this universe the same truth is to be found, for everything is of one piece in God's design. Both from studying the Quran and from investigating the world itself, we become certain that the one essential truth is that there is no God but God. All the other truths are one with this, and they are clearly presented in the Quran and throughout God's creation, for our intellect to examine and become convinced. In this way, through using our intelligence in studying God's revelation and the world, we arrive at iman, certain knowledge, saying with the Quran: "The truth has come, and falsehood has vanished away" (17:81). In this sense, Muslims say, Islam is the natural religion.

Because of the emphasis on each person following only the dictates of his or her own intelligence, Islam does not have any priesthood or religious magistracy that tells Muslims what must be believed. Every Muslim, of course, is duty bound to teach others what he knows; and Islam does have its teachers whom it venerates. But no Muslim is required to accept anything as true just because other Muslims have found it to be true. One must accept only what she herself finds rational, coherent, and corresponding to reality. Nothing is to be accepted by faith without being rationally convinced.

It has been the common experience of Muslims, however, that everything presented in the Quran is certain knowledge, for it corresponds with reality as we know it through our intellect. Further, since the Quran is the per-

fect guide to the truth, the total depth of its meaning can never be plumbed. Each time one studies a passage of the Quran, some new aspect of the truth can be understood. Even a whole lifetime of study of the Quran can never exhaust the meaning of its truth.

Thus iman, certain knowledge, is the first step on the path, the intelligence actively searching and reaching the certainty of truth. Then it is possible, in the arena of free will, for islam, submission, to take place. A choice has to be made on the basis of knowledge. Do we choose the true or the false? If we have not arrived at certain knowledge, if we have instead followed the pseudo-knowledge of reason blind to God's guidance or the superstition of irrational faith, then we cannot choose the good because our mind is trapped in falsehood. But if we have arrived at certain knowledge through our intelligence, then our will can choose the true and we can submit to God.

It is important that this islam take place by virtue of free choice, for that is the only way God's design can be fulfilled. It is said that the reason heaven and earth did not accept the divine trust when it was offered to them is because they have no free will. Humans only accepted this trust because they are free moral agents and can realize the design of God's creation. Knowledge achieved by intelligence on the basis of God's guidance, then submission chosen by free will—this is the path of Islam.

Transformation and the Shari'ah   The attainment of certain knowledge and submission bring about a transformation in humans. This changes the heart and effects a total transformation in human life. If one is a *kafir*, an unbeliever, one is out of harmony with the law of nature and brings disruption and bloodshed into the world. But if one achieves certain knowledge and therefore submits, then one is in harmony with God's will and design, being at peace with the creator and whole creation. Mawdudi describes this state of transformation:

> He has now consciously submitted to Him Whom he had already been unconsciously obeying. He has now willingly offered obedience to the Master Whom he already owed obedience to involuntarily. . . . Now his reason and judgement are set on an even keel—for he has rightly decided to obey the Being Who bestowed upon him the faculty of thinking and judging. His tongue is also truthful for it expresses its belief in the Lord Who gave it the faculty of speech. Now the whole of his existence is an

embodiment of truth for, in all spheres of life, he voluntarily as well as involuntarily obeys the laws of One God—the Lord of the Universe. Now he is at peace with the whole universe for he worships Him Whom the whole universe worships.[2]

The practice of the path of Islam involves studying and learning, teaching, reciting, praying, thinking, and choosing. It is a lifelong path, which continues from birth to death. This path of transformation is based on the Shari'ah, the law or code of behavior in Islam. This law, which is taken from the Quran and the Hadith, provides guidance for the regulation of all aspects of life in the best interests of humans and in accord with God's design. We look at some of the specifics of the Shari'ah later. But here we need to understand that performing the Shari'ah is the following of the path of Islam. It is the means by which the individual person molds and shapes his or her own life into the larger design intended by God. In some respects, the Shari'ah plays the same transformative role for Muslims as the Halakhah plays for Jews. This discipline of following the law is a process of education in the highest sense, for the cultivation and perfection of Godlike qualities.

The Greater Jihad   The path of transformation is a continuous struggle. Although humans are not evil by nature, they are also not perfect by nature. So the path of submission is one that requires constant striving, repenting, studying, praying, and disciplining. One term for this spiritual struggle in Islam is **jihad**. The prophet Muhammad, returning from one of the early wars, said, "We have returned from the small *jihad* to the great *jihad*."[3] This idea of jihad refers to the need for striving and struggling to establish God's design in the world. Sometimes it takes the form of outer struggle or holy war in defense of the law of God. But it also refers to the inner struggle of all Muslims, the lifelong striving to shape one's own life into conformity with God's design—this is called the greater jihad. This is the path: a continual holy war against all God's enemies—unbelievers and evildoers, of course, but also all our own failings, sins, and unbeliefs.

Blessings Now and in the Life Hereafter

Following the straight path brings blessings and rewards. It brings felicity in this world and in the next. As in Judaism and Christianity, so also in Islam, one of the important blessings is simply the following of the path itself. For it is the way of life most in harmony with God and all creation, and therefore it brings peace and happiness to all who practice it. Those who know God's design will always be successful, respected, wealthy, and happy, for they will always choose the right way in all fields of knowledge and action. Since Islam is the natural religion, those who follow it will be blessed by the Creator and will be sources of blessing in the world.

All Muslims consider belief in life after death to be one of the essential truths of existence. This belief includes the ideas of judgment and reward or punishment based on one's deeds. If people follow the straight path, the Quran says, they will be rewarded with the joys and delights of paradise.

> So God has guarded them from the evil of that day, and
>   has procured them radiancy and gladness,
> and recompensed them for their patience with a Garden,
>   and silk;
> therein they shall recline upon couches,
> therein they shall see neither sun nor bitter cold;
> near them shall be its shades, and its clusters hung meekly
>   down,
> and there shall be passed around them vessels of silver,
>   and goblets of crystal,
> crystal of silver that they measured very exactly. . . .
> Immortal youths shall go about them;
> when thou seest them, thou supposest them scattered
>   pearls,
> when thou seest them then thou seest bliss and a great
>   kingdom.
> Upon them shall be green garments of silk and brocade;
> they are adorned with bracelets of silver,
> and their Lord shall give them to drink a pure draught.
> "Behold, this is a recompense for you, and your striving is
>   thanked."
>
> (76:11–22)

Descriptions of the Garden of Paradise, scattered throughout the Quran, vividly combine the delights of body and of soul, the sensual and the spiritual. In keeping with the overall teachings of the Quran about God's creation, even in paradise there is no compartmentalizing of life. God's design for creation is good, and believers rewarded with paradise enjoy both the beatific vision and the pleasures of creation.

Discussion Questions

1 What are the implications, for thought, ethics, and art, of saying "There is no God but God"?

2 While stressing God's transcendence, how do Muslims also emphasize God's immanence? What are some of God's attributes?

3 How does the unity of God mean that the creation has dignity and value?

4 In what sense is the whole world of nature "muslim"?

5 What is the nature and special role of humankind, according to Islam?

6 Why do many people become unbelievers? Are they evil by nature?

7 What are some major sins, in the Muslim view? What results from these sins?

8 Explain how the Muslim path is a "path of knowledge." What is *iman*? How does this lead to *islam*?

9 What is the "greater jihad" in Muslim life?

10 Explain Muslim ideas about punishment and blessing in the afterlife.

CHAPTER 14

Ritual Practices and the Good Life for Muslims

RITUAL WORSHIP AND SACRED TIMES

How can we find new power for life? Muslims believe that how God wants humans to live is totally structured in the Shari'ah, the Law, taken from the Quran and Hadith. God is the Master *(rabb)* and our role is to be the servant *('abd)*. Therefore, all of life is to be service *('ibadah)*, that is, worship of God. This includes both the ritual and the ethical duties of life, since nothing is excluded from God's perfect design. Let us first look at the ritual duties, and then at the ethical part of worship.

The basic idea of worshiping God for Muslims is similar to Jewish and Christian views. As creatures, our primary goal is to submit to God and serve God faithfully. God deserves our praise, and remembering God constantly as we go about our life is our highest good. Like Jews, Muslims believe God has given direct guidance in *how* people should worship, providing specific rituals that are designed to meet their deepest needs as human beings and to bring harmony and well-being into their lives because, performing these rituals, they will be in harmony with God's design. There is no separation of religion from the rest of life; all aspects of common everyday life are lifted up in the continued observances of the worship of God.

Muslim holy days and festivals differ somewhat from those in Judaism and Christianity in that they are not geared to the cycles of nature in the seasons of the year. There are, of course, religious observances in the different months of the Muslim calendar. But this calendar follows the lunar pattern (twelve months of twenty-nine or thirty days each), meaning that each year is some eleven days shorter than the solar calendar. Thus, over a period of about thirty-two years, a particular Muslim festival will move through all the seasonal changes of the year—a sign of God's mercy, Muslims say. Another difference is that not as much stress is placed on one holy day of the week as the special day of rest and celebration. Whereas Friday is significant as the day for congregational noon prayers, that day does not carry the same importance as Sabbath for Jews or the Sunday worship for most Christians.

The Five Pillars

Among the central actions required in the Shari'ah for all Muslims are the so-called **Five Pillars** (*'ibadat,* "worships"). The Five Pillars are Confession, Prayer, Alms-giving, Fasting, and Pilgrimage to Mecca. As the minimum duties of Muslims in ritual worship of God, these Pillars are obligatory on all adult Muslims insofar as they are not excused because of sickness or other such reasons. Muslims believe these Five Pillars are perfectly fit to achieve complete human welfare in God's design. They are performed by each person individually, thus establishing a strong sense of individual personhood. At the same time they create the unity of the whole community, because they are done communally, even throughout the whole world. They combine physical activity with spiritual reflection, thus transforming the whole person. Simple to perform, they at the same

The muezzin sounds out the call to prayer from atop the minaret.

Muhammad as God's final revelation. Saying it, with conviction and intention, makes one a Muslim. The whole universe submits to God's will through the laws of nature. But humans have the great responsibility of testifying to the unity of God and the prophethood of Muhammad by utilizing the special human gifts of intelligence, free will, and speech—and this testimony comes first and foremost in saying the Shahadah.

The Shahadah is constantly on the lips of Muslims; as noted earlier, it is the first thing spoken in an infant's ear and the last thing spoken and heard by a dying Muslim. It is incorporated into every call to prayer and into the prayers themselves, thus sounding forth many times every day in every Muslim community. The Shahadah frequently appears as a visual art form, used as calligraphic decoration on walls and ceilings of mosques, posters, banners, curtains, and the like.

The unity of God also means the unity of humankind. One Muslim thinker, Muhammad Lahbabi, calls the Shahadah "a perpetual crossroads between transcendence and immanence, between the Absolute and finitude."[1] Muslims speak this as a constant testimony and act of submission to God, demonstrating thereby also their solidarity with all other Muslims. Since Muslims live in all lands of the world and in all time zones, the Shahadah is literally a perpetual sound that never ceases.

The Ritual of Prayer (Salat)   According to most Muslims, the Pillar of Prayer is the heart and soul of Muslim life. Since the greatest evil would be forgetting God, it is gracious divine guidance that requires humans to remember God by submitting in Prayer (**Salat**) five times a day, seven days a week. It is difficult to forget God when one's daily activities are so interpenetrated with the ritual of prayer.

Prayer is basically a public expression of praise and submission to God. It is not spontaneous conversing with God—Muslims do use that kind of prayer also, which they call *du'a*. But the required Prayer ritual follows set patterns and uses standard formulas—in Arabic—from the Quran and other prayers. According to Muslims, the ritual of Prayer is perfectly designed to sanctify all of life. It combines mental concentration with vocal expression. It is deeply spiritual but also puts the whole body physically into the service of God. An individual action, it provides a compelling sense of community with fellow Muslims. The

time possess great spiritual profundity. All these rituals center squarely on the unity of God and are practical rituals of submission to God. They are also designed to achieve social improvement and serve effectively in the Islamicization of society.

Saying the Shahadah (Confession)   To Muslims, the brief Shahadah is certainly one of the most important human vocal sounds, chanted out in sonorous Arabic syllables: *ashhadu an la ilaha illa Allah, ashhadu anna muhammad ar-rasula Allah,* that is, "I testify that there is no God but God; I testify that Muhammad is the Messenger of God." This Confession is a testimony, a public witnessing to the unity of God and to the Quran brought through vision of the Prayer is profound: Muslims in every land, representing the whole human race, facing the same center of the world, saying the same Arabic prayers throughout every day, in submission to the one God. That the unity of God means the unity of the human race is powerfully experienced in Prayer.

The Pillar of Prayer takes place five times every day, at early morning, noon, midafternoon, sunset, and evening. It is also required at funerals and recommended to be performed at certain other times. Muslims say prayers in a mosque, at home, or in any clean spot outdoors. It is best to say the Prayer in a group, although praying individually is also valid. When praying in a group, one person acts as the **imam** or prayer leader, standing in front, and the others follow the pattern of the imam, standing in straight lines. It is important to perform the Prayer correctly and in harmony. The signal for Prayer comes when the muezzin sings out the call to prayer from atop the minaret tower (nowadays often a loudspeaker system is used). In a haunting, compelling chant, the muezzin calls out in Arabic, repeating each phrase the required number of times: "God is most great! I testify that there is no God but God. I testify that Muhammad is the Messenger of God. Hurry to Prayer. Hurry to success. God is most great! There is no God but God." Muslims prepare to perform the Prayer first of all by purifying themselves, washing the hands, arms, face, nostrils, hair, ears, and feet with water.

Mental, vocal, and physical actions are united in the Prayer. Standing and facing Mecca, having declared the intention to pray, the worshiper raises the hands to the sides of the head and says, *"Allahu akbar"* (God is most great!). With hands resting on the abdomen, he or she recites the first sura of the Quran together with other prayers and verses. Then the worshiper bows with hands on the knees saying "Glory to my great Lord" and, after praising God again in a standing position, swiftly descends to the prostrate position with knees, forehead, and palms on the floor or ground. In this physical attitude of total submission, he or she says "Glory to my Lord, the Most High!" Then the worshiper sits and finally does the prostration again before resuming the standing position. This completes one cycle of prayers; the cycle is repeated again a number of times, depending on which Prayer it is. There are two cycles of prayers in morning Prayer, four at noon, afternoon, and night Prayer, and three at sunset Prayer. Near the close of the Prayer, the worshiper testifies the Confession, blesses the Prophet Muhammad and his family, and turning the head to both sides says, "Peace be upon you all and the mercy of God"—directed to all fellow Muslims and to all humankind in need of God's guidance.

At the Friday noon Prayer, Muslims are to assemble at the mosque as a congregation (women are not required to attend the mosque). The imam leads the prayer standing in front of the **mihrab,** the niche in the wall showing the direction to Mecca, and the worshipers stand in long straight lines behind. An important feature of this congregational service is the sermon *(khutba),* given by the imam or another recognized scholar from a pulpit (**minbar**), providing guidance for the people.

The Pillar of Alms-giving (Zakat)   Wealth is not viewed as evil by Muslims—God blesses the faithful with prosperity. But all wealth belongs to God, who has directed us to share it with those who are less fortunate, as a sign that all are equal before God and deserve a just and fair livelihood. As a legal religious duty, Alms-giving is not the same as charity; Muslims should also be generous and provide for the needy in other ways. Alms-giving is more like an annual religious tax computed on various forms of wealth, such as money, cattle, and crops.

Alms-giving is required of Muslims who have reached their majority (usually sixteen) and who possess a minimum of each type of wealth. The general rate is 2 1/2 percent annually. It is to be given, according to the Quran, to those who are poor, the needy, those who collect alms, new converts, slaves for their ransom, debtors, those doing good works in God's way, and travelers (*Quran* 9:60). It should not be given to Jews and Christians who live in the Muslim community—they should be given other types of help where needed. It is also not to be used for things like building mosques or burying the dead, nor given to parents, children, or spouses—there are other ways to take care of such needs. Traditionally, Muslim governments collected and distributed this tax, but now in some lands it is a matter of individual responsibility. Alms-giving—or wealth-sharing, as some modern Muslims prefer to call it—is definitely not to be regarded as doing a favor, either by the giver or the receiver. The wealth is God's, and it should not be given in a way that embarrasses the recipient or makes the giver proud. **Zakat** is a way of testifying to the unity of God and of humanity.

Muslims come from all parts of the world to make the pilgrimage to Mecca. Here pilgrims wait at the airport in Senegal-Dakar for transportation to Mecca.

The Pillar of Fasting (Sawm)   One important holy season that comes every year is the month of Fasting, the month of Ramadan. Ramadan is an especially sacred time for Muslims because during this month the first revelation descended on the Prophet. By fasting during the daylight hours, Muslims set apart this whole month as sacred time. It is a time of intense spiritual discipline, for Muslims abstain not only from food and drink but also from evil thoughts toward others. But it is also a joyous time, with opportunities to gather with family and friends at night. Fasting **(Sawm)** is not a means of punishing the body, as in some religions. The bodily needs and passions are not evil; they are good gifts of God and necessary for life. But people sometimes let themselves be controlled by their drives and passions, and Fasting is a time to break bad habits and regain control. By slowing down and withholding things, one learns a richer appreciation of material pleasures. There are physical benefits to Fasting as well, and it helps one feel a deeper sympathy for the deprived and hungry of the world. It strengthens the solidarity of the community, and, most importantly, it provides discipline for greater submission to God.

The practice of Fasting is simple: From first light in the morning until sundown at night, nothing is taken into the body. Forbidden are eating, drinking, smoking, sexual rela-

tions, even taking medicine. Breaking the fast intentionally carries penalties, such as extra days of fasting or giving meals to needy people. However, Fasting should not be permitted to impair one's health, and the sick, the elderly, pregnant women, and small children are excused from the requirement; those who are able should make it up later.

During the nighttime hours eating and drinking are permitted, and Ramadan nights are joyful, communal times. But overall there is a heightened spiritual atmosphere during Ramadan, with many giving special attention to studying the Quran and praying. Restaurants and ordinary entertainments are closed during the day, and the Muslim community revitalizes its spiritual foundations.

The Pilgrimage (Hajj)   The high point of life for many Muslims is the Pilgrimage to Mecca, required once in the lifetime of a Muslim. Muslims may undertake the Pilgrimage only if they are physically and financially capable. One cannot borrow money for this, since all debts must be paid before the Pilgrimage. Nor should one deprive the family in order to go on the Pilgrimage; money should be saved up for many years for this great duty. Women also are equal participants in the Pilgrimage, accompanied by husband or relatives.

The Pilgrimage epitomizes the ritual duty of Muslims. It is a dramatic connection to the sacred story, walking in the footsteps of Abraham, Hagar, Ishmael, and Muhammad. It is an intensely individual spiritual experience, and at the same time a movingly communal experience. Testimony to the unity of God is constantly on the lips of everyone. The pilgrims come from all parts of the world, representing all nations and peoples, yet they come together at the center of the world as one—one human race standing together in submission to the one God. It is a transforming experience of death and new life, and the transformed one returning home from the Hajj is appropriately given a new title, Hajji.

The rituals of the Pilgrimage, as determined by Muhammad in his final Pilgrimage, make use of some of the pre-Islamic practices, but these rituals are transformed in their meaning. For the pilgrim, leaving home is a kind of death. The Muslim enters into a special spiritual state **(ihram)**, symbolized by special garments and vows. All men wear a two-piece white garment, showing that all are equal; women may wear a white garment or their ordinary clothes. All take vows to avoid certain behavior: having sex, cutting one's hair, uprooting living things, wearing jewelry, arguing, and so forth.

After extensive identity checks by the Saudi government (only Muslims are allowed into the sacred area of Mecca), the pilgrims finally see the Ka'bah. For their whole life they have been saying the Prayer in this direction, and now finally it is right before their eyes. The Quran says that Abraham and his firstborn son Ishmael, commanded by God, built the Ka'bah, so the pilgrim feels a closeness to these great prophets of God. A sacred atmosphere is created, with the pilgrims constantly chanting the Pilgrimage formula, "I am here, O God, I am here! I am here! You are without associate! I am here! Praise and riches belong to you, and sovereignty!"

The full Pilgrimage takes place during the month of Pilgrimage and includes many rituals over a period of several days. The first main ritual is the Circling (*tawaf*), walking and trotting around the Ka'bah seven times in a counter-clockwise direction—thus putting the House of God, the center of the world, at the center of one's own life. Circling the Ka'bah, the pilgrims reach out to touch the Black Stone embedded in one corner. This Black Stone, tradition says, was given to Abraham by the angel Gabriel as a sign of God's pleasure, and Abraham and his son Ishmael built it into the Ka'bah. The next ritual is the Running (*sa'y*) between two hills seven times. This is in memory of Hagar and Ishmael. Because Abraham's wife Sarah was barren, she gave her servant Hagar as a wife for Abraham and he fathered Ishmael by her. After Hagar and Ishmael were expelled from Abraham's house because of Sarah's jealousy, they were dying of thirst in the desert at Mecca. But God miraculously provided the well of Zamzam to save them. So the pilgrim acts out Hagar's frantic running in search of water and gratefully drinks from the well of Zamzam.

On the eighth day of the Pilgrimage month, the whole company of pilgrims moves out to the desert, to live in tents for the next several days. The climax of the Pilgrimage comes on the ninth day with the ritual of Standing (*wuquf*) at the Plain of Arafat and the Mount of Mercy. From noon until sunset, all the pilgrims stand together as the representatives of the whole human race, praising and submitting to the one God of all.

In the next days come the rituals of Stoning and the Feast of Sacrifice (*'id al-adha*). The Quran and Hadith tell that Abraham, commanded by God, brought his son Ish-

mael here to sacrifice him. Satan tempted Ishmael to run away, but Ishmael threw stones at Satan to drive off this temptation. God, seeing Abraham and Ishmael's faithfulness, intervened through an angel and provided a ram for the sacrifice. To make this experience of their ancestors real again, each pilgrim performs the ritual of Stoning, throwing forty-nine pebbles at three stone "Satans" in a series of episodes over the next days. The Feast of Sacrifice requires the head of each household to ritually slaughter an animal and prepare a feast, giving some of the food to the needy. This Feast of Sacrifice is observed by Muslims throughout the world, providing a link between those on the Pilgrimage and the world Muslim community.

During these rituals in the desert the pilgrims make a return to Mecca for a second Circling of the Ka'bah, and the required rituals are completed. Pilgrims usually make one more "farewell" Circling of the Ka'bah, and many also go on to visit the holy places of Medina, where the Prophet first founded the ummah of Islam and where he and many early leaders are buried.

Other Festivals and Rituals

Holy Days and Commemorations   The Muslim calendar year does not have a lot of required festivals. There are two "feasts" ('**id**). One is the Feast of Sacrifice already noted. The other is the Feast of Fast-breaking (*'id al-fitr*), which comes on the first day of the month following the Ramadan Fasting, a celebration of thankfulness for having been able to complete the Fasting. After morning Prayer at the mosque and a visit to the cemetery, the feast celebrates the completion of the Fasting and the return to normal life with banquets and other events. In many places, this joyous festival lasts for three days.

A widely celebrated holiday is the birthday of the Prophet Muhammad (*mawlid al-nabi*), on the twelfth day of the third month, Rabi' al-Awwal. In such places as Egypt, this is a major holiday with a festive mood. Reciters chant verses from the Quran and a narrative of the Prophet's life. Merchants sell candies in the shapes of knights on horses for boys and doll brides for girls to celebrate this holiday. Some Muslims, especially under the Wahhabi influence in Saudi Arabia, consider this holiday an innovation and do not celebrate it. For other Muslims, not only the Prophet but also other saints are remembered with celebrations on

The holy Ka'bah in the Grand Mosque at Mecca is one of the important sites visited during the Pilgrimage. It is also the point toward which Muslims throughout the world face during their daily prayers.

their birth anniversaries. Shi'ites especially celebrate the birthdays of Imam 'Ali and the members of his family.

The month of Muharram is the beginning of the Muslim calendar, associated with the Hijra of the Muslims from Mecca to Medina and therefore a significant sacred time. In early times, the tenth of Muharram was a day of fasting called 'ashura (ten), and it is still observed with voluntary fasting by some Sunnite Muslims. Shi'ites have attached another significant celebration to 'Ashura, for it is the traditional anniversary of the martyrdom of Imam Husayn, son of 'Ali. They spend the first nine days of Muharram remembering the tragic events at Karbalah in an atmosphere of mourning. On the climactic tenth day, the drama called Ta'ziyeh is presented. Actors represent Husayn and his family on one side, and the Umayyad forces on the other in the passion play. The theme is the redemptive value of the sufferings and martyrdoms of Husayn and others of the house of Muhammad.

Rituals of the Passages of Life   Although the Quran does not prescribe rituals for birth, Islamic tradition holds that soon after birth the call to prayer should be spoken in the baby's right ear and the summons to perform the prayer in the left ear. On the seventh day after birth, the baby is usually named and a sacrifice may be performed. On the fortieth day, the mother is purified and is able to resume the ritual duties.

Circumcision (khitan) is an important ritual of passage for boys. In some places, like Indonesia, it is performed at eleven or twelve years of age, thus functioning as a passage into adult spiritual status. In other places, it commonly takes place soon after birth or a few years later. Although it is not mentioned in the Quran, Muslims everywhere regard it as an essential purification ritual. The circumcision is the occasion for much festivity, with many guests, special food, and music, and the boy is paraded around in honor and triumph as a little prince. In some localities, a similar operation is performed for girls, cutting away or scarring the clitoris. Muslims disagree whether such female "circumcision" (clitoridectomy) should be performed, but those who practice it consider it a ritual of purification.

The whole Muslim tradition encourages a Muslim to marry as soon in life as possible and to have many children. Since marriage is one of God's good gifts, celibacy and marital abstinence are forbidden, except for exceptional reasons during certain periods of a person's life. Marriage is not a sacrament, as in Christianity, nor is it an unconditional binding together no matter what. The marriage is usually arranged by parents, since it brings two families together into a new relationship. No one may be married without his or her own consent, but in practice the girl is usually represented by a guardian, who interprets her silence as consent. A legal contract is written that spells out the rights and duties of both. Should one party fail to live up to the contract, the marriage can be annulled. One thing included in the contract is the bridal gift (mahr), which the groom must provide for his bride and which remains hers.

The marriage is legally completed by the ritual of signing the marriage contract, by the groom and the guardian of the bride. But after this ritual is completed, the great communal celebration commences, with many guests, special foods, music making, and dancing. The festivities reflect the traditional culture of the people and thus differ widely in the different parts of the Muslim world. In more traditional societies, the men and the women celebrate separately.

The Islamic rituals surrounding death show a realistic acceptance of death as the end of life and a belief in the passage through the grave to resurrection, judgment, and reward. One should be ready at all times for one's own death. Al-Ghazali gave this spiritual advice:

> When you want to go to sleep, lay out your bed pointing to Mecca, and sleep on your right side, the side on which the corpse reclines in the tomb. . . . Remember that in like manner you will lie in the tomb, completely alone; only your works will be with you, only the effort you have made will be rewarded.[2]

Feelings about the grave are also colored by the belief that interrogation by the angels begins as soon as one is buried, and the body may undergo purgatorial punishments in the grave before the general resurrection. True believers, of course, can expect reward and happiness on Judgment Day.

At the onset of death, the dying person's face should be turned toward Mecca and the words, "There is no God but God," should be recited, and also sura *Ya Sin* (36), which deals with death and resurrection. The body should be given the full purificatory washing and perfumed, then wrapped in a simple cotton shroud resembling the Pilgrimage *ihram* garment. The Muslim is now commencing his or her final pilgrimage. It is required that Muslims perform the Pillar of Prayer in the presence of the deceased person, with the entire service performed standing. Special prayers are said on behalf of the deceased, like this one spoken by Muhammad:

> Allah, do forgive him and have mercy on him and make him secure and overlook his shortcomings, and bestow upon him an honoured place in Paradise, and make his place of entry spacious, and wash him clean with water and snow and ice, and cleanse him of all wrong as Thou dost clean a piece of white cloth of dirt, . . . and shield him from the torment of the grave and the torment of the Fire.[3]

After the procession to the cemetery, the body is placed in a grave with a niche carved out on one side; the body lies on its side directly on the ground, with the face in the direction of Mecca. As the mourners drop earth to cover the grave, they may recite the words of the Quran, "Out of the earth We created you, and We shall restore you into it, and bring you forth from it a second time" (20:55). The bereaved mourn for three days after the burial and thereafter remember the deceased periodically with prayer and reading of the Quran.

Art in Islamic Worship and Life

Islamic art reflects the various cultures of the world that have been receptive to transformation through Islam, and thus there is a great deal of cultural diversity. Yet the basic simplicity and universality of Islam radiate through artistic expressions in all parts of the Muslim world.

The Quran and the Hadith repeat the Jewish prohibition of making images and even strengthen it. The Quran insists that nothing in the created world is like God. Thus not only representational art but even metaphoric imaging of the divine in words is prohibited. Generally, Islamic art has avoided not just representations of God, but all forms of representational art. It is said that on Judgment Day God will command those who made images now to bring them alive; failing, they will be punished in the Fire.

There has been some use of representational art in Islamic societies, of course, particularly for secular purposes, such as decorative painting on ceramics or book illustrations. Illustrative painting has been most used in Iran and in India. A special branch of Islamic painting is the depiction of the Prophet Muhammad on his night journey through the heavens, mounted on the steed Buraq; on these paintings, Muhammad's face is usually covered or left blank. The strong sense of avoiding representations of the Prophet and the close companions was demonstrated in a recent film about the career of Muhammad, in which Muhammad and the close companions are represented only by voice, never by visible characters; the action is carried on by characters somewhat distant from the Prophet.

In place of representational art, Islamic culture has richly developed other art forms: decoration, calligraphy, architecture, poetry, and literature. One way to avoid representational art is to give prominence to abstract design, straight lines, angles, and intricate geometrical patterns on a flat plane, giving a sense of clarity and order. An important decorative form is arabesque, lines depicting an endless continuation of leaves, palmettes, and sometimes animal-like motifs growing out of each other. So geometric designs and arabesque are used together, providing an expression of life and growth but an overall framework of order and clear meaning. Geometric patterns and arabesque are often combined with calligraphy, serving well to express spiritual reality rather than the material and concrete world, conveying the rationality, clarity, and universality of the Muslim faith.

Since the Muslim tradition places high importance on the word of the Quran, the art of calligraphy has been richly cultivated, rendering the divine word visible in countless artistic variations of the Arabic script. Calligraphy is the central dictum of Muslim art, preserving and conveying the unchanging, eternal words of God given to humans. The divine words are woven in brocade, carved in wood and stone, painted on ceramics, emerging from mosaics on mosque walls from Baghdad to Cordova. There are many styles of calligraphic scripts, and often the script is combined with arabesques and geometric designs to draw the eye and the mind to the divine word cradled within, calling for thoughtful reflection. For example, the *bismillah* (In the name of Allah) may be written in such a way as to convey the shape of a bird or a beast; and the ninety-nine names of God may form a calligraphic mosque on a poster.

The mosque is the crowning Islamic creation in the field of architecture. The ka'bah at Mecca, the first and primary sacred building, is a simple cubelike structure, and the mosque of the Prophet at Medina was also simple and practical, a gathering place for believers to pray and study. Mosques differ all over the world, but their grandeur expresses the glory of God and their openness and light symbolize the apprehension of God's truth. All mosques have certain common features: a mihrab, a niche in the wall indicating the direction toward Mecca; a minbar or pulpit for the sermon at congregational prayer on Friday; and a minaret, a tower or spire from which the call to prayer goes out to the community.

The arts of poetry and literature have been very heavily influenced by the Quran itself, the supreme example of the artistic word. An early narrative art was the biography of the Prophet, and soon many narratives were produced about the sayings and events in the lives of Muhammad and the saints. Poetry has been an especially influential art in Islam, as, from the beginnings of the Islamic movement, Muslims gave voice to their religious vision in poetry. Especially in the mystical Sufi movement, poets used Arabic, Per-

sian, and Turkish poetry to express emotional, intimate, passionate love for God. The Iraqi woman mystic Rabi'ah (d. 801) and other early Sufi poets gave voice to the mystical longing for God, the pain of separation, and the bliss of union. Perhaps the greatest poetic luminary was Mawlana Jalal al-Din Rumi (1207–1273), who composed some 35,000 lyrical couplets in Persian. The great Arabic poet Ibn al-Farid (1182–1235) developed poetry to a high form of spiritual expression, as in this poetic description of the mystic vision:

> . . . the vision blest
> Was granted to my prayers . . .
> The while amazed between
> His beauty and His majesty
> I stood in silent ecstasy
> Revealing that which o'er my spirit came and went.
> Lo! in His face commingled
> Is every charm and grace:
> The whole of beauty singled
> Into a perfect face
> Beholding Him would cry:
> "There is no god but He and He is the most High."[4]

The impulse of worshiping God frequently in daily prayer and in all aspects of life has led to the cultivation of many other arts and crafts in Islamic communities. To create prayer rugs and decorative cloths, countless artisans across the Muslim world dedicate their days to dyeing fabrics and weaving beautiful rugs and other embroidered cloths. The art of creating beautiful mosaics to adorn mosques and other buildings has been passed down since earliest Islamic times and is still cultivated by artists today. Other artists have worked at manuscript and book illumination, lovingly adorning the sacred Word and the narrations of the prophets and saints. Some Muslim societies, such as those in India and Pakistan, have even cultivated music and song to celebrate religious festivals—though other Muslim societies, such as those influenced by the Wahhabi movement, have tended to avoid music and song in connection with religious activities.

The use of the arts in Islam has given real aesthetic focus to the concepts of the faith and brought these rational ideas into the realm of the everyday life of the people. Overall, the vision of the Quran has inspired Muslims to create a distinctive style of art that is diverse around the world but still unified at its basic core.

An early example of Muslim architecture is the Dome of the Rock in Jerusalem.

THE LIFE OF SHARI'AH: SOCIETY AND ETHICS

How should we live? The Muslim answer is as simple and universal as the Jewish and Christian answer. The Muslim should live as one who belongs to the ummah, the worldwide community of Muslims, following the guidance of the Shari'ah, the Law.

Social Structure of Islam

The Universal Ummah   The word *ummah* is difficult to translate. It has elements of a community, a people, a nation, and a religion. According to the Quran, originally all people were one ummah, but then they fell into variance (10:19). Prophets were sent by God to the different ummahs. The ummah of each prophet received true revelation from God and thus they were Muslims, insofar as they submitted to that revelation and lived according to it. Most of these communities, however, forgot the true revelation and lapsed into unbelief and sin.

God gave to Muhammad, the final prophet, the mission of establishing a new ummah, which would be the social embodiment of God's design for all humankind and which

eventually would reunite all humankind into one ummah. The peoples of Arabia were divided into tribal loyalties, and this greatly hindered Muhammad's work in Mecca. So the decisive moment in the creation of the ummah was the Hijra, the emigration to Medina, where for the first time there arose an ummah that was unified in worship and faith. In making the Hijra, Muhammad and the Muslims were moving against their own kin in Mecca to an alien center outside; faith-solidarity was now sharply pitted against blood-solidarity. The Emigrants had to rely on the assistance of people outside their tribes, the Helpers of Medina. The Constitution of Medina clearly identified the new community as an ummah bound together by faith and submission to God and his prophet, showing that the bond of faith had replaced tribal loyalty.

In Medina, the political and social structure was totally Islamicized, and that set the pattern for the ummah. There is no separation between the secular and the religious in Islam, between the political and the spiritual, between state and church. The ummah is all-embracing, based on the foundation of the Quran and the Law drawn from the Quran.

As Islam expanded under the caliphs, a large territory came under the immediate jurisdiction of the ummah. This is called the Dar al-Islam, the Abode of Islam, inside of which infidels could not be tolerated. But the ummah is not limited to the area of the Dar al-Islam. The ummah is universal, and all who submit to God and recognize the Prophet are equal in this brotherhood and sisterhood of Islam. Equality and unity are of central importance. No one Muslim, no matter in what position, has rights of precedence over another Muslim; all are equal before God. In the days of Caliph 'Umar, the powerful governor of Egypt had a son who, annoyed by an Egyptian commoner in a horse racing contest, struck him, saying, "Don't you know I am the son of the great man?" And the governor imprisoned the commoner for a time. But when he was released, the commoner went to Medina and appealed to 'Umar. 'Umar recalled both the governor and his son, and after they confessed, he ordered the commoner to beat them both. 'Umar spoke to the governor: "By what right do you tyrannize over men? Have they not emerged from their mothers' wombs as free citizens?"[5] Although there may be differences of position or wealth, all Muslims are equal with respect to justice under God's law.

Since God's unity is the bedrock of Islamic belief, the ummah also is an expression of that unity. Ideally, the ummah demonstrates the fundamental unity of the human race. The Quran states, "O mankind, We have created you male and female, and appointed you races and tribes, that you may know one another" (49:13). The rituals of Islam provide dramatic experience of the oneness of the whole Islamic community. Five times a day Muslims everywhere on earth face the same center of the world and say the same prayers. And in the pilgrimage to Mecca, Muslims of both genders and of all races, nations, and language groups come together as one, representing the whole human race. The ummah is not called out to be a special people separate from the whole human race; it is the ideal form that all humankind is designed to be.

Social Structure and Leadership   The ummah is universal and worldwide. But it takes concrete form in the various Islamic nations and especially in the communities of Muslims all over who group themselves together as mosque assemblies. Although Muhammad and the first four caliphs were seen as leaders of the one ummah, down through the centuries Islam has linked together with a variety of nations and empires, so that today there is no one worldwide uni-

fied ruling authority. Muslims today live in a variety of political structures, from Islamic states like Pakistan and Iran to secular states like Turkey; and a significant number of Muslims live in small Muslim communities scattered throughout the Western nations. Yet there is a remarkable unity of Islamic belief and practice throughout the worldwide ummah. Most Muslims consider themselves to be Sunnites, following one of the four orthodox schools of law codified by the Islamic scholars in the generations following the time of Muhammad. The Shi'ites are a significant minority, making up about 15 percent of the world population of Muslims and following their own schools of law. Yet for the most part, Sunnites and Shi'ites recognize each other as equal and true practitioners of the Muslim way.

There is no clergy or priesthood in the ummah. The ruling family of Saudi Arabia has assumed responsibility for the holy places there, exercising some control over who is considered to be a Muslim in terms of who is allowed to enter Mecca on the pilgrimage. But there is no person or body who has authority over the whole ummah. Since Islam is a path of knowledge, the most respected leaders are the scholars, the 'ulama (sing., 'alim), who study the Quran and the Hadith and who are responsible for determining the application of the law. Among the 'ulama, the *mufti* is recognized as a legal expert who can be consulted for a formal legal opinion on a particular question pertaining to, for example, marriage, divorce, or inheritance. Another important figure is the *qadi*, the religious judge who is appointed by the political leader and carries out justice in matters of religious law. The Shi'ite religious scholars in Iran, called **mullas**, are granted an extraordinarily high level of respect and authority in all matters pertaining to religious law— which, in an Islamic republic like Iran, means authority over all matters of human society.

On the local level, most mosque communities contract with a learned Muslim to be the imam, the spiritual leader of worship and teaching in the mosque. Any Muslim has the right to lead prayers and to teach others. But it is helpful if the mosque has a recognized scholar as imam, to teach, preach at the Friday prayers, and give spiritual guidance to the people in a variety of matters.

Women in Religious Leadership   Muslim tradition has been quite strict in separating women from men in public religious activities, so religious leadership has almost exclusively been reserved for men. Although women have equality with men, according to the Quran, the roles of women are understood to be quite different. Laws and cultural customs about seclusion have contributed to keeping women from public activities; instead, their roles have focused overwhelmingly on the family and the home and on the religious training of children. Women do lead prayers when a group of women prays together.

There, of course, have been strong, well-known women religious leaders in Muslim history, starting with Khadijah, Muhammad's strong and resourceful wife. His later wives also were highly respected and talented. Hafsah, daughter of 'Umar, was literate and contributed to the collection of the revelations given to Muhammad. And his beloved young wife 'Aisha was a strong leader, not afraid to enter into the conflicts that developed after Muhammad's death; it was she who supplied many of the *hadiths* (reports) about Muhammad's sayings and deeds. Muhammad's daughter Fatima, married to his cousin 'Ali and mother of his grandsons, was highly revered as a leader in women's spirituality. And there have been numerous women spiritual leaders, saints, and mystics—such as Rabi'ah, mentioned earlier.

In modern times, there are many examples of Muslim women who exercise leadership in a variety of important roles, as political leaders (even heads of state), writers, teachers, scholars, doctors, engineers, and much more. While women have been restricted from public religious leadership positions, they exert much influence in the Muslim community. Some leading Muslim women today are quite westernized. But many other modern women are turning more toward traditional Islamic values to reaffirm their identity as Muslim women. They find vitality not in Western patterns of liberation but within the framework of Muslim tradition. Taking full advantage of educational and professional opportunities, yet choosing to remain within traditional Islamic patterns of society, these women are attempting to express a modern vision of Islamic womanhood distinct from Western models.

The Way of Shari'ah

How should we live? Christianity turned away from the Jewish idea that God's law directly governs and guides all conduct; rather, faith in Christ means that love is the motivating power, following the law in freedom. In many ways,

the Muslim tradition rejects the Christian view and returns closely to the Jewish view of Torah. The Shari'ah is divinely given, complete and perfect in all its details. The highest human good is to follow the path outlined in the law, omitting no details no matter how small. Humans were created to fulfill the divine design, and that design finds its expression in the Shari'ah.

Basic Principles of the Shari'ah The Quran, of course, comes from God, revealed through the Prophet Muhammad. But where does the Shari'ah, the massive religious legislation that governs all aspects of Muslim life, come from? This also comes from God, Muslims say, because it is drawn from the Holy Book. Since law is so important to Muslims, the great Islamic thinkers spent their creative energies elucidating the legal structure of Islam, while Christian thinkers were spending their time on theological issues.

There are actually two basic sources for the Shari'ah: the Quran and the Hadith (the collection of the sayings and doings of the Prophet Muhammad). Many duties of human life find direct, explicit expression in the Quran. But, although the Quran is God's perfect revelation, it is not large enough to state explicitly everything that humans should do in life in all situations. What is implicit in the Quran, or unclear in our limited understanding, is made explicit in the Hadith. Muhammad's close companions reported what he said and did in all circumstances, and these reports convey the example (**sunnah**) of Muhammad as the second source of law. To distinguish the reliable reports from those that are not so reliable, Muslim scholars elaborated a scientific, scholarly method of scrutinizing the "chain" (**isnad**) of people who passed on the report. If the chain can be linked securely back to a close companion of the Prophet, it is reliable and can be used as a basis for Shari'ah.

But even the Hadith does not specify what is to be done in all situations. As new situations arose, the law had to be searched and interpreted to meet the new needs. So Muslim scholars cultivated the method of "analogy" (**qiyas**), likening the new situation to one mentioned in the Quran or the Hadith and thus drawing legal conclusions. Analogy is a very creative undertaking, so finally it has to be checked, verified, and codified by the consensus (**ijma'**) of the recognized legal scholars—for Muhammad had said that his people will never agree on an error. In this way, from the

Quran and the Hadith, by means of analogy and consensus, the whole body of Islamic law was formed and put in place as the divine pattern for human life.

We should not let the process of developing the Shari'ah obscure the fundamental truth that the Shari'ah represents God's total design for life. The Shari'ah has been revealed by the same God who made the whole world for the sake of humans. The guidance supplied in the law is therefore a regulation of life in the best interest of humans, showing us the best way to live to fulfill the highest potential. God has not given anything that is useless or unnecessary; and humans should use all their faculties, powers, and resources in such a way that they can reap the highest benefits from them. Abul A'la Mawdudi explains,

> The fundamental principle of the Law is that man has the right, and in some cases the bounden duty, to fulfil all his genuine needs and desires and make every conceivable effort to promote his interests and achieve success and happiness—but (and it is an important "but") he should do all this in such a way that not only are the interests of other people not jeopardised and no harm is caused to their strivings towards the fulfillment of their rights and duties, but there should be all possible social cohesion, mutual assistance and cooperation among human beings in the achievement of their objectives.[6]

The Shari'ah, then, is the most humanizing force in the world. It is not in conflict with other true humanizing forces of religion and science, but it is the final, all-encompassing, perfect guide.

Because the Shari'ah was worked out by scholars in different parts of the Muslim world, a number of different schools of law developed with slight differences. The Hanafi school, dominant today in central and western Asia, northern Egypt, and India, is the most liberal and flexible. The Maliki school, prominent today in North Africa and southern Egypt, and the Shafi'i school, in Malaysia and East Africa, are generally considered middle of the road. The Hanbali school, dominant in Saudi Arabia, is the most conservative and strict. But in practice, there are no fundamental differences among these schools, and all are regarded by one another as fully orthodox. The Shi'ites have three schools of law, differing from the Sunnite schools mainly in authority of the imam, the recognition of temporary marriage (a limited time of marriage specified in the marriage

contract), a stricter divorce law, and more provision for female relatives in the inheritance law.

Muslim Ethics in Practice   Islamic law is learned, in its basics, by all Muslims so they can live their lives properly. But how can there be definite divine rules about every aspect of human life? The Islamic answer is to classify all acts into five basic categories or principles that allow for a range of shading and flexibility. Some duties and acts are *required (fard)* of all Muslims; performing them brings reward and omitting them brings punishment. Again, some acts are strictly *forbidden (haram),* and doing them brings punishment. Some acts are *recommended* but not required, and performance of them is rewarded. Some acts are *disapproved* but not forbidden or punished. And, finally, some acts are *indifferent,* neither rewarded nor punished. The Pillar of Prayer, for example, is required; drinking alcohol is forbidden. Recommended acts would be, for example, saying extra prayers or visiting Medina after the pilgrimage. The categories of indifferent acts and disapproved acts allow for some disagreement between legal scholars and among the schools of law. An action may be held disapproved by one but indifferent by another; or something considered to be forbidden by one scholar might be thought of as merely disapproved by another.

There are other elements of flexibility in Islamic jurisprudence. The law only applies to those who are *rashid,* that is, free Muslims of legal age and sane. Non-Muslims have complete legal freedom provided they do not interfere with the religious interests of Muslims. Further, a fundamental principle of religious law is intent. Normally forbidden actions are permissible under duress. For example, drinking wine or having illegal intercourse under threat of death is permissible; refusal under these circumstances would be forbidden. Punishments for forbidden actions can only be carried out if very stringent requirements of proof of wrongdoing are met—for example, four eyewitnesses are required in a charge of unlawful sexual intercourse.

A good part of Islamic law is focused on the family, for this is the broad arena in which the individual lives most of her life. In fact, for women in traditional Muslim societies, social contacts outside the extended family are few. Marriage is a duty carried out on the basis of a legal contract consented to by both parties. Sexual expression is considered good and healthy, but it is strictly reserved for marriage. All other forms of sex are forbidden and punished: premarital and extramarital sex, homosexuality, prostitution, bestiality, and so forth. To control the natural sexual urges, Islamic law forbids intermingling of sexes (unless they are nonmarriageable relatives) in any social gathering or even in schools. Further, the law requires modesty in dress; the most conservative law school holds that no more than a woman's face and hands should be visible when she is outside the home. Men are also to clothe themselves modestly.

Divorce is permitted in Islam, although Muhammad said that God considers divorce to be the most detestable of permitted things. Traditionally, the man could divorce his wife by the formula of repudiation, uttering "I divorce you" three times, usually with a prescribed waiting period between the utterances. Once the third repudiation is uttered, it is irrevocable and the man has no more claim on the woman. If they for some reason want to be married again, the woman must first be married to someone else and then divorced.

What is the position of women in Islamic law? Men and women are equal before God, according to the Quran (16:97). The woman, like the man, has standing as a legal individual, retaining her property to use as she sees fit. But women have a different role from men. Whereas the man's role is to work and support the family, the woman's place is in the home, providing care and stability for family life. If a woman must work outside the home, it should be in certain types of occupations appropriate for women, such as teaching or nursing. A Muslim man is permitted to marry four wives, whereas a Muslim woman may have only one husband. Muslims point out that one basic reason for polygamy is to ensure that all women can be married and thus fulfill themselves in family life. Further, in actuality, very few Muslim men have more than one wife, for Islamic law dictates that a man must treat his wives equally both in sexual relationship and in financial support.

There are other aspects of Islamic law in which women seem of lesser value than men. For example, certain legal proceedings require two male witnesses or one male and two female witnesses, and a woman relative generally receives only one-half the inheritance of an equal male relative. Further, a Muslim man is permitted to marry a non-Muslim monotheistic woman, but this permission is not extended to a Muslim woman. The Quran seemingly subjugates

wives to their husbands: "Men are in charge of women, because Allah made the one of them to excel the other"— and men may banish wives who are disobedient from the marital bed and beat them (4:34). Muslims explain these seeming inequalities on the basis of the particular roles of women and men in society and in the family. For example, with respect to inheritance law, husbands are required by Islamic law to support their wives and families, while wives are not required to contribute to the financial support of the family, and so it makes a certain sense that sons should receive a greater inheritance share than daughters. Since men have a more public role while women's activities take place within the family, Muslims say, it is appropriate that the husband should have the role of making decisions and governing the life of the family.

When the question of the status of women in Islam is brought up, Muslims point out that, whereas in Christendom and in most parts of the world, until very recently women were considered little more than property with no legal rights, Islamic law instituted by Muhammad lifted the status of women and gave them equal rights with men. Certainly the Quran presents a strong basic view of the equality of women and men. This does not mean, however, that they should have the same function as men in society, for in God's divine pattern women fulfill their high potential in maintaining the well-being of the family.

Many modern Muslim leaders and governments have brought about reforms in those aspects of Muslim traditional law and cultural practices that subjugated women. Notable among these reforms have been the discouragement of child marriage; restricting the taking of more than one wife, and allowing stipulations about this to be written into the marriage contract; and moving toward more equity in divorce rights for women. Women may, for example, be able to initiate divorce on grounds such as the husband's physical incapacity, desertion, failure to provide support, cruelty, and the like.

As Muslims respond to the pressures of the modern world, some scholars are studying the Quran and the Hadith anew to reinterpret the role of women in modern Muslim society. Women are found in various professions, providing strong leadership in Muslim communities, though not yet in public religious leadership roles. While many Muslim women have become Westernized in dress, there is a tendency among some Muslim women today to reassert their Muslim identity by choosing more traditional dress—to recover their own spiritual sources rather than bowing to Western secular ideas, and to give themselves more freedom and confidence in their new public roles without the sexual innuendos and sexual harassment often associated with Western dress and social intercourse. The role of women—equal with men, but different—is very complex in Muslim tradition. Much thought and care is being devoted to this subject today, and Muslim women will certainly increasingly shape Islamic life and thought.[7]

With respect to personal life, the Shari'ah forbids the use of things that are injurious to one's physical, mental, or moral life. Besides alcohol and drugs, there are forbidden foods, falling into four basic categories: carrion, blood, pork, and anything sacrificed to another god. By carrion is meant beasts of prey and anything that died without being slaughtered properly, such as by old age, illness, or being killed improperly (by another animal or by a hunter, for example). People are required to keep the body clean, and one should not wear excessively costly clothes or jewelry.

The rights of other people in society are especially guarded by the Shari'ah. Lying, cheating, theft, bribery, forgery, and other means of illegal gain at the expense of others are forbidden. And gambling and games of chance are forbidden because, in them, someone wins at the expense of others. Likewise forbidden are various forms of exploitation, such as monopoly, hoarding, black market-eering, withholding land from cultivation, and the like. Usury—that is, charging interest on loans—is also considered a form of gain at the expense of others and thus is forbidden. While this makes capitalistic endeavors difficult, it promotes solidarity and cooperation with respect to the use of financial resources. Islamic banking endeavors have come up with creative methods of providing necessary funding without charging interest, with the lender then sharing in the profits (and the risks) of economic enterprises. Another device by which the Muslim tradition prevents the excessive accumulation of wealth by one party is inheritance law, which requires that the wealth be distributed to all eligible relatives rather than being kept in one estate. Muslims consider wealth as God's blessing, and it is not to be hoarded or squandered, but rather used to the betterment of oneself and others.

Non-Muslims sometimes think of Islam as a religion of the sword, a religion of violence. It is true that certain Mus-

lim political radicals have committed acts of terrorism—but no more than certain political radicals of other religions in other places. The Shari'ah also has legislation on the justification and conduct of war. In general, it may be said that the only permissible reason for warfare is striving in the cause of God—which is what the term *jihad* (often translated "holy war") means. This means that wars for land, resources, power, wealth, and all the rest are prohibited. Striving in the cause of God means enforcing God's law about equality and justice for all. Thus the Muslim tradition has a kind of "just war" idea, in that Muslims are obligated to take up arms in self-defense or in defense of others who are being oppressed and treated unjustly. Such warfare, however, is strictly regulated: negotiations must always be made first with the other side, booty may not be taken, and innocent people may not be injured.

Transformation of Human Society

Muslims have a vision for society, and the contours of that vision find expression in the Shari'ah. Since this law is God's final and perfect design, it is the responsibility of Muslims to implement it for all societies of the world. And since the Islamic principles of faith are the same universal principles that have been revealed by all God's prophets, it is the duty of Muslims to convince all other peoples to submit to this truth of Islam. In other words, Muslims have the duty to engage in *dawah*, missionary activities directed toward the Islamicization of the world, both in the laws of society and in the faith of all people.

But the Islamic vision of the good life under the law has one important difference from the Jewish or Christian vision. To live the Shari'ah in *all* its aspects requires that one live under a Muslim government. In fact, ideally there should be one Muslim ruler (the caliph) who rules over the whole Dar al-Islam. Since the Shari'ah contains provisions that can only be carried out by a government, it is not possible to follow the complete life of Islam while living under a non-Muslim ruler.

Thus, the Islamicization of society ideally means establishing an Islamic government. The notion of *jihad*, "striving" in the path of God, plays a part at this point. It refers to conquering all forces that oppose God's will, starting with one's own sins and unbelief. Since the realms of society not ruled by Muslim governments do not conform to God's law, in theory there is a perpetual state of jihad between the Dar al-Islam and the infidel society, the Dar al-Harb. Some leaders of the Islamic resurgence today would direct that struggle also against modern secular governments in Muslim countries such as Egypt, Algeria, Syria, and the like, since these governments do not rule by the Shari'ah. The Islamic ideal would be for the whole world to come under Islamic rule and Islamic law. This would bring great benefits even for non-Muslims, according to some Muslim thinkers, since it would keep them from forbidden acts and provide a peaceful, orderly society without all the evils of modern, secular society.

The Spiritual Mission of Islam   Spreading Islamic law does not mean religious coercion, which is expressly forbidden in the Quran (2:256). The Shari'ah permits some religions to continue even in the Dar al-Islam. Those who are monotheists and possess a sacred scripture are known as People of the Book—this includes Jews, Christians, and Zoroastrians; although their faith is faulty, they are nonetheless acceptable to God. They can live peacefully within Muslim domains by paying a special tax. But, at least according to traditional law, polytheists must either convert to monotheism or flee; otherwise they face imprisonment or execution.

The missionary impulse in Islam comes from the knowledge that this is the final religion with the final, perfect revelation of God. While God gave revelation of the same faith through prophets in all other lands, the Arabic Quran is the last such revelation and is intended for all peoples universally. Submitting to the divine trust, Muslims feel compelled to share this revelation with all others.

But how should Muslims share this revelation with others? God's great gifts to humans are intelligence, free will, and speech. Speech is the means of sharing the Quran with others. God's gift of free will means no coercion or forcing people to accept Islam. Rather, God's truth should be spread in a rational way, appealing to human intelligence, allowing others to become convinced by their reason and submit to

this final truth. If people really consider Islam in a rational, free way, Muslims believe, they will see that it is the highest truth of God and human existence. Mawdudi says,

> This is Islam, the natural religion of man, the religion which is not associated with any person, people, period or place. It is the way of nature, the religion of *man*. In every age, in every country and among every people, all God-knowing and truth-loving men have believed and lived this very religion. They were all Muslims, irrespective of whether they called that way Islam.[8]

Discussion Questions

1 In what ways is the Prayer the heart of Muslim life? Describe the performance of the Pillar of Prayer.
2 Explain the Pillars of Fasting and of Alms-giving. How do the central motifs of submission to God and the oneness of the Muslim community come to expression in these practices?
3 Describe the various rituals of the Hajj (Pilgrimage to Mecca) and their meaning for Muslims.
4 Describe the traditional rituals associated with the passages of life in Islamic families.
5 Explain some of the basic principles of Islamic art. What are some of the main artistic forms used for ritual and worship in Islam?
6 What is the ummah? What kind of leadership is there in the ummah?
7 What are the traditional views about women in religious leadership roles in Islam? Describe some examples of strong women leaders in Muslim history.
8 On what is the Shari'ah based? How do analogy *(qiyas)* and consensus *(ijma')* fit in?
9 How is it possible for the Shari'ah to govern all aspects of life? Describe how it functions, and give some concrete examples of the Shari'ah in everyday life.
10 What are the basic aspects of Muslim law about the family and the relationship between men and women?

PART THREE

Ongoing Explorations on the Sacred Paths

Religious life is dynamic. Though some traditions seem to stay the same for long periods of time, in reality there always is change and transformation going on, as each new generation accepts the tradition and lives in it under new life circumstances. In certain periods, considerable interaction develops between different communities of people, resulting in much change and transformation in their religious traditions.

Our present age is a time of intensive interaction and communication between all traditional religious communities. And so, religious transformations today are likewise intensive and dramatic. These transformations take many different directions. They may result in significantly new forms and practices, or they may bring about incorporation of new forms within the traditional structures. Yet again, the transformations may be directed toward a regrounding and revitalization of the traditional forms and structures, going back to the roots of the religious tradition.

In any case, the world at the beginning of the twenty-first century (by the common Western calendar) poses critical, intensive challenges to all human communities and thus to all religious traditions. The crises and challenges that have always been there from the beginning of the human adventure seemingly have multiplied and converged in contracting frames of time and space. The search for meaning and hope is an ongoing one, and the paths people follow today often take new and surprising turns.

As we explored the different religious traditions of the Western world in this book, we had occasion to look at some of the continuing concerns and new directions being pursued by people within these traditions. Overall, as we have seen, there is a significant sense of revitalization and heightened relevance in most of the sacred paths today. As we conclude our journey in this book, we highlight the ongoing nature of humankind's religious adventure by focusing on two important dimensions: new religious movements, and increasing dialogue and cooperation between religious communities.

New religious movements are not exclusive to our modern age, of course. It seems significant today that numbers of people have become disaffected with their traditional religious practices and have begun to seek out alternate paths. It would, of course, be impossible to try and look at the enormous number of such new religious movements throughout the world today, many of them quite small in numbers of adherents and others surprisingly large. We can get some sense of the nature of these movements by focusing on some better-known examples from the nineteenth and twentieth centuries in the Western world.

A significant, fairly new emphasis among the world's religious communities today is the attention being given to conversation and cooperation between the different groups. In our shrinking global village, there is increasing information about people of other religions and increasing personal contact. In the face of various social crises, it has become urgent for people of different faith communities to work together for the common good. Many religious people have come to the new realization that deep, sincere dialogue with people of other faiths can be helpful in following one's spiritual path.

New Religious Movements

SPIRITUAL SEARCHING
AND ALTERNATIVE SACRED PATHS

In this study, we have looked at the mainstream of each religious tradition for a basic orientation to the rich landscape of humankind's sacred paths. But each religion is a living, growing, and changing path for people living their lives and looking for spiritual meaning and fulfillment. And so in every age, in every tradition, there have been changes and transformations, new groups evolving, alternative movements vying for people's commitment. Searching, reforming, revitalizing, creating new paths—these tendencies have always been central to the human religious story. Most of the world religions—and many paths that have vanished along the way—began as transformations of the dominant religious path, or as new alternative religious movements.

Today, change and transformation are central characteristics of religion. And so, as we complete our journey of exploration, we pause to take note of some of the new and alternative movements in the contemporary religious world. While many of these groups are small in numbers compared to the major world religions, they often have been highly visible and influential—and controversial, in some cases.

Cults, Sects, and Alternative Religious Movements
Social scientists have developed terminology to describe the role of religious movements within the larger society, using terms like "sect" and "cult." While the dominant religious tradition (the "church," for example) is accepted as mainstream in a society, groups that split off from that mainstream because of their distinctive emphases are sometimes called "sects." They still operate within the basic framework of the religious tradition, but because of their special focus and their tendency to separate from the others they are differentiated from the mainstream.

The term "cult," as used by social scientists, generally refers to an alternative minority within a dominant society, following an altogether different religious structure, alien to the prevailing religious community. Such groups may be transplanted from outside, or they can emerge as innovations based on new religious experiences by charismatic leaders and deeply committed followers. The sociological definition of cult can be helpful in showing the relationship of such a new religious movement to the dominant society.

Unfortunately, the term "cult" is no longer a neutral sociological term but has become highly loaded with other connotations. To some Christian groups, "cults" include all new movements that have departed from orthodox Christian teachings, and are to be condemned. And a secular anti-cult movement has been fighting against many new religious movements because, it is claimed, they practice brainwashing and mind control over their adherents. On these grounds, any religious movement that is different and strange can be dismissed as a "cult" that threatens church and society.

Now it is true that several recent cult movements have turned out to be destructive. One thinks of the People's Temple movement led by Jim Jones, resulting in the mass suicide of 912 adherents at Jonestown in Guyana in 1978. Then there was the recent violent episode of the Branch Davidians, led by David Koresh, resulting in tragic mass destruction at their stronghold in Waco, Texas, in 1993. The Heaven's Gate community shocked the world by group suicide in 1996 in an apparent attempt to reach higher spiritual development by connecting with a nearby comet. And Aum Shinri-kyo, an apocalyptic new religious movement in Japan, shocked Japanese society by a sarin gas attack in the subway system in 1994. Yet these movements, and others with some of the same characteristics, are exceptional, deviant groups, and it is certainly wrong to lump all new religious movements together with them in a single "cult" category. Each new religious movement provides meaning and power that people live by, as do all the established world religions, and our first step is to take a sensitive look inside them and try to understand the vision of sacred life they provide.

Some Characteristics of the New Movements Though new religious movements are found across the whole religious landscape and may vary widely, there are a few typical characteristics that they have in common. They arise in a context of discontent and spiritual crisis. Some people find a loss of meaning in their own traditional path, or perhaps they never felt part of a path and are searching for something to fill the emptiness. The new movements respond to this discontent and searching, supplying a new or alternative meaning, identity, and spiritual purpose. Of course, as we have seen, there are reform and revitalization movements in all the world religions today, but some people are attracted to paths that are more radically new and different, beyond the mainstream traditions.

The new religious movements often tend to be *apocalyptic* in the sense of promising a new age, a spiritual transformation that will meet the crisis and bring fulfillment. Sometimes the promise is for a New Era for all humankind—a future of global salvation, beginning with the new order established by the founder. Often the benefits are not merely spiritual but also concrete and this-worldly. Many new movements focus strongly on individual benefits, promising personal transformation, fulfillment, and growth.

Typically, new movements center on strong founders—charismatic individuals who have had extraordinary spiritual experiences and revelations of higher truths. After the founder dies, the movement often goes through a period of crisis as leadership passes to successors and the original charisma becomes more organized and institutionalized. Schisms may occur, new groups may spin off, and the new movement gradually takes on established forms if it is to endure in passing on the founding traditions.

Some of the new groups are sectarian and thus rather narrowly focused. But most new movements are quite eclectic in their teachings and practices, drawing from a variety of religious sources, putting traditions together in a new way, and incorporating new insights from modern experiences.

While some of these movements are antimodern, preferring traditional views of reality rather than the modern scientific worldview, many of the new movements readily embrace modern life, science, and technology. They often describe their spiritual practices and benefits in scientific, psychological, or even technological terms. They participate rather fully in modern-day structures of politics, economics, education, and the rest, following their spiritual path within the opportunities and demands of modern life.

Most of these groups excel in using all the modern techniques of communication. A striking recent development is the rapidly increasing use of the Internet, with its bulletin boards, discussion lists, and news groups. Adherents, seekers, and interested onlookers can log on and engage in spirited discussions, literally around the globe, about various points of history, doctrine, and practice. Some groups are even experimenting with sessions of spiritual practice conducted via the Internet. This new phenomenon of religious discussion and participation in cyberspace will no doubt have a substantial impact in shaping the future of many religious movements, including the mainline traditions.

Rise of New Sectarian Movements

Sectarian groups are not really *new* religions, but we should take note of this phenomenon in the contemporary religious world. Occasionally, the transformations and new ideas advocated by some are resisted by the dominant religious community, and new sectarian groups have emerged, splitting off from the mainstream. Such sects hold fast to some special aspects of the traditional way but are separated from the mainstream because of their distinctive focus.

For example, a number of sectarian groups have arisen within American Christianity, in some cases becoming rather significant communities in their own right. The **Jehovah's Witnesses,** following a very strict literal understanding of the Bible, have certain distinctive teachings about God and human life that separate them from other Christian groups. They hold that the doctrine of the Trinity is unbiblical—they believe in Jesus as the Son of God but not as Jehovah (God) himself. They meet regularly in "kingdom halls" for study and worship, and they give public testimony to the truth by engaging in door-to-door evangelism. Jehovah's Witnesses follow their distinctive faith and refuse to accommodate modern society—persisting, for example, in being pacifist and refusing blood transfusions.

Another well-established sectarian group within Christianity is the **Church of Christ Scientist,** following the distinctive ideas of Mary Baker Eddy (1821–1910) in interpreting the scriptures. They are thought by other Christians to be nonconventional, even though they consider themselves to be in the mainstream of Christian teachings. Mary Baker Eddy believed her teachings embodied the Divine Science represented in the continuing power of the Holy Spirit, demonstrated in Jesus' miracles, but still operative. God is mind and life principle, she taught, the only reality; matter is an illusion resulting from inferior human thinking. Relying on the Divine Mind leads the believer toward spiritual growth in which the error is transformed and apparent sicknesses vanish.

So new sectarian groups have grown up in many of the world's religions in modern times, as we have noted in earlier chapters, as people struggle with the challenges of modernity and seek to find special meaning in selective aspects of their traditional religious resources. And some of these groups have become strong and international in scope through their energetic evangelistic activities.

Attraction to Alternative Paths in the West

For some people of the Western world, spiritual searching leads them away from their own tradition of Christianity or Judaism to discover the depth of meaning in other traditional religious paths. In Europe and America, recent immigration has brought large numbers of ethnic communities from other parts of the world to live within Western society. People representing all the major world religions are now present, and some Westerners are attracted to these alternative spiritual paths. As Westerners join them and take on their practices and disciplines, new shapes and characteristics emerge. We have already taken note of the Black Muslim movement in America (Chapter 12). To many Westerners, the sacred paths of the East hold a particular fascination.

Hindu Movements in the West   In America and Europe, there has been much interest in traditional and new forms of Hinduism, taught by a large array of masters, swamis, and gurus. Swami Vivekananda (1863–1902), disciple of the Hindu saint Sri Ramakrishna, brought knowledge of Hinduism to America when he came to the 1893 Parliament of World Religions in Chicago, remaining to found **Vedanta Societies** in America and Europe before returning to India to lead the Ramakrishna Order with which the Vedanta Societies are associated. Vedanta temples in the West have been influential in bringing Hindu teachings to many Westerners over the last century, along with instruction in the practices of yoga and meditation.

In the course of the twentieth century, many other Hindu swamis and gurus have made the journey to the West, gathering groups of adherents to follow certain aspects of Hindu teaching and practice. An early yoga master in the West was Yogananda (1893–1952), who came to America in 1920 and stayed for the next thirty years, founding the **Self-Realization Fellowship** with many centers in America and throughout the world. Teaching the basic philosophy of the Yoga Sutras, Yogananda used many modern devices to help Westerners understand and practice yoga—a way of attaining high spiritual energy and evolution by withdrawing life-energy from outer concerns for the opening of one's inner spiritual centers. Teaching that the vision and practice of yoga underlie all the great religions—meaning that Jesus as well as other religious leaders were yoga masters—the Self-Realization Fellowship provides a practical Hindu path accessible to many Western seekers.

A more recent Hindu master who created a large following in America and throughout the world was Maharishi Mahesh Yogi, who studied the nondualistic form of meditation taught by the great philosopher Shankara. Coming to America in 1959, he began to teach the popular, simple meditation technique he called **Transcendental Meditation,** attracting much publicity with his charismatic guru presence. Followers in the 1960s and 1970s included many well-known public figures and entertainers (including, for a while, the Beatles), and the movement established Maharishi International University in Fairfield, Iowa. The heart of TM is to follow the natural tendency of the mind to seek the field of greater happiness, employing meditation to stop external distraction and allow the mind to reach the ultimate ground of reality (in Hindu thought, the Brahman). Practitioners spend a short time each day in meditation, repeating a mantra given to them by their spiritual teacher. Many TM teachers hold that this practice is not really a religion but a scientific technique that can be used by anyone to calm mental and physical anxiety and tap into pure consciousness, leading to greater creativity, mental power, and happiness. While long-term adherents of Transcendental Meditation are perhaps not as numerous as they once were, the influence of this movement has been substantial, considering that hundreds of thousands of Americans and Europeans have studied and practiced TM at least for a short period in their lives.

Many other Hindu yogis and gurus have started movements in America, but one of the best-known recent groups is the **International Society for Krishna Consciousness.** This is a movement that advocates a rather strict form of Hindu bhakti, drawing on the Krishna theistic movement championed by the Hindu saint Chaitanya in the sixteenth century.

Teaching that the Krishna sacred stories are literally true and that Krishna is the supreme personal Lord, ISKCON encourages adherents to devote themselves totally to Krishna through chanting the names of Krishna, dancing, and acts of service. Through love for Krishna, the soul overcomes its ignorant entrapment in material bodies and moves on the path toward supernal bliss. Disciples live in monastic temples and follow a stringent lifestyle of worship and service, with total obedience to their spiritual master; other supporters follow normal careers and join in temple celebrations. Although divisions and scandals have troubled ISKCON in recent years, temples in America and throughout the world continue to thrive as Hindu bhakti centers. In recent years, this Hindu sectarian movement has also been growing in its homeland, India.

Buddhist Paths in the Western World   While many Westerners have been drawn to the various Hindu groups, equally attractive have been the numerous schools of Bud-

Followers of the International Society for Krishna Consciousness prepare for an initiation ceremony in their temple in Brooklyn.

dhism that have made their way to the West and are thriving both in Asian ethnic communities and among groups of Westerners. Among ethnic Buddhist communities in America, largest perhaps is **Pure Land Buddhism,** consisting of tens of thousands of Japanese Buddhists, most belonging to the Buddhist Churches of America and similar organizations. Similarly, Buddhists from Korea, Thailand, Vietnam, and other Asian lands continue their Buddhist practices in America and Europe.

For many years Buddhism has had a strong intellectual attraction for Western scholars, who have translated important Buddhist texts into European languages. But the more widespread interest in Buddhist thought and meditation began with the development of the spiritual counterculture in the 1950s and 1960s, when fascination focused especially on **Zen Buddhism,** popularized by people like D.T. Suzuki and Alan Watts. Some went to Japan to practice Zen meditation, and some Zen masters from Japan started meditation centers in the United States. Zen has continued as a major form of Buddhist practice in the West up to the present, with numerous meditation centers in America, Europe, and elsewhere, comprising both the Soto and the Rinzai traditions. Western disciples have become recognized as priests and masters (roshi) and have taken over leadership roles. Zen practitioners are generally small in numbers in the West, for Zen's austere discipline and anti-symbolism does not appeal to the masses. Emptying the mind in meditation, sitting quietly in long and strenuous sesshin retreats—this is for the dedicated and strong-minded followers of the Dharma.

While Zen Buddhism seems low key and austere to many Westerners, **Vajrayana Buddhism** from Tibet has colorful rituals, mesmerizing chanting, fascinating symbolism, and profound teachings. Although tens of thousands of Tibetans, including the Dalai Lama and many other lamas, fled Tibet in 1959 when China occupied their country, they perpetuated Tibetan Buddhism in exile, in Nepal and India and even in the West. Some young lamas, notably Chogyam Trungpa and Tarthang Tulku, eventually made their way to America and taught Tibetan Buddhism in a way that could be adopted and practiced in Western society. Various centers were established, most notably the Naropa Institute in Colorado and the Nyingma Meditation Center in Berkeley, California. Vajrayana, as Tantric Buddhism, makes use of the full range of mind and body capabilities, using intense meditation, visualization techniques, rituals, chanting, philosophical study, and more. While these forms are practiced in somewhat simplified forms in the Western nonmonastic setting, the Western disciples of Tibetan Buddhism are sincere and energetic in pursuing this profound spiritual path.

One more example of Buddhist paths in the Western world is **Nichiren Shoshu of America.** In Japan, this very large lay Buddhist movement is called Soka Gakkai and claims to number some 17 million members. It emphasizes the chanting of the Daimoku, *Namu myoho renge kyo* (Praise to the wondrous truth of the Lotus Sutra), before a mandala created by Nichiren. Such chanting links one together with the universal Buddha power of the Lotus Sutra and brings great spiritual and material benefits. In the post–World War II era, Nichiren Shoshu came to the United States with American servicemen, their Japanese spouses, and other Japanese immigrants; some Japanese-Americans joined, and some Westerners found this form of Buddhism to their spiritual liking. Nichiren Shoshu of America is well organized, with group meetings and cultural festivals in addition to the daily household worship of chanting and reciting parts of the Lotus Sutra.

NONTRADITIONAL NEW RELIGIOUS MOVEMENTS

The religious paths stemming from the East are not new religions, even though they are fairly newly present in the Western world and represent alternative paths for Westerners. While many of these Hindu and Buddhist movements have developed forms that are adapted to Western needs and characteristics, they still fit broadly into the family characteristics of Hinduism and Buddhism.

But there are also *new* religious movements in many parts of the world—movements that do not fit within any of the traditional paths. Of course, nothing in human culture comes as a totally new entity, and these new religions often use elements from the established sacred paths. But with new sacred experiences, revelations, and teachings, the founders of these movements have created distinctively new paths for their followers.

Some of these new movements have sprung from Western soil, with strong ties to Christian, Jewish, or Muslim tradition, but also reaching back to European roots in antiquity in some cases. Much influence has also come from Eastern religions, as well as from modern secular sources, scientific approaches, humanistic impulses, and modern psychological and therapeutic developments.

To study in depth these newer religious movements would go far beyond this book's purpose and focus. However, to fill out our sense of the vitality of today's religious scene, and to encourage further investigation of some of these interesting and creative movements, it will be helpful to look briefly at several major representatives of these new religious movements.

New Sacred Paths: Nineteenth-Century Roots

Some new religious and spiritual movements have actually been around for many years. The nineteenth century saw the rise of Baha'i and Theosophy, as well as numerous Christian-based movements such as Spiritualism, Mormonism, and many others. Many of these movements have continued and are thriving today as established groups in America and in other parts of the world.

Mormonism: the Latter-Day Saints   In 1823, a young man named Joseph Smith (1805–1844) felt himself led by an angel to the hill Cumorah near Manchester, New York. There he found some golden plates, which he translated with divine help, thus producing the Book of Mormon, which the Latter-Day Saints see as the revealed Word of God. It is this revelatory experience of a new Word of God, to supplement and even supersede the Christian Bible, that makes **Mormonism** into a new religious movement, not just a sectarian offshoot of Christianity.

The Mormon Temple in Salt Lake City with its sharply pointed spires and rows of steep arches.

The newly revealed sacred story tells how some lost tribes of Israel wandered to America, where Christ appeared to them and gave them the true gospel. The promise was made that a New Jerusalem would appear in America. So in 1830 Joseph Smith organized the Church of Jesus Christ of Latter-Day Saints, attracted several thousand converts, and moved westward, first to Ohio, then to Missouri, and then to Illinois, as local people criticized and rejected this new movement. Joseph Smith and his brother were shot by an angry mob in 1844, but then many Mormons followed the new leader, Brigham Young (1801–1877), to their new and lasting center in the Salt Lake valley in Utah. Other, more conservative Mormons, resisting new ideas like plural marriage and a plurality of gods, remained behind and established the Reorganized Church of Jesus Christ of Latter-Day Saints, headquartered in Independence, Missouri.

A strong and visionary leader, Brigham Young was also appointed governor of the Utah Territory. Under his leadership, the Mormons attempted to create the ideal community on earth in preparation for the Kingdom of God.

Although the practice of plural marriage had been revealed to Joseph Smith as part of the new community's life, in 1890 the Mormons abandoned that practice, compromising with the values of American society. Through hard work, solid higher education (centered in Brigham Young University), and participation in American political and economic life, the Mormons have become an established, accepted movement within American life.

In their teachings about the sacred reality and about human life, the Mormons share many Christian-sounding ideas. But the Book of Mormon supplements the Christian scriptures with a more complete view, according to Mormon belief. According to the largest Mormon group, the Salt Lake City branch, there is a plurality of gods—gods who once were human, since humans can become gods. But Mormons worship only the God of this world. They consider the world to be a good creation, so that the kingdom of God can be established here. God created this world out of existing matter, and thus there can be full agreement with modern scientific views about the world, such as its age in millions of years. Through Adam and Eve, humans became alienated from God and thus cannot share in the full measure of life from God. The coming of the Savior makes it possible to regain immortality and live as gods. Since the Book of Mormon shows how to overcome the errors of the previous churches, accepting this new revelation and becoming part of the new church based on it is the path of reconciliation.

Another distinctive Mormon teaching is that this path is also open to the ancestors of each Mormon. One can search the family tree, finding ancestors who would have believed and having them baptized in a sacred temple ritual. Mormons believe in life after death, available at different levels depending on the degree of spiritual development. Marriage is an especially important ritual, celebrated in a temple ceremony, lasting for eternity. Usually, gatherings of Mormon congregations take place in meetinghouses, where they hold simple worship services and other social events. The more important rituals and ordinances take place at temples in the major population centers; only those Mormons who follow the strict rules of conduct can take part in the sacred temple rituals.

Leadership among the Mormons centers on the male hierarchy, with all males involved in religious roles. Young men devote two years to missionary activity, often in other parts of the world. The Mormon vision of the good life includes support for higher education and the various professions. Mormons are expected to work hard and productively, supporting themselves and the church. They have a keen sense of responsibility for one another and for all humans. Here is a new religious movement that is no longer countercultural, as Mormons have retained their special identity while taking an active and responsible role within the modern world.

The Baha'i Sacred Path   The **Baha'i** path arose in nineteenth-century Persia, in the context of the Twelver Shi'ite movement within Islam. As discussed earlier (Chapter 12), the twelfth Imam (successor to Muhammad, in the Shi'ite view) disappeared into the state of occultation, continuing to provide spiritual guidance from a higher sphere, in contact with certain holy leaders and scholars. In 1844, a young man named 'Ali Muhammad Shirazi came forward claiming to be the Bab, the "gateway" to the Imam. Many excited followers gathered around him, but there was much

resistance from the established leaders, and the Bab was executed in 1850. A follower, Mirza Hussain 'Ali (1817–1892), took the name Baha'u'llah ("Glory of Allah") and, in 1863, revealed that he was the Manifestation of God for the present era, whose coming had been predicted by the Bab.

Baha'u'llah spent much time in exile and in house arrest, but in the midst of it all, he wrote letters, taught his followers, and composed sacred texts—especially the *Book of Certitude (Kitab-i-Uqan)* and the *Most Holy Book (Kitab-i-Aqdas),* in which he established the teachings and way of life in this new era for his followers, the Baha'is. His son Abdul Baha (1844–1921) succeeded him and put forth the basic interpretations of these sacred writings. Abdul Baha traveled and lectured in Europe and America, spreading the Baha'i faith and establishing numerous Assemblies. After his death, his grandson Shoghi Effendi (1896–1957) continued as leader for the developing Baha'i community. Shoghi Effendi established the International House of Justice, sitting in Haifa, Israel, to function after his death as the supreme body governing Baha'i affairs worldwide.

Reflecting the influence of Islam, the whole emphasis in Baha'u'llah's teaching is on *unity*—the unity of God and the unity of humanity. There is one God, who is unknowable in divine essence but who has communicated the divine truth to the world through messengers that have arisen in every era. All the great prophets and founders of the major religions have been manifestations and messengers of God—the Buddha, Krishna, Zoroaster, Moses, Jesus, Muhammad, and now Baha'u'llah, the Manifestation of God for the New Era.

While earlier Manifestations of God presented God's truth for their eras, Baha'u'llah's central message for this New Era is the universal truth of the oneness of humanity. And this means the total unity of all races, nations, and classes; it means the total equality of men and women in all aspects of life. Humans are the highest order of creation, with the freedom to realize either their higher or their lower natures. Because of ignorance, errors have entered into the religions and humans have often given in to selfishness and greed, hindering the development of a wholesome humanity in a peaceful world. The truth brought through Baha'u'llah, and interpreted through Abdul Baha and Shoghi Effendi, is the truth for the whole of humankind—the truth that corrects mistakes, overcomes ignorance, and leads the way to reconciliation. This means the essential harmony of all religions, for all religions have taught this truth of unity. It also means harmony between religious truth and scientific inquiry, for all truth is in harmony, whether religious or scientific.

Because of the total unity of God, there can be no separate evil force operative in the universe; what appears to be evil is the absence of good. Religious concepts of the day of judgment and of heaven and hell are not to be taken literally but rather symbolically, in the Baha'i view. Humankind determines the future by actions in the present. The soul is eternal and continues to evolve into different states and conditions after death; when the soul is near to God and God's purposes, that is the condition of heaven, while being distant from God is the condition of hell.

Baha'i worship is simple and is focused on prayer and meditation. Each Baha'i is to pray daily, although prayers do not have to take mandated forms, and even daily work is considered to be prayer. Communal worship is carried on in members' homes, consisting of prayer and readings from the writings of Baha'u'llah and Abdul Baha and from the scriptures of the other world religions. Members gather not on Sundays but for the monthly feast—based on their annual calendar, which has nineteen months, each consisting of nineteen days. Baha'is are supposed to fast during the nineteen-day month that falls in early March, taking no food or drink from dawn to dusk. There are nine festivals during the course of the year, based mostly on events in the Baha'i sacred story.

Most Baha'i activities take place within the local community. When there are sufficient members, the local group elects the local Spiritual Assembly, a nine-member body, to administer the affairs of the local community. Further, each country has a nine-member National Spiritual Assembly elected annually. And the National Assemblies elect the nine-member International House of Justice, whose members serve five-year terms. There are no special clergy, and men and women participate equally in leading worship and in the work of the spiritual assemblies.

The Baha'i vision of life is positive and world-embracing. Work is considered service to God, and justice for all is regarded as the ruling principle in society. In the Baha'i view, there should be universal education for all and a universal language for worldwide communication. War should be eliminated and armaments destroyed, and there should be a world tribunal for solving disputes between nations and for the establishment of a permanent, universal peace.

The Baha'i House of Worship in Wilmette, Illinois.

The Baha'i religion itself, with its International House of Justice, is the blueprint for the new world order of universal peace and harmony. This vision has led Baha'is to spread their faith throughout the world, with some five million followers on all continents.

Spiritualism and the Spiritualist Churches Before the rise of the modern scientific view of the universe, it was widely accepted in Europe and elsewhere that the earth was the center of the universe and that there was a hierarchy of intelligences between heaven and earth, with spiritual forces linking the different elements in the world, within and without. Based on this prescientific worldview, various practices such as shamanism, astrology, alchemy, evocation of spirits, and witchcraft flourished. The new scientific, rationalistic view of the universe and of humanity's place in it shattered all that for most of the Western world. But fascination with the possibility of communication with higher intelligences and spirits, and interest in things metaphysical and the occult, never died out completely. Two movements arising in the nineteenth century that embraced the old, alternative view of reality were **Spiritualism** and **Theosophy**—very different, yet linked in their fascination with communication with higher realities, with spirits, and with masters.

Spiritualism in its modern American form started in 1848 in the home of the Fox family in upstate New York. The two daughters of the family, Margaretta and Kate (eleven and eight years old), puzzled by rappings that had been going on in their house, worked out a code for communicating with the spirit doing the rapping. The story spread like wildfire, great discussions were held, and enthusiasm for spirit manifestations erupted throughout America, Europe, and elsewhere. All over there were rappings sounding out occult messages, tables rising and turning, voices heard from the spirit world, and more. Church attendance dwindled and Spiritualist meetings were packed as people sought communication with the spirits of their loved ones or with great and wise spirits on the other side. Prominent American figures, including Abraham Lincoln, supported the movement. Several utopian communities were founded based on guidance from higher spirits. Some Spiritualist teachers developed an evolutionary view of the soul as traveling gradually higher within the spiritual planes that surround the earth.

After the great enthusiasm of the 1850s, support slackened for Spiritualism, as certain frauds were exposed and as churches and academics ridiculed the movement. The Civil War brought an end to the great popularity Spiritualism had enjoyed, but devoted followers carried on the practice, with revivals in the twentieth century, both in America and in Europe. There are numerous Spiritualist churches and denominations today, although membership and affiliation tend to shift rather easily.

Spiritualist churches center on the spiritualistic powers of the minister, often a wise, experienced woman; she or he is the medium who knows how to contact the spirits and guide the followers in this venture. Rituals and doctrine generally are broadly taken from Christianity and from other religions. In a Spiritualist service, the groups may sing hymns and practice healing by prayer and laying on of hands, but the center point is receiving the spirit messages. The minister-medium goes into a trance, and one of the "control" spirits speaks through her or him, giving a general message and individual messages for the different members of the group. Sometimes a seance is held in a small group, with a guiding spirit speaking through the medium, bringing messages from spirit relatives and friends.

Many of the new religious movements have been influenced by Spiritualism. Here is religious experience documenting the possibility of overcoming the human limitations of space, time, body, and even death. We can expand our minds and our spirits toward higher planes and communicate with the spirits and powers on the other side.

Theosophy   Communication with the Masters, those who know and control the hidden side of reality, the occult—that is a major theme of another movement that arose in the latter part of the nineteenth century: the Theosophical (Divine Wisdom) Society. The guiding light of Theosophy was the remarkable Helena Petrovna Blavatsky (1831–1891), a woman of great charisma and mystery, reputed to have extraordinary psychic powers. Born into a Russian noble family, she tells of some twenty years of fantastic travel all over the world, meeting with masters of the occult in Egypt, Mexico, Canada, and finally even in Tibet, undergoing initiation into the secret doctrine that all the world religions are based on. Coming to America in 1874, she teamed up with Colonel Henry Olcott (1832–1907), a scientist and lawyer who was investigating Spiritualism, and together they founded the Theosophical Society in 1875. They met regularly, often at Madame Blavatsky's New York apartment, to engage in spirited discussion about expanding human mental and spiritual powers through connection with ancient esoteric truths and supernatural phenomena. The discussions were dominated by Blavatsky's own first-hand experiences, and in 1878 she published *Isis Revealed*, transmitting the occult science and wisdom of the ancient Masters for the modern world.

But increasingly, their spiritual journey pointed toward the wisdom of the East, and in 1878 Blavatsky and Olcott set sail for India, establishing the Theosophy headquarters in Madras and more purposefully linking their vision with the truths of Hinduism and Buddhism. They showed great respect for Eastern societies, which were very much under British domination at this time. They were active in social reforms in Sri Lanka, helping Buddhists win benefits under British rule. They interacted with a variety of Hindu spiritual leaders, adopting basic Hindu concepts such as karma and reincarnation in their teachings, and Theosophy came to be respected and supported by numerous Hindu intellectuals. In turn, Theosophical leaders helped Indian people recover confidence in their own spiritual heritage after being subject to colonialism for so many years. For example, Annie Besant (1847–1933), leader of the Theosophical Society in the first part of the twentieth century, worked for social reform, education, and women's suffrage in India and assisted in the movement toward home rule by Indian people.

The most important text for Theosophical ideas, *The Secret Doctrine,* was written by Madame Blavatsky in 1888; she claimed it was based on a lost text, *Stanzas of Dzyan.* A vision emerges here of all of reality emanating from the One, as in Hindu thought, evolving into spirit, mind, and matter, and then withdrawing again back into the One in great pulsing cycles. All of reality is linked together in vast chains of spiritual consciousness, with even the planets and the solar systems controlled by great minds. Humans, each at a different level of spiritual development, have the potential to evolve to the higher levels of spirit. The role of the Masters is to prepare others for expanding consciousness and to initiate them in higher planes of consciousness at the level of Masters, planets, and solar systems. Eventually, Theosophical leaders developed a full-blown hierarchy of spiritual Masters, including the Solar Logos ruling the solar level, with Sanat Kumara residing in Shamballa as Lord of the World, under whom are the Buddha, the Bodhisattva, and Manu. On the next plane, emanating from above, are the Seven Rays governing all areas of earthly life, each Ray ruled by Masters who have appeared numerous times as guides in human history, in personages such as Krishna, Jesus, Ramanuja, Roger Bacon, and many, many more.

Theosophy remained essentially an intellectual movement, without developing ritual worship and other social and practical religious forms. Its appeal was mainly to well-educated middle- and upper-class people in America and England. Although plagued by schisms and struggles for leadership, the Society was quite popular in the first part of the twentieth century and introduced many Westerners to the fascinating realm of Hindu and Buddhist teachings.

Today there are several small organizations that carry on the Theosophy tradition, the largest and most active being the Theosophical Society in America. But Theosophy has had an impact far beyond its current membership. The writings of Madame Blavatsky and others have introduced a great many people to the fascinations of the occult, and a whole variety of new spiritual movements have spun off from Theosophy. These include, for example, the Full Moon Meditation Groups founded by Alice Bailey; the Liberal Catholic Church, a Theosophical group employing a liturgy similar to the Catholic mass; Anthroposophy, founded by Rudolph Steiner, with a larger emphasis on educational activities and scientific study of the spiritual world; the followers of Krishnamurti, who was identified by Annie Besant as the next vehicle of the World Teacher but who left Theosophy to teach his own philosophy of life; the Rosicrucian Fellowship, led by Max Grashoff; the "I AM" movement founded by Guy Ballard, a Theosophical group teaching that humanity began in America and important Masters appeared in the American West; and more. Beyond these various groups, Theosophy, much like Spiritualism, has been a significant influence in the recent upsurge of interest in things occult and in nature spirituality, in the broad religious subculture sometimes referred to as the New Age movement.

New Spiritual Movements of the Twentieth Century

Just as in the nineteenth century, so also in the twentieth century, numerous new religious movements have been spawned in the West and on American soil, some fleeting and diffuse in character, some rather long-lasting and tightly organized. Of the hundreds of such new groups and movements, we can get a sense of the contemporary scene by focusing briefly on several representative movements from different parts of that landscape. We will look at two examples of well-defined and structured groups, namely, Scientology and the Unification Church. And we will survey another broad and diffuse new movement, the nature spirituality movement encompassing Neo-Paganism and Wicca.

Scientology   While many new religious movements draw on ancient occult and spiritualist traditions, and others receive much inspiration from Eastern sources, a few modern groups have their sources solidly within the modern, Western worldview with its scientific mind-set and technological procedures. The spiritual context is still there—the founder has supernormal spiritual knowledge and power and is able to lead initiates into higher levels of personal transformation. But the setting is modern Western society, the language is technological and business oriented, and the goal is personal freedom, power, and happiness within this life. One well-known example of this kind of movement is **Scientology.**

The founder of Scientology was L. Ron Hubbard (1911–1986), a science fiction writer who, receiving a spiritual message through a near-death experience in the Navy, turned to teaching and sharing his new vision and technique for transforming the human condition. He attracted a great deal of interest when he published these ideas in 1950 in his famous book, *Dianetics: The Modern Science of Mental Health,* considered the foundation for Scientology. Four years later Hubbard established the Founding Church of Scientology, and later he moved to England and began the Hubbard College of Scientology in Sussex. Although he stayed out of public view for most of his last years, his picture hangs in all Scientology buildings and his followers continue to venerate him as the chief teacher and master of the new technology.

At a simple level, Scientology considers all human ills to have arisen from experiences of shock in present or past lives (often in the womb) that cause "engrams" or sensory impressions to be recorded in the mind, which then produce psychosomatic or mental disorders and a life of unhappiness. The Scientology technique called "auditing" is designed to enable one to dislodge those engrams and become "clear." In this process, a trained Scientology auditor uses an "E-meter," an electrical device that measures areas of reaction or tension as the "preclear" person responds to questions about the areas of emotional stress. In this way, the engrams are gradually dislodged and the person goes "clear," an experience that is often described as ecstatic, joyful freedom.

Hubbard linked this rather simple therapeutic process with a deeper mythology and spiritual transformation, giving Scientology an aura of the supernatural. He taught about thetans who, millions of years ago, played games and created MEST (matter, energy, space, and time), entrapping themselves in the material universe and forgetting their true nature as eternal and omnipotent thetans. The new revelation Scientology offers is that we are all thetans, having gone through seemingly endless reincarnations, acquiring engrams in all these lives. And so the next stage after becoming clear is to become an "operating thetan" (OT), an initiatory process under the guidance of a teacher who has already reached that stage. The OT is freed from the limitations and toils of MEST. As one moves to the higher levels of OT, there are ecstatic experiences of freedom from body, time, and space.

Scientology is a highly structured, efficient organization that supplies much for its followers in terms of spiritual meaning, social involvement, a close family atmosphere, and a sense of personal growth and transformation. There is considerable cost for the "tech" procedures, but those who pass through these initiatory processes find many rewards.

The Unification Church   A well-known new religious movement that arose from Christian roots and still claims to be a Christian denomination is the Holy Spirit Association for the Unification of World Christianity, better known as the **Unification Church.** This new movement is unlike many of the other new religious movements in that it is strongly anticommunist and pro-America, it advocates sexual purity and family values, and it generally supports conservative political and social causes. Yet it has become one of the more controversial of the new religious movements.

The founder, the Reverend Sun Myung Moon, was born in Korea in 1920, and his family joined a missionary Presbyterian church while he was a child. On Easter Sunday in 1936, when he was sixteen, he had a transforming revelatory experience: Jesus appeared to him, telling him to complete the saving mission that had been interrupted. Over the next years, Moon struggled against Satanic forces and communicated with Abraham, Moses, the Buddha, and God. He came to understand that humankind's relationship with God had been disrupted with a secret crime committed by Adam and Eve, and he felt himself called to restore this relationship and establish the kingdom of God on earth. He began his mission in North Korea in 1945, and his imprisonment and torture by Communist authorities is interpreted as his own "payment" for the sins of the first parents. Finally, in South Korea in 1958, he established the religion of the Divine Principle, as he called his teaching, and he attracted considerable numbers of followers.

A Unification Church missionary, Miss Young Oon Kim, brought this new religion to America as early as 1959, translating Reverend Moon's book, *Divine Principle,* into English. But the movement did not gain much ground in America until Reverend Moon moved to the United States in 1971 and began to spread his teaching energetically through lecture tours, large public rallies, and meetings with public officials and dignitaries. The Unification Church proved adept at raising funds, with converts even canvassing for funds among the general public. Through wise business investments and income-producing enterprises, the Unification Church has generated a flow of income that allows it to carry on its affairs and conduct many activities, such as publishing a daily newspaper, *The Washington Times,* and sponsoring conferences for scholars in the area of religious studies.

Although the Unification Church wishes to be considered a Christian church, and although Reverend Moon puts forth *Divine Principle* as the true interpretation of the Christian Bible, the vision of God, humankind, and salvation set forth in Unification theology is quite distinct from traditional Christian views. Reverend Moon holds that God's basic purpose is to have all humankind live together with God as one divine family, within divine laws of Polarity and the Four Position Foundation. And so God (both male and female) created humans—Adam and Eve—to be the ideal father and mother and to have a child. Thus, the whole human race would be built on the four-unit foundation of God, father, mother, child. But here the secret crime enters in: Satan in serpent form seduced Eve into having spiritual intercourse with him, and Eve in turn seduced Adam into nonmarital physical intercourse. Thus, Satan took the place of God in relation to the first parents, and the proper fourfold foundation was disrupted for all their descendants.

The Bible shows how God attempted numerous times to restore the proper relationship, but unsuccessfully. Even Jesus' mission as the Christ was only partly successful, for God intended him to be the Second Adam and to marry a Second Eve to produce godly offspring and thus restore the human family under God. But, unable to fulfill the divine plan, Jesus could only submit to crucifixion, making payment to God for human sinfulness but only effecting partial salvation for humans. Thus, Jesus appeared to Reverend Moon in Korea, telling him to complete the mission that Jesus failed to fulfill.

A large Unification Church public ritual at Madison Square Garden in New York (1982), as the Rev. Sun Myung Moon conducts a mass wedding ceremony for couples whose marriages he has arranged.

So Unification theology looks toward a Third Adam, the Lord of the Second Advent, who will marry a New Eve and produce pure children, thus bringing purity to humankind and forming the ideal family on which God's kingdom can be built. *Divine Principle* looks for the new Messiah to come from a new country, one that has suffered extreme hardship—and Reverend Moon believes that country is Korea. While *Divine Principle* does not state explicitly that Reverend Moon himself is that new Messiah—the Third Adam—it appears that he has accepted this calling. In 1992, he announced in Korea that he and his wife are True Parents of all humankind, taking on the mission of the Lord of the Second Advent. The Unification Church has placed strong emphasis on the work of reconciliation through the formation of ideal families. Reverend Moon presides over mass marriages for his followers; for example, in 1992 he and his wife held a Blessing Ceremony in Seoul for thirty thousand couples from around the world—symbolically transferring the purity of his own family to the larger family and, ultimately, to all human society.

The Unification Church teaches a strong ethical and moral code, together with a life dedicated to sacrificial good deeds, participating in the general payment for the sins of past humanity. Objections to the Unification Church from Christian churches and anti-cult groups have largely centered on accusations of brainwashing young people and disrupting families; and Unification leaders are accused of living lavishly through the labors of deluded followers. Further, Reverend Moon was convicted on charges of income tax evasion and imprisoned in 1984, dealing a blow to the status of the Unification Church in the eyes of others. However, some of the objectionable practices have been stopped, and it must be remembered that anti-cult sentiment in America does not always have an objective basis. While Christian groups such as the National Council of Churches have generally not recognized the Unification Church as a Christian denomination, there is considerable support for the right of the Unification Church to practice its faith as it sees fit.

Nature Spirituality: Neo-Paganism and Wicca   For an increasing number of people today, the sense of being connected with the sacred and experiencing spiritual transformation is to be found within those ancient paths that were suppressed and replaced by the great world religions—that is, within the nature-oriented religions through which humans were connected with the sacred life flowing and pulsating within Mother Earth. The world religions, particularly the monotheistic ones, dominated by patriarchal structures and ideas of one God totally separate from

nature, downgraded the sacred value of earth-centered life. To recover that sense of sacred belonging and connectedness with nature is the focus of many new movements. The influence of nature spirituality, with its concerns about ecology and holistic human life within our earth-habitation, is being felt across all the religions. Not all people involved in these concerns would think of it as a religious path; but a dedicated and growing group of people today identify themselves specifically with those ancient paths that centered in nature spirituality, and they follow that as their own sacred path. They go by names from the past, such as Pagans, Druids, Witches, and Goddess-Worshipers.

In seeking a common term for this variety of groups, it has become fairly common for many to identify themselves as **Neo-Pagans.** "Pagan," originally meaning a "country-dweller" in Roman times, eventually became a derogatory term to refer to those who practiced polytheistic nature religions rather than converting to Christianity. But most Neo-Pagans today eagerly reach back to those pre-Christian polytheistic or pantheistic religions of Egypt, Greece, Rome, and old Europe for the sources of their spirituality. Though some resonate to Eastern ideas like reincarnation, generally Neo-Pagans have little interest in structured and authoritative Eastern religions like Hinduism and Buddhism. Nor do they identify with other tightly organized new religions like Scientology, Baha'i and the rest. Their inspiration is the "Old Religion" with its goddesses, gods, and rituals; and their focus is on the free and ecstatic experience of transformation within the sacredness of nature—without systems of belief and dogma, without hierarchical rule, without ascetic self-denial.

Instead of the monotheistic idea of one God separate from nature, Neo-Pagans experience a different orientation. All of nature is animate with sacred power—rocks and rivers and dreams alike, with no separation into sacred and profane. Sacred reality is immanent in nature, whether in the sky and the moon, or in the trees and the canyons, or in humans and animals alike. Yet this is no monistic, one-dimensional sacred reality, for Neo-Pagans are polytheists, as they experience the multiplicity and diversity of the sacred in an endless array as boundless as nature itself. Many Neo-Pagans honor ancient pantheons, such as those worshiped by Greeks, Romans, Egyptians, and Celts. Often special emphasis is placed on the great Goddess, widely worshiped in many forms in old Europe, Egypt, and many cultures of the world. Inspiration is drawn not only from the ancient traditions but also from Native Americans, other tribal peoples around the world, literary works like *The White Goddess* by Robert Graves, and even science fiction.

Humans, like all parts of nature, participate in divinity; they are gods and goddesses, reexperiencing that identity time and again through ritual and festival. In the rush of modern life and religion, people have become alienated from sacred nature, and thus from their inner selves. To reform sacred life through linkage with nature, Neo-Pagans focus most of their attention on ritual and ceremony. Many groups try as best they can to reproduce the sacred rituals of the ancient Druids, the Romans, the Egyptians, and others, although little written record of these rituals remains and most oral tradition has been blotted out. They also look to guides from other nature-oriented paths, such as that of Native Americans with their vision quests, sweat lodges, crystals, and medicine wheels. But with a flexible and innovative attitude, they often create their own forms of group ritual, oriented to the changing configurations of nature and human life—the four directions, the seasons, the moon and the sun, the human life cycle. A magic circle may be drawn, creating a new sacred world. With rituals of chanting and dancing, goddesses and gods without and within are evoked, and worshipers experience a deeper sense of how their lives are interwoven with the greater patterns of nature.

Neo-Pagan groups, with their distaste for organization and authority, tend to be flexible, changing movements. One group that was popular in the 1970s was Feraferia ("nature celebration"), founded by Frederick Adams on the basis of an ecstatic experience in which he realized the sacred feminine to be the living, personal unity of all things. The primordial creatrix spins a cosmic dance and all unique realities come into existence, including Mother, Father, Son, and Daughter deities. It is the Maiden Goddess, Kore, who is central, representing beauty, creativity, and desire. Feraferia's celebratory calendar is the life cycle of Kore, including her birth in early spring, her pubescent maidenhood, her nuptials, her retiring beneath the earth in winter. There is much emphasis on play and sensuality in these festivals, for humans need to get in touch with their own sensual nature as part of the rhythmic pulsing of nature.

It appears that many of the Neo-Pagan groups today identify themselves with **Wicca,** a modern renewal of the Old Religion of Witchcraft. The Craft today is a loosely knit movement of people committed to restoring the Wicca traditions of pre-Christian Europe. While some Witches feel this religion has been passed on from ancient times, the modern interest appears to have begun with Margaret Murray's book, *Witch-Cult in Western Europe* (1921), in which she presented Witchcraft as the surviving pre-Christian religion of Europe. Gerald Gardner (1884–1964) later told how he was initiated into one of the surviving ancient English covens in 1939 and then published accounts of how Witchcraft had survived. Other authors added to the mythic history, including Robert Graves in his very influential *The White Goddess.*

The mythic story of Wicca sees it as a religion dating back to paleolithic times in the worship of the god of the hunt and the goddess of fertility, universally practiced all over Europe. Christianity converted the nobility of society and took over sacred places and dates of the Old Religion, though dwellers in rural areas kept to their old practices. Eventually, Christianity turned the god of the Old Religion into the devil and distorted all records, but small family groups went underground and kept the religion alive throughout the Middle Ages until, finally, the Witchcraft Laws in England were repealed in 1951. Most modern adherents of Witchcraft do not take this story as literal history, seeing it more as metaphoric and spiritual truth. While feeling strong ties to the ancient traditions, they believe creativity in practicing the religion today is just as important as unbroken lineage to the past.

Like other Neo-Pagans, Wiccans hold that all of nature is alive with the sacred, and that humans are interconnected with nature, like everything else in the world. Gods and goddesses are present everywhere, in everyone and everything, as the inner spiritual energy of all of nature. In ritual and ceremony, the focus typically is on the Goddess, who appears in triple form, as Maiden, Mother, and Crone, symbolized by the waxing, full, and waning phases of the moon. And there is the Horned God, the male lord of animals, who is born each year at the winter solstice, is the springtime lover of the Goddess, and dies in the fall as the Goddess becomes the Crone for wintertime.

Members of Wicca form their own small groups known as *covens,* typically of twelve or thirteen members, with no hierarchical organization or authoritarian priesthood—all members are Witches. Their main rituals involve the creation of sacred space by "casting the circle," through purification rituals involving the four elements of fire, water, earth, and air, and through demarcation of the four directions. The circle becomes a sacred world, the place where contact with sacred reality without and within takes place. Depending on the tradition of the coven, a variety of sacred implements may be used, such as chalices, wands, and swords. Worshipers chant and dance in circles to raise the energy and then focus that collective energy into a "cone of power," to accomplish some goal of healing and transformation. A powerful ritual in some covens is the "drawing down" of the Goddess (symbolized by the moon) into a priestess of the coven, who thus becomes the Goddess present within the circle.

The usual meetings of the coven are called *esbats,* but they also meet on the great festivals called *sabbats,* which include Halloween *(Samhain),* the Celtic New Year, the winter purification festival *(Oimelc,* February 1), the marriage of God and Goddess *(Beltane,* May 1), and the festival of first fruits *(Lughnasadh,* August 1), as well as the solstices and the equinoxes. Beyond the covens, a recent development in Wicca is the burgeoning of large outdoor festivals, where Witches and Neo-Pagans meet others from throughout the world and feel at home among their true family. These festivals have contributed to creating a national Wicca community with shared dances, chants, rituals, and stories.

An important and invigorating development in the Wiccan movement has been the growth of feminist spirituality. Women have always played prominent roles in Neo-Pagan groups, in contrast with some of the other new religious movements, but in recent years Wicca has become a vehicle of intensified interest in recovering women's spirituality. The worship of the Goddess provides a natural focus, as the rituals, songs, dances, and stories are devoted to the ceremonial exploration of women's mysteries and the renewed experience of the sacred meaning of women's lives. Covens that are restricted to women are called Dianic covens, often focusing exclusively on the great Goddess in all her multiple forms. Some concern has arisen as to whether such exclusive focus on the Goddess tends toward a new form of monotheism, replacing God the Father with God the Mother. But such a development is unlikely, given the multiplicity of forms in which the Goddess appears and functions— sacralizing earth and nature, the natural human functions, the different phases of women's lives, and much more.

It is difficult to estimate membership in the various Witchcraft groups today, given the low-key organization and the atmosphere of privacy, but clearly there is much vitality in the movement. The highly visible presence of several Neo-Pagan and Wicca groups at the 1993 Parliament of the World's Religions in Chicago has stimulated the formation of new groups. The movement has developed to the point where the need for seminaries to train ordained priests is felt—for example, Wiccans would like to serve as chaplains in the military and in prisons and hospitals, but the seminary credentials for that have been lacking for them. At present, most professional religious training for Witches occurs in Unitarian Universalist seminaries, from which dozens of Wiccan ministers have graduated in recent years.

Whatever the numbers of Wicca members today, it is clear that the movement plays an influential role beyond its numbers. Festivals have proliferated to over a hundred each year, with many people participating who are not necessarily members of covens. Many of those attending, women but also some men, are particularly interested in feminist spirituality and Goddess worship. And numerous nature sanctuaries and temples have been established, contributing to something new in Wicca: a group of lay adherents who participate and support the movement but do not consider themselves Witches—a term they tend to reserve for priestesses and priests in the movement.

And Yet More Movements   There is still more. There is the fascinating religious subculture identified in the 1980s as the "**New Age Movement,**" emerging from the counterculture of the sixties, with gurus like Ram Dass and, more recently, Shirley MacLaine. Emphasizing a planetary consciousness in the Theosophical tradition, and reviving Spiritualist techniques of channeling with spiritual realities, this broad movement has brought with it a new emphasis in the metaphysical-occult tradition: personal transformation and growth. And so it moves together with many other interests, such as the Human Potential Movement, the Holistic Health Movement, Native American shamanistic spirituality, healing through use of crystals, astrology, selected Eastern techniques, and much more. It is generally agreed these days that the "New Age" is not really a unified movement in itself but an umbrella term for many groups and movements and eclectic spiritual seekers—a religious subculture with a vague common direction but constantly changing shapes.

But two other new movements with rather clear identity and purpose should be mentioned here, even though they do not necessarily form new religious movements in themselves: the Feminist Spirituality Movement and Deep Ecology.

The **Feminist Spirituality Movement** has leaders and adherents in most or all the religions. To some, Feminist Spirituality itself may be their religion, particularly those involved in Neo-Pagan Goddess worship. But the influence of this movement is being felt as a transforming force across the lines of the different religions—celebrating the feminine aspects of the divine, retrieving women's voices in the sacred stories, and recovering feminine values and patterns of human relationships.

Deep Ecology is a movement seeking to recover the sacred sense of interconnectedness with all of the natural world, humans included. Going beyond the simple science of ecology, Deep Ecology attempts to articulate a comprehensive religious and philosophical view to replace Western anthropocentrism with a "biocentrism," meaning that every living being has an equal right to be. Some Deep Ecologists look to the *Gaia* hypothesis of scientist James Lovelock—the view that the whole earth, with all life and all the surrounding atmosphere, form one living and self-regulating being, Gaia. Gaia thus is our mother and support, but at the same time, if we do not respect the whole balance of life on this earth, the life process of Gaia will pass on, leaving humanity behind. So Deep Ecologists look to a spiritual transformation as essential to human survival on this planet. Again, there are some for whom Deep Ecology is a religion, but the movement crosses religious lines to evoke responses of ecological spirituality among people of different religions. A movement that shares this perspective with Deep Ecology is **Ecofeminism,** holding the ecological crisis to result from patriarchal values that have created a master–slave relationship between humans and nature, just like the one that exists between men and women. The ecological concerns expressed in these movements, linking them together with issues of spiritual transformation and religious commitment, will surely be high on the agenda of all religious groups in the future.

Discussion Questions

1 What do you think are the most important reasons for the rise of new religious movements in recent times? Discuss whether you think these movements will be a long-lasting part of the religious world or will gradually fade from the scene.

2 Discuss the reasons for the apprehension many people feel with regard to new and strange "cults." How would you identify potentially dangerous movements (like the Branch Davidians of Waco) and distinguish them from the other new movements?

3 Discuss the extent to which the Hindu and Buddhist movements growing in the West are still within the mainline traditions from which they stem. Are some groups so Westernized as to become new religious movements?

4 Make a comparison between the Mormon and the Baha'i movements—each arising from a monotheistic world religion in the nineteenth century, each offering a new message for the whole world.

5 Compare and contrast Spiritualism and Theosophy, two movements centered on communication with higher realities. What sorts of interests do they seem to share? What are some of their significant differences?

6 Does Scientology appear to you more as a modern therapeutic technique, or more as a spiritual path focusing on the supernatural?

7 Discuss the extent to which you think the Unification Church should be considered to be within the worldwide framework of Christianity.

8 Give reasons for the rapid growth in Neo-Paganism and Wicca recently in the face of the negative attitude that is prevalent in our culture toward this kind of practice.

9 What kinds of changes and transformations do you think will take place through the burgeoning use of the computer Internet for communication and discussion within religious groups? You might subscribe to one or more such discussion lists to get a firsthand sense of spiritual pursuit through the Internet.

CHAPTER 16

Guideposts
and Crossings
on the Paths

As we reach the end of our study of the sacred paths of the West, we need to remember that our journey has been only a beginning and that a vast store of these paths, and many others, remains to be explored. We have seen that the paths are really a multifaceted human pilgrimage made up of many communities of people, each one with its own path that provides full and compelling meaning for life. We have seen that these individual religious traditions are dynamic, changing homes for communities of peoples, sources of identity and meaning, reservoirs of values, and storehouses of motivation and action. Throughout the many millennia of human life, the various paths have guided, shaped, and inspired the human adventure.

The Religions and the Future of Humankind   It is perhaps important to pause for a moment to reflect on the significance the religious paths of the world might have today. Things have changed; it is a new day in our common human history. Each of us can make our own list of what is new today, different from the past, in the areas of life that are of central concern to religion. Here are some starters:

🌳   As never before, people come into daily contact with those of other religions and cultures.

🌳   As never before, the peoples of the world are bound together into a global village, through interconnections of communications, economy, politics, and concerns of common survival.

🌳   As never before, the peoples of the world are being bombarded with rapid change, unimagined secularity, rampant materialism, and competitive ideologies.

🌳   As never before, people who practice the religious paths are educated in a modern secular way and taught knowledge and value judgments that are often in basic conflict with their traditional worldview.

🌳   As never before, at least in recent human history, women are becoming aware of their own religious experience and religious heritage; and both women and men are recognizing how patriarchal religious traditions have oppressed women and how there is need today to revive the feminine aspects of religious experience.

🌳   As never before, there are forces in the world that have the very real potential of devastating all or most of the human community: overpopulation and starvation; dwindling natural resources and greater competition for their use; and nuclear weapons of awesome and incomprehensible destructive power. Never before (since the early stages of human evolution) has the human race faced such imminent threat of total devastation. Never before has the power to control and drastically affect human destiny been so completely in the control of secular forces far removed from religious visions and values.

Enough—let the reader go on with her or his own list. Given all of this, perhaps the religious traditions of humankind can only be relics of the past! In the view of some, the sacred paths, which in their almost endless variants have nourished the families of humankind ever since the beginning, are in the process of withering and dying. We face, they say, a religionless future. Perhaps, some think, that future will be humankind coming of age, throwing off the shackles of religion and superstition; perhaps, others warn, it will be the Brave New World of totalitarian thought control. Or—more likely—it will be a continuing slide into a one-dimensional, secular, materialistic world culture.

The point of view suggested here, which of course cannot be proved, is that religion will continue to play an important role in the future. To have religious experience appears from our study to be a central dimension of being human, and thus we might suppose that religion will continue in changing and adapting forms as long as there are humans. Religious traditions, as we have seen, possess great adaptability to new needs and pressures. Every religious tradition, in fact, is an organic composite of developments over many years in changing circumstances, always managing to maintain a continuity of identity in the midst of transformations.

So the real question is not whether there will be religion in the future. It is whether the sacred paths can help shape the future of humankind in a creative, beneficial, hopeful way. Each religious tradition has done this among its own sacred peoples and within its own sacred lands. But what of the future of this interconnected global community?

The view taken here is that the religious traditions of humankind provide important resources and guideposts for shaping the future of our human adventure. Most of the religious paths we have studied are "universal," that is, claims are made for some kind of universality for the whole human race. Of course, each religious tradition is bound to its own past, its own claims, and its own mission, and one possible scenario is a bloody eruption of holy wars as people are pressed closer and closer together but revert all the more strongly to fundamentalistic exclusive religious claims. Such a pessimistic outlook, however, is not warranted by our study of the sacred paths. For all the intolerance, conflict, and violence that each of the major religious traditions bears in its history, there is peace and reconciliation at the heart of each. Each one embodies a vision for the welfare and happiness of the whole world, with important blueprints for achieving that. How can these great religious resources be tapped in the common human search for hope and welfare?

There are many ways, and there are dedicated people in each of the religions today who are utilizing these resources in their efforts toward justice, peace, and reconciliation in the world. This book is dedicated to the view that studying, learning, and understanding the different religions will make some contribution toward world peace and reconciliation. The guideposts and crossings on the paths represent high points and interconnections in the common human religious experience, and the better people come to know and understand these, the more consciously they can join others in using these resources to work toward peace and well-being for all. Here are four suggestions as to how the resources of the religious paths could contribute to the common human welfare.

In spite of the increasing globalization of all societies today, world peace and cross-cultural harmony still seem elusive. There is pressing need in our world today for mutual understanding and respect among the different peoples of the world. Although this seems obvious, it still is true that much of the conflict in the world today stems from, or is worsened by, lack of understanding between the peoples involved. Every culture has been influenced by religious traditions, so understanding another culture means understanding the religious vision that the culture is bound up with. Some tragic mistakes have been made—and are still being made—simply by the failure of one people or government to understand and respect the values and religious commitments of another people. As examples of conflict in which religious factors have come into play, one need only mention the treatment of Native Americans, the conflict in Vietnam, the Arab–Israeli conflict, the partitioning of India into India and Pakistan, the strife in Northern Ireland, and the tragic ethnic conflicts in Bosnia and in Kosovo. Sometimes it is said that religions cause conflict, but that is not the case. Most of these conflicts developed over nonreligious issues. It is not religion but rather ignorance and lack of understanding about religion that lends support to the conflict. Conversely, better understanding and mutual respect among the peoples of different religious traditions would contribute greatly to world peace.

A second point of importance is that there is within each religious tradition a compelling vision of the good world, of the ideal goal of peace and happiness for all humankind. No religious tradition advocates evil and destruction on the other peoples of the world—such perversions have indeed occurred at infamous points in the history of each tradition, but that does not negate the honest, peaceful, compassionate motivation at the heart of each. There are many and various approaches, to be sure, to the question of how to create a better world. We might say that the religions from India tend toward pacifism and self-sacrifice; the Abrahamic religions advocate justice, love, and equality; the religions of China and Japan emphasize harmony and reconciliation; and sacred paths of indigenous peoples express community of people and environment. By now we have learned, of course, that such characterizations are oversimplifications, and that within each religious path there are many variant tendencies. But each approach is important and helpful, and through better understanding of one another, these resources can become more effective in our interconnected global village.

A third point is the transnational character of religious commitment. While religious values and commitments, even of people of the global religions, are always located in specific communities and even nations, religious commitment has the quality of transcending national or group loyalties and ideologies. "Is it better to serve God or humans?" (asked by followers of Jesus Christ in a situation of conflict between religious and national commitment) is a question found in some form in all religious communities, especially in the world religions that transcend national boundaries. While religions can be, and often have been, used by the state or other groups to indoctrinate and for selfish, even violent purposes, religious commitment can also be the motivation for people to say no, to pursue values and goals different from those of the ruling authorities. Most governments, in fact, have recognized that religion can be a subversive force. In our world, there are many cases in which people with the same religious commitment are divided into nations or political camps that are hostile to each other.

A fourth, related point is the potential for people of all religious traditions to cooperate across religious, ethnic, national, and ideological lines to deal with our common human concerns, which seem so overwhelming today. The secularization of all values, the great god of materialism, the devaluing of human life, the oppression and exploitation of minorities and women, the rape of our natural resources and degradation of our environment, and the great threat to humanity posed by the militarizing and nuclearizing of our global village—people in each religious tradition do have important things to say in common about all such concerns. A paradigm of such interreligious cooperation might be the worldwide peace movement, in which people from all the different religious traditions

work together to achieve reconciliation, peace, and disarmament throughout the world. It is urgent that those who are steeped in the religious ideal of a peaceful and whole world, rather than those who trade in weapons and conflict, be the visionaries who shape the future of humankind.

Dialogue: Crossings on the Paths   These suggestions about the contribution the sacred paths can make to the future of humankind are based on the presupposition that people will get to know and understand their own religious traditions and the traditions of others better. What is needed is not a turn back to the dark ages of irrational religious dogmatism but a clear and accurate understanding both of the religions and of the modern world. Once, other people's religions (and also one's own, in many cases) were shrouded in mystery and lack of knowledge, and therefore misguided religious prejudices abounded. Today there is no longer any excuse for that, for accurate information and opportunities abound for contact with peoples of the different religions.

In fact, one of the striking developments in recent religious history, at least within some of the traditions, is the increase of meaningful conversation or *dialogue* between people of different religions. Since this has the potential of creating new levels of intercultural understanding, let us look more closely at the attitudes and movements that are involved in understanding through dialogue.

Dialogue can take place on different levels, of course. Important dialogue takes place today between leading scholars and experts in the different religious traditions, each representing her or his own tradition and entering into conversation with those of different traditions on a deep religious–theological level. But dialogue also can take place as ordinary people of the different paths meet each day as neighbors, fellow employees, students, or tourists. In particular, dialogue occurs between people of different paths as they face the common concerns and problems of daily life together, working toward understanding and dealing with the social, political, and economic issues that affect all of us.

Expectations about the results of religious dialogue depend on how one views the relationship between common human religious experiences, on the one hand, and the concrete, specific forms taken in the different religious traditions, on the other. Is there one perennial religious essence shared by all peoples, or is there only a multitude of special forms everywhere different and incompatible? Or is there some view in between?

One approach to dialogue with people of different religions holds that all religions are essentially the same. While outer forms and trappings differ from culture to culture, the real inner essence is all the same. A similar attitude says that, although religions are taking different paths, the goal for each is the same. In practical terms, the result of these attitudes is to look for the emergence of a superreligion, an all-inclusive religion made up of the best of the present religions, that will eventually supersede all the religions today. A related attitude, widespread today, is that we can pick and choose among the religions, adopting elements that suit us and discarding all the uninteresting or unappealing elements. In this way, new religious movements are begun— or at least we develop our own brand of religion.

A major problem with these attitudes is that they neglect the wholeness and integrity of each religious tradition. Our point of view here, as studied in the first chapter of this book, is that each religious tradition is a whole meaning system with its own central and primary symbols. Often it is the unique and different points—rather than the points in common with other religions—that are most important to a particular tradition. That means that to attempt to create some kind of superreligion or arbitrarily to select one symbol or another without regard to the rest is to do injustice to that religious tradition's full integrity.

Another kind of attitude would hold that dialogue is not really possible among people of different religious commitments. This attitude is often associated with religious fundamentalism, the attitude that one's own religion is the exclusive truth and therefore truth claims of another religion can only be argued against and shown to be false. From another perspective, drawing on postmodern thought, certain cultural-linguistic theories of religion also suggest that people of different religions have differing linguistic systems and therefore cannot really understand the vocabulary and semantics of another religion. A Hindu, a Christian, and a Daoist may all use the English term *God*, but the term carries incommensurate meaning for each. If we cannot understand each other's words, real dialogue would seem impossible.

Both of these views remind us of important characteristics of religion. One should remember that claiming to be the *real* truth is essential to any particular religion. And it is also important to realize that each religious tradition is a unique cultural-linguistic system, whose terms and concepts cannot simply be interchanged with those of another tradition.

But it is not necessary to press these ideas to the conclusion that real dialogue among people of different religions is impossible. One can claim to possess the real truth and still listen to, and even understand, the truth claims of others. Our religious traditions are differing cultural-linguistic systems, yet there is a common quality of human experience and rationality that does allow cross-cultural communication and understanding. All humans have lived on the same mother earth, under the same sky and sun, experiencing birth, sex, food production, fellow human relationships, and death in common. It is not necessary to suppose there is a common essence of religion in order to believe that it is possible for humans to communicate their religious ideas to one another.

Furthermore, there have been and continue to be many crossings on the paths—for millennia, peoples of different religious traditions have interacted, learned from others, and adopted elements from other religions into their own. Today, of course, the interaction is more intense and widespread, but there is plenty of evidence from the past that people can communicate across the cultures, and that they can learn and grow through such communication.

The Attitude and Process of Dialogue   The process of meaningful conversation and dialogue among people of different religious traditions has been tried and tested in many settings. Dialogue is going on between Christians and Jews, Jews and Muslims, Muslims and Hindus, Hindus and Buddhists, Buddhists and Christians, and many more. Dialogue often involves more than just two partners, with representatives of three or more religions involved, such as Jews, Christians, and Muslims, or Hindus, Buddhists, and Christians. It is generally agreed that a number of basic attitudes are important, so that the process of dialogue can take place. Among the most important attitudes are the following:

1 Real dialogue presupposes a firm standing in one's own religious tradition. It is interesting to float above all religions, coming down only where something useful is found. But dialogue means to share that which is most essential and innermost to oneself, and that comes from deeply held religious convictions. This does not mean there are no doubts,

questions, or dissatisfactions with one's own tradition—we have seen that such doubt and questioning are essential to change and development within each tradition. But dialogue means "talking through to another," presupposing one sharing her or his religious commitment with one of another faith—not people with no commitments looking around for what suits them best.

2 The goal is to grow in understanding, of the other religions and of oneself. The goal is not to convert the partner in dialogue, nor is it to convince oneself to convert to the other religious viewpoint.

3 Dialogue presupposes a respect for the people of the other religious traditions and a willingness to see how those traditions really make sense to the people who live by them.

4 Dialogue involves the readiness to share at a deep level one's own religious commitments and convictions about truth, yet without arrogance or defensiveness. Such sharing means a willingness to be vulnerable, to let others in on one's inner beliefs and values.

5 Dialogue presupposes a willingness to learn from the other, taking the risk of growing and changing in one's own understanding.

It may seem difficult to bring these attitudes into an area as personal and as subject to strong feelings as religion. It is in the nature of religious belief to make claims to truth. If I were not convinced that my religion is the truth about existence, it would no longer be my *religion*. Each religious person has experienced the sacred by means of a particular religious tradition, and based on that there are certain absolute and irreducible convictions by which he or she lives. The whole issue then of competing truth claims cannot be avoided when two people of different religions talk together: Is one religion true and the other not? Are they both true? Do they both possess partial truth? These are important questions to think about and to discuss.

The experience of people engaged in dialogue today is that it is possible to remain firmly convinced of the truth of one's own religious tradition and still respect the truth claims of others. One can acknowledge the fact that each religious tradition claims to be the real truth about human existence—and leave open the question whether such claims have to be exclusive. The attitude of dialogue is based on the realization that in religion we enter into the sacred mystery of life (remember our definition of religion in Part I), and that the sacred can never be fully grasped or limited by our own understanding or experience. However much we are convinced of the truth of our own religious understanding, we can acknowledge that the sacred mystery is still greater and deeper, and that others may have valid religious experiences, which, if we but listen to them, may be illuminating also to us.

Of course, it is not necessary to give up critical thinking in order to dialogue with people of different religions. Dialogue involves a give-and-take that includes questions and challenges as well as respect and acceptance. Comparing religious ideas and practices calls for accurate information and good critical thinking. But experience has shown that this can be done in an atmosphere of respect and willingness to learn and grow.

The process of dialogue between people of different religious beliefs involves four main movements:

1 It is important, first, to become aware of one's own religious values and commitments. It is possible, then, to "bracket" them so as to enter into the other person's religious world, as much as possible, without preconceived notions and prejudices.

2 Next comes a movement of passing over to enter into the universe of symbols that makes up the other person's religion, seeing it from the inside as the other person does.

3 The next movement is returning to one's own worldview, but bringing new ideas and comparisons from the other person's religious tradition.

4 Now integration and growth can take place, seeing one's own religious ideas more clearly and deeply.

These movements, of course, are essential for learning and growth in all areas of life—moving outside ourselves to experience something new, then returning and integrating that with what we already are, as the process of growth goes on. The four movements listed take place over and over again, sometimes occurring simultaneously, as the dialogue with people of other religions goes on.

The increase of interreligious dialogue today coincides with revival and renewed vitality in most of the world religions. As dialogue between the peoples of the different religions continues and deepens, on all levels, the potential contribution of the sacred paths to the common life and well-being of humankind and of our whole world will become stronger. What this will bring cannot be fully predicted, of course, but it appears as one hopeful sign in the outlook for the future of humanity.

Discussion Questions

1 In what ways is the present age a new critical time for the religions—and for humanity?

2 Sometimes it seems that religions cause divisions and conflict. What are some resources of the world religions that could contribute to the common human welfare?

3 Does what is common and universal to the religions seem more important to you, or do you focus on what is unique and particular to each tradition?

4 Do you see any conflict between holding to one's own religious convictions, on the one hand, and attempting to understand and respect the faith of others, on the other hand?

5 What kinds of attitudes are presupposed for dialogue among people of different religious traditions? What are the main movements by which that kind of dialogue process can lead to deeper understanding?

Glossary

abba   Aramaic term for "father" used by Jesus in addressing God

Abbasids   dynasty of classical Islam, ruling at Baghdad, eighth to thirteenth centuries C.E.

Abu Bakr   companion of the Prophet Muhammad and first caliph (d. 634)

Adi Granth   "original collection," the sacred scripture of the Sikhs; *see also Guru Granth Sahib*

Advent   season of the Christian church year before the celebration of Christmas

aesthetic   concerning beauty or artistic perception, important for religious expression

Agamas   main scriptures of the Jains

Agni   Vedic god of fire

agricultural revolution   the change in human culture when ancient humans learned to produce their own food

ahimsa   "nonviolence," one of the most important Jain principles; also emphasized in Buddhism and Hinduism

Ahriman   the Pahlavi form of *Angra Mainyu*

Ahura Mazda   the "wise Lord," eternal, supreme creator of all, as taught by Zarathustra

Akhenaton   king in ancient Egypt who attempted to enforce a form of monotheism centered on the sun-god Aton

Akitu   New Year festival in ancient Babylon

Al-Ghazali   great thinker (1058–1111 C.E.) who synthesized orthodox Islamic thought and Sufism

'Ali   nephew of the Prophet Muhammad and the fourth caliph (d. 661); considered by Shi'ites to be the first imam or successor to Muhammad

Allah   "the God"; Quranic designation for the one God

Amaterasu   Sun kami, ruler of the Plain of High Heaven, ancestress of the Japanese emperors

Amesha Spentas   in Zoroastrianism, the "Holy Immortals," Good Purpose, Truth, Dominion, Devotion, Perfection, Immortality, and Holy Spirit, generated by Ahura Mazda to aid in the creation of the world

Amitabha   Buddha of infinite light presiding over the Western paradise; Amida Buddha in Japan

Anahita   in Zoroastrianism, one of the Yazata or worshipful ones, the goddess of water and fertility whose cult was widespread in the Roman world

Analects   compilation of the sayings of Confucius

Angra Mainyu   Evil Spirit in Zoroastrian thought, upholder of the lie (druj), cosmic opponent of Ahura Mazda

animism   belief in spirits; theory that religion originated in reverence for spirits of living beings and inanimate objects

Apache   Native Americans of southwestern North America

Apostles' Creed   statement of faith dating from the second century C.E., universally accepted by Christians

arhant   in Buddhism, a perfected saint who has reached nirvana and will be released from samsara at death

Arianism   a teaching advocated by some that Christ was created in time as the Son of God

Arjan   the fifth guru and first Sikh martyr (1563–1606)

Aryans   Indo-European people who migrated into India

Asha   Truth, one of the Holy Immortals in Zoroastrianism; also, the spiritual quality of truth

Ashoka   great Buddhist king in India (r. ca. 272–236 B.C.E.), the "second founder" of Buddhism

ashrama   a stage of life in Hinduism; also a hermitage or place for meditation

atman   in Hinduism, the soul or self, considered eternal

atonement   doctrine of how humans are forgiven and reconciled to God through Christ's work

Augustine   leading theologian (354–430) in the early Christian church; bishop of Hippo in North Africa

avatara   descent or incarnation, especially of the great God Vishnu, as Krishna or Rama

Avesta   the sacred scriptures of Zoroastrians, including the *Yasna* (the Gathas), the *Yashts*, and other sacred texts

Ba'al   storm-fertility god of the ancient Canaanites

Baha'i   new religious movement arising in Persia and spreading through the world, founded by Baha'u'llah (1817–1892), regarded by his followers as the Manifestation of God for this new world era

baptism   ritual of initiation into the Christian church through washing of water, viewed as a sacrament by many

bar mitzvah   ceremony in which a thirteen-year-old boy becomes an adult member of the Jewish community

bat mitzvah   equivalent of *bar mitzvah* ceremony for girls in Reform and Conservative Jewish congregations

Bear Festival   important festival among bear-hunting people such as the Ainu of Japan

Bhagavad Gita   important Hindu scripture containing Krishna's teaching to Arjuna

bhakti   devotion, self-surrender to one's god, in the religions of India

bhikkhu, bhikkhuni   Pali terms for Buddhist monk and nun

Birthday of the Buddha   important festival celebrated in May or April (in Japan)

Blessingway   important Navajo prayer ceremonials that renew the primordial creative actions within life situations today

Bodh Gaya   the place where Siddhartha Gautama attained enlightenment

bodhisattva   being who is to become fully enlightened; in Mahayana Buddhism, one who reaches enlightenment but vows to continue rebirths in samsara to assist others

Brahma   designation for the creator god in Hindu thought

Brahman   Hindu term for ultimate reality; the divine source and pervading essence of the universe

Brahmanas   ritual commentaries, part of the Vedas

Brahmans   highest ranked, priestly class in Hindu society

brit milah   *See* circumcision

Buddha   "Enlightened one"; Siddhartha Gautama (ca. 563–483 B.C.E.) became the Buddha

bushido   "way of the warrior," the Japanese code of self-discipline for warriors, based on Zen, Shinto, and Neo-Confucian ideals

busk   festival at the green corn ripening among the Creek Native Americans

butsudan   in Japan, Buddhist altar in the home

caliph   "deputy," "successor" to the Prophet Muhammad as leader of Islam

Cargo Cults   Melanesian movements in expectation of the return of the ancestors on great cargo ships, a response to Western influence

chado   *See* chanoyu

Chan (Ch'an)   school of meditation Buddhism in China, influential in the arts (Zen in Japan)

Changing Woman   important divine figure among Native Americans of southwestern North America

chanoyu   the art of the Japanese tea ceremony; also called *chado,* "the way of tea"

Christ   Greek title meaning "anointed one" from Hebrew "messiah," applied to Jesus of Nazareth by his followers

Christology   doctrine about the nature and role of Christ

church   the community of all Christians; also specific groups, congregations, and buildings used for worship

Church of Christ Scientist   Christian group founded in America by Mary Baker Eddy (1821–1910), emphasizing reliance on Divine Mind for spiritual growth and for overcoming sickness

circumcision   boys' initiation ritual in many indigenous societies, in Islam, and in Judaism; in Judaism it occurs on the eighth day after birth and is called *brit milah* (covenant of circumcision)

confirmation   a Christian ritual of reaffirming vows taken in baptism; considered a sacrament by some

Confucius, Kongzi   teacher (ca. 551–479 B.C.E.) whose philosophy of life became dominant in Chinese culture

Conservative Judaism   movement attempting to adapt Judaism to modern life by using principles of change within the traditional laws; occupies middle ground between Reform and Orthodox Judaism

Constantine   Roman emperor (ca. 307–337) who legalized and promoted Christianity

cosmic state   perspective in ancient Mesopotamia that the cosmos is governed by great gods of nature

cosmogonic   related to the creation or founding of the world and of basic human realities

Council of Nicea   first great church council, convened in 325 to settle disputes about the nature of Christ

Council of Trent   council convened by the pope in 1545 to reform the church and oppose the actions of the Protestants

covenant (berith)   relationship between God and Israel, enacted on Mt. Sinai, based on Israel's acceptance of God's Torah

crusades   attempts by Christians of western Europe to recapture the Holy Land by force

Cultural Revolution   the period from 1966 to 1976 in China during which fanatical Red Guards attempted to destroy all forms of "old" religion and culture

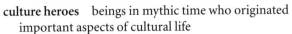

culture heroes beings in mythic time who originated important aspects of cultural life

Daimoku formula used in Nichiren Buddhist worship: "Namu myoho rengekyo" (Praise to the wonderful law of the *Lotus Sutra*)

Dakhma Tower of Silence in Zoroastrian communities, the structure on which the dead are exposed to vultures and the sun

Dalai Lama head of the Gelug Tibetan Buddhist school, traditionally recognized as spiritual and political leader of Tibetans; the current Dalai Lama (b. 1935) is the fourteenth

Dao (Tao) "way," Chinese term for the indefinable source of all reality; the way of nature

Dao de jing (Tao Te Ching) "Classic of Dao and Its Power"; earliest and very influential text of Daoism

Daoism broad term for Chinese tradition based on the *Dao de jing* and the *Zhuangzi;* and also variety of Daoist practices related to priests, scriptures, and techniques for prolonging life

Daoist Canon numerous sacred writings produced in Daoist religious movements

daoshi (tao shih) Daoist priest

Dar al-Harb *See* Dar al-Islam

Dar al-Islam "abode of Islam"; territories of the ummah under Muslim control, whereas the rest of the world is the *Dar al-Harb,* "abode of warfare"

darshana in Hinduism, the ritual act of being granted the "seeing" of a sacred image, person, or place; also, the six "viewpoints" or schools of philosophy

Deep Ecology contemporary movement emphasizing a sacred sense of human interconnectedness with all the natural world

denomination church organization consisting of a number of congregations, having autonomous structure and usually distinctive teachings, especially within Protestantism

dependent co-arising (pratitya-samutpada) central Buddhist teaching that everything is conditioned by something else, that all reality is interdependent

Devi Hindu term for goddess, sometimes meaning the great Goddess, often under many other names

Dharma in Hinduism, the cosmic order, social duty, and proper behavior; in Buddhist usage, the truth; the teaching of the Buddha; *dharmas* also refer to the constituents of all phenomena

dhikr "remembrance"; spiritual exercises in Sufism focusing the consciousness on God

diaspora the dispersion of Jews away from the land of Israel

dietary law Jewish laws pertaining to the proper preparation and eating of food, and the avoidance of certain animal food; see *kashrut*

Digambara "sky-clad," renouncing the use of clothing; one of the two major groups among the Jains

diksa initiation ceremony for Jain monks and nuns

Divali autumn festival of lights and good fortune in India

divination various techniques of reading and interpreting the operation of the sacred forces of nature and of the ancestors

divine kingship notion in many ancient societies, such as Egypt and Mesopotamia, that the king represents divine power to the human realm

Djanggawul Australian culture heroes who created the present world in their wanderings in the Dreaming Time

Docetism teaching by some in the early church that Christ only appeared to be human

Dogen important thinker (1200–1253) and founder of Soto Zen in Japan

Dogon people living in Mali in Africa

Dreaming Time mythic time of the beginnings in Australian tradition

Druj "lie," upheld by Angra Mainyu and the other evil beings, according to Zoroastrian thought

Dukkha "sorrow," characteristic of all conditioned reality as stated in the First Noble Truth of Buddhism

Durga great, fierce Hindu goddess, a form of Devi

earth-diver myth creation of the world when an animal dove into the sea to bring up the first mass of earth, as among the Iroquois

Easter festival celebrating the resurrection of Christ

Ecofeminism contemporary movement that identifies patriarchal values as the cause of the ecological crisis and proposes ecological wholeness through feminist values

ecumenical movement modern movement to achieve understanding, cooperation, and some form of unity between the various branches of Christianity

Eightfold Path the fundamental path toward nirvana as taught by the Buddha

Eisai founder (1141–1215) of Rinzai Zen in Japan

emergence myth story of original people emerging from lower worlds into the present world, as among the Navajo

emptiness *See* shunyata

Ennead the group of nine gods headed by the creator Atum, worshiped at Heliopolis in ancient Egypt

Enuma Elish epic of creation in ancient Babylon, read during new year festival

Epiphany season after Christmas emphasizing the "showing forth" of Christ to the world

eschatology doctrine about the last things: the end of the world, judgment day, consummation of God's plan

Essenes ascetic Jewish movement around the Dead Sea area from second century B.C.E. to first century C.E.

ethics thought and study about moral decisions, on the basis of traditions of right and wrong

Eucharist principal Christian sacrament, using bread and wine as a reenactment or remembrance of Christ's last supper; also called Mass, Lord's Supper, Divine Liturgy, and Holy Communion

Exile the Jewish captivity in Babylon, especially the period from the fall of Jerusalem in 586 B.C.E. until the first return to Jerusalem in 538 B.C.E.

Exodus deliverance of Israelites from Egypt under Moses' leadership

Feminist Spirituality Movement contemporary movement in many religious traditions emphasizing feminine aspects of the sacred and a recovery of feminine values in spiritual practices and in human relationships

feng shui geomancy, the Chinese art of reading forces of yin and yang so as to determine the most beneficial location for graves and houses

filial piety, xiao (hsiao) primary Confucian virtue of respect toward parents and ancestors

Fire Temple main worship sanctuary for Zoroastrians, where the sacred fire is kept burning

First Council of Buddhism held at Rajagriha shortly after the Buddha's parinirvana, where, according to tradition, the Buddha's sayings were recited and compiled

Five Classics the heart of the Confucian scriptures, including the *Shujing* (Classic of History), the *Shijing* (Classic of Poetry), the *Yijing* (*I Ching*, Classic of Changes), the *Lijing* (Classic of Rites), and the *Chunqiu* (Spring and Autumn Annals)

Five Elements Chinese idea of five modes of energy in the universe that mutually influence each other: wood, fire, earth, metal, water

Five Pillars required Muslim rituals of serving God: Shahadah (confession), Salat (prayer), Zakat (alms-giving), Sawm (fasting), Hajj (pilgrimage)

Five Precepts the basic Buddhist moral precepts, to refrain from destroying life, from taking what is not given, from wrongful sexual behavior, from wrongful speech, and from drugs and liquor

Four Noble Truths basic teachings presented in the Buddha's first sermon: the truths of sorrow, of the cause of sorrow, of the overcoming of sorrow, and of the path to follow

Four Sights sickness, old age, death, and a wandering hermit; seeing these motivated Siddhartha Gautama to seek enlightenment

fundamentalism holding to the literal inerrancy of scripture and the authority of doctrines derived from it

Gandhi leader of the Hindu independence movement emphasizing spiritual preparation and nonviolent resistance (1869–1948)

Ganesha son of Shiva, popular elephant-headed Hindu god who overcomes obstacles and brings good fortune

Gathas sacred hymns composed by Zarathustra, part of the *Avesta*

Gemara comments on the *Mishnah;* added to the *Mishnah* to form the Jewish Talmud

ghetto special Jewish quarter in certain European cities

Ghost Dance native revival movement among many Native American peoples in the latter part of the nineteenth century

giri important Japanese sense of social obligation and duty

Gnosticism movements in the Hellenistic world that emphasized a special secret knowledge about God and the world

Gobind Singh the tenth and last Sikh guru (1666–1708), who founded the khalsa

Golden Temple important Sikh gurdwara at Amritsar

Gospels writings compiled in the early church relating the story of Jesus' life and death; the four canonical gospels are *Matthew, Mark, Luke,* and *John*

grace achievement of spiritual goals as given by spiritual powers rather than attained by one's own effort

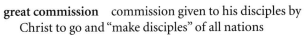

great commission   commission given to his disciples by Christ to go and "make disciples" of all nations

great goddess   feminine sacred being, source of life and power, worshiped at least as early as the Upper Paleolithic period

Guanyin (Kuan Yin)   Bodhisattva Avalokiteshvara, widely worshiped in China as a god/goddess of great mercy (Kannon in Japan)

gui (kuei)   earthly yin spirits; malevolent spirits in Chinese popular thought

gurdwara   temple and meeting place for Sikhs

Guru   leader and guide for Sikhs, through whom God's word is channeled; besides the ten gurus, God and the *Adi Granth* are also called Guru

guru   a spiritual guide and master

Guru Granth Sahib   "Sacred Collection," the Sikh sacred scriptures, with the title Guru; another name for the *Adi Granth*

Hadith   a saying or tradition of the Prophet Muhammad transmitted through a trustworthy chain of reporters; the collection of hadiths

Hagar   wife of Abraham, mother of Ishmael and ancestress of the Muslims

Hainuwele   culture hero in Wemale tradition (Ceram Island in Indonesia) from whose body tuberous plants grew

Hajj   pilgrimage to Mecca

Halakhah   Jewish legal tradition from the Talmud

Han Dynasty   period in China (from ca. 202 B.C.E. to 220 C.E.) during which Confucianism became the state ideology and cult, Buddhism made its entry, and religious Daoism developed

Hanukkah   Jewish festival of lights in December, celebrating rededication of temple in Maccabean times

Hasidim   popular mystical and devotional Jewish movement beginning in the seventeenth century in eastern Europe

Hebrews   ancestors of the Israelites

Hidden Christians   Christians in Japan who continued to practice their religion secretly after Christianity was outlawed in the mid-seventeenth century

hidden imam   in Shi'ism, the last imam (successor to Muhammad) who disappeared into the state of occultation and will return in the future

Hijra   emigration of the Prophet Muhammad and his followers from Mecca to Medina in 622 C.E.

Hinayana   "lesser vehicle," term applied to those Buddhist sects that arose in the first four centuries after the Buddha's death; of these sects, Theravada still survives today

Holi   popular festival in northern India with a carnival atmosphere

Holocaust   ancient Israelite ritual meaning "all-consuming sacrificial fire," used in modern times to denote the destruction of Jews and others under the Nazis

Holy Immortals   See *Amesha Spentas*

Homo erectus   human species from about 500,000 years ago; lived in communities, had many stone tools, and engaged in cooperative hunts

Homo sapiens sapiens   modern human species, dating back to Upper Paleolithic period

Honen   founder (1133–1212) of Pure Land Buddhism as a separate sect in Japan

Hopi   Native Americans of southwestern North America

Huayan (Hua Yen)   a Chinese school of Mahayana Buddhism based on the Garland Sutra

hunters   peoples who live by hunting and gathering, whose religious ideas are especially associated with animal life

Husayn   son of 'Ali, killed at Karbalah (680); considered by Shi'ites as a successor to the Prophet Muhammad and a great martyr

'id   "feast" or festival in Islam; the two major festivals are *'Id al-adha* (Feast of Sacrifice) during the Hajj month and *'Id al-fitr* (Feast of Breaking the Ramadan Fast)

ihram   state of ritual purity and consecration appropriate for entering the sacred precincts of Mecca on the Hajj (Islamic pilgrimage)

ijma'   "consensus"; for formulating Muslim law, consensus among the legal scholars is necessary

ijtihad   independent legal reasoning in Islam; one who does this is a *mujtahid*

imam   Islamic scholar and leader, especially in ritual prayer; for Shi'ites, the proper successors to the Prophet are called imams

iman   "faith," complete certitude about the truth of Islam

impermanence   basic Buddhist doctrine that change is characteristic of everything that arises

incarnation   "becoming flesh"; especially the Christian teaching that the eternal Son of God became human in the womb of his mother Mary

Indra   Vedic storm-warrior god

Indus valley civilization   urban-agricultural civilization that flourished in the third millennium B.C.E. and left influences on Hinduism

International Society for Krishna Consciousness   new religious movement, founded by Swami Bhaktivedanta Prabhupada (1896–1977), drawing on traditional Hindu practices of worshiping Krishna as the supreme manifestation the divine; known as ISKCON, this movement has drawn many Westerners as devotees

Ise Shrine   shrine of Amaterasu, the Japanese Sun Kami

Ishmael   son of Abraham and Hagar, ancestor of the Muslims

isnad   the chain of transmitters for a particular hadith in Islam

Israel   "he strives with God"; name given to Jacob and thereafter to the covenant people; name of modern Jewish state

Izanagi and Izanami   the pair of kami who created the world, according to Japanese mythology

Jade Emperor   supreme god in Chinese popular religion

jati   "birth"; one's caste or closed social group as determined by birth in India

Jehovah's Witnesses   Christian movement arising in America, teaching strict literal understanding of biblical ideas and holding firmly to distinctive views such as pacifism, refusal to accept blood transfusions, etc.

Jiao (Chiao)   important festival in religious Daoism, the Rite of Cosmic Renewal

jihad   "striving" for religious perfection and for God's cause including bearing arms in defense of Islam if necessary

Jina   "conqueror," Jain idea of one who has reached total liberation; *see also* Tirthankara

Jizo   popular Buddhist divinity in Japan known as the savior of the dead and helper of dead children

Judgment Day   the day on which God will judge all according to their deeds

justification by faith   Christian doctrine that justification before God comes by faith, not by works

Ka'bah   the cube-shaped stone shrine in the Great Mosque at Mecca, focal point of prayer and pilgrimage for Muslims

Kabbalah   "tradition," especially the medieval mystical Jewish tradition

Kabir   a poet (1440–1518), an important predecessor of Guru Nanak, founder of Sikhism

kafir   an unbeliever, in Islamic terms

Kali   goddess of death and destruction in Hinduism, a form of Devi, the great Goddess

kami   spirits or divinities in Shinto, including mythological beings, powerful and awesome aspects of nature, and important humans

kamidana   kami altar in the home in Japan

Kannon   Bodhisattva Avalokiteshvara, popular goddess of mercy in Japan (Guanyin in China)

karah parshad   sacred food used in the Sikh worship assembly

Karaites   Jewish sect that rejected oral Torah, relying on scripture alone

karma   "action," law that all deeds and thoughts, according to one's intentions, will have set consequences, in the religions of India

karma   Jain idea of subtle form of matter that clings to the soul because of the soul's passion and desire, causing rebirths

karuna   Buddhist ideal of compassion

kashrut   ritual fitness, suitable for use according to Jewish law; applies especially to dietary laws, what foods can and cannot be eaten, and how to prepare them

kenosis   "emptying out"; in ritual, the movement of separation or doing away with the old state

kevela   the highest state of enlightenment, according to Jainism

Khadija   the first wife (d. 619) of the Prophet Muhammad

khalsa   a major military-type group within Sikhism, founded in 1699 by Gobind Singh, the tenth guru, with a special code of discipline

Kharijites   "seceders"; strict moralistic sect of early Islam

kingdom of God   Jewish and Christian idea of the rule of God; proclaimed by Jesus as a present reality, yet to be fully manifested in the future

kirtan   Sikh practice of singing hymns in worship of God

kirtana   in Hinduism, devotional group worship through song and dance

koan   Zen Buddhist saying or riddle used in meditation (*gongan* in China)

Kojiki   Records of Ancient Matters, earliest writing in Japan, a compilation of stories about the age of the kami and the beginnings of Japan

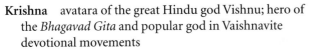

Krishna   avatara of the great Hindu god Vishnu; hero of the *Bhagavad Gita* and popular god in Vaishnavite devotional movements

Kshatriyas   the classical warrior class in Hindu society

Kukai   great Japanese Buddhist thinker (773–835) and founder of Shingon

kusti   the sacred cord given to a young Zoroastrian boy or girl at the initiation ritual (Naojote)

Lamaism   derived from Lama, "master"; the special form of Buddhism in Tibet

langar   Sikh community kitchen

Laozi (Lao Tzu)   legendary author of the *Dao de jing* and founder of Daoism (according to tradition, b. 604 B.C.E.)

Legalists   school of thought in China that emphasized the need for law and order

Lent   Christian season of penitence in preparation for Easter celebration

li   rites, propriety; the Confucian code of ceremonial behavior; *see also Principle*

liminal   in ritual, the state between separation *(kenosis)* and restoration *(plerosis)*

lingam   the phallic pillar that symbolizes the great Hindu god Shiva

literati, ru (ju)   learned Confucian scholars

liturgy   order of prayer, scripture reading, hymns, and exhortations followed in a worship service

Lotus Sutra   important early scripture of Mahayana Buddhism

Lugbara   a people of East Africa

maat   ideal of justice and order in ancient Egypt

Madhyamika   early school of Mahayana Buddhism that emphasized *shunyata* (emptiness)

magic   attempt to control forces of nature through rituals and incantations

Mahabharata   one of the two great epics of Hinduism

Mahavairochana   the great sun Buddha

Mahavira   the twenty-fourth and last Jina of the present world half-cycle, who according to Jain tradition lived from 599 to 527 B.C.E.

Mahayana   the "great vehicle," form of Buddhism that arose in India beginning in the second century B.C.E. and eventually spread to East Asia

Maimonides   great medieval Jewish philosopher (1135–1204 C.E.)

mana   Polynesian word describing the state in which people, places, or objects are especially filled with sacred power

mandala   painting of the sacred cosmos, used especially in Vajrayana Buddhist ritual and meditation.

Mandate of Heaven   in Chinese religion, the expression of Tian's moral will, especially in granting prosperity to virtuous rulers and cutting short evil ones

mantra   sacred word, formula, or verse

Mao Zedong (Mao Tse-tung)   leader (1893–1976) of the Chinese Communist movement and of the People's Republic of China

Marduk   god of ancient Babylon city-state

Marranos   Spanish Jews who were outwardly Christian-ized but who secretly continued Jewish tradition

Masada   mountain fortress near the Dead Sea where Jewish Zealots made a last stand against the Romans

master or mistress of animals   divine being, often a prototype of the herd of animals, who protects the herd and also provides boons for humans

matsuri   Shinto shrine festival

Matteo Ricci   first Jesuit missionary to China (1552–1610)

maya   appearance, illusion, term to indicate that which prevents one from seeing truly

Mazu (Ma Tsu)   widely worshiped goddess of Chinese seafarers; known as the Queen of Heaven

Meiji Restoration   restoration of imperial rule in Japan in 1868

Mendelssohn, Moses   Jewish Enlightenment thinker (1729–1786)

Mengzi (Meng Tzu; Mencius)   leading thinker (ca. 372–289 B.C.E.) whose writings shaped the Confucian tradition

messiah   end-time king, descended from King David, expected to redeem Israel; Christians identified the messiah (Greek christos) with Jesus

mihrab   niche in the mosque wall indicating the direction to Mecca

minbar   pulpit from which the sermon is given during the Friday prayer in the Islamic mosque

Mishnah   code of Jewish oral law compiled ca. 200 C.E. by Judah the Prince

Mithra   one of the Zoroastrian Yazata, guardian of light and giver of wealth, widely worshiped in the Roman empire

mitzvot Jewish term for commandments; acts in obedience to God's will

moksha liberation from bondage to samsara and karma; the goal of Hindu spiritual practice

monasticism the way of life of monks and nuns, usually celibate, without personal possessions, and dedicated to meditation, prayer, study, and service

monism view that all reality is one unified divine reality

monotheism belief in one almighty God, separate from the world

Mormonism new religious movement founded in America by Joseph Smith (1805–1844) on the basis of the Book of Mormon, also known as the Church of Jesus Christ of Latter-Day Saints, with headquarters in Utah

Moses leader of Israel in the Exodus from Egypt and the founding of the covenant on Mt. Sinai

mosque (masjid) place of communal worship in Islam

Motoori Norinaga leading scholar (1730–1801) of the National Learning movement that advocated the restoration of Shinto as Japan's central religion

Mughal Muslim dynasty established by the Mongols in India

mulla Persian word for learned Muslim teacher and expounder of the law

Muslim one who has surrendered to God in accepting the authority of the Quran

Mu'tazilites school in the classical period of Islam that accepted reason as a primary criterion for establishing beliefs

mysteries secret ritual cults in ancient Greece in which initiates could experience union with a god and promise of life after death

myth story about sacred beings in the beginning of time, telling how existence came to be as it is and providing the pattern for authentic life

Nagarjuna important philosopher (ca. 150–250 C.E.) of the Madhyamika school of Buddhism

Nam in Sikhism, the Name of God, the total divine presence in the world

Nanak founder (1469–1539) of Sikhism and the first guru

Naojote the ritual of initiation for young Zoroastrian boys and girls, in which they are invested with the sacred shirt and sacred cord (kusti)

Navajo Native American people of southwestern North America

Ndembu people living in Zambia in Central Africa

Neanderthal human species ca. 100,000 to 35,000 years ago, with clear archaeological evidence of religious activities

Nembutsu formula of calling on Amida Buddha: *Namu Amida Butsu,* "Praise to Amida Buddha"

Neo-Confucianism revival of Confucian thought in the eleventh century C.E., with emphasis on the underlying principle of all things

Neolithic period beginning after the last ice age (ca. 10,000 years ago) when planting was discovered and villages and cities founded

neo-orthodoxy modern Protestant theological movement reasserting orthodox tradition about human sinfulness and divine grace

Neo-Pagans broad new religious movement emphasizing nature spirituality on the basis of pre-Christian traditions about gods, goddesses, and sacred nature, including various groups such as druids, witches, goddess-worshipers, and more

New Age Movement broad term sometimes used to identify the religious subculture that emphasizes personal transformation and growth through spiritual techniques like channeling, planetary consciousness, shamanism, astrology, use of crystals, and much more

New Religions in Japan, term used for new religious movements, often drawing on and combining aspects of Buddhism, Shinto, and folk religion

New Year festival important annual festival in many societies, a time of purging out the old year and bringing renewal

Ngaju Dayak agricultural people living in Kalimantan, Indonesia

Nichiren Japanese Buddhist sect based single-mindedly on the *Lotus Sutra,* founded by the monk Nichiren (1222–1282)

Nichiren Shoshu of America new religious movement in America based on the lay Buddhist Soka Gakkai movement in Japan, emphasizing chanting and meditation as taught by Nichiren (1222–1282)

Nihon Shoki chronicles of Japan, compiled shortly after the *Kojiki* and containing stories about the kami and early emperors

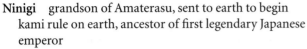

Ninigi grandson of Amaterasu, sent to earth to begin kami rule on earth, ancestor of first legendary Japanese emperor

nirvana "blowing out" the fires of life, liberation from suffering and rebirth, the spiritual goal of Buddhist practice

no-action (wuwei) basic Daoist principle of not doing anything contrary to the flow of nature

no-self (an-atman) the basic Buddhist doctrine that there is no permanent, absolute self

noble person, junzi ideal Confucian goal, a noble person defined by moral character

Noh classical Japanese theater, closely linked to the religious traditions, especially Zen

nondualism view that ultimate reality and the phenomenal world are not different

Norito ancient Shinto ritual prayers

Obon (Ullambana) festival of the seventh month in Japan welcoming the ancestors

Old Testament Christian designation for the Hebrew scriptures

Olorun supreme god among the Yoruba

Olympian gods powerful gods of ancient Greece thought to rule from Mt. Olympus

ordination (upasampada) important Buddhist ritual marking the beginning of life as a monk or nun

original sin Christian teaching that the fall of Adam and Eve represents a basic condition of sinfulness that all humans share

orisa divinities in Yoruba belief that control life in the world

Orthodox Church term referring to the historic Eastern Christian churches, including the Greek, Russian, Armenian, and other traditions

Orthodox Judaism modern movement continuing a strict traditional belief in the binding character of the Torah and Halakhah

Osiris god of the dead in ancient Egypt, important for the afterlife

Ottoman dynasty ruling much of the Muslim world from Istanbul from the fifteenth to the twentieth centuries C.E.

Paleolithic Old Stone Age; in the Upper Paleolithic period (ca. 35,000 to 10,000 years ago) the modern species of Homo sapiens sapiens appeared

Pangu (P'an Ku) in Chinese tradition, mythic primordial person out of whom the whole universe developed

parables stories by which Jesus taught his disciples about the Kingdom of God

parinirvana full nirvana; complete liberation attained at the death of a Buddha

Parshva the twenty-third Jina of the present world half-cycle, who lived in the mid-ninth century B.C.E.

Parsis communities of Zoroastrians in India

passion story the climax of each of the four Gospels, telling of the suffering and crucifixion of Jesus

pastoralists peoples who live by raising herds of cattle or sheep and whose religious ideas are associated especially with their herds

Path of Action (karma-marga) Hindu path toward liberation based on acting according to Dharma, without desire for the fruits of action

Path of Devotion (bhakti-marga) Hindu path toward liberation based on devotional practices directed toward one's god

Path of Knowledge (jnana-marga) Hindu path toward liberation based on knowledge, emphasizing meditation

path of transformation practice in a religion that changes one from the wrong or inadequate state to the ideal state

Paul leading apostle who brought the gospel of Christ to non-Jews and whose letters form part of the New Testament

Pentecost Christian festival approximately seven weeks after Easter, celebrating the coming of the Holy Spirit upon the church

Pesach (Passover) Jewish spring festival commemorating deliverance from Egypt

peyote religion modern Native American revival movement, called the Native American Church, with ceremonial use of peyote (small hallucinogenic cactus)

Pharisees party in ancient Judaism teaching the oral Torah along with the written Torah, resurrection of the body, and application of the law in everyday life

philosophy humanistic, rational thinking that developed especially in ancient Greece

pietism a Christian reaction to the rationalism of the Enlightenment, emphasizing the experience of God's grace and emotional dedication

plan of salvation   Christian idea of God's design for the salvation of the world foretold through prophets and accomplished through Jesus Christ

planters   peoples who cultivate plants for food and have religious ideas associated especially with vegetation and the fertility of the earth

plerosis   "filling up"; fulfillment or restoration movement of ritual

pollution   in the Shinto view, anything that hinders life and fertility by causing separation from the kami

polytheism   belief that many divine powers share in the world's operation

prehistoric   before written records

Principle, li   neo-Confucian concept of the underlying source of all phenomena

prophets   in Judaism and Christianity, inspired people who spoke God's word and advocated reforms in Israel, especially from the eighth to the fourth centuries B.C.E.

prophets   in Islam, messengers through whom God has given revelation to all peoples, culminating with Muhammad as the Seal of the Prophets

Protestantism   broad designation in the Christian tradition for the main churches of the Reformation

puja   in the religions of India, ritual worship of the image of a god by offering food, flowers, music, and prayers

Puranas   late Hindu scriptures that developed from popular theistic devotional movements

Pure Land   school of Buddhism focusing on worship of Amitabha Buddha, with hope of rebirth in the Pure Land paradise, founded in Japan especially by Honen and Shinran

purification   rituals, important in Shinto, to remove pollution and reinstate harmony and communion with the kami

Purim   early spring festival in Judaism remembering events of the Book of Esther

qi (ch'i)   material force, breath, flowing vital energy, in Chinese traditions

Qing Ming (Ch'ing Ming)   "clear and bright" festival; spring festival of visiting and renovating ancestral tombs in China

qiyas   "analogy" in legal argumentation and decision making in Islam

Quran   "recitation," primarily the revelation sent down by God upon the Prophet Muhammad; the Holy Book

rabbi   "my master"; title for Jewish teacher of the law; spiritual leader of a congregation

Rabbinic Judaism   designation for Judaism as it developed under the teachers of the oral Torah (Mishnah and Talmud)

Rain Retreat (vassa)   important three-month time of study and discipline for Theravada Buddhist monks and nuns, when lay people also make offerings and perform service for the monastics

Rama   avatara of Vishnu, divine hero of the *Ramayana*

Ramanuja   Hindu philosopher and advocate of the Vaishnavite bhakti tradition (ca. 1017–1137)

Ramayana   story of Rama, one of the two great epics of Hinduism

rebirth   in the religions of India, belief that after the death of its body the soul takes on another body

Reconstructionist Judaism   modern movement founded by Mordecai Kaplan (1881–1982), emphasizing Judaism as a civilization

rectification of names   Confucian program for the development of a moral society by properly structuring social relationships

Reform Judaism   modern movement attempting to conform tradition to conditions of modern life, allowing changes in the Halakhah

Reformation   reform movements in the Christian church, especially the reform of the European church through the work of Luther, Calvin, Zwingli, and others

religious Daoism   general term for the variety of Daoist practices related to priests, scriptures, and techniques for prolonging life

ren (jen)   humaneness, an important ideal in Confucianism

restraints   the Jain vows of nonviolence, not lying, not stealing, refraining from wrong sex, and nonpossession or nonattachment

resurrection   rising from the dead; in Christian belief, Christ's resurrection as the first fruit of the resurrection of all

Rig Veda   the earliest and most important collection of Vedic hymns

rites of passage   rituals connected with the critical changes of life

ritual   activities of many kinds that connect people with sacred realities, including prayer, sacrifice, chanting, pilgrimage, festivals, disciplines of meditation, and much more

Roman Catholic church   the historic Western church as it has continued under the leadership of the pope, the bishop of Rome

Rosh Hashanah   Jewish New Year, first day of Tishri (usually in September); beginning of High Holy Days (which include Yom Kippur)

Sabbath   seventh day of the week, sacred day of rest and study for Jews

sacraments   Christian rituals that convey God's grace, such as baptism and the Eucharist

sacred space   space that is made special by connection with the sacred, providing orientation and rootedness for a people

sacred story   master story of a religion, providing identity for the adherents; *see* myth

sacred, the   general term for what is experienced as ultimate reality, the mysterious Other that is the ground of ultimate value and meaning

sacred time   special time of ritual and festival, when mythic events are made present once more

Sadducees   conservative party of temple priests and sympathizers in ancient Judaism who rejected the oral Torah and the idea of the resurrection

Safavid   Muslim dynasty in Iran, featuring rule by the shahs

Saicho   founder (767–822) of Tendai Buddhism in Japan

Salat   required Muslim ritual of prayer five times daily

Samhitas   "collections" of early Vedic hymns and verses; there are four collections: *Rig-Veda, Sama-Veda, Yajur-Veda,* and *Atharva-Veda*

Samkhya   one of the classical schools of Hindu philosophy stressing an absolute distinction between matter and spirit

samnyasin   one who has renounced the cares and concerns of the world; samnyasa is the fourth stage of life in Hinduism

samsara   in the religions of India, the rebirth cycle of existence

samskaras   in Hinduism, rituals performed at the critical changes and passages of life

samurai   the Japanese class of warriors influenced by Zen and Neo-Confucianism

sandpainting   Navajo ceremonial art used in healing rituals

sangha   the assembly of Buddhist monks, nuns, and laity

Sawm   required Muslim fasting during the month of Ramadan

School of National Learning   Shinto restoration movement during the Tokugawa period

Scientology   new religious movement founded by L. Ron Hubbard (1911–1986), emphasizing scientific-type techniques to remove mental and physical disorders and bring spiritual transformation

Self-Realization Fellowship   modern religious movement founded in America by Yogananda (1893–1952), teaching various Hindu yogic practices

Shahadah   the Muslim formula bearing witness to the unity of God: "I testify that there is no God but God; I testify that Muhammad is the messenger of God"

Shakti   in Hinduism, divine energy, personified as a goddess; female aspect of a god, especially of Shiva

Shakyamuni   a title of the Buddha: the wise one of the Shakya clan

shaman, shamaness   person who undergoes special training and can go into trances, communicate with the spiritual world, and bring healing and special benefits

Shang Di (Shang Ti)   supreme god worshiped by the Shang rulers in ancient China

Shankara   great philosopher of Advaita (nondual) Vedanta (788–820 C.E.)

Shari'ah   Islamic law, based on the Quran and on the sunnah of the Prophet

Shavuot   Jewish Feast of Weeks (Pentecost), commemorating the giving of the Torah on Mt. Sinai

Shema   Jewish statement proclaiming the unity of God, based on Deuteronomy 6:4–9, beginning, "Hear, O Israel, the Lord our God, the Lord is one."

shen   in Chinese tradition, heavenly yang spirits; benevolent and honored spirits, including ancestors

Shi'ites   the "faction" of 'Ali who believe that 'Ali and his descendants are the proper successors of the Prophet Muhammad

Shingon   esoteric (Tantric) Buddhism in Japan

Shinran   disciple (1173–1262) of Honen and founder of the True Pure Land Buddhist sect in Japan

Shinto   Chinese term shen-dao used to designate the Japanese "way of the kami"

shirk   "association"; Muslim term for the great sin of idolatry or associating something else with God

Shiva   the great ascetic Hindu god symbolized by the lingam; focus of the Shaivite devotional movement

Shotoku   prince regent (573–621) who advocated Buddhism as one of the pillars of Japan

shrine (jinja) Shinto sacred place focused on the presence of a kami; usually has appropriate buildings where a symbol of the kami is housed and where worshipers can consult priests

Shruti "that which is heard," the eternal truth, that is, the Vedas

Shudras classical servant class in Hindu society, the fourth class

shunyata "emptiness," Mahayana Buddhist teaching that all things are devoid of any substantial or independent reality

Shvetambara "white clad," accepting the use of clothing; one of the two major Jain groups

Sikh "disciple," that is, one who follows the gurus

Singh surname taken by men who join the Sikh khalsa

skandhas "heaps" or aggregates; the Buddhist teaching that a person is really a changing process in five aggregates

Smriti "that which is remembered," the tradition, that is, the scriptural writings after the Vedas

Soka Gakkai largest New Religion in Japan, based on Nichiren Buddhism

Son of Heaven title of Chinese emperor

soteriology theory of salvation

Spenta Mainyu Holy Spirit in Zoroastrianism, closely identified with Ahura Mazda, creator of world, opponent of Angra Mainyu

spirit writing in Chinese religion, writing on a tray of sand or on paper by a spirit who moves the pen

Spiritualism broad religious movement begun in America in the 1840s, focused on methods of communicating with spirits of the dead; some groups are organized as Spiritualist Churches

stupa memorial Buddhist shrine or reliquary

Sufi one who follows the mystical path of Islam

Sukkot Feast of Booths, autumn harvest festival in Judaism

sun-god divine being manifested through the sun, important especially in ancient Egypt

sunnah "custom" or "way of acting," primarily of the Prophet Muhammad; the Prophet's *sunnah* is known through the hadiths

Sunnites term for the Muslim majority, those who acknowledge the first four caliphs and the interpretation of the Quran and the Prophet's sunnah by the orthodox ʻulama (religious scholars)

supreme god the god with final authority, usually the creator, often associated with the sky

Susanoo storm kami in Japanese mythology, unruly brother of Amaterasu

sweat lodge special lodge among some Native Americans constructed for purification ceremonies

symbols words, pictures, ideas, rituals, and so on, that evoke deep meanings by connecting with sacred reality

synagogue Greek term translating Hebrew "house of assembly"; Jewish place for prayer and study

tabu Polynesian word indicating someone or something is full of sacred power in a volatile, contagious (and therefore potentially harmful) way

Taiping Rebellion (T'ai P'ing) abortive popular movement in the mid-nineteenth century in China, based on religious ideas, attempting to change the hierarchical structure of society

Talmud Jewish "oral Torah," comprised of the *Mishnah* and *Gemara;* exists in a Palestinian and a Babylonian version

Tanakh Hebrew scriptures comprised of *Torah* (the Pentateuch), *Nevi'im* (the Prophets), and *Ketuvim* (the Writings)

Tantrism movement in Hinduism and Buddhism (also called Vajrayana) using initiation, rituals, imagination, and sexual symbolism as spiritual practices leading toward liberation

Tathagata title for the Buddha meaning the "Thus Come One," that is, the perfected one

tawhid Muslim term for maintaining the unity of God

temple place of worship in many religions

Tendai important school of Buddhism in Japan (Tiantai in China)

Tenrikyo the oldest of the existing New Religions in Japan, founded in 1838

theology thinking about God and God's work

Theosophy new religious movement founded in America by Madame Helena Blavasky (1831–1891) and Colonel Henry Olcott (1832–1907), integrating Hindu and Buddhism ideas with notions of communicating with higher spiritual masters

Theravada an early Hinayana sect that survives today; term generally used for the type of Buddhist tradition and practice followed in South and Southeast Asia

Three Ages of the Dharma   Buddhist teaching of increasing decline and degeneracy in humans' ability to follow the Buddhist path: the Age of the Perfect Dharma, the Age of the Counterfeit Dharma, and the Age of the End of the Dharma

Three Body Teaching   Mahayana teaching of three dimensions of the Buddha: the Dharma Body, the Bliss Body, and the Transformation Body

Three Pure Ones   designation for highest gods summoned by Daoist priests

Three Refuges   the Buddha, the Dharma, and the sangha; many Buddhist prayers and declarations begin with the Three Refuge formula

Tian (T'ien)   "heaven," from ancient times in China considered an ultimate power that rules especially through the moral order

Tiantai (T'ien T'ai)   a school of Mahayana Buddhism in China, based on the *Lotus Sutra*

Tipitaka   *See Tripitaka*

Tirthankara   "ford builder," Jain idea of one who has reached total liberation and shows the way across the ocean of suffering; *see also* Jina

Torah   first five books in the Hebrew scriptures; also the whole of scripture; also the whole corpus of revelation, including oral Torah

torii   characteristic gateway to the Shinto shrine

Tower of Silence   *See* **Dakhma**

tradition   "passing on" of the sacred story and basic ideas of a religion

Transcendental Meditation   Hindu meditation movement founded in America by Maharishi Mahesh Yogi (b. 1917), emphasizing simple meditation techniques for practical benefits

transformation   reaching the ideal state of wholeness, perfection, or salvation

Trinity   the Christian doctrine that God is revealed in three persons—Father, Son, and Holy Spirit

Tripitaka (**Pali:** *Tipitaka)*   the scriptures of the Pali Canon of Buddhism, meaning "Three Baskets"; they include the Vinaya Pitaka, the Sutra Pitaka, and the Abhidharma Pitaka

Tudigong (T'u Ti Kung)   local earth god in Chinese religion

Twelvers   the largest group within the Muslim Shi'ites; those who hold there have been twelve imams

'ulama   the class of learned Muslim legal scholars who study and apply the religious sciences

Ullambana   Buddhist festival in China and Japan worshiping the souls of ancestors and providing for souls temporarily released from purgatory; called Obon in Japan

'Umar   the second caliph in Islamic history (d. 644)

Umayyad   dynasty ruling Islam from Damascus from 661 to 750 C.E.

Ummah   a community having a common religion; especially the Muslim community

understanding   "standing under" another's way of thought and life, comprehending it by reference to one's own experience

Unification Church   new religious movement founded in Korea by Rev. Sun Myung Moon (b. 1920), based on Christian ideas but teaching a new Messiah to form the ideal human family

Upanishads   secret teaching; collection of teachings about the self and ultimate reality that makes up the last part of the Vedas

Uposatha   fortnightly Buddhist holy day when temple meetings for teaching, ritual, and meditation are held

'Uthman   the third caliph in Islamic history (d. 656)

Vaishyas   the classical producer-merchant class in Hindu society

Vajrayana   Diamond Vehicle, the Tantric tradition of Buddhism, represented especially in Tibet and Japan

varna   "color," term for the classes in the classical system of Hindu society

Varuna   Vedic god of the heavens

Vedanta   "end of the Vedas"; influential school of philosophy based especially on the Upanishads

Vedanta Societies   Hindu groups in America and Europe following the teaching of Swami Vivekananda (1863–1902) and Sri Ramakrishna (1836–1886)

Vedas   most important scriptures of Hinduism, the Shruti; they consist of the Samhitas, Brahmanas, Aranyakas, and Upanishads

Vinaya   texts containing rules for Buddhist monastic life and discipline

Vishnu   great Hindu god manifested in avataras, including Krishna and Rama; focus of the great Vaishnavite devotional movement

vision quest   Native American tradition involving individual purification and several days of fasting and praying in a remote sacred place to attain spiritual powers and direction for life

Wahhabi strict reform movement founded in Arabia in the eighteenth century and influential throughout Islam

way of art in Japan, practice of an art (such as poetry, Noh drama, or the tea ceremony) as a way of self-cultivation

Wicca one of the Neo-pagan new religious movements, emphasizing traditions of witchcraft as nature spirituality, focused on the powers of goddesses and gods of nature

Word of God in Sikh thought, God's presence that reverberates throughout creation, channeled especially through the gurus

worship respectful ritual activity in special times, directed toward sacred beings or realities of ultimate value

Xunzi (Hsün Tzu) important Confucian thinker (ca. 300–238 B.C.E.) who advocated a realistic understanding of the human inclination toward evil

Yahweh special covenant name of Israel's God as it was probably pronounced; written YHWH in the Hebrew scriptures; at a certain point, Jews stopped pronouncing this sacred name and substituted the name Adonai

Yazata worshipful ones, Indo-Iranian gods who continued to be objects of worship in Zoroastrianism, sometimes called angels

Yijing (I Ching) the *Classic of Changes,* an ancient Chinese divination manual based on sixty-four hexagrams (each of six unbroken and broken lines)

yin and yang Chinese idea of polarity of forces in the universe; yin is the passive, earthly force, and yang is the active, heavenly force

Yoga techniques of spiritual discipline for overcoming bondage to samsara, often emphasizing breathing and meditation exercises; one of the classical schools of Hindu philosophy

Yom Kippur Jewish Day of Atonement on the tenth of Tishri, a solemn day of repentance

yoni in Hinduism, a circular sacred image representative of the female reproductive organ, often associated with the lingam

Yoruba a tribal people living in Nigeria

Zakat the required Muslim practice of alms-giving or wealth-sharing

Zao Jun (Tsao Chun) God of the Cooking Stove in Chinese religion

Zarathustra the founder of Zoroastrianism, who lived perhaps around 1000 B.C.E., reformed the Indo-Aryan religion, and composed the Gathas

zazen "sitting in meditation," central practice in Chan (Zen) Buddhism

Zealots Jewish religious party in the Roman period that advocated resistance to Roman occupation

Zen important school of meditation Buddhism in Japan (Chan in China)

Zeus sovereign over the Olympian gods in ancient Greece

Zhou Dynasty (Chou) long dynasty (ca. 1123–221 B.C.E.) during which the classics were compiled and the Confucianist and Daoist traditions developed

Zhu Xi (Chu Hsi) leading thinker of the Neo-Confucian movement (1130–1200 C.E.)

Zhuangzi (Chuang Tzu) important early teacher (ca. 369–286 B.C.E.) whose writings have been very influential for the Daoist movement

Zionism modern movement to secure a Jewish homeland in Palestine

Zionist churches independent Christian groups in Africa that have attempted to combine African traditions with Christianity

Zoroaster Greek form of the name Zarathustra

Note: The glossary includes terms from both volumes, *Sacred Paths of the West,* Second Edition, and *Sacred Paths of the East,* Second Edition.

Notes

PART 1   EXPLORING THE SACRED PATHS

Chapter 1   Perspectives on Religious Experience

1. Ruldolph Otto, *The Idea of the Holy,* trans. John Harvey, 2nd edition (London: Oxford University Press, 1982).
2. Joachim Wach, *Sociology of Religion* (Chicago: University of Chicago Press, 1944), pp. 17–34.
3. Mircea Eliade, *The Sacred and the Profane: The Nature of Religion,* trans. Willard R. Trask (New York: Harcourt, Brace & World, 1968).
4. The terms *kenosis* and *plerosis* are used by Theodor H. Gaster, *Thespis: Ritual, Myth, and Drama in the Ancient Near East* (New York: Doubleday, 1961), pp. 23–49.
5. The structure of the rites of passage was first analyzed by Arnold van Gennep, *The Rites of Passage,* trans. Monika Vizedom and Gabrielle Caffee (Chicago: University of Chicago Press, 1960).
6. Eliade, *The Sacred and the Profane,* pp. 20–65.

Chapter 2   Beginnings of the Human Religious Adventure

1. Daniel L. Pals, *Seven Theories of Religion* (New York: Oxford University Press, 1996).

Chapter 3   Sacred Paths Among Indigenous Peoples

1. Eliade, *The Sacred and the Profane,* p. 95; *Myth and Reality* (New York: Harper & Row, 1963), pp. 6–7.
2. Sam Gill, "Nonliterate Traditions and Holy Books: Toward a New Model," in *The Holy Book in Comparative Perspective,* eds. Frederick Denny and Rodney Taylor (Columbia: University of South Carolina Press, 1985), p. 226.
3. Frank Waters, *Book of the Hopi,* reprint edition (New York: Viking Press, 1985), pp. 114–115.
4. See John Middleton, *Lugbara Religion: Ritual and Authority Among an East African People* (London: Oxford University Press, 1960), especially pp. 230–238.
5. Adolf Jensen, *Das religiöse Weltbild einer frühen Kultur* (Stuttgart: August Schoeder Verlag, 1949), pp. 33–40.
6. See J. Omosade Awolalu, *Yoruba Beliefs and Sacrificial Rites* (London: Longman, 1979); William Russell Bascom, *Ifa Divination : Communication Between Gods and Men in West Africa,* reprint edition (Bloomington: Indiana University Press, 1991); and Baba Ifa Karade, *The Handbook of Yoruba Religious Concepts* (York Beach, ME: Samuel Weiser, Inc., 1994).
7. Sam Gill, *Sacred Words: A Study of Navajo Religion and Prayer* (Westport, CT: Greenwood Press, 1981), pp. 50–55; *The Portable North American Indian Reader,* ed. Frederick W. Turner III (New York: Viking Press, 1973), pp. 175–205.
8. Sam Gill, *Native American Religions: An Introduction* (Belmont, CA: Wadsworth, 1982), pp. 20–22; *North American Indian Reader,* pp. 36–39.
9. Ronald M. Berndt, *Djanggawul: An Aboriginal Religious Cult of North Eastern Arnhem Land* (New York: Philosophical Library, 1953), pp. 24–28.
10. Marcel Griaule and Germaine Dieterlen, *Le renard pale* (Paris, 1965); see the briefer account in Griaule and Dieterlen, "The Dogon," in *African Worlds: Studies in the Cosmological Ideas and Social Values of African Peoples,* ed. Daryll Forde (London: Oxford University Press, 1954), pp. 83–89.
11. John S. Mbiti, *Concepts of God in Africa* (London: SPCK, 1970), pp. 171–177.
12. Gill, *Sacred Words,* pp. 61–84.
13. Leland C. Wyman, *Blessingway: With Three Versions of the Myth Recorded and Translated from the Navajo by Father Berard Haile, OFM* (Tucson: University of Arizona Press, 1970), p. 465.
14. *The Sacred Pipe: Black Elk's Account of the Seven Rites of the Oglala Sioux,* ed. Joseph Epes Brown (Baltimore: Penguin Books, 1971), p. 50.
15. Arthur Amiotte, "Eagles Fly Over," *Parabola,* I, no. 3 (1976), 34.
16. Mircea Eliade, *Shamanism: Archaic Techniques of Ecstasy,* trans. Willard Trask (Princeton, NJ: Princeton University Press, 1964).

17 Vilmos Dioszegi, *Tracing Shamans in Siberia* (New York: Humanities Press, 1968), p. 62; quoted in John A. Grim, *The Shaman: Patterns of Siberian and Ojibway Healing* (Norman: University of Oklahoma Press, 1983), p. 46.

18 Eliade, *Shamanism,* pp. 115–120.

19 Amiotte, "Eagles Fly Over," p. 29.

20 Eliade, *The Sacred and the Profane,* pp. 68–72.

21 Ruth M. Underhill, *Papago Indian Religion* (New York: AMS Press, 1969), pp. 77–79.

22 Hans Schärer, *Ngaju Religion: The Conception of God Among a South Borneo People* (The Hague: Martinus Nijhoff, 1963), especially pp. 27–38, 94–97, 131–141. These rituals are interpreted by Sam D. Gill, *Beyond "the Primitive": The Religions of Nonliterate Peoples* (Englewood Cliffs, NJ: Prentice-Hall, 1982), pp. 81–85.

23 See John Batchelor, *The Ainu and Their Folklore* (London, 1901); Kyosuke Kindaichi, *Ainu Life and Legend* (Tokyo, 1941); and Joseph M. Kitagawa, "Ainu Bear Festival (Iyomante)," *History of Religions,* I (1961), 95–151.

24 John Batchelor, "The Ainu Bear Festival," *Transactions of the Asiatic Society of Japan,* 2nd Series, IX (1932), 42.

25 John Witthost, *Green Corn Ceremonialism in the Eastern Woodlands* (Ann Arbor: University of Michigan Press, 1949), pp. 52–70.

26 K.H. Basso, *The Cibecue Apache* (New York: Holt, Rinehart and Winston, 1970), pp. 53–72. The quotations here are from pp. 65, 66.

27 Victor Turner, *The Forest of Symbols: Aspects of Ndembu Ritual* (Ithaca, NY: Cornell University Press, 1967), pp. 151–279.

28 Knud Rasmussen, *The Netsilik Eskimos—Social Life and Spiritual Cultures* (Copenhagen: Gyldendalske Boghandel, 1931), pp. 15–16, 321; quoted in Sam Gill, *Native American Religions,* pp. 42–43.

29 John S. Mbiti, *African Religions and Philosophies* (New York: Doubleday, 1970), p. 141.

30 Awolalu, *Yoruba Beliefs,* pp. 69–91, 108–126.

31 Baldwin Spencer and F.J. Gillen, *The Arunta,* vol. I (London: Macmillan, 1927), p. 388.

32 *The Sacred Pipe,* pp. 31–43.

33 Ibid., pp. 41–42.

34 From J.W. MacMurray, "The 'Dreamers' of the Columbia River Valley in Washington Territory," *Transactions of the Albany Institute XI* (Albany, 1887), pp. 241–248; quoted in Sam D. Gill, *Native American Traditions: Sources and Interpretations* (Belmont, CA: Wadsworth, 1983), pp. 156–157.

35 John (Fire) Lame Deer and Richard Erodes, *Lame Deer: Seeker of Visions* (New York: Washington Square Press, 1972), pp. 254–255.

36 Jonathan Z. Smith, "A Pearl of Great Price and a Cargo of Yams: A Study in Situational Incongruity," *History of Religions,* 16 (1976), 1–19.

37 James Mooney, *The Ghost Dance Religion and the Sioux Outbreak of 1890,* abridged (Chicago: University of Chicago Press, 1965), p. 181.

PART 2   RELIGIONS ARISING IN THE MEDITERRANEAN WORLD

Chapter 4   Religions of Ancient Egypt, Mesopotamia, and Greece

1 *Ancient Near Eastern Texts Relating to the Old Testament,* ed. James B. Pritchard (Princeton, NJ: Princeton University Press, 1950), p. 407.

2 Ibid., p. 164.

3 Ibid., pp. 434–437.

4 *Ajax,* lines 126–133, trans. John Moore in *Sophocles,* vol. II of *The Complete Greek Tragedies,* eds. David Grene and Richmond Lattimore (Chicago: University of Chicago Press, 1959), p. 219.

Chapter 5   The Zoroastrian Tradition

1 *Textual Sources for the Study of Zoroastrianism,* edited by Mary Boyce (Totowa, NJ: Barnes & Noble Books, 1984), pp. 38–39.

2 Ibid., p. 42.

3 Ibid.

4 Ibid., p. 34.

5 Ibid., pp. 28–29.

6 Ibid., p. 35.

7 Ibid., p. 45.

8 Ibid., p. 39.

9 Ibid.

10 Ibid., p. 35.

11 Ibid., pp. 56–57.

12 Ibid., pp. 58–59.

13 Ibid., p. 61.

14 Jacques Duchesne-Guillemin, *Symbols and Values in Zoroastrianism: Their Survival and Renewal* (New York: Harper & Row, Publishers, 1966), pp. 91, 95.

15 Ibid., p. 151.

Chapter 6   Jewish Sacred Story and Historical Context

1 Translated in Judah Goldin, *The Fathers According to Rabbi Nathan* (New Haven: Yale University Press, 1955), p. 34.

Chapter 7   Jewish Worlds of Meaning

1 Quoted in Louis Jacobs, *A Jewish Theology* (New York: Behrman House, 1973), p. 62.

2 C.G. Montefiore and H. Loewe, comps., *A Rabbinic Anthology* (New York: Schocken Books, 1974), p. 217.

3 Jacobs, *A Jewish Theology*, p. 93.

4 Jacob Neusner, *The Life of Torah: Readings in the Jewish Religious Experience* (Belmont, CA: Dickenson Publishing, 1974), p. 19, reprinted from *Weekday Prayerbook,* ed. by Rabbi Gershon Hadas (New York: Rabbinical Assembly of America, 1961), pp. 42–43.

5 Milton Steinberg, *Basic Judaism* (New York: Harcourt, Brace & World, 1947), p. 86.

6 Montefiore and Loewe, *Rabbinic Anthology,* p. 305.

7 Neusner, *Between Time and Eternity: The Essentials of Judaism* (Belmont, CA: Dickenson Publishing, 1975), pp. 79–80.

8 Steinberg, *Basic Judaism,* p. 58.

9 Neusner, *Between Time and Eternity,* pp. 77–78.

10 Steinberg, *Basic Judaism,* p. 61.

11 Abraham J. Heschel, *Between God and Man: An Interpretation of Judaism,* ed. Fritz A. Rothschild (New York: Free Press, 1959), p. 72.

12 Howard R. Greenstein, *Judaism—An Eternal Covenant* (Philadelphia: Fortress Press, 1983), pp. 31–32.

13 Jacobs, *Jewish Theology,* p. 256.

14 Neusner, *Between Time and Eternity,* pp. 91–94.

15 Heschel, *Between God and Man,* p. 164.

16 Montefiore and Loewe, *Rabbinic Anthology,* p. 140.

17 Ibid., pp. 607–608.

Chapter 8   Ritual Practices and the Good Life for Jews

1 Jacob Neusner, *The Way of Torah: An Introduction to Judaism,* 4th ed. (Belmont, CA: Wadsworth Publishing Company, 1988), p. 79.

2 See, for example, Judith Plaskow, *Standing Again at Sinai: Judaism from a Feminist Perspective* (San Francisco: Harper, 1991); Tamar Frankiel, *The Voice of Sarah: Feminine Spirituality and Traditional Judaism* (San Francisco: Harper, 1990); Ellen Frankel, *The Five Books of Miriam: A Woman's Commentary on the Torah* (San Francisco: HarperSanFrancisco, 1998); and Lynn Gottlieb, *She Who Dwells Within: A Feminist Vision of a Renewed Judaism* (San Francisco: HarperSanFrancisco, 1995).

3 Isadore Twersky, "The Shulhan Aruk: Enduring Code of Jewish Law," in *Understanding Jewish Theology: Classical Issues and Modern Perspectives,* ed. Jacob Neusner (New York: KTAV, 1973), p. 146.

4 Heschel, *Between God and Man,* p. 183.

5 Ibid., p. 164.

6 Montefiore and Loewe, *A Rabbinic Anthology,* p. 433.

7 Ibid., p. 535.

8 Ibid., p. 200.

9 Ibid., p. 108.

10 Ibid., p. 536.

11 Ibid., p. 226.

12 Jacobs, *A Jewish Theology,* pp. 292, 300.

Chapter 9   Christian Sacred Story and Historical Context

1 Henry Bettenson, ed., *Documents of the Christian Church* (New York: Oxford University Press, 1947), pp. 72–73.

Chapter 11   Ritual Practices and the Good Life for Christians

1 See, for example, Elisabeth Schüssler Fiorenza, *In Memory of Her: A Feminist Theological Reconstruction of Christ Origins* (New York: Crossroad Publishing Co., 1994); Rosemary Radford Ruether, *Sexism and God-Talk: Toward a Feminist Theology* (Boston: Beacon Press,

1983); Pamela Young, *Feminist Theology/Christian Theology: In Search of Method* (Minneapolis: Fortress Press, 1990); and Elizabeth A. Johnson, *She Who Is: The Mystery of God in Feminist Theological Discourse* (New York: Crossroad Publishing Co., 1993).

2 John Burnaby, *Augustine: Later Works,* vol. 8, in *The Library of Christian Classics* (Philadelphia: Westminster Press, 1955), p. 316.

Chapter 12 Muslim Sacred Story and Historical Context

1 A. Guillaume, trans., *The Life of Muhammad: A Translation of Ishaq's Sirat Rasul Allah* (London: Oxford University Press, 1955).

2 Passages from the Quran in the chapters on Islam, unless otherwise indicated, are from Arthur J. Arberry, trans., *The Koran Interpreted* (New York: Macmillan, 1955).

3 Guillaume, *Life of Muhammad,* pp. 69–81.

4 Ibid., p. 106.

5 Ibid., pp. 106–107.

6 Ibid., p. 552.

7 Ibid., pp. 651–652.

8 Ibid., p. 682.

9 Ibid., pp. 682–683.

10 Margaret Smith, *Rabi'a: The Life and Work of Rabi'a and Other Women Mystics in Islam* (Oxford: Oneworld Publications, 1994), p. 50.

11 Ibid., p. 126.

12 Louis Massignon, *The Passion of Al-Hallaj: Mystic and Martyr of Islam,* abridged edition (Princeton: Princeton University Press, 1994), p. 285.

13 W. Montgomery Watt, *The Faith and Practice of al-Ghazali* (London: Allen and Unwin, 1953), pp. 56–57.

14 Mohamad Jawad Chirri, *The Brother of the Prophet Mohammad (the Imam Ali),* Vol. I (Detroit: Islamic Center of Detroit, 1979), pp. 128–133.

Chapter 13 Muslim Worlds of Meaning

1 Seyyed Hossein Nasr, *Ideals and Realities of Islam* (Boston: Beacon Press, 1975), pp. 18–21.

2 Abul A'la Mawdudi, *Towards Understanding Islam,* trans. by Khurshid Ahmad (Plainfield, IN: Muslim Students' Association of the U.S. and Canada, 1980/1400 A.H.), p. 19.

3 See Nasr, *Ideals and Realities of Islam,* pp. 73–74, 116–117.

Chapter 14 Ritual Practices and the Good Life for Muslims

1 Kenneth Cragg and R. Marston Speight, eds., *Islam from Within: Anthology of a Religion* (Belmont, CA: Wadsworth, 1980), p. 50.

2 Watt, *Faith and Practice of al-Ghazali,* p. 115.

3 *Garden of the Righteous: Riyadh as-Salihin of Imam Nawawi,* trans. Muhammad Zafrullah Khan (London: Curzon Press, 1975), p. 176, quoted in Frederick Mathewson Denny, *An Introduction to Islam,* 2nd ed. (New York: Macmillan Publishing Company, 1994), p. 289.

4 R.A. Nicholson, *Literary History of the Arabs* (Cambridge: Cambridge University Presss, 1914), p. 397.

5 Chan et al., *The Great Asian Religions,* p. 377.

6 Mawdudi, *Towards Understanding Islam,* p. 101.

7 See, for example, Leila Ahmed, *Women and Gender in Islam: Historical Roots of a Modern Debate* (New Haven: Yale University Press, 1992); Yvonne Yazbeck Haddad and John L. Esposito, *Islam, Gender, and Social Change* (New York: Oxford University Press, 1998); Barbara Freyer Stowasser, ed., *Women in the Qur'an: Traditions and Interpretations* (New York: Oxford University Press, 1994); and Amina Wadud, *Qur'an and Women: Re-reading the Sacred Text from a Woman's Perspective,* 2nd ed. (New York: Oxford University Press, 1999).

8 Mawdudi, *Towards Understanding Islam,* p. 26.

Suggestions for Further Reading

PART 1   EXPLORING THE SACRED PATHS

Perspectives on Religious Experience

Brockman, Norbert C. *Encyclopedia of Sacred Places.* New York: Oxford University Press, 1998.

Brown, Frank Burch. *Religious Aesthetics.* Princeton, NJ: Princeton University Press, 1990.

Carmody, Denise Lardner. *Women and World Religions.* 2nd edition. Englewood Cliffs, NJ: Prentice Hall, 1989.

Christ, Carol P., and Judith Plaskow, eds. *Womanspirit Rising: A Feminist Reader in Religion.* Revised edition. San Francisco: Harper & Row, 1991.

Comstock, Gary L. *Religious Autobiographies.* Belmont, CA: Wadsworth, 1995.

Cunningham, Lawrence, et al. *The Sacred Quest: An Invitation to the Study of Religion.* New York: Macmillan, 1991.

Denny, Frederick M., and Rodney L. Taylor, eds. *The Holy Book in Comparative Perspective.* Columbia: University of South Carolina Press, 1985.

Doniger, Wendy. *Splitting the Difference: Gender and Myth in Ancient Greece and India.* Chicago: The University of Chicago Press, 1999.

Eastman, Roger, ed. *The Ways of Religion: An Introduction to the Major Traditions.* 3rd edition. New York: Oxford University Press, 1999.

Eliade, Mircea, ed. *The Encyclopedia of Religion.* 15 vols. New York: Macmillan, 1987.

———. *A History of Religious Ideas.* 3 vols. Translated by Willard R. Trask. Chicago: University of Chicago Press, 1981–1988.

———. *Patterns in Comparative Religion.* Translated by Rosemary Sheed. Lincoln: University of Nebraska Press, 1996.

———. *The Sacred and the Profane: The Nature of Religion.* Translated by Willard R. Trask. New York: Harcourt, Brace & World, 1968.

Falk, Nancy Auer, and Rita M. Gross, eds. *Unspoken Worlds: Women's Religious Lives.* Belmont, CA: Wadsworth, 1989.

Ferguson, Marianne. *Women and Religion.* Englewood Cliffs, NJ: Prentice Hall, 1995.

Graham, William A. *Beyond the Written Word: Oral Aspects of Scripture in the History of Religion.* New York: Cambridge University Press, 1987.

Hall, T. William, Richard B. Pilgrim, and Ronald R. Cavanagh. *Religion: An Introduction.* San Francisco: Harper & Row, 1985.

Holm, Jean, with John Bowker, eds. *Rites of Passage.* London: Pinter Publishers, 1994.

———, eds. *Sacred Writings.* London: Pinter Publishers, 1994.

Kinsley, David. *The Goddesses' Mirror: Visions of the Divine from East and West.* Albany: State University of New York Press, 1989.

Livingston, James C. *Anatomy of the Sacred: An Introduction to Religion.* 2nd edition. New York: Macmillan, 1993.

Lovin, Robin W., and Frank E. Reynolds, eds. *Cosmogony and Ethical Order.* Chicago: University of Chicago Press, 1985.

Paden, William. *Religious Worlds: The Comparative Study of Religions.* Boston: Beacon Press, 1988.

Pals, Daniel L. *Seven Theories of Religion.* New York: Oxford University Press, 1996.

Sharma, Arvind, ed. *Religion and Women.* Albany: State University of New York Press, 1994.

———, ed. *Today's Woman in World Religions.* Albany: State University of New York Press, 1994.

———, ed. *Women in World Religions.* Albany: State University of New York Press, 1986.

Sharpe, Eric. *Comparative Religion: A History.* 2nd edition. Chicago: Open Court Publishing Company, 1991.

Smart, Ninian. *Dimensions of the Sacred: An Anatomy of the World's Beliefs.* Berkeley: University of California Press, 1996.

Streng, Frederick J. *Understanding Religious Life.* 3rd edition. Belmont, CA: Wadsworth, 1985.

Weaver, Jace, ed. *Native American Religious Identity: Unforgotten Gods.* Maryknoll, NY: Orbis Books, 1998.

Wilson, John F. *Religion: A Preface.* 2nd edition. Englewood Cliffs, NJ: Prentice Hall, 1989.

Beginnings of the Human Religious Adventure

Adams, Richard E.W. *Prehistoric Mesoamerica.* Revised edition. Norman: University of Oklahoma Press, 1996.

Bahn, Paul G. *Journey Through the Ice Age.* Berkeley: University of California Press, 1997.

Carmody, Denise Lardner. *The Oldest God: Archaic Religion Yesterday and Today.* Nashville: Abingdon Press, 1981.

Clottes, Jean, et al. *The Shamans of Prehistory: Trance and Magic in the Painted Caves.* Translated by Sophie Hawkes. New York: Harry N. Abrams, 1998.

Davidson, Hilda R. Ellis. *Gods and Myths of Northern Europe.* Harmondsworth, England: Penguin Books, 1964.

Fagan, Brian M. *People of the Earth: An Introduction to World Prehistory.* 9th edition. Reading, MA: Addison-Wesley, 1997.

Gimbutas, Marija. *The Goddesses and Gods of Old Europe, 6500–3500 B.C.: Myths and Cult Images.* Berkeley: University of California Press, 1982.

———. *The Living Goddesses.* Edited and supplemented by Miriam Robbins Dexter. Berkeley: University of California Press, 1999.

Marler, Joan, ed. *From the Realm of the Ancestors: Essays in Honor of Marija Gimbutas.* Manchester, CT: Knowledge, Ideas, and Trends, Inc., 1997.

Scarre, Christopher. *Exploring Prehistoric Europe.* New York: Oxford University Press, 1999.

Sharer, Robert J. *The Ancient Maya.* Stanford, CA: Stanford University Press, 1994.

Wenke Robert J. *Patterns in Prehistory: Humankind's First Three Million Years.* New York: Oxford University Press, 1990.

Sacred Paths Among Indigenous Peoples

Barnes, Sandra T., ed. *Africa's Ogun: Old World and New (African Systems of Thought).* 2nd edition. Bloomington: Indiana University Press, 1997.

Berndt, Ronald M. *Australian Aboriginal Religion.* Leiden: E.J. Brill, 1974.

Black Elk, Wallace, and William S. Lyon. *Black Elk: The Sacred Way of a Lakota.* San Francisco: HarperSanFrancisco, 1991.

Blakely, Thomas, et al. *Religion in Africa: Experience and Expression.* London: J. Currey, 1992.

Brown, Joseph Epes. *The Spiritual Legacy of the American Indian.* New York: Crossroad, 1988.

Carpenter, Edmund. *Eskimo Reality.* New York: Holt, Rinehart and Winston, 1973.

Carrasco, Davíd. *Religions of Mesoamerica: Cosmovision and Ceremonial Centers.* San Francisco: Harper & Row, 1990.

Dorson, Richard M., ed. *African Folklore.* New York: Anchor Books, 1972.

Eades, J. S. *The Yoruba Today.* Cambridge: Cambridge University Press, 1980.

Eliade, Mircea. *Shamanism: Archaic Techniques of Ecstasy.* New York: Pantheon Books, 1964.

———. *Australian Religions.* Ithaca, NY: Cornell University Press, 1973.

Evans-Pritchard, Edward E. *Nuer Religion.* Oxford: Clarendon Press, 1956.

Gill, Sam D. *Beyond "the Primitive": The Religions of Non-literate Peoples.* Englewood Cliffs, NJ: Prentice-Hall, 1982.

———. *Mother Earth: An American Story.* Chicago: The University of Chicago Press, 1991.

———. *Native American Religions: An Introduction.* Belmont, CA: Wadsworth, 1982.

———. *Native American Traditions: Sources and Interpretations.* Belmont, CA: Wadsworth, 1983.

Hudson, Charles. *The Southeastern Indians.* Knoxville: University of Tennessee Press, 1977.

Hultkrantz, Ake. *Native Religions of North America: The Power of Visions and Fertility.* San Francisco: HarperCollins, 1987.

———. *Religions of the American Indians.* Translated by Monica Setterwall. Berkeley: University of California Press, 1979.

Kehoe, Alicia Beck. *The Ghost Dance: Ethnohistory and Revitalization.* New York: Holt, Rinehart and Winston, 1989.

King, Noel Q. *African Cosmos: An Introduction to Religion in Africa.* Belmont, CA: Wadsworth, 1986.

Lanternari, Vittorio. *The Religions of the Oppressed: A Study of Modern Messianic Cults.* Translated by Lisa Sergio. New York: New American Library, 1965.

Lawson, E. Thomas. *Religions of Africa: Traditions in Transformation.* San Francisco: Harper & Row, 1985.

Levy, Jerrold E. *In the Beginning: The Navajo Genesis.* Berkeley: University of California Press, 1998.

Lewis, I. M. *Ecstatic Religion: A Study of Shamanism and Spirit Possession.* 2nd edition. New York: Routledge, 1989.

Lewis, Thomas. *The Medicine Men: Oglala Sioux Ceremony and Healing.* Lincoln: University of Nebraska Press, 1990.

MacGaffey, Wyatt. *Religion and Society in Central Africa: The Ba Kongo of Lower Zaire.* Chicago: University of Chicago Press, 1986.

Olupona, Jacob A. *African Traditional Religions in Contemporary Society.* New York: Paragon House, 1991.

Powers, Maria. *Oglala Women: Myth, Ritual, and Reality.* Chicago: The University of Chicago Press, 1986.

Ray, Benjamin. *African Religions: Symbol, Ritual, and Community.* Englewood Cliffs, NJ: Prentice-Hall, 1976.

Reichard, Gladys A. *Navaho Religion: A Study of Symbolism.* Princeton, NJ: Princeton University Press, 1990.

Rice, Julian. *Black Elk's Story: Distinguishing Its Lakota Purpose.* Albuquerque: University of New Mexico Press, 1991.

Schele, Linda, and David Friedel. *A Forest of Kings: The Untold Story of Ancient Maya.* New York: William Morrow and Company, 1990.

Steinmetz, Paul B. *Pipe, Bible, and Peyote Among the Oglala Lakota.* Knoxville: The University of Tennessee Press, 1990.

Stewart, Omer C. *Peyote Religion: A History.* Norman: University of Oklahoma Press, 1987.

Sullivan, Lawrence E. *Icanchu's Drum: South American Religions, an Orientation to Meaning.* New York: Macmillan, 1988.

———, ed. *Native American Religions: North America.* New York: Macmillan, 1989.

Turner, Victor. *The Forest of Symbols: Aspects of Ndembu Ritual.* Ithaca, NY: Cornell University Press, 1967.

Zuesse, E.M. *Ritual Cosmos: The Sanctification of Life in African Religions.* Athens: Ohio University Press, 1979.

PART 2 RELIGIONS ARISING IN THE MEDITERRANEAN WORLD

General

Corrigan, John, et al. *Jews, Christians, Muslims: A Comparative Introduction to the Monotheistic Religions.* Upper Saddle River, NJ: Prentice Hall, 1998.

Peters, F.E. *Children of Abraham: Judaism/Christianity/Islam.* Princeton, NJ: Princeton University Press, 1982.

Religions of Ancient Egypt, Mesopotamia, and Greece

Beard, Mary, John North, and Simon Price. *Religions of Rome. Volume I: A History.* New York: Cambridge University Press, 1998.

Black, Jeremy, and Anthony Greed. *Gods, Demons and Symbols of Ancient Mesopotamia : An Illustrated Dictionary.* Austin: University of Texas Press, 1992.

Blundell, Sue, and Margaret Williamson, eds. *The Sacred and the Feminine in Ancient Greece.* London: Routledge, 1998.

Burkert, Walter. *Greek Religion.* Translated by John Raffan. Cambridge, MA: Harvard University Press, 1985.

Clark, R.T. Rundle. *Myth and Symbol in Ancient Egypt.* London: Thames & Hudson, 1991.

David, Rosalie. *Handbook to Life in Ancient Egypt.* New York: Facts On File, 1998.

Faraone, Christopher A., and Dirk Obbink, eds. *Magika Hiera: Ancient Greek Magic and Religion.* New York: Oxford University Press, 1991.

Ferguson, John. *The Religions of the Roman Empire.* Ithaca, NY: Cornell University Press, 1985.

Frankfort, Henri. *Ancient Egyptian Religion.* New York: Harper & Row, 1961.

———, et al. *Before Philosophy.* Baltimore: Penguin, 1949.

Garland, Robert. *The Greek Way of Life: From Conception to Old Age.* Ithaca, NY: Cornell University Press, 1990.

Guthrie, W.K.C. *The Greeks and Their Gods.* Boston: Beacon Press, 1955.

Jacobsen, Thorkild. *The Treasures of Darkness: A History of Mesopotamian Religion.* New Haven, CT: Yale University Press, 1986.

Kerenyi, Karoly. *The Religion of the Greeks and Romans.* London: Thames & Hudson, 1962.

Kramer, Samuel Noah. *Summerian Mythology: A Study of Spiritual and Literary Achievement in the Third Millennium B.C.* Rev. edition. Philadelphia: University of Pennsylvania Press, 1998.

Martin, Luther H. *Hellenistic Religions.* New York: Oxford University Press, 1987.

Morenz, Siegfried. *Egyptian Religion.* Translated by Ann E. Keep. Ithaca, NY: Cornell University Press, 1973.

Parker, Robert. *Athenian Religion: A History.* New York: Oxford University Press, 1996.

Price, Simon. *Religions of the Ancient Greeks.* New York: Cambridge University Press, 1999.

Ringgren, Helmer. *Religions of the Ancient Near East.* Philadelphia: Westminster, 1973.

Shafer, Byron E., ed. *Religion in Ancient Egypt: Gods, Myths, and Personal Practice.* Ithaca, NY: Cornell University Press, 1991.

Turcan, Robert. *The Cults of the Roman Empire.* Translated by Antonia Nevill. Oxford: Blackwell, 1996.

Vernus, Pascal. *The Gods of Ancient Egypt.* Translated by Jane Marie Todd. New York: George Braziller, 1998.

Zoroastrianism

Boyce, Mary, ed. *Textual Sources for the Study of Zoroastrianism.* Manchester: Manchester University Press, 1984.

———. *Zoroastrians: Their Religious Beliefs and Practices.* London: Routledge & Kegan Paul, 1985.

Choksy, Jamsheed K. *Purity and Pollution in Zoroastrianism: Triumph Over Evil.* Austin: University of Texas Press, 1989.

Clark, Peter. *Zoroastrianism: An Introduction to Ancient Faith.* Brighton, UK: Sussex Academic Press, 1999.

Duchesne-Guillemin, Jacques. *Symbols and Values in Zoroastrianism: Their Survival and Renewal.* New York: Harper & Row, 1970.

Nigosian, Solomon A. *The Zoroastrian Faith: Tradition and Modern Research.* Montreal: McGill-Queens University Press, 1993.

Pangborn, Cyrus R. *Zoroastrianism: A Beleaguered Faith.* New Delhi: Vikas Publishing House, 1982.

Judaism

Baskin, Judith R. *Jewish Women in Historical Perspective.* Detroit: Wayne State University, 1991.

Borowitz, Eugene B. *Choices in Modern Jewish Thought.* New York: Behrman, 1983.

Braiterman, Zachary. *(God) After Auschwitz: Tradition and Change in Post-Holocaust Jewish Thought.* Princeton, NJ: Princeton University Press, 1998.

Bulka, Reuven P. *Dimensions of Orthodox Judaism.* New York: KTAV, 1983.

Cantor, Norman E. *The Sacred Chain: The History of the Jews.* San Francisco: HarperSanFrancisco, 1994.

Clendinnen, Inga. *Reading the Holocaust.* New York: Cambridge University Press, 1999.

Cohen, Shaye J. D. *The Beginnings of Jewishness: Boundaries, Varities, Uncertainties.* Berkeley: University of California Press, 1999.

Cohn-Sherbok, Dan. *Judaism.* Upper Saddle River, NJ: Prentice Hall, 1999.

Donin, Hayim. *To Be a Jew: A Guide to Jewish Observance in Contemporary Thought.* New York: Basic Books, 1972.

Dorff, Elliot N., and Louis E. Newman, eds. *Contemporary Jewish Ethics and Morality: A Reader.* New York: Oxford University Press, 1995.

———, eds. *Contemporary Jewish Theology: A Reader.* New York: Oxford University Press, 1998.

Dosick, Rabbi Wayne. *Living Judaism: The Complete Guide to Jewish Belief, Tradition, and Practice.* San Francisco: HarperSanFrancisco, 1995.

Encyclopedia Judaica. 16 vols. Jerusalem: Keter, 1972.

Fishbane, Michael. *The Exegetical Imagination: On Jewish Thought and Theology.* Cambridge, MA: Harvard University Press, 1998.

Frankel, Ellen. *The Five Books of Miriam: A Woman's Commentary on the Torah.* San Francisco: HarperSanFrancisco, 1998.

Frankiel, Tamar. *The Voice of Sarah: Feminine Spirituality and Traditional Judaism.* San Francisco: Harper, 1990.

Fuchs, Esther, ed. *Women and the Holocaust: Narrative and Representation.* Lanham, MD: University Press of America, 1999.

Goldscheider, Calvin, and Jacob Neusner, eds. *Social Foundations of Judaism.* Englewood Cliffs, NJ: Prentice Hall, 1990.

Gottlieb, Lynn. *She Who Dwells Within: A Feminist Vision of a Renewed Judaism.* San Francisco: HarperSanFrancisco, 1995.

Greenberg, Irving. *The Jewish Way: Living the Holidays.* New York: Summit Books, 1988.

Greenstein, Howard R. *Judaism—The Eternal Covenant.* Philadelphia: Fortress Press, 1983.

Grossman, Susan, and Rivka Haut, eds. *Daughters of the King: Women and the Synagogue.* Philadelphia: Jewish Publication Society, 1992.

Hertzberg, Arthur, and Aron Hirt-Manheimer. *Jews: The Essence and Character of a People.* San Francisco: HarperSanFrancisco, 1998.

Heschel, Abraham J. *Between God and Man: An Interpretation of Judaism.* Edited by Fritz A. Rothschild. New York: Free Press, 1959.

Heschel, Susannah, ed. *On Being a Jewish Feminist.* New York: Schocken Books, 1983.

Jacobs, Louis, ed. *The Jewish Religion: A Companion.* New York: Oxford University Press, 1995.

———. *A Jewish Theology.* New York: Behrman House, 1973.

Johnson, Paul. *A History of the Jews.* San Francisco: HarperSanFrancisco, 1988.

Levenson, Jon D. *Creation and the Persistence of Evil: The Jewish Drama of Divine Omnipotence.* Princeton, NJ: Princeton University Press, 1994.

———. *Sinai and Zion: An Entry into the Jewish Bible.* New York: Harper & Row, 1985.

Matt, Daniel C. *The Essential Kabbalah: The Heart of Jewish Mysticism.* San Francisco: HarperSanFrancisco, 1996.

Montefiore, C.G., and H. Loewe, comps. *A Rabbinic Anthology.* New York: Schocken Books, 1974.

Neusner, Jacob. *The Life of Torah: Readings in the Jewish Religious Experience.* Belmont, CA: Dickenson, 1974.

———. *The Way of Torah: An Introduction to Judaism.* 4th edition. Belmont, CA: Dickenson, 1987.

Plaskow, Judith. *Standing Again at Sinai: Judaism from a Feminist Perspective.* San Francisco: Harper, 1991.

Schiffman, Lawrence H. *From Text to Tradition: A History of Second Temple and Rabbinic Judaism.* Hoboken, NJ: KTAV Publishing House, Inc., 1991.

Scholem, Gershom G. *Major Trends in Jewish Mysticism.* New York: Schocken Books, 1961.

Seltzer, Robert M. *Jewish People, Jewish Thought: The Jewish Experience in History.* New York: Macmillan, 1980.

Sered, Susan. *Women as Ritual Experts: The Religious Lives of Elderly Jewish Women in Jerusalem.* New York: Oxford University Press, 1992.

Sherwin, Byron. *In Partnership With God: Contemporary Jewish Law and Ethics.* Syracuse, NY: Syracuse University Press, 1990.

Solomon, Norman. *Judaism: A Very Short Introduction.* New York: Oxford University Press, 1997.

Strassfeld, Michael. *The Jewish Holidays: A Guide and Commentary.* New York: Harper & Row, Publishers, 1985.

Wiesel, Elie. *Souls on Fire: Portraits and Legends of Hasidic Leaders.* Translated by Marian Wiesel. New York: Random House, 1972.

Wylen, Stephen M. *Settings of Silver: Introduction to Judaism.* New York: Paulist Press, 1989.

Zborowski, Mark, and Elizabeth Herzog. *Life is with People: The Culture of the Shtetl.* New York: Schocken Books, 1962.

Christianity

Atiya, A.S. *A History of Eastern Christianity.* London: Methuen, 1968.

Baly, Denis, and Royal W. Rhodes, *The Faith of Christians: An Introduction to Basic Beliefs.* Philadelphia: Fortress Press, 1984.

Barrett, Charles D. *Understanding the Christian Faith.* Englewood Cliffs, NJ: Prentice-Hall, 1980.

Barton, John, ed. *The Cambridge Companion to Biblical Interpretation.* New York: Cambridge University Press, 1998.

Boff, Leonardo, and Clodovis Boff. *Introducing Liberation Theology.* Translated by Paul Burns. Maryknoll, NY: Orbis Books, 1987.

Borg, Marcus J. *Jesus: A New Vision.* San Francisco: HarperSanFrancisco, 1991.

———. *Meeting Jesus Again for the First Time: The Historical Jesus and the Heart of Contemporary Faith.* San Francisco: HarperSanFrancisco, 1994.

Brown, Robert McAfee. *The Spirit of Protestantism.* New York: Oxford University Press, 1965.

Carmody, Denise Lardner, and John Tully Carmody, *Christianity: An Introduction.* 3rd edition. Belmont, CA: Wadsworth, 1995.

———. *Roman Catholicism: An Introduction.* New York: Macmillan, 1990.

Cragg, Kenneth. *The Christ and the Faiths.* Philadelphia: Westminster Press, 1987.

Crossan, John Dominic. *The Historical Jesus: The Life of a Mediterranean Jewish Peasant.* San Francisco: HarperSanFrancisco, 1991.

Davies, W. D. *Christian Engagements With Judaism.* Harrisburg, PA: Trinity Press International, 1999.

D'Costa, Gavin. *Theology and Religious Pluralism.* Oxford, England: Basil Blackwell, 1986.

Dombrowsky, Daviel A. *Christian Pacifism.* Philadelphia: Temple University Press, 1991.

Doran, Robert. *Birth of a Worldview: Early Christianity in Its Jewish and Pagan Context.* Blue Ridge Summit, PA: Rowman & Littlefield, 1999.

Eckardt, A. Roy. *Jews and Christians: The Contemporary Meeting.* Bloomington: Indiana University Press, 1986.

Fasching, Daniel J. *The Coming of the Millennium: Good News for the Whole Human Race.* Harrisburg, PA: Trinity Press International, 1998.

Gonzalez, Justo L. *The Story of Christianity.* 2 vols. New York: Harper & Row, 1984.

Grant, Robert M. *Gods and the One God.* Philadelphia: Westminster Press, 1986.

Gunton, Colin E., ed. *The Cambridge Companion to Christian Doctrine.* New York: Cambridge University Press, 1997.

Gutierrez, Gustavo. *A Theology of Liberation.* Maryknoll, NY: Orbis Books, 1994.

Helm, Thomas E. *The Christian Religion: An Introduction.* Englewood Cliffs, NJ: Prentice Hall, 1991.

Herrin, Judith. *The Formation of Christianity.* Princeton, NJ: Princeton University Press, 1987.

Johnson, Elizabeth A. *She Who Is: The Mystery of God in Feminist Theological Discourse.* New York: Crossroad, 1993.

Johnson, Luke Timothy. *Living Jesus: Learning the Heart of the Gospel.* San Francisco: HarperSanFrancisco, 1999.

King, Ursula, ed. *Feminist Theology From the Third World: A Reader.* Maryknoll, NY: Orbis Books, 1994.

Kraemer, Ross Shephard, and Mary Rose D'Angelo, eds. *Women and Christian Origins: A Reader.* New York: Oxford University Press, 1998.

McBrien, Richard P. *Catholicism.* Revised edition. San Francisco: HarperSanFrancisco, 1994.

McFague, Sallie. *The Body of God: An Ecological Theology.* Minneapolis: Fortress Press, 1993.

———. *Metaphorical Theology: Models of God.* Minneapolis: Fortress Press, 1997.

McKenzie, John. *The Roman Catholic Church.* New York: Doubleday, 1971.

Meeks, Wayne A. *The First Urban Christians: The Social World of the Apostle Paul.* New Haven: Yale University Press, 1983.

Meyerdorf, John. *The Orthodox Church: Its Past and Its Role in the World Today.* 3rd edition. Crestwood, NY: St. Vladimir's Seminary Press, 1981.

Neville, Robert Cummings. *A Theology Primer.* Albany: State University of New York Press, 1991.

Niebuhr, H. Richard. *Christ and Culture.* New York: Harper Torchbooks, 1956.

Pelikan, Jaroslav. *Jesus Through the Centuries.* New Haven, CT: Yale University Press, 1985.

Ramshaw, Gail. *Under the Tree of Life: The Religion of a Christian Feminist.* New York: Continuum, 1998.

Riley-Smith, Jonathan, ed. *The Oxford Illustrated History of the Crusades.* New York: Oxford University Press, 1997.

Rowland, Christopher, ed. *The Cambridge Companion to Liberation Theology.* New York: Cambridge University Press, 1999.

Ruether, Rosemary Radford. *Sexism and God-Talk: Toward a Feminist Theology.* Boston: Beacon Press, 1983.

———. *Gaia and God: An Ecofeminist Theology of Earth Healing.* San Francisco: HarperSanFrancisco, 1992.

Sanders, E.P. *Jesus and Judaism.* Philadelphia: Fortress Press, 1985.

Schüssler Fiorenza, Elizabeth. *In Memory of Her: A Feminist Theological Reconstruction of Christian Origins.* New York: Crossroad, 1994.

———. *Searching the Scriptures: A Feminist Introduction.* 2 vols. New York: Crossroad, 1997.

Sobrino, Jon. *Christology at the Crossroads.* Maryknoll, NY: Orbis Books, 1978.

Sölle, Dorthee. *Thinking About God: An Introduction to Theology.* Philadelphia: Trinity Press International, 1991.

Sundkler, Bengt, and Christopher Steed. *A History of the Christian Church in Africa.* New York: Cambridge University Press, 1999.

Tillich, Paul. *Dynamics of Faith.* New York: Harper & Row, 1957.

Walker, Williston, et al. *A History of the Christian Church.* 4th edition. New York: Scribners, 1985.

Ware, Timothy. *The Orthodox Church.* Baltimore: Penguin Books, 1984.

Weaver, Mary Jo. *Introduction to Christianity.* 3rd edition. Belmont, CA: Wadsworth, 1998.

Welch, Sharon D. *Communities of Resistance and Solidarity: A Feminist Theology of Liberation.* Maryknoll, NY: Orbis Books, 1985.

Wiggins, James B., and Robert S. Ellwood. *Christianity: A Cultural Perspective.* Englewood Cliffs, NJ: Prentice Hall, 1988.

Wilson, Brian. *Christianity.* Upper Saddle River, NJ: Prentice Hall, 1999.

Islam

Ahmed, Leila. *Women and Gender in Islam: Historical Roots of a Modern Debate.* New Haven, CT: Yale University Press, 1992.

Arberry, A.J. *The Koran Interpreted.* New York: Macmillan, 1955.

———. *Sufism: An Account of the Mystics of Islam.* New York: Harper & Row, 1970.

Armstrong, Karen. *Muhammad: A Biography of the Prophet.* San Francisco: HarperSanFrancisco, 1993.

Bloom, Jonathan, and Sheila Blair, eds. *Islamic Arts.* London: Phaedon Press, 1997.

Choudhury, G. W. *Islam and the Contemporary World.* Des Plaines, IL: Library of Islam, 1991.

Cohn-Sherbok, Dan, ed. *Islam in a World of Diverse Faiths.* New York: St. Martin's Press, 1991.

Cragg, Kenneth, and R. Marston Speight. *The House of Islam.* 3rd edition. Belmont, CA: Dickenson, 1987.

———, eds. *Islam from Within: Anthology of a Religion.* Belmont, CA: Wadsworth, 1980.

Denny, Frederick Mathewson. *An Introduction to Islam.* 2nd edition. New York: Macmillan, 1996.

———. *Islam and the Muslim Community.* San Francisco: HarperSanFrancisco, 1988.

Eickelman, Dale F., and James Piscatori. *Muslim Politics.* Princeton, NJ: Princeton University Press, 1996.

Elias, Jamal J. *Islam.* Upper Saddle River, NJ: Prentice Hall, 1999.

Esposito, John L. *Islam: The Straight Path.* 3rd edition. New York: Oxford University Press, 1998.

———. *The Islamic Threat.* 3rd edition. New York: Oxford University Press, 1999.

———, ed. *Voices of Resurgent Islam.* New York: Oxford University Press, 1983.

Esposito, John L., and John O. Voll. *Islam and Democracy.* New York: Oxford University Press, 1996.

Gibb, H.A.R., et al., eds. *Encyclopaedia of Islam.* New edition. Leiden: E.J. Brill, 1960–.

Guillaume, A., trans. *The Life of Muhammad: A Translation of Ishaq's Sirat Rasul Allah.* London: Oxford University Press, 1955.

Haddad, Yvonne Yazbeck, ed. *The Muslims of America.* New York: Oxford University Press, 1991.

———, and John L. Esposito. *Islam, Gender, and Social Change.* New York: Oxford University Press, 1998.

———, and Jane Smith, eds. *Muslim Communities in North America.* Albany: State University of New York Press, 1994.

Haneef, Suzanne. *What Everyone Should Know About Islam and Muslims.* Des Plaines, IL: Library of Islam, 1985.

Hathout, Hassan. *Reading the Muslim Mind.* Plainfield, IN: American Trust Publications, 1995.

Haykal, Muhammad Husayn. *The Life of Muhammad.* Plainfield, IN: Islamic Book Service, 1995.

Hodgson, Marshall G. *The Venture of Islam: Conscience and History in a World Civilization.* 3 vols. Chicago: University of Chicago Press, 1974.

Holt, P.M., Ann K.S. Lambton, and Bernard Lewis, eds. *The Cambridge History of Islam.* 2 vols. Cambridge: Cambridge University Press, 1970.

Hovannisian, Richard G., and Georges Sabagh, eds. *Religion and Culture in Medieval Islam.* New York: Cambridge University Press, 1999.

Kandiyoti, Deniz, ed. *Women, Islam, and the State.* Philadelphia: Temple University Press, 1991.

Kurzman, Charles. *Liberal Islam: A Sourcebook.* New York: Oxford University Press, 1998.

Lawrence, Bruce B. *Shattering the Myth: Islam Beyond Violence.* Princeton, NJ: Princeton University Press, 1998.

Lings, Martin. *What Is Sufism?* Berkeley: University of California Press, 1981.

Madelund, Wilferd. *The Succession to Muhammad: A Study of the Early Caliphate.* New York: Cambridge University Press, 1998.

Malik, Ghulam. *Muhammad: An Islamic Perspective.* Lanham, MD: University Press of America, 1998.

Martin, Richard C. *Islam: A Cultural Perspective.* Englewood Cliffs, NJ: Prentice Hall, 1982.

———. *Islamic Studies: A History of Religions Approach.* 2nd edition. Upper Saddle River, NJ: Prentice Hall, 1996.

Mawdudi, Abul A'la. *Towards Understanding Islam.* Translated by Khurshid Ahmad. Plainfield, IN: Muslim Students' Association of the U.S. and Canada, 1980/1400 A.H.

Mernissi, Fatima. *Beyond the Veil: Male–Female Dynamics in Modern Muslim Society.* Revised edition. Bloomington: Indiana University Press, 1987.

Metcalf, Barbara Daly. *Making Muslim Space in North America and Europe.* Berkeley: University of California Press, 1996.

Momen, Moojan. *An Introduction to Shi'i Islam: The History and Doctrine of Twelver Shi'ism.* New Haven: Yale University Press, 1985.

Nakash, Yitzhak. *The Shi'is of Iraq.* Princeton, NJ: Princeton University Press, 1994.

Nasr, Seyyed Hossein. *Ideals and Realities of Islam.* 2nd edition. London: Unwin Hyman, 1985.

Peters, F.E. *The Hajj: The Muslim Pilgrimage to Mecca and the Holy Places.* Princeton, NJ: Princeton University Press, 1996.

———. *Muhammad and the Origins of Islam.* Albany: State University of New York Press, 1994.

Pinault, David. *The Shi'ites: Ritual and Popular Piety in a Muslim Community.* New York: St. Martin's Press, 1992.

Pullapilly, Cyriac K., ed. *Islam in the Contemporary World.* Notre Dame, IN: Cross Roads Books, 1980.

Rahman, Fazlur. *Islam.* Chicago: University of Chicago Press, 1979.

Renard, John, ed. *Seven Doors to Islam: Spirituality and the Religious Life of Muslims.* Berkeley: University of California Press, 1996.

———. *Windows on the House of Islam: Muslim Sources on Spirituality and Religious Life.* Berkeley: University of California Press, 1998.

Savory, R.M., ed. *Introduction to Islamic Civilization.* New York: Cambridge University Press, 1976.

Schimmel, Annemarie. *And Muhammad Is His Messenger: The Veneration of the Prophet in Islamic Piety.* Chapel Hill: University of North Carolina Press, 1985.

———. *Islam: An Introduction.* Albany: State University of New York Press, 1992.

———. *Mystical Dimensions of Islam.* Chapel Hill: University of North Carolina Press, 1975.

Siddiqi, Abdul-Hamid. *Life of Muhammad.* Chicago: Kazi Publications, 1991.

Stowasser, Barbara Freyer, ed. *The Islamic Impulse.* Washington, DC: Center for Contemporary Arab Studies, Georgetown University, 1987.

———. *Women in the Qur'an, Traditions and Interpretation.* New York: Oxford University Press, 1994.

Trimingham, J. Spencer. *The Sufi Orders in Islam.* 2nd edition. New York: Oxford University Press, 1998.

Waardenburg, Jacques, ed. *Muslim Perceptions of Other Religions: A Historical Survey.* New York: Oxford University Press, 1999.

Wadud, Amina. *Qur'an and Women: Re-reading the Sacred Text from a Woman's Perspective.* 2nd edition. New York: Oxford University Press, 1999.

Williams, John Alden, ed. *The Word of Islam.* Austin: University of Texas Press, 1994.

PART 3 ONGOING EXPLORATIONS ON THE SACRED PATHS

Contemporary Alternative Religious Movements

Adler, Margot. *Drawing Down the Moon: Witches, Druids, Goddess-Worshippers, and Other Pagans in America Today.* Revised edition. Boston: Beacon Press, 1997.

Albanese, Catherine. *Nature Religion in America: From the Algonkian Indians to the New Age.* Chicago: The University of Chicago Press, 1988.

Beckford, James A., ed. *New Religious Movements and Rapid Social Change.* London: Sage Publications, 1986.

Bednarowski, Mary Farrell. *New Religions and the Theological Imagination in America.* Bloomington: Indiana University Press, 1989.

Berger, Helen A. *A Community of Witches: Contemporary Neo-Paganism and Witchcraft in the United States.* Columbia: University of South Carolina Press, 1998.

Bergman, Jerry. *Jehovah's Witnesses and Kindred Groups: A Historical Compendium and Bibliography.* New York: Garland, 1984.

Brandon, Ruth. *The Spiritualists.* Buffalo, NY: Prometheus, 1984.

Brown, Karen McCarthy. *Mama Lola: A Vodou Priestess in Brooklyn.* Berkeley: University of California Press, 1991.

Bruce, Steve. *Religion in the Modern World: From Cathedrals to Cults.* New York: Oxford University Press, 1996.

Campbell, Bruce F. *Ancient Wisdom Revived: A History of the Theosophical Movement.* Berkeley: University of California Press, 1980.

Chryssides, George D. *The Advent of Sun Myung Moon: The Origins, Beliefs, and Practices of the Unification Church.* New York: St. Martin's Press, 1991.

———. *Exploring New Religions.* London: Cassell, 1999.

Corbett, Julia Mitchell. *Religion in America.* 3rd edition. Upper Saddle River, NJ: Prentice Hall, 1997.

Ellwood, Robert, and Harry Partin. *Religious and Spiritual Groups in Modern America.* 2nd edition. Englewood Cliffs, NJ: Prentice Hall, 1988.

Fisher, Mary Pat. *Religion in the Twenty-First Century.* Upper Saddle River, NJ: Prentice Hall, 1999.

Galanter, Marc. *Cults: Faith, Healing and Coercion.* New York: Oxford University Press, 1999.

Hansen, Klaus J. *Mormonism and the American Experience.* Chicago: The University of Chicago Press, 1981.

Hatcher, William S., and J. Douglas Martin. *The Baha'i Faith: The Emerging Global Religion.* Revised edition. San Francisco: Harper & Row, 1997.

Huddleston, John. *The Earth Is But One Country.* London: Baha'i Publishing Trust, 1988.

Hurst, Jane. *The Nichiren Shoshu and Soka Gakkai in America: The Ethos of a New Religious Movement.* New York: Garland, 1992.

Kerr, Howard, and Charles Crow, eds. *The Occult in America: New Historical Perspectives.* Urbana: University of Illinois Press, 1983.

Kim, Young Oon. *Unification Theology.* New York: The Holy Spirit Association for the Unification of World Christianity, 1980.

Lewis, James R., ed. *The Gods Have Landed: New Religions from Other Worlds.* Albany: State University of New York Press, 1995.

Lewis, James, and J. Gordon Melton. *Perspectives on the New Age.* Albany: State University of New York Press, 1992.

Melton, J. Gordon. *Encyclopedic Handbook of Cults in America.* Revised edition. New York: Garland, 1992.

Miller, Timothy, ed. *America's Alternative Religions.* Albany: State University of New York Press, 1995.

———, ed. *When Prophets Die: the Postcharismatic Fate of New Religious Movements.* Albany: State University of New York Press, 1991.

Moore, Rebecca, and Fielding McGeehee III, eds. *New Religious Movements, Mass Suicide, and Peoples Temple.* Lewiston, NY: Edwin Mellen Press, 1988.

Murphy, Joseph M. *Santeria: An African Religion in America.* Boston: Beacon Press, 1988.

Palmer, Susan Jean. *Moon Sisters, Krishna Mothers, Rajneesh Lovers: Women's Roles in the New Religions.* Syracuse, NY: Syracuse University Press, 1994.

Pearson, Michael. *Millennial Dreams and Moral Dilemmas: Seventh-Day Adventism.* New York: Cambridge University Press, 1990.

Richardson, James, Joel Best, and David Bromley, eds. *The Satanism Scare.* Hawthorne, NY: Aldine de Gruyter, 1991.

Robbins, Thomas, and Dick Anthony, eds. *In Gods We Trust: New Patterns of Religious Pluralism.* New Brunswick, NJ: Transaction Publishers, 1991.

Rochford, E. Burke. *Hare Krishna in America.* New Brunswick, NJ: Rutgers University Press, 1985.

Sered, Susan. *Priestess, Mother, Sacred Sister: Religions Dominated by Women.* New York: Oxford University Press, 1994.

Shipps, Jan. *Mormonism: The Story of a New Religious Tradition.* Champaign: University of Illinois Press, 1985.

Silberger, Julius. *Mary Baker Eddy: An Interpretive Biography of the Founder of Christian Science.* Boston: Little, Brown, 1980.

Sjöo, Monica, and Barbara Mor. *The Great Cosmic Mother: Recovering the Religion of the Earth.* San Francisco: Harper and Row, 1987.

Smith, Peter. *The Babi and Baha'i Religions: From Messianic Shi'ism to a World Religion.* Cambridge: Cambridge University Press, 1987.

Starhawk. *The Spiral Dance: A Rebirth of the Ancient Religion of the Great Goddess.* New edition. Boston: Beacon Press, 1988.

Stockman, Robert H. *The Baha'i Faith in America.* Wilmette, IL: Baha'i Publishing Trust, 1985.

Tabor, James D., and Eugene V. Gallagher. *Why Waco? Cults and the Battle for Religious Freedom in America.* Berkeley: University of California Press, 1995.

What Is Scientology? Los Angeles: The Church of Scientology, 1992.

Guideposts and Crossings on the Path

Bryant, M. Darrol, and Frank Flinn, eds. *Interreligious Dialogue: Voices from a New Frontier.* New York: Paragon House, 1989.

Chapple, Christopher Key. *Ecological Prospects: Science, Religion, and Aesthetic Perspectives.* Albany: State University of New York Press, 1993.

Forward, Martin. *Ultimate Visions: Reflections on the Religions We Choose.* Oxford: One World Publications, 1995.

Ingram, Paul O. *Wrestling With the Ox: A Theology of Religious Experience.* New York: Continuum, 1997.

Kinsley, David. *Ecology and Religion: Ecological Spirituality in Cross-Cultural Perspective.* Englewood Cliffs, NJ: Prentice Hall, 1995.

Kosmin, Barry A., and Seymour P. Lachmin. *One Nation Under God: Religion in Contemporary American Society.* New York: Harmony Books, 1993.

Küng, Hans, ed. *Toward a Global Ethic (An Initial Declaration).* New York: Continuum, 1993.

Sharma, Arvind, and Kathleen Dungan, eds. *A Dome of Many Colors: Studies in Religious Pluralism, Identity, and Unity.* Harrisburg, PA: Trinity Press International, 1999.

Smith-Christopher, Daniel L., ed. *Subverting Hatred: The Challenge of Nonviolence in Religious Traditions.* Boston: Boston Research Center for the Twenty-first Century, 1998.

Swidler, Leonard, ed. *Toward a Universal Theology of Religion.* New York: Orbis Books, 1988.

Thich Nhat Hanh. *Living Buddha, Living Christ.* New York: Riverhead Books, 1995.

Tucker, Mary Evelyn, and John A. Grim, eds. *Worldviews and Ecology: Living Sustainably on a Fragile Planet.* Maryknoll, NY: Orbis Books, 1994.

Twiss, Sumner B., and Bruce Grelle. *Explorations in Global Ethics: Comparative Religious Ethics and Interreligious Dialogue.* Boulder, CO: Westview Press, 1998.

Van Voorst, Robert E., ed. *Anthology of World Scriptures.* Belmont: Wadsworth, 1994.

Acknowledgments

TEXT

From "Eagles Fly Over" by Arthur Amiotte, in *Parabola* I, No. 3 (Summer, 1976). Reprinted by permission of *Parabola Magazine*.

From *Papago Indian Religion,* by Ruth Underhill. Copyright © 1946 Columbia University Press. Reprinted with the permission of the publisher.

From *Literary History of the Arabs* by R.A. Nicholson, © Copyright 1914 Cambridge University Press. Reprinted with the permission of Cambridge University Press.

From *Weekday Prayerbook,* edited by Rabbi Gerson Hadas. Copyright © 1961 Rabbinical Assembly. Reprinted with permission of the Rabbinical Assembly.

From *The Fathers According to Rabbi Nathan* by Judah Goldin. Reprinted with permission of Yale University Press.

From *Towards Understanding Islam* by Abul a'la Mawdudi, translated by Khurshid Ahmad. Copyright © 1980 by the Islamic Foundation, UK. Reprinted with permission of the Islamic Foundation, Leicester UK.

From *A Rabbinic Anthology* by C.G. Montofiore and H. Loewe. Copyright © 1974 by Schocken Books Inc. Reprinted by permission of Schocken Books, a division of Random House, Inc.

From *Blessingway*, by Leland C. Wyman. Copyright © 1970 The Arizona Board of Regents. Reprinted by permission of the University of Arizona Press.

From *Rabi'a: The Life and Work of Rabi'a and Other Women Mystics in Islam* by Margaret Smith. Copyright © 1994 Oneworld Publications. Reprinted with permission of Oneworld Publications.

From *The Faith and Practice of al-Ghazali,* by W. Montgomery Watt. Copyright © 1953 by Allen & Unwin. Reprinted with permission of Oneworld Publications.

From *Lame Deer: Seeker of Visions* by John Fire/Lame Deer and Richard Erdoes. Copyright © 1972 by John Fire/Lame Deer and Richard Erdoes. Reprinted by permission of Simon & Schuster, Inc.

From *The Koran Interpreted* translated by A.J. Arberry. Copyright © 1955 by George Allen & Unwin Ltd. Reprinted with the permission of Scribner, a division of Simon & Schuster, Inc.

From *Between Time and Eternity: The Essentials of Judaism,* 1st Edition, by Jacob Neusner. © Copyright 1975. Reprinted with permission of Wadsworth Publishing, a division of Thomson Learning. Fax: 800-730-2215.

From The *Complete Greek Tragedies,* Vol. II. From Sophocles, "Ajax," in Grene and Lattimore, eds. translated by John Moore. Reprinted with permission of the University of Chicago Press.

From *Textual Sources for the Study of Zoroastrianism,* by Mary Boyce. Copyright © 1984. Reprinted with permission of Mary Boyce.

From *Ancient Near Eastern Texts Related to the Old Testament* by James Pritchard. Copyright © 1950 by Princeton University Press. Reprinted by permission of Princeton University Press.

From *Hallaj: Mystic and Martyr* (abridged edition) by Louis Massignon. Copyright © 1994 by Princeton University Press. Reprinted by permission of Princeton University Press.

From *The Life of Muhammad: A Translation of Ishaq's Sirat Rasul Allah* translated by A. Guillaume. Copyright © 1955. Reprinted with permission of Oxford University Press, Karachi, Pakistan.

IMAGES

All Maps illustrated by Carto-Graphics.

Chapter 1: Page 5, Air India Library; **p. 9,** Israel Ministry of Tourism, North America; **p. 15,** AP/Wide World Photos; **p. 20,** The Metropolitan Museum of Art, NY. Harris Brisbane Dick Fund, 1939.

Chapter 2: Page 27, Gunter R. Reitz, PIX Inc., **p. 28,** Museum of Natural History.

Chapter 3: Page 37, American Museum of Natural History, **p. 45,** Bernard Wolf, Monkmeyer Press; **p. 53,** Marc & Evelyne Bernheim, Woodfin Camp & Associates; **p. 56,** George Holton, Photo Researchers, Inc.

Chapter 4: Page 66, The Metropolitan Museum of Art; **p. 70,** The Oriental Institute Museum of The University of Chicago; **p. 71,** Charlie Waite, Tony Stone Images.

Chapter 5: Page 77, Jehanair Gazdar, Woodfin Camp & Associates; **p. 81,** Magnum Photos, Inc.; **p. 83,** E. Norman Issott, Barnaby's Picture Library.

Chapter 6: Page 89, Uffizi Gallery, Florence, Italy, Corbis; **p. 97,** Israel Ministry of Tourism, North America; **p. 104,** Bill Aron Photography, PhotoEdit.

Chapter 7: Page 110, Israel Ministry of Tourism, North America; **p. 112,** PhotoEdit, **p. 116,** Heribert Proepper, AP/Wide World Photos, Inc.

Chapter 8: Page 121, Barbara Alper, Stock Boston; **p. 123,** Leonard Freed, Magnum Photos, Inc.; **p. 129,** Paul W. Liebhardt.

Chapter 9: Page 135, Erich Lessing, Art Resource, NY; **p. 139,** El Greco, "Agony in the Garden" Toledo Museum of Art, Toledo, Spain, Corbis; **p. 152,** AP/Wide World Photos; **p. 155,** Jim Hollander, Corbis.

Chapter 10: Page 160, Corbis; **p. 165,** The Metropolitan Museum of Art, Fletcher Fund, 1933.

Chapter 11: Page 174, Katrina Thomas, Photo Researchers, Inc.; **p. 177,** Pastor Jean Holmes; **p. 181,** Paul Sakuma, AP/Wide World Photos.

Chapter 12: Page 186, Kingdom of Saudi Arabia; **p. 189,** Corbis; **p. 204,** Fritz Henle, Monkmeyer Press; **p. 206,** Dorothy Littell Greco, The Image Works.

Chapter 13: Page 212, The Metropolitan Museum of Art, Harris Brisbane Dick Fund, 1939; **p. 217,** Charles Gatewood, Stock Boston.

Chapter 14: Page 222, Ewing Galloway Inc.; **p. 224,** Eugene Gordon, Pearson Education/PH College; **p. 226,** Robert Azzi, Woodfin Camp & Associates; **p. 229,** Israel Ministry of Tourism, North America.

Chapter 15: Page 241, Margot Granitsas, Photo Researchers, Inc.; **p. 243,** United Airlines; **p. 245,** Santokh Kochar, PhotoDisc, Inc.; **p. 249,** Ken Karp, Pearson Education/PH College.

Index

a

Abba, 137
'Abbas, Shah, 203
Abbasid dynasty, 195–196
'Abd al-Malik, 195
'Abd al-Muttalib, 187, 190
'Abduh, Muhammad, 205–206
Aborigines, 31
    art, 53
    Dreaming Time, 34, 43
    revival of traditional religious
       identity, 61
Abraham, prophet, 186
Abraham religions, 12
    See also Christianity; Islam;
       Judaism
    historical development of, 8,
       63–64, 88–89
    human failure and evil, 14
Abu Bakr, 189, 193
Abu Lahab, 190
Abu Talib, 189, 190
Abu Yazid, 199
Achadmenid dynasty, 75–76
Achilpa, 56
Acts of the Apostles, 140
Adams, Frederick, 251
Advent, 172
Aesthesis, 19
Africa/Africans:
    Christian-African movement,
       60–61
    creation myths, 43–44
    indigenous peoples of, 32
    location of selected groups, 40
    rites of passage, 51–52
    sacred stories, 34

Yoruba vision of sacred reality, 39,
    41
Aggiornamento, 156
Agricultural revolution, 29
Ahriman, 76, 78–79, 109
Ahura Mazda, 74, 75, 76, 77–80, 85,
    109
Ainu, 31, 38, 50
'Aisha, 231
Akbar, 203
Akhenaton, 66
Akitu, 70
Al-Amin, 188
Albo, Joseph, 115
Alexander the Great, 65, 71, 76
Al-Ghazali. *See* Ghazali, al-
'Ali, 193–194, 205
'Ali, Amir, 206
'Ali, Mirza Hussain, 244
Allah, 186, 187
    meaning of, 210–212
Allah, Wali, 203
All Saints' Day, 173
All Souls' Day, 173
Alms-giving (Zakat), 223
Amaterasu, 21
Amesha Spentas (Holy Immortals),
    75, 77, 79
Amida Buddha, 15
Amiotte, Arthur, 47
Amos, prophet, 94–95
Anabaptists, 153–154
Anahita, 78
Ancient religions, 25, 29–30
Angra Mainyu, 75, 76, 109
Animals, master/mistress of, 38
Animism, 26, 36
Anthroposophy, 247

Antiochus IV, 96, 121
Apaches, 51
Apostles' Creed, 143, 144
Aquinas, Thomas, 150, 151
Architecture, 20
    See also Temples
    Christian, 176
    Islamic, 228
    Judaic, 125
    Zoroastrian, 84
Arianism, 147, 167–168
Aristotle, 73
Art:
    Aborigines, 53
    cave paintings, 28
    Christian, 175–176
    Egyptian, 67
    figurines (Willendorf Venus), 28,
       29
    indigenous peoples, 52–54
    Islamic, 227–228
    Judaic, 124–125
    Navajo sandpainting, 53–54
    sacred, 19–20
    Zoroastrian, 83–84
Artaxerxes, king, 75, 76
Asha, 75
Ashanti, 32, 44
Ash'ari, al-, 197
Ashkenazim, 102
Ash Wednesday, 172
Athanasius, bishop, 147
Atonement, 166
Augustine, Saint, 5, 147–148, 163, 164
Augustine of Canterbury, 148
Aum Shinri-kyo, 239
Averroes, 198
Avesta, 74, 76, 78

291

d

k

 l

 m